ANTHOLOGY

Volume I
1994 - 1997

Takilma Common Ground Anthology
Volume I • 1994 - 1997

Published by Takilma Common Ground with the support of
Left Fork Books of O'Brien, Oregon
Cover design by Alan Laurie
Book layout by Ryan Forsythe

Anthology created in celebration of 100 issues
100 Issue Logo Copyright © 2015 by Alan Laurie

Design, layout, and pre-press production of individual issues
by Takilma Common Ground staff

Created in 1994 to increase community communication
and stimulate discussion, Takilma Common Ground is
published seasonally in conjunction with the
solstices and equinoxes (more or less).

The editors of TCG gratefully acknowledge the ongoing support
of the Takilma community, all past and present volunteers and staff,
and all writers, artists, and photographers who have contributed.
Special thanks to Greg Walter and Patricia Mersman
for contributing archival copies for this project.
(This truly wouldn't have happened without you!)

Please consider a subscription
4 issues $13, 8 issues $20
Make checks payable to Takilma Commmunity Association
and mail to Takilma Common Ground,
9335 Takilma Road, Cave Juntion, OR 97523

CONTENTS

* When the staff realized they skipped making a #24, they followed #25 with a "25 1/2" (so that issue 26 was truly the 26th). See this note from issue 25 1/2: *Although we assumed that most folks contributing to our ever rotating staff were schooled in basic math, logical numerical continuation should never be taken for granted. (what happened to #24?)*

INTRODUCTION

I remember when something called **Takilma Common Ground** first arrived in my mailbox. It had articles by people I knew, classified ads for some local and some imaginary products, and an offer for free aura polish if I paid for a subscription. I noticed how well it had been proofread. Pre-internet, and pre much prevalence of home computers, it had been put together somehow and printed by IV Printing, a Cave Junction business run by Mike and Linda Hughes. The group of friends who had thought of a Takilma newsletter wanted to have payment on the public radio model; people could receive free subscriptions and would pay voluntarily to support the effort. There was also a lot of interest in **Sun Magazine**, which survives without advertising. Some people did subscribe and some donated generously and the paper continued, with publication dates on the Pagan calendar centered on the Solstices and Equinoxes and for a while, on the cross-quarter celebrations. The astute reader of this anthology will spot this brief high-energy period when not four but eight issues per year were published. This, or any productivity was due to the relatively large number of people involved. At some point I got involved because I had an early Mac.

Besides the Mud Council which met regularly to make decisions, which were sometimes remembered and followed up on, there were meetings attended by non-Mud Councilors as well for each issue where each article was read aloud and commented on. Each issue had a facilitator who was responsible for calling around to ask people to write, following up with them, getting all the handwritten and typed pieces of paper retyped into the then new word processing programs, laying out the issue and then following up through printing, folding and mailing. This was all done through amazing community support. Typing parties at Cedar Gulch got scraps of paper into computer documents. Community members came forward to facilitate issues. IV Printing charged very little and Mike and Linda were infinitely patient. Marjorie Reynolds helped (and still helps) get the complexities of bulk mailing right. We also had a few friends at the Post Office who bent the rules for us.

But this great creative endeavor, like many others, was steadily going broke. Internet had arrived, making publication easier, we were recording Takilma history, but we had lost people and money. Many of the original TCG people got bored, or got too busy with their real jobs, or became Takilma FM DJs or moved. It seemed like **Common Ground** should fold when a surprising number of people showed up for a meeting about its future. Suddenly we had a layout person, a new treasurer, people with interest and ideas. We had display ads. We had more meetings.

Today **Common Ground** is a sustainable resource that still needs your support. It is still well proofread. It still needs your subscriptions and submissions. Our email is tcommonground@ gmail.com, we have a PayPal site on Takilma.org and our physical address is 9335 Takilma Road, Cave Junction, Oregon 97523. Try out a subscription for $13 for four issues, $20 for eight (checks to Takilma Community Association) to see what Common Ground is like now and how you can participate. Have fun with the anthology!   *- Rachel Goodman*

ANTHOLOGY

Volume I
1994 - 1997

Takilma
Common Ground
A community newsletter

Issue #1   Jan-Feb '94

WHAT IT'S ALL ABOUT OR WHO IS WE

COMMON GROUND, a newsletter for Takilma, was born out of a desire to broaden and deepen our connections as a community. Our mission is to present a forum for information, ideas and debate on issues of concern to our community. We support diversity, encourage debate, promote creative expression and actively seek common ground. We honor the Earth we inhabit here at the headwaters of the Illinois River.

This newsletter is being mailed to all addresses on Takilma road and to others whom we have identified as a part of our community in the Illinois Valley and Ashland. Anyone wanting to be added to our mailing list may fill out the form on the back of this issue. As support grows, we will publish monthly, with a deadline for submissions of articles, announcements, classified ads, art, calendar, poetry, etc. on the last day of each month. The cost of each issue for printing and mailing to about 300 addresses is about $300. per issue. So we count on your support. We will not take paid advertising but will charge $3.00-6.00 for classified ads.

Our policy-making body, the Mud Council, operates by the principles of non-hierarchy and consensus process. We are grateful to the Takilma Community Association for financial and moral support in getting started, to the Siskiyou Project for office facilities and technical expertise and to all those amongst us who have made contributions to get us off the ground. Please send us your articles, graphics, calender events, poetry or stories to POB 2016 before Feb 28, 1994.

Contributors to this issue are Adrian, Barry, Dave H, Jill, Felicity, Heller, Dave T., Kayla, Kerry, Laurie, Miguelo, Robin.

MAGICAL MYSTERY TOURS

Takilma Transit is a new bus service available for group outings to various events and adventures. Bruce and Eve recently acquired a 20-passenger older (yet spiffy) school bus and they are making it available for occasional use to transport Takilma folks to special events in S. Oregon. The driver will be carefully selected.

Takilma Transit is taking reservations now for its maiden voyage on Saturday, February 12 to the Mardi Gras Celebration at the Armory in Ashland. Etoufee, an exciting, high-energy Louisiana swamp rock band out of Eugene will be headlining. There will also be African music. Costumes and masks are in order.

The bus will leave Takilma late afternoon and stop for dinner. There is room for up to 20 merry-makers on this 'tour'. The transportation fee is $5.00 to $10.00 sliding scale. For more information and reservations, call Bruce evenings: 592-2872.

SALMON CEREMONIES

Many of you attended one or both of the Salmon Ceremonies held in Takilma in 1993. Agnes Pilgrim, friend and supporter of the Siskiyou Project, created these ceremonies as her way of giving thanks to her Creator and the salmon. For her, it was a homecoming to return to Takilma, land of her ancestors.

The first Ceremony was held in May at Out & About with many thanks to Michael and Jude. About 100 people attended including members of the press. Agnes displayed many of her crafts and was seen that evening on several local TV stations dressed in her full regalia. The atmosphere created was one of reverence and thankfulness. Agnes' husband, Grant, created the fire pit and cooked the salmon. His traditional Native American fire starting method of using a propane blow torch added humor to a wonderful day.

The second Ceremony was less formal. Perhaps this was due to the rain we had in November. Or perhaps Agnes had gotten to know us and feels comfortable here with us. Again, Grant built the fire pit and cooked the Salmon. About 150 people filled the Dome School. Many younger Native Americans from the Ashland area attended and brought their ceremonial drum. Many of us danced ritual dances including the Friendship Dance. The feelings again were of warmth, friendship and kinship.

Agnes' ancestors once lived in the Rogue and Illinois Valleys without destroying the wild. She teaches us a lot about giving thanks, creating culture & ceremonies. Perhaps there is more we can learn.

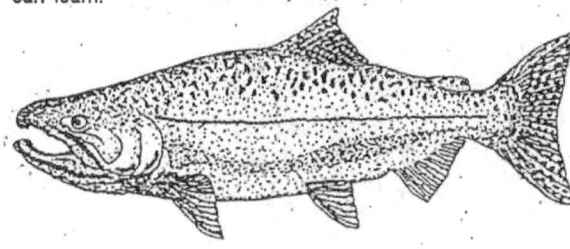

A STORE OF OUR OWN

"Hon, would you run down to the store for some half-n-half. We're running dangerously low." Yes, this will be an option soon here in Takilma. Bruce and Eve are deep into plans for a new store at the site of the old one in 'downtown' Takilma. Construction is expected to be underway this Spring. They are getting lots of enthusiastic support from friends and neighbors which definitely helps move this ambitious project along.

The plan is to build a 24 by 36 foot two-story building with a porch surrounding it. The first floor will have a kitchen, coolers, bulk food bins and shelves. The upstairs will have tables and be a community space with a coffee-house atmosphere.

People who want to help in building and landscaping will be called upon when the time arrives. Your suggestions are welcome.

OPINIONS

In search of...
COMMON GROUND   by Dave Toler

At long last, the dreams and aspirations of many has come to fruition with this first issue of COMMON GROUND. For many of us, the inception of COMMON GROUND is long overdue. For too long, our community has been paralyzed by the hypnotic grip of a Corporate media whose version of " reality " often seems to sharply contradict our own daily experiences.

A central tenet of mainstream media is upholding the myth of competing interests among brothers and sisters within our community and across the globe. For example, the concept of " National interest" is a favorite. Supposedly, you and I have more in common with " fellow-American " corporate executives who pull in a cool $10 million a year than we do with working families in Japan or China who also confront the daily struggle to make ends meet.

Meanwhile within our own communities, the media consistently bombards us with the notion of interests between neighbors so divergent they are beyond understanding and compromise. Blacks vs. whites, straights vs. gays, young vs. old, environmentalists vs. loggers, poor vs. middle class, the list goes on and on.

Yet in real life, at one time or another, many of us find ourselves straddling the artificial line between two " competing interests". It is then we discover there is plenty in common between the two. What we thought were inseparable differences are found to be mere misperception fostered by an effective media shower of lies and distortions.

With economic and political power their exclusive domain, Corporate America benefits greatly from the fragmentation of our communities. United we stand, divided we have fallen! In order that our children might inherit something better, we must search vigorously through a web of myth, to find our own COMMON GROUND.

BEYOND GENDER   By Shannon Rose

The birth of our new baby has been an incredible, special time for us. I imagine every parent of a newborn hopes their child won't have to experience prejudice and discrimination, or be subjected to archaic, limiting beliefs about themselves

The programming that results in gender discrimination begins at birth. Not disclosing the gender of our baby is a statement in support of Awareness... Awareness of the fact that people react differently to the exact same behavior depending on gender. They offer babies different toys, they use different words, and they touch and hold babies differently depending on their gender. It's a statement in support of Awareness of the limitations of gender assumptions.

I wish that people would release from their minds any and all thoughts about gender and see that any individual has the capabilities and the potential of any other human being. A world without gender programming would be a better place for children to grow.

If you'd like to share your thoughts or comments I'd be happy to hear them.- PO Box 1070, CJ 97523.

HOME IMPROVEMENTS   by Miguelo

Even before press time of this tabloid, the holidaze will be behind us, gone. That is till the next Madison Avenue Day of Hype or importance. Gone the celebration, gone the re-union, gone the added food consumption, gone some of the decadence. Today in this column the topic will be that which is not gone. The nightmare that consumer antics create, that is landfill!

I went to two gatherings where either paper or plastic conveniences were used, while washable counterparts sat on nearby shelves. We've all heard those not so intellectual but oh so poignant quips 1) if you're not part of the solution, you're part of the problem; 2) we have met the enemy and they are us; 3) out of sight , out of mind; and 4) asleep at the wheel. Upon examination, this Takilma based reporter sees much truth in all the aforementioned.

Takilma has bonded around fire, medicine & education. All worthy tasks. The purpose of community is to help community. The mid 90's are upon us. New tasks, new areas for application of our strengths are upon us as well. Today's issues like landfill should be met with the same gusto and the same intent to solve the issue at hand.

Once the Kerby landfill becomes a transfer station the price of a dump run will skyrocket! I wonder of those Takilma 'style' abodes that push the word rustic to the limit. How, in already 'wallet chakra' deficient homes will more money be earmarked for dump runs? What in our community constitutes visual inappropriateness? Where is the fine line between rustic and run down? Takilma is a community of artisans, anarchists, parents, teachers, children, elders, sages and fools. Each of us a consumer, each of us with consumer responsibilities! Along with water quality, landfill should be at the vanguard of our immediate and long term issues.

Here are a few easily applied steps that can be useful today. 1) buy bulk or local whenever possible, 2) Each home should have a picnic style basket for pot-lucks, both of which we're fortunate to have lots of, 3) go the extra step to wash and recycle, 4)cut down on consumption period!! Keep in mind Madison Avenue spends millions on strategies and psychology to inform us of what we 'need', and most of the time we do not really need it.

Now with the creation of a local rag Common Ground we have a sound board for local issues long and short term, a forum for local input (your input), a way to coalesce, to express, to challenge, to effect the change. Our pride in Takilma will continue to manifest the strengths necessary for today's community needs.

A PROPOSAL FOR STEWARDSHIP
by Michael Garnier edited by Kayla Starr

Historically, we have had two distinct groups in opposition regarding uses of our forests in the northwest. One group has focused on saving the environment, the other on developing industry.

The E. Fork Illinois is a unique situation. Many of the people who moved to this valley 20 years ago brought sensitive environmental awareness with them. Many of us turned to the forest for our livelihood, establishing a tree-planting co-op, Greenside Up, Inc. Trees were planted, stands were thinned and cones were picked. Stewardship was born.

Now most of us live in wood houses, some of us still rely on the forest for our livelihood, we all depend on the forest ecosystem for our well-being. Without water, no living thing survives. It is in our, and our children's best interest to protect our environment and our economy here. We have a vested interest in what happens here.

Let's explore establishing a formal Stewardship to direct forestry practices in our watershed under the auspices of Option 9. Please contact me for further discussion at 592-2208.

MEET Jim Nordahl, M.D

Our new doctor at Siskiyou Community Health Center (aka Takilma Peoples Clinic) moved to the Illinois Valley last fall with his family . He is now a regular member of our health care team.

Birth place: Salem, Oregon, 1958

Family: wife Ginger, 2 sons, Daniel age 18 months, Celilo, 4 months

Work experience: 2 years working in a lumber mill, a summer flying sky divers

Education: B.S. U. of Oregon, Eugene, Medical school Portland Health Science, 1986, Family Practice Residency,University of Wyoming, Casper, WY.

Interests: Playing with his kids, rockhounding, wood-working, hunting, fishing, knife-making, spinning and reading

Favorite movie (currently): Pow Wow Highway. Diva

Favorite Book (currently): The River Why

Favorite Cartoon: Calvin and Hobbes

Favorite music: Manheim Steamroller, Classic Rock.

Why he chose to live here: Appreciated the dedication of the staff at our health center, familiar with the area, loves living close to nature.

Causes: Helping people assume responsibility for keeping fit and healthy.

Pet peeves: Working on cars, being asked to magically fix the consequences of poor health habits.

ADOPT - A - ROAD

The community clean-ups are going great! New people are joining the program and folks in the community have commented on how much cleaner the roadsides are. It's nice to hear that positive feedback.

It really works to our advantage to do all the cleaning of county and state roads during one 4 day weekend each quarter. All those bags along the roadside have a visual impact, broadcasting a simple advertisement. It's also very helpful to the county and state in organizing the pickup of the bags afterwards. We thank you for promoting solidarity during those 4 selected clean-up days.

The state has asked us to remind each group cleaning state highways to be sure to call in on the following Monday morning to confirm that there are bags for the state to pick up in your adopted section. The phone number is 474-3149.

The trash bags will continue to be available at each gas station the Wed. before the weekend clean-up.

If you know a section of road that needs a caretaker, we hope you won't be shy about spreading the word to friends, groups and organizations.

You're the one that makes this program such a success. Thank you!

NEXT CLEAN-UP   *APRIL 21,22,23 & 24*

NEW YEARS RESOLUTIONS 1994
by Adrian Murillo

Think of your passion as a work of art
with the power to heal & liberate trapped souls.
A thing of beauty & wisdom becoming polished
and perfected over time through continual
expression.

Think of your varied, migrant, episodic life
as a vision of songs & murmurs standing far
apart from the bitter jealous voices
telling you why you must stop. Remember:
Solitude is the root note in a compositional life.

Think of time as the education of your senses
blossoming fresh beginnings from the friendship
of your body guiding you back to a graceful
state of being.

Think of your love - so large and continuous
only sound can fill it - and be true to it.
Sing with the mother tongue of tenderness of the
brutal yet simple facts of your life so others
may gain strength to live fearlessly & love openly.

There is no growth without desire. No juice as
sweet as human connection.
Enjoy living. It's the essence of life.

GREEN BRIDGE   by Adrian Murillo

Everyone is naked, moving with balanced wildness.
A young mother & baby sit at waters edge.
Boys and girls play jump and dive off boulders.
A slender young man, a cosmic bamboo sort,
meanders in, meanders out.

Their freedom seduces the pain from my eyes.
Like an alien from another universe
or a scientist of revolution consumed with research.
I shamelessly search their bodies,
reading their histories, their quiet thoughts,
like sheet music.
Hungry to hear my secret language
coming back to me.

My language improvises meaning into my pain.
Smooths it out like river over rocks.
My life is a glittering bridge of golden moments suspended in
    space,
connecting nothing.

6

GARDENING by Beth Peterson

Gardening in the Upper E. Fork Illinois River (aka Takilma) can present some special challenges. Whether you have the widespread Takilma cobbly loam or the more widespread Takilma loamy cobbles your soil will definitely need some work. Then there are those pockets of clay that turn to cement if tilled while wet and sometimes won't dry out until summer. Whatever your soil is like, even the best dirt will yield disappointing results if crops are not planted on the right date, so we'll focus here on planting dates that experience has shown to give good results in our area. Dates recommended herein do not relate in any way to astrological considerations such as moon sign phase, etc. Whatever the benefits of such methods may be its tricky to put them into practice. While waiting for the moon sign change, your nice dry tillable ground can be turned to muck by a spring rainstorm.

Even though the gardening season is at its low point and days are at their shortest, our climate is mild enough that with some planning there can be vegies out there all year. Big over-wintering cabbages and kale resist all but the worst of winters as do the leeks, beets, parsnips and carrots.

One of the easiest ways to extend the gardening season through the winter is to grow salad greens in an unheated coldframe or greenhouse. Even a small (15-20 Sq. foot) area planted on October 1st with looseleaf lettuce (Black seeded Simpson, Ruby) pac choi, spinach, cilantro, parsley and endive will produce significant salads all winter long. This fall planting of greens does become a bit threadbare and tends to go to seed towards spring, so one needs a second planting in an additional area to maintain vegie continuity. New Years day is a good target date for this second planting and these plants will be growing vigorously just as the first ones are fading away. If you grew a supply of 'longkeeper' tomatoes last summer you can now have homegrown lettuce and tomato salads all winter long and into April!

Other worthy wintertime agricultural activities include: Pruning all woody perennials (fruit trees, berries, grapes, ornamentals) hopefully before March 15th. Cover compost and manure piles to shield them from winter rains which can quickly leach out the majority of available nutrients.

Refrain from tilling or cultivating during winter months. Bare soil is vulnerable to intense storms and much of the available nutrients can be lost in a short time during heavy rains. Even weeds make a good cover crop that help lock in fertility.

TAKILMA GOOD FOOD NEWS
by Marcy Tilton
Marinated Tofu

I first experienced this version of marinated tofu at Green's restaurant in San Francisco where it is offered grilled in a sandwich or in vegetable brochettes. Firm tofu is recommended, but the soft variety absorb flavors beautifully and break up into small succulent bits in a stir fry, soup or sandwich. Marinate up to 5 days for the "big taste", but even a few hours add a delicate tang. The marinade can be strained and used again after short soaks. Marinated tofu is good baked whole, sauted whole or in cubes, and reaches the sublime whine grilled on a barbecue. Cubed tofu is fabulous in a stir fry or added to fresh vegetable soups.

Ingredients:
1-2 pounds tofu
1/2 ounce dried wild mushrooms (shitaki, porcini or black.)
  Note: This pricey ingredient adds a subtle yet rich flavor, but can be eliminated.
2 teaspoons dried oregano or marjoram (if fresh, use more)
1/2 cup olive oil

1/2 cup sherry vinegar	4 whole cloves
1/2 cup red wine	1/2 teaspoon salt
1/2 cup tamari	black pepper to taste

Begin with 1 inch slabs of tofu. Drain, set on a board or plate, cover with another weighted plate for 1/2 hour or more to remove excess water. This allows the marinate to penetrate. Prepare marinade while tofu is draining. Simmer mushrooms in water to cover for 15 minutes. Presoaking mushrooms is optional. If you do, strain and re-use soaking water to simmer. Toast the oregano or marjoram in a small heavy skillet until fragrance is released but not burned. Add to remaining ingredients, bring to a boil and simmer slowly 5 minutes or more. Mushrooms may be chopped or left whole.

Place drained tofu in a glass, ceramic or stainless flat pan, one layer deep. Pour marinade over tofu. Cover with plastic or lid and refrigerate. If the weather is cool, room temperature works. Marinate the tofu for 3 hours to 4-5 days.

This is the basic formula. Try these variations and combinations: Sherry vinegar and sherry instead of wine. 1/2 sherry, 1/2 mirin (Japanese cooking wine), rice wine vinegar, canola oils and sesame oil and red pepper flakes. 1/2 red wine vinegar, balsamic vinegar, lots of slivered garlic.

RUNNING BROTHERS WEATHER
by Robert, Doug and Kerry

This column will be dedicated to the "fools and Californians" among us who try to predict the weather. The Running Brothers, who make appointed rounds at 7:20 AM a couple of times a week are certainly among these people since what is happening to the atmosphere at that moment occupies a major portion of their conversation. Also look for the semaphore railroad signal as you round the curve heading out of town. A foolish station master, who ought to know better, sets green-arm extended upward for fair, sunny skies and red-arm outward for rain. Fortunately, there is a mid-point yellow for that partly cloudy, partly sunny, with periods of partial clearing weather which tends to prevail more than any other.

Finally we would appreciate feed back as to whether the drought years brought a decline in summer grasshoppers or not. Doug thinks there is a correlation, Kerry isn't sure, and Robert just hasn't ever had enough of a hopper invasion to notice one way or the other.

Coming soon to this space, various theories concerning the origin and effects of El Nino

6

6

HERE COMES THE SUN, LITTLE DARLINGS
By Felicity Elworthy

Trips to the drive-in, dances at the community building and twice yearly treks to our local medicine circle satisfy most of my ritual needs.. None of these venues has much to recommend it from the strictly religious point of view, but I haven't been strictly religious for about thirty years now. Ever since I was baptized, aged 12, in the lukewarm waters of the baptismal pool concealed beneath the sober sisal matting of the chapel on Hampstead Road. Dripping wet, surrounded by the assembled brethren and sisters, none of whom made eye contact with anything but their hymn books, my heart expanded with horrified, exultant knowledge. Transcendence is smoke and mirrors. God, who is love, is also an irretrievable male and He will continue to be, at best, emotionally unavailable and at other times, royally pissed off.

For the next two decades I bumped into ecstasy in exclusively secular contests. Dropping acid for the first time, alone in a funky trailer on a wild Welsh night of storm; I crawled under the eiderdown, fearing fear, and crawled back out in time to watch the heavens boil, radiant, apart. I learnt touch at the hands of an apricot colored fertility goddess from Oakland and taste and smell in a multitude of vivid kitchens from the boiled cabbage and bangers of home to saabzi and abgusht in the Tajrish bazaar at the noisy end of Ramadan. I learned to look at things--water, shadows--for a long time, in order to see where they began or ended. Transcendence was great sex, the first wood anemones in spring, the more incisive whine of Bob Dylan.

Later on I met Dianne, the angel of tofu, who magicked perfect cloudlike curds night after night in the noisy commune-factory in St. Ignatius, Montana. She had arrived there from Teaneck, New Jersey where she had a whole other black-and-purple life. There was a church she wanted to go to in Missoula, so I tagged along, just to be with her. She has steady eyes the size of jawbreakers and her spirit is like the color of a light spring breeze. We all sat in a circle on ugly fold-up chairs and translated the gospel according to St. John as if it were in a foreign language, or someone else's dream. "There is a light", it said, "which lighteth every one that cometh into the world". That needed no translation and was straight out of my own dream. Must have read it a hundred times before without knowing it was there. I cried hard, dazzled by healing fireworks as the past lost it's hard edges and gave something back.

I was curious about these middle-class, middle-aged, blissed-out people who acknowledged no contradictions in their behavior. Who were welcoming and sincere with hippies, fundamentalists, Buddhists, criminals. They seemed to think you could have your cake and eat it too. They believed love to be more powerful than evil. They didn't actually believe in evil at all. I tried it out, tentatively and for several months was convinced there was no danger in the world. This was long enough to fall in love, and everything after that was life threatening. Babies, and wholly falling in love with babies. Marriage; I will love you, and only you, forever. Despair: I chose to do this. Pain: this is real pain, again. Mystery: there is mystery at the heart of everything. Emerging from this deep dream, I concluded that the mystery at the heart of everything and the periodic table of elements had much in common. Every day I remade god in my own image, mineral, female, mostly water, irreducible, whatever.....

Twice a year now in June and December, some of us walk to the top of a ridge in Takilma to observe the sun rise on the summer and winter solstice. The medicine circle as it is called, has at it's center a small ring of stones and a crouching tree. Over the last ten years people have taken a variety of quaint, beautiful, humble objects up there and left them, along with candle stumps and garden produce. For the last few years I have rasped my way up the ridge, wondering what might happen. It's always a little different. This year the circle has been in the news. Some people we don't know went there and changed things around a bit. My friends straightened up the terrain and had a few laughs, then a week or two later more things were disturbed or disappeared. My friends left in place the old T-shirt that has been there for years, but is now inscribed in charcoal with this text--"Bind the devil in you through the Lord Jesus Christ". It is still hanging there.

This solstice there was a big crowd; amazing what a little publicity can do. We jiggled and hugged; cracked jokes, were silent; smiled. This group re-makes ritual, spontaneously, often. We faced east and watched the trees on the horizon sizzle like a burnt film as the sun rose behind them. It was still cold. We took tobacco ties to release the past and someone else served wish-water, thinking more of the yet-to-come. A Ziploc bag of dried fruit made the rounds. The dates were especially well received. We chanted a catchy native american number and sang the first two lines - memory loss - of "Here Comes the Sun". Comfortable, silent people, and at least one who left in the middle of something, without a ripple. People stomped and shuffled and talked about death, the weather; all my relations. I pinned a tiny flying angel, probably plastic, on the T-shirt in the tree. I had no thoughts about the past or wished for the future. I watched the faces of my friends and neighbors and children and I saw the sun come up in glory.

Up there no-one inquires what you believe in; it matters utterly, and it matters not at all. Down here, I am curious about who saw fit to add to and take from our circle, and why. Toleration is most potent when it knows in detail what diversity it is that it encompassed and remains openhearted notwithstanding.

THE ASHLAND CORNER by Heller

Ashland, or Takilma East, as I think of it, has it's own social orbit, but one that often intersects with the one around Takilma.

The fund-raising drive for Holly Sincerny is a little over half-way to it's $200,000 goal. Holly has received bone marrow transplants to help her overcome the rare cancer that attacked her body. She has responded incredibly well, and looks healthier everyday. We're thinking of you Holly.

We have some world travelers in our midst. Gloria will be off to Vietnam in January, Roxy and Aja to Bali, Leslie Van Gelder is applying for a stint in the Peace Corps and will go in Sept. if accepted. Her 1st choice is a Spanish speaking country. Janie and Neal are vacationing in Mexico for a couple of weeks, and Mary Beth, Ry and I just came back from a trip to Costa Rica.....a very beautiful country, especially the Northern Highlands around the volcanoes. Unfortunately there is a feeling that Americans are slowly turning it into their playground and in the process will probably destroy a lot of the native charm. What else is new!

And the next generation: Obie, Ester's son is off to work in Antarctica until March, when he will explore the South Pacific. It is rumored that mom may spread her wings and head South also to check out the Penguins. Molly, Jenica, Ben and Zephyr are all seniors in high school this year and are starting to figure our which college to aim for— Good Luck you guys!! Molly was Student of the Month for November. She and Jenica are planning a summer graduation spree through Europe.........ahhh those were the days.

The Parker-Shames, aside from colds, are doing well. Jim is taking medicine to treat his Gauchiers disease (it affects joints and bones). The twinkies are growing big and strong. Big brother Simon is looking at the prospect of being the starting soccer goalie maybe this next season at Ashland High. Wear a face mask Si.

In January Mary Beth will be starting her second year at the Hahneman College of Homeopathy. Dr Paul is back at school going for a Masters in Public Health......oh those perpetual students!

Couple of good reads: The Brothers K by Duncan. and The River Why. A good mystery is "Lizardskin" by Carsten Stroud.

Upcoming Ashland Events:

Barn Dance....Second Saturday of every month at Walker Elementary School.

Tumbadora....Feb.5 Local Conga drummers at Community Center on Winburn Way.

One World-Performances from around the World.

Obo Addy.....Feb. 26, Saturday SOSC Recital Hall

Carlos Nakai....Mar 31, Thurs. SOSC Recital Hall

For tickets to one World Performances call 503-552-6461

SREP by Barry Snitkin

1993 was a year of many changes and accomplishments for Siskiyou Project (SREP). In June we moved our office to the former Takilma People's Clinic site. We invite you to stop in and visit us soon. Sadly we said goodbye to Shel Anderson, who did such a wonderful job of keeping our office together. We will miss her. Beth Howell is also leaving our staff but we hope she'll return in the spring. Kelpie Wilson and Lou Gold have traded in their staff status and are now serving on our Board of Directors. We welcome our newest staff member, Steve Marsden. He will be the Project Coordinator. The remaining staff include Cathy Hocker, Rich Nawa, Barbara Ullian, Barry Snitkin, Debbie Lukas and Marjorie Reynolds. Additionally, Romain Cooper and Dennis Eucalyptus have joined our board.

As we begin 1994 the future of both the Ancient Forests and the Siskiyou is still uncertain. The Clinton administration has promised to "protect spotted owls and other species" while also promising to "deliver the timber volume". It is difficult, if not impossible, to do both. Scientists from across the country came up with 8 proposed forest plan options. None of them proposed a high enough timber volume for the Administration so they came up with 2 more options and selected Option 9. Under it, much of our roadless areas are not protected and up to 40% of the remaining old growth can be cut down. In response to Option 9 the Forest Service received more than 100,000 comments. Our grassroots network generated about 10% of these comment letters. It is safe to say that no other area received this level of support.

In spite of tremendous nationwide support, the Siskiyous remain at imminent risk under Option 9. However, we are determined to keep the Siskiyous wild! We also intend to remain active in the local community working for the restoration of the Illinois River and the salmon. In both of these arenas, we need your help.

We recently received monthly pledges of between $5-10 from several local community members. This is an almost painless way to support us. Please join these folks by calling Cathy or Barry at 592-4459. Remember, your donations are critical and enable us to continue working for the forest.

We also need of volunteers in our office. Please call Barry.

Enclosed is my contribution of:

$10. ◯ 1 year subscription

$25. ◯ 1 year subscription + Takilma mug + one bottle of Aura Polish

$50.+ ◯ 1 year subscription + Takilma mug + we'll omit the Aura Polish

◯ I'm broke but literate. Please send me the newsletter

☐ Please remove my name from the mailing list

Name_____

Address_____

_____

TAKILMA COMMON GROUND   POB 2016   Cave Junction, Or 97523

KID'S WORLD

FLOWERS by Shanti Birmingham (age 5)

Roses are red
Airadee said.
Flowers grow
Flowers sing.
Flowers glow in the dark,
Flowers grow in the night-
Sing!

I'M SCARED by Ida Madsen

Not scared because I'm alone in the world
Not scared because my parents caught me sneaking out
Not scared like a child whose mother
forgot to close the closet door before
she turned out the lights and is now
about to be engulfed by the terror of his own imagination

But just scared that I will someday
be in eternal darkness, always wondering,
and never knowing what's right in front of me.
Scared that I'm not alone in this world
and that some crazy bastard will have a bad day
and take it out on me by blowing
my brains out.
scared that even if I sneak out and my
parents catch me, they don't care
enough to do anything about it.
scared that even if I try my hardest
to do everything right, I will still
turn out just as stupidly insane as
the next person.

MUSIC REVIEW by jon jeans

I'm enjoying a rainy day listening to Bruce Marsh's wonderful tape, "Siskiyou". The cassette comes complete with liner notes written by George Shook who tells us that these are "first of all songs of place". The songs smoothly alternate between slow and fast. Bruce is backed instrumentally by HiJinks, long time friends who are a must to see whenever possible. The instrumentation consisting of acoustic guitar, stand up bass, mandolin, fiddle and banjo is excellent throughout. The solos are melodic and building, leading the songs between verses like old friends hand in hand. In particular, the mandolin and fiddle are exquisite.

Bruce wrote all of the songs with the exception of "Takilma Shuffle" which was written by George Shook. The songs carry strength and melodic opportunities for both the musicians and Bruce's personable singing. "Hippo Park" is a biting & rollicking comic tale of a young entrepreneur. On a more serious local note is the "Fire of '87" which creates enough ambience to make me feel as if I was there (as most of you were). A Cowboy's Lullaby" is a beautiful tune with the enchanting chorus regarding belching bovines. The fiddle solo toward the end of the song takes me back to a time when life was slower. Finally, Smokey and Bigfoot" contains a little of it all, a wonderful song structure, environmentally potent lyrics, a confident vocal and great string work by HiJinks.

Overall, this is a vibrant and important collection of songs. The tape is well produced and packaged. Treat yourself to this one and pass one on to your loved ones. It is available at The Barn, 9710 Takilma Road or through Siskiyou Project.

DOME SCHOOL by Oshana

The Dome School's major fundraising events have been quite successful this year, with our Holiday Bazaar proceeds exceeding all previous years. Miguel and River helped the kids make great crafts to sell. If you have special talents that you would like to share with some really neat kids, come in and let's talk about who we can work together.

Currently our enrollment stands at 13 children in preschool, with Helen and Alison teaching. Helen, Laurie and Oshana are working with 18 kids in the full kindergarten class, and Deborah and Katherine are team teaching 15 students and the multi-aged elementary class. Robin comes in on Thursday afternoons to explore many dimensions of drama and creativity with the elementary class.

Friday afternoons we have music classes with Judy Axtell. If you haven't been to the Community Building recently, come over and take a peek at our remodeled kitchen and office. Special thanks to Robin for the inspiration and coordination overseeing these wonderful building improvements. Our upcoming events are listed on the enclosed calendar. We are always happy for your help with coordinating these events.

CLASSIFIED

'57 Chevy Pick-up w/camper shell parts $150.00 592-4196

Delicious organic canned fruits, grape juice, organic fruit pies and honey to order   592-3783 Celesta

Glass front woodstove, takes small logs, heats small space $150 592-2492

Kawasaki 400 Motorcycle, not running, parked 2 years, needs minor mechanical $150   592-2492

Handyman seeks to expand Takilma Clientele. Good work, merciful rates. Beaucoups references. 5 9 2 - 2 4 9 2 Dave

Office space for rent, downtown Takilma call Cathy at Siskiyou Project   592-4459

Investment opportunity: 1937 O'Keefe & Merritt gas stove. Needs restoration. $150. Potential value- $800.   592-4275 Kayla

Exciting cooking classes by Chef Sandi Richardson. Studied at Cordon Bleu, France. Feb. 5th Hearty Soup, Feb 12th Northwest   Cuisine,
   $50 ea. class plus food fee. Lots of samples to take home. 592-2669

PERSONALS

Arachnaphobia support group now forming. Call Charlotte Webb 592-7000

Active straight comic strip couple seeks same. Color or Black & White. Send photos or drawings. Herb & Yoni ICU 81, c/o Common Ground P.S. Gumby or Dick Tracy types need not apply.

SWM, mini talents, into flying, telekinesis, good-samaritanism: Kent Clark 592-8765.

ANNOUNCEMENTS

I'm stuck in prison. Please write me and let me know what is happening in the world, if anything. It's lonely here.

Write to : Michael Menge
7251106
Oregon State Penitentiary,
2605 State St.
Salem Or 97310-0505

Announcements are services rendered for free or people needing help. We will print them for free.

COMMON GROUND
POB 2016
CAVE JUNCTION, OR 97523

Issue #2

A community newsletter

March-April '94

STOP BEAR AND COUGAR KILLERS
by Debbie Lukas

VOLUNTEERS ARE NEEDED! Hunting black bears and cougars with dog packs and bait stations in the early spring are all lawful and common practice in Oregon. Colorado voters recently approved a referendum to ban the practices of houndhunting, baiting and spring hunting for black bear. If this can be stopped in Colorado, we can do it in Oregon. According to the Oregon Department of Fish and Wildlife, 1,150 black bears were legally killed by sporthunters in 1991. Many wildlife experts assume that at least that number were poached during the same time period, primarily for black market exportation of bear parts to Asia. Houndhunting, using packs of dogs equipped with radio-telemetry collars, is the "most effective method" of hunting bear and cougar, according to ODFW. This unethical method often separates mother bears from their cubs, usually dooming those cubs to death by predation or starvation.

From a biological perspective, current black bear and cougar hunting management in Oregon is unsound for two obvious reasons. First, hunters and poachers do not emulate natural selection. Generally, the biggest and strongest animals are killed for trophies and body parts, leaving the weaker animals to restock the gene pool. Black bears and cougars are not preyed upon in the wild, except in extremely rare situations. Second, the ODFW has no concrete population data on black bears and cougars at this time.

The Oregon Bear and Cougar Coalition is working to place an initiative on the November Ballot that will ban bear baiting and the use of hounds in hunting bears and cougars. Volunteers are needed. Contact Debbie Lukas at Siskiyou Project, 592-4459 before March 30.

TEENS
by Marjorie Reynolds

We need to get together all interested parties who would like to offer our teens direction and skills to start their own cottage industry or get employment and training. Robin Wren has already begun a process where crafts people share their skills. Perhaps we can join this process and organize apprenticeship and craft workshops Please call or write Marjorie if interested in this project . 4443 Waldo Rd., Cave Jct., Or. 97523   592-6733

TO YOUR HEALTH
by Kayla Starr and Meadow Martell

The Oregon Health Plan is finally in effect. You may be eligible for its benefits. This health plan is the outcome of a grassroots organizing effort begun six years ago by the southern chapter of Oregon Fair Share. The much publicized national health reform plan that the Clinton administration is pushing aims for the same goal as the Oregon plan and is encountering massive resistance from the entrenched and powerful insurance, hospital and physician lobbies. Hopefully, the new Oregon Health Plan will show the rest of the country that health care is a social responsibility that can be addressed by public agencies.

How can you plug in? Applications are available at Siskiyou Community Health Center and staff member Nancy Lyford is there to answer your questions. You may also call the State's information number to learn more and have applications sent at 1-800-359-9517. During the first week of operation, they received over 16,000 calls. As one might predict, the agency is overwhelmed already.

.   The first stage of the program is designed to cover only 120,000 new people, far fewer than the number who need it. However, all who want to apply are encouraged to do so in order to demonstrate the real level of need.   There are special application forms available for the self-employed. Eligibility includes all those already covered by Medicaid plus any individual or family whose income is below the Federal Poverty Level. For a family of 4, this amount is $1195 per month; for an individual it is $580 per month. Pregnant women and families with children under age 6 with an income of less than 133% of the Federal Poverty Guidelines are also eligible. You must be a U.S. citizen or a resident alien--(that should include lots of us!)

The Plan covers most medical expenses including diagnosis and treatment of most disorders (excluding those which get better without medical intervention and those for which there is no useful treatment), preventive services, family planning, vision, hearing and dental care, prescriptions, hospice and emergency services. All services will be administered through approved Managed Care Organizations. You choose a primary care physician within the Organization who treats you and refers you to the other services you may need. Our own Siskiyou Community Health Center is an approved provider under Family Care and although the staff is still gearing up, they are there to steer us through the new system. You may reach Nancy Lyford at the clinic, 592-6444 . Also the state is holding an informational meeting on March 29 at 2:30 at the City Hall in beautiful downtown Cave Junction.

DIGGIN' IN
Gardening tips by Mark 'n Beth

Frequent late frosts make growing fruit in our watershed a real challenge. There are some types of trees that can be productive if planted on a good site and given care. Trees that we feel are worth growing here are: apples; European plums (green gage, French prune, Italian prune); sour or pie cherries (Montmorency); and pears (Bartlett). On best sites; frost and curl resistant peaches and Japanese plums (Satsumas). Forget about sweet cherries, apricots, figs, persimmons and citrus unless you just want to experiment and/or enrich the nursery industry.

Apples are the only fruit trees that are unquestionably productive in Takilma. We think the all around best apples for this area are those which exhibit a growth habit called "tip-bearing." These varieties open their flowers a few at a time over a 2 week stretch. Often some blooms get lunched by a frost but the long bloom period greatly increases the odds of a crop. Tip bearing varieties such as "King" and "Melrose" seldom fail to produce a crop for us. They also produce high quality, large fruit that keep well and have some tolerance to scab. Some varieties which are totally immune to scab and several other diseases are "Prima," "Priscilla", and "Liberty". Though they are not as late blooming as the tip-bearers, they ripen earlier and so lengthen the apple harvest season.

It may be controversial, but we recommend the planting of full-sized (standard) trees. Dwarf and semi-dwarfs are trees that never really grow up and are proportionately dependent on you for their survival. Standard trees develop adult-tree root systems for probing deep for water and nutrients, far more capable than their dwarfed cousins. Several varieties can be grafted onto each tree and it's not difficult if done at the proper time of year (just before buds open). We have scion wood for many kinds of apple (free) and even some seedling trees. If anyone is interested they can call us at 592-2311.

ASHLAND CORNER
by Dan Heller 2-26-94

So here we are, Ashland Corner, round two.

Well, Roxy and Aja are back from Bali with stories and great tans. . .

Some of our next generation (a Majeski and a Parker-Shames) are working on another "Odyssey of the Mind" project with Jim Shames as advisor. It's called Fur, Fins and Feathers. The kids have to write and perform a script around an animal they have created. They chose Sassy the dog (a perverted Lassie). They will compete locally and hope to advance to the state level and maybe beyond. Kate and Nathan: Keep barkin' up the trail.

Talked to Rabbit the other day. She says she's almost 100% healed from her skydiving fall. . . she claims that good sex and lots of it (only with her boyfriend, of course) has helped her make a quick recovery. Don't wear him out, Rabbit!

Here's a tip for you urban dwellers on how to save a few bucks. Paul and Janie, neighbors on 8th street, have become garbage mates, sharing the same garbage can and splitting the $12 a can price. Janie says its the cleanest relationship she's ever had.

By the way, Larrissa Stewart is now a married woman. She and her man Stu tied the knot a few months ago.

A sighting has been made - who is the tall, dark and handsome package that Esther has been seen with recently? If you know, drop me a card.

And the younger generation. . . Asa Van Gelder is snow-boarding and working in Telluride, Colorado this winter with ideas for a Europe trip this summer. Maybe he'll run into Molly and Jenica.

Paul, Priscilla, Mary, Dan, Nancy, Ben, Patti and Paul all just came back from a big ski trip to Utah. I hear they had a great time on the slopes.

Heller went in for knee surgery on March 1st. OH, BOY!

If you like the macabre, check out Ann Rice's Vampire Series. And Skookum by Shannon Applegate is a wonderful read about our pioneer ancestors.

POP'S 911 SALAD DRESSING from Paco's Dad through Marcy

This could not be easier to make. It's delicious, contains very little oil, and kids love it. Use in any salad combination.
9 parts rice wine vinegar (sweetened in the original, unsweetened is good too)
1 part sesame oil
1 part Hoisin sauce
Grated ginger; 1 - 2 knobs, peeled. More if you like ginger, Pop says it is almost impossible to use too much.
Mix and refrigerate. Flavors blend and improve over time.

HISTORY, CULTURE, AND NATIVE WISDOM: AN INTERVIEW WITH AGNES PILGRIM

By Barry Snitkin

The following conversation took place on December 19, 1993. This is the first in a two part series.

B.. Aggie, please tell us who you are.

A.. I'm a registered member of the Confederated Tribes of Siletz which obscured my identity as to my Tribe because I'm a Rogue River Indian of the Takelma band. Many people thought that the Takelma Indians were no more. My grandfather, Chief George Harney was the last full blood. He and his people lived all along the Rogue River, the Illinois and parts of the Applegate.

B..Why were your people killed or forced to leave their land?

A..In the early 1850's there was an issuance to exterminate the Indian people because the miners had found gold along these rivers which my people occupied. This created quite a problem for my people. We were put into a reservation between the upper and lower Table Rocks, then moved to Agnes. The last major war occurred at big bend on the Rogue. Many tried to escape and they were killed instantly. My grandfather signed a treaty at Agnes. He said "We'll fight with you no more if you let us stay on our land." He was told "This is not your land." Then they were surrounded and taken to reservations, they weren't allowed to go home or get any of their things, they could only take one bag. Quite a few of my people walked on that "trail of tears" over rough terrain in all kinds of inclement weather to Port Orford. Many died from sickness and exposure. In Port Orford many tried to escape. The men were killed, the women were chased down in the streets, raped and murdered. Then they were taken north to the Siletz Reservation, a 200 mile trip. Many drowned and many died of thirst and starvation. Reaching there, they were promised land, housing, food and clothing, which was very little. They were out in the cold, there was no homes for all of them. They were surrounded at all times by cavalry and told that if they tried to escape they'd be shot. It was very hard for them to survive where there was no deer and the food was scarce. Much of the food was inedible. There were about 32 bands there at that time. They elected my grandfather, George Harney, Chief of the Confederated Tribes of Siletz. He worked for the people to get them to stop warring and fighting other wise I wouldn't be sitting here today. He met with the Priest out of Grande Ronde. He thought that maybe this was a way to save the people. He took them to be baptized in the Catholic Church and he was the first convert. Then they built the Church at Siletz.

B.. How did this affect the people and the culture?

A.. Many of the people didn't like it and was sad. My mother also thought going to the church would be a better way. When she was a young lady her parents told her to forget her language and her culture because the world would be easier for her if she did that. We went to the Catholic Church and the Indian school where we were forbidden to speak our language, do our culture or have anything to do with it. That made it very difficult for me to come back and reconnect with a culture that was taken away

B.. How did your tribe's cultural ways reemerge ?

A.. When I was young the cultural ways came back to Siletz. Many people were concerned with hanging on to the old ways. Some of the old people were still alive and knew the way to dress and to make these things and so we began to make our things. When I was just a teenager, I came on to some of our culture. *But to this day it has been very difficult for me to speak of my ancestors. I know they thought they were doing right but the thing that really hurt me was that we weren't allowed to hang on to our language.* The church and schools wouldn't allow it. I kept up with the culture over the years and all my children are kept in with the culture and in the traditions. I am very happy to say that my people, the old ones, left us with a great heritage. I feel rewarded that when I pass to the other world that they will continue to keep the traditions and the culture growing; this is very important to me.

B..How did you end up in California?

A..I came to Crescent City to take care of my older sister. I met my husband and we got married. I'm still over there but who knows, maybe soon I'll be moving back to my tribal grounds. I love my tribal grounds. It's a peaceful thing that comes over me when I'm back where my people used to live. I belong there. I didn't really feel like I belonged in Siletz.

B.. How do you see your role in the world?

A.. I am like Johnny Appleseed spreading culture and talking about the environment. We are caretakers and mother earth needs us to watch out for her because if the environment goes, so goes all people. We have to take care of our mother earth or we all perish. We have to back up and stop thinking about finances and think about what we are destroying. We're all connected , the trees, the rocks, the rivers, the earth, and all life. We depend upon one another for survival and we need to keep that foremost in our minds at all times. I have a sense that when my people lived here it was very pristine and the rivers were the same, you know they were unchallenged by man, they were left in that natural setting. They only took what they needed. We've become a throw-away society. We think something is good for us, or profitable so we use more and more and forget that there is a saturation point.

B.. How do you feel being an elder of the Takelma tribe?

A.. I feel fortunate to have grown up to be grey headed and an elder. Not many of my people a long time ago lived that long. I hope that I have many years to give to this world the gifts the Creator has given me. I'm older now than my mother was when she passed away. There's only two brothers I have left. There used to be nine of us. We're kind of shrinking but I don't feel bad and I don't feel frightened of the other world. I feel like I have so much left to offer, so much to give to the people. Not only to the people but to my own children and my great-grandchildren that are coming. I want to point them in a direction in a good way and a good path.

PIECES OF SOUP
by Jon Jeans

Timothy, the one-eyed laideler, poured me a steaming bowl of gruel out of the giant cast iron brewing pot. "Thank you" I quietly let slip as I grabbed a spoon out of the adjoining silverware compartments. I rushed back to my table to share my bowl with my friend Brian.

Brian has been clinically, socially, and emotionally insane for the past four years. His visit had been disturbing, a break in the continous flow of happy go lucky days I had become so accustomed to. His blonde hair shone clean, as if the chemicals he ingested everyday to help him think somewhat straight, to sedate him, also acted as a bleach. His head was constantly bobbing back in forth in rhyme, ticking like a grandfather clock.

"Hope ya like the soup." I offered. He nodded and drifted off back into another time and space when thinking wasn't so difficult. The soup was chicken noodle, full of carrots and celery, a surprisingly hearty meal for the college cafeteria renowned for its thriftiness.

Brian kept the spoon in rotation, bowl to mouth, bowl to mouth, and back again and again in perfect timing. He blew on each of the first ten spoonfuls until assured that the soup had cooled in the bowl. The taste of the hot soup and the cold milk beside it seemed to bring a smile to his face.

"Do ya remember, do ya remember Jonny?" He begged me with urgency and a curled lower lip.

"What?" I awoke, startled, "Remember what?"

"The chicken soup, the fine chicken soup we slurped down on the beach in Florida, do ya remember?" He pleaded. Memories had become painful to him, offering hope that often went unfulfilled. His memories had become distorted with dreams and hospital hallucinations; reality rested somewhere in between but the middle ground had long since been mowed.

"I remember, my friend." I assured him. "Down at the Sebastian Inlet, Mikey Z surfing the days away, us just sitting, getting tan between riding the waves. I remember the good times my friend, we were there together."

Brian said "Yea" over and over again before drifting back to the soup coagulating on the table. "Ya know Jonny, I'm gonna go thank that man, the chef brother, for making this kickin soup." He gleamed.

That look was back in his eye, the look of old when he was simply funny and eccentric, not purely crazy. Perhaps simply before we realized his condition. He got up and took the bowl back for more, his hands were pasty and trembling, the medication often gave him the jitters.

As he took his next few steps the bowl slipped and fell, smashing into hundreds of pieces all over the floor of the cafeteria. Faces turned, pumpkinlike in their glaze. Brian's jaw just dropped, his composure leaked and dripped like too many faucets. I tried to offer assistance but he was gone, long gone into past memories. Memories swirled into dreams and back, his mind became blank. Brian was hopeless, begging for help, help only he could offer to himself. But he was unable and simply sat on the floor and counted the many pieces, saying "Yea" over and over again before finally asking for glue. But the pieces were too scattered and numerous to ever come perfectly together again.

ADVICE TO TEENAGERS
by Felicity Elworthy

Do not sell drugs at school. You face expulsion.
Buying them is safer.
Did we forget to tell you, knowledge is responsibility?
Did we forget to ask you, what is it safe for you to know?
We are not as street smart as we used to be
And neither do we have the wisdom
We assumed would come with age
After the rules changed
After the dreams came true
After the shadow came out of the bag
When our bodies would become our selves
When our selves would be our own
When our revolution would be over
When the cops would know less and the people know better
Now the cops know more and the judges care less.
We are living in the wild west, wearing cheap sunglasses,
Pretending to be Indians, working for the government
With one foot in the grave
And one foot in our mouths
And one foot following the other down the garden path.

You are out there in the drug and sex war of your time
AIDS and addictions are your adversaries
You are correspondents in a foreign language
Sent out blithe with a handful of rubbers
And a pocketful of home truths.
Your fond parents evade some taxes
Do illegal drugs in moderation
Build additions without permits
Recognise an unjust law at twenty paces
And sniff out vile dictatorships an ocean and a half away.
They know how to steal this book
But insist you pay full price
And look the cashier in the honest eye.
We are something less than true and more than half alive
Forgive us, for we do not know, we trust in things half seen.
The truth we thought would set us free
May yet bind all our children.

Negative Speak
by Chris Casas

Can'ts and Won'ts
Doubts and Fears
Tell such a tale
Over the Years
It's easily read
In furrowed brow
In piercing eye
And hardset jaw.

TAKILMA COMMUNITY BUILDING

MAINTENANCE: Last summer a wonderful group of about twenty people participated in a much needed maintenance day at our community building. The numerous projects they undertook ranged from felling trees to fixing the water fountain, and everything else in between. In addition, thanks to Robin Wren , Kenny Houck, Kerry Holman, Dave Hocker, Dave McKechnie and Michael Heon, the kitchen and office were also completely renovated.

In spite of all this great energy, wear and tear on the building continues to create more maintenance work and there are several large and splendid new projects that will require our time and resources over the next five years.

The newly re-activated Takilma Building Committee is addressing both of these concerns as part of its new agenda. Part of the mission is "to maintain and enhance the Takilma Community Building. To raise and administer funds for the maintenance and enhancement of the building and to create a community based volunteer force to oversee the maintenance of the building. We are a support group for the Dome School Board which has the responsibility of maintaining the building."

The group has generated two major proposals . One is a way to fund new projects and the other is an on-call system of volunteers. The on-call system would mimic the old clinic's on-call system. From a pool of 20-30 people we could break down into sub-groups of 4-6 people. Each sub-group would be on-call to survey maintenance needs for a 4-6 month period. The amount of time per month each person would contribute might be from one to four hours. Each sub-group could decide how to structure themselves but there would be a basic outline of responsibilities posted in the janitor's room. The committee is considering funding these projects by adding on to event admission charges, and they are eager to hear other suggestions. If you have input for the on-call system please call Beth Meadows at 592-2311, evenings before 9p.m.

FUTURE: The big news on new construction is that the Committee is recommending the addition of a new office and storage space on the S.W. corner of the existing building. Doug Kendall has drawn up plans and estimated the costs of this addition. Once the office is relocated, the kitchen can be totally finished. The kitchen porch also needs a roof to stop water damage which is currently buckling the floor. Other projects envisaged during the next five years are, in suggested order of priority, acoustic tile ceiling, new tables,opening windows, janitor closet expansion, stage facility and new solarium. Other suggestions from the community are encouraged.

In order to complete the first stage of this work, namely the office addition, kitchen porch and heating system repairs, we need to raise $15,000. The committee plans to complete this stage during the summer of 1994. A party in April is expected to boost this fund by $2500 . The rest will come from donations, grants, and from the community which uses the building.

For more than twenty years Takilma has been willing to explore and develop a sense of community. The Building Committee invites your participation. Feedback on all issues relating to these projects can be sent to: Takilma Building Committee, c/o Common Ground, P.O.Box 2016 , CJ.,OR 97523. Contributions can be made to Takilma Community Building Fund, SOFCU, Cave Junction.

WEST ELEVATION

TAKILMA COMMUNITY ASSOCIATION
by Bill Gray

The phone rings off the hook and I am accosted on the streets by people anxious to know what TCA is up to. All right, already! Here's an update.

The stated purposes of the TCA include "to provide a forum for discussion of matters of importance to...., hold real property in trust for....,and service the needs of, the Takilma community". Lately, its primary business has been to purchase - and struggle to pay for - several pieces of property in the community. Its financial situation has been uniformly dire: up to the ears in delinquent property taxes, way over its head in land payment obligations.

Last year brought a monumental change. The "Clinic" building was rented to the Siskiyou Regional Education Project (SREP). This new income, combined with a Spring fundraising campaign, enabled TCA to pay property taxes up to the present, stay current on land payments, cover several maintenance projects, contribute to start-up costs for this newsletter, and still have a little left over!

But TCA is seven and a half years and about $18,000 away from paying off its property and there are more maintenance projects in the offing. SREP is facing significant revenue reductions, making continued rental uncertain. This, of course, makes TCA's revenues unreliable, while expenses continue to be high.

To those of you who donated to TCA last year, thank you. To those of you who have committed to an annual contribution, it's about that time again. To those of you who have rarely or never donated, stop for a moment and reflect on the importance of open space, permanently protected from any development not sanctioned by the community as a whole. Then send a contribution, as generous as you can, to: TCA, P.O.Box 1127, CJ. OR 97523.

TCA Board meetings are open to all community members. They deal with routine finances and legal matters as well as more topical issues such as recycling, group health insurance and watershed rehabilitation. Board meetings are held the third Thursday of each month, 715 p m at the SREP office.

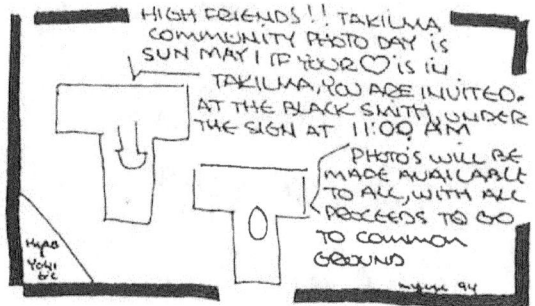

JO. COUNTY HUMAN RIGHTS ALLIANCE
by Shel Anderson

Many people in this community are familiar with Josephine County Human Rights Alliance, but for those who are not, a little background might be useful. JCHRA was first formed to combat the anti-gay initiatives of the Oregon Citizen's Alliance (OCA) here in Josephine County. JCHRA's statement of purpose is "to act as a non-partisan alliance of groups and individuals promoting and preserving equal rights and freedom from discrimination for all persons in Josephine County. This group is dedicated to peaceful social action."

Many of us are concerned about the attack on gays as a minority, and wonder where this right-wing agenda will lead. We know that the OCA has an anti-environmentalist agenda, but who else will be on their agenda next if they are increasingly successful? Welfare moms? Feisty women? Pagans and all non-Christians?

Since it is difficult for many of us to drive to evening meetings in Grants Pass, we've asked the JCHRA to meet with us here in the Illinois Valley. We're calling for an initial meeting to talk about our concerns, the special issues that arise out here. Several JCHRA Board members will be present, and Sky Blue will tell us about the Rural Organizing Project and some ideas she has for positive actions. Bring your ideas, concerns, and your friends. The meeting will be Monday, March 21, at 7 pm at the IV High School. For further information, call Adrian (592-2629) or Shel (592-6521).

DOME SCHOOL
by Oshana

We are rounding the last bend in the school year, keeping busy with classes and special events at the Dome School. During the last school year the Dome School awarded $630.00 in tuition discount scholarships, assisting financially needy families in meeting tuition costs. Oshana recently submitted a grant to the Slade Child Foundation in Washington D.C. hoping to increase the scholarship funds we have available. We would gladly accept any donations towards the education of children in our community.

We are about to embark on our annual fundraising letter campaign, one of our best fundraising efforts of the year. We will have a variety of letter styles to choose from, from serious introductions to the more humorous versions we all love. If there is anyone out there in the reading audience who knows of people, businesses, or groups who might contribute to our school, let us know! All contributions are tax deductible....

Katherine and Deborah have received the balance of an $800.00 grant from the Oregon Parks Foundation Diack Ecology fund. The money has been used to buy tools, books and equipment for class field trips and nature studies in the Siskiyous and Kalmiopsis areas. The children are going to plant hundreds of trees on the banks of the Illinois River again this year, helping our area's riparian ecosystems. Way to go class!!

LETTER FROM SETH

I am thankful to have been born in Takilma. Growing up with all the special people in this community has helped to make me a stronger person. The support I have gotten from the people around here in the last six weeks has made me realize how unique this community is compared to a city environment. In the city you may not even know your neighbor, and if you do, they might not go out of their way to help you. Some people in our community have gone out of their way to call or write a letter for me.
It is a great feeling of support to have so many people respond.

Our community is starting to spread. More and more people are learning how special this place is. Many have moved away but they always come back and visit and even bring more people into our community. This place is strong for its individuality and friendship. I am glad to have been born here and this is where my heart will always be.

Thank you to all who have given me support throughout my life.   Seth Sarrett

---

ENCLOSED IS MY CONTRIBUTION OF:

$10 ___ 1 YEAR SUBSCRIPTION

$25 ___ 1 YEAR SUBSCRIPTION +TAKILMA MUG + ONE BOTTLE AURA POLISH

$50 ___ 1 YEAR SUBSCRIPTION + TAKILMA MUG + WE'LL OMIT AURA POLISH

___ I'M BROKE BUT LITERATE. PLEASE SEND THE NEWSLETTER.

___ PLEASE REMOVE MY NAME FROM THE MAILING LIST

Takilma COMMON GROUND
PO BOX 2016   CAVE JUNCTION, OR 97523

NAME_____

ADDRESS_____

_____

KIDS WORLD

CUPID IN PEACE AND HARMONY
by Solomon age 9

MADD ESSAY written for Mothers Against Drunk Driving
by Ananda Floyd age13

"I'm sorry!" cries the driver, staring at the car crumpled against the wall, "I'm sorry, I didn't mean to . . . I'm sorry, I'm sorry. It was a mistake . . . I mean . . ."

The emergency personnel work quickly, efficiently, talking in clear, calm sounding voices.

The line of cars moves slowly, directed by the flaggers. As the people see why they are slowed, they shake their heads sadly or become angry and shake their fists at the driver who stands to one side repeating:

"I'm sorry . . . I'm sorry . . . sorry . . . "

The mother lies white and still on the stretcher as it is lifted on to the ambulance. The child cries as she watches, not understanding.

Her older sister picks her up and tries to comfort her. Then she walks slowly, like someone very old, over to a rock and sits down.

As the day fades the scene becomes a moving confusion of colors with the child's cries echoing slightly in the night.

"Momma . . . momma . . . momma . . ."

The driver walks slowly past, handcuffed. Turning his head to the crying child and her older sister, he says, "I'm sorry . . . Truly I am. I didn't mean to!"

The older sister looks up slowly, "You could have just gotten a ride."

The driver opens his mouth then shuts it and is pushed into a waiting police car.

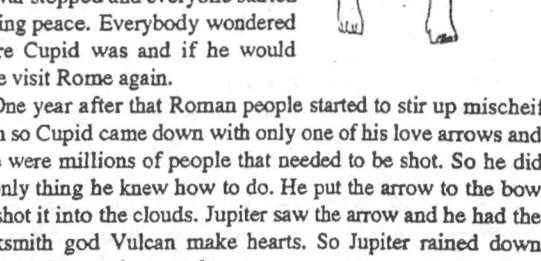

Once upon a time there was a boy named Cupid. He was the god of love and friendship.

There was a war in Rome. Cupid was sad because his Roman friends were all fighting in the war. So Cupid went up to a special place in the woods and shot his arrows of love into the animals and trees there.

Cupid made friends with the trees and the animals. The trees let him make a shelter up in their branches with the birds and bees. One day he found out that his tree was hollow. He found that it was a cave and he could live in it.

The war went on down in Rome for 10 years. So Cupid remained in the cave for 10 more years. Finally the war stopped and everyone started making peace. Everybody wondered where Cupid was and if he would come visit Rome again.

One year after that Roman people started to stir up mischeif again so Cupid came down with only one of his love arrows and there were millions of people that needed to be shot. So he did the only thing he knew how to do. He put the arrow to the bow and shot it into the clouds. Jupiter saw the arrow and he had the blacksmith god Vulcan make hearts. So Jupiter rained down hearts on the warring people.

Then the people stopped warring. There was a little chipmunk that was caught in the war and all the weapons came to him. Jupiter sent down a giant heart that was a shield for the chipmunk and that stopped the war forever.

RUNNING BROTHER'S LATE WEATHER-
by Doug, Kerry, and Robert

"Well what's going on with this droughtie winter"? Robert thinks its the worst he's ever seen. Kerry says the IV Rag reports 1/2 total rain to date as last year. Jonny compares it to '91. His records show similar rain amounts by Feb. 1.

"What about 'El Fucking Nino'? Haven't heard much blame attached to that lately."

"Who started El Nino anyway?"

"El Nino (the child) is so named in Peru for a yearly weather affect that happens right around Christmas. It seems that contrasting temps in the ocean currents stir up their weather around Christmas. In 1927 they had a Super Nino bringing in torrential rains washing everything from alligators to Aztec ruins out to sea."

"But what does that have to do with our weather?"

"Maybe there's some ripple effect that causes the equatorial currents to rub elbows and disturb Northern Pacific weather."

"Nah! The media uses the term 'El Nino Effect' to describe similar types of weather changes in our hemisphere, causing things like those 2 years of Texas rains or the Mississippi floods."

LATE WEATHER rain amounts, totals to date: 2-27-94, J. Klein-29.2", Dg. Kendall -24.65".

Here's a footnote about El Nino from Alyce's science teaching notes: Scientists are not sure what causes El Nino, but most scientists think that the cause has something to do with how winds blow across the ocean. One large belt of winds, called trade winds, usually blows over the ocean towards the west. If the trade winds stop blowing, the warm currents of El Nino begin to drift to the east. When this happens, major changes in weather take place in many parts of the world.

YA NEVER KNOW-YA KNOW!

ANNOUNCEMENTS

Newman is planning to be here with his dell'Arte friends during the Spring Bazaar on May 7th at the Dome School , 3pm. Their student touring show will be presented for FREE. It will be in the interactive, archetypal, wickedly humorous style of the original commedia dell'Arte. It's expensive to bring the big equipment trucks over here so we need some angels to help cover costs. Talk to Robin Wren 592-3159.

"Every understood dream is like a slight electrical shock into higher consciousness." -Marie Louise Von Franz
Dream group starting late March. Join us in learning to translate the symbolic language of your dream into understandable meaning for you in your life. Bring one dream to delve into for seven weeks. Call Hollis at 592-2476 or Pat at 592-3563.

We need someone(s) to help with Ian on Saturdays for 2-3 hours, and an occasional day or eveni.ng so we can get out. Please phone Mar and Leo at 592-4436 if interested.

The annual tin can and glossy magazine recycling event will be April 23, 8am -2pm, at the recycling center at the Junction Inn.

Phases and Stages: A Menopausal Workshop for Women
April 23, 11am-4pm (Registration at 10:30)
Takilma Community Building. Sliding scale $5-$10.
For more info call 482-5156 or 592-4269.

CLASSIFIEDS

FOR SALE : 1978 Chevy Suburban, sm block 400 auto trans. Exc. for towing or hauling+/or family or recreation vehicle. $1500 or trade for smaller vehicle. Randy 592-2308

1974 SUBARU DL SEDAN FOR PARTS. All parts in good shape as she was treated with TLC for 17 years by a single owner. Call Grace at 479-8505 before 8pm.

WANTED TO TRADE : Clean cabin in Hawaii Rainforest near black sand beach. Organic garden, solar electricity. Trade for nice place in Takilma area so our family can expand. Bruce and Lisa, Box 1175 Panoa, HI 96778 (808) 965-6487

EMPLOYMENT WANTED
Glassblower's apprentice seeks supplementary odd-jobs. Strong, hardworking, local. Call Mark, 592-2214.

Intelligent, reliable woman with years of retail, wholesale and cooking experience seeks part-time work. Flexible hours. Kate 2214.

Announcements are for free services or for people in need of help. We will print them free of charge. Classifieds and Personals require payment: 1-25 words-$3.00, 25-50 words-$6.00. First come, first serve. Deadline next issue-April 30

COMMON GROUND, a newsletter for Takilma, was born out of the desire to broaden our connections as a community. Our mission is to present a forum for information and ideas on issues of concern to our corner of the world. We support diversity, encourage debate, promote creative expression, and actively seek common ground. We honor the Earth we inhabit here at the headwaters of the Illinois River.

This is our second issue- for those friends who do not live in Takilma, we need to hear from you, merely by replying with good wishes or money, in order to keep you on the mailing list. After the third issue, only those who have replied will be retained.

We encourage submission of articles, letters, graphics, and announcements. We prefer them typewritten, double-spaced, and in triplicate, but if the content is stellar we will tolerate funk. Submissions deadline for our next issue is April 30. Please send your comments or submissions to Takilma Common Ground, PO Box 2016, Cave Junction, OR, 97523.

The Mud Council consists of Laurie, Kayla, Adrian, Jon, Felicity, Jill, Robin, Kerry, Dave Hocker and Dave Toler. The editorial staff for this issue was the same folks, minus Dave H., and with the addition of Kate. Dave Toler was our facilitator.

Takilma COMMON GROUND
Post Office Box 2016
Cave Junction, OR 97523

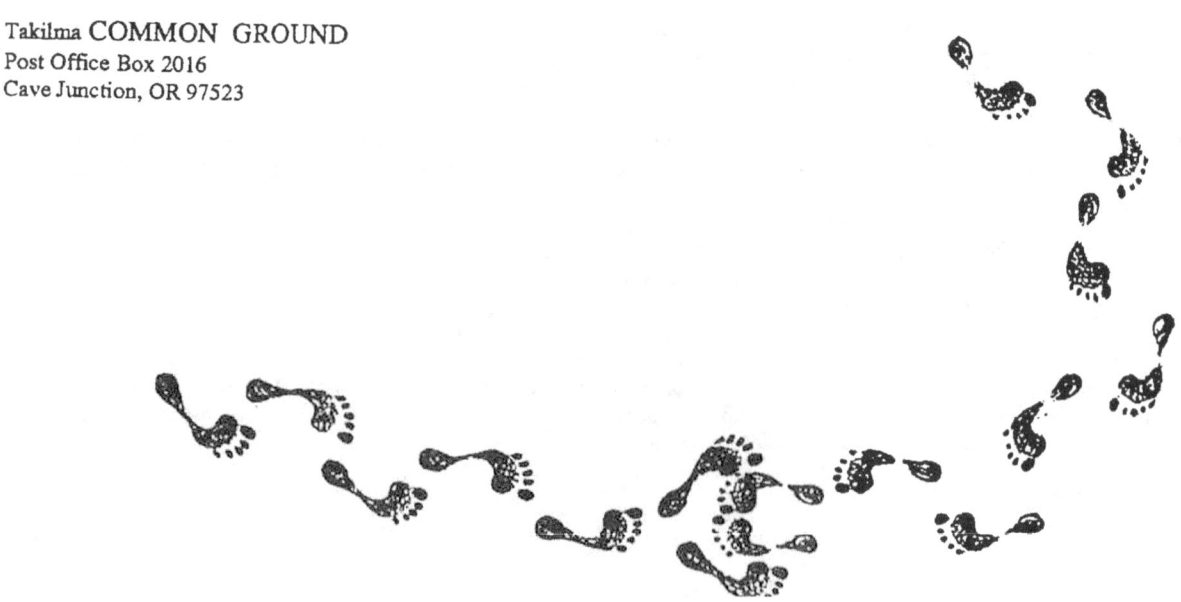

Takilma Common Ground
A community newsletter

Issue #3   May-June '94

CAVE FUNCTION

"The seminal event of the season! "- Steve Marsden
"Cool, Cat!" - Joy Shinerock
"Intimate!" - Lisa Kelz
"The most fun we ever had at a party in Takilma!" - Roy &
Leslie
"Phantasmagorical!" - Marjorie Reynolds
"Wow!" - Meadow Martell

This is a sampling of what various critics are saying
about the Cave of the Nine Cats, a fundraising party held April
30 at the Community Building. The food and drink were
marvelous, the entertainment dazzling. Twenty-eight original
works of art were donated by attendees toward a silent auction.
Wonderfully crafted poetry was shared by party-goers
throughout the evening. A jazz fusion band and other stars
provided music.

The Le Show "Party People" labored for weeks to put together
this annual community event to encourage new friendships and
talents to emerge. These parties are generally theatrical in
nature, and provide a fun way to raise funds for our community
building.

At this writing net proceeds were not available, but were
estimated to be between $2000-$3000. This is a great start
toward our $15,000 goal. Thanks for the support, Takilma!
Seating was very limited, and one had to be quick to get a ticket.
If you were inadvertently left off the mailing list, WE
APOLOGIZE ! Our aim is to include all community members in
these events. Please call 592-2492 and leave a message for
Cathy if you would like your name and address added to the file
so we can include you next time ! -*Dave Hocker*

JOSEPHINE COUNTY, WEED CAPITAL OF THE WORLD?

Our brothers and sisters over in Williams have found
themselves in the forefront of the local debate over roadside
herbicide spraying to the degree that they have incurred the
wrath of the commissioners and their brown-shirted varlets. I
would like to see Takilma follow another path on the way to a
future free of chemicals.

If we don't want herbicide sprayed on our road frontages, we
can maintain our vegetation ourselves. A homemade "no spray"
sign does "no good." We must enter into a contract with the
Public Works Dep't. This assures that the work will get done,
and covers legal questions regarding liability. It IS a hassle, but
a system exists for us dissidents to play the game. Let's learn the
rules of the game, and then try to win it. Here's how.

You must go in person to the JoCo Public Works Dep't in
Grants Pass. Take Hwy 199 past the Fairgrounds to Ringuette
St., turn left. Go a block to River Heights Way, turn left.
Proceed to the office. See any clerk. Request your "Owner
Maintains Roadside Vegetation" signs; the bureaucrats will take
it from there. There is no charge, but the paperwork, as always,
will take a chunk out of your day. Annual renewal is required.
All of this sucks, but it IS better than using herbicides OR getting
arrested.

The Powers That Be are content to use sprays. According to
them, it's cheap and it works. Those of us who are concerned
about this issue need to let our actions speak louder than our
words. GET the signs; this lets the County know how we feel.
POST the signs; this makes a political statement on your street.
DO the work; this keeps our roadsides pleasant for bicyclists and
keeps public maintenance costs down. And remember the folks
in Williams; they have taken the lead on this issue, and they
deserve our support. -*Dave Hocker*

BACK TO THE WOMB

A Takilma tradition is being reborn. Our community is
once again privileged to birth our babies at home with the
professional support of a skilled midwife. Karen Beesley, CNM,
will offer comprehensive prenatal, birthing, infant care and
family planning services as an independent provider, beginning
this summer. Karen comes from work with the Frontier Nursing
Services in Kentucky and the Garden of Life Clinic in Michigan.
She has visited here several times , worked (and played) with
clinic staff, hiked and biked our mountains, and finds Takilma
just the place she's been wanting to call home. She will also
offer women's health services at the SCHC (aka Takilma
People's Clinic) in CJ, and be affiliated with obstetricians in GP.
Welcome home, Karen. - *Kayla Starr*

HOW YOU CAN HELP THE CLINIC SURVIVE THE OREGON HEALTH PLAN

You've heard about it (many times), maybe you even thought about applying. And now it is time to act. Siskiyou Community Health Center needs you to sign up for the Oregon Health Plan if you think you qualify. The clinic gets $14 a month per enrollee to provide all the primary health care to a person under the Oregon Health Plan. The theory is that the pool of people receiving care will contain a balance of people who are sick and healthy and the money received by the clinic each month will cover all the services provided. So far we are seeing mostly sick people who have been waiting a long time to receive care. The $14 we receive a month for someone enrolled who doesn't need health care services immediately helps subsidize someone who does. The enrollment process is fairly simple and the income levels for qualifying have been raised. Julie Ferguson at the clinic can help with the paperwork. Her number is 592-6444. If you think you may qualify for the Oregon Health Plan , give her a call. Please don't wait until you get sick. You can be reassured that you will have health insurance when you need it and the clinic will benefit by your participation.

-Meadow Martell

LEGALIZED? HEMP

Seven Thunders Productions, a multi-media video production company, recently opened an office in downtown CJ. Its three principals are Neriah, Jubal and Donna.

Our first meeting at the TCB on April 16 was a success. We plan to continue to have "Town Hall" type meetings regularly in town, with occassional guest speakers.

In addition to working with all types of professional people and private citizens, Seven Thunders has taken on two very important projects: Legalizing Hemp for food, fuel and fiber, and the Forfeiture Laws - What is the Law? Our research is extensive and thorough, in order to provide the truth when educating the people.

At a later date our office will have a "Library" system where you can check out books, materials and tapes, and we will have an Audio/Video Viewing Room. COMMUNITY SUPPORT IS ENCOURAGED.

Our office is located at 140B Redwood Hwy. (next to Dan's Books.) Office phone is 592-4545. We ask that you stop by and check us out. However, please keep your personal visits brief, as we are a working office with lots to do. Thank you for your support. *-The Three Principals*

THE SISKIYOU PROJECT

There's plenty going on at SREP these days. Thanks in part to the wonderful volunteer energy of Steve Siegel and "Jay Kay," we have many projects in process at this time.

The "Save Our Siskiyous" campaign we launched many months ago in response to Option 9 has been pronounced a huge success. Of the 100,000 letters sent to the federal government about the President's Forest Plan, we estimate that more than 10,000 were generated by Siskiyou Project networkers. Thanks for expressing yourselves in favor of protecting the Siskiyous! 100,000 additional acres from our region have been added to the Ancient Forest Reserves. We think that all those letters of support made a statement to the Clinton Administration about how the public feels about the Siskiyou Roadless Area.

There is much public land surrounding Takilma. The land managed by BLM is in the matrix and available for clear-cutting. The land managed by the Forest Service on the East Fork Illinois appears to be largely protected in the reserves, at least for now. Please come see us if you wish more detailed information about specific areas. We have maps and can help answer your questions.

We joined forces with more than a dozen other environmental groups and recently asked the Federal government to provide Endangered Species Act protection for all West Coast Wild Steelhead runs. Federal agencies have three months to decide on this petition.

SREP recently received a grant to fund a comprehensive study of biodiversity in the Klamath-Siskiyou Region. This study will take more than a year to complete and will provide recommendations on how to protect the unique qualities of the area.

There is growing concern about the health of our beautiful Port Orford cedars. They are threatened by a fatal disease introduced from Asia that has spread steadily through most of the cedars' range.This disease is called Phytopthora lateralis (commonly called "root rot") and has been reported on the East Fork of the Illinois River. The spores of this fungus are spread by logging and roadbuilding equipment, and by vehicles that use these logging roads. The Forest Service is responsible for the activities that have spread the pathogen, and has been aware of the consequences for decades, but is moving slowly to change the practices which further spread the disease. To raise our voice in defense of these trees, we filed two appeals on proposed projects of the Forest Service. These projects would have encouraged more vehicle travel in areas where this tree grows. In both appeals, the USFS has agreed to change plans to protect the trees.

We are providing technical support and networking skills to help the East Fork Illinois River Watershed Council protect the river and its inhabitants, both human and non-human.

We have helped to distribute copies of CLEARCUT, a "coffee table" book filled with photographs of some of the horrors of modern logging techniques in the U.S. and Canada. If you have not yet seen this book, there are copies on display at our office, Coffee Heaven, and the Public Library in Cave Junction. You owe it to yourself to view a photographic essay of what lies beyond the "beauty strips" that border what's left of our public lands.

This is just a sampling of what we're up to at the Project. If you would like to volunteer your energy for a worthwhile cause, consider "The Wild." We are working to protect wild places and wild things and could use many different kinds of help. Please call (592-4459) or stop by. Our office is housed in the old Clinic Building, next door to the Dome School. *-SREP*

Salmon

LETTER TO THE EDITORS:

To da editors:

One does not need to leave Takilma to see the very obvious signs of the timber interests' current approach to keeping up the flow to the mills. Their tactic of a nice "on the hoof" price has been far too successful. The "back yard" private sector for "fiber" is the current beast of exploitation. What will be the tendencies of Takilma locals when personal needs outweigh the effects of extraction?

At my end of the road (Green Bridge area), many were surprised by the visual experience of one such local decision. Trees assumed safe because of local ownership are now stumps akin to those of the National Forest variety.

What can be done? I believe that inquiry, though not a deterrent, can at least protect one from surprise. It is not politically correct to assume anything about anybody ... anymore. The treachery of a failing system will, with its highly sophisticated psychological and political ploys, attempt to divide and conquer us, and through its whining, teasing intimidation and lies, will continue its pursuit of perversion. (As seen in the rise of "snitches" on the herb side of things.) We must all be responsible for what we know!! Power to Takilmans and indigenous peoples of the world!

In crucial times,

Miguel

"LE SHOW"

Thanks, family and friends, for working, celebrating, producing, executing and completing, hauling, (breaking down), getting left behind, cooking-entertaining, presenting, offering, buying-singing, playing-risking
honoring.....
and cleaning it all up.
Thanks to the all of" 'Le Show'
Caves of the Nine Cats",
Robin Wren.

TAKILMA POLICE BLADDER (Things that could be true)
As reported to the editors.

April 20-Five elderly tourists in a Cutlass with Alberta plates got lost in the 12,000 block of Takilma Rd. looking for Peter's Vista.....April 21- Caller complained of Dijuary Doo disturbance in Hogues Meadow.....April 23- Dogs cited for no tailights throughout Takilma.....April 24-Early swimmers cited at Green Bridge for parking in Handicap Zone.

April 25- Full Moon sighted in Takilma at 12:43 P.M.
.April 27- Children held and released.
..April 28- Full moon sighted again in Takilma at 12:43 P.M.
...April 28- Three people cited for bad drumming.
....April 30- Middle-aged goateed gang cited for excessive finger snapping. Fined.
.....April 31- Hallucination witnessed in the Compound district.

support

May 1.More than 200 people, feared to be anarchists, suspiciously gathered near Takilma Rd.....May 1- Purported semi-nude mob complains of speeding Cutlass with Alberta plates leaving Takilma.....May 1- Complaint of Dijuary Doo disturbance in 8,000 block of Takilma Rd....May 3- At 10 PM, driver complains of mysterious midnight sun on the Barn in 9,000 block of Takilma Rd.

May 4-Loose horses complain of speeding traffic in 10,000 block of Takilma Rd.
.May 4- Kids rescued from tub of Gack, rinsed, held and released.
..May 5-Pre-dawn joggers collide with pack of dogs.
...May 6- Woman licking slug reported near Meadows Bridge.
....May 6 -Couple making love, observed, held and released.
.....May 7- Crying trees reported in the 12,000 block of Takilma Rd.

ANOTHER MEANING OF THE FLOWER

The world was different 200 million years ago. There were no flowers and so there were no fruits. Only the mosses, ferns, and conifers stood steadfast in the huge forests that stretched across the continents. The animals had merely leaves, stems and wood to eat, and so they moved with little energy through the landscape. Nothing could move as fast, or with such bursts of energy garnered through the chain of life from the sun, as our stealthy predators and prey of today. Dinosaurs lumbered along in their glory, the first bird was trying to fly, and the few little mammals that had recently evolved were staying safely hidden beneath the forest canopy.

And the world stood on the brink of the most wondrous revolution.

Somewhere in a hidden grove along a meandering stream there grew a plant that began our very own crazy experiment. For some reason it made the leaves near its ovules and pollen into showy petals. The petals attracted an insect and employed it to bring pollen from other plants to its own ovule (containing the egg) and to carry pollen (with sperm) away to another plant's ovules. It was a brilliant idea. Instead of making tons of pollen and hoping the wind will carry it to another plant, just make a little and have a precise vector distribute the goods. That same plant wrapped its seed in a tasty coat, a coat that we would later name a "fruit." It was a first. No one had ever done it before. The fruit was, and still is, an efficient package of energy with lots of sugars to burn. Thus, the flowering plant was born.

Among all the creatures on earth at the time, mammals were the best equipped to find and utilize these little morsels of the forest. What they found and ate gave them huge amounts of energy - energy to move, grow, and multiply. And so for the first time in history our ancestors began to flourish. Their numbers grew and their tribes diverged into a multitude of species, including our own.

Without flowers we would not be. Is it any wonder then that we take such delight in the blooms of spring? It is the flower that creates the fruit, and it is the fruit that provides the gift of the sun with enough strength that we might feel such joy. -Eric Jules

HISTORY, CULTURE, AND NATIVE WISDOM: AN INTERVIEW WITH AGNES PILGRIM. PartII -*by Barry Snitkin*

B .. Aggie, you spoke last time of returning to your ancestral lands. Given American History, is this really possible?

A .. The U.S. Government could allow some land to be given back to the Native American people. That would be a wonderful healing between all types of people to see the original owners have a little spot along the areas where they used to live, to know these were once the lands of the moccasined feet of the ancient ones, to know what they did, to learn the ways of how they thrived and how they lived in moderation and took only what they needed. We know how to take care of a forest in the old way, to revere it, to know that the trees have life and all things have life, to cherish and respect that.

I still say that the biggest disgrace in the history of the USA is the treatment of American Indians. And I'll always say that. We've been abused. Not only abused but we've been used. We've been hurt and we've been trampled upon. There were those people who did trick us, teach us how to sign our names to sign away this property and we didn't know we were signing away our property because we couldn't read or write and so distrust seeped like an ink blotter into the lives of the people. We are wary. The BIA gave us things and took it away. They stripped us of the land. We got nothing.

B..Will things be better for individual Native Americans?

A..I pray that things will become in a better way and a better understanding of the treatment of the Native American Indians. Indian people need to accept who they are and create their own personal identities of acceptance that gives them the feeling that they can move over and share. At least I feel like that.

B Have you seen this to be true? Have you seen changes coming?

A I think that when Indian people put up the big fist, the power is education. We have no choice. We cannot go backwards, we have to go forward. And we can do this role like a pendulum swinging. We can take the best of both worlds and fly. I've done it. I worked in the business world and gone over to the Indian world. I am proud of who I am. I'm proud that I could step out into both worlds and still keep my identity as a Native American.

B .. How do you feel about Native Americans sharing traditions and values with white people?

A.. I have nothing to hide. I walk a good path, the best I can. I look to my creator for guidance, I really believe that my life in my church is every day. It's not just on a Sunday. Like being apprehensive about this interview, I prayed today , 'Grandfather tell me what you want me to say and let the words go out in such a way that maybe good things will come of it to whomever reads or sees or hears it. ' They have the same opportunity I have to walk a better road and a good road. And they have a gift, all people have a gift, be it Indian or whomever.

B..How do you keep such a positive attitude?

A....I believe in the spirit of all things and I recognize the spirit of all things. If you have a good spirit then your mind is healthy and your body comes along so I would say I try to keep my spirit up by making my connections to the creator. I like to make my expression upon the world and leave a place in history to my people, to my children and my grandchildren. I contribute willingly when I bead, when I sew, when I dance, anything. I do it with a good heart that something's going to come out of it, something's good, something's accomplished. Everyone needs to experience accomplishment ,be it reading a book, helping a child or helping an old lady across the street. Every day I do what I can to the best of my ability for my family and for those around me to embellish their lives with the gifts I have.

B .. You and Grant come and do ceremonies for the people here. Why Takilma? Why now?

A..This has been a calling I've wanted to do for a long time, to go back to the land of my people. My people lived over here in Takilma and they lived in the Ilinois Valley and along the Illinois and the Rogue. We've done services in these different places in honor to the spirit world. In honor to these people who now walk along the land and live the land and I think it's a blending of cultures, it's again an opening the teepee flap of understanding to the people that we do too care, I do too love. I think maybe it's because the Creator told me to do this, maybe it's because the Ancient Ones are speaking to me to do these things. I feel that's what it is. To come back and honor these people and the old ones at the same time. To be their representative. I feel like people need to know that to honor the world of the old ones gives them a piece of contentment and a feeling that they fit and that they belong and it's all right to live there and honor the Spirit world.

B.. How do you feel coming to Takilma?

A..It was like returning home. It was like being surrounded by all my people. I felt like they were all smiling because I was there. As we cooked I could feel like they were all watching me, they were all standing and nodding their heads and feeling great about it. I still feel I need to come back periodically to do that because of them. They also enjoyed my return. I represent them to the people. It's not ego or anything. It's something like when the wind pushes me, the door opens and there I am. I like to honor the old ones. This land, this street, once my people walked and I know they hear. It feels comforting, like a place of peacefulness, an understanding to acknowledge them.

B..You have a lot of history here.

A..Agnes, Oregon was named after my Aunt. Some of my uncles signed the treaty over at Table Rocks. Chief Limpy was one of them and Chief Joe. Limpy Creek is named after my Great Uncle. It's really good to be able to walk around the land where they walked. It makes me feel very honored to stand there, to feel their presence, for them to know I know they were here. That makes the connectedness, for me, to the land and to the people. I feel an obligatory thing to come back and do these things with the people, to share. It's kind of like a supplication together, to be able to sit down, to enjoy the history or the stories or the songs or the drumming or the dancing or the sharing of food in honor of the unseen ones.

B..Aggie, I feel that there is some purpose for our meeting.

A..Barry, I really appreciate our paths crossing. I always feel like the Creator has a message or a reason why people's paths cross. I've been at death's door so many times that I feel greatful to fill my day as best I can with everything I accomplish and by the time I go to bed at night I feel good about what I have done. I thank the Creator for all he has given to me. To come back to the people in the valley it's been very very good, a healing thing not just in my life but in their lives. They were there, they shared, they cared. Their smiles were there, their compassion was there. The feeling of open arms to the Native Americans was there. Their warmth and their love and their sharing and their diligence to carry on the feeling of welcoming. Not only welcoming but wanting us to come back again is really a warm feeling in my heart to always know there's people here who welcome us back year after year. For my peoples' spirit still walks the land. Their presence is known and other people realize that. What cheers me is that people know why we are doing this and that's okay with them. I think that's really great.

B..You often go share with the kids.

A..The little ones at the school were awed and I thought how wonderful to see those kids. Sharing our culture with them was gobbled up. It warmed my heart to be able to be there with them.

B..If there is one last message you'd like to share with folks, what would it be?

A..There was a time when I was young that they had signs on the doors of restaurants and places that "Indians and dogs not allowed". How degrading and how humiliating! Now, I'm accepted. People have to make their own acceptance too. You've got to be a friend yourself before you can have a friend. I believe if you want to have a friend you have to work at it. Friendship is like a fire, you have to stick wood on it every once in a while.

THINK FIRST OF THE EARTH THEN THE GRANDCHILDREN

Takilma

SHIT HAPPENS

Spring is the time of year when some of us turn our thoughts to fertilizer. By any other name (Manure, animal waste, poop, etc.) it's still the same old shit. Here are some gleanings from years of shitty experiences.

Shit is simply plants that have been run through an animal. The animal grinds up the plants and adds bacteria from its guts, making the end product very biologically active. The same, or more, fertilizer value can be obtained by applying the plants directly to the soil (green manure) or by composting them first. Helen and Scott Nearing, authors of "Living the Good Life," gardened for more than 60 years without using a single scoop of poop!

The advantage of shit is that it is concentrated material often available for free to those willing to get down and dirty. For an earthy experience, Beth recommends shoveling fresh cowshit while naked and bloody from one's period - sort of a spring fertility ritual..

Don't be prejudiced as to what species the stuff comes out of. Only shit from our fellow humans should be verboten in the vegie garden. If you must use it, compost it first and apply to flowers and fruit trees away from the garden..

Usually, the sooner the shit is applied to the soil the better. The longer it sits around, the more nutrients go elsewhere. Fresh shit does not harm or burn most crops when applied properly, even in large amounts. Either till it in before planting or top dress the crops with a mulch of shit that avoids direct contact with plants. A few crops like potatoes and strawberries really do like to have their shit aged or composted first. And blueberries don't like shit at all in any shape or form. (They prefer Pee, but that's another story...)

Happy Shoveling !   -Beth & Mark

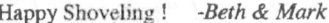

DOME SCHOOL

The Dome School is planning on extending its elementary program to the 4th, 5th, and 6th grade level. It would offer a unique opportunity for students to work with community members. We are looking for people to offer academic, vocational, and arts and crafts workshops with 6-8 students. Time commitments can vary from one day to six weeks. Schedules will be discussed with interested individuals. We are looking for people to work on a voluntary basis and we will offer stipends. This is an excellent opportunity for all. Remember, it takes a whole community to raise a child!!!! For more information, contact Katherine at the Dome School, 592-3911.

HUMAN RIGHTS ALLIANCE FORMING IN VALLEY.

People concerned about human rights violations gathered last month to share common concerns and work toward solutions.

The group will work on the following issues: discrimination upon race, sexual identity, class or religious beliefs and the civil rights inherent in the foreiture laws (as) enforced in the Illinois Valley.

Openness and inclusiveness of all people and problems is a goal of the group; hopefully all of the individuals factions will be able to present a united front and be strong, not devisive.

The group' vision is to be a non-profit, pro-active alliance of people that will work to raise conciousness and protect the rights of all people in the valley.....especially people who fall outside the mainstream of the population. A "formal" name has yet to be decided upon, but one acronym suggested is SAFE (Siskiyou Alliance for Freedom and Equality).

The human rights alliance welcomes new members with new ideas. People are asked to think about how we can bring about positive change in the valley, and to attend the next meeting with ideas for action. -Mary Wertz

TURKISH CAKE   by Marcy Tilton

Easy to assemble, in two bowls or a food processor, this cake has a crisp crust and nut topping that toasts as the cake bakes.

Combine in a bowl or food processor:
2 cups flour
2 cups brown sugar
1 tsp. freshly-grated nutmeg (the pre-ground variety is a poor but acceptable substitute)
2 Tbs. grated orange or lemon rind
OPTIONAL (not in original recipe) I add 1 tsp. powdered vanilla and/or 1tsp. powdered almond.

ADD 1/2 cup (1 stick) sweet butter, chilled.
Mix with above as for pie crust, until it is like cornmeal.

Separate mixture into two equal parts. Press one half into buttered springform pan with fingers.
Then, in a small bowl, mix:
1 tsp. baking soda
1 cup sour cream (may use part or all yogurt)
This combo will react immediately. Stir together. Add
1 egg and beat it all up. Add to remaining crumb batter. Beat well by hand, mixer, or food processor. Pour this mixture on top of crumb batter in pan. Sprinkle top with raw nuts (walnuts, pine nuts, slivered almonds hazelnuts.)

Bake in a 350 oven for 45 minutes or until cake pulls away from sides of pan.

WHO IS WE

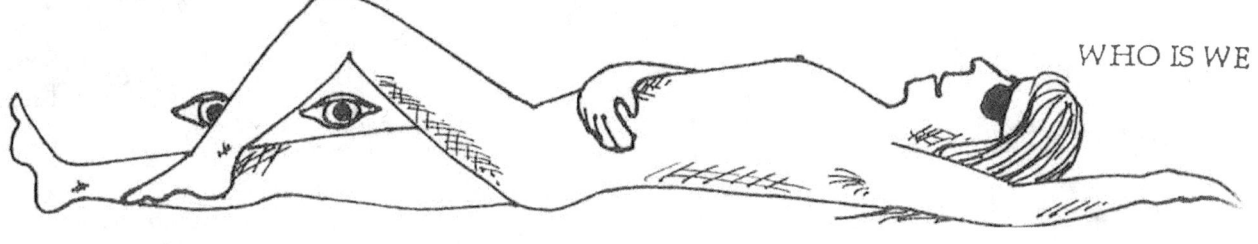

THE FIRE HYDRANT
A Column for Dogs by Dogs

Hey, pups, beware of that woman who keeps Pan. She throws rocks. Zeus and Bear are hosting a game of chase the cat at DooDah every Thursday. All are welcome and extra cats are appreciated. Ralph reports a lovely party for Paco's birthday. Delicious tidbits were dropped on the floor. Maxi and Sambo proudly announce a new concrete slab at the gulch. They invite all to sun themselves. Youngsters, remember to get spayed before it's too late or watch your pups go to Shop Smart in a box! Speaking of town, Western Family kibble is on sale this week so we'll be seeing a lot of it. Until the research crew gets the Canopener Project off the ground it will have to do. The traffic slowing crew is doing beautifully, especially at the blind curves between Page Creek Road and the forge. Way to go, guys! Finally, we'd like to remind you that there's a full moon on the 25th. Happy howling!

-X

BAHIA DE CONCEPCION

back to the bay of conception
where life begins before dawn
waiting for the sun to creep
up and over the hills
encompassing the eastern horizon.
we rest on the southern shore
accepting and feasting
on a gentle bay breeze
carrying the salty scent
of its travels,
telling stories as it rustles
the shade of these tiny trees.
under them I sit
staring to sea,
watching for more dolphins,
basking in the memory
of six playful dark figures
cresting at dawn,
waiting for their return
or a visit from a new guest
come to revel in and reveal
their passing of the time,
time carefully disguised
as creation
in the bay of conception.

Jon Jeans

WATCHUNG

A native American tribe called Watchung are now gone- have been for some time. In their day the women and children grew vegetables, and the men, with hand-crafted weaponry, killed deer, birds, and fish. On special nights the people danced and sang to the beating of drums and the light of a fire. This tribe worked to live and celebrated life. They paid no rent or taxes. They did not labor in random offices or shops making random salaries. The hills they lived in are named after them, but it's much different there now - has been for some time.

To secure their place in the Watchung hills, today's warriors, adorned in customary suits and armed with briefcase, travel daily by car or train to a city or corporate facility. On an island called Manhattan - also named after the tribe who once lived there - people of the hills work, detached from family, community, and the land many miles away that they are striving to maintain as their home. These people are in the process of fulfilling a dream shared by many Americans. A large enough house on a green acre in a safe peaceful suburbia, children playing on a weed-free lawn with the family dog, cars in the garage, weekends off from work, and perhaps a week or two a year spent vacationing. The people of Watchung were more fortunate than others - and still are.

Down out of the hills and just across a highway there were people whose lives weren't as favorable. There wasn't much green and few big yards with big houses. In the nineteen hundred and sixties the people here rioted, burning and looting just blocks away from the base of the Watchung hills. In a large group ready to explode, edged on by the shadeless summer sun and the growling of police dogs, the wrathful crowd could gaze upon the cool, rich foliage, that ascended into a world that could offer them no sanctuary from their asphalt reality. It could for those managing to ride the American dream - those with careers, a landscaped yard, a hammock, and perhaps a pool or lake to spend a hot Sunday. The man in the hammock - shoes off, socks on, cold drink in hand - is certainly not to blame when the angry crowd is refreshed only by a jet of water being shot from a firehose, humans sliding across slick pavement to the accompaniment of bullhorn and barking dog. A mother weeps seeing her son and husband taste the club and the blood. She wonders whose fault it was. Why hadn't her family and their people prospered? Her husband worked hard, when he had work. Her son had quit school to earn money, and he did find jobs from time to time. Now she can only wait and hope for change or luck, anything that could bring a better life. She thinks of trees and hammocks and cool drinks. The man in the hammock thinks of Monday and a computer, stacks of papers, forms, figures, buses, trains, cars, clocks, bills, bosses, and the American dream. He sobs and tries to think of next Sunday and cool fall breezes. *-Mike ZonFrilli*

Soul Garden

I embrace the feminity
   in my life right now.
I swoon and smile and
   soak in it.
That Yin energy
That Sisterhood
That Motherhood
That very Core of Spirit
   reaching into the soil
   of Mother Earth
   bringing forth Life
   and beauty
   growth and wisdom.
I nourish and bless
   my Self
   so my Self
shall nourish and bless
   others. *-Chris Casas*

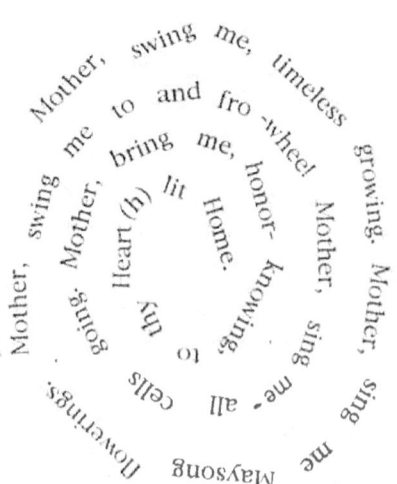

by Sandra Newell.

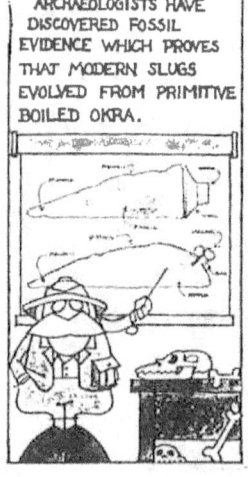

ARCHAEOLOGISTS HAVE DISCOVERED FOSSIL EVIDENCE WHICH PROVES THAT MODERN SLUGS EVOLVED FROM PRIMITIVE BOILED OKRA.

Jack Vaughan's
Weird Humor

creative expression

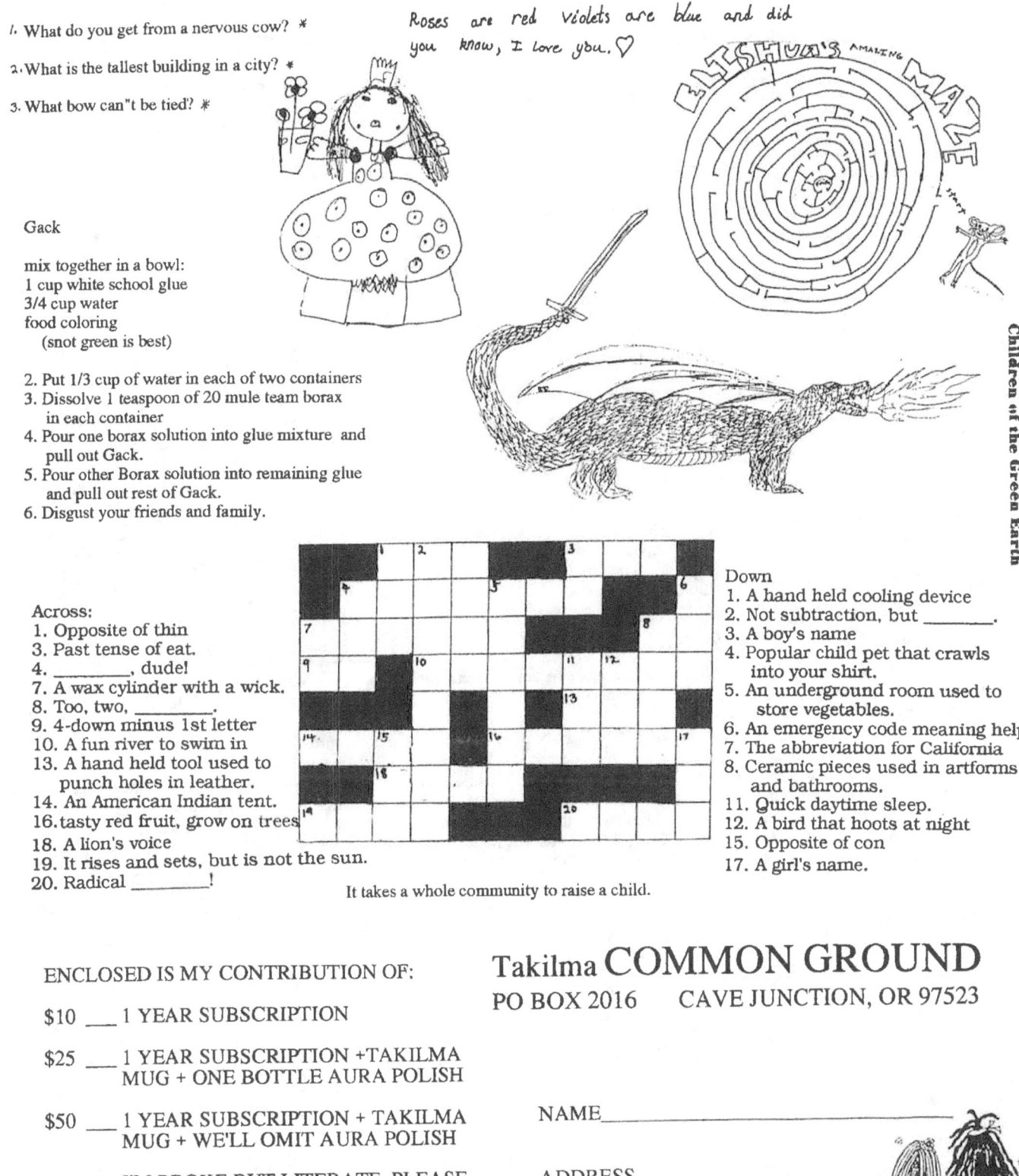

1. What do you get from a nervous cow? *

2. What is the tallest building in a city? *

3. What bow can"t be tied? *

Roses are red violets are blue and did you know, I love you. ♡

ELISHUA'S AMAZING MAZE

Children of the Green Earth

Gack

mix together in a bowl:
1 cup white school glue
3/4 cup water
food coloring
   (snot green is best)

2. Put 1/3 cup of water in each of two containers
3. Dissolve 1 teaspoon of 20 mule team borax
   in each container
4. Pour one borax solution into glue mixture and
   pull out Gack.
5. Pour other Borax solution into remaining glue
   and pull out rest of Gack.
6. Disgust your friends and family.

Across:
1. Opposite of thin
3. Past tense of eat.
4. _____, dude!
7. A wax cylinder with a wick.
8. Too, two, _____.
9. 4-down minus 1st letter
10. A fun river to swim in
13. A hand held tool used to
    punch holes in leather.
14. An American Indian tent.
16. tasty red fruit, grow on trees
18. A lion's voice
19. It rises and sets, but is not the sun.
20. Radical _____!

Down
1. A hand held cooling device
2. Not subtraction, but _____.
3. A boy's name
4. Popular child pet that crawls
   into your shirt.
5. An underground room used to
   store vegetables.
6. An emergency code meaning help.
7. The abbreviation for California
8. Ceramic pieces used in artforms
   and bathrooms.
11. Quick daytime sleep.
12. A bird that hoots at night
15. Opposite of con
17. A girl's name.

It takes a whole community to raise a child.

ENCLOSED IS MY CONTRIBUTION OF:

$10 ___ 1 YEAR SUBSCRIPTION

$25 ___ 1 YEAR SUBSCRIPTION +TAKILMA
       MUG + ONE BOTTLE AURA POLISH

$50 ___ 1 YEAR SUBSCRIPTION + TAKILMA
       MUG + WE'LL OMIT AURA POLISH

___ I'M BROKE BUT LITERATE. PLEASE
    SEND THE NEWSLETTER.

___ PLEASE REMOVE MY NAME FROM
    THE MAILING LIST

Takilma COMMON GROUND
PO BOX 2016   CAVE JUNCTION, OR 97523

NAME_____

ADDRESS_____

_____

1. A milk shake.
2. The library. It has so many stories.
3. A rainbow.

Remember that unsightly pile of junk at the corner of Rockydale and Waldo? Well, it's GONE, thanks to the Earth Day efforts of the Dome School kids. Now that's community service!

Please note this correction: Oregon Bear and Cougar Coalition volunteers are needed through November (not "before March 30th," as previously reported.) Please contact Debbie Lukas at the Siskiyou Project (592-4459) as soon as possible to add your energy to this important effort.

The Running Brother'sWeather

This time of year we seem to receive an endless parade of nasty cold fronts which spin off the Gulf of Alaska and land right in the Illinois Valley. Yet any rain we getnow can be termed "too little too late". Going into May, we have received less than half of our rainfall to date last year and probably one of the lowest totals since we came to the valley twenty five years ago. Here we go again with "water wars" and extreme fire danger. *Robert Hirning*

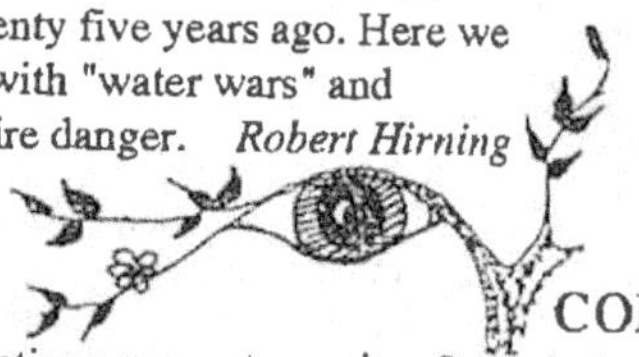

ANNOUNCEMENTS!!!!!

To all people who brought poetry offerings to "Le Show" but forgot to leave them after their readings, please call Joya, 592-4619.... and Jack- Robin says - He's so sorry.....

On Friday, May 27, at 6:00 PM, Agnes Pilgrim will conduct a Salmon Ceremony at Out and About for local residents, public invited. Pot Luck. Bring dishes and silverware. Come earlier if you'd like to participate further. For more information call Barry at SREP, 592-4459.

Do you want to stop smoking? Let's do it together, call Robin, 592-4459.

We are organizing a Takilma softball tournament for the afternoon of Sunday, July 3rd. We hope to have enough players to create 4 teams. Anyone interested in playing, helping, or being a part of rebuilding the TCA softball field, please call Jon Jeans, 592-2831, or Miguel, 592-2549.

honor the Earth

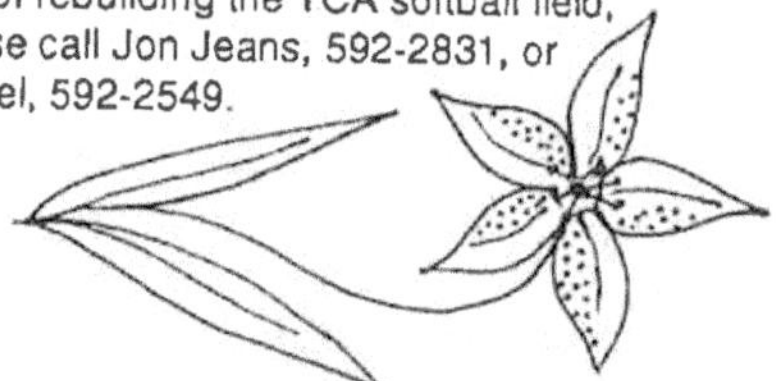

COMMON GROUND, a newsletter for Takilma, was born out of the desire to broaden our connections as a community. Our mission is to present a forum for information and ideas on issues of concern to our corner of the world. We support diversity, encourage debate, promote creative expression, and actively seek common ground. We honor the Earth we inhabit here at the headwaters of the Illinois River.

This is our third issue- for those friends who do not live in Takilma, we need to hear from you, merely by replying with good wishes or money, in order to keep you on the mailing list. After this issue, only those who have replied will be retained.

We encourage submission of articles, letters, graphics, and announcements. We prefer them to be brief, typewritten, double-spaced, and in triplicate, but if the content is stellar we will tolerate funk. We reserve the right to edit. Submissions deadline for our next issue is June 7. Please send your comments or submissions to Takilma Common Ground, PO Box 2016, Cave Junction, OR, 97523.

The Mud Council consists of Laurie, Kayla, Adrian, Felicity, Jill, Robin, Dave Hocker and Dave Toler. The editorial staff for this issue was Jon(facillatator), Kerry, Jill, Kate, Laurie, Felicity, and Dave Hocker. Art by JIll, Robin , Kate, Randy, Mary.

COMMON GROUND
POB 2016
CAVE JUNCTION, OR 97523

WHAT IT'S ALL ABOUT

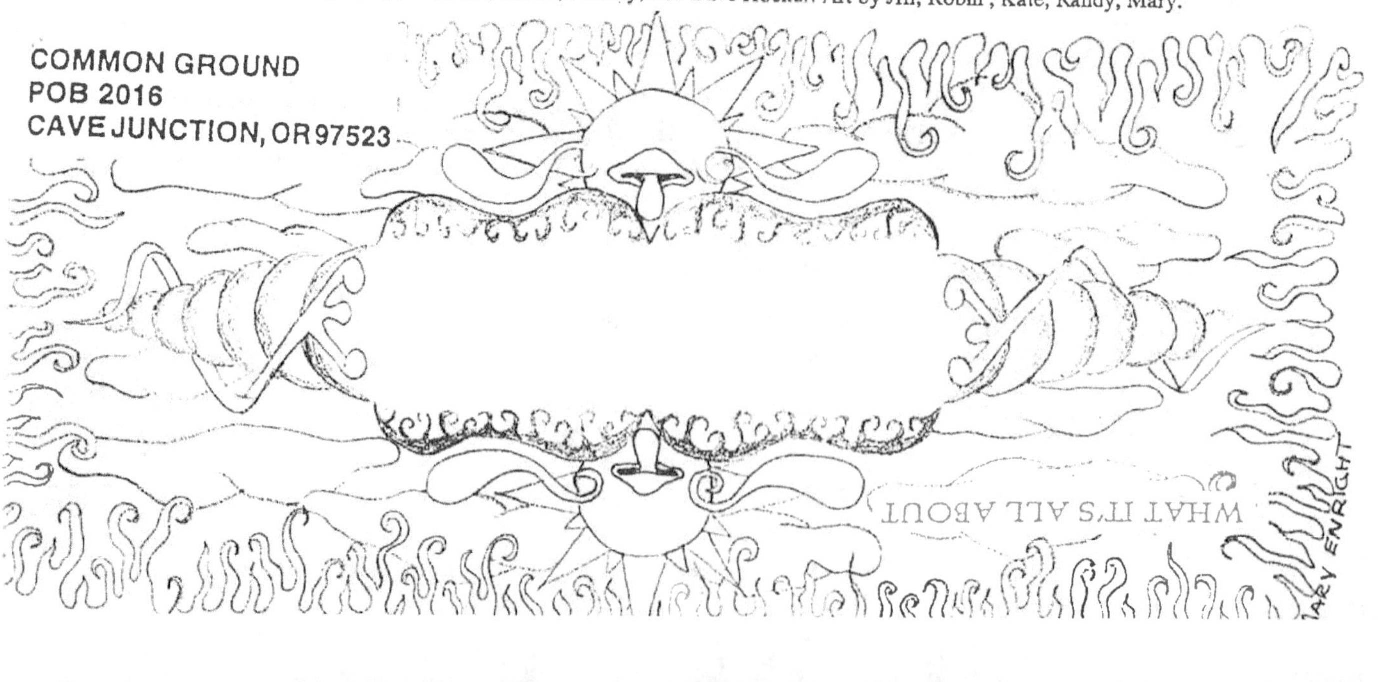

Issue #4   A community newsletter   June-July '94

DRUG WAR : LORNA BYRNE STUDENTS CAUGHT IN THE CROSSFIRE

In the last few weeks the government's ever expanding War on Drugs has spilled over into territory many here in the valley thought safe haven from the cross fire. In two unrelated incidents local police have recently entered the Lorna Byrne Middle School and interrogated students.

Concerned that violations of student and family rights may become routine within the halls of public schools, representatives of the local Siskiyou Alliance for Freedom and Equality [SAFE] are investigating the situation and addressing their concerns to school officials.

According to SAFE, one of the interrogations at Lorna Byrne involved no illegal activity at the school as police showed up uninvited. They were apparently seeking information from a child to be used for a case against the child's parents. When asked by a SAFE representative about this policy, a deputy replied that the police can informally question anyone at any time as long as they have "lawful presence".

According to school officials, because the school is public property, any attempts on the part of the school principal to deny police entry could lead to an "obstruction of justice" charge. Under such charges, Jann Taylor [LBMS Principal] could lose her job.

In a meeting with school officials, members of SAFE expressed their concern that current school policy may encourage an increase in police interrogation at the school where children lack the support of family members or some other legal advocate. For example, SAFE pointed out that current school policy does not call for parent notification even when the police show up for reasons unrelated to the school. Also, school policy states that the principal may or may not be present during interrogation of the student.

In another incident, the police were requested by Lorna Byrne to interrogate a child who had brought sterilized hemp seeds to the school. Although the seeds are a legal substance, the child was interrogated for several hours. Apparently, information extracted from the child was used by the police to acquire a search warrant for the child's home.

After the incident, the child involved repeatedly expressed the fear experienced throughout the entire affair, stating "I no longer feel I can trust my school". This lack of trust, say SAFE members, is exactly what the community should avoid.

"A school policy that ensures a stronger advocacy role for the student needs to be developed if the school wants to retain a relationship of trust with the students and with the community at large. As legal parent in absentia, schools should ensure that a trained legal advocate always accompany the student during police interrogations. Our children need support when confronted with fearful situations like this. All we want the school to do is ensure a Constitutional process. By protecting students' rights we achieve the trust our community must have with its public schools". *-unAssociated Press*

STUMPS DON'T LIE

Now is the time to express your opinion on the proposed Sugarloaf timber sale. This area is in the Grayback watershed in the Kangaroo roadless area adjacent to the Oregon Caves National Monument and was deemed an Ancient Forest Reserve in the Clinton Forest Plan. The Forest Service is blatantly contradicting its own experts in stating that this area is not Old Growth and is ignoring the fact that similar terrain has failed to be reforested, that it is spotted owl habitat, and that this is the only part of the drainage that is not yet infested with Port Orford cedar root rot. The Grayback Creek drainage is also singled out in the Forest Plan as a Key Watershed, critical to the restoration of salmon and steelhead .

The Sugarloaf sale has been controversial from its inception, subject of a lawsuit, public protests and many confrontations with U.S. Forest Service personnel. The Forest Service at one point even tried to close off a large area of the National Forest surrounding the sale blocking a major connecting route between Cave Junction and Williams.

The Siskiyou Regional Education Project organized a mass meeting with Forest Service personnel in Grants Pass on June 14th so that concerned residents would be able to express the degree of opposition that exists toward this sale. We have succeeded in the past in stopping over-logging in our bioregion. We can do it again. Please call TODAY : JACK WARD THOMAS , U.S. Forest Services Chief at 202-205-1055. Also, there's MIKE LUND, Supervisor of the Siskiyou Forest locally at 503-471-6507. For more information, check with the folks at Siskiyou Project who are working hard to save our forests at 592-4459. Call one, call all....call NOW! *-Kayla*

ROCK-N-ROLL RETIREMENT HOME

"Will you still need me, will you still feed me, when I'm sixty-four?"

Our community building/Dome School certainly has been a wise investment of time and energy, serving our needs as a place to educate our children and to celebrate and party. As time goes on , we will have more and more need for a place where we can take care of ourselves, our friends and family members who, due to illness, injury and old age, are unable to fully care for themselves. Many of us are starting to see our elderly parents and even some of our contemporaries needing residential care. Do we want to leave our homes to go and stay with our folks for extended periods of time? Do we have room and the amenities they would need to live in our homes? Do we want to depend on our grown children when we need this kind of help? Although it will be some time before most of us are in this predicament, it behooves us to plan ahead so we can be comfortable when and if that time comes. The residential care facilities out there are not always pleasant and loving places. They probably don't serve the kind of food we like or offer the entertainment and diversions we've come to value in our community.

When I envision the rock-n-roll retirement home, I see a house in a beautiful Takilma setting where myself and my friends spend casual time togetether in the living room, talking, listening to music, watching the latest videos, having parties and live entertainment. There is a big, fully equipped kitchen and dining room where we enjoy meals together, and a separate bedroom for each resident with bathroom access. The place is managed by someone who hires help for cooking, cleaning and health care, thereby providing work opportunities for local people. We will still do for ourselves as we are able and our friends and families will volunteer since we'll be right here in Takilma. We will have good, healthy food, choices in our health care and loving respectful treatment from the staff and our loved ones.

Can we create this in Takilma? Financing may come from renting our homes. Possibly, government programs will have progressed in the future to a place where funding will be available. Those of us who help build it and staff it will earn our care in advance. We will need to surmount all the regulatory restrictions governing such an endeavor, and learn by doing. How much autonomy are we capable of achieving, what is it worth to have more control over our later years? Can we pull together the resources to complete such a project?

The first step is for people who are interested in exploring this project to get together for preliminary discussions and research. Anyone interested , call Paco at 592-4196. *-Paco Despacio*

In line with our stated purpose of encouraging debate and providing a forum for the exchange of ideas within our community, these letters have been printed as originally submitted. We encourage all our readers to write to us.

Dear Folks,

Very nice rag-especially the Takilma Police Bladder. That's the best part of the local papers. And I like the art work. Maybe a cat column instead of a dog one? Just asking.

Thanks for the Earth, J.K. Canepa

Dear Takilma,

"Common Ground" is real nice, but far away. Thanks for the copies, but I can't subscribe. I'm the guy who wrote an Oregonian Sunday Magazine article about Takilma.

Thanks, good luck, peace & joy, hello to any who remember my passing ----- Rick Rubin

Dear Folks of Takilma,

I'm writing this letter to clarify that the driveway I put in on my property was not put in for the purpose of any logging or anybody's logging concerns, particularly for profit. Since I'm somewhat new to the area as a resident and homeowner, I want to squash any rumors that I have anything to do with the so-called "forest management" that has been going on around both my property and my innocent neighbors', who also had nothing to do with this mess.

My road, or driveway, if you will, was put in with either direct or indirect misinformation or miscommunication. I gave my word to John Jones, the former owner of my place, that I would buy his land and protect it; not so much for him but for myself and the community of Takilma. If the persons doing the logging do not wish to consult with the people who live around this land, unfortunately that is his or their business.

But I want to make it clear to all concerned that I am not in any way a part of this logging. I unfortunately have had to put "no trespassing" markers on my place to further make a point. I do welcome any concerns or criticisms from anyone who lives here in Takilma, whether they own land or not. I just feel it's a shame to cut down so many trees for a profit at the expense of the community, again who live here. I certainly didn't come here to make enemies of the people who live here, or the environment. It's unfortunate again as it is in so many situations that the term "forest management" is a lie.

Sincerely, J. D. Smith

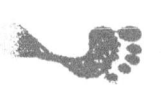     

Eco-management in Progress

In response to a letter to the editor in the May/June publication, I find it fairly arrogant that Miguel should assume to know the reasons behind my decision to do selective timber harvesting on my property, and somewhat immature to negatively influence others by his assumption. If Miguel can't see the difference between what I'm trying to accomplish and the destruction of our public lands by various government agencies, then there's not much I can say. I assure the readers, however, that my decision had zero to do with any goals to perpetuate the affairs of the lumber mills. Neither was money my primary motivation. But, since I'm the one who has worked all these years for the right to manage this property as I see fit, I don't feel the need to justify my actions to negative people.

I also find it in bad taste for this newsletter to add credence to his complaint by drawing pictures of tree stumps, and making light of the report of trees "crying." For every cull tree harvested, a hundred healthy trees have been left standing, and a countless number of fruit and ornamental trees and shrubs have been planted. And all you can focus on is tree stumps? Now that's tunnel vision! I've been cleaning up all spring, and all I ever hear (besides people, etc.) is the river, wind, and birds. Maybe you can teach me how to hear trees crying...and after that, you can teach me how to walk on water.

I would like to thank those who have been patient and neighborly. I know there's a lot of you out there.

Andre Peter S.

Takilma Logger Succeeds?

_Logging in Takilma-

Without written permission and doubtfully having proper environmental concerns, Jim (2%) Dougherty and Peter have successfully carved through the horse, bike & people trail, removing moderately small and medium trees. They are now progressing up this very fragile hillside towards the old growth in the northeast corner. Will they make those big bucks and live happily ever after or will they spend their money on bigger equipment & go for 4% gains? Dwight Smith has temporarily slowed the progress by denying easement. Thank you very much Dwight. Leo is very concerned as is the rest of the enviroots community. Please talk...amongst yourselves. As for those who are in favor of this commercially motivated plan-- you must go through the proper channels or suffer the consequences. Remember: Your mother is watching...and so am I.

John Jones
Port Townsend, Washington

Editor:

In the last edition of "Common Ground", I read the letter to the editor by Miguel. He wrote about logging activity near the Green Bridge in Takilma and about herb informants.

As logger/operator I reflect that some of the people I met in passing were very polite and genuinely interested. I appreciated their interaction. Many, however, were rude, double minded, unforgiving and outright hateful. Some shouted from their cars, one notified the sheriff's office concerning possible action against me, another notified the State Forestry, to realize that I am in compliance. Few people took initiative to contact myself or the owner to settle differences or offer constructive comment or action.

I conclude that most people from that end of town are uninterested in community healing but content to gossip and ridicule, allowing their imaginations to run amuck, while knuckling to local social pressures.

Please, people, be honest and think for yourselves. Communicate your feelings as responsible civil folk.

About police - they are not my foundation, strength, fortune or deliverance.

About trees - get to know them, get involved, petition a tree one at a time, if you must.

About herb - look at the sadness around you. Face your pain!

-James R. Dougherty

CORRECTION
More WOMB SERVICE
Karen Beesley has asked that we clarify that she is establishing an independent midwifery service and will refer and consult with other health care providers in Josephine County.

ALL WATER IS RIVER WATER

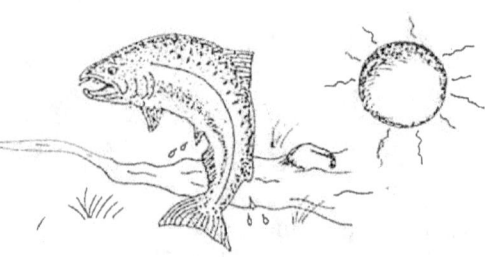

Salmon and Steelhead die when water temperatures approach 80 degrees Fahrenheit. Much of the Illinois River will no longer support salmonids during the summer months. While there are many contributing reasons for this phenomenon (logging, mining, etc.,) there is general consensus (among those who recognize it as a problem,) that by far the largest factor in the dying of our river is water withdrawals, i.e. irrigation. As water flows downstream it absorbs energy from sunlight. The less water there is in the stream, the slower it flows and the hotter it gets. ALL water is river water. Whether creek, spring, or well, it's all destined for the water table and hence affects river levels. Now that every little draw has an increasing and thirsty human population, the river can no longer afford wasteful water practices. We are once again in the midst of the drought. The wet season just over was the driest one in recent memory (just over 40" of precipitation in our Takilma rain gauge - about half of "normal".) Drought makes it critical that we all practice water conservation if we want to continue to live near a live river.

Some things to consider when deciding how or whether to water:

-We have a (mostly) unconscious cultural bias towards over-watering. Our urge to keep everything green probably comes from deep within our northern European dominant cultural roots. Takilma is definitely not Merry Olde England or the Emerald Isle.

-Over-watering is not just wasteful, it's harmful. It promotes fungus diseases and slugs and leaches away the soluble nutrients you have so laboriously applied to your soil.

-Little, if any, water applied to crops finds its way back to the streams via the water table.

-Most garden crops need no more (often much less) than one inch of water per week during the growing season. Since sprinklers deliver wildly different quantities of water, (from 1" per night to 1' per hour,) get to know yours by measuring their outputs with a rain gauge.

-To figure out when to water, don't judge by how plants look or how dry the soil surface is. Instead, stick a finger or shovel several inches down and feel for moisture there.

-Deep, thorough, infrequent waterings are more efficient than shallow, frequent ones.

-Sprinkle only at night or in early mornings if at all possible. Up to HALF the water can be lost to evaporation by sprinkling on hot dry afternoons.

-Mulching crops in the heat of summer can greatly reduce their water needs.

-Minimize water to non-food areas once the really hot weather sets in. Lawns, roads, paths, woods and meadows don't need much (or any) extra watering during the summer. Cultivate a "Brown is Beautiful" mind set.

-Use alternate watering systems where appropriate. Drip and soaker systems lose less water to evaporation but are more expensive and labor intensive than sprinkling. They're best for small separate plantings in hard to sprinkle spots (around buildings, etc..)

Would the Illinois River be better off if everyone ceased all irrigation? You bet! But perhaps if we all practice smart, minimal water use we can have fresh veggies and a live river, too. *-Beth Peterson*

BISCOTTI

Biscotti simply means cookie in Italian, and there are many interpretations of this variety of twice baked cookie. Traditionally served to be dunked in wine or strong coffee, this makes a simple dessert with fresh fruit. This version is 'short', and I have doubled the original recipe and embellished it. After testing many recipes for biscotti, from Chez Panisse (ed. note: a four star up trend spot in Berkeley) and other renowned cooks, this it the best, and according to Italian authorities/friends, the most authentic. I'm still looking for a recipe which makes the dry crunchy biscotti, described by my sister Kathy as "those things which look like rocks, but taste pretty good".

MAGICAL BLEND

2 cups sugar
1 1/2 cups sweet butter
6-8 eggs (depending on size of eggs)
1 Tbsp. vanilla
6 cups flour
2 Tbsp. baking powder
1 Tbsp powdered vanilla (optional-gives stronger-subtle flavor)
1/2 tsp salt
2 cups toasted chopped nuts
1 cup currants (optional)
2 Tbsp. brandy or other liqueur

Preheat oven to 350. Cream sugar and butter-by hand,mixer or food processor. Add eggs, 1 at a time, beating until mixed, then add vanilla and brandy. Mix the flour, baking powder, salt, and powdered vanilla in a separate bowl. Mix in slowly with butter-sugar/egg until it forms a nice medium soft dough. Add the nuts and optional currants and mix for 1 minute more. Turn dough out of bowl onto a lightly floured surface. A slab of marble is ideal, but wood cutting board or pastry cloth works well, too. Divide into 8 portions. Roll each piece of dough into a log shape 1 1/2 inches in diameter and 14 inches long. NOTE: the size can be varied, adjust baking time to accommodate. Butter and flour cookie sheets. Place logs 3 inches apart and bake 25-35 minutes until puffed and golden brown. Remove from oven and let cool about 5 minutes. Place slightly cooled logs on a cutting board and slice diagonally into 3/4 inch wide slices. Place slices on their sides on the same cookie sheets and return to the oven and bake 12-15 minutes until lightly toasted-a rich golden brown. I prefer more crisp. Remove from pans and cool on racks. Store in an airtight container. Biscotti will keep up to three weeks. *- Marcy*

MOLLY MCBRIDE'S ESSAY

I grew up on a commune in southern Oregon. It was there, on a 33-acre piece of land we called Magic Forest Farm, that I learned much of what I know about both the natural and the social worlds around me. I learned to love the cool shadow of a deep forest and to tell the difference between a common and a death camas flower. I learned to swim in the ice cold Illinois River and to grow a Senaca garden with corn, beans, and squash.

There were up to 25 people living on The Farm at a time. I learned to trust other people to help me accomplish things, and I learned, in turn, to help others as well. There was no need for locks on our doors because all members commonly respected that some property was communal and some property was personal. Through this universal trust I learned to be respectful of others and to expect the same in return.

Conversation at The Farm reflected everyday matters like who was going to be on the work party to fix the pipes, how many quarts of string beans were frozen, and who was going to make ice cream for a kid's birthday party. I remember discovering that some people differentiate between women's work and men's work; I was shocked. At The Farm, women turned manure into the soil, fed children, went on wood runs, swept floors, and built log houses. And so did the men. In fact, they all did it together. The dynamics of the situation allowed for joint child rearing, so I had the benefits of a large family. I had multiple role models and plenty of opinions to take into consideration. I had lots of practice with human relations and how to get along with others. The highest form of praise among us was the desire to be in company to celebrate, to laugh, to make music, and to enjoy the family sense of being together.

When I was writing this essay, my mom told me not to use the word "commune". I asked her why and she told me, "Because it's one of those loaded words people get scared of." but somehow, any other word just wouldn't have told where it was that I grew up. The word "commune" is at the heart of "community", which is exactly where I was born and raised. There is something beautiful to me about people from all kinds of backgrounds coming together to create a way of life for themselves. It's important to me that people who interact together make a conscious effort to work together, to play together, to care about each other, to be brave together, to succeed together, to resolve conflicts with each other, and to do more than merely acknowledge each other's existence.

Molly graduated as President of Ashland High's senior class and as one of the twelve Valedictorians. This essay was submitted to one of the six colleges she applied for.

Haiku by Dave

SITTING IN MEETINGS
MASTICATING VEGETABLES
REDUNDANCY REIGNS

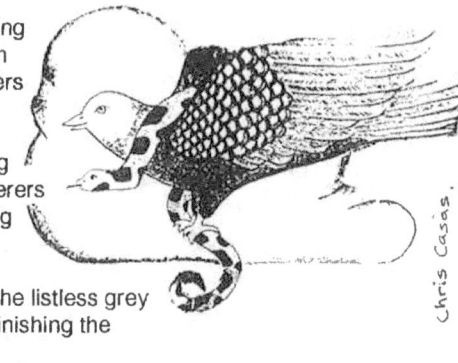

Morning gathering
Enduring search
Passing strangers
[unmet friends]

workers hurrying
late night wanderers
homeless hoping
renters lonely

sounds invade the listless grey
sun's delaying finishing the
previous day.
        Robin Wren

Chris Casas.

PETITION FOR STATE INITIATIVE MEASURE:
BEARS AND COUGARS

Well, I wheedled, needled, wheeled 'n dealed
Coaxed, cajoled, beguiled, smiled, sidled, sighed,
Seduced, induced, prattled, embattled,
Peeked 'n sneaked, prayed, inveighed,
Expunged, expurged, explained, exposited,
Shrilled, trilled, bargained, barged in,
Walked, stalked, and talked and talked
Baited, waited, traded, impeded, repeated, depleted
Walked some more, talked some more
And got them to sign.
Then I went home and took off that damn uncomfortable human skin
And howled and growled late into the night
Til the alarm clock went off and on went the disguise, another day.
        J K Canepa

HO NOW

One of the more powerful sounds in the Universe is the syllable HO. Most Americans may be reminded of Santa Claus and his HO HO HO, but the significance of HO encompasses much more. As a Native American affirmation, HO is used to signify assent to profound statements. Things which are sacred are said to be HO-ly. The name of the HO-pi tribe means "peaceful ones." Navajo dwellings were called HO-gans. These days, weary travelers seek HO-tels.

Our survival depends on water, H2O. Early settlers in this area named one community Holland, or HO-land. Many names reflect the power of HO, particularly HO Chi Minh. Others with HO power: HOlly, HOllis, HOlman, HOuck, HOhm; HOcker, HOlton, HOwell, HOvelman, HOelzle, HOusel, HOoey, and HOback. Many of us have used HOse, HOes, or HOe-dads. The pioneers cried "Westward HO!"

Personally, this HObo is going to HOle up in HOgues Meadow to HOg out on HOstess HO-HO's. HOpe to see you there!   *Dave HOcker*

KIDS WORLD

Nicole

The following essay won statewide honors for its author, Chelsea Hocker, a 6-year old from Della Meengs' first grade class at Evergreen Elementary School. We did not correct her spelling.

I would like to be a librarian when I grow up. I would like to be a librarian because I love to read and there are very many books in a library. A librarian can help people of any age, That is very specail. Anyone can use a library. In a library there are lots of books. A library has cooking books and picture books and creativity books and coloring books and school books and math books and books about the world and ABC books and number books. There are books about just about anything you can think of. You can check out books from a library or sometims you can buy them from a library. There are card catologs that can help find the book we want. A library can be very specail if you love to read and you don't have any books at home. There can be librarys in towns or librarys in schools.

IF I WERE IN CHARGE OF THE WORLD

If I were in charge of the world,
I'd cancel the male race when it's under 10,
math and spelling, homework,
and early morning school.

If I were in charge of the world,
There'd be cute boys my age,
no book reports,
and never fight between friends.

If I were in charge of the world,
You wouldn't have divorce,
or "You didn't pass math!",
violence,
or broccoli.

If I were in charge of the world,
A cavity would be a good thing,
candy would be health food,
and a person who doesn't always turn their
work in, and doesn't always get A's, could still
be in charge of the world.
                    -Mirya, age 12

A HAIRY MAZE

THERE WAS A YOUNG LADY OF FIRLE
There was a young lady of Firle,
Whose hair was addicted to curl;
It curled up a tree,
And all over the sea,
That expansive young lady of Firle.

Snow is
so white
I can't
Believe it.

-Janaki, age7

ASHLAND CORNER barely makes another deadline........... Graduation is in the air everywhere. In Ashland, Molly, Jenica, Zephyr and Ben have their day. Hard to believe, but it seems like just yesterday that they were kids playing at the Dome School. They have all done exceptionally well. Molly is off to Smith College in Massachusetts, Jenica will be going to Hampshire, also in Mass., Zephyr will go to Pacific in Oregon, and Ben is going to work in Colorado to establish residency. Good Luck you guys!!!!

Lots of changes in Ashland these days. Besides the seasonal rush of tourism, we have the opening of the new *Natural History Museum* on July 5th. Along with all this, the railroad district is getting a new park -- development everywhere. Takilma sure looks sweet right now.

If you are in town and hungry, check out the new Indian restaurant, *Five Rivers,* above the Pub in downtown.

And of course if you need a good read....*The Meadow* by Galvin, beautifully written, about the lives of intertwined families over a long period of time living in a meadow in Colorado. Darrel "the movie maven" Pearce recommends *Babette's Feast* and *Flirting* for all you video freaks *-Heller*

POLEEZ BLADDER

May 21 10:00pm: Tipped off by smoke. Group of sisters caught hot-footed. Warned for playing with fire and self endangerment. Ring Leader sought.

June 10 3:00pm: Exodus of students towards various swim holes on Illinois River-No problems.

June 11 Noon: Wayward Mormon Lesbian returns, held and released repeatedly.

June 11 10:30pm: Restless youth, TCB vicinity, tough guy/booze combo. No arrest made though parental counseling suggested.

June 13: Thespian Giant, unmasked, harmless, questioned and released. Results pending.

June 13: General alarm from gardeners attacked by freak frost at 2 am.

June 14: Odd frocked campers with trippy hairdos, sighted near Sunstar .

ENCLOSED IS MY CONTRIBUTION OF:

$10 ___ 1 YEAR SUBSCRIPTION

$25 ___ 1 YEAR SUBSCRIPTION +TAKILMA
          MUG + ONE BOTTLE AURA POLISH

$50 ___ 1 YEAR SUBSCRIPTION + TAKILMA
          MUG + WE'LL OMIT AURA POLISH

      ___ I'M BROKE BUT LITERATE. PLEASE
          SEND THE NEWSLETTER.

Takilma COMMON GROUND
PO BOX 2016   CAVE JUNCTION, OR 97523

NAME_____

ADDRESS_____

_____

COMMON GROUND, a newsletter for Takilma, was born out of the desire to broaden our connections as a community. Our mission is to present a forum for information and ideas on issues of concern to our corner of the world. We support diversity, encourage debate, promote creative expression and actively seek common ground. We honor the earth we inhabit at the headwaters of the Illinois River.

With this, our fourth issue, we are making a couple of changes in our publication schedule and distribution practices. Instead of printing every two months we will be publishing the paper EIGHT TIMES A YEAR, to coincide with the solstices, equinoxes and the mid-points in between. Our next deadline for submissions will be July 19th, for publication of the fifth issue on August 2nd.

Friends who do not live in Takilma or the Illinois Valley and who have not so far responded, with either bucks or greetings, will not be receiving any further issues. Just contact us and we will be happy to reinstate you on the mailing list.

We encourage you to send us your articles, letters, graphics and announcements. We prefer them to be brief, typewritten, double-spaced and in triplicate, but if the content is stellar we will tolerate funk. We reserve the right to edit. Please send all material to Takilma Common Ground, P.O.Box 2016, Cave Junction, OR 97523. The Mud Council consists of Kayla, Adrian, Felicity, Jill, Robin, Dave, Dave T. and Laurie. The editorial staff for this issue was Dave, Kayla, Kate, Laurie, Felicity, Jill, Dave T., Robin and Kerry.

TAKILMA CROSSWORD

If you get stuck, call Dave 592-2492

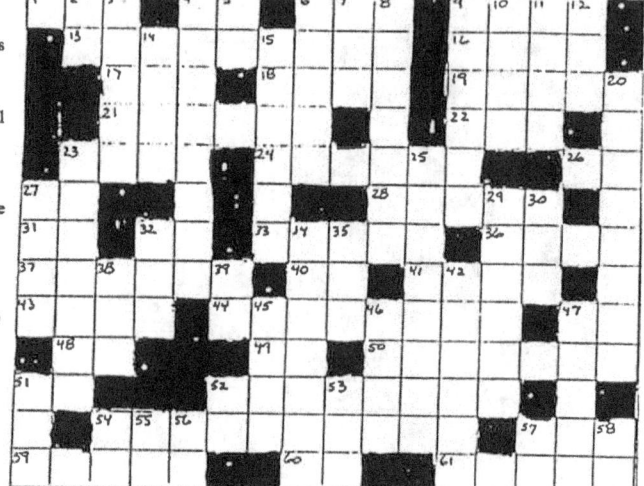

DOWN
2. STOP - not!
3. Cedar _____
4. Nuclear Protester
5. Hell's sister city
6. Indolent variety of potato
7. Public Utilities Commission
8. Eager for a drink
9. Takilma ballpark site
10. Ancestor of slugs?
11. Moms opposed to inebriates in traffic
12. Potato part
14. Miguel's medium
15. No matter what color, it will always be green
20. Jesus, or a coupon user
23. Center of the Universe
25. Famous artist with unique geometric perspective
27. Take a hit
29. Calls like a crane
30. Affirmative vote
32. Poem intended to be sung
34. I would be more sober if I drank this (2 words)
35. Swiss mountain
38. Ho HO Ho Chi Minh _____ is gonna win
39. Blvd. - NOT!
42. A break or interruption in continuity
45. Entrance - NOT !
46. Askew
47. 39.37 inches
51. Sitting artist
52. Seek you?
53. Higher than a king
54. Off - NOT !
55. Mrs. Allan's initials
56. Do too many crossword puzzles
57. 3.14159265
59. Are we having fun yet

ACROSS
1. One gets laid
4. Betty call me this
6. Accountant's initials
9. Everyone's favorite school
13. T-town B & B
16. Feelin' allright
17. Held a match to
18. Barter Fair site
19. Request food from buying club
21. It may be SREP now, but it will always be this
22. Paternal hep cat ?
23. Now—NOT !
24. Kerouacian bums
26. Take too many drugs
27. Famous/infamous local writer
28. "Uh" sound with odd consonant grouping
31. How are you?
32. Want a hit?
33. Make happy
36. Jekyll-NOT!
37. Bush's gentler America
40. Elevated railroad
41. Hippie footwear - not
43. Fashion mag. with French name
44. Slowly in Spanish
47. You, to yourself
48. Initials for a commonly deleted expletive
49. Extra small
50. Williams roadside spray opponent
51. District Attorney
52. Coffin nails
54. Okay, cutey I see, why are you?
57. Implement not recommended for this puzzle
59. Gratuitous sexual reference
60. Southwest - not
61. Political "household word" 25 years ago

Takilma COMMON GROUND
POB 2016
CAVE JUNCTION, OR 97523

Entertainment for the outhouse. #5

WALK WILD IN THE SISKIYOUS

Come join a diverse group of forest lovers for a weekend of day-hiking around the threatened Sugarloaf Mountain forest. Enjoy scenic vistas, learn about forest ecology and celebrate the Wild!

As you read in our last issue, this site is up for logging, even though it is designated in the new forest plan as Ancient Forest Reserves, is at high elevation, the only part of this forest not infested (yet) with Port Orford cedar root rot, is spotted owl habitat, and the watershed has already been cut to ribbons. But, because this sale was awarded five years ago, the Forest Service claims they don't have to abide by the new rules. Gov. Barbara Roberts has written to the Regional Forester, John Lowe, expressing her concern that allowing this logging of an Ancient Forest Reserve would undermine the whole Clinton forest plan. The Forest Service claims that this is a tree thinning and that they will not cut many trees over 21" in diameter. In fact, 59% of the trees over 21" are marked for death!

You can still call or write John Lowe, Reg. Forester to tell him what you think about this plan. The address is U. S. Forest Service, P. 0. Box 3263, Portland OR 97208 or phone 503-326-2971 and tell him not to award this sale. (By the way, our calls and letters do seem to be effective sometimes; the Canyon sale that many of us wrote about last year has just been withdrawn from consideration.)

The Sugarloaf camp-out will begin on Friday evening, August 26th with music and meals, hiking and workshops on Saturday and Sunday. Breakfasts and Saturday dinner will be provided. This is all being sponsored by Siskiyou Regional Education Project. Call the office at 592-4459 for the details and to loan equipment for this adventure.

We need propane stoves, large cooking pots, spoons and knives, chopping blocks, coolers, hand pump fire extinguishers, shovels, pulaskis, 2-way radios, first aid supplies. water barrels, tents and tipis. We also will need people power to help with parking, children's activities, food prep. And lots of folks to join in the fun. - *Siskiyou Project*

EXPANDING SPACE

It's summer and what a hot one........speaking of hot....here's some hot news!! Have you seen what's happening at the Dome School, this 20th anniversary summer? Notice the foundation for the new office storage and special needs space. It's a happening!! We received a grant from the wonderful folks at "The Carpenter Foundation" for $4,000, plus we raised $2100 from Le Show. The projected cost of the new space is between $12-15,000........and we are halfway there. Loans from community members are available to finish the structure. This will free up our kitchen space, thus starting a new chapter in Takilma style entertainment. Look forward to those exotic meals just waiting to happen........OK, here's the pitch.........we have to raise a few (6-7) thousand dollars in order to pay back loans. Let's see.....300 people at $20.00 each, that's $6,000 not bad! Have you paid your Community Tax yet???

We are looking for folks who would like to contribute to the labor in this project...Bobby Mannix has taken on being our hired general contractor and could use some help. By the time this paper is mailed, the foundation should be poured and hopefully materials will have been delivered to start the construction. During the first two weeks of August is when we'll being needing volunteers.......skilled and unskilled. Please call Robin for more info. 592-3159.

Please send any contribution $5.00 to $1,000. to:
Community Building Fund
c/o Common Ground
P.O. Box 2016
Cave Junction, OR 97523

AUGUST 26 - 28
SUGARLOAF MOUNTAIN

"...TO BE INDEPENDENT OF PUBLIC OPINION IS THE FIRST FORMAL CONDITION OF ACHIEVING ANYTHING GREAT." G.W.F. HEGEL

Gail Borod has returned to Takilma after a year at Brown College in Rhode Island where hard work earned her a Masters in Teaching. She will begin her teaching career at Lorna Byrne Middle School this fall.

Gail originally migrated to Takilma to visit Melissa Chauvin, whom she met as an undergraduate at Princeton. She camped out on the Chauvin lawn for several weeks, and realized she and her partner, Jon, had found their new home in this valley.

During her first couple of years here, Gail explored the natural beauty of our area and got to know many of our colorful characters. She taught in the Dome School and initiated a volunteer tutoring/counseling service at I.V. High School . With these endeavors, Gail found that she needed more advanced training to be the educator she wanted to be and so made the tough decision to go away to school ,hoping that she would find a job here when she was finished . Those of us who know her also hoped that she would return, although it seemed a long shot at the time. Gail chose Brown College for itts unique program of national school reform which has developed effective methods for advancing our nation's education system to meet the needs of the 90's. The focus is on developing creative and critical thinking skills in students rather the the rote learning required by the industrial mass production machine of the past century.

Gail, who grew up in the deep south (Memphis!) and went to college in the deep Northeast (New Jersey), chose the Illinois Valley because of the natural beauty, ancient forests, clean rivers and the wealth of human resources here. She loves to garden, drum and spend time in the wilderness... right out her front door. She relishes communal living at the Magic Forest Farm where the pooling of individual energies and skills challenges and stimulates personal growth. The spirit of community here in Takilma is a big plus in her active life. She is impressed with the diversity of life styles here in the Valley with traditional and alternative values co-existing in relative harmony. Usually! - Kayla

IT'S A ZOO OUT THERE

Match the names in the first column with those in the second column.

1. Ron	A. Dove
2. Robin	B. Eagle
3. Sitting	C. Horse
4. Gray	D. Raven
5. Luna	E. Hawk
6. Sky	F. Dog
7. Rabbit	G. Cat
8. Bird	H. Wren
9. Robyn	I. Tromier
10. New	J. Woman
11. Bunny	K. Man

LETTER TO THE EDITOR

Dear Common Ground,

The only grounds we have here are in the kitchen and thank the Lord they're not common! Your newsletter has brought a smile to this ol' face each time it arrived. But, alas, all good things must come to an end, and it's true with Common Ground for me. My celly is being paroled from OSP and with him goes the newsletter.

I have noticed that on your subscription form you have a spot for those of us who are 'broke but literate'. That describes me, so I marked it! Currently the State is paying us a buck per day but this will be reduced to twenty-five cents per day, beginning July 1st,1994. Measure five, cost of living (on the outside) and Clinton's Health Care plan are but some of the rumored reasons. Who knows for sure, but I will send you as much as I can.

I'm hoping you'll continue to send Common Ground to me so I can keep the smile on my face and know there are really people out there somewhere.

Sincerely

Ronald S. Meadows

HOT-FOOTED RINGLEADER SPEAKS UP

Fire walking has been a community ritual around the globe for thousands of years. This ancient rite has always been used in the context of healing, celebration and a deeper connection with the divine.

Tibetans hold a community fire walk in which the priests and monks hold the energy and invite the community to walk. It is a fast paced, high energy walk where participants go over the coals 108 times. In Greece, the believers of St. Constantine dance in a pit of hot coals until the coals are ground to ash. The community onlookers become reunited with the power of faith. In the Fijian Islands the fire walk is a coming-of-age ritual for the seven year old girls of the community and in the Kalahari desert, the Kung tribe has an all night ecstatic ritual during which the healers dance, eat and roll in the red hot coals, with the energetic support of the community. In the morning, the healers use their rekindled energy in the laying on of hands for their tribe.

The western fire walk movement began seventeen years ago and has been used for personal empowerment, group cohesion, goal setting and to become reconnected. I was trained by Peggy Dylan, the female originator of the western movement. I recommend her training to anyone interested.

What is fire walking to me? Alchemy! It is the heat source required to change the base metal of what we are, into the gold of who we are. I have a vision of a Takilma Community Fire Walk, to heal our old wounds and create a new vision for our community. This would be a tribal event and a healing experience. The fire walk will be a Dome School benefit and take place at the community building. I wanted to hold it in connection with the 20th anniversary celebration but due to the severe drought conditions have decided to hold off until October. I'll keep you posted.

-Hollis Abraham

a few innings of ritual

the 'stress test was behind us
ahead the equally important 'diamond'
gypsum boundaries mark the arena where
slow pitch would bring together tribe
in an exchange of hits, runs, throws and catches

slowly the crowd gathered
all the while energies moved in the air
gland and mental activities uncontrolled
re-discussion of before-hand challenges
many had their opinions, most had a favorite team

potatoes of youth, strong legged and quick
rallied their hopes around last year's victory
and envisioned a repeat
the elders slower, yet honed with years of experience
nursed their lifetime's aches and "owies"
while flashbacks of past athletic achievements
danced in their present thoughts...
as if today, old ways will again be 'new' ways
hopes of imminent victory were everywhere

the day was clear, the sun had its place in deep left field
there would be no excuses of blindness today
the grass was mowed, watered, and mowed again
manicured as a field of dreams
spectators eager, jubilant as the elders took the field
[indeed] this year's challenge had been accepted
and history was to unfold

few could have imagined, many were amazed
knowing the importance of early inning manifestations
the elders struck quickly, the old crowd cheered
talk of lopsided victory circulated the bleachers
then, equally as quick they were caught and fell behind
'elders' become 'geezers', breathes shortened
feelings of despair rose in the ranks.

[and] across the landscape potato fans smile in relief
they were happy, they were confident
they were mostly young
then, as if by magic
the elders put forth the nearly forgotten
......eighth inning stretch and chant
the miracle was about to unfold-

a hit here, a hit there, an error in the field
a hit, a run, another
that little train that could.......was back!!
in that last inning a puff of smoke
clearly marked the elder's dug-out
they knew the scenario, they've been here before
their victory was as close as their leg cramps
hold 'em, score and they win
the potatoes in the field were wide-eyed in disbelief
the elders were humble in their pursuit
and on this day would not be denied
 - anon. 1994 a.d.

JULY 4.1994

Glorious, sparkling defense, thrilling suspense, the long ball, sportsmanship and camaraderie across team lines, community spirit played out on a horse pasture freshly mowed and lined for THE SOFTBALL GAME. The rematch. Payback time for the Over 35 team. This was a beautiful game, transcending its simpleness.

On July 4th, 1994 the Over 35 Geezers won in extra innings, justice I suppose. Those who lay seeds will eventually reap the harvest. That I grant. Miguel again took the mound, threw the same junk, but to different results, earning his team the victory. The Under 35 Potatoes came back from a 6-0 first inning to shut down the powerful older lineup for six straight innings. Impressive defense stunned the crowd into an uneasy silence. Two homeruns in the 8th vaulted the Geezers into a sudden 9th inning lead. A lead wiped away with a Potato homer in the top half. Then two runners on, two outs, bottom of the 9th, tie score. Drama or a tease. A tease, a groundout. Extra innings.

Bottom of the 10th. The end. Dave Toler lofts a fly ball to a hole in centerfield. And as I stood out in shallow centerfield, watching Erik Jules' throw rise toward the infield where Steve Marsden was scoring the winning run, I watched Miguel's lanky figure leap towards the heavenly blue sky in utter jubilation and I shared a slice of that joy. For what we did, all of us, to build that field, play a thrilling game, a show of our community's vitality. I felt blessed.

But out in centerfield I felt useless, having to walk off the field. "The game's not over is it?" asked a teammate. "It is." I said. But it isn't, this game wasn't the whole story. The game is part of a new tradition which has brought us all even closer. Congrats to the Geezers, sip the sweet nectar of victory, for 1995 shall be the year of the Potatoes!! It will be glorious, see ya there.....-Jon Jeans.

'ANOTHER' INNING OF RITUAL

20th ANNIVERSARY of the DOME SCHOOL

Big time for us all!!!!! Hard to believe it was 20 years ago our little darlings began their schooling in the DooDah Dome! We have all come a long way from a Dome to a 40'x60' building. Thanks to much appreciated energy and time from all community members. This year we will celebrate the anniversary at our annual Carnival, Sunday, Aug. 14th beginning at noon. This is our BIG fundraiser--games, dunk tank, food booths, raffles and talent show. We welcome all alumni to participate in the talent show. This year we even have beautiful 20th anniversary T-shirts that will be for sale. We do need help with donations for baked goods, tostada ingredients and raffle items. If you can help with donations or energy, please call Helen 592-2327 or Susan 592-3632. We need your help!! We would like to thank and congratulate Helen Kauffman for her many years of love and dedication to the school and our children and for making these great carnivals happen. -Laurie

SPICY SUMMER FRUIT COMPOTE

The combination of macerated fruits, wine and herbs and spices is luscious, easy and fat-free. Great alone or with fresh fruit sorbet or biscotti. Use any combination of soft fruits and berries; include dried fruit if you wish - dried cherries soaked in brandy or liqueur are spectacular.

Pit two each: peaches, plums, apricots, 1/2# cherries, pitted and cut in half, plus 1 cup berries. Place all the fruit in a bowl and sprinkle with 15 cilantro leaves on top. NOTE: the world is divided into those who love cilantro and those who loathe it; cilantro can be omitted or passed separately, but it adds a subtle flavor combined with that of the seed.

Combine: 1 cup of white or red table wine, 1/2 cup water, 1/2 cup sugar, 2 Tablespoons grated ginger, 8-12 crushed peppercorns and 8-12 coriander seeds. Bring to a boil and simmer 15 minutes. While still hot, strain out the ginger and spices and pour the syrup over the fruit. Refrigerate and allow to macerate at least 1 hour before serving. Yields 8-10 servings. -*Marcy*

ASSUME THE POSITION

This new column is for brief comments, quotes, even vignette , that remind us of the harsh realities of life in post-modern Amerika--**and how we rise above it!**
So....SUBMIT,SUBMIT, SUBMIT. (next deadline is Sept.7)

Hippy/Hippie {defined in the '93 edition of Merriam Websters Dictionary}: "A usually young person who rejects the mores of established society (as by dressing unconventionally or favoring communal living) and advocates a non-violent ethic; broadly: a long-haired unconventionally dressed young person."

Since the U.S. government spends more on the military in 5 hours than it does on health care in 5 YEARS, it's a good thing we have alternatives here in Takilma (consider the proposal for our rock-n-roll old age home).

Hey, we're not doing so bad getting our priorities on straight: In Japan last year two guys earned a profit of $96,000. selling girls' used underpants from vending machines.

STOP KILLER WEED!

INFACT, the organization that conducted the boycotts of Nestle (the infant formula fiasco) and General Electric (nuclear weapons production) has now taken on the tobacco industry. Tobacco is still, strangely, legal to smoke, though it is the leading cause of preventable deaths in the U.S., killing 419,000 annually.

The industry, desperate to build markets due to reductions in the smoking population, is now promoting tobacco to youth and the third world in a big way. INFACT has targeted Phillip Morris, the world's largest tobacco company (makers of Marlboro), and RJR Nabisco (makers of Camels). The campaign is heating up with nation-wide actions to remove the macho Joe Camel ads from markets. There is also a consumer boycott of subsidiary products including Kraft, Maxwell House, Oscar Meyer, Miller, General Foods and Post. Well, most of us here don't use tobacco and many of us already avoid these food products as they are not the healthiest of vittles. However, we can be sure to avoid these products and tell others about the boycott.

For more information , literature, buttons, decals etc. contact Kayla at 592-4275. We have more power to change the world than we realize! We succeeded in getting GE out of the Nuke business, so watch out tobacco pushers!- *Kayla*

RUNNING BROTHERS WEATHER

Well, the weather has finally stabilized into that hot and dry pattern which characterizes our summers. This may be good or bad depending on how a person feels about heat. According to Kerry Whitehead (who is a Canadian, runs in shorts all winter and heats his house only to keep Sheila happy) , "We're doomed." Robert, on the other hand, loves it. "I can finally take off my third shirt" he said, as the mercury climbed to 101. When asked about the pros and cons of hot weather, Doug exclaimed, "We won district championship!! Now it's off to Hermiston for State Championship." Referring, of course, to Jessame's stunning pitching performance in the Senior Little League Softball, ages 13-15, and Illinois Valley's great undefeated season. This is payback to Doug for pitching to Jessame all these years.!! -*Robert*

Love someone

Our quality control staff is on summer vacation.

HOW ?
(with apologies, apologies, apologies to Allen Ginsberg)
by Jack

I saw the lots better than average minds of my generation
    mundaned by busy ordinariness,
dragging their bedwarm cellulited asses through rough paneled
    kitchens looking for the rice cream fix,
who busytired and projectmired and burntwired had stayed up
    past kidroar leafing through alternative catalogs,
mothballed revolutionaries damply smoldering with
    untappable zeal,
visionaries variably clouded with a slight chance of
    reigning in a new day,
who once fled deadleadered and dedicated piney lots of
    rural refuge to inner transformation chosen community
    saved world and global gloriosity,
who trusted groovy dealers more than agricorporations and
    bet their stomachs and brains and genes on that trust and
    were often right and sometimes treated and released,
who seeking harmony with natural body needs examined their
    own shit, dangled crystal pendulums, ate organic
    concoctions impossible to assemble before the New Age
    of longhaul trucking,
who built lawnless cabins and squat toilets their parents
    wouldn't use and were disappointed if they did and
    later planted lawns but no diachondra and put in
    flushtoilets too but still peed outside,
who were refused service and joyously serviced themselves
    and whoever else would allow them,
who rock and rolled and balled and swallowed and smoked
    neuroscramblers until the daylight bad dreams and
    sundry bodily dysfunctions just said whoa,
who hopped up on dope and sprouts crammed swaddled families
    into ratty pickups and were turned away from drive-in
    theaters showing The Ten Commandments
who benudely frolicked free in pristine pools, dallied
    bareassed in dandelion-bowers until the kids got wise,
who doubtless screwed up by their parents raised free to
    be you and me children still screwed up but
    this time by Richard Nixon and Sylvester Stallone,
who went west and turned East, angry cats preferring dogmas
    from anywhere elsewhere, moaning dancing chanting,
    singing anything but onward christian solders,

who flaunted hairy tie-dyed badges of scornful difference
    and were surprised when treated differently,
who fought bulldozers with bare bodies presscovered, or
    who came to fight with justice for vocabulary
    adjustments and world beat CD's and the letters
    letters letters lying unsent in drawers unread in
    the offices of the powerful,
who thrust through sexual taboos and boundaries and so did
    everybody, and everyway, and got herpes and scared
    and tossed at night wide-eyed and alone listening for
    he/she/it to come and fill the gaping bed,
who found themselves telling their children to turn their
    music down or grooved along until the kids
    begged them to stop,
hardworking bums, responsible spongers, libertine ascetics,
    mystical dogmatic freethinkers and other paradoxes
    when grouped as lumpen hippitaritat or even in lumpy
    individuals,
who spoke to they of oneness but lived in we-theyness and then
    acknowledged the difference and so began to learn oneness,
who bravely went on ushering in the recalcitrant New Age
    or declared it already here or turned off their
    flashlights and quit ushering except to shush those
    who talked of it,
who soothed the poor and sick and self-destructive, and
    healed and taught and marveled how there could be more
    and more poor and sick and self-destructive pouring
    through the doors,
who saw that needs would outlast efforts, despair outlast
    hope yet worked and hoped,
who poured love into community and trees, little plots of
    soil and little soiled hands and were amazed at their own
    thirst as the love worked full circle,
who made peace with their parents at home, in the grave,
    or inside themselves,
or who like me got early straight and loyaled to the working
    class bill payers and always wondered, watching with
    admiring scorn and derisive envy and open amazed love
    as my generation thrashed out the timeless new and
    profound silly of countless newly encountered cultures.

Jupiter's in retrospect.

The Mud Council (our ersatz Board of Directors) consists of Adrian, Jill, Dave, Laurie,
Kayla, Felicity, Dave T., Marcy, Robin and Kate. The editorial staff for this issue was all
the same people with the exception of Kate and the addition of Kerry and Jon. SPECIAL thanks to
Mr. TRACY

ENCLOSED IS MY CONTRIBUTION OF:

$10 ___ 1 YEAR SUBSCRIPTION

$25 ___ 1 YEAR SUBSCRIPTION +TAKILMA
MUG + ONE BOTTLE AURA POLISH

$50 ___ 1 YEAR SUBSCRIPTION + TAKILMA
MUG + WE'LL OMIT AURA POLISH

___ I'M BROKE BUT LITERATE. PLEASE
SEND THE NEWSLETTER.

Takilma COMMON GROUND
PO BOX 2016   CAVE JUNCTION, OR 97523

NAME_____

ADDRESS_____

Q. How can you tell if a Deadhead has visited you?

A. They're still there.

KIDS PAGE

THE SHARING GAME

Have a little time? What to do? Have fun with your kids! Play the sharing game! Print each activity on a card or matching pieces of cardboard. Turn them over and shuffle; spread cards face down and choose a card. Share the activity. ENJOY!
Feel free to make up your own activities.

Take a walk
Read a story together
Invent a game and play it
Make a collage
Make or bake a treat
Play a card game
Write a story together
Sing some songs
Have a treasure hunt
Dress up
Look through old photos
Go on a bike ride
Explore nature together
Draw, color or paint
Play with water (hoses, bath, swim, water balloons etc.)
Play with earth (plant something, dig, play in sand etc.)

MAXIE AND SAM ANNOUNCE THE SLAB

One day Max and Sam invited a whole bunch of dogs and people to go to a barbeque at the slab. Tilly tried to shoot a hoop and made a whoosh and Pan comes at the exact time before any of them(except Max and Sam) and rolled on the new big spool that they were going to have the barbcque on. But they did not mind that he was rolling on it because all of them together could push it straight up. Mish and Jessea came on their bikes and rode around on the slab and then they played tic-tac-toe with the new chalk. And there was a whole bunch of people coming to the barbeque. They then played a big basketball game and nobody cared if they won or lost. The end.
- *jessea , age 6*

OK KIDS-

THIS IS YOUR PAGE, 100'S OF PEOPLE READ YOUR OPINION, DO YOU HAVE ONE? HOW ABOUT YOUR OPINION ON: LIVING IN TAKILMA, WHAT WOULD YOU CHANGE, WHAT DO YOU LIKE?.... SEND US "YOUR OPINION" IN 50 WORDS OR LESS FOR THE NEXT ISSUE...COPY DUE SEPT 7,1994 . SEND YOUR DRAWINGS, POEMS, PUZZLES - THOUGHTS AND DREAMS

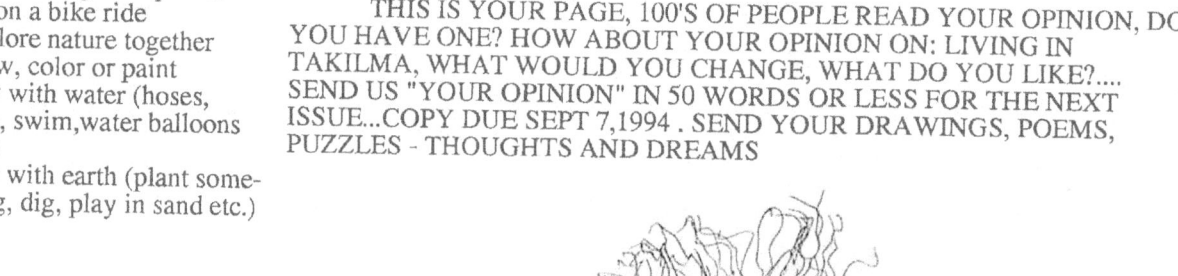

Illustrators on Kids Page. Jessea, Kristen, Mirya, Mishael, Nicole, Shanti.

The Mystical

In a realm, half asleep
half awake, in a land of dreams.
Sun shines down on this rocky place
Water so green in a land of peace.
Foolish plans for pirate's gold
Careless thoughts that must be told,
Clues abound from yesteryear
Dreamy words that we must hear.

I believe in the mystical
Reds seen in the color blue
Changin time, endless scenes
Glories that I have seen.

The rocks rise up, the tree twist round
The water rolls in without a sound,
Birds fly by they sing to me
Looking for food in the shallow sea.
Contented space I dream upon
Completing tasks I've just begun,
With a prayer in a silent way
Giving my mind to the day.

I believe in the mystical
Reds seen in the color blue
Changin time, endless scenes
Glories that I have seen.

Lie with me in emerald pools
In this dream there are no rules
Twist thru canyons as you ride
In deep shadows the truth does hide.
Deep between this dream I weave
The magic of springs fallen leaves,
Lies hopes among the castaways
Who beautifully give the past away.

And I believe in the mystical....

    Jon Jeans. Baja 94.

TAKILMA POLICE BLADDER
-THINGS THAT COULD BE TRUE

June 25: Missing: Sign from Green Bridge swimming hole - 'No Alcohol'. Also missing: Naked Lunch.

June/July: Numerous vehicles reported dead, dying or damaged. Jupiter charged retrospectively. Resisted arrest.

July 4: 62 plastic deputies go out on a limb near Page Creek. Got high and heavy. Passed stress test.

July 4: Potatoes whipped. Revenge promised. No problem.

July 5: Still missing: Naked Lunch.

July 5: No potluck on Rockydale Road. Narco-terrorists eat and run.

July 7: Takilma quiet and calm after eco-herd stampedes north. House-sitters request waterbed maintenance training.

July 8-10: Large numbers of normally reclusive persons crawl out of woodwork. Held and released, but not too much.

July 12: Still missing: 'No Alcohol' sign at Green Bridge. Women intervene successfully with drunks. Women held. Drunks released.

July 14: Marjorie skips through Mud, wearing a skirt. Emerges unsoiled.

July 14: Great rave on Rockydale Road.

July 15: Women, children and men patrolled the scene around the dance at Community Building. No problems. Wayward Mormon lesbian sighted at 2 a.m. taking care of naked youth in downtown Takilma.

July 16: Missing: naked youth's memory.

July 19: Quality control staff of local rag leaves town. Investigation reveals it makes no difference.

July 22: 9a.m.-4p.m. Noisy airborne narco-terrorists observed flying low over all parts of listening area. Neighbors disgusted.

July 22: Slab-happy fool moon celebration in 12000 block. Neighbors happy.

July 23: Takilma migrates to California for fiesta.

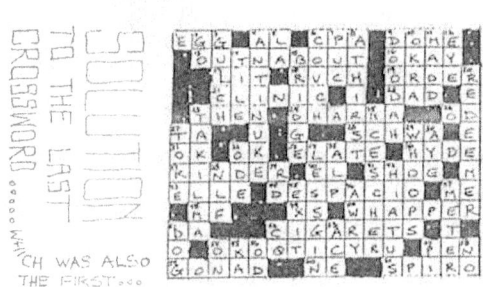

SOLUTION TO THE LAST CROSSWORD ...WHICH WAS ALSO THE FIRST...

the gift

since one can only
give that which is wanted
finding the true gift
is a blessing given

to one who would give
himself and find love
wanted in return sees
the nature of grace

one cannot give freedom
but only honor flowing
and cherish the unbound
spirit that chooses to stay

in truth we are one
being given to ourselves
the reflection it sought
when the mirror was made

let me serve you tea
sit in a place here
you are the gift that is wanted

    -River

COMMON GROUND, a newsletter for Takilma, was born out of the desire to broaden our connections as a community. Our mission is to provide a forum for the exchange of information and ideas about issues that concern our readers. We support diversity, encourage debate, promote creative expression, hunger for humor and actively seek common ground. We honor the earth we inhabit here at the headwaters of the Illinois River.

    The paper is mailed to all the addresses we can find in Takilma, and to our friends in the Illinois Valley and points beyond who have responded with bucks or greetings. If you are reading this in somebody else's outhouse, and wondering what happened to your own copy, you now know what to do. We publish eight times a year, to coincide with the solstices, equinoxes and the mid-points in between.

    Out of respect for our depleted forests, we have changed our policy on submissions. We still crave stellar content, but we'll accept single copies on Mac-compatible software, carved in stone, or anything in between.

    Due to a critical typo in the crossword, we have had to fire one typist. We are on a quest for volunteer helpers in the production of this newsletter. If you can fold, staple, peel or stick, we need you. If you are into spindling or mutilation, you are unwelcome. If you like to lick, please come in for a personal interview.

    OUR NEXT DEADLINE FOR SUBMISSIONS WILL BE SEPTEMBER 7TH, FOR PUBLICATION ON SEPTEMBER 21ST. Please send articles, cartoons, letters, announcements and stunning artwork to Takilma Common Ground, P.O. Box 2016, Cave Junction, OR 97523.

Q. How do you starve a Deadhead?   A. Hide their food stamps in their work boots.

Q. What does a Deadhead say when the acid runs out?

A. This band really sucks.

CLASSIFIEDS:

MFF announces opening of wiffle Golf course, 18 holes, cost is 1 beer to Jon or Eric; Potatoes, the movie, rental $2. contact Jon 592-2831.

Whirlpool almond fridge; frost free!! $125.00   Rebecca 592-4677.

Printer Wanted: Mac compatible...cheap but fast...trade $ or ? Kayla 592-4275.

You've been lied to about Cannabis Sativa! Learn the truth about Hemp in the new entertaining video "Let My People Grow" based on the best seller "The Emperor Wears No Clothes" by Jack Herer. The video is available for $19.95 plus $4.00 for ship/hand. at Seven Thunders, PO Box 2067, Cave Junction, Or 97523. Call 592-4545 for more information.

ACROSS

1. Ms. Emerald
6. Modern LP
8. Native American affirmation
9. Ms. McCoy
11. Northeast IV
13. Lincoln's phone greeting ? (2 words)
16. Mirth
17. Maine to a postman
18. Midnight sun ?
19. Mr. Dunnit
21. China and cherry
22. Elementary teacher (init.)
24. Better than hell
26. Monthly pain
28. Awry
31. Honda---NOT!!
32. Less aged
33. Suffix used to turn liquid into a verb
34. Appalling
36. His magazine bears his name
37. Extra Large
38. Whip Inflation Now slogan
40. Before HST and DDE
43. Stateline to Hays
44. Dog's first trick
46. Create landfill---NOT !!
49. SREP and many local businesses
52. King of Norway
54. Native American named after bird
55. Meditation mantra
56. In the direction of
57. Why am I ?
58. Lady Chatterly's author

DOWN

2. Famous party hostess
3. Ms. Abraham
4. Approached
5. Mr. Gore
6. A large, important town
7. _____ Moines
10. Bud not common in Takilma
11. Like most local wells
12. Magazine with angry name
14. Big name on campus
15. mr. cummings
18. Drum-maker extraordinaire
19. In what place ?
20. To chop a tree
21. LI + LI
23. Beth's brew (2 words)
25. Ms. Starr
26. Freedonia art form
27. Neil's forte
29. Rank of Bilko
30. Coffee king
32. Why you?
33. 1986 special effects movie
35. Barter _____
39. Why elephants die
41. Make a hole
42. Every one
44. I spy backwards
45. Frog's cousin
47. Gratuitous sexual reference
48. Vitamin advice for cold sufferers (2 words)
50. Where 57,000 died
51. Trio after CDE
53. Enemy
55. Where rust is State Gem? (abbreviation)

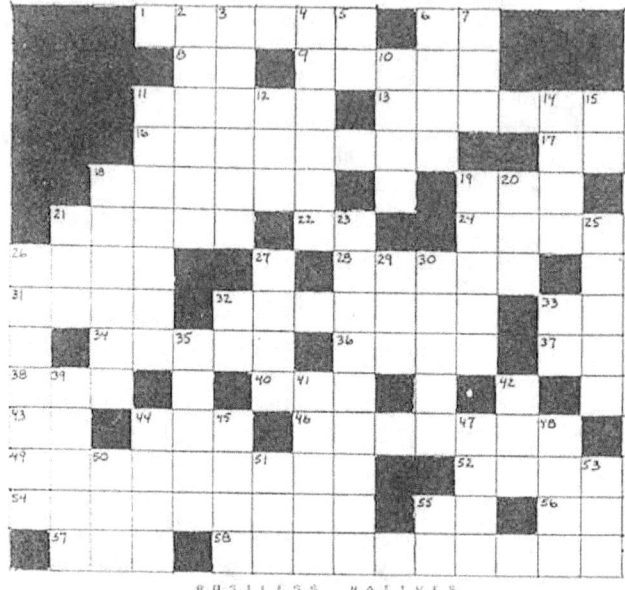

RUSTLESS NATIVES

ROSTLESS   NATIVES

Takilma COMMON GROUND
POB 2016
CAVE JUNCTION, OR 97523

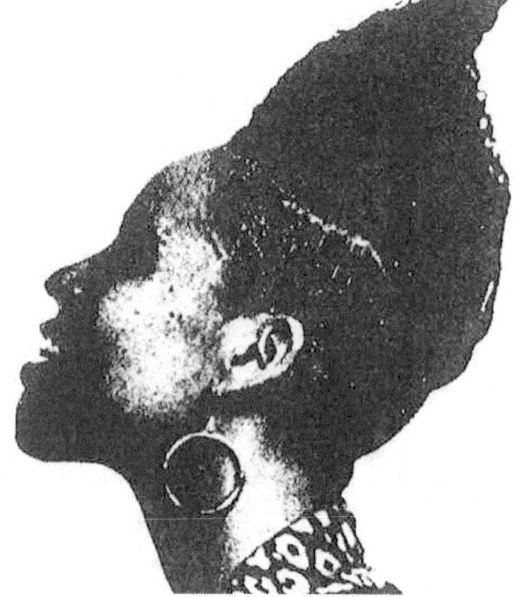

TAKILMA COMMON GROUND

September-October 1994   Issue #6

serving the Takilma Spirit Family

A WATERSHED WITHOUT A COUNCIL

Efforts to begin state funded recovery projects for a declining Illinois River watershed have come up against a political dam.

About $470,000 of project funding is now held up in a struggle between Oregon state officials and Josephine County Commissioners.

Recognizing the need to take action on critically impacted watersheds throughout Oregon, the 1993 legislature passed a bill to channel lottery funds into two major water basins, the Grand Ronde in the Northeast and the South Coast/Rogue Basin, which encompasses the Illinois. These funds are designed to help "demonstrate watershed recovery through projects that improve watershed health."

While the primary objective is to rehabilitate fisheries in the Illinois River, many in the valley also see the $470,000 as a welcome shot in the arm for this economically depressed community.

However, without a state approved local watershed council, these, and potentially hundreds of thousands more dollars in future projects will have to bypass the Illinois Valley.

Local watershed councils are the "cornerstone" of the state's recovery strategy. Council members are appointed by local governments with final approval coming from the Oregon Strategic Water Management Group, known as SWMG (SWiMGee).

According to Jerry McCloud of the Oregon Watershed Health program there are some fundamental guidelines which local agencies must follow in forming local councils. McCloud points out that the councils must "represent the diverse nature and elements of watersheds" in order to ensure a "reasonably balanced" voice.

The Illinois Valley Watershed Council appointed by Josephine County Commissioners has not been accepted by SWMG due to a question of balance.

According to Corky Lockard, project director for the I.V. Soil and Water Conservation District (SWCD), the I.V. Watershed Council proposed by commissioners is made up of 13 members, eight of whom are SWCD board members. Lockard figures nine of the 13 members are agricultural or mining irrigators. He points out that Carl Summers represents environmental concerns.

But County Commissioner Harold Haugen thinks this is pretty good representation. He says Josephine County is being unfairly scrutinized by the state.

"In no other case throughout the state have other councils been questioned about their composition," he claims.

"Flat not true," responds McCloud. "Like Josephine County, there have been two other cases in the state where councils initially proposed by local governments were made up of already existing water user groups.

"In both cases, they were rejected by the state. The local agencies adjusted their councils to include other watershed interests like fishing advocates, biologists, recreationalists and environmentalists and were then approved by SWMG. So far Josephine County has refused to make acceptable adjustments."

Asked if the county might be willing to make some adjustments to appease SWMG, Haugen said that commissioners have already made their choice and its the only one he thinks the state needs to recognize.

While some see the gridlock as a missed opportunity for the river and project dollars, Haugen says he's "not so sure that the (SWMG) stamp is worth a whole hell of a lot anyway.

"There are other options to getting these projects funded, like the Forest Service and Bureau of Reclamation," he says.

Economic development advocate Meadow Martell, on the other hand, says she's concerned not only with losing much needed project dollars for the valley, but "more importantly, the divisiveness which has characterized the Watershed Council issue could be detrimental to future funding projects for the valley.

"Funders are looking for projects that have broad based support, and unfortunately the word gets around if a community is seen as divisive.

"If this valley is going to attract funding from outside sources," Martell says, " we will have to pull together and develop a model process where inclusiveness is emphasized."

But for now, it appears to be up to county commissioners to determine whether or not the Illinois Valley Watershed Council will ever provide such a model.   *- unAssociated Press*

LETTERS

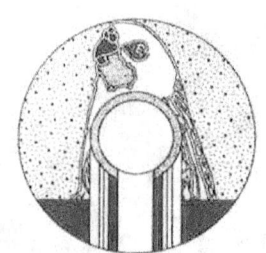

Dear Editors and Friends:

Election time is nearing again and I'm writing to tell you that there is a local election which can be important to all of us, with candidates who deserve your support.

There will be several openings in the local Soil and Water Conservation District to be filled in the November election. Generally these are posts that only have once candidate running. The Soil and Water Conservation District is a local group of a national organization. The intentions are good, but its interests are in helping agriculture more than preserving or restoring watersheds.

As many of you know, the issue of how to use our forests and rivers is hotly debated. The Soil and Water Conservation District is at the heart of this issue, because the Josephine County Commissioners have appointed them as the Watershed Council for the Illinois Valley. They will make decisions about how to spend some of the $3 million which the Oregon legislature set aside for watershed restoration in the south coast.

Also, as Commissioner Irv Whiting publicly stated, many of us who are conservation activists were deliberately excluded from this council. We're making a fight of it with the help of state agencies, but another way to be included is to be elected to the Soil and Water Conservation District.

I recommend to you several candidates for these offices. June Robinson and Fred Mittleman have been involved with river issues since the first Illinois Valley Interest Groups symposium. They have put hundreds of volunteer hours into learning about forest and river issues and doing projects like the treeplanting efforts. Tom Middleton is also running; he is a long time resident of the area, runs an organic farm, and is very concerned about water issues.

These candidates would all represent a real change from the Business-as-Usual politics of this valley and county. Voting for them could actually mean something to the health of the river and our lives.

Thanks for your attention,

Shel Anderson

Dear Common Ground,

I want to thank all the staff of the T-town Rag for including my poem "the gift." Inspired by the book Mutant Message, it really wrote itself. Actually, if One is One, this poem was penned by you. On your copy, please capitalize the "I" in "it."

Thank you so very much for all the great response as well. So much processing Onegether. I encourage you to write for the paper too. This is the gift that is wanted: the scent of your flowering.

Love,
River

To the Editor:

The last couple of months have truly been hard ones for me. I just want to thank all those wonderful friends who have encouraged me and let me lay on their shoulders. I love you all so much.

Robin

Dear Takilma,

I want to thank all the people who helped make the 20th anniversary of the Takilma Dome School very special. Although I was not here 20 years ago I felt very close to those pioneers who were. It was very touching to see the photographs of the students and families and to read some of the essays. Mollie McBride's essay summed up what most we would want and hope for our children to glean from growing up in a community. It gave me chills.

Debbie Murphy.

POETRY

Someone

One early morn,
a child is born.
A child sent wandering,
always wondering,
"Where will I go?...
Will I ever know?"

Ananda Floyd

bring me an ember
from the still coals
warming the ash
holding my fire
let the flame
brighten the night
with an unheard sound
heard tonight

J.S.

NOTES FROM THE NEWSROOM

Editors note:

Felicity: A quality or knack of appropriate and pleasing expression in writing and speaking.-Webster's New World Dictionary

Takilma Common Ground was conceived in a field and born at home, in a borrowed bedroom. It is thus culturally appropriate and may even be politically correct. Putting out the rag gives those of us with more talent than ambition (or vice versa) a chance to get into print and stay out of trouble. It encourages computer illiterates to play and learn at no expense to the government and provides opportunities for those with a penchant for raucous meetings and chaotically productive work environments to indulge their vices at our expense, for we are they.

We have debated our political stance and adopted a position flat on our backs, somewhere to the left of left. Idealistic distribution policies, capitalistic display advertising, marginal graphics and tasteless jokes have all been discussed for as long as it takes. Now this baby is close to a year old and proceeding at a fast crawl. Like toddlers everywhere, we are looking for other kids to play with, so here is the step-by-step guide to the infrastructure of our sandbox vox populi, in case you care to romp.

The Mud Council is roughly like a Board of Directors in the straight world. Its job is to make decisions about money and policies. It consists of seven to ten people (at the moment all ten spaces are filled) who are also active participants on the project. This could mean anything from gathering aura polish at the Green Bridge swimming hole to selling subscriptions in front of Hammer's or wearing a green eye shade and writing every article on the front page. There are some minimalist policy statements that no-one except the Mud Council members themselves will have the slightest interest in, though we will happily print them if anyone asks us.

The Mud Council meets one week post-publication to review the latest issue and snag at least one euphoric member willing to be on the Editorial Staff of the next issue, five weeks away in the non-threatening future. As most of the Mud Council always has been, is now and possibly for ever will be the same damn crowd as the Editorial Staff, this is a somewhat redundant exercise, though it can establish someone as the overall facilitator of the upcoming issue. But anyone can do this. It could be you next time.

The Editorial Staff is all those people, Mud members and others, who work together during the two-week period from the submissions deadline - always featured on the natty calendar insert intended for the adornment of your icebox - to the publication date. These folks start by perusing the tattered and immortal contributions that have come their way. Some don't make it; some they keep for later, some they mess around with before printing, though it is now a policy to consult with authors (notoriously touchy, here as elsewhere) before doing anything more drastic than tweaking with the spelling. Then the anarchic brouhaha begins and the creative genius of our current crew gets in gear. This is probably the juiciest part of the process, involving the transformation of a sheaf of assorted papers into the slick document you have in your hand. Why pass up a good thing? Sign here, right now, you'll love it and the rest of us need a break. Just joking.

Here's the bottom line. All those folks without last names who have been putting out the broadsheet up till now seem to be quite happy with the way things are, but sooner or later every group needs fresh roadkill. We know who you are but we want you to come willingly. Don't make us hunt you down later when we're really mad.........

If you have even a fleeting interest in joining this playgroup, in whatever capacity - staff reporter, fund-raiser, data entry person, proofreader, editor-in-chief, guest artist, stamp licker - please write to Common Ground, P.O. Box 2016, Cave Junction, OR 97523, or call one of these folks for more specific information:

Kayla 592-4275; Kerry 592-2549; Robin 592-3159; Jill 592-4695; Jon 592-2831; Dave H. 592-2492; Dave T. 592-3098; Marcy 592-2629; Kate 592-2214; Laurie 592-4399; Felicity 592-4245.

P.S. Thanks to Cathy H. for your excellent hard work as treasurer. We welcome T.A. to our editorial staff!

Submissions deadline for our next issue is October 20.

ENCLOSED IS MY CONTRIBUTION OF:

$10 _____ 1 YEAR SUBSCRIPTION

$25 _____ 1 YEAR SUBSCRIPTION + TAKILMA MUG + ONE BOTTLE AURA POLISH

$50 _____ 1 YEAR SUBSCRIPTION + TAKILMA MUG + WE'LL OMIT AURA POLISH

_____ I'M BROKE BUT LITERATE, PLEASE SEND THE NEWSLETTER.

Takilma COMMON GROUND
PO BOX 2016 CAVE JUNCTION, OR 97523

NAME _____

ADDRESS _____

ANNE FRANK EXHIBIT COMES TO GRANTS PASS

Almost 50 years after the Holocaust ended in Germany, the Josephine County Human Rights Alliance has arranged for the showing of the "Anne Frank Exhibit" at the Grants Pass Museum of Art.

At the same time, the Oregon Historical Society's exhibit on "Differences and Discrimination: An Oregon Perspective" will be available for public viewing at the Museum. In conjunction with these, the "Courage to Remember" exhibit from the Simon Wiesenthal Center in Los Angeles will be displayed at the Illinois Valley High School from November 1st-9th.

RCC will be the location for the opening ceremony on October 19th. These exhibits will run until Nov. 9th through the closing candlelight ceremony remembering "Kristalnacht" (the night in Germany, 1938, when many Jews were killed and many Jewish shop windows broken, signaling the beginning of the reign of terror). There will be many speakers in between, including: an Auschwitz survivor, a camp liberator, a Schindler Jew, a former member of the Aryan Nation, and our own Agnes Pilgrim speaking about the American Holocaust. All will be free of charge to the public.

Why, may you ask, in the Land of the Free and Home of the Brave New World should we need to view the pictures of a travesty that happened long ago and discuss discrimination, fear, hatred, and abuse? Perhaps the answer lies in the fact that the OCA along with others on the Religious Right would like to legalize hatred in Oregon and all across this great land so that no one different from them is excluded from their discrimination.

So, what can you do? You can always give money. There is no free lunch and this shindig is expensive. You could become a Docent for the exhibits at the Museum. This means being at the exhibit at specific times to answer questions and help viewers (a short training will be required). Or you could volunteer to help staff the "Courage to Remember" exhibit at IVHS. But, if your schedule does not allow any of these things, you can always remember to discuss and confront discrimination whenever you see it and vote in November against Measure 13, the OCA's new initiative to legalize discrimination. For more information on how to help or where to send money, call Barry at SREP at 592-4459.

- Barry Snitkin.

See Calendar for dates; call Barry for list of speakers. See you there. -editors

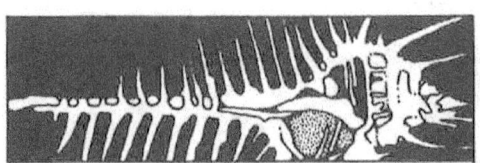

THREE DAYS OF KNIGHTS

Hear Ye! Hear Ye! The shire of Glyn Dfwn and Cavern's Gate Freehold cordially invite you to come and revel with them on the lush green lawns next to the beautiful Illinois River.

The Society for Creative Anachronism will be holding a free medieval tournament and revel at the Illinois River State Park on Friday 9/30, from 4pm-dusk, and Saturday and Sunday, October 1 and 2 from 9:30 am.

At 10 am on Saturday, SCA will present a tournament of knights in armor. Prizes will be awarded for style, costuming, character and chivalry. 50 and 100 foot archery contests are open to all (no compound or crossbows, please.)

Merchant's booths will be selling blown glass, wrought iron, armor, pottery and baked goods. Stone-skipping contests and a storytelling hour will be sure to amuse children of all ages.

The SCA is a thirty year old international organization which encourages people to learn about history, handicrafts and art. Members make their own armor and costumes, and often develop their own medieval personas, thus bringing their favorite bits of history back to life. To this end, many learn and share their knowledge of metalwork, spinning, sewing, woodwork, and more skills needed for medieval life.

Glyn Dfwn (pronounced Glen Dubin) is the name given to the shire of Ashland. Cavern's Gate Freehold is the name chosen for the shire here in our valley. All interested can attend monthly shire meetings at the Pizza Deli(what a strange name for a medieval tavern!)

Come one, come all, fair lords and ladies! Join us in chivalry, celebration and song! For more information about this and other events, please contact Ross and Lydia Welcome (a.k.a. Marlon Legatto and Giovanni Aguilari) at 592-6868.

-Mark Dwyer (a.k.a. Cedric Barca)

WALK FOR THE WILD SISKIYOU A HOWLING SUCCESS!

Over 250 people showed up to the Wild Siskiyou Camp (between Mt. Elijah and the Oregon Caves) on the weekend of August 26-28 to hike, howl, sing, dance and eat for the Wild Siskiyou. Many people hiked to the Sugarloaf sale area and saw the Forest Service lies for themselves: over 1000 trees greater than 4 ft. in diameter are marked for cutting in a sale the USFS claims is a "light thin."

The communities of Takilma and Williams really came together to build the camp. Mucho-mega thanks to Bridge and David Baker, whose super organized kitchen tent kept the masses well fed and happy. Without you, we would have been eating dust sandwiches! The constant supply of nourishing food, herbal teas and coffee gave us the energy to hike all those miles. Thanks to Chi, Tom Tap and other organic growers for those delicious veggies. The Takilma Buying Club, Coffee Heaven, Sunshine Cafe, the Ashland Food Coop, the Arcata Food Coop, Royal Blue Organics and Great Harvest all donated food. Thanks! And thanks Spencer for sharing your birthday keg with those of us who forgot to BYOB!

Evelyn Roether and Debbie Lukas worked hard on organizing logistical details, and Mark Thomas lugged all those water barrels up to the site for us. Marjorie Reynolds was gentle but firm in keeping the parking scene together. Kayla Starr, Lisa Kelz and Naomi D'Abbracci brought up a first aid tent and responded quickly to our one medical emergency, a bee sting reaction. Katherine Roncalio and Alison Gutshall provided a fun kid's tent and activities to keep the younger generation happy - the kids seemed to be as blissed out as the rest of us. Robin Wren did a neat mask making workshop for kids, and Jennifer Beigel took them on an exciting mud-between-your-toes wildflower walk to Bigelow Lakes.

Thanks also to Public Forestry Foundation for sending forester Greg Harty down to talk to us about Sugarloaf. John Roth of the Oregon Caves led a fun hike down to the caves. Hawk enthralled dozens with his knowledge of edible and medicinal plants, and Julie and Bobcat were there to fill everyone in on the history of the Sugarloaf sale. Kerry Holman and company drummed for world unity on top of Mt. Elijah - we sure need it! Rebecca and Newman brought the mysterious presence of Coyote to the gathering. Tom Ness and Sophie Sparks ran all kinds of folks 90 ft. up a tree in their tree climbing workshop. Ken Vance-Borland spoke about the Biodiversity Study that he is doing at Oregon State University, funded by the Siskiyou Project. Lou Gold led a group of hikers up to his new vigil site, overlooking the Sugarloaf forest. He is up there now and welcomes visitors. Please call Siskiyou Project for directions. He needs people to hike up and bring him drinking water.

There are many more people to thank, but I don't have room. Folks have been thanking me for organizing this event, but it was really one of those self-organizing phenomena. It was our community organism bringing itself to life! On Wednesday after the Walk, about 75 of us showed up at the Boise Cascade mill in Medford to ask them not to cut Sugarloaf. Though they wouldn't meet with us, we got some excellent media coverage. Please keep calling and writing them at: Mr. George Harad, CEO, Boise Cascade Corp., PO Box 50, Boise, ID 83728-7298, (208)384-6161. Also write to President Clinton, The White House, Washington, DC 20500. We are awesome and we will stop Sugarloaf!   - *Kelpie Wilson*

SUGAR LOAF SALE—ALERT

True to form, the Forest Service did award the Sugarloaf sale to Boise Cascade. Despite a massive telephone campaign and demonstrations in five cities, Boise Cascade signed the contract, and could make upwards of $5,000,000 laying to waste this precious area of roadless ancient forest east of the Illinois Valley. So now it's time to consider direct action! Call Debbie at 592-3386 or 592-4459 to get involved. You are REALLY needed now.   -*Kayla*

FOREST SERVICE ABUSES SCIENCE

The leaders of the United States Forest Service are currently building a new agenda that will greatly abuse any knowledge we might use wisely concerning forest practices in the Pacific Northwest. Their agenda is insidious — with the sole purpose of pleasing the timber industry and (therefore) keeping the politically appointed positions of high-ranking Forest Service employees intact. Their tool is equally insidious — they are actively fueling the public's fear of forest fire so they may justify the cutting of old-growth trees in our last remaining roadless areas. These cuts, their scientists profess, will lessen the threat of fire and the degree of destruction in the event of a fire.

We need to be aware of several points if we are to influence what happens in our forests. First, all of our forests will burn at some point in the future; we cannot stop forest fires; we should not be so arrogant. The Siskiyous, as compared with the Cascades for example, have an especially high rate of forest fires because of the long dry summers, and these fires have been one of the major natural roots of the beauty and biological complexity we cherish here. Secondly, fires have been suppressed (but not eliminated) over the past century, and so a build-up of fuel material is occurring in our forests. Certain logging practices may reduce the risk of a fire that burns extremely hot, killing all the trees and rendering the soil temporarily lifeless at a site. The third point, and perhaps most important, is that the Forest Service does not know how to reduce the potential of intense fire in old-growth forest ecosystems. The Forest Service is once again determined to experiment on the last gems of our region.

Here in the Siskiyous, the Forest Service is planning such an experiment with the Sugarloaf sale. Forest Service scientists insist that not only can they accomplish their goal of reducing the risk of fire, but that they can log without harming biological diversity. The U..S.Congress mandates the Forest Service to maintain biological diversity. In truth, we have no idea what the consequences of selective forestry will be in the Sugarloaf area although the safe bet is that leaving the forest alone is the best way to maintain diversity. Scientific information about the nature of old growth forests is inadequate to justify cutting in the Sugarloaf area or in any other roadless area. One can only conclude that the Forest Service is once again abusing the authority of "science" to further the goals of powerful people and industries.   - *Erik Jules*

48

The following is a response to the article "Stop Killer Weed," written by Kayla, which appeared in the last issue.

TOBACCO THE SACRED

 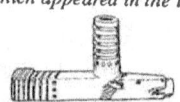 

It has been less that a century since Phillip Morris and other megacorporations began to create preblended, packaged cigarettes. Before this brief period of time, tobacco *(nicotiana tabacum)* has been used for centuries by North America's indigenous peoples. It is a sacred herb used in all aspects of life. It is used in prayer, all major ceremonies and family events. It is an expected gift when visiting elders and attending hosted events. At the Sundance, it is an integral part of the five day ceremony and is used to dress the wounds of the dancers when the dance is completed.

Just 150 years ago, a wild form of tobacco *(lobelia inflata)* was considered one of the most important medicines known. If administered properly (usually by indigenous people,) it was an effective remedy for whooping cough, croup, and asthma. Unfortunately it also had dangerous alkaloid properties which were misused particularly in some of America's early quackery medicine shows. Tobacco has also been used as an insecticide. Tobacco now almost universally carries a virus which is harmful to tomatoes and related plants (so don't use it in your garden.) This virus is viable even after the cigarette making process.

Tobacco has been adulterated to such an extent it is no wonder that it is now a killer. Many people believe if left in it's natural form without additives, tobacco is not harmful. Perhaps if it were seen more as the sacred, it would not be so potentially dangerous. And perhaps it would not be smoked carelessly and its remnants thrown on the ground.

Care to differentiate between the wrong and the instrument is most important now. Mega corporations adding harmful chemicals to tobacco, and controlling the marketing of the herb is most certainly not helpful or healthful for the public. To outlaw tobacco itself would add yet another substance controlled by the government, and another law with which to control the people. It would also be detrimental to those who still believe and use it for it's sacred properties.

If there were no market, Phillip Morris, RJR and others would not stay in the cigarette business. Their interest is solely profits, not the plant. It is possible the destruction by processing could end. Perhaps we should awaken the sacred herb tobacco, bring it back into our gardens and reconsider its uses and its place in community and culture.   -Kim Clough

Kayla responds: As a responsible anarchist, I did not mean to imply that tobacco should be outlawed. INFACT calls for economic boycotts of the mega tobacco corporations. With 1 in 4 deaths in Oregon directly due to cigarette smoking, we all pay the consequences of corporate greed. Enough is enough!

 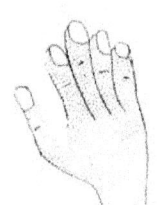

REALLY GOOD TIPS
From Ewing Brewing

The greatest strides forward in home brewing have been in the availability of prime yeast cultures. Yeast imparts far more flavor to the beer than any other ingredient. By-products of zymurgy are alcohol, carbon dioxide and yeast, and the flavor of the beer is dependent on the quality of your yeast.

For centuries, brewers have contracted laboratories worldwide to culture "their" yeast strain. This insures their *very specific* yeast will be safe in case of disaster at the brewery. Most of the world is familiar with Louis Pasteur and his sterilization of milk. While heating dairy products does kill off potentially hazardous bacteria, Louis was, in his time, more widely appreciated for his purification of yeast strains. Pasteur was hired by virtually all of Europe's finest breweries to isolate and culture their individual yeasts.

To culture yeast one must raise and grow the yeast over and over. Until recently, these labs had been required by contract to discard excess yeast. Now, these yeast cultures have been made available to home brewers. They are for sale by mail and at local home-brew shops, and also in the bottom of bottles of micro-brewed beer.

To use this yeast: A day or two before you plan on brewing, make up a 3/4 gallon batch of beer, usually a ladle or two of malt extract boiled and poured into a clean and sterile gallon juice bottle. While you prepare and cool this wort, have a six-pack of your favorite micro-brewed beer on hand. This beer should have obvious sediment in the bottom of each bottle. Pour most of each bottle into a glass, (you know what to do with this,) and shake and pour the last inch of each and all bottles into the clean and sterile gallon and cover with aluminum foil or a fermentation lock. In a day or two the yeast culture has doubled and redoubled and is ready to be added to your beer batch, as with any yeast packet. To compare the yeast you've been using to this reclaimed micro-brewer's yeast, use an old recipe with which you are familiar. I'm sure you'll like the difference.

P.S. Beer making is 80% clean-up, so here's some help.

"Clean" means the absence of *all* foreign matter and films..

"Sterile" can be attained by immersing everything that will touch the solution of 1Tbsp.chlorine bleach per gallonof water for twenty minutes. Any cloudy plastic siphon tubes should be *replaced*.

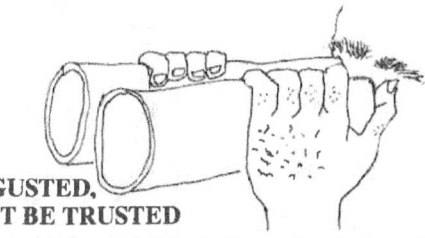

BRINGING IT ALL BACK HOME

As we fight the Sugarloaf timber sale, we find fault with the Forest Service for mismanaging and over cutting our precious forests. However, we often overlook the impact of a more hidden threat: the logging of private lands.

Back yard logging usually happens on small scales. Frequently the cuts are permitted as "selective," which could mean thinning and fire prevention or might be "high grading," in which the largest and most valuable trees are logged for profit. Even on small parcels, these cuts add up quickly and can spell serious danger for our watershed.

Private and residential lands have been so encroached upon by human settlement that they can be extremely sensitive to timber removal. Where will the wildlife go when the neighboring lands have been logged?

Each large tree in a residential area becomes critical to wildlife, the water cycle and the stability of the tree stand. With timber prices soaring, each of these trees becomes more at risk.

Public information about private land logging is limited to what is asked in permit applications, which is very little. Therefore, we cannot know the true state of logged private lands around us without extensive questioning of landowners.

All we really know is how many permits have been issued. According to data compiled by the Oregon Department of Forestry, in five "townships" of the Illinois Valley (39S-41S; 12 ranges) 339 permits have been issued in 137 sections, adding up to tens of thousands of acres.

The cumulative effect these cuts have on our watershed must be taken into account when we decide how to manage our woodlots.

To determine that one's back yard can sustain a money yielding high grade cut based solely on the timber volume within one's own property lines is dangerously inaccurate. To do so denies the connectedness of all our back yards and the ecosystem they compose.

Any private land cuts should be viewed in the context of the **cumulative** effects on the land. Thinnings and forest management should be overseen by a highly experienced forester with an environmental focus.

(For thinnings, some eco-foresters will mark trees for a modest fee, allowing the landowner to proceed knowing the tree choices are wise.)

The decision to reap cash from the trees in one's back yard cannot be made in the false belief that a few acres won't matter. They will.

Furthermore, each person saying "yes" to cash for their trees makes the idea more acceptable to others. They may say "What the hell!" and cut their trees for profit too.

Because our back yards are connected, they comprise a community forest, of which we are all stewards. What we accept and promote on our own parcels must be something we can accept for the whole.

We each set standards for community behavior, and we each are a miniature forest service, with the fate of an ecosystem in our hands.

-Kate Dwyer

BUSTED, DISGUSTED, AGENTS CAN'T BE TRUSTED

Unless you've been out of country, living under a rock or don't speak English, you've probably heard about the rude visitors Kat and I had last Spring.

They came while we were out, tore up the house, took many things and terrorized our poor kitties with a vicious dog.

They took family photographs, a video tape of an east coast vacation, a bunch of personal papers, what ever cash they may have found and, they say, some marijuana.

They arrived right around 10 that morning and stayed until well after midnight. When they arrived they had a search warrant for the vacant cabin on the land next to ours. The warrant was achieved, according to the affadavit, through information provided by the tax assessor. They had no warrant for our house until at least four hours after initial penetration.

Two days later, Kat and I were arrested. We're charged with 12 crimes each, including two each for child neglect and endangering the welfare of a minor because they allegedly confiscated pot that was in an unlocked room, therefore "available" to the children.

It has caused and continues to cause major emotional upheaval for all of us.

The two lead detectives, narcs both, are Walt Markee and Ken Smith. In addition to invading and ransacking our home, they later went to the schools and harassed our children.

Still not satisfied, the impotent little dicks recently subpoenaed both kids to testify against me. That's not going to happen.

Our trials are set for January. Mine begins the morning before Kat's fortieth birthday, hers is the following week. Kat has a docket appearance at 8 a.m. the morning after the big FOUR, OH!

At this time we are soliciting letters to attest to our character, involment with the community and quality of parenting. We are also researching case law to support various pretrial motions.

—T.A.

SUPPORT THE HOSERS

What do Jim Shames and Mike Meidinger have in common?

That's right, they're both doctors: Dr. Jim and Dr. Cemento! But let us not forget that they were also once volunteer firefighters for the IV Fire District. So was I. We all retired for one reason or another, but I have remained connected to the department by serving on the budget committee for the past several years.

This does not make me a dreaded government official, just another community volunteer.

Once a year the five elected directors meet with five appointed committee members to review and approve the annual budget, which is prepared by the fire chief.

Detailed expenditures are analyzed: salaries, insurance, utilities, maintenance, hose replacement, radios, protective clothing, etc. And, of course, a fund for reimbursing the volunteers, a whopping $3.00 per firefighter response.

Okay, to the point: the fire district is requesting a tax base increase in the fall election. Modern standards of equipment and training are far more costly than 20 years ago, when the last tax base was established. The department is relying on engines as much as thirty years old and other trucks more than 40 years old.

The time is right for the citizens of the Illinois Valley to support the fire district with a yes vote on this request.

Tax increases are always controversial. If you would like more information from someone who hates taxes but understands the need for this one, please feel free to call me at 592-2492   *- Dave Hocker*

50

CLASSIFIEDS

LOCAL ARTISANS: Booths available for indoor "Last Minute Christmas Gift Show" at County Bldg. Dining Rm. Sat. Dec. 17th. Call Mariana for info. 592-4890

PROFESSIONAL BAKER will trade home-baked goods for home-grown produce. Also, birthday cakes made to order. Special diets no problem. Kate 592-2214

18" CANONDALE 21 speed mtn. bike. New bearings and tires, overhauled. $340. Robin 592-3159

I.V. SHOTOKAN KARATE CLUB Adult/Advanced class Wed. 6-8pm. New kids' class Wed. 5-6 starts Oct. 5. RCC Belt Bldg. in Kerby. $10/mo. ; Family rates. Info: 592-6868

PROFESSIONAL CATERER with food allergy experience will prepare meals for your family. Packaged for freezer and micro-wave. Very affordable. Kate 592-2214

LOOKING FOR ART for gallery wall. Excellent Grants Pass location, Booking monthly. Call Robin at 592-3159

SAY, DID YOU KNOW that for THREE DOLLARS, you can make $10,000 in JUST ONE WEEK? Try our classified ads!

Joe ran one ad and has received so many orders he had to go to Taiwan!

Rebecca advertised her refrigerator; now she owns a Kenmore appliance center!

Robin tried to sell a Subaru and he still has it. (This is just a cheap way of advertising it again.)

O.K., let's get real: This paper goes out to 300 or more people of like spirits and minds. Classifieds help you; announcements are free. Take advantage of this opportunity. Feel free ($3 worth of freedom) to use them and use them often. This is your community poster board.

Need a ride? Need a rider? Advice? Sell a used pump, yard sale, need work, know of a party, lost something, found something, want to find someone? It's so nice to receive mail from you.

Send your copy to:
Takilma Common Ground
P.O. Box 2016, Cave Junction.

RUSTLESS NATIVES

ANNOUNCEMENTS

Floating around somewhere in Takilma: Red wool shirt (my favorite), Medicine cards and book cards in marbleized fabric case. To return, call Gloria at 592-4269. REWARD. Thanks.

On Saturday 10/2, STONE CRAZY (blues-rock-jazz-soul) will play a benefit boogie for the Dome School. A delicious home cooked meal will be served from 6:00-8:30 for only $2! Our usual excellent desserts will be there, too! Please come eat dinner, dance, celebrate autumn and help support the Dome School!

TO HELP SAVE THE LIBRARY, CALL DEB AT 592-2866!!!

If you missed "Phases and Stages, a Menopausal Workshop for Women," don't miss the repeat performance to be held Sat. Oct. 8, in Ashland's First Congressional Methodist Church, 10:30-4:00. Sliding scale, $25-$45. For more info, call Gloria Stone (592-4269 or 482-5156) or Deb Murphy (592-2866.) Watch for flyers!

Community Firewalk will be at Takilma Community Building on Oct. 22, unless fire danger too extreme. Potluck at 5 PM, firewalk at 7 PM. Anyone interested in co-ordinating child-care, please contact Hollis, 592-2476. $7-$25 sliding scale. If you can't afford $7, talk to Hollis about trade. Benefit for the Dome School, to heal the past and create a new vision for our community.

Thanks go out to Miguelo and Jim for helping build the climbing dome at the Dome school.

LASER MOZART

Come see a classic LASER LIGHT SHOW
a tribute to MOZART
Illinois Valley High School, Cave Junction
Saturday, November 5, 1994
Doors open 7 PM, show starts 8 PM
NO LATECOMERS
(The room must be kept as dark as possible to achieve maximum impact.)

Joint benefit between The Dome School and the Illinois Valley High School Drama Club

For more information
please call The Dome School 592-3911

Children must be closely supervised and stay in their chairs for the duration of the show.

8

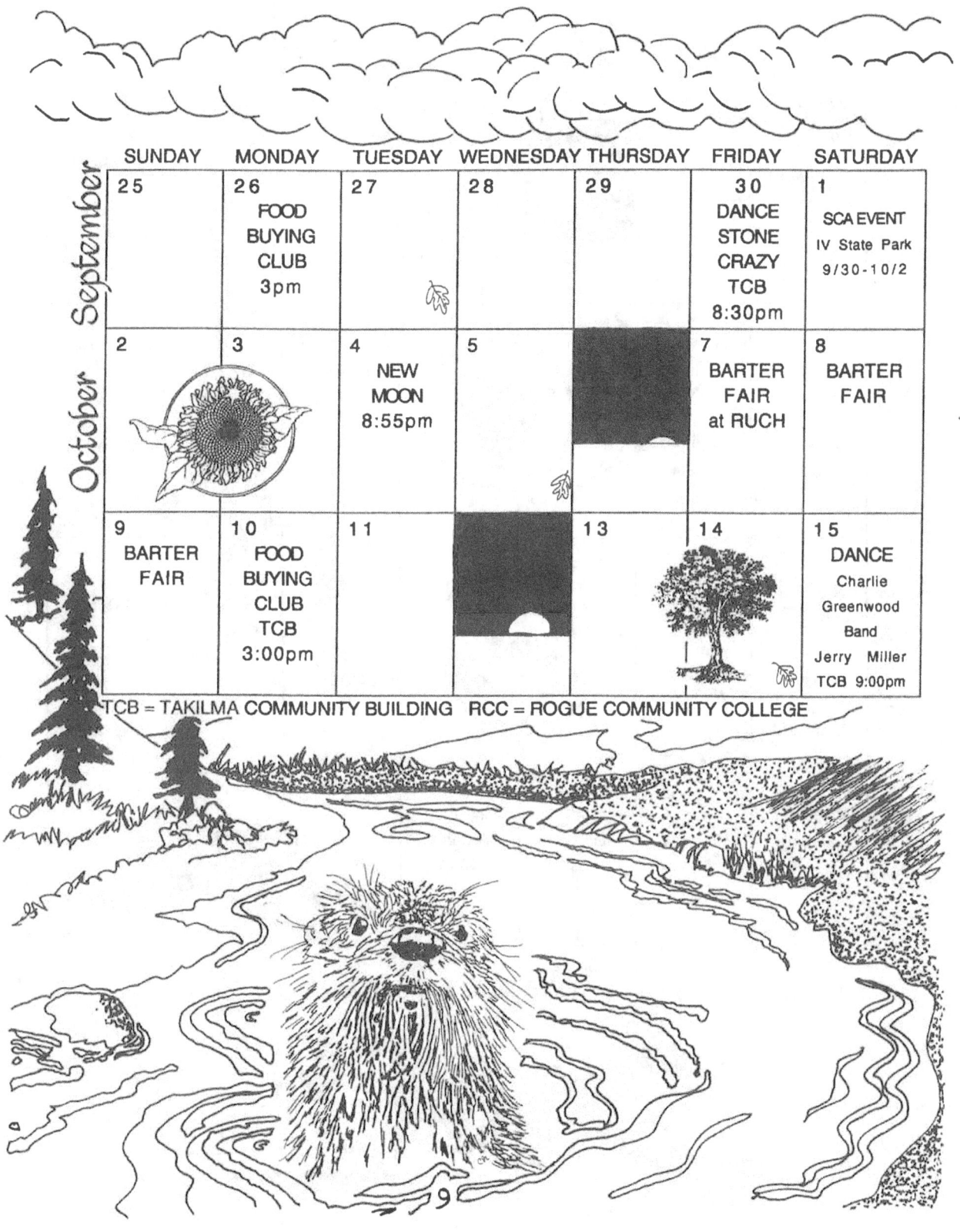

	SUNDAY	MONDAY	TUESDAY	WEDNESDAY	THURSDAY	FRIDAY	SATURDAY
September	25	26 FOOD BUYING CLUB 3pm	27	28	29	30 DANCE STONE CRAZY TCB 8:30pm	1 SCA EVENT IV State Park 9/30 - 10/2
October	2	3	4 NEW MOON 8:55pm	5		7 BARTER FAIR at RUCH	8 BARTER FAIR
	9 BARTER FAIR	10 FOOD BUYING CLUB TCB 3:00pm	11		13	14	15 DANCE Charlie Greenwood Band Jerry Miller TCB 9:00pm

TCB = TAKILMA COMMUNITY BUILDING   RCC = ROGUE COMMUNITY COLLEGE

SUNDAY	MONDAY	TUESDAY	WEDNESDAY	THURSDAY	FRIDAY	SATURDAY
16 QUEEN SALMON Oct 15·8PM Oct 16·2PM Ashland H.S.	**17**	(full moon image)	**19** Anne Frank Opening Ceremony RCC 7pm FULL MOON 5:18pm	**20**	**21** Anne Frank Exhibit RCC 7pm	**22** COMMUNITY FIRE WALK at TCB Potluck 5pm Firewalk 7pm
23 Anne Frank Exhibit RCC 7pm Sun Scorpio 8:36pm	**24** Anne Frank Exhibit RCC 7pm BUYING CLUB 3pm	**25** (triangle image)	**26**	**27** Anne Frank Exhibit RCC 7pm	**28** COMMON GROUND Submissions DUE	**29** Anne Frank RCC 7pm DANCE: Dr. Ross & the Soul Twisters TCB 8:30pm
30 Halloween Hay Ride (call Robin) Daylight Savings Ends Fall Back	**31** HAPPY HALLOWEEN (ghost & pumpkin)	**1** (mask image)	**2**	**3** SOLAR ECLIPSE NEW MOON 5:35am	**4** Anne Frank Exhibit RCC 7pm	**5** Anne Frank Exhibit RCC 7pm Laser Light Show IVHigh School 7:00 pm
6 Anne Frank Exhibit RCC 7pm	**7** BUYING CLUB 3pm	**8** ELECTION DAY! Menopausal Workshop 1st United Methodist Chuch Ashland	**9** Anne Frank Exhibit RCC 7pm	**10** (bear image)	**11**	**12**

October

November

TCB=TAKILMA COMMUNITY BUILDING   RCC = ROGUE COMMUNITY COLLEGE

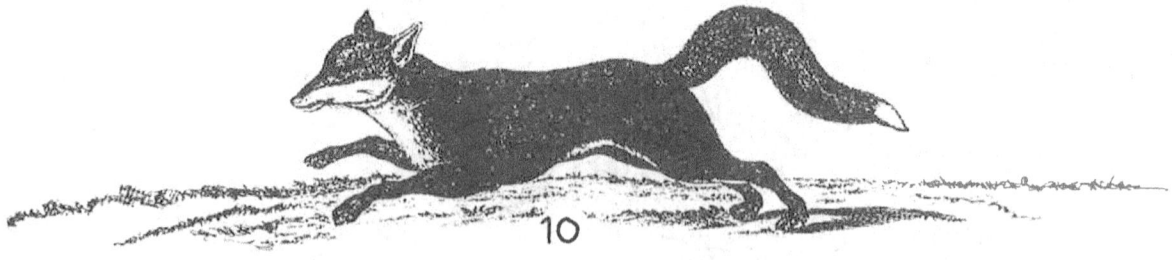

MARIJUANA THEN AND NOW

Once upon a time, a long time ago, there lived a tribe of happy hippies. They ate, they laughed, they loved, they worked, and they grew their gardens. Cucumbers, tomatoes, corn, potatoes...and pot.

Boy did they grow pot! It was part of their spiritual culture, and almost everyone took part. Some were known to throw some "to the gods" each time they indulged. No community function was held without it.

Some people grew for money, but most grew for the love of growing, using and sharing.

In those days, when the sheriff came upon someone's "garden," they pulled the plants and left a calling card with a gentle reminder... "It is still illegal to grown marijuana in the state of Oregon. If you should care to turn yourself in, please call the sheriff at this number..."

In the days when the "convention" was still being held, the main questions of the day were "What strains did you cross? What fertilizer did you use? Can I trade you for some of those seeds?"

My how things have changed! Little RICO, $5,000 a pound, halide lighting, secrecy, mistrust, greed and "Just Say No" have all combined to make this a very different world. Growing the stuff carries repercussions that we never imagined in the seventies.

Information, education and awareness have led to many making the choice not to indulge, which brings us to the present day. The questions have changed.

Do we still think its okay to smoke with/around our kids? What are the messages we are sending them?

Are we modeling behaviors they will need to "make it" in the next century?

Is it fair for children to bear the burden of having to hide what their parents do?

Does the negative energy generated by drug busts in our community make our children proud to live here? Is the cost (in terms of disruption of family life) worth it?

Perhaps it is time for contemplation and reflection...Koyaanisquatsi—a way of life that calls for another way of thinking?

Concern for the children of our community has prompted this forum. We encourage you to share your feelings and your ideas. Remember it truly does take a whole community to raise a chid. *- Dolores & Inez*

Those were the days...

i just watched my daughter, jenica, climb on an airplane. she is off to college. that memory seems no more close or distant than watching her climb the stairs to the doo dah dome so many years ago.

a couple days before she left we were trading stories about when she was a kid. jenica said,

"...these things i remember, or are they remembered about me, and were told to me so often that now i think someone else's memories are my own..."

this is how fragile our recall is, how little we trust, what our memory reveals; how much is revealed by our trust in memory.

like so many other folks with roots in takilma who have been transplanted to ashland, i am somewhat torn. i love my life here, it works for me, but some part of me lingers in the illinois valley. i can feel the river flowing

through me, the stars are overhead and the quiet of a summer evening rests deep inside me.

even now, sitting in the realm of sirens and noisy neighbors' kids, there is peace borrowed from an earlier, simpler, incarnation when absolutely everything came back, somehow, to getting an axe.

when i am in the presence of one of so many dear friends from the early days in takilma, there is always the temptation to swap tales: an hallucinatory summer solstice party in the big meadow or the time abdul got dumped in the clinic waiting room with a hole the size of a hubcap in his gut.

those days can take on a relevance in the vicarious eye of remembrance that they never had in the present tense. there is danger there. there is peril in putting down our emotional kickstand and dwelling on some perceived, golden, time and not allowing

ourselves to move forward. the trick is in honoring the past without becoming mired in it; in learning from the river how to be still and move on at once.

as is sit here, in takilma east, someone is jumping naked into the illinois, someone is harvesting tomatoes and someone is deciding what to wear when they go back to the dome school on tuesday. someone is getting an axe. it all goes on and changes and remains the same.

when jenica flew off in that plane, i walked back to my car, with my arm around my sweet friend and a hollowness inside. i cast my mind back to another time jen was about to go away for the summer. i said

"remember, jen..."

she looked back, with a question mark on her face,

"remember...everything."

these are the days...

darrel

GOOD NEWS FROM JANESVILLE, WISCONSIN

People from all corners of the earth are engaged in a pilgrimage, paying homage to a special birth.

A sacred white buffalo has been born in the middle of Turtle Continent, near a place called Beloit, Wisconsin. These homelands of the Winnebago tribe are at the heart of the Turtle.

According to Mato, one local source, "This birth means pure innocence is available for the heart, so there is hope. This is proof from the Father that pure innocence is available, that Christ energy is here. Now everything unfolds, offering hope, but we will have to wait to see what Man does with it."

There have been white buffalo born before, but there are so few remaining buffalo, a white calf is particularly significant. At one time 80 million buffalo roamed the plains. The number was reduced to 500 by the end of the 1800's. Presently the north American herd numbers 135,000. The odds of a white buffalo have been calculated at one in ten million. The last true white buffalo was born in 1933 and died in 1959.

Much lore exists among the Red Nations concerning this event. We regret that we were not able to further research this incident in time for our printing deadline. Watch, pray, and meditate for more information and direction on this amazing topic.

TAKILMA COMMON GROUND
P.O. BOX 2016
CAVE JUNCTION, OR 97523

Takilma Common Ground

A Community Newsletter

Issue #7   Nov.-Dec. '94

DOES IT MAKE SENSE TO VOTE FOR CANDIDATES?

Dave Toler and Shel Anderson are local activists who enjoy an on-going discussion of politics. Both find our present political and social structures to be threatening, that there is an essential need for change, and that grass-roots activism is important. But how to accomplish these changes is where Shel and Dave take different paths. While Shel believes the ballot box is an essential tool, Dave sees movement organizing outside of electoral politics as the key to success. We thought you might be interested in hearing about it...

SHEL: Dave, we agree, I think, that in this election we're offered candidates in many races where the choice is one between "bad" and "worse". Where we differ is that I think that we should vote for the better candidate, even though she or he may not be anyone we're excited about.

DAVE: Yeah, Shel, some of these races really epitomize the absurdity of "democracy". I mean, the Commissioners race is a choice similar to Hitler vs. Stalin! I think those of us working for meaningful social change need not waste time with electoral garbage and get on with organizing "in the streets".

SHEL: You make it hard for me to argue that we should vote for one of the two candidates, but I will. Really bad office holders make a lot of difference to activists, not only because of how they vote and work with the public, but because of the long-term effects of appointments to bureaucracies and committees. It gets very depressing when you can't even talk to an office holder because they froth at the mouth.

DAVE: Well Shel, I'd certainly agree that "bad" office holders can pose a barrier to change, but let's face it: the electoral process won't produce the politicians we need because it's a process bought and sold by the powers that be. The only way to affect politicians is effective organizing outside the electoral game where they make (and break) all the rules. Just look at the positive changes throughout our history, they were accomplished by movements in the streets. Womens' suffrage, for example.

SHEL: I don't agree that all office holders are bad, but I also don't expect anyone to be perfect. I often find a candidate who is great on some issues, and terrible on others. We each have to know our own priorities; for example, I always vote for women if I can, and never would vote for an anti-woman candidate. What I'm concerned about with this election is candidates supported by the radical Right. THEIR election will really be a disaster.

DAVE: We're already facing disaster Shel, and the difference between Right and far Right is a lost cause. The point is, politicians serve the powers that put them there, Democrat or Republican. But with effective organizing, we can force these politicians to work in our interest. For example, most of our major environmental laws were signed by Nixon. There was a loud and effective voice in the streets that couldn't be ignored, even by a conservative Republican. It's the kind of energy that we need to generate today.

SHEL: I certainly agree with that last point, and I'll continue as an activist to try to manifest the world I want my daughter to live in. But, I'll also hold my nose and vote for the best person offered in most of the races. It does make a difference.

DAVE: Today, we're on a train to disaster. By voting you may slow it down a bit Shel. But for this and especially future generations, we've got to derail this train and set a new course. To do that, we'll have to step outside the narrow confines of electoral politics and become what we can be, a movement too loud to be ignored.

MEASURES 13(State) and 17-27(Grants Pass) ANTI-GAY DISCRIMINATION

State measures, if passed, are unlikely to stand the test of constitutionality. However, they are damaging to our state and citizenry. We must send a message to those who would legitimize discrimination against gays and lesbians that Oregon will not sanction intolerance! Measures #13 and 17-27 reflect the Oregon Citizen's Alliance exploitation of people's confusion and discomfort about homosexuality. Gay people contend with this confusion, often turning it on themselves. Gay youth struggle with self-esteem issues; the result is suicide rates much higher than for heterosexual youth. While doing nothing to protect children (though fraudulently titled the "child protection act") these measures send the message that hostility toward gays and lesbians is acceptable, even desirable. This harms all children; while they cannot be taught to be homosexual (another OCA myth), they can be taught discrimination and hatred.

At what point will the OCA be satisfied? Even though we voted NO on 1992's Measure 9, they continue to shove their bigoted agenda down our throats. Oregon has been subjected to a divisive, disruptive, ugly campaign to eliminate gay rights. We must register a loud enough NO that there can be no question that Oregon does not support discrimination against anyone. There certainly are not enough homosexuals to fight groups like the OCA, it will take fair-minded heterosexuals to oppose them. "You do not have to be gay to be outraged about these measures. You have only to wonder, Who's next?" Please, join us in voting NO on Measures 13 and 17-27.

MEASURE #19 –

Obscenity. Measure #19 opposes the application of free speech laws to cases against obscenity. Currently, the constitution protects the right to "speak, write, or print freely on any subject...but every person is responsible for abuse of this right". Measure #19 says that if a community determines something to be obscene, this protection would not be available. It is yet another attempt by the Right (along with Measures 7, 13, and 17-27) to dictate their morality on all of us. Measure #19 plays upon fear by focusing on child pornography. It purports that child pornography is somehow made legal by free speech laws. In reality, it is already a felony to use a child in a display of sexually explicit conduct, or to possess, distribute, duplicate, or import such depictions. We do not intend to trivialize the true problem of violence and exploitation of women and children. Measure #19 promotes censorship, without dealing at all with the underlying issue of exploitation. Free speech laws do not cause violence! Defend your right to free speech. Vote NO on Measure #19.**This position also endorsed by the American Civil Liberties Union, the League of Women Voters of Oregon, the National Organization of Women, the Oregon American Association of University Women, and the Oregon Coalition for Free Expression.

MEASURE 20: NOT EQUAL, NOT 2%

When it comes to politics, I used to think " conservative " was the belief that government should have it's hand in our wallet as little as possible. But the way many conservatives are rallying around the so called 2% tax, I'm increasingly convinced that any tax relief refers only to a small , wealthy minority while the rest of us foot the bill. Such is the case with the Measure 20 Unequal tax which would be a lot more than 2% for most of us.

Orton's recent letter in support of Measure 20 was basically an admission that this is no tax cut, merely a tax shift. Orton states the measure will " decrease taxes " while at the same time " it stands to provide even more money for government services ."

It doesn't take an economics degree to see that if this is true, some will see a tax cut while others a raise. Any small business or average Oregonian should be concerned about who will be carrying the heavier load under Measure 20.

Unfortunately, like Measure 5 (which was authored by a Portland area businessman, not the legislature) the Measure 20 Unequal tax is a dream come true for Corporate Oregon. Like Measure 5, Measure 20 is no real tax cut for most Oregonians, just another welfare program for big business. Measure 20 literature states that the " Tax is imposed on each transaction between persons in state including: retail, wholesale sales, purchases of labor and services....".

So when the Walmart chain retails a product in Grants Pass, they will most likely purchase outside the state, no 2% tax. When they warehouse it outside the state, no 2%. When the outlet purchases from the warehouse, still no 2%.

Now, when a small business in CJ produces a product, it's more likely they will sell to another Oregon firm, that's a 2% tax. If it's trucked in Oregon, that's another 2%. If it's warehoused in Oregon, 2% more. Trucked to an Oregon retailer, 2% again. Sold to a customer in Oregon? Yes, 2% more.

A product manufactured and retailed within Oregon could easily see a 10% tax ! It's already tough for small business to compete with the big Corporations, the Unequal tax is only going to make it tougher...

The Unequal tax will conveniently lift what little tax burden these corporations have left after Measure 5, and dump them on individuals and small businesses. Not only will the Unequal tax be easier for Mega chains to avoid, the measure will also wipe out the minimal corporate taxes they pay today.

And can you imagine the bureaucratic nightmare in attempting to tax every single transaction that occurs in the entire state of Oregon? It will be far more encompassing than a sales tax. Instead of more tax shifts onto the backs of over-taxed Oregonians, JUST SAY NO TO MEASURE 20 and call for a shift back to the wealthy corporations that benefitted so disproportionately from Measure 5.

MEASURE 7   DISCRIMINATION

Measure #7 would amend the Oregon Constitution by adding a new section to the Bill of Rights (1) Equal protection of the laws shall not be denied or abridged by any public entity...on account of race, color, religion, gender, age, or national origin... Why would a human rights advocacy group be opposed to such a measure???? Currently, the Oregon Constitution states that equal protection under the law is available to all people . This equal treatment cannot be denied on account of anything. By specifying particular groups, Measure #7 erodes the concept and application of equal rights for all. Therefore, we urge you to vote NO on Measure #7.**This position also endorsed by the American Civil Liberties Union, the League of Women Voters of Oregon, the National Organization of Women, the Oregon American Association of University Women, and the Right to Privacy PAC.

MEASURES 10, 11, AND 17. MORE JAILS, LONGER SENTENCES, SLAVE LABOR

Our steering committee recommends a NO vote on all three of these measures. **Measure 11** sets mandatory sentences for certain violent or sex crimes, with no early release or reduced sentence. It would treat juveniles from the age of 15 as adults, with the same sentence. **Measure 10** would keep the Legislature from changing this mandatory sentencing by amending the state Constitution to require a 2/3 vote to reduce sentences. **Measure 17** requires all prisoners to work a 40 hour week, with no minimum wage or Workers' Comp. It sets up another bureaucracy to manage the program. Products and services from this program are available to both public agencies and private businesses. The money earned (what do you guess? $.50/hr?) by each prisoner will be used to pay prison costs, pay victim restitution, support his/her family, and pay fines, court costs, and taxes.

I support the initiative process; it makes law-making available to citizens. However, we've seen how a measure which seemed great on its own can have many unintended consequences. I suggest that you always look very carefully at any measure which amends the state Constitution, and ask what will be the impact of any law. Measures 10 and 11 together would mean that the state budget will need to allocate $462 million over the next five years to build prisons, plus $100 million per year after that to run them. Where will that money come from? Since Oregonians don't want to pay more taxes, probably it would be taken away from schools, health plans, old age assistance, social services, libraries. Do we really want to commit our limited state budget to prisons?

Don't forget, Measure 11 would also **require** 15 year-old kids to be treated as adults. Under present law, a juvenile may be tried as an adult, depending on age and severity of crime. And this set of measures does nothing about plea-bargaining, which is the source of many lesser sentences. If passed, these measures would cause even more pre-trial adjustments to happen.

We know that people of color and poorer people make up the bulk of the prison population. With these three measures, we would have virtually a slave population. Commit a crime? Go to jail for twice as long as at present, and work while you're there to pay for the costs of keeping you. Your services can be sold far below the cost of wages for a non-prisoner, both to private companies and government. What do you think this will do to the job market?

"First they came for the Jews, and I did not speak out - because I was not a Jew. Then they came for the communists and I did not speak out - because I was not a communist. Then they came for the trade unionists and I did not speak out - because I was not a trade unionist. Then they came for me - and there was no one left to speak out for me."

— **Pastor Martin Niemoeller**

MEASURE 15 - KIDS FIRST? NOT!

The Kids First Committee is promoting **Measure 15 as the** solution to fix what's wrong with public education. IT WON'T.

Kids First claim that measure 15 will relieve overcrowded classrooms, IT WON'T; that classrooms will receive the educational materials which have been in short supply- THEY WON'T. and that the money captured by measure 15 will sit in a slush fund to be spent on special projects- NOT TRUE.

The KIDS FIRST COMMITTEE really has nothing to do with putting our children first. While education should be a high priority for us, Measure 15 will take huge bites out of other state programs, many of which serve kids.

State funding for mental and physical health care will be cut. Programs addressing domestic violence and abuse will be cut. Funding for disabled children and troubled youth will also see severe cuts under the Measure 15 axe.

Yes, Oregon needs solutions to its budget problems, but these solutions will have to take a holistic approach in order to avoid such negative impacts. Measure 15 is a money grab to protect the status quo of one bureaucracy with total disregard for the devastating consequences on other programs. Vote NO on 15!

MEASURE 8: THE 6% DILEMMA

Our steering committee is unable to reach consensus on Measure 8, which would amend the Oregon State Constitution to require public employees to pay 6% of their salary toward their pension. Presently, the state, and some local governments and school districts, pay the full cost of contributions to employee pensions. Also, employees may increase their pension from unused sick leave, which would be prohibited under this measure.

PRO: The arguments for the measure include large savings to the state and local districts: those supporting this measure estimate a savings of $300 million per year to governments and $140 million per year to school districts. Public employees now enjoy better retirement benefits than most private employees. Another argument in favor is that the high cost of paying for full time employees causes government to use many part time employees with no benefits.

CON: There are several arguments against this measure. First, some argue that we shouldn't scapegoat workers who have a decent retirement plan, but instead work to extend the same benefits to everyone else. Second, this measure would put what should be a law into the state Constitution, so that the legislature cannot change it. Third, public employees have been working since 1979 under this plan, and this measure will reduce retirement benefits they counted on, as well as produce a 6% cut in present pay. Opponents ask, "How would you feel?"

"YES!" Measures 14 & 18 - Mining restrictions, Bear and cougar hunting restrictions "YES!"

Measure 14 and Measure 18 are the only positive environmental protection measures on the ballot. They need your support and your vote. Measure 14 seeks to protect us from the damage that large multi-national mining companies have caused in other states. Open-pit cyanide mines turn mountains into gigantic pits in the search for microscopic amounts of gold. What they leave behind is a legacy of poisoned drinking water and dead wildlife. Current regulations are not strong enough. Take off your gold and say YES on measure 14. Measure 18 deals with ethics, the ethics of slaughtering bears and cougars by baiting them and chasing them with dogs wearing radio controlled collars. It just isn't right. **Please vote YES.**

SOME OPPONENTS OF MEASURE 18 SAY IT IS UNNECESSARY BECAUSE MOST HUNTERS USE THE "TREE AND RELEASE" METHOD.

Vote NO on Josephine County initiatives 17-22, 17-23 and 17-24.

These measures are part of a larger "wise use" agenda that has been seen throughout the West. The "wise use" movement is an astro-turfroots movement paid for by the extractive industries and which seek a laissez faire approach to natural resource issues. Their true agenda is to defeat environmental laws such as the Endangered Species Act, privatize the use of public lands by doing things like drilling for oil in National Parks, do away with safety regulations and labor laws, and destroy the ability of governments to maintain positive social agendas.

The interesting phenomenon researchers have found is the close link between the "wise users" and the OCA. Just as interesting are the links to the Unification Church and the Korean CIA. Strong support of the wise users come from Joseph Coors and the John Birch Society. Imagine Lon Mabon with an Uzi.

The overall intent of these measures is to supersede the State and Federal governments' enforcement of constitutional issues. The measures are clearly unconstitutional and unenforceable and will create an incredible financial burden by increasing the number of lawsuits County Government is involved in.

17-22 The right to Bear Arms. Already protected by U.S Constitution. This would prohibit the enactment or enforcement of waiting bills such as the Brady Bill. Vote NO.

17-23 Due process and just compensation for private property. It sounds good at first, especially for anyone concerned about the government seizing their personal property. Sorry, it won't help if you're dealing with the drug nazis. This measure is designed to allow continual environmental degradation without regulation. This is a takings bill. Under the Constitution," takings" means that private property shall not be taken without just compensation. However, the use of property can be regulated so that it shall not be injurious to the community and so that proposed uses that may be a public nuisance can be forbidden without compensation. This means that if you take my pen you have to compensate me for having taken my private property. But even though this is my pen I don't have the right to poke you in the eye with it. Takings bills say that I can do anything I want with my pen. I can go right on poking you in the eye. If you want me to stop, you'll have to pay me. Got the picture? The river and the forest will continue to be destroyed, health and safety regulations would end but profits would rise. It's dangerous, unconstitutional, unenforceable and is guaranteed to cost you money. Vote NO.

17-24 Non-advocacy of forfeiture of constitutional rights. Public officials will be prohibited from speaking about reasonable measures such as the Brady Bill. So in the guise of freedom this measure would restrict public officials' freedom of speech. I understand wanting to shut up certain public officials but it is unconstitutional. Vote NO.

4

CANDIDATES FOR PUBLIC OFFICE:
RECOMMENDATIONS   By Shel Anderson

In another article in this newsletter, I make an argument for voting against truly terrible candidates by voting for a candidate who is not so bad. If you agree with this strategy, I would like to make some recommendations in several races. These are my personal choices, not necessarily supported by the Mud Council or the I.V. Human Rights Alliance. My choices are made from a commitment to feminism, human rights and social justice, and a passion to keep a place for the wild in this world.

In the local election for the I.V. Soil and Water Conservation District Directors: vote FOR June Robinson in Zone 3; Tom (James T.) Middleton in Zone 2; and Fred Mittleman, Director at Large.

For governor: vote **against** Denny Smith. I will vote for John Kitzhaber; two other candidates are running.

For Representative, 2nd district: Vote **against** Wes Cooley. I will, reluctantly, vote for Sue Kupillas.

For Commissioner of the Bureau of Labor and Industries: vote for Mary Wendy Roberts.

For State Representative, 49th District. Vote for Eleanor Edmondson.

For Commissioner: Vote **against** John Tefteller, in my opinion a real disaster for the County. Reluctantly, I will vote for Fred Borngasser.

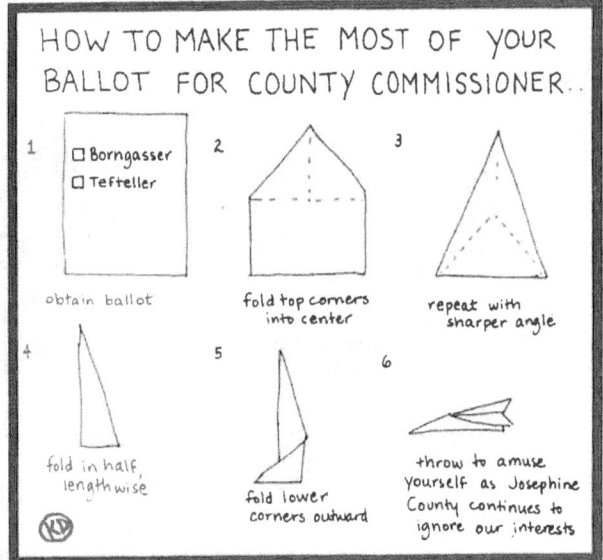

IF VOTING WORKED, THEY'D MAKE IT ILLEGAL

The myth that we live in a democracy is trotted out once again as the November election revs up. It's so comforting to believe that we can change things simply by marking ballots. Yet, what I've noticed as a player in the 'democratic 'process, is that even when we 'win', we lose. In the '80's, we won the Freeze, which asked Congress to stop producing and deploying nuclear weapons. It was ignored in Washington. We elect a Democrat president and see him bow to the military-industrial power elite as did his Republican predecessors. We don't even get a candidate on our ballots unless that individual has already sold out. We are told that there's just not enough money to pay for environmental clean-up, national health plan, decent public education, etc.; yet there's billions for the military forays, weapons systems, and S&L bail-outs the Big Boys want. After a while the chorus imploring us to vote, to have a voice in the future, sounds a dissonant note. No wonder only about 30% of those eligible, actually vote.

Let's face it: our government was established to protect the propertied, to maintain the status quo, at all costs. If people had political power in this system, would we accept the unequal distribution of resources that keep the elite super-rich and the multitudes scrambling to survive? The myth that this is a government of the people, by the people, and for the people comes in handy here. Stage elections every two years, and business goes on as usual.

But what alternative is there? True, as Churchill once so succinctly observed, democracy is lousy, but its the best we've got. Well, representative democracy may be the best form of government we have so far, but it's not good enough! Not with people still starving and dying in our dirty little wars, not with the environment nearly destroyed and our cities imploding. We can do better!

Let's consider anarchy. The government propaganda defines "anarchy" as synonymous with chaos and violence, insisting that the social chaos we have now is security and order. Not true. There are many examples of peaceful, well-ordered anarchic systems. Anarchy worked in Spain and the Ukraine for several years early in this century. The 30,000 member worker collective, Mondragon, in central Spain is based on anarchic principles of voluntary association, cooperation and non-hierarchy. Holland and Norway under Nazi occupation during WW II, many international organizations like the International Postal Association, several large worker collectives such as United Airlines, are all examples of anarchy in action. The anti-nuclear movement in the '80's was consciously organized on anarchy precepts. Decisions were by consensus, representatives to regional councils were ad hoc, not permanent positions, the tactics were creative and non-violent.

Our own community uses anarchic principles, as a matter of fact. Most of our groups value consensus decision-making, the freedom of each individual to make her/his own choices, a deep spirit of active cooperation is evidenced by the way we responded during the Fire of '87 and other crises, we have an aversion to using authorities to solve our problems, we appreciate (or at least tolerate) diversity and personal empowerment. We have created this community within the larger system of corrupt power and exploitation. We are part of similar experiments happening all over the world.

Most anarchists recognize that changing our social order on a grander scale will not be accomplished by the customary methods: neither violent uprising nor slow electoral reform (urged by traditional liberals) will succeed in changing hearts and minds as well as institutions.   Each time we take back our own power to accomplish good for ourselves and our community, each time we refuse to be intimidated into doing what is against the common good, each time we establish a group process that empowers all members, each time we withdraw our participation in systems employing power of the few over the many, we are demonstrating the courage of resistance and imagination that can create such change.

Specifically this may involve refusing to register for the draft and to pay federal income tax, economic boycotting of businesses engaged in evil for profit, creating alternative housing, credit unions, health and legal services, growing our own organically, birthing and dying at home and stopping business as usual when that business involves raping our environment. Tens of thousands are doing these and other such actions every day.

Come election day, most anarchists I know will probably vote, knowing what we know, on the chance that some local issues can be impacted this way. But, pragmatically, we do not waste much energy in this charade, when we can do much more to create change by letting this system crumble under its own evil weight, while we actively seek a better way.   - *Kayla*

5

A Guide to Oregon's 1994 Ballot Measures

Statewide Measures

Measure 5 Tax Votes - NO
Measure 7 Discrimination- NO
Measure 9 Campaign Finance Reform -YES
Measure 10 Mandatory Sentences- NO
Measure 11 Crime- NO
Measure 12 Prevailing Wage- NO
Measure 13 Anti Gay Rights -NO
Measure 14 Mining Restrictions -YES
Measure 15 Education First- NO
Measure 16 Assisted Suicide -YES
Measure 17 Prison Work- NO
Measure 18 Bear and Cougar Hunting Restrictions- YES
Measure 19 Obscenity -NO
Measure 20 2x2x2% Tax- NO

County Measures

Measure 17-19 JuvenileJustice Center No Recommendation
Measure 17-20 Computers Yes
— Measure 17-21 Increase Fingerprinting fee NO
Measure 17-22 Bear Arms NO
Measure 17-23 Takings NO
Measure 17-24 Prohibits Advocacy of Forfeiture of Rights NO
Measure 17-25 Mandates Animal Control NO
Measure 17-26 IV Fire District YES

Grants Pass Measure

Measure 17-27 Discrimination NO

These recommendations come from the Illinois Valley Human Rights Alliance who, with the help of other Common Ground volunteers, compose the editorial staff of this issue. We evaluated these measures on the basis of human rights and environmental concerns as well as looking at the impacts of the potential laws with a basic sense of economic fairness. Remember, in times where we have a limited pie to share, when the pie gets reduced, someone loses and it's usually the poor and powerless.

EXPATRIATE GAMES by Dave

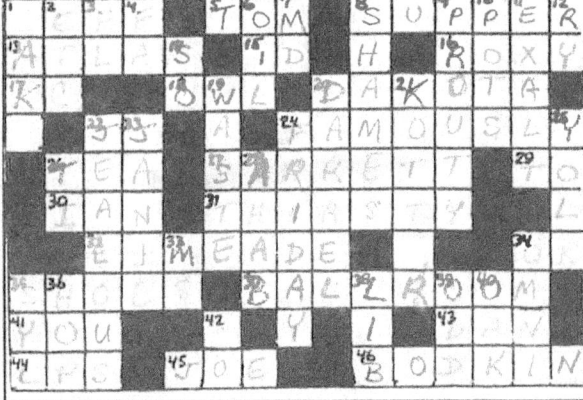

ACROSS

1. Expatriate Coach "Duffy" Campbell
5. Expatriate Smokejumper Troop
8. Some sing for this
13. World-class hold-up man
15. Show this for drinks
16. Expatriate Foxy rhymer
17. Former home of Athletics
18. Indicator species
20. Homelands of Rocky Raccoon
22. On Common Grounds owner, initially
24. How friends got along
26. See homonym
27. Expatriate lab tech
29. Not fro
30. Mar's son has Leo rising?
31. Needing a Margarita
32. Frozen Margarita ingredient
34. All right
35. Charlie Two _____
37. Found in hotels, ships, and baggy pants
41. Not me!
43. Expatriate Ashland mason
44. Collectibles from Listen Here
45. Expatriate Santa Barbara father of twins
46. Odd word for hairpin, needle, dagger, or awl

DOWN

1. Expatriate McGroom
2. And so forth
3. Everglade State (abbr.)
4. "A long long way to go"
6. Kuwaiti commodity
7. Maryland doctor's toilet paper
8. Expatriate Ashland father of twins
9. Expatriate Rowdy Sisters
10. What Roy throws
11. Praise, glorify, extol
12. Mar's first son
14. ___ what?
19. Squander
20. Expatriate midwife/movie maven
21. "Welcome Back _____"
22. Resentfully envious
23. Expatriate Stewart
24. Thank God for this
25. Non-white?
26. See homonym
28. Wished for Moby Dick
33. A grown-up miss
34. Science/future magazine
35. She and Gene walk a Fine Line
36. Make like a bunny
38. Women's ____
39. Not even
40. Source of acorns
42. Expatriate cone-picker extraordinaire

ANNOUNCEMENTS

West African Dance classes with Simbo. We are really privileged to have the quality and experience of this teacher come to us in Takilma. Alternate Mondays starting November 14th. $12/class includes building rental fee at the Takilma Community Building. 6-8 pm We need a minimum of 10 people per class to bring Simbo here from Ashland. PLEASE PRE-REGISTER . Commitment through the end of '94 means only three classes - a good opportunity to experience this for first-timers. No experience necessary. Please call Beth at 592-6970.

TCB ADDITION Since our last printing, close to a thousand dollars have been raised to finish the addition to the Takilma Community Building. About 12-15 people have responded thus far and we sincerely thank them for their generous gifts. If you have not responded, please mail checks to "Common Ground" now, so that we can get on to stage three. Thanks.

CLAN DYKEN. This time it is for real... YES! The CLAN DYKEN DANCE will happen on Saturday, November 19 at the TCB at 8:30 p.m.. Food will be served beforehand. The Clan is on their BIG MOUNTAIN TOUR and are collecting useful items to carry to the Hopi and Din'e people. The band has decided to go in a couple of different directions for a while and has agreed to come together with special friends and play once more...Let's complete the circle and say good-bye to our friends. This dance will benefit Robin's Defense Fund. Thanks you all...

BEAUTY IN THE BEAST. The Pacific Northwest Museum of Natural History in Ashland is opening a new exhibit, "Beauty in the Beast". Trace the results of human customs which jeopardize the world's most exquisite creatures. Explore the alternatives for the future. November 6,1994 - March 31, 1995. Info: 488 -1084,

DELL'ARTE THEATER will present "Journey of the Ten Moons" Saturday, December 10, at 7:30 p.m. at Lorna Byrne Middle School. Admission: Adults $5, Teens $3, Children $1. This is a benefit for the Dome School and Lorna Byrne Middle School Drama Clubs. This performance interweaves the adventure tale of the discovery of Humboldt Bay in 1849 by the Gregg-Wood expedition with a Native American tale about Coyote's Defeat of the Winter Moons. This will be performed in Dell'Arte's acclaimed physical comic style with live music and an amazing array of masks.

TAKILMA COMMUNITY BUILDING ADDITION BENEFIT. The Stickmen will perform at the TCB on Saturday, December 10 from 9 p.m. to 1 a.m.. The group consists of local resident J.D. Smith on guitar and vocals, Dan Curren on keyboard and vocals, Dave Hand on bass and vocals, and Mike Penman on drums and percussions. They have played with some very well known bands such as Moby Grape, Van Morrison and Paul Butterfield to name a few. The music is vocal oriented rock with some original music and some definitely original arrangements of classic rock songs. They will also be playing at the Talent Club in November and the Mark Antony Hotel in Ashland on December 15. The TCB performance will be recorded on digital tape . Come support the completion of our Community Building while hearing some great music!

TAKILMA COMMUNITY FIREWALK has been rescheduled for November 12 due to an extended fire season. The Firewalk has been practiced for thousands of years, always in the context of healing and celebrating life. Let's join together in this ancient ritual which includes drumming, dancing, and singing, to heal old wounds and renew our vision for our community.

Potluck starts at 4:30 p.m. and the firewalk begins at 6:00 p.m.. Sliding scale: $7 - 25 . At the Takilma Community Building. The Firewalk is for adults and children who are mature enough to participate. Child care for younger children is available on a pre-arranged basis. Call Hollis at 592-2476 or Beth 592-6970

Kayla Starr wants to let her clients know that she will be working in Hawaii for three months and will be home again in late February. In the meantime, she is referring people wanting massages to Robin Hawk, L.M.T. (formally Robin Hawkins of Takilma) at 476-2563 in Grants Pass.

If you have jewelry-making tools to loan for a one-month class that Marjorie is teaching the students at the Dome School in November, please call her at 592-6733.

CLASSIFIED ADS

DRUM LESSONS in your home with a group of your friends or in my space. I'll supply all drums, claves, shakers, bells etc. We'll work on Haitian, Cuban, African rhythms, some of which are thousands of years old. Left brain/Right brain endeavors, fun and empowering.Sliding scale. Classes now forming, call Miguelo 592-6970, 592 2549.

WELCOME BRYNAN!

BRYNAN ADAMS was born October 5th, 1994 at 9:28 a.m. at our home. He weighed 8 lbs 5 oz. and was 21" long. It was a wonderful birth, assisted by Karen, Joya and Lisa. We are so thankful for Brynan. We would like to send a huge thanks to all those who brought us dinner, did laundry, went to town, checked on us and helped out in other ways. A big thanks to Kate who organized the dinners and so much help. Our community is so blessed to have not only wonderful midwives, but such an incredible support network. We feel that our family is so incredibly fortunate to live in Takilma. Thanks again to the Takilma Tribe. With much love, Julia, Jonathan and Brynan.

LETTERS

RESPECT OUR ELDERS

Who are the elders in our community circle? How can we council with them and honor them once they are identified? Lately I have found myself befuddled with paths to choose on my earth Planet walk that will lead me to balance and to clarity. In the community of Williams where I have built a log home with my husband Snow, I am Maya Many Moons; relationship dances have been out of focus as far as people changing partners within the circle and what to do with the sistar that is LEFT AND how to embrace the new happy weds or unweds? How do we humans, hopefully developing compassionate hearts, deal with more separation in our families and especially with the hurt and the SHADOWS: which probably lead to the switching of partners so quickly. Onto the Elder Council. I believe if we set up an elder council in our communities, or have a shared council for Williams and Takilma, this will be a positive step in helping to restore harmony and balance to our lives and to the lives of our children and benefit our communities vastly. Anyone or everyone with knowledge and interest in this concept please contact me. I know I have read an article in a new age magazine about this concept being established in these seemingly upside down times and spaces so—let's go for it! i come to you in peace *i am maya*

SEEING IS BELIEVING

A simple idea and some take-charge tendencies can lead to the accomplishment of quality community endeavors. And not only will you see these results, but you can take some of the magic home with you, at this year's Dome School Winter Bazaar. Yes, once again Jim Shames has gone beyond the call of duty, taken time out of his busy, busy schedule to move forward with the completion of "our" community photo. That memorable day in May has been captured in two(2) large format size photos. All $ will go to this rag and the TCB Building Fund. The photos came out wonderful. So come to the Bazaar, look for the Common Ground booth and check it out. Thanks again Jim for nurturing our bodies and our souls.
-Miguelo

IT TAKES A WHOLE COMMUNITY

Sarah and Edie Tramontana lived in Takilma in the 70's and 80's, across from Four Sum One. Edie was the pre-school teacher for many years at the old Log Cabin School. They moved to Ashland when Sarah was fourteen. Two years ago, Edie, Sarah's mom, died suddenly and unexpectedly of a brain tumor. It was the day before Sarah graduated from high school. Last month Sarah turned twenty and started nursing school at Linnfield College in Portland.

I've known Sarah since she was three. Some of you know her too, or remember. She was quiet, shy. Now she is a lovely young woman, soft spoken, self-possessed, gentle, compassionate and hardworking. She has wanted to be a nurse since she was ten. Sarah is a good student. She is motivated and excited to be following her dream.

These past two years haven't been easy for Sarah. No mom, no dad. She started at Lewis and Clark College. It was too much, too soon, so she decided to hold off on college for a while. Now she is ready.

I want to help her. I believe that it takes a whole community to raise a child. If my son was left without parents I would want our community to help him. I'm starting a scholarship fund for Sarah at Ashland Community Hospital and out in the community. I'd like us to give support to Sarah over the next four years. It will mean a lot to her. Financially , she is strapped. She has financial aid, but so much is in loans that her counselor has advised her not to take any more. Whatever we do will make a difference.

There is an account set up at Valley of the Rogue Bank, 250 N.Pioneer, Ashland, OR 97520. Make checks out to Sarah Tramontana Scholarship Fund. Or you can give them to Helen Kaufmann. In a few months I will send Sarah a check. Next year I will start collecting funds again in the summer. Thanks.
-Nancy Fisher, Takilma East

MODEL CITIZEN

Bold, self-assured and empowered.

TO THE EDITORS:

(Dear Felicity - This is the only freebie, sweetie. I really liked reading your article; in fact, it was the only thing that held my interest.)

Here are a few thoughts on the rest of the rag, from Baja Takilma. First - who are Dolores and Inez? I can assure you that in the " old happy hippie" days of Takilma Ward a gentle reminder from the cops was definitely not a "little gentle note".

And as far as Gloria Stone is concerned - if I had her favorite red sweater the only reward I would take is a free evening of eavesdropping on her women's support group.

Also, if I hear any more about menopausal workshops I'll puke. How about some workshops on penis envy, penis comparing, scrotum differences, erection prophylaxis, loss of bowel fantasy and male menopausal sightings.

Please reinstate the Police Bladder - my only favorite. See you at the Firewalk.

-Christina Henning

PS. Barry..........remember Albert Einstein's favorite word: "eschuchen" - lighten up.

PPS. And to Dan Heller....if you're so ready to talk about other people's sex lives why not start with your own?

FAREWELL MESSAGE FROM LIBBY GOINES

Thank you Takilma for all the years of learning, giving, taking, creating, receiving and most of all, the soothing peacefulness of this tiny Valley, which has healed me and all who stay long enough to receive the blessings built into this location.

My heart will always be here in this place no matter where my Goddess sends me on this planet! I will never forget or regret one moment.

Love and Peace Always,
Elisabeth Horn

DEAR EDITOR,

I loved Darrel's article in the last issue. He did such a wonderful job putting into words the feelings of so many of us Takilma folk, both young and old. As a parent of two children born and raised in Takilma, who have gone away to college, I too have heard many of the same memories and feelings expressed. Thank you Darrel!!

Cathy Dunham

TO COMMON GROUND: IN RESPONSE TO DOLORES AND INEZ

This is my second attempt to respond to your article "Marijuana Then and Now". My first was far too rhetorical and you don't deserve that, since I believe you are sincerely concerned for us and our children's welfare. I do, however, believe that your information, education and awareness has a slight bureaucratic taint to it.

You mention that it was part of the spiritual culture and that no community function was held without it. My! I haven't noticed this to be different today.

I also want to respond to the suggestion you made that the sheriff was so easy on the folks who grew it. Is that why the community got together and blocked the road with trees and rocks to stop this same sheriff's department from busting a whole group of gentle hippies? I wish this same consciousness still existed. How powerful and explicit that message was.

I checked close to fifty articles I have on the subject of marijuana, to see what the government has concluded to be dangerous or harmful. After that, I called the local clinic and asked about cases stemming from the use of marijuana. This is what I found out:

Question: Do you know of any medical complications arising from the use of marijuana that have come to the attention of the clinic over the years? Answer: Perhaps a few cases of bronchitis and one or two cases of someone ingesting a high dose and having to ride out the effects. They did come down and go on with their lives.

Question: Do you know of a case in which someone's sperm count was lowered? Answer: No.

Looking around this community it seems that quite a number of children were conceived after a night of smoking or tripping. No lack of sperm here, although I bet a few mothers wish there were. From looking at these children (including Inez' and Dolores'), they have ten fingers, two arms, two legs and have produced progeny to continue the species. Most of these children have exceptional beauty that radiates from within to the rest of the world

I have seen no men with large plump breasts, that weren't caused by an excess of pork, cakes or pies, and I haven't noticed any women with long beards, though I have met a few with muscle. More power to us; and I have a feeling that the spiritual use of the EVIL WEED had something to do with this elevated and strengthened position women are achieving. Thank you.....

I moved here because I felt people here worked hard to create a community where individual rights were important; where children were raised to be aware of the life spirit around them and the outside forces that surround them. I believe that children here are given the tools to live in that "other world". Those tools keep the lies at a distance.

You are right about the consequences of indulgence in this herbal medicine, or from living in this time. 300,000 people, one every two minutes, are arrested for the use of marijuana. A higher percentage of the American populace is in jail than any other nation in the entire world. Hundreds of millions of dollars are being pumped into the "Law and Order" scam. More prisons, more police, more guns and more propaganda. Notice how this coincides with the reduction of a military force. Teenagers are presently in jail for ten to twenty years for possessing as little as 100 hits of acid. Good people in our community have lost their homes and life's work for growing the magic herb.

I could go on and on here. We all know this stuff and have been personally involved. Terence McKenna said "They are keeping cannabis illegal because it causes people to question the social values that they are being programmed with".

Perhaps one of the things that we can teach our children is that we are not "getting stoned", but rather we are "turning on". Our personal attitudes might help change the perspective of our children. It is not the consequences of marijuana that we must be concerned with, but rather the consequences of ignoring what the government is slowly doing to our rights as human beings on a spiritual quest to save ourselves and our planet. Our children have a right to this perspective. They have a right to look for themselves. We must teach them how not to buy into the program. They have plenty to fear out there; let's give them the anchor of love and good information to go forth. Let's hide nothing and teach our children to respect the diversity of life and fight that which impedes spiritual progression.....

I might add that if you have not read "The Emperor's New Clothes" that you do so. It will make you angry and give you something to work with. Remember, it's not marijuana we're talking about, it's hemp. Big money interests continue to hide behind the government and the War on Drugs. - *name withheld by request*

TO ALL MY RELATIONS,

I was unfamiliar with your journal and related projects until recently, when I received the Sept/Oct. issue and a letter of goodwill from Cathy. I thank you very much for the correspondence that adds to what has amounted to me for an astonishing network of support for me while I've been in jail. As you may or may not know: I've been found guilty of 3 federal misdemeanors stemming from my involvement with direct action protests last year on International Wild Rockies Wilderness Day, Aug. 17th, celebrated annually around the world as a day in action in homage to the Rocky Mountain ecosystem. I also failed to appear for the original trial, declaring my contempt for and lack of faith in the U.S. judicial system. This, of course, is the main reason I face a possible 14 month sentence when the decision comes down Oct. 19th. I've been denied bail, and will have served 5 months come sentencing...

At this point, I must respond to Dolores and Inez and their article, "Marijuana then and now." They sound prepared to abandon the herb that has given so much. While I agree with the fact that the simple procurement of this ancient medicine has in many ways become a disgusting and dangerous affair, cannabis is absolutely essential to environmental recovery and social health. What is needed is respect. The article contains references to indulging. Like tobacco, this is a sacred thing that should not be abused. Every single entity in the universe is composed of energy. Some entities by their nature contain more sensitive or volatile energy. If we continue to disrespect every powerful force, we shall suffer repercussions in perpetuity. It is not information, education and awareness that has led to neglect of the herbs. Rather I assert it is fear, propaganda and fascism. This is the same plant that can replace fossil fuels for gasoline and plastics, halt the destruction of forests for most timber products and all paper, stronger than cotton, a more digestible protein than soybean, a medicine for cancer, AIDS, glaucoma, arthritis, countless afflictions. This is a sacrament to those who approach it with all due respect. If we aren't willing to sacrifice the security from possible persecution or are unprepared to teach our peers and children the necessary steps to proper reverence of the sacred, then we definitely should not partake of the sacred or we are bound to learn some tough lessons. But that's life, isn't it? I for one am not willing to trade off my desire for spiritual and evolutionary progress for a mundane life of servitude and compulsion as dictated by a special interest government and its robot police force. One does not avoid rape by professing abstinence, nor does one avert violence by submitting to a lynching. Resist til the end and have faith in others continuing the struggle.

Yours truly,
Scout Walkingflower
c/o Latah County Jail
Box 8086
Moscow, ID 83843

GATHERING OF THE TRIBES

The 1994 Southern Oregon Barter Faire was a wonderful gathering this year. Drawn to a natural meeting place overlooking the Upper Applegate Valley, the tribes came from far and wide. This was a celebration of a lifestyle and also a demonstration of our collective power.

The S.O.B.F. almost didn't happen this year. Although details are unclear, there was a concerted effort to stop the fair. Some of the local residents don't like the event and organized against it. All summer long the news came in bits, with conflicting forecasts. An eleventh hour desperation injunction was simply made inoperative when the sheer force of our arrival couldn't be stopped. Score one for us.

There was much merriment, with the Takelma tribe well represented. With the "Illuminated Fools" anchoring the daily parades, and a well received puppet show, the magic side came alive; a good balance to the trade-and-sell part of the fair.

The Mud People parade was especially powerful. Primitive in nature, a glorification of the Earth Mother was presented on Sunday afternoon. Picking up inspirited pagans along the way, the group circled up, drums throbbing. The ritual climaxed when a statuesque woman was lifted up on the men's' shoulders. Dressed only in mud, and feeling the part, she bestowed love on all. The chant, "Ursa, Ursa!" matched the beat that quickened until finally all stopped onegether. A spirited cheer arose and they all ran for the showers!

Fun as it was, there was an undercurrent of a problem that flowed beneath the surface of events: what will happen next year?

Some feel that the business community of Ruch will convince a few people of the major gain that the fair brings to the area. Most of us just wish we could find a good place - that could stand a little uncomfort - to host a remarkable and crucial happening.

I also visited the Okanogan Barter Fair a week later. Filled with a love of our way, going north was like a pilgrimage. I was proud that I and my friend, Chad's Dad Dave, were representing our tribe here. I am glad to report that they are alive and well up there, and many connections were established. All the women were beautiful, the men strong and the children, above average. Being at these gatherings was empowering, creatively and spiritually, and charged my being.

I see a lot of potential for an event like this, staged in Takilma, to generate all the money we need for our Rock'n'Roll Retirement Fund. Using our experience of other Fairs, we have all the skills to design and contain a great event while at the same time enriching our lives, both now and later.   *River*

EDITORS:

While visiting my family in Takilma last month, I had occasion to see the last issue of Common Ground. I enjoyed catching a glimpse of the community portrayed in its pages. I want to respond to the article about the effects of marijuana use on the children of parents who smoke the herb. As the child of parents who are socially responsible professionals, who provided a secure and loving home for their children and who smoked marijuana with many of their friends during social occasions in our home, I was stimulated by the questions posed in the article.

It is clear to me that it is the "repercussions" not the herb that is the real danger. This danger is imposed on our society by repressive unnecessary laws against the use of a substance that is not addictive and far less dangerous than alcohol, tobacco and various chemicals added to our foods and environment -with the ready approval of our government. My parents taught me to question authority, to take responsibility for myself and to be a productive citizen. It would be surrendering to the corporate Big Brother's intimidation to forfeit this herb based on police state threats and tactics. No one in my family is addicted to any substance. We are all college graduates pursuing our careers. That we had to be secretive about the plants growing in our garden and our parents' use of herb was simply a graphic example of what's wrong with our criminal justice system and the economic injustice that is its basis.

We live in a society that constantly bombards us with pressures to conform to many values that are harmful; to deny our feelings, to support military intervention in other countries, to shave our legs and wear high heels, and to waste our natural resources, for example. I am glad my parents taught me to think for myself.

-Anonymous

THIS EDITION OF COMMON GROUND IS COMING TO YOU EARLIER THAN USUAL SO THAT YOU COULD TAKE ADVANTAGE OF THE FACT THAT SOME OF US READ ABOUT AND DISCUSSED THE VOTERS INITIATIVES AND THE CANDIDATES. WE HOPE YOU FIND THE INFORMATION USEFUL.

THE EDITORIAL STAFF FOR THIS ISSUE CONSISTED OF BARRY, SHEL, ANDREA, ROCHELLE, KATE, KERRY, JILL AND DAVE T. SOME OF US PARTICIPATE IN THE ILLINOIS VALLEY HUMAN RIGHTS ALLIANCE.

AS USUAL, WE ENCOURAGE YOU TO WRITE TO US, FOR US, AND BECOME PART OF THE EVER EVOLVING AND CHANGING STAFF. THE DEADLINE FOR SUBMISSIONS FOR THE NEXT ISSUE IS DECEMBER 7, 1994.

The Illuminated Fools are offering home-dyed, block printed T-shirts. Creative choices: "Takilma Tribe," "Takilma - Hippies Rule," Fools shirt. Proceeds to benefit troupe projects and continuing foolery. See you at the bazaar or call 592-4677, 4695, 6183.

10

KIDS PAGE

MY IMAGINARY ANAMAL
by Chelsea Hocker (age 17....just kidding.....age 7!)

My imaganary animal has ears that hang down to her feet, it is very difacult for her to walk becuse she is always stubling over trhem. by the way she has 20 ears. She is a girl. She has a tail 100 feet long. She can also shrink her self, make her self bigger, or she can tem her self invisabal. She eats fried grass hopers, throw up, berned lasanta, brockaly cookis, pepper cookis, pigs eye balls, cows noses, brocken down bisecats, char coles, and its favrit thing is, cats, dogs, cow, horses, pigs, fishes, and there tails. She has 2000 eye balls. She also has 9000 noses. Here is a story about her. Once a pont a time there was a land full of wild thngs me and all of my second grade budies saild there. We all picked out a anamal. I picked out the one I'v bene discribing. She is a very good pet! She is also related to ms Meengs, so ms Meeings is hafe MONSTER.   The end

Harvest time

MY FRIEND AND ME
by Nicole Birmingham and Elizabeth Johnson

We were friends since we were small,
Now we're big, strong and tall.
We used to play with little toys,
Now we go for all the boys.
When we were small, we played with barbies,
Now we go to all the parties.
We can go out late at night
Without carrying a flashlight.
Now that our little poem is done,
You can see that our life is Fun.

The pumpkin patch had a cat wearing a hat.
And the cat met a bat.
The bat was fat, and so was the cat.
They didn't know where they were at.
The end.

-Shanti, Age 6

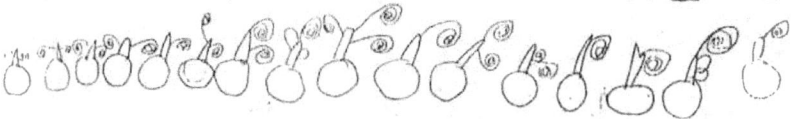

TAKILMA TIME

The sun will soon rise over the dense green eastern hillside framing Hope Mountain. The dust will soon subside from our long country driveway, a trail of morning goodbyes, goodbyes to loved ones and a way of life. Working in Cave Junction or in Grants Pass forces many Takilmanites to hit the road in the predawn. Kids are waiting on the roadside for the sun only to climb aboard a school bus instead. Only the roosters and the hour reveal the impending dawn as the alarm clock jolts too many from dreams and passions left unfullfilled.

This is a commuhity built upon sharing and openness and love, connections that were created through a simple luxury, the abundance of time spent together working and playing. Yet time has become too tight, squeezed and strangled until we have little say over its uses. With the demands of the 8 to 5 workday, one has just enough hours left in the day to foster personal needs, to keep grounded and balanced, to keep sane, perhaps an hour or two to spend with one's partner or children. These are real needs, essential to our quality of life. One needs to feel individual balance in order to be capable of functioning and sharing within any broader contexts. This leaves little time for relaxed community building.

I moved to Taklima for its community. True, Takilma is beautiful, the dense conifer forests and dripping orange winter madrone reveal signs of mystical magic. We dance with reckless abandon, appreciating our uniqueness. Cabins and houses and saunas and orchards and gardens offer pride in human ingenuity and the glory in handmade work. But these will all fade into separate memories if we cannot sustain the time to maintain community. Here we have the opportunity to live within meager means, the enlightenment to realize that chosen families within extended community offer support we all need.

America lacks community; American families too often falter. Takilma is a successful lesson regarding the essential communal value in offering American refugees an extended family. Someone to eat breakfast with, someone to share a hug with on a difficult day, a neighbor to bounce ideas off, a group that can organize projects that better everyone's life, the idea that, through the health of the group, we sustain our own health.

The dust has settled on the driveway, the sun has cleared the hopeful crest and shines with all its strength on our tiny tucked away village. Trails are revealed carving between our cabins in the woods; a two-lane road looks weary under its heavy burdens. Stay off the roads, maintain the foot paths and the community they have built, save your time, share yourself with your extended family, offer a balanced healthy self for everyone's benefit.- *Jon Jeans*

66

BOYCOTT BOISE CASCADE

CALL BOISE-CASCADE ON THEIR DIME & TELL THEM WHAT YOU THINK ABOUT THE SUGARLOAF SALE!

Please call these regional reps. and find out who the distributors are in your area. Encourage your friends, family and <u>all</u> businesses that you support to stop purchasing Boise Cascade paper and office products (including the Reliable Corp., a B/C subsidiary). Join the boycott and protect this priceless ancient forest!

Boise Cascade Office Products
Portland, OR 800-626-1044 FAX 503-283-1494

Boise Cascade Shareholders Services
800-544-6473

For more numbers or information call Debbie at 592-3386.

TAKILMA **COMMON GROUND**
PO BOX 2016
CAVE JUNCTION. OR 97523

BULK RATE
U.S. POSTAGE
PAID
Cave Jct., OR 97523
Permit #16

Address Correction Requested

Takilma COMMON GROUND

ISSUE #8
WINTER SOLSTICE 1994

A FOCUS ON TEENS AND FAMILY

**"The best lack all conviction, while the worst
Are full of passionate intensity."**

So said Yeats shortly after the Great War, and so I find myself saying seventy-four years later, as I write about today's youth.

Apocalypse Now? I doubt it. Too many generations have identified themselves as standing on the brink of "mere anarchy," projecting ruination based on temporary trends. It's always been easy for old curmudgeons like me to detect shortcomings in the latest batch of young whippersnappers. We're probably not headed straight to Hell. History would suggest that the journey is more cyclical.

Nevertheless, I feel like something bad is happening to our society in general, and to youth in particular, and Yeats says it pretty well. Statistics on youth crime, suicide, and poverty; the mood in pop music; the punitive rage our country's in– pretty scary stuff.

I've been teaching here for twenty-odd years, and I've gotten to know so many kids that it feels dishonest to generalize. I know exceptions to everything I will be saying. But I will be talking basically about two groups, the achievers and the alienated, those who say "yes" and those who say "no," and ignoring the many in-betweeners, because I think the tone and feel of youth culture, and perhaps their assumptions and values, are determined mostly by the edges, not the middle.

In brief, I believe a large portion of kids today in this valley are alienated from the community and the country. And their anger, their "passionate intensity," affects most of their peers, helping to rob them of their "conviction".

Why do so many kids thumb their noses at society? They know the rewards they lose and punishments they risk. Mass media makes this clear, and no generation has ever been so bombarded with media. Get the grades, the careers, the fancy cars and houses. Please the parents and get better treatment, more pocket money, less hassle. Conversely, step too far out of line and go hungry, lose your home, or go to jail. The message from the electorate is neither kind nor gentle, but is quite clear.

Moreover, this increasingly insidious media bombardment has molded most young people into unquestioning consumers. Their most common answers to the questions of favorite pastime and goal in life are "shopping" and "getting rich." As materialists, they must have money.

So today's kids know what's at stake. Thus, most of the kids who believe they can be part of the next generation's elite – the higher-skilled achievers with manageable or even good family situations – still go for it. They're embarrassed at times about their academic pursuits and compliance with their parents, just like some of their parents were. It's never been cool to be a goodie-goodie, and as I'll discuss below, increasingly it has connotations of sell-out and betrayal. So they affect rebellion and study ironically, but they study hard enough to be successful.

Seeing these achievers go for the gold, one might wonder why other kids choose school failure and wars with their parents. Why set yourself up for zombie jobs, low status, poverty, jail, and the gamut of destructive possibilities found in drugs and alcohol, terrible driving, violence and other antisocial behaviors, non-lethal STD's and AIDS? Why do so many kids end their adolescence by becoming unwilling parents, or by killing themselves? [Continued on page 3]

1

GERALDINE SPEAKS ON PERFECT PARENTING

STAY MARRIED if at all possible. With even a limited amount of imagination, one can have a variety of lovers over the years. Put a bag over his head if all else fails.

HUMOR is your friend, your ally, your first and last resort. Don't let a single day go by without abusing this valuable tool.

NEVER tell them they were "planned". You say "you were all mistakes". I believe and practice all forms of birth control; well, three for sure. Tell them they are here only by your good graces. That way, they'll never beat you to death with "I wish I was never born".

ALL the years, all the ages are great fun. However, they're not very cute in the 6th grade, the whole miserable year of it. The first six months that they drive, wreck and dent your car is a picnic for sure. Is there anything they don't know at sixteen?

NEVER say "your home, your room," unless you're referring to shit work you don't care to do your-self. Remind them daily who pays the rent. We want grateful, grateful, grateful. For the roof over your head, for the food on the table, the puppy at your feet, the pony in the barn etc. etc. etc.. Life itself is pointless without the "be-nevolent ones", mummy and daddy in this case.

GOOD COP, BAD COP, an art form. You can't possibly spoil them rotten without it. Reward the pleasing, crush without mercy the unacceptable. You'll never tire of this team sport.

BE PREPARED to live in your car. As we reside in the country side, without the benefits of pub-lic transportation, you will drive them every-where, all the time, for the rest of your life, or so it seems at the time. Learn to knit, write the great American novel, while you wait. Everywhere. All the time. Soccer, softball, ballet. This system, unfortunately, precludes anything resem-bling extended vacations. We waited twenty years for our honeymoon, but remember paragraph five, boy were we grateful.

CHILD SWAP, why day care doesn't work. Anything's easier than just your own. Tuesday Thursday my house; Monday Wednesday yours. The skill your child learns is "do unto others". By being a good hostess one learns how to be a per-fect guest. When children only play in neutral territory, day care or preschool, cooperative skills are not learned. You have lovely homes; share them with those messy buggers.

For more fun facts, you may wish to purchase my two new publications. "I've Barfed Away A Year of My Life", or "A Guide For The Useless Fluff In You".   *Geraldine Davidson*

END OF THE TRAIL, HO CHI?

The liveliest topic of last month's Takilma Community Association meeting concerned a sym-bolic remnant of the Takilma Clinic: the Ho Chi Minh room. When the clinic pulled out of its former home one and a half years ago, the Ho Chi Minh room was left with medical equipment intact, leaving the possibility for some type of limited medical facility to develop in Takilma.

After eighteen months of quiet dormancy, the Siskiyou Health Center is ready to put the equipment back into service with plans to remodel their emergency room in Cave Junction. Expressing her respect for the historical ties betwqeen the Clinic and the Takilma community, Meadow Martell approached the TCA board for its approval.

While opinion was somewhat diverse among Board members, a consensus arose to tentatively approve the release of clinic equipment to the Siskiyou Health Center. The TCA felt it was appro-priate that the equipment should serve our commu-nity in C.J. rather than continue collecting cob-webs for memory's sake.

Unless a persuasive proposal is presented to the TCA board at its next meeting, the approval will be finalized at that meeting. The next TCA meeting will be at the Siskiyou Project office (former Clinic) on Thursday, January 19th, 7:15 p.m.
                                                    - TCA Board

THE BEST LACK ALL CONVICTION continued from p.1.

As soon as you ask the question, you know that "choose" is not the right word. They're either in too much pain, or too numb, or too benighted to do otherwise. Confidentiality does not allow me to describe in detail the personal horrors many of my students face, but they often have lives like soap operas: raising themselves, coping with parents who are so often alcoholic/abusive/ incapacitated, or simply irresponsible, or overwhelmed/ single/ poor, or stunted/blighted/ignorant/bitter.

Raised by TV and their peers because they have no strong, healthy relationships with adults, these alienated kids at best learn to cope, at worst to lash out, but never to belong.

Some of the paths we have chosen, like environmentalism, seem hopeless to most young people.

They are angry, and really haven't much to be grateful to adults for. They develop a hard veneer of pseudo-sophistication, and brandish the defiance that comes from a sense that they have nothing to lose. Having only peers for companions, they are fully immersed in teen culture, and usually become its experts. They have the inherent strength of cynicism: nothing to defend. All these attributes make them fascinating, exciting, and authoritative to their peers. Thus they do much to set the tone of what is cool, curbing those who are too positive or exuberant, and punishing those guilty of the cardinal sin, Nerdism.

Also, they absorb the energies of individuals and institutions that could be spent enriching a larger number of their peers. In groups, their negativism sometimes reaches critical mass and chain reacts, in classrooms and parking lots. They lower our expectations. They wear us out.

Alienated kids have always been around, but I think they have more influence than ever. For one thing, there's more of them now; about eight to ten percent of LBMS kids raise themselves, with nominal parents (or surrogates) who have abdicated their responsibilities. Much of pop culture endorses their anger and cynicism— Beavis and Butthead, Bart Simpson, many rap lyrics. And perhaps because they are victims, like blacks in the Sixties, their more fortunate peers feel some need to support them.

Kids have a network, so they know far better than their parents and teachers who slept in a ditch or with Mom's boyfriend last night. Kids see a friend, coming back to school from a hellish weekend in an otherwise hellish life, get scolded or embarrassed for not playing the school game right. In the next instant the more fortunate kids are asked to demonstrate how good they are at this game. Their natural urge to excel and learn runs counter to the need to have compassion and show solidarity. The most common compromise is to do the game well, but show a subtle contempt for it.

I believe in the value of education to enrich life, so why do I call it a game? Perhaps because the liberal arts rationale for education is almost never invoked. Why is an education important? So you can get a good job. Even for the achievers, it's been reduced to that, a competitive jockeying for position in the breadline of life. This brings us to the central problem with kids today: us.

We Boomers used to believe we could roll back injustice, take control of our government, save the environment, establish peace, and live in harmony with the planet. I don't think most of us, let alone the kids, believe that stuff is really happening. The "best" lack conviction because we lack conviction.

We haven't communicated to them a clear set of ideals they could build meaningful lives on. Some of the paths we have chosen, like environmentalism, seem hopeless to most young people; perhaps they see incremental approaches like recycling as merely postponing the inevitable cataclysm. Other paths, like Native American and other alternate forms of spirituality, seem irrelevant to the life of the American teen, swept along in the media mainstream.

Nor have our generation's choices always been helpful. Our drug involvement has often been damaging to young adolescents. Our desire to be considered cool by our kids has led us to enable them. Our sexual revolution is clearly dangerous in the days of AIDS but continues to be all kids see, in their homes or at the movies.

Finally, just how would our kids go about making a difference? We joined with the right wing to discredit what were once thought to be the major tools for progress in our society: public schools and other governmental agencies. As for establishing peace and harmony one consciousness at a time, kids just aren't buying it.

What's to be done? First and foremost, establish close one-to-one relationships with kids; the most at-risk kids don't have an involved adult in their lives. Kids must receive if they are to feel like giving something back. Only adults in a close relationship can do this giving. Believe and persevere; they'd probably rather hang out with their friends or watch a video, but they need the kind of foundation for ethics and values that only adults can give.

Kids must receive if they are to feel like giving something back.

Help with programs that provide activities for groups of youth, such as school, RAPP, and the Boys and Girls Club. But remember that just keeping the kids grouped, busy and amused is not the solution.

Politically, fight the increasingly anti-kid tide that is sweeping the U.S. Culturally, resist the violent, materialistic mind numb-ers who seek to entertain us, and subvert the message they give our youth.

And in this community, we must search out, proclaim, and embody a set of ideals that offer a path for kids, a rationale for ethics and service and reverence and belonging that can stand up to the nihilism around us. - *Jack Dwyer*

70

Letters from our readers:

Thank you to all those who participated or sent good thoughts for our community firewalk. It was an amazing experience. As I mentioned that night, we did not get a chance to talk about our visions for the future of our community. I invite you to use the Common Ground as a forum for your creative ideas and a means for expressing your needs and desires.

One thing I would like to see is a child care cooperative. If you are interested in this, give me a call at 592-2476.

Many people have expressed their desire for another Firewalk soon. If you really want it to happen it is up to you, the community, to pull it together. This means:

1. 1/4-1/2 cord of dry fir and oak.
2. Make arrangements with Helen for the use of the building and cover building rental costs.
3. Make sure there is a hose to the fire site.
4. Break down school and put back together and clean.
5. Get the word out to the entire community.

If you have the energy to put it together I would be happy to show up and facilitate on purely a donation basis. If it doesn't happen soon I will definitely put together a Takilma Community Firewalk in the early spring.

I look forward to joining with you all in the sacred circle again.   *-Love and Blessings, Hollis*

I would like to give thanks to Hollis and all who were present, for creating an incredible heartfelt healing ceremony of body and spirit, "The Firewalk".

May we continue to grow and awaken our spirits to all elements of earth, life and love.   We Are Alive !!!
-Randy

Thank you Takilma, and all my friends, from far and near for attending the Clan Dyken benefit, It certainly made my life a little easier. I love you, as schmaltzy as it sounds... hugs ,kisses, laughter and good sex for ever.   *-Robin Wren*

Dear Staff,
Thank you for providing a counter-culture digest of the voter's handbook. It felt good to join our own sort of Political Action Committee and put some purpose in the process.

I feel we must vote. The moral minority are vocal and mobilized (they vote). Pro-choice and human rights are in jeopardy. To remain apathetic (doesn't vote) seems to play into Big Brother's hand. Truly, we haven't seen the darkest hour if we continue to give our power away to people that don't seem to have our interests in mind. Please vote with us. *- Michael Rusich*

A letter to the teens;

The only place I am aware of that provides dances for all ages is the Dome School. Up until this last year I always saw teens, adults and children participating together at the Dance. A year or so ago I began to notice that outside the school there were as many people as inside and 90% of those outside were teens. During this last summer, cars were broken into, car windows were smashed, graffiti of an offensive nature was sprayed on the pump house and at least three teens were injured in fights that ocurred. Large numbers of beer bottles and cans were left on the grounds and recently bonfires were lit, using the school's wood, even when I asked that the wood not be used. I had no objection to the fire, because it was so cold. The teens hang out outside, use the facilities, try to sneak in, ask to use the phone but will not often pay the usual fee of $3.00 for the dance.

I do not speak on behalf of the school, though I know other folks there who share these opinions. Many people in the community are concerned. We cannot have drinking or rude behavior around the school. We want you to participate. We love you and think of you as a part of the community. We want to share these evenings with you.

I sponsored one dance especially for teens and had music that I thought you wanted. Very few of you went in and spent the three or four dollars admission for the three bands and light show brought in for the evening.

Question: What do you want to happen, in order to come in to the dance? Do you want to have some of your own dances? If so, who will be willing to help? Put yourself in the school's place and ask yourself what you think the school should do. Please pull your act together and participate with us. We want you at dances. You do not have to spend all your time indoors, but you need to participate and you need to pay the two or three dollars that is asked, in order for the school to continue to provide this form of entertainment...   *- Robin Wren.*

LOADED SUBJECT

Okay - we've got the lid off - now let's stir the pot!!!!!!!

Isn't there anyone out there who remembers the sheriff's department's notes but us? (I still have one - D.) Yes, they (police) got much heavier very quickly, but that's not the way it was in the beginning.

Police persecution is not right or fair, *but it exists*. We don't agree with the criminalization of marijuana - but that's what we are having to live with - and while working for change, each in his/her own way, we want to raise questions about how we can best deal with the current system while minimizing its impact on us, our kids and our community.

First - let's address some comments from your letters:

1. We did not profess abstinence *or* submission.

2. We never suggested it was an "evil weed".

3. We never suggested anything physically dangerous about pot (but we WOULD love to meet a couple of guys with low sperm counts and large breasts!).

4. We never suggested that our kids were somehow abnormal because we smoked.

5. We are not concerned about plants in the garden, but plantations in the garage.

We are concerned about kids being pulled out of class and interrogated without lawyers or parents present; about the effect on families and lives when people get busted. I don't believe any of us plans on "..surrendering to corporate big brother's intimidation to forfeit this herb based on police state threats and tactics". (WOW!)

But how do we deal with this?

When we talked about the "message we are sending to our kids" by smoking with, or in front of them, we were wondering if any of us advocates encouraging our young ones to smoke *anything*, period? We are also concerned about young kids having to be protective of their parents' life style, while being inundated with confusing "just say no" and "squeal on your folks for their own good" messages away from home. We are concerned with the conflicts they must deal with as they try to balance appropriate behaviors in two cultures (home and elsewhere). Is it fair to put the burden of that responsibility on them? Twenty years ago, it was no big deal if a kid was found with pot at school; the principal dumped it out, and they sent a note home, or requested a parent conference. Today they might send the DEA home!

We make a great effort to educate our kids about sex without 'doing it' in front of them or sharing it with them. We suggest that the same care needs to apply to drug education (Oops! Should that be 'herb education'?).

The comment about hemp (re: The Emperor's New Clothes) is valid, but we are talking about marijuana. How many of us would be happy smoking fibrous, stringy hemp?

Those were some good responses, but we want more! We'd like to hear from some of you other folks - WE KNOW YOU'RE OUT THERE! How about some of you who have had to deal with getting busted? How about some of the other kids who started smoking at a young age? Would you do anything differently? Why? Why not?

Yours 'til the pot boils.....*Dolores and Inez*

Dear Friends,

I attended a parenting class at the Dome School last week and would like to share part of my experience with you. Mavis Cloutier came a great distance, on a Friday night, to share her knowledge with us. She came at the request of someone in the Takilma community. I don't know her impression of the evening, but I left feeling frustrated and hostile. Once again Takilma's public relations had been blighted by a few ill-mannered, insensitive people. We were enlightened many times on parenting technique and listened to a personal critique of our obviously lacking skill of raising children by someone who does not have, or ever had, children. We politely listened while our sitters counted out the dollars and our backs became stiff. We must not infringe on anyone's freedom of speech. What happened to our rights? Why was this tolerated? We would never have allowed this blowing wind from any of our children or politicians.

Another person showed up so stoned they could not even speak on the subject at hand. This, however, did not keep them from sharing their opinions on other subjects. They even went so far as to join Mavis at the front of the class to write us a note on her teaching chart. This person then sat behind me, lit a huge sage stick and fumigated the whole front row. So much for second hand smoke, so much for the No Smoking signs, so much for the rights of others. This was to be the tone of a three hour meeting.

Why didn't I say something? I don't live in Takilma. The people around me who do live here acted like it was a nuisance that just had to be tolerated. No one from the school spoke up, this was a school sponsored event. Who was I, an outsider, to say anything? No, I didn't want to look like some narrow-minded, tight ass bitch who should just stay away. Why do you invite the outside world into your nest and allow these types to spoil your public events and your reputations? Why is it not OK to say "Hey, you are being rude, obnoxious, insensitive, when it is obvious to the dead that it is the truth? Thank you Dome School, for trying. I smelled to high heaven of sage but I still learned a lot. Next time, though, I will probably wait until the class is held in town. Please accept my apology if I've insulted anyone.

- Sincerely, Debbie Messerli

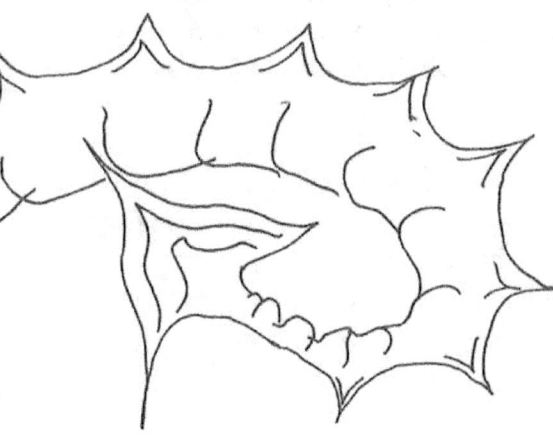

PLAY DOUGH

This is a recipe for making clay ornaments that you can bake in the oven and have as keep-sakes or use as gifts.
Mix together:
2 - 2 1/2 cups all-purpose flour (not self-rising)
1 cup table salt
Slowly add:
3/4 cup cold water

Knead this mixture for about five minutes and add more flour if mixture is too sticky, or a tiny bit of water if it's too dry. You want it to be firm.

When the dough is workable you can form shapes and place on a cookie sheet. Bake at 350 F for 45 minutes or so, depending on the thickness of the items.

Objects can be painted with water colors or acrylics after they are dry. Or you may choose to add food coloring to the water when mixing.

If you want to make a play dough type clay, for playing but not baking, use WARM water and add two tablespoons of vegetable oil. This will make a pliable dough that will not dry out quickly if sealed in a plastic bag when not in use. We keep our extra dough in the refrigerator - BUT IT IS NOT EDIBLE!

Cookie cutters make great stencils for orna-ments. Have fun! We've used this recipe to make stars, moons, angels, candy canes and animal to-tems to adorn our Solstice/Christmas trees.
-Oshana

Green rolling hills slowly reaching up to a
snow crusted mountain. A doe drinks from an icy
mountain stream : her fawn peers at its crystal
clear image in the running water. Hikers stop to
record the picture with their memory. In the
distance the Siskiyou Mountains loom large and
forbidding. In the fall leaves tumble down in
great bouquets of color: everything from a deep
brown to the brightest yellow, from rust to
flaming red.
Oaks, madrones, pines, firs all standing strong
in the winter winds.
Meadows unfolding into a bountiful landscape
full of plants, flowers, and wildlife.
The Illinois River tumbling down to seep into
the Rogue , full of power, yet gentle.
- Mirya, age 13

KIDS

WHEN ASKED "HOW WOULD YOU CHANGE THE COMMUNITY FOR THE BETTER ?"

Lorenza,age 9, said: " If I could change the community I would want kids dances with clean rap and no violent music. Kids would not be around violence and bars, school would have no grafitty and no gang related clothes, violence kills people. Ther would be no cigarette smoking. My dad was shot because of racial problems. Ra-cial problems can happen in any community things like nigger are used as names for people of color. I would stop sexual abuse, and child abuse. I would band police from using batons to beat people with.

Dani,age 11, said: " How I would change the com-munity, Since not very many kids go to community dances they usually stay home or something.
I think the commu-nity should make a kids' dance. Alot of kids I know go to Evergreen. It seems like they learn how to be gang members and smoke pot and be racial. They don't have good homes. Their parents wern't ready to have them. So they go shhot each other. Young female teenagers get pregant. The baby have Birth Defects. "

Sol,age 10, said" I wish people would get along People would share. Here people are nice and some are mean. Me and my friends usually get along but sometimes we can't. Usually we don't mind. Adults don't get along sometimes people are glad they live here. "

HOW TO REALLY

Be there. Say yes as often as possible. Let them bang When they're unlovable, love yourself. Realize how importa books out loud with joy. Invent pleasures together. Remember no when necessary. Teach feelings. Heal your own inner chil a cake and eat it with no hands. Imagine yourself magic. Mak own dreams. Search out the positive. Keep the sparkle in you your garden. Open up. Stop yelling. Express your love. A

SPEAK

WHEN ASKED "HOW WOULD YOU CHANGE THE COMMUNITY FOR THE BETTER ?"

Mike,age 10, said:" If I could change the comunity I would have kid dances and to have mixed dances for kids and parents, together for awhile. and parents to take ther kids to places that they go so they would be together more often. And if parents woodent yell at them if they forgot to do a chore.'

Paul,age 11, said: " Leave the kids alone if they want to be left alone. Have more music classes available to kids. Have sport activities planned for after school. Have Art and other fun game stuff rec. room or something.. Need parents to help and plan ways to keep kids together. Kids get bored after school because they have no planned activi-ties. We need a rec room with activities for all ages. "

Aaron, age 10, said;" I wish people would be a more friendly type. Seeing each other more often. Being with other people more often . He or She. No different. We are all people. No matter where. He or she is black, white, who cares. that is the problem. no one cares much about each other. Even your x wife you should care about. 'Even your x hus-band. everybody. "

We think that these letters are pretty clear in what they would like to have. Anyone know how to make it happen? A Saturday afternoon dance could be fun.

LOVE A CHILD

⊃n pots and pans. If they're crabby, let them play in water. ıt it is to be a child. Go to a movie in your pajamas. Read ıow really small they are. Giggle. A lot. Surprise them. Say Learn about parenting. Hug trees. Make loving safe. Bake lots of forts with blankets. Let your angel fly. Reveal your eye. Mail letters of love. Encourage silly. Plant licorice in ot. Speak kindly. Paint their shoes. Handle with caring.

TODDLER'S CREED

If I want it, it's mine.
If I give it to you and change my mind later, it's mine.
If I can take it away from you, it's mine.
If I had it a little while ago, it's mine.
If it's mine, it will never belong to any body else. No matter what.
If we are building something together all the pieces are mine.
If it looks just like mine, it's mine.

JESSEA'S WORD SEARCH

```
R W Y P S G N I L W O B G L L R
B A L S M B G H J A K R U O S E
Y E K R U T Y T R A H R L O Z M
X T O P R H K E I X A M C H B M
A R C A D E C S V D D A H C R U
R A N Z Y C O T E D O M E S I S
T U E E O N R C R E R L C V S P
F L T S M I R Y A B K I W I C P
O E I C D L G A M E S K X Q O O
P G K H C A E B A C J A N I E O
T O S C M B B A S K E T B A L L
```

DOME SCHOOL	ARCADE	MIRYA
TAKILMA	FUN	BRISCOE
CEDAR GULCH	RIVER	TURKEY
DRUMS	JANIE	SOCCER
BASKETBALL	GAMES	BOWLING
KITE	ROCKY	POOL
MAXIE	PETEY	LEGO
SUMMER	BEACH	BALI
KIWI	SAM	SETH

WHERE EVERYTHING IS

THE SKY WHERE THE ANGELS OF HEARTS ARE
AND FLOWS WHERE
LOVE IS. and
WHERE NOUTHING CAN GO WRONG.
BUT THE BEST OF ALL IS
WHERE YOUR LIFE IS AND
WHERE YOU ARE.

Janaki, age 8

BITTERSWEET BURDEN OF YOUTH

Hicks and Stoners
Town and Gown
Sticks and Stones
Wound to the bone
Cops and Robbers
Us and Them
Serene Buddha, Merciful Jesus
How do we stop the pain?
How do we teach the beautiful young to soar
on first flight wings?
How do we start the change that heals the pain?

Shop Smart Madonna and Child
push a cart down a dead end aisle
filling life's holes with soft sweet salty crunch
Wannabe hipster Hammerheads
while away hazy afternoons
passing the pipe they hope will make things
right, bright, full.

Everything we fear, all our dreams come true.
What have we done to you?
How do we start the change to heal the pain?

Rainier Ale, large Fattie, Tofuburger, Big Mac,
Ancient forest
Job and paycheck
Who wins? How do we all stand to lose?

Frazzled teachers, hassled cops,
Loving blundering parents.
Road to confusion paved with innocent intentions.
Kill the messenger, jail the sinner,
keep your sights small, erase the vision.
Be safe, stay clean, keep your room neat,
rent a movie, stay in line.
Take risks, get down and dirty,
seek out great thinkers.
Become one.
Be brave. Stay open. Have fun.

Make your life your art. Create yourself.
Love yourself.

See us, your elders, look us in the eye.
We see the you in you, the us in you,
the best in you.
Surpass us. Surprise us.
Dazzle yourselves at how well, how high,
how deep and wide you can
soar.
And when you fall, as you will, as you must;
we are here to dress the wounds,
and take part in the healing that restores us
all.

-Marcy Tilton

MOM

Each tear I shed today
is for ALL those words
we never did say
Each smile parting my lips
is for those moments of laughter
we shared so long ago
Each surge of anger through my veins
is for those white men in white coats
who brought you so much pain
And each time I pause and think of you now.
I'm so thankful you're free at last
I love you Mom........
-Dave Toler

A SECRET PLACE

When a cold wind rattles your house in April it
startles you
The shutters flap helplessly, the doors power-
less
Coming in from all sides
Disorienting chill bites hard
At friendships once thought honest
At habits once thought too old to break

Facing the storm with closed eyes
Instinct deftly guides you
On journey to your secret place
A short quest to somewhere very far away
The mind your only carriage

Ringed by sentinel pines
A humble brook nurtures
Tall verdant grasses and countless
Flowers proud with abundant color while
Vigilant jays keep silent watch

Nestling into a smooth warm rock
Apprehension and worry melt like ice in spring
thaw
Streams clogged with fear and self doubt
Break free in a rush of insight
Soul water flows deep cool and steady

Viewing with a fresh hopeful perspective
That reflects the natural order
Every action is a purposeful link
Each step nearly a jump for joy
And that harsh April wind?
A cooling breeze after the glow of sweat
-Marcus Kauffman

Let's make Swedish heart baskets

Let's see. You start by folding two sheets of glossy paper (construction paper will work), one red and one white. Then you cut out two half-heart shapes, like the one in the drawing.   They'll be easier to weave if you make them larger than the pattern.

Then, holding one color in each hand, weave white strip number 1 through red strip number 6, around red 5, through red 4, around red 3, and so on. It's a little trickier to do the next white strip, but you can push the first one up out of the way to give yourself more room. Weave white strip number 2 the same way, but start by going around red 6, through red 5, and so on. Continue weaving until you've used all the strips. Try it. It's a lot easier than it sounds. Next, cut out a strip of paper for a handle and glue or tape it on the inside of your heart basket. Now you can fill it with nuts and hang it on the tree.   *-from Linnea's Almanac*

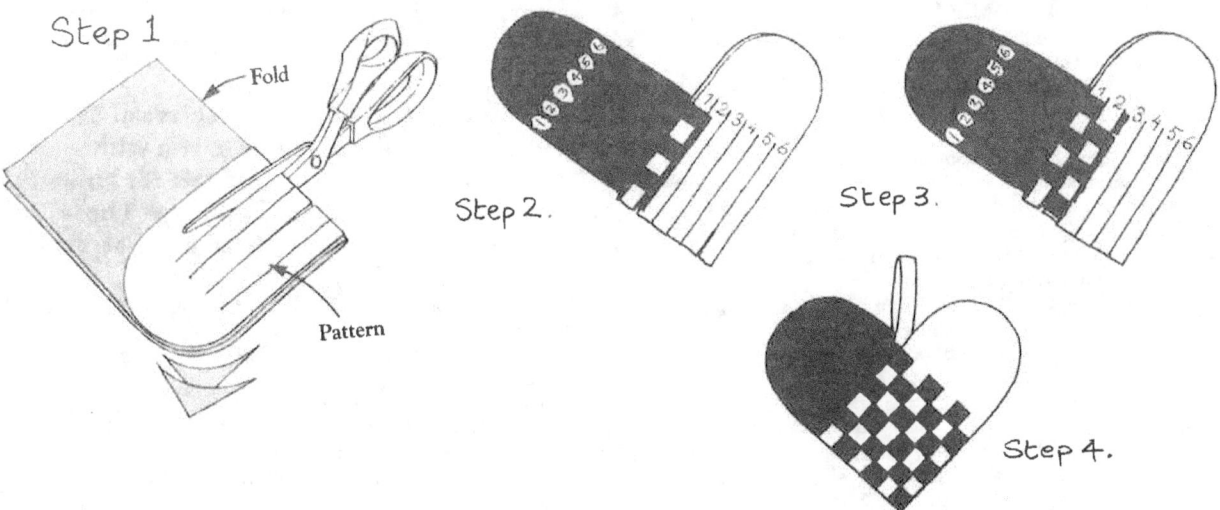

Step 1

Fold

Pattern

Step 2.

Step 3.

Step 4.

HOLIDAY GIFT WRAP

You only need a few simple materials to make beautiful gift wrappings. This process is euphoria producing.....kids and adults love it, and your packages will look like small works of art.

Gather a few materials:
* plain white tissue paper
* brown wrapping paper - or use the inside of grocery bags...press with a warm iron or crumple, then press for a handmade paper effect
* candle
* paint brushes: artist brushes, fan brush, small/large
* paint - fabric paint, watercolors, acrylics. A few basic colors. Metallics are good too.
* small jars or plastic artist's palate for paints
* jar of water to clean brush between colors
* rags to wipe brushes

Cover your work area, table, floor, with a plastic tarp.

1. Tissue paper spatter paper: use two sheets of tissue. Thin paint to consistency of cream. Dip brush in paint, a few inches from the paper, snap to spatter by holding the end of the brush with one hand, and snapping with thumb and forefinger of the other hand. Layer colors. Add random designs. Allow plenty of time, once you start you'll want to play. Let tissue dry completely.

2. Brown paper "resist": Mark with a white candle on brown paper. Random markings, regular patterns, drawings. Then paint a wash of color/ colors over it.

3. Combine these techniques, invent your own.

RIBBONS: make ribbon from fabric by cutting into strips with a pinking shears - a yard or two of fabric goes a long way. Use plain cotton, shiny sleazy, scraps. Paint ribbon as you paint the paper. *- Marcy Tilton*

CAREER CENTER NEWS

At I.V.H.S., budget cuts, staff reductions, and shifting priorities have made extinct that part of high school called guidance counselling. Encouragingly, a local volunteer group has formed to respond. Here is their report to our readership, and an invitation to join.)

If you are a caring, enthusiastic individual who enjoys listening and communicating with young adults, we welcome your energy and talents at the I.V.H.S. Career Center. This volunteer-based center is now open 5 days a week at lunch, and from 12:45 - 3:00 P.M. at the Illinois Valley High School Library. Trained parents, community members, and students keep the "World of Opportunities" center open every day in order to assist students with individual goal-setting and career focus. Our career team shares in privately interviewing students, teaching them to access the C.I.S. (Career Information System) computer, and preparing them for higher education and post-graduation life. The interest, enthusiasm, and encouragement of people (like you for instance) helps to deepen personal committment (for student and volunteer alike).

One of the Career Center's main goals is to develop students' self-esteem and respect for personal accomplishments. Each student will acquire a portfolio/folder with news coverage, certificates of accomplishment, personal recommendations, outstanding poems, art work, and essays which reflect their talents and build a comprehensive account of who they uniquely are! This material can be used for resumes, scholarships, job interviews, college entrance, whatever their personal needs are after high school.

We have great faith in the potential of these creative young people, and hope that they can appreciate their own unique talents and capabilities. If you would like to become involved with our career team, please call Andy at 596-2550 or Karen at 592-4205.

WHEN IN DOUBT WHACK IT OUT

Trees in a wild natural forest environment are genetically programmed to bear only as many fruits (seeds) as they can nutritionally afford to produce. Evolution has long since eliminated those strains that bear too much, thereby weakening themselves and becoming susceptible to insects and diseases.

In growing agricultural tree and bush crops, however, we humans have (as usual) attempted to bypass evolution by selecting just those varieties that have tendencies to bear large crops every year. To counteract the detrimental effects of overbearing we've come up with two strategies: fertilization and pruning . Fertilizer gives the tree more nutrients than would be naturally available. Still, many cultivars, even if optimally fertilized, will commit suicide or bear tiny, low quality fruit unless some pruning is done. Pruning is the tool that keeps a tree's bearing in balance with its nutrients and growth habits thereby making it "thrifty".(Continued)

Some cultivars need far more pruning than others. Most pear and apple varieties will survive and bear some fruit without any pruning at all (though fruit is often small and scabby). Others, such as peaches, <u>need</u> to have at least half or more of each year's growth removed to bear quality fruit (or even to survive).

Volumes have been written about the best way to prune and there are many, sometimes conflicting, theories and systems. Here are a few aphorisms that, from our experience, sum things up and may give you the courage to get out there and start whacking.

Don't let the fact that you haven't read 85 books on the subject paralyze you with inaction. You don't need to meditate for hours on the perfect way to shape each tree. Those trees want - no, need - you to hack away at 'em.

Prune all wood that falls into any of the "4-D" categories:

1. <u>DEAD</u> Dead wood is fairly obvious. Get rid of it.

2. <u>DAMAGED</u> Did a bear help you harvest your apples last Fall, thrashing some branches in the process? Remove any broken ones. Make cuts flush to trunk or large branches leaving no short stubs.

3 <u>DISEASED</u> Eyeball every branch including the trunk, especially crotches. Are there any odd-looking necrotic or discolored patches of bark? Are there holes or wounds exuding gummy sap or sawdust? If so, cut 'em out. If such areas are found in the trunk itself they should be carved out with a knife or gouge.

4 <u>DUPLICATE</u> This category accounts for your largest volume of pruning. It consists of any branches that touch, cross, or shade each other. That is, branches occupying or heading towards the same space.

It's easier to under prune than to over prune. We try to remind ourselves to be brutal...

One other reason to prune is for convenience. Shape the tree so you can take care of it easily. Long leggy branches that make you teeter on the highest step of your ladder to pick and prune are dangerous and should be shortened.

When you're done pruning, two jobs remain. First paint all large cuts (larger than 2 1/2 " diameter) with white interior latex paint or other tree dressing. Second collect and burn all prunings as they harbor insects and diseases.

Your trees and bushes should reward your efforts with years of high quality fruit. -*MARK*

CLASSIFIEDS

INNER CHILD TAROT, by phone or in person. Short session - $10; long session - $30. Trades welcome. Let your dreams come true. Sandy Newell 596-2983.

FOR RENT 2 bedroom house, washroom, pantry, fenced yard. $375/ month. Leave name and number , 592-3535.

HOWDY FOLKS. I need work - wood cutting, stacking, yard cleaning, rock moving, window cleaning, anything available. Reasonable, negotiable rates. Call your friend, Randy. 592- 2308

TWO DREAM GROUPS starting in January. Mondays 2:30 - 4:30 and Thursdays 6:30 - 8:30. Must be committed for 7 weeks. Entire cost is $35. Come and learn what messages your dreams are bringing you from your unconscious. For registration and information call Hollis 592-2476,by December 30.

FREE PROPANE STOVE; needs repair. FREE wood stove. You haul. 592-2476

ONE HUNDRED AND EIGHTY THREE PEOPLE you probably know in Takilma Photo; Available now in 81/2"x11" format, later on in the larger size. $10 small; $20 large; includes delivery/postage. All proceeds to Common Ground and the Takilma Community Building. Send orders to PHOTO, Common Ground, P.O.Box 2016, Cave Junction, OR 97523

ANNOUNCEMENTS

PHOTO
THANKS, HUGS AND KISSES to Jim Shames for another piece of fine documentary black-and-white photojournalism. We love the picture; we love you; we appreciate all the energy put out and all the green energy coming back in.
THANKS AND PRAISES to Miguelo for the Idea and the co-ordination and to Laurie Prouty for helping in the dark room.
THANKS TO ALL who showed up at the Forge on May Day (now turn to the Classifieds for important ordering information.....).

COMMUNITY BUILDING UPDATE
Work is continuing on the addition to our Community Building. The wiring and the heating work has been done. In late December/early January people will be needed to work on installing insulation. Several individual contributions have been made recently and we received an anonymous donation from a group of people who are known to be fond of egg nog. We have raised close to $10,000 from our numerous, generous friends. If you would like to help us reach our goal please contact Robin at 592-3159 or the Dome School at 592-3911, P.O.Box 812, C.J., OR 97523. We still need money and workers! Thanks!

WOMEN'S CAFE
This year the Women's Cafe will be held on Saturday, March 11. We would like to expand the concept of celebrating March as Women's History Month by putting on some other events. If you would like to participate, or simply offer ideas, contact Deb Murphy at the Dome School 592-3911 or at home 592-2866. An organizational meeting will be held on Tuesday, January 10 at 7.00 p.m. at th Takilma Community Building.

HELP YOURSELF!
An action alert is being sent out throughout the community to help you respond to the BLM Ten Year Plan proposal. We hope you'll take 20 minutes to fill it out and send it in. Any questions, call Romain (592-2311) or Dave T. (592-3908).

LIBRARY LOVERS UNITE As you all know, our library system is in dire straits. Our funding has continually been reduced, leaving us with old books, few hours of service and only a couple of librarians in the whole system! With the tax situation in this county, funding is not going to increase due to our tie-in with decreasing O&C funds. To alleviate this there is a plan to put a library levy on the mail-in ballot on March 28, 1995.

If this passes we would be in a semi-acceptable position according to library standards. As it is now we are considered to be operating on a sub-standard level. The Waldo voting precinct has always been a strong supporter of our library. It is hoped that this spring it will once again vote for this important community service.

The levy will not be tied to any other department, such as the Sheriff's department, as was done in the past. This money will ONLY go to fund the Josephine County Library.

For further info or input: France Osborne is President of the IV Friends of the Library, 592-6381. Mary Jo Weber is Vice-President, 592-2873. Deb Murphy is a trustee on the Jo.Co. Library Board, 592-2866.

COMMON GROUND, a newsletter for Takilma, was born out of the desire to broaden our connections as a community. Our mission is to present a forum for information, ideas and debate. Poetry also turns us on. Humor is crucial. We support diversity, encourage debate, promote creative expression and actively seek common ground. We honor the earth we inhabit here at the headwaters of the Illinois River.

The paper is published eight times a year, on the solstices, equinoxes and the mid-points in between. We distribute freely to all the people we can find an address for in Takilma; all those who identify themselves to us in the Illinois Valley; all our friends and relations in the rest of the world who cough up some bucks. We will send three free issues to anyone, anywhere in the forty-eight contiguous states (OK, and the others) but after that we need some sign of continued life from you, dear far-flung reader.

Please keep sending us your immortal prose, lyrical verse, tiny little line drawings and scurrilous opinion. Investigative reporting excites us madly; agitated letters convince us that you are out there, and you care. Our computer is a Mac; we will return your disk to you, should you be technocratic enough to send us one. We deal calmly with messy bits of paper. We reserve the right to edit, though we will endeavor to let you do it yourself.

PLEASE SEND ALL MATERIAL FOR ISSUE #9 TO COMMON GROUND, P.O.BOX 2016, CAVE JUNCTION, OR 97523, BY JANUARY 19,1995 FOR PUBLICATION FEBRUARY 2.

The Mud Council bids farewell and happy trails to Adrian Murillo and welcomes Jack Dwyer.

Editorial staff for this issue were Kerry Holman, Dave Hocker, Kate Dwyer, Felicity Elworthy, Jill Birmingham, Deb Murphy. Our facilitator was Robin Wren. Thanks to Margarita and Ina. And Elishua.

TO THE WILLIAMS TRIBE!

Hi and hello to our sister city over the mountain! We'd like to include more folks from the Williams community on our mailing list. We'd love to see letters and articles from that neck of the woods too. We'll be handing some copies of this issue to Maya and folks at the Horizon School so they can pass round the news. If you like what you see (or even if it makes you puke) please fill out the subscription form so that we can talk to each other.

```
SUBSCRIBE NOW!
    $10 ___ 1 Year Subscription            Name _____
    $25 ___ 1 Year Sub + Takilma Mug
        ___ Broke but Literate.Please include me.  Address _____
```

TAKILMA **COMMON GROUND**

PO BOX 2016
CAVE JUNCTION, OR 97523

BULK RATE
U.S. POSTAGE
PAID
CAVE JUNCTION
OREGON 97523
PERMIT #16

Water and the Spirit

Common ground

Issue #9   Feb.- March '95

BADGES BEYOND BOUNDS?

While Josephine County has christened the New Year as Murder Capitol of the west coast and crime has taken yet a higher profile, some recent cases are beginning to draw attention towards possible criminal activity within the Sheriffs' Department itself.

One case, involving Darvin Paape has drawn the attention of a Josephine County Grand Jury. Grand Jury assistant foreman Frank Gladson is a former law enforcement official. He spent several years as an investigator in the District Attorneys's office and on a sheriff's patrol in Kansas. Gladson states that he saw " enough irregularities in the case to ask Paape to testify."

According to Paape, he was initially cited for possessing a small amount of marijuana which is not a crime in Oregon. However, Paape alleges when he refused to provide police with information concerning his source of the pot, the cops hit him with three felonies including manufacturing and delivery.

Aware that police personnel were taping the arrest, Paape requested the tapes for his defense. According to Paape, " I had my lawyer request the tapes, but my attorney returned to inform me that the DA had acknowledged the tapes were destroyed."

It was the destroyed tapes that caught the attention of Grand Juryman Frank Gladson. " Our jury saw 45 cases and in every one of them the DA presented tapes to secure an indictment, but then I kept hearing about cases reaching trials and the tapes were never presented by the prosecution."

After hearing Paape's case, the Grand Jury instructed the DA to further investigate the improprieties of the case. The DA has responded that it can not legally investigate itself. With no apparent watchdog to keep local police in line, Paape and many others are convinced that the Sheriff's department operates above the law.

In the hope that others who have been victimized by the cops will speak up along side him, Paape knows that bringing attention to what's going on is the only way we'll ever correct such blatant injustice.   *-Kermit*

AND IN THE SCHOOLS...

Despite forging new policy on police interrogation with the local school district, the Illinois Valley Human Rights Alliance is disappointed to learn that interrogation of students for non-school related incidents may still be taking place. According to an Alliance spokesperson " this forces us into a position where we may have to take legal action. It's unfortunate that the basic legal rights of these children and their parents has to be so diligently defended".

Representatives of the Alliance met with a school district official last May to address the problem. Alliance representatives " expressed to him the concerns of many parents in the Valley who feel that the school should be a sanctuary for the kids, safe not only from criminal activity, but also from harassment by law enforcement officials who seem to find it more convenient interrogating children at school, where their lack of legal knowledge leaves them somewhat vulnerable, and frightened".

The Alliance asked for two things: that law enforcement be excluded from interrogating students on non-school related issues and, secondly, that in school related cases where the police are brought in to interrogate, parents would be notified in advance and a trained advocate for the child shall be present.

Last June the school District responded with a new policy stating " we (the district) will be counseling our administrators (principals) to question the deputy in detail and IF THE INCIDENT IS NOT RELATED TO SCHOOL THEN WE WILL REQUEST THAT THE INTERROGATION TAKE PLACE ELSEWHERE."

The Alliance " responded in praise of the new policy and has attempted to continue a dialogue to ensure that on school related matters, the kids will have either a parent or some advocate at their side. But since last June, the district has been unresponsive."

Alliance representatives have repeatedly expressed to District officials " their support for law enforcement to enter the schools to ensure that the youth of this valley are provided a safe environment that is conducive to learning. But using the schools to fish for information against their own parents has terrified these kids. We think creating such fear is counterproductive to a learning environment".   *-HRA*

ALL THAT IS NECESSARY FOR THE TRIUMPH OF EVIL IS FOR GOOD PEOPLE TO DO NOTHING. -Edmund Burke

BEARS AND COUGARS STILL UNDER FIRE- WILL MEASURE 18 SURVIVE?

Several powerful legislators in Salem are attempting to repeal Measure 18, passed last November by Oregon voters. Volunteers gathered over 90,000 signatures to qualify this initiative for the ballot. Despite the well financed opposition, Measure 18 passed by a margin of 44,000 votes! Now, however, Representative Bill Markham (R, Riddle) is insulting Oregon voters by introducing legislation to reinstate hound hunting of bears and cougars, and bear baiting.

Contact your sentator and representative immediately.

For Josephine County contact Senator Brady Adams, Rep. Bob Repine State Capitol, Salem OR 97310 (503)986-1180 or leave a message on their voice mail (800)332-2313.

Also, urge the governor to veto any legislation to modify Measure 18. Gov. John Kitzhaber, State Capitol, Salem OR 97310 ,(503)378-3111. For more information contact Debbie Lukas 592-3386 .

ADOPT-A-SPECIES

Wanted: Oregon environmental and civic organizations, businesses, campus groups, religious organizations, school classes, health professionals and others to adopt one of the 925 federally listed endangered species. "Foster parents" will receive a certificate of adoption, fact sheets about their species and the Endangered Species Act (ESA), and an action checklist to help reauthorize the ESA and protect endangered species.

Part of the campaign is a WALK FOR THE WILD endangered species parade through the streets of Portland on March 11, 1995. Every endangered and threatened species will be represented in the parade which will culminate in a candlelight vigil for extinct species and a press conference calling for a strengthened ESA.

To adopt a species or volunteer on this campaign, contact Monica Bond at the National Wildlife Federation, 921 SW Morrison, Suite 512, Portland, Oregon 97205. (503) 222-1429. For more information, call Debbie Lukas, 592-3386.

BE A PART OF THE PACK

Wolf lovers have been delighted by the recent triumphs of a lengthy campaign to re-introduce the grey wolf to Yellowstone Park and Cenral Idaho.

The US Fish and Wildlife Service is picking up the tab for most of the initial expenses, but the long term success of the project may depend on selective radio-collaring and monitoring of the packs. These costs are being shouldered by the Wolf Education and Research Center in Boise, Id. and the Wolf Recovery Action Fund . They need our help.

If you, your school, or organization would like to help by sponsoring a wild wolf, please contact Jill Birmingham at 592-4695.

WATERSHED COUNCIL- THE MONEY FLOWS BUT DAMN THE RIVER

At the December meeting of the Strategic Watershed Management Group (SWMG) the Josephine County Commissioners proposed that their version of the Illinois Valley Watershed Council be formally recognized. Having been denied official status since August, because we claimed it was a non-representative council, they enlisted the Rogue Valley Council of Governments (RVCOG) in their drive to control the purse strings of local watershed restoration

RVCOG essentially testified that the commissioners had been making progress. How they could know this without bothering to call the people who felt excluded and unrepresented ,I'll never know. We have traveled t o Salem to testify several times; they know who we are. The Watershed Health Team testified that they knew we were right but that they needed to trust the commissioners. They said that we should feel comforted because the irrigators, who helped create the problems and who screamed two years ago that the only problem with the Illinois River was the damned environmentalists, are now in charge of restoration dollars.

Now the Watershed Council will have to produce a Watershed Assessment and a Watershed Action Plan which will assess the problems and set a course of restoration. No, the Watershed Council won't do these tasks. They will have Corky Lockard, the Soil and Watershed Conservation District's paid staff do it. So much for getting the local citizens involved.

Feel free to call Mr. Lockard at 592-2731 to give him your recommendations about what needs to be done to help the river. Specific recommendations regarding road closures, changing irrigation practices, screening diversion ditches and pumps, in-stream water rights and conservation easements would be helpful. If you'd like to discuss any of this, call us at the Siskiyou Project: 592-4459.

Kamots
"to go free"

Matsi
"Sweet and Brave"

2

LITERACY AT RISK - UNFUNDED LIBRARIES MEAN UNOPENED MINDS

There will be a measure on the March 28 mail-in ballot which will fund the library system at $1.1 million for each of the next 3 years. It would restore services to 1993-'94 levels and provide some additional money for books and programs. The library as a whole would be open more hours. The IV branch would go from the 12 hours it is currently open to at least 27 hours per week. Children's story time and class visits would be resumed. Telephone reference service would be restored. Library customers would be able to request books from libraries outside the county system and outside the state of Oregon. Books and new reference materials would be purchased.

In 1992 the county charter was amended to mandate support and maintenance of library services but it did not include funding levels. The library depends on local tax dollars and on federal O & C Timber revenues, which have steadily declined in the last five years. Total property tax receipts for ALL county services in 1994 were about $800,000.

In July, 1994, the Library's budget was cut. The book budget was reduced by 50%, the staff by 38%, and hours were drastically slashed. The Josephine County system is now considered below standards for a library system that serves a county of our population. The cost of the Library levy to taxpayers with property valued at $100,000 would be $33 per year in 1995, $31 in 1996 and $29 in 1997. That's less than ten cents per day!

I do not favor more taxes but I urge you to support this levy. We need a viable, healthy Library in this community. We need services whereby we may access information from beyond this county's boundaries. We need stories for our children and ourselves. We need to be able to use the Library for more than just a few hours a week. We do without many things here but a Library should not be one of them. — *Deborah Colette Murphy*

ASSUME THE POSITION:

Legislative Outlook: Eye on the Newt

Republicans, in a transparent attempt to fool most of the people most of the time, created their "Contract on America". Not to be confused with a Mafia style contract, it nevertheless would render many people virtually alive (or I suppose virtually dead).

Public opinion polls show that most Americans are fed up with big government. They overwhelmingly want cleaner air, safer drinking water and want more participatory community planning- and they are willing to pay for it.

The Newt would have you believe that he can do it all for you. He will get government off the corporations' back and into your bedroom and your wallet. And forget about wild places, public lands, clean air or water. He will do his best to eliminate welfare for the poor and elderly and increase the subsidies for mill owners, ranchers, miners, corporate farmers and the like.

So what, may you ask, can I do? We need to participate in the process. We need to organize progressive coalitions and alliances and work together to oppose their shortsighted vision and offer our long term vision. We might need to become school board members, go to city council and county commissioner meetings. We might need to call our representatives often and tell them our views. We need to influence or change the government or we'll certainly be disappointed in the way we're governed. When Jesse Jackson said "We must keep hope alive" he intended us to work at it, not wait for someone else to do it. Now is the time.

-*Barry Snitkin*

Toxic Trucking

Forty years after touting nuclear energy as "too cheap to meter," the feds are closer to finding a more permanent home for radioactive nuclear waste. Their proposed site is the Yucca Mountain nuclear waste repository near Las Vegas, Nevada. The nuclear waste would be transported from reactors all over the country.

For example, the nuclear waste from Eureka is projected to come up 101 and along 199 to I-5. No waste could or would likely be transported until the end of the decade. Therefore we still have time to kill this plan.

Remember last year's paint spill into the Smith River? Can you imagine *nuclear waste* trucks travelling through the Smith River canyon? Think of the consequences that a spill would have on the valley and on the river system.

Supposedly, all shipments involving nuclear waste are accompanied by an emergency team and supposedly they have a better safety record than other toxic waste shipments but it hardly makes me feel better. Especially considering that it took half a day just to begin the cleanup of solvents spilled on I-5 a year ago.

It is time to call Mark Hatfield's office and tell him how you feel about having nuclear waste travelling through the Smith River canyon and the Illinois Valley. Call him at (202) 224-3753. Or write at U.S. Senate, Suite SH-711. Washington D.C. 20510.   -*Barry Snitkin*

OUR READERS RESPOND:

Dear Friends,

The staff and the Board of Directors of the Dome School would like the community to know that if there is a problem with a school sponsored event that you please first come and deal with us to resolve it.

We want people to know that we are available and are willing to work things out, if we can. We would appreciate your cooperation and the opportunity to communicate with anyone who participates in our events and programs. Thank you.   - *The Dome School Board of Directors.*

To Everyone Concerned,

I, too, attended the parenting class mentioned in last month's newsletter. Indeed, there were some distractions, but I had no idea where these people were from nor what their input might be; it didn't matter. I came not to judge but to share information which could help me to become a better parent.

I fail to see what being from Takilma or not being from Takilma had to do with anything. "Accepting blowing wind" whether from children, politicians, or anyone else is a part of the learning process: tolerance. Sometimes ignoring a disruption is the quickest way to end it. Besides we were all attending as equals, not as teacher/police or Takilmaites/trouble-makers or Townies/our way or no way but people wanting to learn about the most dynamic segment of our population- our children.

Remember, children learn from example. How can one label "outside worlds"? To my knowledge we all live in one world. It is up to all of us together to pass this one on to our children with as little hate and negativism as is possible. Sincerely,   - *Barbara Mabry*

Thanks to you, Takilma tribe, our way was made easy. You were the shock troops, the ones to take the heat, the ones that stood up to the sheriff when he came for your plants. You are an inspiration to us. From the Dome School to the clinic, we see the possibilities of hippies working together; we honor your achievements. You are the Alpha, we are the Omega, together we can do anything. Let our children marry, let our blood flow together, let us beat the same drum.

We invite you all to journey to the Rainbow Gathering in New Mexico to form one-camp of southern Oregonites. June 5 to July 15. Maya, Myray, and I plan to arrive June 25, Please come camp, play and pray with us.

The tree as an art medium...We are pleased to announce that we are developing a different kind of topiary. Inspired by the work of Axel Erlandson, who died in 1964, we bend and graft tree whips into various forms like chairs, tables, spirals, and peace signs.

I am also researching a book on the subject. I am looking for applicable information, especially trying to find others who are doing similar things with trees. Any Internet surfers out there? Call if you can help. Snow and Maya, 846-7188. *-From Snow of the Williams Tribe*

Dear Common Ground,

I was offered a job working for an electronics repair service in Cave Junction. During my employment, I discovered my boss was dealing crystal meth to children through his business. He told me he has an inside connection with our police department. Twice during my employment J.O.I.N.T. task force showed up to search the premises for drugs. Both times they came up empty handed. Why is it that every other day and every other hour of the day there was mass drugs? But by the time the cops showed up to search the place, it's clean!

I asked my boss to take his drug business somewhere else several times. But he said the business was a perfect cover for all the traffic, so I wound up quitting.

I spoke to half a dozen members of the community and asked them: " if you knew someone who was dealing meth to 13 year old kids, would you report it to the cops?" They all said " YES ."

So I anonymously did so and 2 days later I was confronted by the dealer. The only people who might have known I had told were the cops. So how did the dealer find out? Was it the inside connection he had mentioned?

An inside connection would indicate that the cops are assisting the drug trafficking in our valley. What would the cops be gaining from this? Perhaps a cut of the action? Perhaps the cops are trying to keep themselves in business.

Two to three days later I called the DEA and the Oregon State Police and told them about the leak in our Police Dept. They stated they were going to dry up the leak. Two days later I was busted! They brought charges of possession, manufacture and delivery of a controlled substance. The latter two I have never been involved with. They had no physical evidence to support their case. I was not breaking the law, I was exercising my Constitutional rights! Mushrooms are used in religious ceremonies of the Druidic religion that I practice.

The Constitution guarantees freedom of religion, but it seems that if it isn't Christian, it's not legal! What ever happened to the great American melting pot? We can melt races together but not religions? What about our rights to life, liberty, and the pursuit of happiness?

And I still can't figure out why I'm the one that gets busted. I wasn't the one dealing crank to kids. I don't have a problem with consenting adults using meth, but selling to children or seeing children deprived of the necessities because of the parent's addiction is unacceptable to me! I hear people here in Takilma bitch about the meth scene, but nobody does anything about it. Maybe now, others will begin...

- *Tom Yattaw*

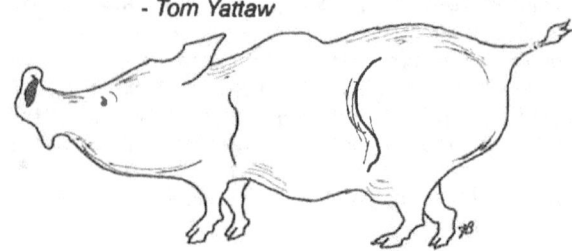

4

Dear Common Ground,

Okay, about the lead article in last issue on today's youth. The Yeats quote, used way out of context, threw me for a while. What's so bad about "passionate intensity?" What's so great about playing the mainstream game without "conviction"? Is it really peer alienation that "robs the achievers" of their conviction? Or is it the pervasive hypocrisy and evil that riddles the fabric of our culture? And aside from the 5-10% of kids who must "raise themselves" and wind up in serious trouble, and the 5-10% who climb the ladder of material success, what are the remaining 80-90% of our kids doing? It often surprises me that there isn't more rebellion, given the irrelevance of our archaic public education system, the despair and confusion felt by most adults, and the uncertainty of a viable future which our kids face. I can only honor their cynicism and passion as they set sail on such perilous seas. I did appreciate the suggestions given at the conclusion of the article, but I'd emphasize listening to the soul questions of our kids over telling them what they should do. We can only look a little foolish standing here on shore handing out instructions on how to do it as they embark on their uncharted course.

It was sad to learn that no use has been found for the Ho Chi Minh room; good to hear that the community building continues to expand and that our little newsletter is growing stronger and more vital with every issue. Keep warm Takilmaites, see you soon -*Kayla*

A THOUSAND CRANES

Another renaissance is about to flower at Hammer's Model Market, scene of many energy exchanges in the past lives of our community.

A year ago, it was difficult to accept that Carl Hammer wanted a change of life. We trembled and quaked at the thought that our general store might go the way of all flesh and turn into....what?

A Seven-Eleven? An empty lot? Now that Chas (or *Jazz,* as he prefers to be called) and his partners (thanks and praises, y'all) have successfully steered the business through the whitewater, it seems we are about to get an even more delicious treat in the shape of Robin Wren's "A Thousand Cranes".

This deli-style eatery will be opening in Hammer's on February 6th for light breakfasts and sophisticated lunches. Simplest pizza for the hungriest adolescents and epicurean take-home dining for the working stiffs amongst us.

Just as appealing as the cosmopolitan menu - featuring lots of ingredients ending in vowel sounds - is the notion that Hammers will once again be hopping with faces. Look for major-domo Robin making magic behind the deli case and that lunch time hostess with the mostest, Ms. Geraldine Davidson. Other crew members with wide-ranging culinary histories are Holly Shinerock, Patty Dalegowski, Sandy Kaminsky, Mike Z. and Margarita Schladkohl. Tracy Taylor will be baking specialty breads to die for. Raya Light and Sean Welcome will be there after school and who knows which other personalities will find meaningful employment in this brightly soulful environment. Marilyn and Kenny Houck will, bless them, be running a mini espresso operation during the morning java hours.

Good-bye nostalgia - bring on the new - Go Robin!

Community Question:

What do all of the following Friends, Mothers, Fathers, Children, and Neighbors have in common?

Beth H.-Beth P.-Kate-Hollis-Shannon-Paco-Meadow Diane F.-Zu-Zu-Connie-Kerry H.-Mirya-Raya-Jolna-Ina

Greetings from Paradise

An island of transformation, where molten red lava forms brittle black land, highways become rippling walls of black rock overnight and Pele's steaming breath rises from the ever changing encounter of land and sea.

All the while, bursting papaya drop at my doorstep, macadamias and breadfruit beckon, passion fruits ripen sour-sweet, and for dessert the custard-like spoon-meat of early coconut and succulent strawberry guava. These are generously shared with shy mongoose, a brilliant array of winged-ones and creepy crawlies (NO SNAKES HERE THOUGH). We fall asleep to the sounds of chirping geckoes and the waves; waves that are rocking the sea turtles and cradling the dolphins to rest from their day's spinning play.

From this balmy vantage point I reflect on life in Takilma, the "Common Ground" on the lava rock that is my ground now on the Big Island of Hawaii.

I've learned, first of all, that We ARE Everywhere! Dancing to Zap Mama and B 52's in the kitchen between sets of dishes, mind expanding, soul unfolding and ego tripping through jungle/forest/'burbs - it's all the same trip. With long hair or shaved head, we fly our freak flags still; diving deep, flying high, keeping on.

Restoring the Balance, *-Kayla*

Sacred Grandmother

My roots reach deep into the core
    of this earthy body.
I am a treetop dancing in the wind
    of my own sigh.
My blood is flowing in the rivers.
The dewdrops are my sweat.
The ocean is the tears I have shed
    and caught in my cupped hands.
In prayer, I raise them up
    to merge with the cloud of my mind.
And tears fall like rain
    washing me clean of thought.
I am able to just Be,
    Be all of everything to everyone.
May all Beings hear the beat of my heart
    and know that I still am
    and always will be
    Sacred Grandmother.
        -Ina Kipanna

The Land

Look on this land
and see the mud
and the dirt and the sand and the clay.
Did you ever behold
such things to hold trees?
Did you, to this very day?

Sleep on the land
and drink night potion.
Drink the moon and the clouds and the ocean.
Have you lain on the ground
without ceilings or walls
and smiled and watched the stars fall?

Travel the lands
and go just for wondering
and pass passes and rivers and woods.
No reason to stop
for snows when they drop.
Push on, with mittens and hood.

Look quietly, still,
and spy a shy critter,
That slithers or soars or lopes.
Have you squawked at a dodo,
or wrestled a bear,
or joked with spry jackalopes?

Find a spot
Where no one has stood,
just critters, trees, dirt, sky, and you.
And there things are quiet.
Your spirit can sigh,
no should haves and really must dos.

Savor the land.
It's a land like no other.
Winds sweet, plains wide, and sky blue.
So guard the land
With strong and wise hands.
Keep it happy, and it shall for you.
        -Ben Fisher

ASTRIDE THE KALEIDOSCOPE

Poor words try vainly to explain
Kaleidoscoping conferences of earth and soul and brain.

Wild ponies in a pen;
Water flowing through a photo;
Vast heavens cast in mathematical formulae.

Limited at best, omitting all the rest.
Perhaps (if one is blessed) the truth is somehow guessed.

And I, for lack of courage, lie stagnant as these words.

But hush. Be still.

Without rhyme or reason unlock the gates;
Ride roiling rapids;
Dance naked under moonless summer skies.

Wild horses may run away forever,
Wild rivers rave to parts unknown.
But sooner or later, sleepy star-filled skies ignite.

A fleeting flash.
A falling, dying, celestial body.

Do not be alarmed, nothing will be harmed.
Believe your life is charmed.

This is no time for wishes. Just do it.
                                                    -Jake

        SILENCE, precious SILENCE i know where you dwell;
it's how to navigate myself to you often enough to quench
my thirst for you-Oh SILENCE- you are one of my cherished
elixirs. I give thanks for you SILENCE and to those moments
when Myray is off on "her own", quietly in dreamland; and "I"
Maya Many Moons Reames wade slowly into your peaceful
waters, passing through the ripples of my daily life's dance-
and with a relaxed body and mind I embrace my entire feminine self into you- oh sweet sister SILENCE.

WET DREAMS

This week the earth's a swollen water bag,
The sky an upturned bowl
Dumping the gravy-colored flood,
Indiscriminate and prodigal.
By day we breathe water,
Our senses grown amphibious enough
To navigate the squelching air.
Reciting at night the ceremonious names
Of new astonishing quantities of rains.

Monday, sploshing to the boiling river,
Here come our neighbors,
Pink and excited as the new-washed worms,
Flushed out from underground.
Stout trees bounce gaily by upon the surfing broth,
Scummy with forest droppings, flailing branches.
Underneath the hollow bridge, boulders grind and detonate;
Earth's teeth, wrenched from deep sockets, dark as Hades.

Wednesday, in a dripping pause between deluges,
Two people disappear into the night-blind trees.
Wet branches slap and stroke their cheeks.
The ground's a labyrinth of rivulets, not there before.
Once-quiet brooks have found their epic voice
And roar new stories, dark, wild and arcane.
Sudden as tears the rain begins again.
Crystal percussion, hammering at thin scalps
With gorgeous excess.
They drip new silver, rich as old Venetians.
Later, in the steaming torrents of the shower,
The cell walls of their bodies saturate, dissolve and tear.
Lips melt through flesh
Wet as a crushed persimmon.
The dissolute tissues slide apart
And tongue caresses bone.

By Saturday the elements have quit their dizzy reel.
Beaten sunlight clatters on the lake
Like a bright tin shield,
And furry hills crouch round, replete,
Streams trickling from their sodden flanks.
Thunder returns below the earth
And stars resume their wheeling.   -
                                    -Felicity Elworthy

7

More Ballot Measures by Red Kneck

(Editor's note: The Common Ground has been criticized as being too exclusive: first name by-lines, inside jokes, etc. To cover a wider spectrum of opinon, we have asked "Red" to represent the rest of the valley, and are considering a regular column called "Red Knows.")

We'll be exercising our right to vote this spring, and in this county we're especially privileged. As usual, the government's going to have to beg us if they want to buy so much as a paperclip. It sure was smart to make that bunch subject to the collective wisdom of the electorate— who elected those yo-yos anyway? But this election we also get the chance to compel all householders in the county to own guns, unless they don't want to.

I can almost hear you bleeding heart liberals whining about violence and your precious "right to choose." Wring your hands all you want; we're putting guns in them. Think how safe we'll feel after everybody in the county is armed and dangerous! Tired of those teenagers crossing your field? Want to put a little scare into those weirdo neighbors? Fed up with meter readers and Jehovah's Witnesses?

Put together by our local constitutional experts, this ballot measure's got those ACLU pinkos buffaloed because it lets off those who don't have the money or those with some kind of religious excuse. Case closed. And anyway, who wants those kinds of people to have guns? It's mostly the poor we want protection from, and the philosophical types might hesitate to shoot, which is a waste of good firepower.

Common Ground readers don't generally write ballot measures (b.m.'s for short), which seems kind of un-American, so I asked around for ideas and got the following:

1. would prohibit any public employee or pointy-head lawyer from saying or doing anything that would interfere with any body's right to misquote the Constitution, enforce heterosexuality, or pave their land (I like this one!)

2. would legalize cannibalism for home consumption (not sure I got this one right—this person rambled on and on about rope.)

3. would prohibit people from identifying themselves as members of the "People" unless they are "Taxpayers" who "belong to a church or some other right wing organization, and who fly the flag." "Taxpayers" would be defined as "those who pay taxes AND as a result feel enormously sorry for themselves."

4. would prohibit native-born Oregonians from interbreeding.

5. would establish a complicated system of Common Sense Credits and Demerits and would require those with low scores to fund public broadcasting.

6. would require every household to have an unabridged dictionary unless all occupants are illiterate or watch more than seventy hours of TV a week. Research indicates that about nine percent of county households would have to get those dictionaries.

The guy who was pushing this b.m. supplied arguments, which I wrote down as fast as I could: "dictionaries would promote better understanding, reduce ugly domestic altercations like Scrabble fights, create jobs at bookstores, and most importantly aid English teachers in their struggle against the rising tide of language abuse. The Valley is threatened by nonstandard verbs, the apostrophe epidemic, and just plain crumy spelling."

Well, those are the submissions thus far. Please send your ideas to me, no matter how stupid they are. I want to see your b.m.'s. (Editor's note: make sure to clearly mark your proposal if you're being ironic, as it's otherwise impossible to tell.)

A Foolshirt Story

For all you Fool watchers out there who are wondering, "What's the story behind foolshirts?" Here it is...

Whilst visiting the Bread and Puppet's Domestic Resurrection Circus in Vermont last summer, Newm and Rebecca Fool learned not only some new ways to make puppets and some new things to do with them, but also a nifty way to make posters, banners, and T-shirts, using hand-craved masonite(cheap!). Unfortunately they didn't discover the most important rule of this technique until after a grueling 4 hours of carving....C.B.S.!

Carve it Backwards, Stupid!

Thus was born the now famous "Backwards Fool" Logo

For a while they tried to hawk the logo on T-shirts, telling folks that when they looked in the mirror to check their image, the logo would read true. Thus this was a design created especially for their "image"... Nobody bought the story, but they did buy some shirts.

Mike, Jill and Newm Fool have formed the core group of printers. The Fools have since produced many banners to decorate their performance spaces and homes, and many T-shirts. Proceeds from the sale of these fine block prints swell the coffers of the Illuminated Fools puppet troupe of Takilma.

Oh, and if you happen to be around Takilma, and someone says it's print day, and you like a party, you should go!

8   *-Newman*

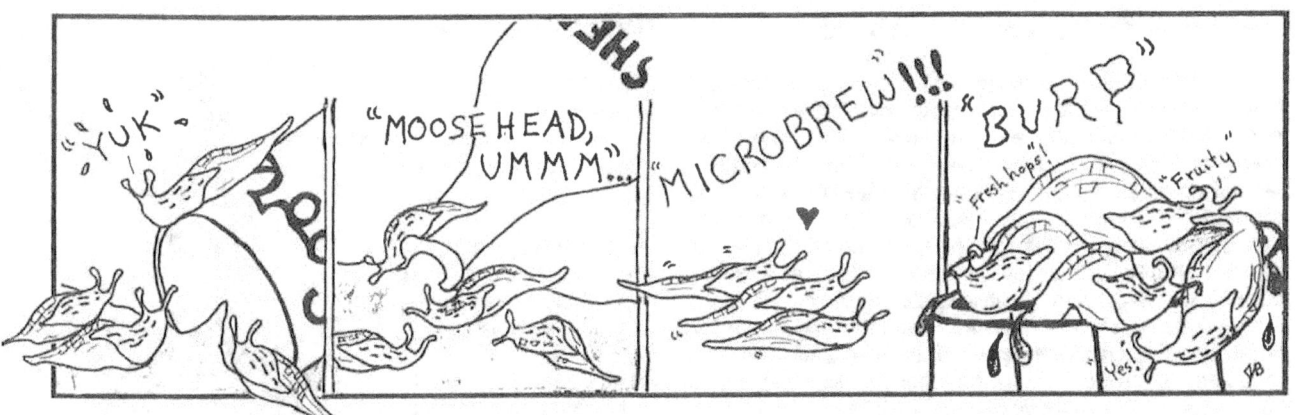

The Brew Review

This is the culmination of frivolous fantasy, devotional surrender to duty, the results of recent travels in this beautiful region. The Brew Review, a critique of the region's microbreweries, a guide for when you find yourselves out of the Pizza Deli comfort zone and looking for a tasty microbrew.

The tour starts in California, the coastal run. In festive Arcata rests the Humboldt Brewery. It has a nice open atmosphere, many tables and a large light dining room, a bar complete with ten stools, a backroom for sporting events, and three fine beer selections. The Oatmeal Stout is heavy, bitter, hinting at coffee with molasses. I found it to drink smoother over the course of the glass. The Goldrush Ale was an average if not sour ale. The selection here though is the Red Nectar Ale. It is fruity, light, and sweet. It won the silver medal at the 1993 Great American Beer Festival. Worth the trip! All of their beers have high alcohol content, Red Nectar is 5.5 %. Pitchers are $6.50, glasses $2. The food is mid-range, $5-10, seafood being the specialty. There is live music Friday and Saturday and always bottles to go.

Keep heading south to Eureka. On is a tall room, bar stools, upstairs, pool beer selections, a pale ale, amber ale, I found all the beers to be slightly wa- enough for refills. Pints are $2 and preferred the stout and the wheat (with Brown for its mild flavor. The bar has good happy hour prices.

Highway 101 stands the Lost Coast Brewery. It tables, reasonably priced food. There are five harvest wheat, downtown brown, and stout. tery, lacking true full body, but decent pitchers are $6.75. Pick your preference, I lemon); my party chose the Downtown a festive atmosphere that evolves from

South again, North Coast way. They are closed until 4 PM so I to be a dinner restaurant, prices are class than previous breweries. They do steep.

Brewery in Fort Bragg, again on the high- have yet to sample. This appears primarily high range and the interior seemed higher sell bottles of their brew but prices are

Then cut east to Hopland for the gem: the atmosphere was pleasantly al- dark, moody, sensual, and friendly. There is

Mendocino Brewing Company. This was my ternative, live acoustic and electric music, a bar, outdoor deck with picnic tables, and booths

inside. They have five fine beer selections, Red Tail Ale, Blonde Ale, wheat, stout, and light ale. The Red Tail Ale is my selection for beer of the region, smooth, full-bodied, fruity, and comfortingly strong. But the real uniqueness of Mendocino brews is their blends, the black and purple, strawberry blonde, and others. Prices are the same as Lost Coast with the pleasant addition of cheap 4 oz. tasters that quickly transform into your own personal mixing center. Try a few rounds of the tasters, all flavors, find your favorite individual or blend, and order away.

Adios, California. Adios, sales tax, back to Oregon.

Grants Pass, 5th Street, the Blue Pine Brew Pub. Alternative tie-dyes, musical atmosphere complete with two homebrews, Rip Roarin' Red and Big Barley Brown. Both are smooth and tasty, not great but worth the venture. Pints are $2 and glasses $1.50. There are no pitchers. The small room is full of nice long picnic like tables, perfect for larger gatherings. Food is cheap, there is great cheap fresh juice for designated drivers and do not miss the homemade Ale Toast!

Eugene's 19th Street Cafe boasts the finest selection of Oregon microbreweries on tap in addition to their numerous beers brewed on location. They offer many ale selections, wheat, and porter and specialty beers. For stout fans, their Terminator Stout is a prize. It would take a few nights to become familiar with all of their brews, an interesting challenge. A good place to sample other Oregon beers to direct future adventures.

Good tasting! More reviews? Send them in or tell me your tales over a smooth ESB or sweet tangy Snug Harbor or thick stout at my favorite brewery, the Pizza Deli in downtown Cave Junction   .- *Jon Jeans*

The Weird Butterfly by Chiara Casas, age 9.

Once there was an egg laying on a leaf. A few days later it hatched. And out came a caterpillar. It was a small one. One day a bird passed by and said "Hello". The caterpillar was frightened he hid behind a leaf. Then the caterpillar started eating he got big. Then he made a cocoon and climbed in. In a few days he climbed out. There wasn't much of a change except he had wings. At first he couldn't fly but he tried and tried. One day he jumped off a leaf and flew through the forest after a while it started to rain he didn't know where to go. After that he started thinking of the fun times when he was a caterpillar. Then he got an idea. The idea was that he would make a cocoon and turn back into a caterpillar so he could have fun again. So he did. He made a cocoon, climbed inside and stayed there. A couple days later he was ready to come out. At first he felt a little weird but he got used to it. The day after that a bird passed by and said "Hello". The caterpillar said "Hello". He did not hide under a leaf.

And from that day on the caterpillar or butterfly changed back and forth being a butterfly and caterpillar. His friends got very confused. The End.

Dome School Haiku

TREES
Towering giants
Laced with bark and dressed in green
Reaching toward the sky
-Sol

Birds flly in the sky
Turtles walk slowly on ground
Sun shines on the waves
-Kristine

Rain is very wet
It is raining and flooding
It is still raining
-Jacob

We study Japan
I like tofu and sushi
I like Japan now
-Geno

Here we go again, girlfriends and boyfriends. NOW we're having some fun! Takilma Common Ground is all those things we told you it was in the preceeding issues--broadening, connecting, informative, opinionated and funny. We aim to honor the Earth, make a joyful noise, prod ourselves and give pleasure.

Please keep sending us your goodies. Our computer is a Mac. 3" disks, accompanied by paper copies, please. First drafts are met with some grumbling. Please revise your gems into coherent legibility.

PLEASE SEND ALL MATERIAL TO COMMON GROUND, P.O. BOX 2016, CAVE JUNCTION, OR 97523. Deadline for Issue #10 is March 7th for publication March 21st.

SPECIAL GRATITUDE is due, retroactively and in triple measure, to Cathy Hocker who performs, impeccably, all the duties of Treasurer, while Dave still carries the nominal title, comes to meetings, looks sage, and signs checks. This division of labor is acceptable to them (they just celebrated anniversary #10. Breathless hush. Major congratulations, Hockers) and we give thanks.

Mirya Holman also gets flowery accolades for allowing this wordy mob to invade her bedroom, coming between her and her CD ROM with relentless regularity. Thanks Mirya.

Editorial staff for this issue is Kerry Holman, Dave Toler, Claire Sierra, Deb Murphy, Jon Jeans, Jack Dwyer, Dave Hocker, Jill Birmingham, Ina Kipanna, Mirya Holman, and Felicity Elworthy. Kate Dwyer was our facilitator.

ANNOUNCEMENTS:

A SWEETHEART OF A SALE: The Illinois Valley Friends of the Library are holding their 20th Annual Book Fair on Saturday, February 11 from 10 am.- 4 pm. at the IV County Building in Cave Junction. Choose from thousands of books. There will also be a silent auction for select items. To donate books, records or puzzles stop by the Library or call for pickup at 592-3581.

A WOMEN'S FIREWALK: is scheduled for Saturday, March 18 as a way to celebrate Women's History Month. It will begin at 4 pm. A potluck will follow. The cost is based on a sliding scale $10-25. Trades are possible on a pre-arranged basis. Call Hollis at 592-2476 or Beth at 592-6970. No child care arrangements have been made as yet. It would be great if someone would like to organize that.

OREGON ENVIRONMENTAL LAW CONFERENCE: will take place at the U of O in Eugene from Thursday, March 2 - Sunday, March 5. For info call the Siskiyou Project at 592-4459.

I LOVE MY LIBRARY POSTER CONTEST: will be held for children of all ages during the month of February. Check out the IV Library for details.

SOME MONTHLY COMMITTEE MEETING DATES FOR OUR AREA:
The 2010 Community Response Team: 2nd Thursday of the month, 6:30 pm. at the IVHS Cafetorium.
The Water Conservation District: 2nd Wednesday if the month, 7:00 pm. at the IV County Building.
The Consensus Coordinating Committee Meeting: 1st Tuesday of the month, 6:30 pm. at the IVHS Cafetorium.
The Real Library Committee will meet weekly on Thursdays at 7:00 at the Main Branch of the Library in Grants Pass in the Ben Bones Meeting Room, located in the back of the Library. Weekly meetings to work on the Library Levy campaign will take place from now until Election day. If you would like to send a donation: The Real Library Committee 900 Lathrop Rd., G.P., OR 97526.

VOLUNTEERS NEEDED: Are you in need of adventure? Tired of your routine? Stuck in the slow lane? Here's an opportunity to fulfill yourself and serve this wondrous bioregion by spending a few hours a week helping Siskiyou Project keep up with an information overload. We need persons to read elevating environmental periodicals, absorbing newspaper articles and fascinating faxes...and then file them! Your skills can be put to good use, so call us or stop by Ye Olde Clinic Building, downtown Takilma. 592-4459.

ENVIRONMENTAL ACTION DAY is on the 14th of February at the State Capitol in Salem, 10am - 4pm. Workshop lobbying. Environmental lobbying, Contact Barry 592-4459

WHERE'S MY PHOTO? It's an idea in the mind of God, folks. We've got your cash; we're off to Hawaii....
Seriously, it took several months to coordinate production of the first, smaller batch of Takilma photos. It may take a few more to get' round to the big ones. Jim Shames is a busy guy and he doesn't have free access to darkroom facilities. Anyone who lives in Takilma East and wants to help out should talk to him.
Meanwhile we still have plenty of smaller (8-1/2x11) photos for $10 each. Available through Common Ground, POB 2016, Cave Junction, Or. 97523.

WOMEN'S CAFE: To celebrate Women's History Month the Dome School will present a "Women's Cafe" on Saturday, March 11 from 5-11 pm. Artwork and food will be available form 5-7 pm. . Homemade soups, salads and sweets will be for sale, as well as, non-alcoholic beverages. Beginning at 7 there will be a variety of performance by talented local women The event is open to all, but young children are discouraged. Admission is based on a sliding scale form $3-5. If you would like to participate, donate time, food or talents please contact the Dome School at 592-3911. There will be an organizational meeting on Tuesday, February 28 at the TCB at 7 pm.

ANSWER: They are ALL part of the newly forming Takilma Drum and Dance Troupe and you too can be a part. It's a lot of fun. Left/Right brain challenge, and community. What more could a person want? Opposite Mondays from the Food Buying Club, 6:00-8:00. Very reasonable sliding scale. Committment requested but we realize life goes on. Please come be a part of this on-going vision.

Classifieds

MIGUELO will show up with bells, claves, drums and rhythms. All you need is a place, 2-3 hours, and 5-8 friends. Very sliding scale. 592-2549

VALENTINE'S TREATS made to order: Cream puffs, eclairs, raspberry shortbread cookies, chocolate cakes, whatever you fancy! Strictest secrecy observed for maximum surprise. Kate 592-2214.

WANTED: 2 Nice-looking area rugs or carpets. Will trade massages. Call Ina 592-2308.

SILVER FABRICATION: Enameling, cloisonné and plic-a-jur. KIDS' CLASS Saturday 10-1. Sliding scale $2.50-$5/hr. plus metal cost. Marjorie 592-6733.

1979 VOLVO 242 auto. New steering rack, new battery, electrical system. Good tires. Reliable. Needs transmission. $500 OBO. Marjorie 592-6733.

HOUSING FOR RENT in Kerby. Unique secluded setting. Call Dave for details, 592-2492.

RESPONSIBLE woman looking for peaceful abode to rent in Takilma. Kim 592-4275

HORIZON HERBS of Williams has seeds for hundreds of medicinal plants. Call Richo 846-6704

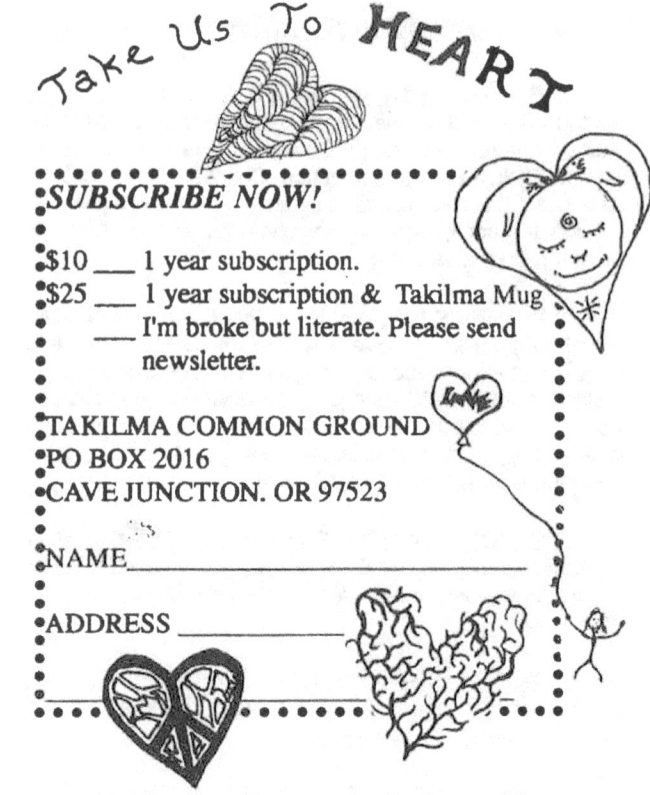

Take Us To HEART

SUBSCRIBE NOW!

$10 ___ 1 year subscription.

$25 ___ 1 year subscription & Takilma Mug

___ I'm broke but literate. Please send newsletter.

TAKILMA COMMON GROUND
PO BOX 2016
CAVE JUNCTION. OR 97523

NAME ____________________

ADDRESS ____________________

____

TAKILMA COMMON GROUND
PO BOX 2016
CAVE JUNCTION, OR 97523

BULK RATE
U.S. POSTAGE
PAID
CAVE JUNCTION
OREGON 97523
PERMIT #16

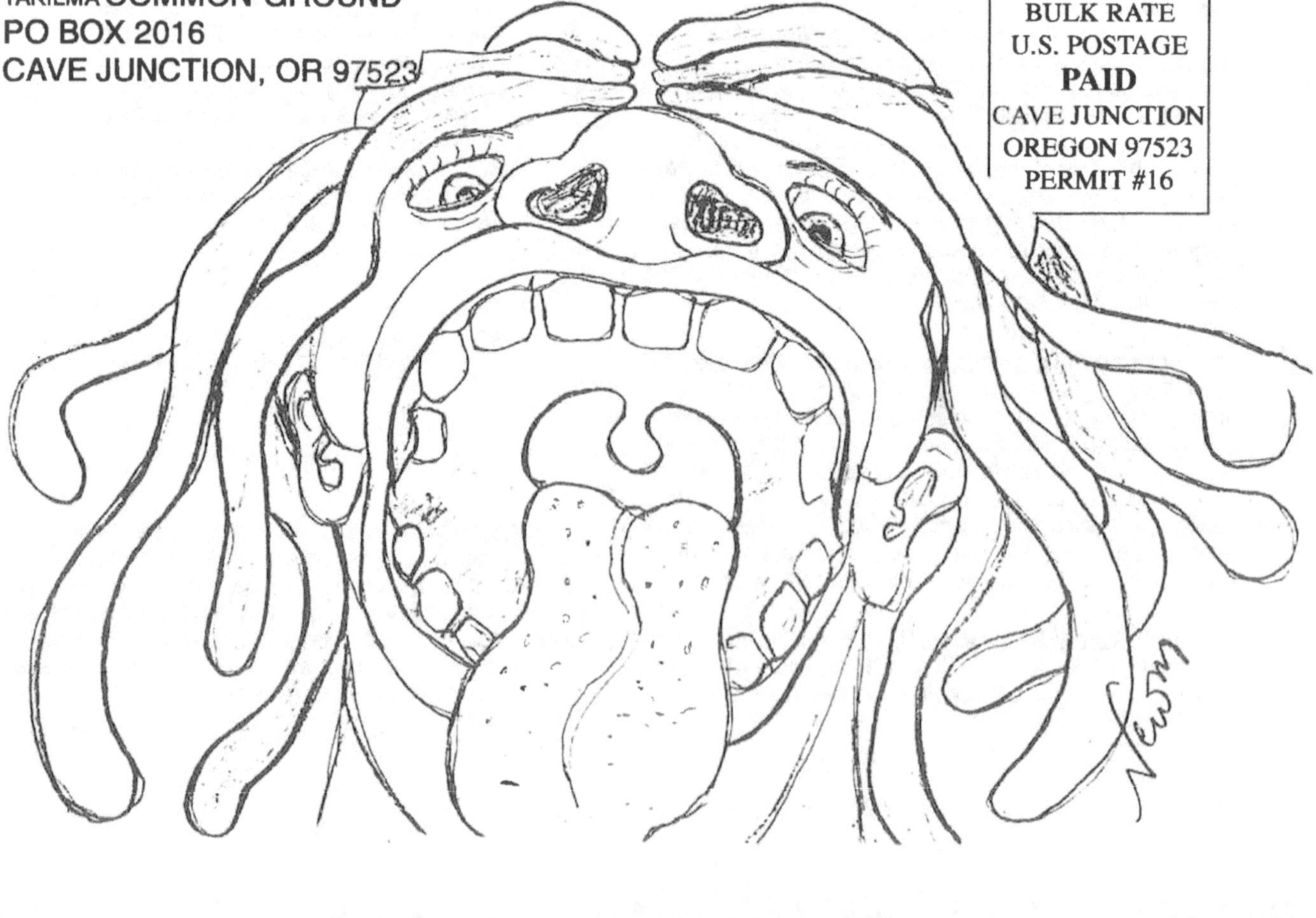

Takilma Common Ground

March, April '95

LOOKING INTO WOMENS' HERSTORY

#10

Rosie

Herstory isn't just a handful of famous women whose deeds are finally becoming publicized. Each of us knows a woman whose deeds will never be publicized, but whose life borders on the heroic. My great-aunt Rosie was just such a woman. The eldest of seven sisters, she was a heroine her whole life through. At age 13 she left her Lithuanian home and family for the promise of America. When a Jewish couple took her in as a "housegirl" she was thrilled to live with someone who came from the Old Country and understood her native tongue. Unfortunately, they were abusive and impossible to please; a rude awakening to the facts of immigrant life. Still, besides scrubbing their floors, and cooking their meals, she began to work at a factory. Like many girls of her ilk, she sent her earnings back home to her family and eventually was able to accumulate enough money to bring them all to America.

One can imagine what a woman worker must have had to put up with in her day. Sexual harassment on the job is not a modern phenomenon, but Rosie's response seems before her time. One day, when the shop-boss fondled her once too often, Rosie unflinchingly stabbed him with long-bladed shears. It's a family controversy whether she actually killed him or not. I do know she was shuttled off to remote Billings, Montana to avoid prosecution for her "crime".

Rosie was an independent thinker, and doer. When she found her first husband was sleeping with another woman, she promptly divorced him, at a time when this action was strongly discouraged. She always encouraged me to "go my own way" and make my own traditions. She lived a long (90+ years) and heroic life. While too outspoken and crotchety to be well-loved, she was always well-respected.

Rosie's life was the stuff that herstory is made of. She was strong in the face of adversity and always willing to speak her mind. I feel blessed and honored to carry on the legacy of my great-aunt Rosie. - *Rochelle Desser*

Promises To Keep

March - spring time, a time for renewal, the month that is dedicated to Women's History. As Mother Earth comes alive again, it is a time to celebrate ourselves and the women that came before us, those we did not get to learn about in school.

This year's theme for the National Women's History Project is "Promises to Keep." We do have promises to keep, promises we make to ourselves- to reach within for the songs that want to be sung, for the poems that need to be written, the dances that need to be done or the drawings that long to be drawn- any work we choose to express what is deep within our hearts. We have promises to keep to our mothers, grandmothers and all those who came before us, the ones we know about and the ones whose voices were never recorded and willl never be known. We have promises to pass on to our children so that they know WE HAVE A HISTORY and it is well worth celebrating. -*Deb Murphy*

BECAUSE....

WOMANS' WORK IS NEVER DONE AND IS UNDERPAID OR BORING OR REPETITIOUS AND WE'RE THE FIRST TO GET THE SACK AND WHAT WE LOOK LIKE IS MORE IMPORTANT THAN WHAT WE DO AND IF WE GET RAPED IT'S OUR FAULT AND IF WE GET BASHED WE MUST HAVE PROVOKED IT AND IF WE RAISE OUR VOICES WE'RE NAGGING BITCHES AND IF WE ENJOY SEX WE'RE NYMPHO AND IF WE DON'T WE'RE FRIGID AND BECAUSE WE STILL CAN'T GET AN ADEQUATE SAFE CONTRACEPTIVE BUT MEN ARE WALKING ON THE MOON AND IF WE CAN'T COPE OR DON'T WANT A PREGNANCY WE'RE MADE TO FEEL GUILTY ABOUT ABORTION AND.... FOR LOTS OF OTHER REASONS WE ARE PART OF THE WOMENS' LIBERATION MOVEMENT

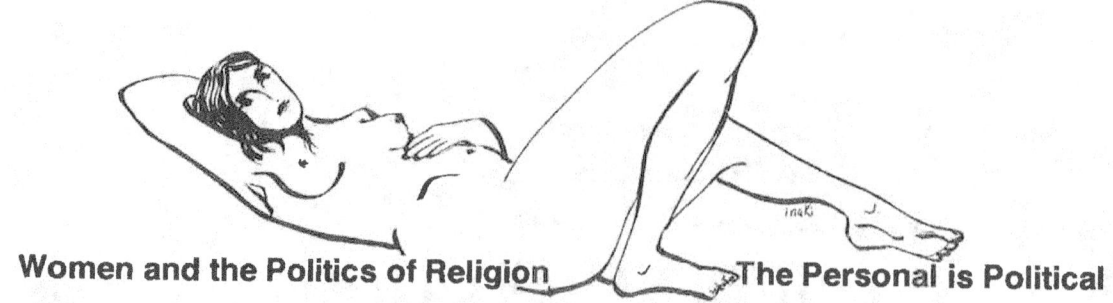

Women and the Politics of Religion

religion "The spiritual or emotional attitude of one who recognizes the existence of a superhuman power or powers."

religionism "Overdone or affected religious zeal."

I am an astrologer. The I Ching is my teacher. The Runes are guides to me in uncertain times. I deeply love the Goddess, in all her manifestations. I believe in a Spirit inherent in the Universe, whose voice I hear in the rivers, trees, mountains about me. I believe in magic.

So, all right already, what is this, an ad? you ask. No, this is, in the times we live, a courageous political statement. When the Takilma drummers appeared at a City Council meeting in Grants Pass - another courageous political act - a letter appeared in the Courier which said that though minority beliefs may have their rights, they shouldn't offend the majority belief system by public practice. Wow.

There is good evidence that a Christian Right minority is attempting to destroy public tolerance for the expression of "deviant" practice. Like being gay, pro-choice, or being a pagan or goddess worship per. They don't have to take away our rights. They just have to make it scary to be public about what we do.

So what does this have to do with women?

I know, and I hope you do, that women are special targets when they exhibit "deviant" behavior. Millions of women have been killed in the periodic witch hunts in the Western world. Women who dare to be "modern" and educated are being persecuted in the Islamic world today. Women who dare to be fat, or solitary, or old, or feminist, or assertive may be freely despised and reviled. Part of being a woman is to fear the consequences of being different.

I have come to believe in reincarnation. Once, doing breathwork, I had a deep and compelling memory of being stoned and burnt as a witch in medieval Germany. Other women I know have had similar experiences. I think the bodies of women hold this kind of memory. When Christian religionism begins to attack our religion, small events can trigger this deep fear. Patriarchal Christianity has a long history of violence towards women.

It is in honor of Women's History that I declare my religious practice. And I honor all of us who are open in non-Christian religion. But it is also time for us to abandon innocence, to understand that religious practice can become a major political act. The Aryan Nations didn't choose Josephine County as a base because they love the beauty of the Siskyous, you know. So- live dangerously! Love the Goddess! And do it out _loud!_ -Shel Anderson

The Personal is Political

Giving birth was the strongest thing I ever did. From being clamped to a cold table-like hospital bed in Newark, New Jersey, writhing, shaved and coated with brown iodine from bellybutton to knee, to a circle of women and children in the Takilma Clinic birthing room, early in the morning, birds singing, storm winds howling, surrounded by warmth, love and strength.

The first to the last, the yin to the yang, my eighteen year old daughter's birth to my nine year old son's.

When I first came to Takilma, I was eight months pregnant and eighteen years old. Getting to the Green Bridge, my husband and I noticed a bunch of naked hippies by the swimming hole. Curious, we went down to the beach and were warmly welcomed. Seemed half the ladies there were midwives. They all felt my belly and asked me if I was going to birth at the Clinic. Amazed to find out about the Clinic and available home birth, we thanked the gods and goddesses and waited for the moment.

Early in the morning on August 25, my waters broke and we rushed down the road to the Clinic. In the barnwood sided birthing room, I panted, holding Cory back until Dr. Jim and the midwives got there. As soon as they did I pushed him out. The birth was incredibly easier than the Newark hospital birth of my eldest daughter. Cory was born with a cleft lip and palate. Dr. Jim got out a large book and read a portion of it to us explaining the birth defect. It was sad, but beautiful, as this amazing dark-haired boy lay warm and wet in my arms surrounded by caring love and compassion. Meanwhile, the midwives cooked up the placenta. A vegetarian, I delighted in the idea of a meat offered by birth, not death.

Azlan was born next to the Van Duzen River in Humboldt County. His dad caught him, cut the cord, and cooked the placenta. When Azlan's head was out, he looked at everyone in the room. He was blue. He looked like E.T. This time there were no doctors or midwives, but lots of angels. The room glowed pink with fluttering rose-colored wings. We weighed him on the post office scale the next day.

Ivy was born in a hospital in Medford. She came early. The midwives drove me to the hospital in the new, improved birth mobile. Although I had the baby in the hospital, it was better knowing about breathing, and being strong. Ivy was so tiny, and jaundiced. They put her under lights and took blood samples. I slept in a bed next to her. Once, in the middle of the night, I woke up and saw a nurse tying Ivy's tiny arm off and preparing to take her blood with a big syringe. I was so mad. Before they had just pricked her heel. I told that nurse to stop. She did. Phew. (Continued on page 6)

Wholy and Spirit

Like an ocean
Forever turning,
Always yearning
Toward the edge of the land
And back out again
There's no choosing.

I've been sailing
The water's calm
Before the dawn.
Gray on gray
All the same
There is motion.

No direction
The ebb and flow
Spirit which grows
As much as we dare
The lives we share
Underwater.

Where's the Spark!
Show me the Spark that makes me.
Feel s like a bad dream
I want freedom from my bad dreams
They shake me.

I woke up feeling like a wave on a rock
Slammed to the surface, like birth it's a shock
I woke up feeling the sting of the spray
Edges undefined in the encompassing gray
Where do I draw the line
Between the sensual and the sublime
In bondage and also free
Drowning in the currents of morality

I'm a dolphin, I'm a snake
That I walk with two legs must be some
kind of mistake

What a coward
Stand on the pier, harbor my fears
Look out over the water
Forget what I sought here
Innocence?

Dreams forsaken
In the day to day
Thrills and the pain
While neither deep nor resounding
I can still feel the pounding
Lifeblood.

I rise like a goddess
Smooth as stone
Molten as earth core
Solid as bone

A witch by moonlight
Woman by day
Always knowing
Ignorant still
The differences fade away.

Still as sister
To the wind and the sea
Half fluid half full
I'm feeling her pull
Around and inside of me.

And I will choose my fate
Though the salt may sting my fate
In the ebb and flow, vision which grows
Whole and holy.

-Rochelle Desser

Me

Understand me,
Believe in me,
Trust me.
Even though
I may not
Be all you:
Expected,
Hoped for,
Needed.
I am all
I can be...
Myself.
- Ananda Floyd

  **"Prolife"?**

In the last few years, the anti-abortion movement's"" right to life " message has effectively seized the moral high ground. Holding up life as their sacred cause, the movement has created a climate in which young women and teens in this community are increasingly defensive about opting to abort unwanted pregnancies. It seems "right to life " has enabled the anti-abortion movement to spin itself an ethically impenetrable cocoon.

However, the results of a recent survey of Illinois Valley residents calls to question the authenticity of the " right to life" message used so effectively by the anti- abortion movement.

In an attempt to achieve scientific randomness, the COMMON GROUND interviewed nearly 150 individuals in front of the Cave Junction Post office. Respondents were asked whether they supported keeping abortion legal; whether they supported the death penalty; and third, whether they supported our government's policy in the Persian Gulf War where American forces killed over 500,000 Iraqis, many of them civilian women and children.

74% of those polled were pro-choice. While only 25% came out against legal abortion, their opinions on the other issues were quite interesting. Over 86% of the " Pro-lifers" were in favor of the death penalty. About 50% of the "Pro-lifers" expressed support for our government's Iraqi War policy. These results clearly contradict the Pro-life image as defenders of sacred life.

Many who expressed the need to illegalize abortion made additional comments to support their opinions. In every case these comments contained a uniform message: that the result of pregnancy was the responsibility of the woman and that she should have to deal with the full impact of its consequences. Herein lies the heart of the anti-abortion movement.

Rather than holding life as sacred, the heart of the anti-abortion movement beats upon the notion that sexual freedom is the exclusive domain of men and that the burden of unwanted pregnancy lies solely with the woman. If she would get married and stay at home, there would be no such thing as unwanted pregnancy!

An unwanted pregnancy leaves no easy answers and we must strive as a community to help young women and teens to avoid it. Pro-choice is much more than just having the option of abortion, it is the assurance for all women that like their male peers, unwanted pregnancy need not stand in the way of their life's dreams and aspirations.   *-Dave Toler*

IF YOU HAVE AN UNWANTED PREGNANCY, WHERE DO YOU GO HERE IN JOSEPHINE COUNTY? You can go to either the Siskiyou Clinic, Cave Junction 592-4111 or Planned Parenthood, Grants Pass 474-2784 and they can refer you to providers. There are several in the Medford -Ashland area.

At Risk

The impact of teen pregnancy on the lives of young people is dramatic and far-reaching. Bearing a child while a teenager usually drastically limits the possibilities for the parents' future. Young women who choose to continue their pregnancies are forced to abandon their own personal needs, goals,and dreams, often never to be reclaimed. This is not an easy sacrifice, nor is it short-lived, as the commitment to a child is life-long.

Young fathers are also called upon to step into a role of great responsibility, often before they are mature enough to do so. Over 84% of fathers of children born to adolescents do not live with the mother and child. 60% of teen marriages end in divorce within 5 years. Thus the major resonsibility of raising the child typically falls upon the young mother and her support system, if she has any.

Health risks to teen mothers and their newborn are much greater than for adult pregnancies. These include 40% increased risk of prematurity, birth defects, retardation and even death. Stresses of teen parenting include financial difficulties, academic demands, social and family problems, isolation and logistical complications, e.g.: how to get your sick baby to the doctor when you aren't old ehough to have a driver's license, or are too poor to own a car.

According to recent statistics, the U.S. has the highest teen pregnancy, abortion and birth rates in the developed world. At least 43% of our adolescent girls will experience an unintended pregnancy before the age of 20. Teen moms are much less likely to finish high school and are more likely to experience life-long poverty, earning on the average about half the income of women who first gave birth in their twenties.

The United States is a sex-saturated society. However, unlike other countries with lower teen birth statistics, we are a sex- silent society. Exposure to sexual imagery is pervasive in T.V., movies, books, advertising-but most families don't talk about it at the dinner table. How can we expect teenagers to talk with their boyfriends and girlfriends about sex and protection if we adults can't even broach the subject with them?

Some recent studies looked at the characteristics of young people who were successful in delaying childbearing, and found several common elements

1. A sense of purpose, hope, future goals.
2. Self-esteem . Parents are the key role models.
3. Low use of alcohol and dangerous drugs, which can impair judgement and affect normal brain development in teenagers.
4. Freedom from sexual abuse, since sexual abuse impairs personal boundary development and often leads to increased use of alcohol and drugs.
5. Involvement in activities such as school, sports, church, clubs, service groups.
6. Practice of communication skills
7. Easy access to a full range of family planning services.

I really have no conclusion. This is an enormous and ongoing problem. Congress wants to blame teens with punitive legislation, adults want to blame the schools and vice versa and the teens...who do they blame? I often see young girls struggling so hard, being so brave, trying their best to change the world in maybe the only way they feel they can, trying not to make the same mistakes their parents made, wanting to make up for all the things they missed when they were younger, struggling hard against the odds to do the right thing.

This is not just a teen problem. All of us need to look at our responsibilities to our planet, to each other, and to ourselves when considering bringing a new child here. We are all at risk. *-Lisa Kelz*

Legislative Blues

I am sure by now that you have been inundated daily with bleak news about what the New Majority in Congress is doing. Let me share with you one of the worst bills the Congress is considering. HR-925, masquerading as the Private Property Protection Act is really the Federal Takings legislation, which, if passed by the Senate and not vetoed by President Clinton, will require the government to "compensate an owner of property whose use of that property has been limited by an agency action that diminishes the fair market value of that property by 10% or more". One sponsor of the 1994 takings legislation, Rep. Billy Tauzin of La., admitted his legislation would "bankrupt the government" unless Congress rolled back environmental protections. Landowners would be free to do whatever they want no matter what the consequences are to others. For example, if your neighbors wanted to place a toxic waste dump next to your property the government would have to pay them to not do it. This legislation would enact into law the principle that the government must pay corporations not to pollute, not to damage the health or safety of others and not to harm their neighbors or the public. The House has already passed this bill as part of their Contract on America. Please call your Senators and the President today. The White House switchboard # is 202-456-1111. The Congressional switchboard is 202-224-3121.

On a statewide level the Legislature is trying to equal the Congress' level of absurdity. SB 305 is the Oregon Takings bill requiring we the taxpayers to pay for any net loss of property from environmental regulations. The same man introducing this bill also introduced a bill to limit the leasing or selling for instream use to only 50% of a person's water right. So my right to sell & make a profit from my water right would be limited. In their words this is also a taking. SB 279 would weaken Oregon's plastic recycling laws. SB 628 would provide additional water for the Grants Pass Irrigation District in order to save the dam. HB 2612 would preempt local governments from regulating pesticides applications. And there are many others. The one thing these things have in common is that they jeopardize either environmental, health or safety rules. Or the legislators are wanting to help their friends. Call us at the Siskiyou Project if you want to help and\or need more information. To contact your senator, representative or the governor see Deb's Wildlife Update. *-Barry Snitkin*

"Beast of Exploitation" to Offer Big Reward

In a past issue of this worthy publication, I was curiously attacked by two individual members of this rare community and would now like the opportunity to shed some light on this "whatever". Knowing that talk is cheap, I would like to offer them 100 per line if they are able to contradict me as I am about to contradict them now.

The first is J. Jones...1(No. I am not a logger... If anything, by fighting fires all summer I contribute to the opposite effect. 2) No. It was not "Leo and his friends" who stopped my progress. It was the fire season. 3) No. It was not me who flagged a road across the horse trail. It was Mr. Smith. Done for his own personal good reasons. (I can't bet on this one. It was told to me by J.D. the dozer operator. 4) No. I did not cut any virgin trees, mark any for cutting nor am I heading in that direction. Maybe someone can show you the difference between a 50 year old stump and one cut last year. Finally, 5) YES!. I DO HAVE MY PERMITS! HOORAY!!! now everyone is happy. But you would be crying if I cut everything allowable on this permit... Believe me!

Did I ask you what you doubted?? Here's what. I doubt that you will have the integrity to apologize to all those readers that you've misled with your letter to the editor. The only thing I will concede to you is that someone's mother is watching me. If I was worried about that, John, I would have built a fence all around my property and marked "NO TRESPASSING" everywhere like you guys did. Some members of the community might even appreciate this.

And to J.D. Smith: It wouldn't be prudent for me to take seriously the opinion of someone who has never worked a day of his life in the woods. Be advised that I have been living here longer than you, J.J before you, and that other "innocent" party that was mentioned COMBINED. (As if it mattered.)   *- Peter. S.*

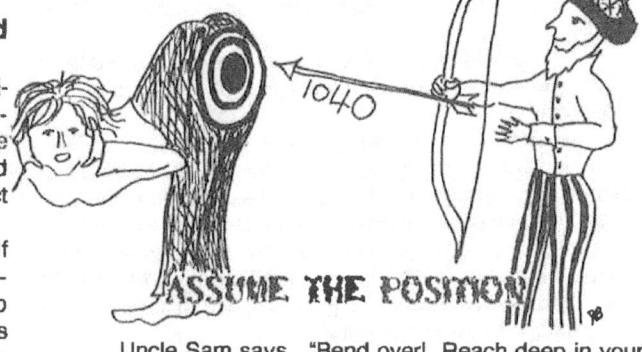

Uncle Sam says, "Bend over! Reach deep in your pockets, you fools, scrape together your cash, pay up!" Yep, your government needs money, your money. Two hundred fifty billion dollars more to the Pentagon-for "defense," ya' know. Then there's the little adventures into Grenada, Angola, Panama, Kuwait, Haiti etc. that cost a pretty penny. And we gotta subsidize the tobacco industry, big oil companies and pay agribusiness not to grow food.

Oh, and by the way, there's the $1 million on the national debt. That goes to the financial moguls who loaned the money to Uncle Sam. Hey, there's not enough to pay for decent education, health care, housing or environmental cleanup, folks. But there's sure gonna be plenty for the S&L bailout, more missiles and bombers, more CIA fun 'n games, more NASA space research...

All because we, the people, are too scared to refuse.-

Not all of us- at least 30,000 U.S. citizens are openly federal tax resisters-are refusing to pay all or part of federal taxes in protest- and we're not in jail. We refuse to be intimidated into participating in evil! Want more info on how to do it? Call Peace House in Ashland, 482-9625.)

-Kayla Starr

My Blue Heaven

For us, no place on this planet so closely approximates paradise as a lush, well tended blueberry patch in late July (except maybe the top of a persimmon tree in late November...).

Hybrid highbush blueberries, humankind's most recently domesticated fruit crop, have lots of advantages: no thorns, easy picking, frost proof blossoms, long lifespan (100 years plus), and freedom from serious pests and disease. They are also just plain yummy.

They also have a few disadvantages: Their yumminess means that they are fair game for every critter with any sense of taste including birds, possums, coons and kids. They need to be netted or fenced if you are to expect any for yourself. Blueberries are also a bit fussy about their soil nutrition but stay tuned for how to deal with that.

Here are a couple of myths about blueberries: "It's too hot and dry around Takilma to grow blueberries." Witness our many thriving 6 foot bushes. And: "Sawdust , oak leaves or pine needles will make the soil acid enough for blueberries." Maybe in 30 years if you'd care to wait that long.

Most soils around Takilma are only slightly acidic. To satisfy the blueberries' need for emphatically acid soil here's a recipe for starting and feeding them organically that really works:

— Dig holes 18" deep x 30" wide in a well-drained fairly sunny location about five feet apart. Or 3' as a single hedgerow.

— Refill each hole halfway with peatmoss.

— Add: one quart of either bloodmeal, fishmeal or soymeal (for nitrogen (No manure—the pH is too high!) One quart of soil sulphur (granules or powder). It's derived from ground sulphur rock, usually from the Yellowstone region. Sulphur reacts with soil, making it more acidic. One half pint rock phosphate or bone meal (for phosphorus). One half pint Kelp meal (for trace elements)

Stir the mixture thoroughly then add the soil you removed and stir again.

Plant the bushes. Small younger plants are cheaper and do as well as big older ones. Two or more varieties will aid pollination. We like Berkeley, Earliblue and Blue crop but most available varieties are excellent.

Mulch the bushes a foot thick with sawdust (the older the better). But—fresh is O.K. The shallow roots can't stand cultivation so sawdust keeps down weeds and conserves moisture.

After mulching, sprinkle another quart of blood, fish or soymeal around each plant, and another pint of sulphur too. -Beth and Mark

Personal is Political (continued from page 2.)

Another time they wanted to take her temperature rectally. I said, "Can't you take it under her arm?" Authoritatively, the nurse said, "This is much more eficient." I knew Ivy wouldn't like that and she didn't. She scrunched up her face and cried and pushed hard. The baby poop sqirted all over that nurse's white uniform. All Right Ivy!

Zach was born on a winter morning. All night I labored with him, my once tight stomach muscles now loosened like an old rubber band. The wind howled, all four of my children were with me on the futon in the new birthing room at the Clinic. Katy and Cory rubbed my feet. Cory said it sounded like the ocean in my womb when we listened with the stethoscope. Ivy dozed off and on and Azlan perched by my knee watching intently as his brother entered the world. It wasmorning. Children were walking up the hill to the Dome School. Someone asked me if I minded if they watched. I said, no, it's fine. When I pushed Zach out, the room was full od faces, mostly women and children. Dr. Jim took pictures. I still remember forgetting what to do in the intensity of the transition right before it's time to push. I asked one of the midwives. She said to take a deep breath and push.

Now I realize how fortunate I was to be able to experience these cosmic high-energy, spirit-filled births. It's nice to know that thanks to Karen Beesley and Joya there is a new midwifery service starting up in Takilma. What a precious and right experience to birth our babies naturally...in peace without the walls, halls and regulations of hospitals. One of the reasons we are here is to live a simpler life, closer to the earth. All women in good health deserve the choice of a home birth. -Mary Wertz

Where's the Bucks?

For some of us the COMMON GROUND is a breath of fresh air amidst the sterile and mundane, for others it's an oasis of useful information in a desert of trivial "news". What is it for you? If you value the COMMONGROUND, you should know that it does take some $bucks$ to keep it rolling. With printing, paper,postage, etc., COST OF EACH ISSUE AVERAGES $223. BUT SUBSCRIPTIONS FOR JAN. AND FEB. TOTALED ONLY $120. Can you say DEFICIT! Please support your local rag with a timely renewal or new sub.

A RED STICKER ON YOUR COMMONGROUND MEANS IT'S TIME TO RENEW!

ANNOUNCEMENTS

March 25 @7 pm. Artis, "SPOONMAN," performer extraordinaire, winner of a 1995 Grammy award, will perform at the Dome School. Admission is based on a sliding scale; adults $3-5, teens and seniors $2 and children under 12 are free.

March 26 @ 7 and 9 pm, " 'C'est la Vie," a masterpiece of a film about a girl coming of age, will be shown at the Varsity Theatre, Ashland. Two showings only . General admission $5. Tickets available now.

March 27 @7:00pm. Peg Millet concert at the Dome School. Come hear Peg sing and tell her experiences of being part of the Earth First FBI sting in Arizona which earned her 2 years free room and board at the Federal Correctional Institute. Suggested donation $2.00-5.00

April 5 @6:00pm. IV Human Rights Alliance pot luck dinner meeting at Rivendell Farm (David Atkin's big red barn at the end of River St). On tap: "Teaching Tolerance" video. Please join us.

April 12 The Siskiyou Project and the Southern Oregon Land Conservancy will be sponsoring a seminar about conservation easements at the Butler Bldg. on the Forest Service complex. Speakers include Dan Kellogg and Bob Hunter. for info. call Barry 592-4459.

April 25 @6:00pm. Floyd Cochran, former recruiter for the Aryan Nations will be here to share his experiences. In his words, "I left the Aryan Race and joined the Human Race". Join the IVHRA at Rivendell Farm for a pot luck dinner. $2.00 donation requested to help pay expenses. 592-4459

May 6 @10:00am. Hike the Wild Siskiyous along Rough & Ready Creek with Steve Marsden. This moderate hike might require a creek crossing, depending on the flow of the creek. Please call the Project the week of the hike for details. Bring lunch, water and meet at the OBrien Store. 592-4459

May 7 @ 2:00pm. Salmon Celebration. Join Agnes Baker-Pilgrim at Out N About for a pot luck feast. $2.00-5.00 donation requested. Feel free to come at noon to help.

Don't forget to vote! It's not too late. Ballots due by Mar. 28th. VOTE YES FOR LIBRARIES!

"Women and War, Women and Peace around the World": Drumming, singing, and stories from Freedom Singers and others. Sponsored by Peace House, held at the Congregational Church, 717 Siskiyou Blvd., Ashland.

River Appreciation Day Clean-Up
A project to clean up junk and garbage by the river and the road will be dicussed at the next T.C.A. meeting March 30th. A large truck is being lined up and the county is being asked to help with dump fees. If you would like to donate time, energy, ideas, or garbage please come to the meeting. The date of this project is tenatively on or around Earth day, April 24. For more information you can call 592-2872.

Be on the lookout for the EARTH WEEK calendar put out by SOSC with all the activities that will be taking place in Southern Oregon.

Parenting Workshop: To nurture childen through the teenage years. This will focus on communication, conflict resolution, normal adolescent development and how to recognize serious problems. This will be sponsored by the IVHS Student Health Center Advisory Board in cooperation with the Family Coalition, and Josephine County's Mental Health and Juvenile Departments. It will take place at IVHS on Monday, April 3 from 7 to 9 PM. Refreshments will be served.

R.A.P.P. (Reduce Adolescent Pregnancy Program) meets the 2nd and 4th Wednesdays of the month from 3 - 4:30 PM at the Library at LBMS. Due to Spring Break, the next meeting will be April 5. Meetings are open to the public. For more info call Lisa at the Siskiyou Community Health Center, 592-4111.

CLASSIFIEDS

The COMMONGROUND is published to provide you a vehicle for expression and absorption of information, feelings, ideas, even nonsensical whims, that constantly flow through our community. We invite your perspective via 3" disk (or typed double spaced), or creative drawing; send it to: COMMONGROUND POB 2016, CJ,OR.97523. Deadline for issue #11 is Apr.21. Editorial staff for this issue was Deb Murphy, Kayla Starr, Dave Hocker, Kerry Holman, and Jill Birmingham. Dave Toler was our facilitator. Printed on recycled paper. Thank you, Ina, for your beautiful graphics.

ACROSS

2. First 4 term lady
6. Feminist Author, Marilyn _____
11. Southern state
12. 1932 Olympian
14. Grease a car
15. Mayflower descendents
17. Songwriter Laura _____
18. Underground railroader
20. Not them
21. Songwriter Reynolds
22. Shade Tree
24. Be in debt
25. FeetxFeet
26. Grown-up sappling
27. Mantra
29. Desire
30. Birth control rights activist
    and local mountain

DOWN

1. Native American guide
2. Pioneering flyer
3. Finale
4. Type of tampon
5. First Congresswoman
6. 1984 VP candidate
7. Elevated railroad
8. Where you find young
   plants or young children
9. Two-way radio
10. Platwright during the
    "scoundrel times"
13. Next to
16. Some women try to avoid
    playing this
21. ____-24 tea
23. Onion's cousin
28. Famed anthropologist(init)

CROSSWORD

by Rochelle Desser

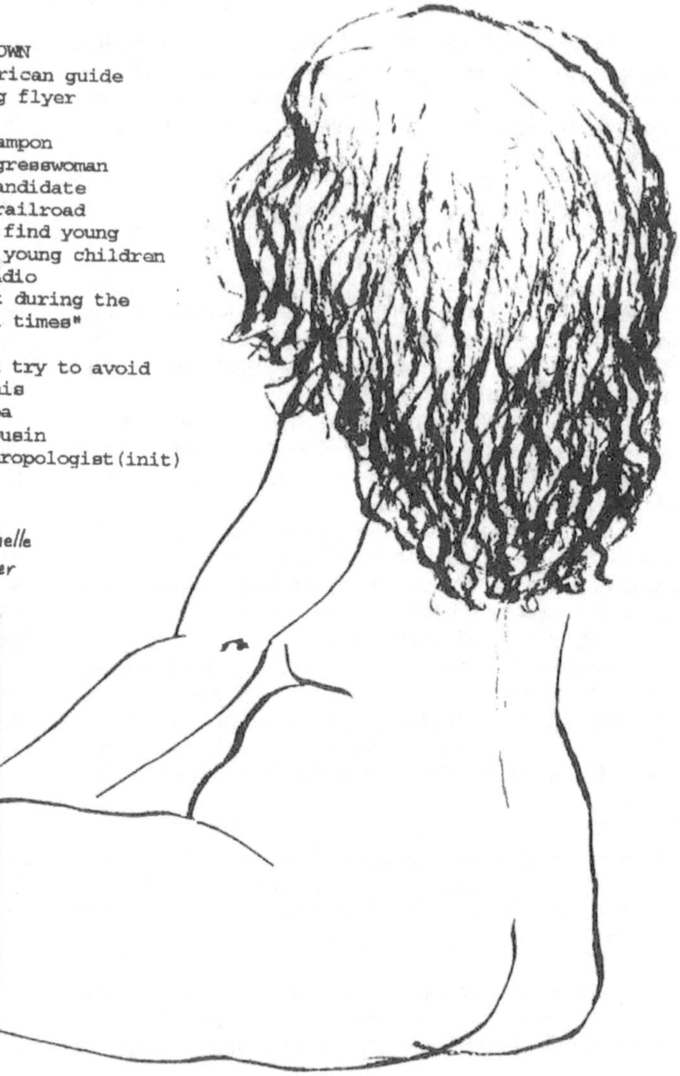

TAKILMA COMMON GROUND
POB 2016
CAVE JUNCTION, OR. 97523

BULK RATE
U.S. POSTAGE
PAID
CAVE JUNCTION
OREGON 97523
PERMIT #16

Takilma Common Ground

#11 May-June '95

For this issue, we asked for views on our economy. We hope these articles stimulate more thinking and bright ideas. How do you experience the economics here and how do you 'make do'?. The Takilma COMMON GROUND is a cauldron for expression and absorption of information, feelings, ideas, and whims that flow through our community. We invite your contributions (preferrably on 3 1/2" diskette), Send your creations to Common Ground, P O Box 2016, C,J.,OR. 97523.

Deadline for the next issue is June 7th. Editorial staff for this issue : Kayla Starr (facilitator), Deb Murphy, Kerry Holman, Rachel Goodperson, Jill Birmingham, Dave Hocker, Claire Sierra, Dave Toler, Mirya Holman and Kate Dwyer.

EVOLUTION OF AN ECONOMY

Twenty years ago the economy of our (Takilma) valley presented a much different face that that which we see today. In addition to widespread horticultural endeavors, now largely curtailed, our community offered three basic venues of employment: Green Side Up, the indigenous tree-planting cooperative; the Takilma People's Clinic, another indigenous endeavor, run as a collective, and Delbert Kauffman Wood Products, whose enterprise accommodated all levels of equine and woods skills.

To someone such as myself arriving from the outside world, the Clinic was by far the most remarkable institution: all collective members — doctor, nurses, midwives and a cadre of lay health workers — received the same monthly salary, about $150 per month if recollection serves me. In addition to standard AMA-type allopathic medicine, a menu of various alternative treatments or therapies were available depending on the clinic's current staff resources and the desires of patients. Those who mistakenly referred to the "free" clinic were quickly corrected: all patients were expected to pay something; firewood or other types of barter if not cash. The low salary levels were made possible by the communal living arrangements of many of the clinic staff members. As communal institutions weakened (or evolved), the clinic folk gradually accommodated themselves to salary differentials to meet rising living costs.

CONTINUED ON PAGE 3

RIVER RESURRECTION

The TCA-sponsored riverbank clean-up day was a big success. They lost count of the number of truckloads of trash that went to the dump on April 29th as a result of this effort to beautify our community and keep the river free of human debris. Much gratitude to the many who braved chilly wet weather to help out, including: Bruce, Patrick F., Gail, Jon, Christie, Romain, Debra, Randy, Chipper, Tom, Bill G., Bill S., Mike Z., Andrea, Adam, Kim, Alan N., Gloria, Robert, Beth, Mark, Paul K., Russell, Ina, Pauli, Don, Lance, Steve, Jennifer, Diane, Dave T., Michael M., Lydia and perhaps others whose names were missed by this reporter. Anyone who is inspired to sponsor another such event to clean up their neighborhoods around Takilma may contact TCA members for assistance in organizing it. Let Earth Day be everyday

While we're at it, here's a belated 'THANK YOU' to Norm Hoskins for his great backhoe work on the Community Building driveway in the nick of time before the floods, *-Kayla*

IT'S GET TOUGH TIME

We've tried all the usual methods to stop the logging of the sacred SugarLoaf ancient forest on Greyback mountain: participating in Forest Service planning and public input processes, hundreds of letters and calls to elected representatives, meetings with Forest Service officials, attempts to meet with Boise-Cascade management, (who bought the logging rights), public protests...Now it's time for ACTION!

We must show our determination to save this last remaining unlogged area in our watershed. All people who are commited to protecting the last 5% of our ancient forest are invited to attend the strategy session, non-violence training and benefit performance in Williams, Saturday, May 13. Non-violence protest training session will be from 11 - 5pm followed by a pot-luck dinner hosted by Williams folks, and performance by Takilma's own Illuminated Fools Puppet Theater, songs by Alice DiMiceli, and dancing to the Williams Band. All these events will be at the Provolt Grange. Carpooling from Takilma meets at the SREP office at 9:30 a.m. Sat. May 13. Call Marjorie for more info: 592-6733 evenings. LET'S JUST DO IT!

CHILDREN AND POVERTY

Adults have some choices for themselves, hopefully. Children do not.

If poverty exists in their home, they have no recourse. Growing up without the basics is very hard. For many young people in this valley the basics simply do not exist. For them inadequate food, clothing and shelter are the norm.

It is hard to have children grow up happy and healthy when their essential needs are not met. The sad statistics tell us that those children become the ones labelled "at risk." They are at risk to have low self-esteem, to do poorly in school, to have troubled teen years and to become parents too young.

When children do have their basic needs met they are free to go beyond a survival level. They are able to dream a different path for themselves and to find the way to make those dreams come true. *- Deborah Collette Murphy*

NO PLACE LIKE HOME

We all know the economy of our fair valley is depressed. Lack of jobs. lack of job training. Look around. What is there? The schools, the banks, the Clinic, restaurants, food stores, a smattering of shops and services along 199 and Caves Hwy, some professional offices, not many. Services are to be found in Grants Pass.

I work at Headstart, have for the last nine years as a family advocate-social worker. Most of my clients are receiving Aid to Families with Dependent Children, otherwise known as Welfare. These folks are having a hard time making ends meet, harder yet with the Republicans controlling the purse strings of the county. I used to wonder why folks choose to settle here. Well, lots of them grew up here, families still here, roots run deep here in Southern Oregon where the Illinois River flows. Housing is cheap as well, when you can find it.

It costs a lot of money to make a change. Scary when you have to come up with first, last, and security deposit. Scarier still when you have kids, and maybe, single. Takes all the energy just to get through the day...kids to school or child care, go to school or search for a job in order to keep getting your welfare check, keep the old car running with no skill and no money.

Welfare gives 47-49% of the poverty level. This means that if the poverty level for a family of 4 is $15,000 a year, well, then a welfare family is making about $7,000. Not much these days!

I went to Grants Pass yesterday. It's really booming. Lots of traffic at all hours. Lots of buildings going up, ugly ones taking away my horizon. I was glad to get home to my depressed valley where trees still make great neighbors. *- Ellie McCoy*

CHANGE IS

Where once was open meadow to the north of my home, pristine forest to the south and three households as neighbors, now is post-logging debris and stumps, makeshift sheep, goat and horse pens, a dozen trashed vehicles and 5 or 6 new households living in vehicles and tents. Poverty and its accompanying blight encroaches on the natural seclusion which many of us once enjoyed in our valley. How many of us are listening to the ugly sounds of chain saws as neighbors log their properties? How many of us are tempted to do the same when we have bills to pay and not enough money to cover the basic costs of living? Is it fair to live on 5 or 10 acres while others have nowhere to go?

Our diseased socio–economic system fails to provide the education, emotional stability and the jobs which are the basis of a self-sufficient society. No wonder so many people are out of work and homeless. No wonder so many turn to crime and drug addiction to cope with the futility of dead-end lives. The squalor and devastation growing around us are simply the most visible signs of the times.

So, what's to be done? One of my neighbors has decided to plant trees and beautify her own place in reaction to the clearcut next door. Some are building fences (using cut down trees, of course, to do this). Others are selling and moving to places where the poverty is less obvious. A few are attempting to pressure government agencies to provide better education and social support services and new jobs in our area. Some are engaging in community clean-up efforts; trying to help neighbors keep it together... by providing water from their wells to neighbors who have none for sanitation and fire safety, offering firewood, loaning tools, assisting with vegetable gardens, clothing and transportation.

Such band-aid efforts are better than doing nothing, I suppose. However, it is clear to me that only a profound overhaul of our economic system that equitably distributes basic resources can cure these ills, locally and globally. When will we stop grovelling for our crumby piece of the pie and be ready to heal ourselves? *- Kayla*

EVOLUTION ... CONT. FROM PAGE 1

The watershed year for change was 1987, the year of the Longwood fire and the clinic's evacuation to Cave Junction while the Takilma building became the headquarters for the fire fighting effort. The move, intended to be temporary, became permanent when the new location brought an unanticipated increase in the number of patients seen and in income, an irresistible combination to those whose growing families made voluntary povery less and less attractive. To those of us who were not around to witness the gradual evolution of a Maoist collective into the Siskiyou Community Health Center, the connection of the two institutions might be hard to imagine.

For those unable to subsist on clinic salaries, there was Green Side Up. An outgrowth of the early efforts to deal with the effects of the truly horrendous logging practices of the 40's, 50's & 60's, reforestation was often just window dressing for a lost cause, but if some units would need multiple replantings to remain on forest service smokescreen lists of successfully replanted units, this made more work. A combination of intelligent bidding and a dedicated workforce made Green Side Up a truly valuable economic resource for its many members. Hourly wages in excess of $12 were not unheard of, a wage usually applied to all members of a crew including the cook, regardless of individual productivity, the latter often a bone of contention. GSU gradually faded as more and more contractors brought in outside minimum wage laborers with whom no one cared to compete. The most tenacious GSU workers found a niche in cone-picking, an area not open to competition with low-wage unskilled labor.

Nor was the Kaufman enterprise immune to evolutionaly forces. Pole peeling piece-work was available to virtually anyone and could be well-paying for those willing to deveoop a skilled hand with a spud, but this avenue dried up for all but a few with the advent of the mechanical pole-peeler. For years an endless succession of big mules, miniature mules and big horses required drivers, skilled and not-so-skilled, to move logs and poles down skid trails to landings. Many have memories, fond and otherwise, of Jack, Jake and Jude (the big mules), Dick and Doc (the gray Percherons), Lucifer and Beelzebub (the miniature mules), Bud and Babe, etc., all memories now that logs and poles are purchased rather than harvested. Fence crews and barn crews remain at work with the addition of the pole furniture crew at the new Kerby location of Kaufman Wood Products.

With the changing economy came the exodus to Ashland in search of better jobs and better schools. Many of us who remain in Takilma can't help but think of Ashland as a Takilma annex, so many familiiar faces do we see there.

Omitted here are the many individual craftspeople, artists, professionals and entrepreneurs who still make their homes and livelihoods in Takilma and environs, and the Dome School, whose history and evolution is a story in itself. What will the future bring? Continued evolution, certainly, but in what directions we will have to wait and see.

-Jim Rich

A VIEW FROM PROJECT BABY CHECK

As a parent trainer and outreach worker for Project Baby Check, I have become all too familiar with the dire economic situation in the Illinois Valley.

We provide outreach support and parenting education to our families, as well as growth and developmental assessments of their children aged birth to four. Year after year we face additional challenges to our program due to drastic budget cuts in Josephine County services. I see the struggles our families must endure. The economic picture in the Illinois Valley continues to worsen. The Republican "Contract On America" threatens the welfare of all our families, as does the recent deceitful debacle of the law enforcement levy no one in the county really understood, obviously. There is now talk of cutting all immunization services for children in the Illinois Valley, which are only minimal now (twice a month). Who knew they were voting to do away with this program when they voted against the sheriff's department wasting more of the taxpayer's money?

Most of the families we see in our project receive public assistance. They are primarily young parents, often single. We see many of our parents coerced into attending JOBS Program, Jobs Council, or the JOBS club, under threat of being cut off from any public assistance. The Republican notion of limiting Aid to Dependent Children to two years, with all recipients being trained for employment is a wonderful concept, but once all these people are trained where are they going to find a job? Many people in the valley do not own cars and cannot afford insurance or gasoline if they did. The distances they must travel to even look for employment are prohibitive. They do not have a safe, caring place to leave their children all day long, especially a place they can afford, working for minimum wage.

Many of our parents have been trained and retrained. Are they now working? No; there are few jobs available. Some are on long waiting lists hoping to be called for an apprenticeship, a job, anything to improve their finances and way of life. I would say of the fifty families we work with approximately 75% would love to work if the conditions were favorable.

I see families living in substandard housing in our beautiful valley, with no power or running water, trying to keep up with feeding, cleaning and clothing their children. Just getting to the Clinic is a major task, with sick children and no transportation. People cannot get ahead, they can barely live, on public assistance. The little cash benefits they receive are not enough to cover rent and uility payments, as well as other luxuries such as a telephone, laundry soap, baby diapers, shampoo, etc.

When state, county, and local funds are allocated for social, educational or medical programs, rarely does it positively affect our valley. Little of the available money ever seems to make it over Hayes Hill. And when budget reductions are necessary, our minimal services always seem to be the first to go. Unfortunately, I do not see any hope for improvement in the Illinois Valley's economic situation in the near future. I see more budget cuts, more loss of services, and no increase in available employment.

-Nancy Lyford

LETTERS

Dear readers,

Smokers at Community Building events are generally considerate and smoke outside, often on the porches. On a cold night, with an interesting event, a little social smoking occasionally creeps up closer, maybe just barely inside the doors. This doesn't matter much when you're smoking, and most people around you seem to be too. Everybody's happy. The problem I experience is that I'm a former smoker who's trying to avoid smoke and its associations for me. Smoke smells a lot stronger when you haven't been smoking for a while, and the clouds extend quite a bit past their source. So smokers have a greater effect on the immediate area than they may realize. Beyond those who just don't like the smell, smokers provide secondhand smoke to children, pregnant women, and people who have respiratory problems or are allergic to smoke. All these kinds of people may show up at events open to the general public.

In the interests of harmony and compassion I suggest a specific smoking area at Community Building public events. The back and side porches are one possibility. I realize that they are smaller than the front porch, but since they are not the general entrance the smoke would stay with the people who choose and enjoy it. We could have metal containers there to prevent litter and fires, and smokers could still hear the music. Peacefully, *Rachel*

Dear Common Ground,

I certainly have great appreciation for the efforts of the Illinois Valley Human Rights Alliance to protect the rights of children in regard to in-school interrogation. Illegal in-school interrogation is certainly an abuse of police power and in my opinion, another form of child abuse! This topic upsets me greatly, because it happened to me.

Back when I was in school, I was illegally interrogated in regards to a non school-related issue. The police told me that if I didn't cooperate I would be arrested and taken away from my family, and in this process they violated every constitutional and Miranda right that I had! Under the pressure of the situation, and the fear of being removed from my family and placed in state custody, I divulged information about some people in this area. I regret most of what I said, because I didn't know that the authorities would rob people and destroy lives. My parents were very straight and conservative, they never said that the system is screwed up. How could my parents teach me to see the truth when they couldn't see the truth themselves?

If I only knew then what I know now. I regret that I had to learn a lesson at the expense of others. The only truths I claim I have had to find out on my own. Everyone makes mistakes, especially in youth. If people wish to hold against me my mistakes from my childhood, then the problem is theirs, not mine. I have spoken with those who were affected by what I have done and I have been honest. I am not ashamed of my mistakes because I have learned from them and I have grown from them, and they have made me who I am.

I would do whatever I could to set things right and I don't expect to be forgiven, but I do expect honest people to understand the pressure children can be placed under. As far as I am concerned, illegal in-school interrogation is another form of child abuse and another form of molestation, mental molestation. I will never forget what they have put me through, on all levels.

I will forgive... but I will never forget...

Tom Yattaw, aka Charles Pullen

EDGES

Living is richest on the edge. Edges are so alive. That's why I love it here. Natural edges everywhere. So much life.

You know how it is under a rock, that edge between the rich earth and a warm stone? Pick up the rock. Watch that instinctive dash for other edges, the race to those safe, dynamic places that sustain the work of making food and love and new generations. The mad race looks for a moment like rush hour in the city. But that's because we interrupt. We've destroyed the edge. We changed the nature of things.

Look under a stone this time of year. You'll likely catch in their act those tiny armadillos that roll up into troll-sized marbles at a touch. When we leave them alone, they go about their work, busily creating and taking care, enhancing the world, with their lives and with their deaths. Life on the edge is intensely, yet so often, to our eye, not much is going on. Kind of like city folks and their food. Or suburban children and their parents' labor. Or watching a garden grow. We see the scene, perhaps even appreciate it with sense or thought. But we miss the living of it. We are on the outside.

We put up fences and call them edges. But most fences are only knives to slice and serve up the earth or way to shield us from what's on the other side. Good fences do not make good neighbors. They separate. They try to wall us in and others out. They embody the idea that your interests and mine are different and so we must live on different earths.

That's the trouble with the city, not enough real edges. So people make fences instead. Like opaque walls between neighbors and invisible walls between neighborhoods. Asphalt and building between people and their earth. Supermarkets between folks and their farms.

But edges make good neighbors. Nature's edges nuture life. They provide a profusion of contact among the living as all work to sustain life. Like communities with footpaths leading from home to home and fences that let people through to one another, edges are rich in variety and full of networks where people engage one another and the rest of life in the enterprise of living.

I love it that between the air and the earth, the edge that changes stone to dirt and clods of clay and rotting hay to gentle garden loam. Months of constant invisible change beneath rolling waves of weather—the lacy frosted landscape turning to dazzling winter sun and back to softest rain—alter the very ground we walk on, grain by grain. Then at the sharp edge of spring, creatures and plants burst forth again with living's magic, working together in all our different ways to regenerate a fertile world.

I love this valley because of its real, living edges. Bird song is most diverse at an edge. So is human discourse. And if you look and listen well here, every human argument alive echoes through this valley's conversations—in homes, on common grounds and through our media. We, like every other living thing in our valley, come out of hibernation in the spring, full of the energy to create the world anew again. We come forth to meet at the edges, where friction generates heat, where the democratic swords of argument and the historical tests of everyday practice mix it up to evolve and create new designs for our future, designs that are tested by living at the edge.- *Joyce Abrams* copyright 1995

LE SHOW

Love was the theme—daunting to many—but surprise! Love was what happened last Saturday night when our community building became an up-trend night club. Guests were entertained and entertaining in unexpected ways. "Connie" and "Tina," an omni-gendered glamour duo reminiscent of "The Crying Game" had the crowd entranced; lovers of Chocolate, Springtime, the Tropics, Pepe le Pew and his kitty consort, Kermit and Miss Piggy, Lady Godiva in the goose-pimpled flesh, as well as two hapless haploid strands of DNA toasted to the various faces of love.

On stage, Sue-Patsy Kline-Norman wowed the crowd, piercing our hearts with her plaintive song, leaving us begging for more. Pat, the love doctor gave advice on safe sex and the tao of multiple orgasm. Harley, aka Marcus, was our favorite rejected suitor...we'd peruse his copy of Easy Rider anytime! Sunny and Cher(also known as Barry and Meadow) proclaimed their love—after all these years. And the Ashland Love Handles were hilariously inept as love's cheerleaders.

Love was magic on the dance floor with faces glowing, energy flowing to the provocative beat of the Rhythm Kings. Four a.m., the last of the hard core straggled out to post-love, 4-poster love scenes of their own.

Anyone wanting to get on the mailing list for invitations to next year's extravaganza may notify the Le Show Committee at P.O. Box 2016, Cave Junction. Proceeds from the event will be donated to the Community Building Fund. Thanks to all who made this possible. -*The Skil'd-'lerts*

PROTECT WILD STEELHEAD

The National Marine Fisheries Service provided a ray of hope for lovers of wild steelhead and rivers when, in March, they proposed to list steelhead populations in the Klamath mountain province as threatened under the endangered species act. But within a month misinformation and opposition to the listing threatened to dim that hope. It is important that the NMFS receives a simple letter of support for the proposed listing from each and every one of you. These are our fish and rivers.

Please write the National Marine Fisheries Service and tell them that you fully support the proposed "threatened" ESA listing of the Klamath Mountain Province steelhead. Comments must be received by May 15th. Write to the Environmental and Technical Services, NMFS Northwest Region, 911 NE 11th Ave. Suite 620, Portland Oregon, 97232. Send a copy or your letter to Mark Hatfield, 711 Hart Senate Office Building, Washington, D,C. 220510.

-*Barbara Ullian*

ANNOUNCEMENTS

•COMMUNITY FIREWALK: SATURDAY, MAY 20 7:00 pm. Hollis' finale before departing for Maui. The ritual will pass on the Firewalk to the Community. Sliding scale $7-25. If you are interested in trading your labor instead of paying money, we need help setting up. Call me to make arrangements. For childcare, call ahead, 592-2476.

As my time of departure draws nearer I find myself wanting to "officially" say my parting words to you, Takilma Community. Your arms opened wide to welcome me when I arrived and seemed to smile on me and support me as I changed and grew and blossomed. Then I felt very much received as I was now able to give back with the Firewalk and Dreamwork. I treasure the moments we've shared and in retrospect wish we weren't all so "busy", that the moments could have been hours. To the drummers I have had the privilege to drum with ... The drum beat, keeping us together, though an ocean apart — one drum! -*Hollis*

•OPEN HOUSE: THURSDAY, MAY 25 The Dome School will host an Open House for its families and the public. Children from the Kindergarten and Elementary Programs will perform from 7-8:30 pm. Children's artwork will be displayed.

•CULTURAL ARTS FAIR: Evergreen Elementary School is presenting its third annual Cultural Arts Fair, Thursday, May 25 from 6-8 pm. in the gym. Many wonderful, diverse artists, adults and children, will perform. Children's artwork will be presented. Support diversity in our local public schools.

•KARATE: Self- Defense for Women. Martial artistry may paint a picture of safety and self confidence for you. D. Saito, Sixth Degree Blackbelt, National Director of the International Karate Federation, will hold a free class on Wednesday, May 31 from 7- 8:30 pm. Sponsored by the Three Rivers Community Hospital & Health Center. It will be held in Conference Room A on the Washington Campus. For further info: 479-9401.

•THE REAL LIBRARY BLASTS-OFF: On March 28th the voters of Josephine County passed a 3 year levy providing stable funding for its library system for the first time in 15 years! This means increased hours, more staff, the restoration of the interlibrary loan system, a full summer reading program and new books! The IV Branch will be increased to 30 hours including Saturday afternoons. Thanks to all those who helped in the campaign In celebration, the IV Friends of the Library will host a special day on Saturday, July 1. With poetry readings, storytelling, entertainment, food and a storybook parade. If you would like to participate, please contact Deborah Murphy at 592-2866.

•S.R.E.P. AS PENPALS: The Sisikiyou Regional Education Project has a computer terminal available to the public to be used to write letters for environmental and social issues. To arrange for time or further info call 592-4459.

•CLEAN UP/CLEAR OUT: MAY 30 and MAY 31 are work days for the Dome School families and Takilma Community members to help put away school and get the building ready for summer. The staff would appreciate any offers of help!

POETRY

REMEMBERING THEIR BEAUTY AND MAJESTY
I CRAWL OVER THEIR CORPSES
I CAN'T FATHOM THIS DESTRUCTION
ONE MAN HAS WROUGHT
OM MANI PADME HUM I CHANT AS
TREE AFTER TREE CRASHES TO WHAT
USED TO BE THE FOREST FLOOR
NOW A GREAT PILE OF PICK UP STICKS
                        - Marjorie Reynolds

ADVICE FOR TEENS

DOING STRANGE THINGS CAN BE COOL.
DOING COOL THINGS CAN BE STRANGE.
BUT THE BEST IS DOING COOL THINGS
IN A STRANGE PLACE.
DON'T DO STRANGE THINGS JUST TO BE COOL.
IF YOU FEEL KINDA STRANGE SOMETIMES,
THAT'S COOL,
BECAUSE WE ALL DO.
                        - Sequoia's brother, *Marcus*

SPRING STORY

Spring air
Spring rain
Spring sun
Spring snow

Spring buds
Springs flowers
Spring greens
Spring glories
                - *Miz Moons*

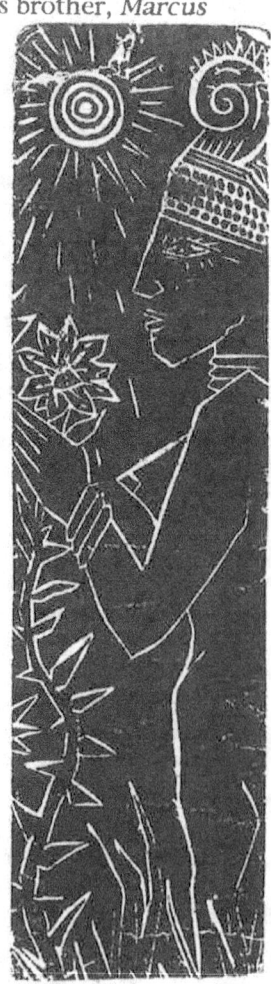

GULF WAR JUNKIES

GULF WAR JUNKIE
OUR MILEAGE
indicative
of an artificial
pump price
NOT our 'real' desires
Takilma to town
town to Takilma
Solstice to Equinox
Equinox to Solstice
groovy us
the gulf war junkies
                - *miguelo*

I was inspired to write this after experiencing the ritual with the Shaman at the Community Building on March 9th. I want to share it to help us remember that important event.

MESSAGE FROM THE ANDES

With deepest respect,
The feet of the Shaman
Walk slowly in the earth.
Traveling over mountains,
Crossing rivers, flying through skies
Passing beyond borders,
To bring this message:
We have the same Mother,
Our Mother Earth.
Hear Her cries!
Listen to her voices:
In the stones, the birds, the trees
The lizards, the worms, the breeze.
We, who are humanity
Must open our hearts wide,
And take better care
If we want to survive.
Don't ask questions
Think! the answers will come.
Listen to the voice of the Spirit
Which dwells within each one.
Pay close attention-
Listen to Her call!
Always follow your heart,
Say "Thank you" for all gifts,
With Love, embrace All.
                        - *Zandra*

OBEDIENCE

THE BOY STOOD ON THE BURNING DECK
JUST LIKE HIS FATHER SAID.
DAD LEFT IN A LIFEBOAT.
IT LEAKED.
IT SANK.
HE'S DEAD.

THE BOY STOOD ON THE BURNING DECK
HIS FACE WAS BLISTERED RED.
ALONG CAME THE COAST GUARD
AND NOW
HE'S SAFE
IN BED.   - *GOOD DOG*

KIDS PAGE

MY FAVRIT FORT

I haf to woc uhcros a brich and a log an I wil be at my forte. Thas my favrit spot and I feel lic I want to gow swimen and I here the rivr flote by me and I love it thar. It has a swing and a rivr and a chare and a hamoc and I sleep in it and it is comderbl. I luf it thar! and it is miy favrit spot to slep in. It is bootifl.

by Shanti   age 6

SAVE THE WORLD!

The environment is being destroyed. These things have CFC's that destroy the ozone; a refrigerator, plastic foam, air conditioners and aerosol spray cans. Every time a space shuttle takes off, 75 tons of chlorine ((the chemical that destroys ozone) are deposited in the ozone layer. More ultra-violet rays are reaching the ocean and killing the one celled plants and animals. That hurts big fish in the chain. Some things you can do: stop using air conditioners, use fans. Stop buying styrofoam and plastic. Try not to use cars, walk or run or bike. Plant a garden.

by Jacob Lukas   age 8

VELVET SKY

Stars shine against the black velvet sky.
The moon glows with passion and   power.
I wonder,
if I wish,
my dream will spring to life.
Love and joy fill my mind
And I feel like I'm floating
in the midnight sky.

by Nicole Birmingham   age 11

A CHILDS HEART

A childs heart can never be broken from a mother because a childs mother is some body speshel to a child. somebody so spechel.

by Janaki   age 8

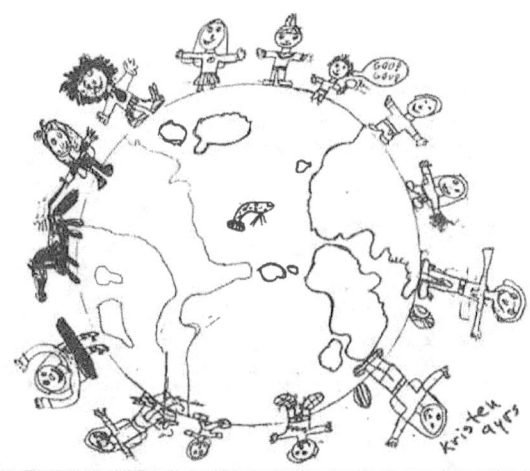

Hey kids, young and old: send in your stories, poetry and art. How about a teen advice column, by and for teenagers? Deadline for the next issue is June 7.

ASHLAND CORNER

When I drive the 80 or so miles between my two homes, I am amazed thatthings can change so radically, so quickly. The drive connects an area that feels like a desert sometimes, to one of lush vegetation. The elevation of Ashland and Takilma is relatively the same, but that is where the similarity stops. From a growing hustle-bustle to a quiet, laid- back feeling, each place certainly has its appeal. But my heart rests in Takilma, and when I haven't been over for a while I yearn for the peace and quiet of my homeland.

Usually it is climbing Hayes Hill that triggers all sorts of trips down memory lane, probably because it is here that things seem to change...the road is more clearly guarded by trees and has the feel of the Oregon that I came to know 22 years ago. I hope when I finally get it together to move back over it will still be there in most of the ways that I hold in my heart's eye. Until we meet again... *Heller*

LOST & FOUND

LOST HAT: I left my felt cap at the dance at the Dome School when "Higher Ground" played on April 8. It is shaped like a ski cap and is white with black threads mixed in. The edge is turned up and has a scalloped cut. It is very special to me. If anyone finds it or knows where it is, please leave a message at 846-7563 for Jimmy. Thank you.

LOST NECKLACE: A pipestone, serpentine, and bone necklace was lost at the Community Building at Le Show. Intense sentimental value! Please return to the Blacksmith Shop or call Heather or Jim at 592-2681.

SUBSCRIBE NOW!

A 1 year subscription is only.................................$10____

A 1 year subscription and a Common Ground
  T -shirt (block-printed by Fools).....................$25____

A 1 year subscription while you are getting
  your economic trip together.........................$0-10____

Send to: TAKILMA COMMON GROUND
           POB 2016
           CAVE JUNCTION, OR 97523

CLASSIFIEDS

GARDEN WORK MY SPECIALTY: Do brush cleaning, firewood cutting and other yardwork & projects. Al Karger 597-2205.

INNER CHILD TAROT: by phone or in person. Short session - $5 ; long session - $10; in-depth session - $30. Trades welcome. Weddings, donation. Rev. Sandy Newell 596-2983.

LOVING HOME WANTED: for loving large (very large) 8 year old Malamut/Husky? Great with children, loves to travel, is slower moving these days so he sticks close to home. He is fixed, lives outside and is very bearlike. Please, if you have room in your heart and yard, it would save his life. Also need a home for 4 cats. They don't need to stay together. Call Hollis 592-2476.

GOLDEN DAWN: Gardens and Botanicals, Bedding Plants, Perennials, Vegetable and Herb starts, Container Gardens, Cut Flowers, Dried Flowers and Flowers Essences. 4275 Waldo Road, Cave Junction. Connie Hayes 592-6312.

SUPER BLUE GREEN ALGAE & MULTI-PURE WATER FILTER SYSTEMS: Call Connie Hayes at 592-6312.

HEART & SOUL CENTERED PSYCHOTHERAPY: Expressive art, sacred movement meditation, guided imagery, breath/body awareness. Compassionate listening. Adults & teens. Sliding scale. Claire Sierra, M.A. 592-6254

TAKILMA COMMON GROUND
POB 2016
CAVE JUNCTION, OR. 97523

TAKILMA Comm☯nGround

"NEW" Tee Shirt available

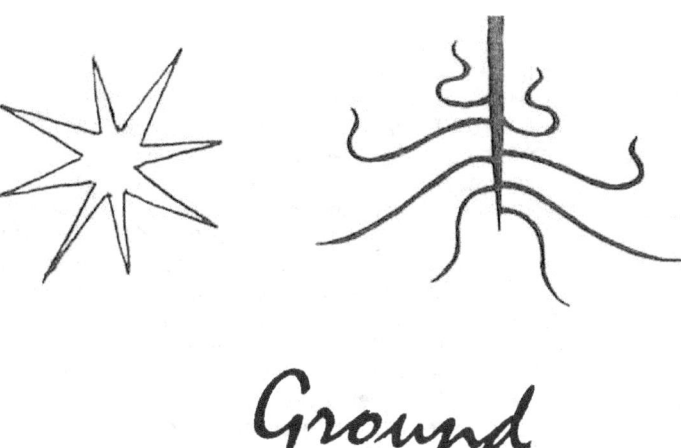

Common
Takilma
Ground

JULY · AUGUST · 1995 ✳ INDEPENDENCE AND FREEDOM ISSUE ✳ NUMBER 12

ISN'T IT TIME TO C.A.R.E. ?

Last April, the Illinois Valley Human Rights Alliance(IVHRA) invited Floyd Cochran, former White Aryan Nations leader, to speak out against racial hatred in our public schools. A white supremacist organization based in Idaho, the Aryan Nations' goal is simple: to rid the world of people of color and non Christians. Last spring, White Aryan Nation recruitment flyers began appearing in Cave Junction and in Lorna Byrne and I.V. High.

While the presence of the Aryan Nations in our community is surprising, far more shocking has been the response of our public school district. Josephine County was the first District in the nation to ban Cochran's message from our county schools. When asked why Cochran's anti-hate message was censured from the schools, head honcho Carol Ricotta said "it's not fair to impose this on students who might not want that information."

While the Cochran issue has subsided for now, many in the community are left pondering how Cochran's message against the Aryan Nations could ever be construed as "controversial." A more comprehensive look at District policies on various issues reveals some interesting patterns.

In a recent presentation by the the Josephine County AIDS Support and Prevention (ASAP) program, Sabrina Clanton expressed her frustrations with the school district. According to Ms. Clanton, AIDS appears to be growing at epidemic rates in southern Oregon. While AIDS was virtually nonexistent in the area five years ago, she now estimates 1 out of 168 people in Jackson County are HIV positive. Yet, in a survey of Josephine County high school students conducted by ASAP, 80% of females responded that their partners refused to use condoms. Apparently, many of the students don't seem to feel that AIDS is a real threat in our community.

The urgent need for AIDS education is clear to the ASAP. However, getting the information to the kids in school has not been easy. Like the anti-hate message, AIDS education is often deemed "too controversial" by the District. Ms. Clanton points out "it's kind of difficult when we aren't even allowed to say the word penis in some of the high schools!"

CONTINUED ON PAGE 2

SPIRIT WALK FOR SUGARLOAF
WALK FOR THE WILD SISKIYOUS

Come join us for the third annual Walk for the Wild Siskiyou, Spirit Walk for Sugarloaf. After a Thursday campout at Sugarloaf, this interdenominational, 46 mile peace and prayer walk will begin on Grayback Mountain (above the Oregon Caves) at the sacred site on Friday morning, July 14. Walkers will bring the message of this sacred place to Boise Cascade's Medford mill.

Support vehicles will follow the walk for those who are unable to hoof it the full 15 mile daily distance. Dinner and camp space will be provided by people in Williams, Ruch, Jacksonville and Medford.

Walkers will hike for three days, arriving near Medford on Sunday, July 16. There will be a chance to join the walkers for the last three miles, a walk through downtown Medford, on Monday morning, July 17. Meet at 9 A.M. at Alba Park.

At the mill we will join Agnes Baker Pilgrim, surviving elder of the indigenous Takelma people. Together we will tell Boise Cascade that we must protect this sacred place.

In the spirit of non-violence, please do not bring drugs, alcohol or weapons.

YOUR HELP IS NEEDED! If you can contribute food, first aid, tents or other supplies, your time, energy , money, or if you would like to sponsor or register for this event please contact us! Checks should be made out to the League of Wilderness Defenders, and are tax-deductible.

Debbie (503)592-3386 or Marjorie 592-6733
Spirit Walk for Sugarloaf
P.O. Box 2093
Cave Junction, OR 97523
siskiyou@igc.apc.org

Freedom only for the supporters of the government——only for the members of one party, however numerous they may be——is no freedom at all. Freedom is always and exclusively for one who thinks differently.
Rosa Luxemburg, The Russian Revolution (1918)

108

CARE   (Continued from page 1)

Similar horror stories are heard from the Reduced Adolescent Pregnancy Project(RAPP). RAPP was born out of the need to address an epidemic of teen age pregnancy in our community. Unfortunately, RAPPs' attempts to to get comprehensive sex education into our schools have been stymied by administrators who fear the potential for "controversy." This is especially disturbing since high pregnancy rates are a strong indicator of the potential spread of AIDS.

Recently, RAPP received a grant to bring a young HIV positive speaker to IV High. Students have expressed the need to hear about the dangers of AIDS from their peers. When approached about the project, a District official said that this is a "sensitive issue" and that even though AIDS education is mandated by Oregon law, " Josephine County does not always follow recommendations by the state." RAPP remains hopeful that the project will not be blocked by the Distrtict.

Sex education in our high schools remains in the Dark Ages with reproductive charts of vas deferens and uterus linings. Sex relations topics that could, for example, empower young women in their relationships are rejected as "too controverisal." So what is keeeping our schools in the dark? Why are these important issues kept from our childrens' ears?

According to the Ricotta regime it's because " our parents have made it clear that they want (just) the basics taught in the public schools." For those of us confused by the source of "controversy", this is a truly enlightening statement. "Our parents" refers to a vocal minority of parents in the county who want public education minimized to the 3Rs: Readin', Ritin', and 'Rithmetic. Eventually, perhaps public education would give way to private church-related schools. It's no accident that the last school levy failed. It appears the Ricotta regime has aligned itself with the very people who oppose the public education system she was hired to protect.

Today, those who oppose a well-rounded curriculum in our schools are in control. It is not because they are a majority. Quite simply, they are organized, active, and effective. The time is ripe for advocates of quality public education to stand up and be heard. This is the intent behind the formation of The Citizens Advocates for Real Education (CARE), now forming in Josephine County.

CARE will push for passage of a school bond that reflects the priorities of parents throughout the community. CARE will work to impress upon our school Board members the need for a well-rounded education. Our youth need preparation for the 21st century, not the 18th! Advocating free, quality education for all children, CARE should be a natural ally of any school district. Our success will depend on support from throughout the county, including Takilma.

Without the voice of Takilma, positive change in our valley and throughout the county is a much steeper hill to climb. Isn't it time the spirit of Takilma was felt in our community and in the halls of our schools?

Support does NOT mean big time commitments. It just means you CARE. For more info please call 592-3908 .
    - Dave Toler

CENSORSHIP AT IVHS

One of the most prominent aspects of censorship at IVHS that I have noticed is the continuous denial or lack of acknowledgement of the teen pregnancy rate. At a recent meeting of the "Pride Group", a group primarily focused on discussion of any problems arising at our school, it was addressed that the two most pertinent problems at our school are that of drug use and weapons, with no regard to teen pregnancy. It is true that those are problems in our school, more so in other more populated schools, but the issue of teen pregnancy was not even mentioned until a concerned member of the Pride Group questioned its status.

A recent survey conducted by RAPP (Reducing Adolescent Pregnancy Project), has shown that IVHS has one of the highest pregnancy rates in the county. It makes one wonder why we should be having this problem. After all, we were one of the first schools to provide students with a student-based healthcare center and an on-campus daycare center. The daycare center was established first and logic would suggest that if you provide something for the consequences of pregnancy, you would also provide something for prevention.

But that must not be acceptable at IV High, because approximately one and a half years ago, before the healthcare center was put in, Mrs. Hoback emphatically stated that condoms would not be distributed on campus. She said they would be available within close access to campus, but that was never made very evident since no one knows their whereabouts.

It is probably widely known, but supposedly classified information, that Mrs. Hoback also receives four thousand dollars per pregnant girl. The four thousand is not for everyone either. Programs such as band and choir receive very little money or support. You would think that with that kind of income, more could be spared for other programs. I guess the moral here is, if you are irresponsible you receive more support and money than if you aren't. Either way you get screwed. - Jackie Parker

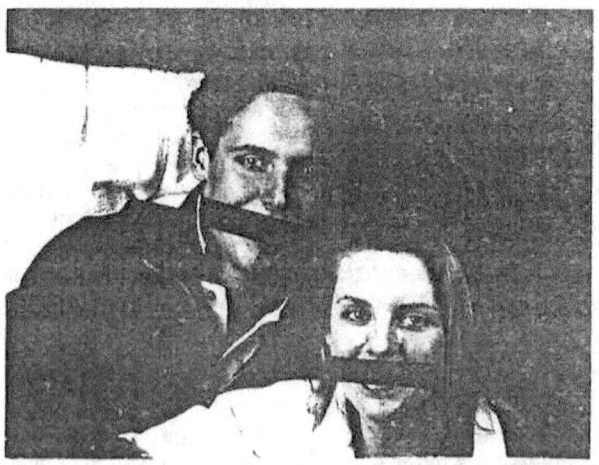

Men would rather be starving and free than fed and in bonds. - Pearl Buck, What America Means to Me (1943)

FREEDOM OF MOVEMENT

Exploring the notion of freedom inevitably leads me to the vast possibilities of the open road. A highway traversing shadowy Rocky Mountains, back roads through red sandstone monoliths reverberating wishes from above, the exuber-ant cluttered streets of New York City, even the miniature replica from an airplane window. This is freedom of movement, a form of independence from place, a belief in transcendence and the glory of escape. The fact that anything is possible, any location reachable, that we CAN get there from here.

And today, more than ever, we can get there quickly. The world has become increasingly smaller as new inventions change our relation to distance. We can cough and sputter at cars and buses, professing their evils to our almighty conscience, but we can no longer deny their impact. Roads scrawl across the American landscape, offering refuge or intriguing adventures to those simply bold enough to begin. Turn the key, follow your senses, search for mysteries still unsolved, explore cultural differences that exist from region to region. Discover a new world around every bend. Or we can fly. I can only admit, with environmental disgrace, that planes have brought the world closer to my door. What was once foreign and distantly separate is now simply a short flight away. A day in the air, with a relaxing drink and movie, and we transfer to the other side of the world. Visit Asia, Australia, Africa or exotic islands at any time of the day, on command from the random demands of our will.

America is naturally accomodating to travel. Many native American cultures were/are dependent on migration for survival and identity. This is not a new freedom, nor a luxury of excess, but a new means to rekindle important experience. Despite a fringe of vagabond hippies and seniors spending their children's inheritance in souped up RV's, much of mainstream American culture has become so rooted as to deny itself migration, the two week sunny vacation a poor substitute. We must see the opportunities that now exist. Migrate with the birds from season to season, challenge our rooted possessiveness, open ourselves to new cultures and their interpretations of this world. The freedom of movement teaches flexibility, adaptation and cultural understanding by offering a view of ourselves. Our own values lose their root and become easier to examine. Yank the rug from below and watch the feet dance.

We know this exists, but we temper our desires for this freedom with an understanding of community. In Takilma we treasure our community, our shared togetherness that affords security for the confident, expressive individual. How can we maintain our connections with increased freedom of movement? Do we become a nation of wanderers, lost on separate trips that pass at high speeds? A healthy community must require commitments; improvements do not simply happen, we work together to accomplish our common goals. Can we construct social frameworks that create commitments that will ￼ w the individual the freedom of motion? This is the challenge. The solution rests in our ability to adapt, to accept our ￼ doms with an understanding of their consequences, with pledges to help bolster community locally or globally, with the assurance we can create home wherever we land, and that life is an adventure we are blessed to have stumbled upon.
  -Jon Jeans.

Dear Takilma,
  Four years ago I took to the road, winding my way from there to here, east to west, to somehow land in Takilma for a visit that has been a joyous extension. I fell in love with the river, the meadows, the trees, and our commitment to them. But ￼ I must move on. Change is natural. I want to thank all of you for making me welcome, giving me loving support, for ￼ ￼ring meals of homegrown foods, sharing your arts, talents and energies, for being my extended family. May Takilma continue to nurture its community, protect its surrounding forests, and always strive to offer our children an idylli place to grow up. This is a magical, beautiful place. I will miss it and all those who bring it to life; hope to see you again soon, dancing under the moon, with love,   - Jon Jeans

Kenaf is a short-day annual herbaceous plant originating in Western Sudan. It may have been domesticated as early as 400 B.C. Russian varieties grow well in northern latitudes. An intensive research program on kenaf was initiated by the U.S. Department of Agriculture (USDA), which presently funds kenaf research.

The kenaf plant has a wide range of adaptation to climate. It grows well and produces high fiber yields when grown on a wide range of soils. The principal requirement is that the soil has good drainage. Kenaf will thrive in dry climates for it needs little water.

Kenaf is safe for the environment (no pesticides or herbicides are needed), and can be grown organically.

Processing trees into paper releases dioxins causing air and water pollution. No chemicals are needed in the manufacture of kenaf paper. One acre of kenaf will yield 7-9 tons of paper pulp with a net worth of $3,500. That is four times as much paper pulp per acre as one acre of fifty year old trees. Kenaf paper is stronger and can be recycled 4-5 times more than tree paper pulp.

The woody core is ground and pressed to make fiber board superior to that of trees. The chips can be used for livestock bedding or mulch for the garden. Kenaf is composted to make ethanol and other clean burning bio-mass fuels. The protein-rich leaves and shoots can be harvested early for livestock feed, and the kenaf will still grow enough to harvest again for fiber and cellulose. Even fertilizer is made from kenaf.

Plastic bags, cellophane wrap and complex polymers are made out of the plant's core. Composite plastics made from kenaf are fire resistant, shock absorbent and stronger than steel. Spray-on insulation made from kenaf is fire resistant. Polyester-like plastic yarns are made into 'non-woven' spray-on mats which are used to stop soil erosion and are completely bio-degradable.

Kenaf's fiber is used to make woven products such as rope, cloth and baskets. The plant grows up to 18 feet tall and will make a perfect wind barrier.

With all the known uses for kenaf, there should be a market. Instead, the USDA continues to subsidize and stockpile corn for export. Why not make fuel out of surplus crops?

The American Petroleum Institute and the National Petroleum Refiners Association challenged the EPA requirement to use ethanol as oxygenate in fuel. As a result, petroleum suppliers can add a petroleum based methanol derivative (MTBE) instead of ethanol. When burned, MTBE releases carbon dioxide that plants and trees cannot convert into oxygen, thus adding to global warming.

Kenaf could solve many problems related to deforestation and pollution. The environmental community can work with the timber industry to find solutions everyone can accept. We are sending kenaf information and seeds to timber corporations and environmental organizations to generate interest in this commercial cash crop.

For information and seeds, write to TEST (Try Environmental Solutions Together), PO Box 545, Cave Junction, OR 97523.

-Aaron Isenagle

Hello fellow tree planters, environmentalists, and people who care for our Mother Earth:

This letter is a kickoff for a new fundraiser. The Tree Planter's statue is dedicated to the people of a profession which is very important to the future of Mother Earth and our childrens' childrens' survival. Tree planters are widely unrecognized by the majority of our nation's people.

This statue will be a tribute to these people of such great physical and spiritual strength who have worked in all types of weather and terrain from predawn to dusk. Quietly, rhythmically, they have worked, trying to heal the Mother Earth's cuts, scars and gouges.

We owe great gratitude and thanks to these early environmentalists of the '40s and '50s and to the counterculture (as we were labelled) of the '60s, '70s and '80s. Planting side by side, men and women who cared for the earth did this positive and arduous labor for a living. And thanks to the growing number of Hispanics planting trees in a trade of work and cultural exchange.

Thanks to ALL who plant a tree. Think if all the population planted a tree on the same day. Think of the multiplied understanding of positive and thoughtful energy, of giving back to the very life Mother Earth has given us and all creatures, the life from the beginning.

Walk softly- listen to the trees. Sing and listen to them scream. Drum for the trees.

- Wayne FitzPatrick

P.S. Donations and ideas welcomed. Please call (592-2286) after July 1st. I very much regret not being at the Tree Planter's Reunion. My only excuse is that I'm on a planting contract; 420,000 trees in Flathead National Forest in Montana, or 400 acres in John Day, Oregon, or in Wyoming for a mere 28,000 tree job. Thank you for your support.

Dear Takilma community:

What a wonderful gift we were given when Takilma got its own safe bike path! Few communities have anything like this sheltered path we negotiated for in the aftermath of the Longwood fire so our kids could be safe from logging trucks. Now this much-used haven for joggers, horse riders and even bikes is neglected-it's overgrown and littered and really needs maintenance . Come on folks, let's get together and take care of it- or chip in money and pay our teenagers to do it. We can keep our kids busy and help our community too. Think about it- it's for all of us!

- Mike Meidinger

GARDENING TIPS FROM THE MAGIC FOREST FARM

We cannot overemphasize the importance of daily communication with one's potatoes. Encourage! Eight to ten inches of mulch will also help. Corn plantings can continue through the 20th of July; plant every ten days and be patient and hopeful. Over-wintering carrots can be planted before the 15th of July. Sand can be added to dense soil to offer improved mobility. Beware, though; once sand is added it cannot be removed. Carrot seed beds MUST be kept moist. Try planting in a few inches of sawdust to retain moisture. Fall and winter greens can also be planted around the 15th of July. Kale, rutabagas, chard, beets and your own favorites can be planted directly in the soil. Cabbage, broccoli and cauliflower can be started in flats in a greenhouse by the 15th of July. They can be transplanted out when mature enough, any time after the 1st of August. Shady spots in the garden may be ideal, depending on the heat. On August 1st, fall lettuce and spinach rotations may begin. Keep moist and plant new plantings every ten days.

With the August heat arrives the harvest. Enjoy to its fullest, try new recipes, invite friends over to dinner, arrive for dinner at a gardening friend's home, eat outside, trade veggies. But don't forget..... harvest the garlic before it goes to seed; August 1st often works for us. Prepare your garden beds for the winter by continuing the hardworking shit runs, planting cover crops in late August (early? Try buckwheat). If possible, prepare a cold frame for fall lettuce and spinach. Keep up the backbreaking weeding where needed, jump in the river for survival and don't forget to enjoy the flowers. -Mr.Potatohead

Dear Common Grounders-

I read with pleasure about the TCA riverbed clean-up, and spent some time waxing nostalgic, remembering the first winter I spent in Takilma-'69-70- with the Mirage Garage/River Rats crew: J.D. and April (who remembers the Mayflower?), Joyce and Charlie Two-shoes, Scorpio Karen, Jack Quinn, Suzy Creamcheese, Mary and Randy Hughes, T. Nicholas...we spent a lot of time that winter gathering the debris left along the river by the army of passers-through during the previous summer (who came, camped for a week or a month, and went on their way, leaving their trash-and various dogs-behind) and hauling it to the dump in Delbert's truck...

It's good to know that so many of you are still there, still care, still clean up after the rest; and in thinking about this, I'm reminded of a poem written beside the river, down by the ford, some time ago, now. I've enclosed a copy-if you would, please share it.   Yours , *John Whiteside.*

FACES IN THE RIVER

Full moon passing; sensitive sister Cancer, gone in Leo's fire.
Coyote sings in it, shrieking in the cold light;
Moonbeams flickering ghosts on the river;
Memories flooding me, mirrors of the bright night
Moonlight images, shining on a dead fir.

I cannot stop this feeling of hopelessness, as I think of
All the people who have died here.
I think of how they lived,
How they learned what the earth could give,
How they grew with everything that grew around them;
How they knew about the magic in the moon by the river,

But they died at the hands of men who stole their land,
Though they tried, tried in vain.
To stop the tide that even then
Had spread too wide for them to ever live again
As they had lived- all their lives- the way of peace.

My friends, those that live here with me now, by the river,
Share much in the spirit of the ones that lived here then.
We seek to learn the ways they knew of living gently on the land;
We come to hear the river song as they do, seeking peace.

So fill us, Leo moonlight, with your fire,
That we may have the strength
to try again, as they tried then,
To teach the song of hope and freedom
That the river sings.

J.Whiteside 1976

WE'RE LATE! Did you even notice? Our intention is to print the newsletter eight times a year, at Solstices, Equinoxes and the mid-points in between. We veered from the straight and narrow this time to land in your mailbox with some thoughts on freedom and independence just in time for your barbecued tempeh burger/dead beast picnic salon. As you will have observed, most of us are already so free and independent that we don't feel bound by some old theme, and write about whatever we damn well please. We approve of this behavior.

OUR MISSION! Is to provide a forum for debate and a bulletin board for the old fashioned transmission of information. We support diversity, love art and crave humor. As far as we can tell, we honor the earth and use recycled paper.

EDITORIAL CREW for this issue: Jon(we just hate to see you go) Jeans,Dave Toler, Kayla Starr, Jill Birmingham, Dave Hocker, Mister Tracy, Marcy Tilton, Rachel Goodman, Jack Dwyer, Kerry Holman, Mirya Holman, Laurie Prouty and Felicity Elworthy, who facilitated the production. Thanks too, to Indica

SEND US A PICTURE! WRITE US A LETTER! Next submissions deadline is July 31st for publication on August 17th. Give or take a day or two.

COMMON GROUND, P.O.Box 2016, Cave Junction, OR 97523.

" 5 "

COMING TO AMERICA-
OR, IT'S A PITY ABOUT THE POOR IMMIGRANTS....

I've always been an alien; I never quite fit in.
My bible thumping parents still deplore my yen for sin.
In Iran I was a woman and a Christian (so they thought).
Any blonde in skimpy dresses is fair game for Muslim sport.
In college, I regret to say, I thought the girls were stupid.
I wore men's clothes, drank beer in pints and sneered at poor old Cupid.
And later on at Oxford, where the great tradition rules,
I hung out with only radicals and lesbians and fools.
Coming to America, us Limeys have it made:
You say five words, they think you're quaint. No problem getting laid.
I married a fanatic so I'd feel extremely sane.
I fell in love with anguished souls, to minimize my pain.
Now I'm here amongst the affluent, who seem to think I'm poor;
I pay state taxes, pick up food stamps, feel detached from urban war.
But lately I've discovered that there just might be a hitch
In this scene of disaffection, by the name of Newt Gingrich.
For though legal, I've no franchise. That's to say I cannot vote.
And to all intents and purposes this could mean I've missed the boat.
Though I do good work for Head Start and have kept my nose quite clean,
If all goes well for Newt and co., my future's looking lean.
So here is my dilemma; listen closely, I'll be brief.
In order to get citizenship, you must lie between your teeth;
Say you'll never rock the government and fight in all their wars,
That anarchists are full of shit and communists are boors.
All this to exercise the right to cast a dubious vote
And lose my precious status as a foreign anecdote?
What irony, by relinquishing my resident alien status
To also leave the cozy ranks of all those folks who hate us.
Forgive my rude ungraciousness. Accept this sad lament.
I love this country, and may join, but FUCK THE GOVERNMENT.
                    -Felicity Elworthy.

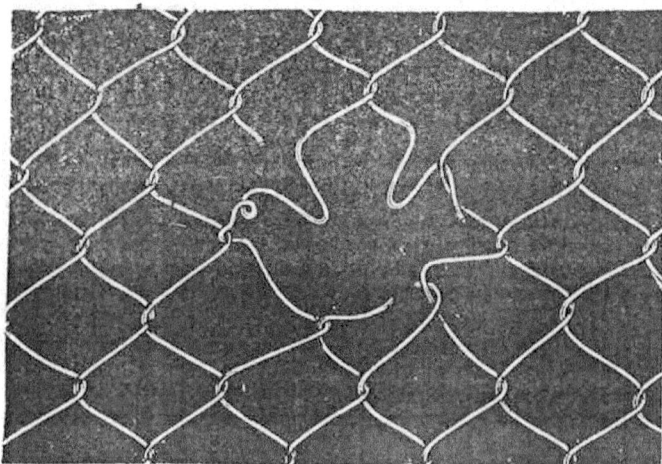

He who believes in freedom of the will, has never loved and never hated.
        -Marie von Ebner-Eschenbach, Aphorisms. (1905)

HOW TO BE FREE

here in the land
    of friendly fascism
where camo'd jack-boots
    of sex-,race-, n' classism
divide and confuse us;

where economic survival
    and commodity fetishism
salaciously seduce us;

where truth and pleasure,
    and herb and deviance
threatens an empire
    that relies on obedience.....

I pledge allegiance to the truth
    within each soul
and to real freedom
    by which it stands;
may no coercion undermine us
    incorruptible,
with courage and play-time for all.
                    --kayla

TO LUNA:

Behind a veil of misty clouds
you reach gentle fingerlings out
to entrance all that are aware.
Slowly your white light
creeps out to touch me.
Beautiful, yet so strange,
you enhance my every delight
with your atmosphere.
Stay,
radiant friend,
stay,
for you make my every worry
fade away.
Half the night I gaze upon you;
half the night I sleep under
your watchful eye.
With you no nightmare
may touch me.
No horror may wound
my memory of the darkest hour.
I sleep with no idea
of what I will awake to,
but with you it may
surprise and appease me.
Thank you for your beautiful
face that pleasantly scars
the night sky.   -Mirya Holman

The Polize Bladder

Licking boots
Grovelling like dogs
And smelling other's dresses,
Turning lezzy
Growing shrooms
And dyeing green your tresses,
Life at Common Ground is strange
Folks are getting madder
Time to lighten up our act
And resurrect the Bladder.

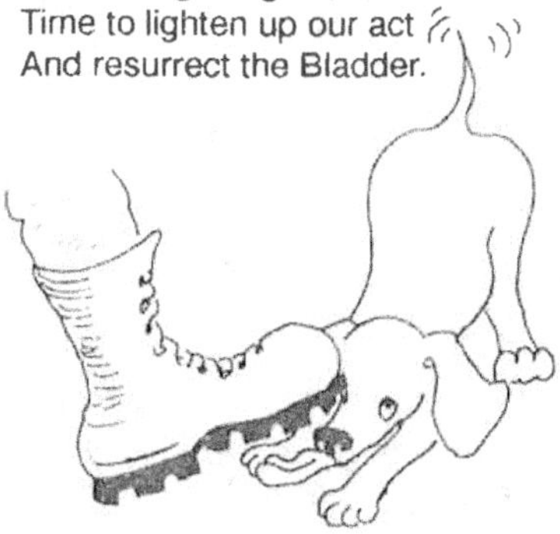

May 15-Bald Mountain hermit napalms face. Clear cut, but unscathed.
May 16-Mobile monsters march further into Takilma, leaving tick brush and local charm in ruin.
May 17-Smelly dress taken to cleaners.
May 25-What's going on with the Frickin' pool?
May 29-Naked hippies missing in Takilma.
May 30-New chef discovered at Grants Pass Probation Center. Inmates shocked at discovery of garlic.
June 1-Smelly dress owner taken to cleaners.
June 2-Stacks of unused bologna mass outside GP Probation Center.
June 8-Suffering artist Trish becomes heroine, preventing desecration of Alex' historical art work on the now defunct Head Start building.
June 9-Thin man squeezes through the flames in 9000 block of Takilma Rd.
June 14-Prisoners flee in yellow buses only to be randomly released in the valley.
June 16-Aging ex-tree planters trade tendonitis remedies, gaze tearfully through bifo cals at fading photos, dance arthritically to the Tin Apple Baroque Ensemble.
June 17-County Commissioners hypnotized by swaying tree houses before finally coming to senses.
June 18-Hippy bladder blockage at end of the road.

SPEAK OUT! FOR VALLEY FORESTS

It's summer and the heat is on. Cruisin' down Rockydale, that southern end is so nice and cool. That's BLM forest and it runs continuously from the East Fork Illinois, around the French Flat open savannah, and on to the Logan Cuts. Its tall, majestic firs are now quivering at the threat of a BLM ax. The Noreast Sale is one of the first Sales being put back on the block since the Court injunctions were lifted. Noreast may provide an indicator for things to come for other mature BLM stands around Takilma.

The Rockydale Neighborhood Assoc.(RNA) has submitted an alternate plan to the BLM proposal. RNA's plan retains recreational and ecological values compatible with providing a sustainable supply of timber product. The BLM appears stuck in the all or nothing mode. In response to our plan, the BLM has stated " you can't do everything on the same site." The Rockydale community believes we can, and knows we had better learn how.

Convincing the BLM to adopt the RNA plan will prove beneficial to future Sales in our community. We can do it with your help. If you give a damn, take 15 minutes to finish the letter below, or write your own letter. Need a copy of the RNA plan? call 592-3908. Thanks! (send copies to IV News, Courier etc!!!) -*Dave Toler*

BLM Medford Dist.
3040 Biddle Rd.
Medford, Or. 97504

Bob Korfhage;
I would like to convey my support for the Rockydale Neighborhood Association (RNA) plan for the Noreast Sale. The RNA plan advocates "compatible forestry" techniques that allow for sustainable timber production and retention of important ecological values.

The differences between the BLM proposal and the RNA plan seem clear. The BLM will be taking twice as much timber per acre as the RNA plan. While the BLM proposal will remove a significant portion of larger trees, the RNA plan will ensure that mature stands are always represented in these forests. Finally, I understand the BLM will be regenerating with shelterwoods, a watered down clear cut.

Haven't we learned to reject mismanagement of our forests? We have very little mature forests left on our valley floor. We must protect what we have and ensure that more mature stands are left to grow in the future.

Sincerely,

ANNUAL DOME SCHOOL CARNIVAL Saturday, August 19, 4:00 - 9:00p.m. This year's theme is Dr.Seuss. We'll need lots of help from community members, including kids and teens! Your ideas are welcome too. Space outside for craft and rummage booths, $5 minimum. P.O.Box 812, Cave Junction, OR 97523. SEE YOU THERE!

SISKIYOU PROJECT NEEDS your help this summer. Please help us answer the phones, file, type, do mailings, tend the grounds, etc.... No experience necessary. We will help train you on computers. Please contact Debbie Lukas or Cathy Hocker at P.O. Box 220, C.J. OR 97523, 592-4459 or siskiyou@igc.apc.org

DO YOU OWN LAND along the Illinois River or one of the tributaries? Siskiyou Project is willing to help you permanently protect the riparian area with a conservation easement. For more information call Barry at 592-4459.

THANKS TO MARY JO and Mountain People, Buying Club is back to its every two week schedule. July 3 is the next order and pickup day.

ON TUESDAY JULY 4TH the 3rd Annual Takilma Softball Challenge will take place at Out 'N' About. The first game will be the rematch between the Under 35 Potatoes and the Over 35 (and the hill) Geezers. The teams are practiced and prepared. The game will begin at 1:00. A second game will follow, its teams to be filled by those interested at the moment. Come early . . . . Stay late to dance to live music. A community affair; be there!

There are only two kinds of freedom in the world; the freedom of the rich and powerful, and the freedom of the artist and the monk who renounces possessions.
-Anais Nin, The Diary of Anais Nin, vol.3 (1939-1944)

SUBSCRIBE TO COMMON GROUND!

____ $10   1 YEAR SUBSCRIPTION   NAME   _____
____ $25   1 YEAR + COMMON GROUND T-SHIRT   ADDRESS   _____
____ $?   SEND WHAT YOU CAN .   _____
            SEND TO : TAKILMA COMMON GROUND POB 2016 CAVE JUNCTION, OR 97523

It is easy to be independent when you've got money. But to be independent when you haven't got a thing—that's the Lord's test.   - Mahalia Jackson, Movin' On Up. (1966)

Takilma Common Ground
pob 2016
Cave Junction, OR 97523

REGISTER NOW FOR FREEDOM NOW

September~ October 1995 ♥   Issue ♥ #13

RELATIONSHIP:

In this issue, Common Ground looks at relationships with our. . . selves, loved ones, Mother Earth, and . . .

With Our Community

Everywhere one goes, it seems the conversation merges into one: There is a real need for strong community if we are to effectively face some very challenging times on the not-so-distant horizon. Yes, the shit is gonna hit the fan and where will Takilma be? Have we drifted along with the rest of America in believing we can ride the storm alone, isolated in our nuclear family household?

The notion of an economic system mortally wounded by its inherent insanity need not be negative truth. A conscious community finds hope beyond such insanity and forges ahead to prepare for a much brighter future for our children.
How can we begin to build stronger community? The answers surely exist in our collective wisdom. Where do we begin?
One important place might be to define our own sense of what is right or wrong. Our community is alienated by the present "justice" system. The long arm of the law ensures the filthy rich get richer raping the earth while imprisoning those who dare to seek a decent livelihood outside the clutches of Corporate America.

A Takilma "justice council" would provide our youth a model amidst all this confusion. They need to know a set of values does exist that is important to live by. The Council would address various conflicts that arise between residents in the community. The Council could also address incidents where individuals within the community have been accused of violating laws which our community may not recognize. Perhaps in such cases the Council would play a supportive role for the individual.

Rather than the western notion of all or nothing, guilty or innocent, it seems our sense of justice would often recognize the value of compromise and mediation. With the Sheriffs Department our only recourse today, many contentious issues begging for some resolve are left simmering, further splintering our

community. A Takilma Council would provide a meaningful alternative to the Sheriffs Department that would strengthen our community. Formation of a Council is but one dimension of a stronger Takilma community.

Growing our own food, raising our children, building our homes, and providing our entertainment all take a conscious community effort. This effort can not be delegated to just a few people. Too few bodies left responsible leads to burnout and lack of support. Perhaps a community potluck meeting every month would serve as a vehicle for community building. Each month, we could recognize an individual for the community work they have done. If we are to have community, many more people will have to step up and give just a little time. Only together will we muster the strength required to face the challenges that lie ahead.

And speaking of community effort, a big thank you should be extended to Leslie for all her work in organizing the OJ EKEMODE Concért.

With Our Mother Earth

Sugarloaf Mountain

A man and woman stood here, with copper colored skin
They listened to the wind here, and to the Voice within

The Voice said
I am the Spirit of all that you see
This mountain is my Home and I guard these ancient trees
I bless you and I thank you for coming here to me
Now hear my prophecy:

Teach your children well
For you do not have much time
Barbarians are coming
They will take your people's lives
They will drive you from this forest
They will kill with guns and hunger
Only a few will survive

They will give this place a new name
They will call it Sugarloaf Mountain
And the sacred grove you stand in
Will not die
One day your children and the children
Of those who come to kill you
Will defend Sugarloaf Mountain
As one tribe

For the strength of a people, grows in the trees
The trees make the rain that cools the summer breeze
The rain is the life that sprouts the waiting seed
So the people will not hunger, they will feed.

O send your spirit to them
When they stand on Sugarloaf Mountain
Make them calm, Make them strong, Make them wise
They will stop the murder
They will end the plunder
So let their anger rise...
And let their spirits rise...
And let their courage rise!

Lindi Anne Sarno

Tree Lovers

Visit the Selma Cemetery on Lake Shore Drive 3 miles east of Hwy 199. Although the Selma area has been logged constantly over the last 150 years, the Cemetery has not. There are no stumps there. There are some beautiful large firs and the biggest Madrones I've seen anywhere. Stand back and admire the size of the firs. While you are there, go to the Northeast section of the cemetery as there are some very old and thought provoking tombstones from the mid-eighteen hundreds. There are no gates, the cemetery is open to the public.

Al Karger   2

Are We Mad??

I 've been thinking about the relationship between the destruction of the earth and our collective insanity. Our relationship with the earth has become increasingly disjointed. We have treated the earth as we've treated women, poor folks and people of color throughout history, as objects to be exploited for personal and monetary gain. The last 50 years has seen the earth being destroyed at an ever intensifying rate.

Perhaps it started with the explosion of an atomic bomb at Alamogordo, New Mexico followed by Hiroshima and Nagasaki. This past weekend marked the 50th anniversary of the Hiroshima bombing. In Grants Pass the Doctors for Disaster Preparedness annual conference featured Edward Teller, alias Dr. Strangelove, and Sam Cohen inventor of the neutron bomb, a bomb which only destroys people, not property. They were hanging out with local civil defense advocate, Art Robinson, who advocates that with enough shovels we'll all be saved. Robinson also claims there is no connection between draining the river and the near extinction of salmon and steelhead.

And why was Lew Krauss of Rough & Ready Mill there?? Does the timber industry have a plan similar to the one we had regarding the Soviets, mutually assured destruction (MAD)? They destroy the forest using a corporate welfare plan sponsored by Mark Hatfield. When there are no trees left to buy, they sue for compensation under the takings laws enacted by Congress. Once again they get the mine and we get the shaft and their workers take a permanent hike.

I recently viewed the Cascade Mountain range from the top of The Middle Sister in the Three Sisters Wilderness Area. We could see from Mt. Shasta to Mt St Helens. It was awe inspiring. However, looking west we saw the work of the Forest Service, clearcuts too numerous to count. We who live in the Siskiyous don't have to go that far from home to see the destruction. The Siskiyou National Forest is working to destroy what's left of our forest under the guise of forest health.

Which brings up an interesting question, does the neutron bomb kill forests too? If not, you could say that Sugarloaf would be better off in the hands of Cohen than the forest service. Speaking of Sugarloaf, do the words forest health, salvage logging, and regenerative harvests remind you of the nuclear double-talk such as mutually assured destruction and a survivable nuclear war? How did these old growth forests survive without us?

There must be a close correlation between our detachment from the earth and the increasing craziness we see in the news. I have lived most of the last 50 years. I have listened to most of the rhetoric the polluting, earth killing, people degrading, leaders of government and industry have spewed in the name of the all mighty dollar bill. I refused to join the collective insanity. -My relationship with friends and family continues to get me through the hard times. I worry, not for myself, but for the children who will have to clean up or live in the mess our society has made. What will there relationship to the earth be in the future if the air isn't fit to breath and the water isn't fit to drink?

Barry

With Our Significant Others

Geezers

Your beautiful, grown up successful daughter will never make you feel as old as your own personal geezer. Don't deny it, our life partners, husbands, old men, significant others, have rounded the bend. Long in the tooth, as we say at the barn. They come in all shapes, sizes, and dispositions; geezers none the less. Hippie geezers, by far my favs, way-gone vitamin junkies. One more "the benefits of organic ginkgo biloba gold by the pound, versus, ginkgo bilboa extract, or take your multiple before, after, during meals." I especially hate the way they borrow one another's reading glasses, everywhere, bars, restaurants. "Check out those heart-healthy specials Mike." "Pass the specs, and I just will."

Geezer bikers. These guys come in two categories. Blue collar, Hondas, with matching helmet. Or the doctor, pediatrics, real estate lawyers from Las Vegas. They own Harleys and BMW's that they cart around in the back of their really fine vintage pickups, usually to campgrounds with full hook-ups. Golf geezers, these same gentlemen used to refer to golfers in terms we reserve today for child molesters. Bicycle geezers, big seats with 20,000 pound springs, flat terrain only please..

Geezer sex, it's been so long since there was somebody else, who can remember anyone but wifey These guys never say die, but we are talking the ultimate in safe sex here. He insists all the really fine women desire him because, well, damn, you still like me sweetheart so there ya go. Besides, everyone knows the only people gettin' any are married people. Obviously he hasn't been to a singles bar in at least a decade.

Geezer music, gads if Jimmy Hendrix had lived we would have had to suffer him un-plugged too. Geezer babes, they really do like us, so grateful too. Such sweet liars, "you look terrific, gray hair is so becoming," just another laugh line, honey. They like that we're older too, security in numbers.

Gay geezers, these guys get no respect, just ask them; or better to save your time, don't ask. And of course all they want is a life mate, but would settle for a boy toy in a heart beat. Childless geezers, they can do a much better job raising your children than you ever dreamed possible, but not now thanks. Geezers poker. I swear the same $100 has gone from house to house. for years, same good fellows, same $100. At my house you overhear "Damn women, half the money and all the pussy, hardy har har."

Fashionably dressed geezers have all moved on to the "relaxed fit jean." They still have a 32 inch waist and I'm still a size 9. New Age Geezers, still trying to find themselves, still can't find their ass with both hands. Hot rod geezers, these men are always named Mike, and are usually fire chiefs in small towns.

My mother's generation either divorced these guys by now, and got it all, or, out-lived them, got it all and his best friend. These gentlemen are lovingly referred to as geezer number two. Not my luckless generation, they'll be here after dirt's gone, when Hootie and the Blowfish are singing Sinatra. Thank god, security in numbers. —Geraldine

---

We're still tardy but gradually we're returning to our Pagan time frame. With luck, the next issue will be out fall equinox. The next theme will be **alternative health with** Rachel Goodman as facilitator. Our Mission is to provide a forum for debate and information. We support diversity, honor the Earth and cause trouble whenever possible.

We encourage, actually beg, for your submissions by September 13. New energy will be greatly appreciated for graphics, production or facilitation. Volunteer NOW..

Graphics: Cathy H, Jill, Claire.
Production: Barry - *Dave Toler*
Facilitator: Dave T

Breaking the Mold

My Mum and Dad celebrated their Golden wedding anniversary this year. In an atmosphere approaching gaiety, friends and relations whom I hadn't seen for decades listened to my father announce that he wasn't going to deceive them, and that he and my mother had in fact exchanged some cross words during the preceding half century. In my family this sort of admission amounts to searing honesty. He also stated that nothing less than the grace of God had kept them together, which was the unquestioning belief of almost everyone in the room. My brother Paul and I were impressed by his candor though hardened to the ubiquitous kow-towing to Almighty God. Paul responded to Dad's frankness by congratulating our parents on their forbearance and observing, not without relief, that neither he nor I were likely to achieve this Olympic pinnacle of marital tenacity ourselves. He is a few years into his second marriage, and pushing fifty, while I am a veteran of three long-ish episodes of serial monogamy, now single, and my lover is a woman.

I had some complicated feelings during the bash. My parents have a stoic frame of reference and personify all the best and worst qualities of the Puritan work ethic. Their fidelity to each other is beyond question, as are a good many other things in their house. That they love their offspring is equally evident, and I thank them for this. I know enough to realize that you can't take love for granted, and even parental love is not guaranteed. I can honor their achievement as well as remember the seamy, bitter, boring side of their life together. Thinking about the long years of their marriage makes me feel bone tired. That they stuck it out long enough to have this jolly party with graying aunts and fat cousins and great-uncles in open-necked shirts, dancing country dances they haven't attempted since they were bony kids in primary school, -this makes me heart-happy. Out of 70 people in the room, only my brother and I and our cousin Rowena have been divorced. My mother's friend Pat bends towards me as she says good-bye; "I hope you find a good man for your boys, dear.," nodding sagely and looking concerned. Her husband is tall and beige with large, careful teeth. He looks like a lobotomized Bugs Bunny and I feel weary and misunderstood and amused.

The bosom of my family is not the only palace in the world here I don't feel as if people are seeing me in focus. The Christian Right doesn't have a corner on the market when it comes to judging relationships. Our culture's bias towards heterosexual, long-term relationships is not just a mainstream preoccupation. There is subtle tendency in most of us to view the lifelong mating of a man and a woman as the acme of a personal quest for love and stability and growth. I am getting ready to challenge this assumption and have to start with myself.

Trying to heal one of those under-the-bridge relationships, I went to a therapist and she said "All relationships are an accommodation." She said it twice, slowly, casually, and some diligent section of my psyche has since devoted itself to weighing up the pros and cons of every relationship I've ever been in, and each one I consider entering into. I no longer view this behavior as callous and self-serving, but as a necessary step in safeguarding my relationship to me. The same woman once asked me to describe my Ideal Relationship. What came out was an

impassioned thumbnail sketch of every romantic arrangement of soul mates from Heloise and Abelard to Popeye and Olive Oyl, whose union may not qualify as soulful, but is certainly intense and durable. There is such a burden of unconscious yearning attached to my dream of what a marriage could be that every time I get involved in one it inevitably founders under the weight of it own sail. Add to this a growing belief that men and women are indeed from two different cultures, and might do well to learn and respect each other's language and customs instead of trying to merge, and you can see I might be ready for a change.

I've spent a big chunk of my life trying to accommodate myself to others' needs and desires so that I could get and give the relationship I wanted more than anything else in the world, but the truth of the matter is, it takes too much time, energy, unselfishness tongue-biting, late night anguish and patience to achieve, so at least for now, I quit. At least for now, I am promised to myself. I am done with pro-creation, so I do not need a mate. I have a whole village to help me raise my children. I can make a decent living all by my self, so I don't need a partner to bring home the bacon. Sometimes the joy I feel at being thus liberated from the old script, inch by mental inch, is unholy. I have loved some men deeply, and been deeply loved, but I have suffered from being stuck in a role that, for all its magnificent possibilities, no longer serves me well. There are places to go with in the framework of same-gender relationships, that may not exist for me, at present, in the well-worn groove of hetero-partnerships. I claim my right to love a woman or a man or to be alone and love my single life, or the earth that holds me, or spirit that mystifies me and for each love to be its singular self. I want my relationships with all living things to be judged by their fruits, not their forms, or duration. I don't want to be ranked on some ancient scale of values we assigned a long, long time ago when the union of the woman and the man was sacred and the longevity of the relationship might guarantee the survival of the species.

All relationships come with a built-in tutorial; each is unique and mysterious. All relationships are sacred, amazing opportunities to expand the limits of our existence, and learn how to love. We are alive at a time when the old forms are undergoing molecular rearrangement. Wish us well, Mum and Dad, and thanks for letting us go our own way. It was a great party.

Felicity

4

Defined (?)

Facing the Struggle

In our throw-away society, it comes as no surprise that so many divorces arise. When the 'issues' come up, rather than 'doing the work' the tendency is to run to the relationship 'mall' looking for a new smile, a new smell or an all together new 'version' of the problematic older version. However, in this scenario the issues inevitably rise again somewhere down the road, bringing with them more pain and frustration. Get the picture? This is not "Leave It to Beaver", where Ward and June lived their shallow, phoney existence, where the only issues were what was going to be served for dinner. This is real life folks and in reality relationship is work. Our 'culture', for lack of a better word, has many well thought out technique to push its plan of B.S. on us. Television in its perversion advertises with these techniques, and one easily sees it in its programming too. It doesn't take a PHD.. to see the dysfunctional history of Ozzie and Harriet ousehold.... (where's Ricky?) A friend mentioned that in the Sundance ceremony one is advised to dance into the pain, not towards the pole. Only through facing the pain can real growth come. Its time to wake-up and hear what the Aquarian age is so clearly whispering. Things that used to work no longer work. Things like technology and avoidance are Picean in nature and worked well in a Picean age, but that was then and this is now. Ever see fish bumping into things? Exactly! Then was being 'numb', smokin' herbs all the time, avoiding pain, dodging issues, throwing away relationships etc. etc. Whether one looks at the Mayan calendar or merely looks around our community or tribe, things are exhilarated... very exhilarated. A change and feel of unfulfillment are in the air. Transformational relationship is one of the key elements in coming to peace with-in ourselves and bringing peace to the planet.   Miguel

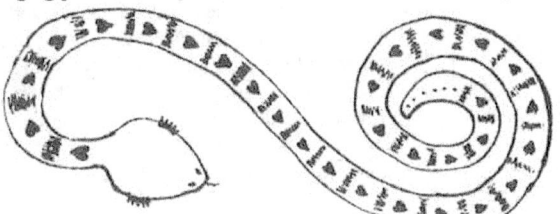

One Way to Relate

There are times when an intimate relationship needs work that may or may not be forthcoming. It may seem too hard to do; one person may not be available, or understand the other's point of view. Sometimes it feels painful to begin directly. At those times I try to remember that I am in relationship to everything, not just to our lover. I can practice love and care with a plant or a child. I can care lovingly for myself. I can pour out anger by throwing rocks in the river, feeling total anger, letting it out without abusing the person I hope to communicate with.

I have a lot of relationships. How is my relationship to my father, sister, etc. mirrored in the intimate relationship I am trying to cultivate? It may become easier to talk to the other person now that I have become more balanced in myself. Even if the communication never happens, I'll still be balanced.

Buddhist wanna-be

Relationship Puzzle

In this test, choose the answer which best completes the analogy; for instance,

nail is to hammer as screw is to --------------.
a . yew b. this c. screwdriver d. wrench

the answer would obviously be a., b., or c.

for answers to test, send SASE and $100 to :
Stupid Test
P.O. Box 2016
Cave Junction
Attn: Hugh Else

1. Woman : man :: fish: ----------
   a. bicycle b. eel c. worm d. chips
2. Cabbage : /brussel sprouts :: Bagel : -------
   a. lox b. cream cheese c. Cheerios d. toast
3. cedar : leaf :: pine : -------
   a. needle b. sol c. cone d. apple
4. dive : swim :: cook :-------
   a. compost b. eat c. burn d. vomit
5. banana : split :: balloon : -------
   a. condom b. pop c. prick d. payment
6. FBI : CIA :: TV : -------
   a. OJ b. NFL c. NPR d. OCA
7. carry : shell :: cat : ------
   a. mip b. dog c. nap d. skin
8. hip : hippie :: arm : ------
   a. army b. armoire c. armadillo d. nipple
9. yellow : submarine :: purple : ------
   a. rose b. deep c. haze d. acid
10. apples : oranges :: potatoes : -------
    a. Dan Quayle b. O'Brien c. tomatoes d. geezers

dave hocker

Revenge of the Tater Tots

On Tuesday, July 4th, the third annual game of the Ages was played on the bumpy ballfield at Out'n'About. The rubber match, the over-35 Geezers (Elders) again challenging the under-35 Tater Tots (Potatoes). The field well-trimmed, watered, beaming under the afternoon sun. Fans expectantly waiting in the shade; a scoreboard lazing under the wild rose. Hendrix's national anthem blares from dusty car speakers. Stage set.

There had been much talk over the year, the Elders still riding high after last year's victory, ruminating the ecstasy of each day's rights, Potatoes ready for revenge. Enough talk! Game begins with silent bats; 0-0 into second inning.

BUT POTATOES RALLY TO 5-0 LEAD; they would never trail. The game well played, few errors, decent hitting, the ball always kept in play by strong outfield winds. The tension building as game crept on, sun wearing holes in stamina, beer soaking the viral Potatoes.

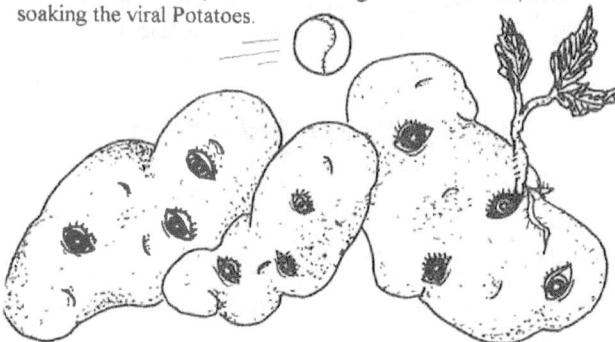

Drama: the ninth inning, the essence of baseball, the home team's last up. Down 9-7 with three outs to go. Was not the scene set for destiny? This is their town, their homeland; we but the insurgent youth reveling in, and reviling, their designs. The first two runners reach, then a single scores a run, then another; First and second no outs, tie game. Next run they win. Eric grimaces at me "Now this is pressure!" Yes indeed. Home team and home crowd joining, momentum willed, how could I have ever thought we'd win? The next hit through the infield's legs, runner coming in, the throw, runner tries to return, in a pickle, finally out at third. One out! Then line drive out to third base, two outs, runners on second and third; same exact situation as last year. Deja vu, like fried potatoes for breakfast.

The ball lofts in the air, Amy below, Potatoes clustered around, everyone expecting their private demons and desires. The ball in, then out of the mitt, but nestled safely against chest like and infant. She leaps with happiness, teeth flashing to blue skies; a moment to live by

The tenth inning hot and scoreless, again Potatoes survive Destiny's knocking. In the eleventh, Chad Meengs scores go ahead run, 10-9. Potatoes take field, Marcus tossing magic from his tired fingers. With one out, runner on first, ball hit sharply on ground to Amy, throw to me at second, out, then back to first, OUT!. Double play, game over.

Beware of flying mitts. Somehow we had been spared; perhaps destiny, just a roll of the dice. Elation and relief, handshakes and friendshakes, the ritual bring us together. The youthful potatoes escape, earning respect from their elders. Will miracles ever cease? Jon Jeans

A Diamond Jubilee 1920-1995: WOMEN WIN THE VOTE

This August 26 will celebrate the 75th anniversary of Women's Suffrage. Referred to as the Susan B. Anthony Amendment the following was certified as the 19th Amendment to the U.S. Constitution: "The right of citizens of the United States to vote shall not be denied or abridged by the United States or by any State on account of sex."

That is a seemingly simple statement but it took decades of relentless campaigning to attain ratification. Hundreds of campaigns were waged to get Legislatures to submit suffrage amendments to voters and 19 campaigns with 19 successive Congresses to get the word male out of the Constitution.

"Millions of dollars were raised, mainly in small sums and expended with economic care. Hundreds of women gave the accumulated possibilities of an entire lifetime, thousands gave years of their lives, hundreds of thousands gave constant interest and such aid as they could. It was a continuous, seemingly endless, chain of activity. Young suffragists who helped forge the last links of that chain were not born when it began, Old suffragists who forged the first links were dead when it ended...." (Carrie Chapman Catt and Nettie Rogers Shuler) Woman Suffrage and Politics 1923.

To honor those women and their accomplishments there will be a celebration on the steps of the Courthouse in Grants Pass from 10am-noon Saturday, August 26. "Blue Lightning", an all woman band will play rock, blues and country music from 8:30 to 11pm at the Dome School.. Part of the proceeds will go to benefit the Women's Crisis Support Team. To help please contact Laurie Prouty at 592-2549 or Deborah Murphy at 592-2866.

Dear editor,

Siskiyou Project announced a riparian conservation easement program in the last Common Ground with no explanation. I'd now like to explain the program. Conservation easements are voluntary agreements permanently restricting the use and\or development of property. They are often used to keep property in its current condition yet may allow for some limited development, depending on the needs of the owner and the land to be protected.

Often people want to protect their land after they die or sell it. They can put deed restrictions on the land or instructions in their will but neither can guarantee the fate of their land. Conservation easements provide a unique opportunity to protect the land because a 3rd party (such as a land trust) maintains the right to monitor the easement and enforce it if necessary. There is normally a fee charged to hold a conservation easement because they have the responsibility of monitoring and enforcing the easement forever. Problems may arise with the next owners of the property who decide they want to cut the trees or do whatever it is you decided to protect against. The enforcement fund then needs to cover the court costs to prevent the damage, or in the worst case scenario, force the restoration (if possible). The IV Watershed Council recently included $5,000. for conservation easements for the valley. We need to take advantage of the money out there to pay for monitoring and enforcement fees. Call 592-4459

Barry Snitkin

The Birds and the Bees in the 90's

by Rachel Goodman

ACROSS

1. A deception; "with" in Spanish.
3. Self-pleasure device aiding in abstinence or 24 across.
5. ...and behold!
7. Preposition.
8. National M.D.'s organization. (init.)
10. Past tense of do.
11. Officially suggested way to avoid pregnancy or disease.
12. Preposition.
14. Same as 6 down.
16. One syllable chant.
18. Rhode Island. (init.)
21. Sexually explicit art; major Internet product.
24. Dr. Elders was fired for suggesting this.
27. Teeny little (with "bit".)
28. Abbr. for N.Y. aboveground train.
29. 12-step organization for recovering alcoholics.
31. Said at marriage ceremony.
32. Magical effect, as in first stages of romance.
35. With "job," one way to create 32 across and/or seduction.
38. Pre-computer word spacer.
39. DR.
40. Forced sex; sometimes linked to 3 down.
42. Greek god of love.
44. Underwear for breasts.
47. Same as 10 across
49. (A) male sex organ not always mentioned in H.S. classes.
51. Add "safe" or just say 12 down
53. Traditional formal address for fathers or other males.
54. Microscopic squiggles restrained by condoms.
55. Those who perform 24 across are these, in Judaical-Christian tradition.

DOWN

1. Teenage balloons; latex barrier device.
2. Preposition.
3. Friendly rendezvous or prelude to?
4. Victims of coat-hanger abortions have done this.
5. Tell an untruth; 1 across.
6. Lethal result of unpredictable drug combination.
8. Surgical embryo removal.
9. Not Miss or Mrs.
10. U.S. capitol city; with "and" part or 8 down.
11. Preposition.
12. Just say ---.
15. Preposition.
17. First sound babies call parent.
19. Contraceptive device.
20. Ward of hospital where future Moms are found.
21. Oral Contraceptive.
22. Sound of pleasure, perhaps during sexual encounter.
23. Init. of gene ingredient or local neighborhood organization.
25. Preventable with condoms (initials)
26. Persons between ages 13-19.
30. Major lethal S.T.D.
33. Diaper soaking liquid.
34. Small people possibly overproduced by Or. teens.
36. Sexual release (but is unnecessary to make 34 down.)
37. Sound made by unhappy 34 down.
39. Women with a child are called this.
41. Those exerting pressure on teens and others
42. Hesitations in speech.
43. CD--M
45. ___-837, morning-after pill.
46. Heavy wood cutting tool.
50. With r2 =3.14, geometry formula. (Gk. letter)
52. _____ e _____, bygone significant others.

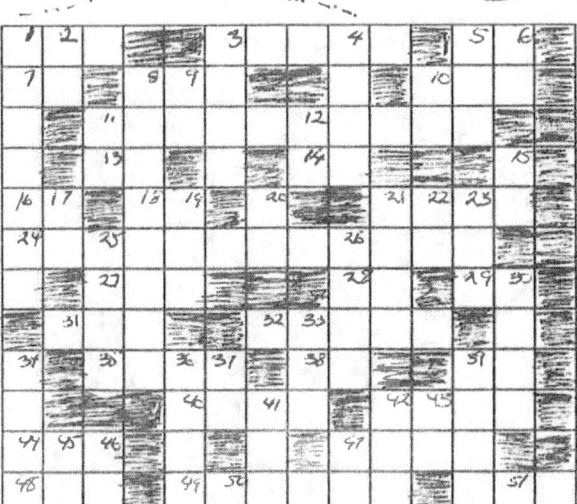

Ten Tips for a Trouble-Free Lifestyle

1. Right is tight; left is loose, except
2. Propane bottles have left-hand threads (so do toilet handles, Ford Courier lug-nuts, and New York City subway light bulbs)
3. Shit flows downhill
4. Stovepipe should be installed male end down
5. Clean your flue twice a year
6. Might as well check your gutters while you're on the roof
7. If you don't understand electricity, don't even try to work on it
8. Smoke detectors save lives and indicate when dinner is ready
9. Poly pipe sucks
10. Your sprinkler isn't broken; it just has a rock jammed in it

Dave Hocker

Classifieds

Quality, Interactive child care by Ananda. call 592-3908

The Dome School has openings available in Kindergarten, to begin in September. Ages acceptable are 4-6 years. 592-3911 or 592-3632

Anyone wanting to donate raffle prizes to the Dome School Carnival raffle, please call Helen at 592-2327 or Susan at 592-3632. Thank you. Carnival will be Saturday, August 19 4-9 pm.

BIRTHDAY CAKES for any number, any diet. Kate 592-2214

Garden & Yardwork my Speciality. I follow directions well and I am able to assist in other projects. Al Karger 597-2205

Wanted- House to rent within a 15 mile radius of the Dome School. Please call Heidi at 592-2123

WANTED: Feet for Reflexology. Let us touch your soles to relieve stress and tension. First two sessions at introductory rate $5.00 Diane 592-3908 Mar 592-4436

KATE'S BAKERY ON WHEELS is back for Fall! Do you wish to be added to the route? Call with address/directions and for info on delivery days and geographical limits. 592-2214

WANTED: single bed in good condition. Used garage door and automatic opener for sale. Call 592-2693.

Return of the **Naked Lunch** at the Green Bridge. Noon thirty on Aug. 30. *Be there!*

Community Building Addition

The new addition should be complete and ready to move into by September. The sources of funding were as follows:

$4,000   The Carpenter Foundation of Medford (Thank you Oshana, for writing the grant.)

$3,728   Donations- from our immediate community, as well as the larger community from as far away as New York and Florida. This includes money donated in memory of Amethyst Schaefer, a former student.

$4,565   Community fundraisers- including Cave of the 9 Cats, Stickmen dance, Artis snack bar, Le Show '95 and marimbas snack bar.

$617   Dome School

$100   Western Bank

$3,500   Ben B. Cheney Foundation of Tacoma, WA (Thanks _____ again, Oshana.)

$16,510 Total

We estimate that there has been approximately $5,000 worth of donated labor on this project. Many thanks to everyone.
Susan

The community photo will be availabale at the Dome School Carnival !!

Takilma Common Ground
P.O. Box 2016
Cave Junction OR 97523

Bulk Rate
U.S. Postage
PAID
Cave Junction
Oregon 97523
Permit # 16

Takilma

Common Ground

Sept.- Oct. 1995   *Alternative Healing*   Issue #14

A FOCUS ON ALTERNATIVE HEALTH CARE

In this fall Equinox issue, just in time for winter sneezes, Common Ground focuses on alternative health care. From a cup of herbal tea to complex discussions of mind, body, and soul, alternative health care is not a new topic, but currently it's a hot one. It's worth remembering that the medicine now called alternative is actually traditional, with documented roots reaching into human antiquity. The changeover to a treatment system basic on antibiotics, immunizations and technological equipment is quite recent, basically beginning in the 20th century. Traditional methods, never entirely forgotten, are now in an exciting renaissance, with new research to prove their validity. Alternative and modern methods have tended to lead parallel and sometimes antagonistic lives. One article explores the new partnership that is beginning to emerge between these sometimes very different concepts of health care. After you read on, you may wonder how any alliance at all is possible- but you wanted your thinking stimulated, didn't you? Maybe that's why you read Common Ground...

Divisiveness, is, of course, not limited to issues of health care. Racism has a long history in Josephine County. Following the health articles, the community section covers a recent painful racist episode in need of healing.

Response to this issues's topic has been fantastic and exciting. Sit back, sip your favorite comforting brew, and read on...

HEALTH CARE AND HEALING

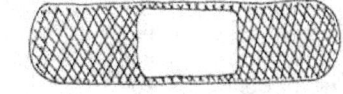

My last two years have been an odessey of total immersion in the study of our miraculous bodies and the multiple philosophies of assisting the healing process. During my Physician's Assistant Program I was honored with the op- portunity to intern at the Warm Springs Reserva- tion in Central Oregon. Connecting with the cul- ture and the individuals there was one of those peak life experiences that change you forever. One theme underlies these people's philoso- phy: we are not isolated single beings. Health is the harmonious balance of life's condition. Agnes Pilgrim advised me to, "Remind them of the right order of things. Spirit comes first, then mind, and then body..." On the Reservation, the chal- lenge is much the same as we all face... how do we achieve a balance between our appreciation of the spiritual chal- lenge of dis-ease and the highly scien- tific technological approach to medicine in the nineties? Days I worked with state of the art computerized diagnostics, lab x-ray and research statistics. Nights I prayed in the sweat lodge and pulsed with heartbeat drummings.

I've worked with dozens of practi- tioners and seen as many solutions of- fered for the same problem. Medicine is truly an ART, a creative blend of theoreti- cal knowledge, experience and intuition, ap- plied to unique situations with sometimes unpredictable results. To label one approach as "conventional" (and therefore toxic, tech- nical, impersonal) or "alternative" (and therefore harmless, natural, wholistic) does a disservice to our individualized needs. Our bodies are an intri- cate blend of genetics, environment, daily habits, spiri- tual and mental health. We each have our own personal response to injury, illness, medications and treatment. Each therapy may assist the healing process, but we are each responsible for our own healing.   *CONTINUED PAGE 2*

CONTINUED PAGE 2

124

HEALTHCARE From page 1   My recent AMA approved education focused wholistically on the personal, social, emotional and spiritual needs of our patients as well as physical symptoms and medical history. It is established knowledge in the medical world that 80% of all clinic visits have stress-related causes. With no release of the stress's fight or flight energy, our hearts overwork, blood pressure rises, body chemistry and hormones change, muscles tense and the immune system slows. This altered state is an opportunity to slow down, reevaluate. What is happening here? Each state of dis-ease offers a potential for learning about ourselves.

At each moment, millions of miracles inside us give us our existence. Consider this illusion of dense matter, molecules of carbon and hydrogen, really atoms of spinning, orbiting twinkles of electricity, marvelously arranged to look and act like us. We are plumbing, electrical wiring, cables and pulleys, at the same time that we are emotional, loving and learning soulful spirit beings, awkwardly bumping and delicately dancing with each other through this life.

Though we are all unique, I do suggest one cure-all remedy. It is harmless, non-toxic, totally natural with proven benefits. Whether you see physical, mental, or spiritual pain, reach out to your fellow human creature. We each possess the potential for healing through the gift of a touch, a listening ear, a comforting word, a bowl of soup. The laying on of hands works. We're all here together in this journey through our bodies. It takes a whole community to raise each one of us.
    -Sue Terran

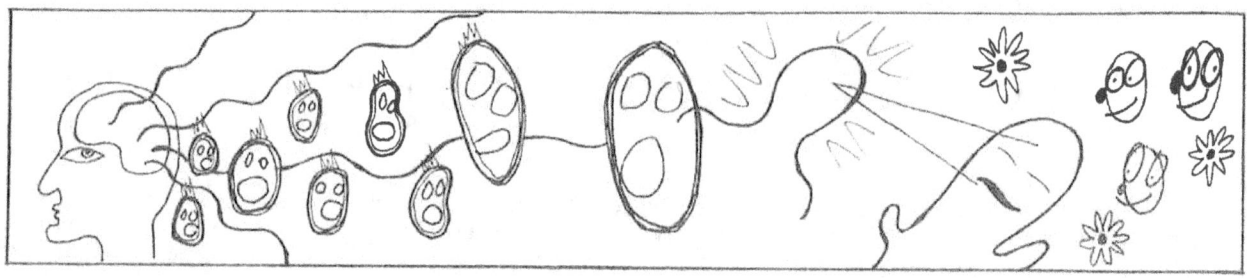

MIND/BODY CONNECTION

Darn, i missed the deadline on the last issue. Relationships, now there's a subject close to my heart. Imagine my delight when i realized i could still write about a powerful relationship, the one between mind and body.

Being in the healing profession for 20 years, observing and helping everywhere from nursing homes to rock concerts, i believe we can and do make choices about ourbodies and how they behave. Many well known healers; Louise Hay, Bernie Siegel, and Deepak Chopra are all visionaries in this type of thinking.The combination of good genetics, a healthy life style, quality diet, and regular exercise are extremely vital; however, what about the power of the mind? Can it keep us healthy, restore us when a virus or bacteria attack? Will it help to shorten the duration of an illness or injury? On the flip side, does the way we choose to think and feel about ourselves create dis-ease and injury?

I know when i am stressed, overly tired, worried or sad, i need to be hypervigilant to keep myself accident and illness free. If some naughty little virus sneaks in, it's usually a time to have a chat with both the bug and my body. "OK, you can indulge for 2 or 3 days tops, then you're out of here". Let's face it, if we get a strep throat, it's probably better to take Penicillin than risk heart or kidney problems later. Allopathic medicine can be of great benefit in a myriad of ways; the same goes for homeopathy or naturopathy. When touted as the ONLY way, any avenue of healing can have grievous results.

Two year ago while in Viet Nam, I visited many hospitals along the way. I saw Western surgery being performed in one room while acupuncture treatments were being performed in another. The patients were offered a choice of herbal remedies or Western pharmaceuticals. The physicians and nurses there understand the value in keeping an open mind.

One wonderful July i was dancing with wild abandon at the Oregon Country Fair—Whoops! into a hole i stepped. My ankle twisted so badly it started to swell and turn colors immediately. My first-line treatment was ice and elevation. Soon a small child came and handed me a balloon and told my foot to get better. Then a woman sat down next to me, flung away the bag of ice, announced her physic healing abilities, and proceeded to hold both hands inches away from my foot and ankle for 30 minutes. The heat radiating from her hands was incredible. Left alone again, i replaced the slightly melted bag of ice.

No sooner did i get into whining about being hurt at the OCF when an acupuncturist asked if he could rub a healing liquid into my obviously bruised appendage. "Sure, I'll try anything. I have to work in 2 days." All this attention was amazing. To think i had to hurt myself to get it. Two days later i was working an 8 hr shift in a busy Emergency Room with only a slight limp and minimal pain!

For years I wondered which of those healing techniques was the source of my rapid recovery. Finally i decided it didn't matter, in fact it was probably the combination, each one playing its part. All the people who kindly helped me that day understood my need to heal quickly.

So, my friends, what's the point of all this? I believe that understanding how each system works and interrelates with the entire body/mind paves the way to health and wellness. It also creates a well informed consumer. As a community, we have the unique opportunity to grow old, not only with grace, but with a clear vision of remaining strong, healthy, and feisty as hell. Be Well.'   ♥ *Gloria*

2

ABOUT AYURVEDA

"With the full knowledge of who we are, we can accomplish anything. We are spirit. Life force itself. . . As a result of our misconceptions about life, we have literally squeezed ourselves into the volume of a body and the span of a lifetime. Yet, this is not who we are. We are eternal, limitless life. If we conceive of something and believe it, it becomes real."—Deepak Chopra.

It was inspiration like this, which came at critical turning points in our lives, that led us to the study of Ayurveda, mind-body healing, and meditation. What began as the pursuit of knowledge has literally changed our lives. Delving into the study of Ayurveda, we discovered that the more we learn, the more there is to learn. We offer to you this humble introduction to the vast art of Ayurveda.

Rising from the same Vedic tradition as yoga, meditation, and astrology, Ayurveda is a system of healing that came out of India 3,000-5,000 years ago. *Ved* means "knowledge", and *Ayus* means "daily living" or "longevity". So Ayurveda is the knowledge of life. It is a health care system which acknowledges that all beings come from Nature. Ayurveda recognizes that our physical well-being is directly connected with our environment, our relationships, the biological cycles of nature, and the universe and its laws.

The three main factors in the Ayurvedic system of healing are: to instill a sense of connectedness to all life; to balance the system through the integration of body, mind, spirit, and emotions; and to promote the free release of beneficial chemicals into the bloodstream through the experiences of deep relaxation, love, and faith in life itself.

Everything that exists in the universe is composed of five elements: Ether, air, fire, water, and earth. The combination of these elements form what are called *doshas.*, which govern all biological processes. Ether and air combine to form Vata dosha, responsible for all the body's activities and sensations. For example, blood circulation, breath, and the movement of thought through the mind. Fire and water comprise Pitta dosha, "that which digests things", governing all chemical and metabolic transformations. Included here is our ability to digest ideas as well as food. Water and earth unite to form Kapha dosha, "that which holds things together", giving strength, stability, and support, both physical and psychological. Together the three doshas govern all activities of life: catabolism (Vata), metabolism (Pitta), and anabolism (Kapha). A harmonious state of the three doshas creates balance or homeostasis, the foundation of good health.

Ayurvedic practitioners help you determine your unique constitutional make-up through pulse diagnosis, physical characteristics, and mental and emotional patterns. They will help you recognize imbalances and correct them through the use of counseling, massage, herbs, diet, and daily regime, including meditation, yoga, and other practices to increase the vital life force and instill a sense of connectedness to the whole of life.

Our studies have included some training in the Ayurvedic cleansing and rejuvenating treatments. These are luxurious, involved treatments using copious amounts of warm sesame oil, steam, aromas, and herbal pastes. A few examples are *Abhyanga,* a vigorous yet soothing warm oil massage designed to loosen and separate impurities from the cell structure. In *Shirodara* , a continuous stream of warm herbalized oil is poured slowly and gently across the forehead, profoundly settling and balancing the nervous system. One of the most elaborate treatments is called *pizzicilli*, which means "royal treatment." Used by the royalty of India to ensure long life and perfect health, *pizzicilli* is a two-person full body massage with a continuous stream of warm oil flowing over the body during the entire massage. For those of you who loathe the idea of so much oil, there is *Udvartana*, a massage with herbalized paste to stimulate the underlying tissues for weight reduction. Or *Swedana*, an herbalized steam bath to open the channels of the body to allow loosened impurities to move to the digestive tract for elimination. After receiving an *Abhyanga-shirodara*, Beth H. said that she felt like she had experienced pre-trauma, life before anything traumatic had ever happened. Others have had equally moving experiences.

Ayurveda recognizes that the disease process begins quietly in the body/mind and grows slowly from there. A full-blown disease does not happen overnight. Deepak said, "Every bite of food, every breath, every thought, is like laying a brick, even if we aren't aware that we are building." Our bodies are not frozen sculptures, standing still for all time. In fact, the body is more like a river, ever flowing, ever changing and renewing. In fact, the physical matter in our bodies is completely renewed every 2 years. Based on our beliefs about who we are (individually and collectively), we re-create the same version of ourselves that we had last year.

Ayurveda is a simple and graceful health care system, unfolding to the mind the laws of Nature. A wonderful complement to any other healing modality, it offers support and comfort and brings us back into balance.   *- Myrica and Mar*

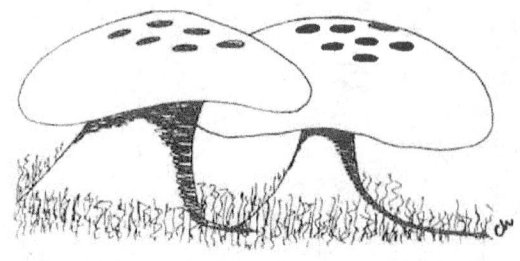

ANOTHER "MAGIC" MUSHROOM

In the Orient, several species of mushrooms have been used for centuries to maintain health, preserve youth, and increase longevity. We are finally giving acknowledgement to the potent healing properties of the legendary Maitake (My-tah-key) mushroom.

Medical research over the last twenty years has shown the Maitake, also known as *Grifola frondosa* or 'Hen of the Woods', to have an adaptogen or tonic effect on the body. Adaptogens are substances that have a balancing effect on us.

A common denominator among mushrooms and herbal adaptogens are the presence of the complex polysaccharides in their structure. These active components act as immunomodulators and have thus become a central focus of cancer and AIDS research. The polysaccharide found in Maitake has a unique structure and is one of the most powerful to be studied to date. A property of Maitake that sets it apart from other mushroom extracts being studied for anti-tumor activity is its ability to remain active when consumed orally.

Once again we are back to food as a medicine. It is both a delicious and beautiful mushroom. The Maitake, often growing as big as a watermelon in the wild, has shown to lower blood pressure and stabilize blood sugar. Testing revealed that Maitake inhibits a rise in blood glucose levels while re-straining the insulin production.

Much cancer research has been done studying its anti-tumor effects on inhibiting or reversing tumorous growths. Maitake is also being studied for its effectiveness on weight loss without change of diet.

The claims made in this article came from articles and books by Dr. Hiraki Nanba, who has done extensive, award-winning research on Maitake mushrooms in Japan. He is a member of the Japanese Cancer, Immunology and Pharmeology Societies. -*Sue Krisa*

ALTERNATIVE HEALTH OR CRACKPOT PANACEA?—YOU DECIDE!

The editorial staff for this issue of Common Ground has solicited and printed several articles from our community on health issues. We have not tried all the therapies mentioned herein, and we make no claims as to their effectiveness for every individual. We have included contributors' names so that our readers can research for themselves the validity of these practices.

REFLOGY--FEET IS WHERE ITS AT

For the last 25 years Alice Brinkley has been the Illinois Valley's reflexologist. Her mentor was an 80 year old Swedish man from Chico, California, who worked on her husband Vern when no one could figure out what was wrong with him in the mid-1950's. Working on Vern's feet, he began to teach Alice to do the treatments. Vern regained his health, and Alice continued to work with her teacher for 5 years. It wasn't until they moved to Oregon in 1970 that she actually began taking in clients. She's had clients from all over the world and has many regulars from around Southern Oregon. Still going strong at 79, Alice says, "We don't really know exactly why reflexology works, but it does. It's a complete therapy of the body."

Reflexology is a method for activating the healing powers of the body. Its roots go back thousands of years. Used by early Chinese, Japanese, Indians, and Egyptians to promote good health, reflexology is based on established principles of energy zones, along which the body's energy flows. There are ten zones that run the length of the body, five on each side beginning in the head and ending in each finger and toe. The zones pass completely through the body from front to back and incorporate all organs, glands, and parts of the body.

The feet are a perfect microcosm or minimap of the entire body, each foot representing half of the body. The toes look like little heads; the ridge beneath them resembles the neck and shoulder line. Even the inside curve of the foot corresponds to the natural curves of the spine. Each part of the body is reflected in points in the feet (and hands) called reflexes. Reflexology is a unique and specific method of using the thumbs and fingers on these reflex areas. Stimulating any part of the foot by applying pressure with the thumbs and fingers affects that entire zone throughout the body, revitalizing and balancing it. For example, working the kidney zone on the foot will affect not only the kidneys, but will also release vital energy that may be blocked somewhere else in that zone, such as in the eyes.

Reflexology stimulates more than 7,000 nerves in each foot and encourages the opening and clearing of these neural pathways. In Alice's words, "All the nerves come down into the feet and end in a reflex. If there's anything wrong with any part of the body, it will have a crystal on that reflex. We work the crystal off in order for that reflex to go back to work in the body." Crystals are believed to be calcium deposits which settle in the feet. Working the crystals off happens over a series of treatments.

A large percentage of our health problems today is believed to be caused by the incredible amounts of stress and tension present in our daily lives. If we don't handle the stresses well, our body's defenses become weakened. Reflexology reduces stress and tension by inducing a deep, tranquil relaxation.

Another important benefit of reflexology is improved circulation. By reducing stress and tension and deepening relaxation, reflexology allows the miles of cardiovascular vessels to conduct the flow of blood naturally and easily, causing all systems of the body to function more efficiently. As circulation improves, blood flows more smoothly, and oxygen reaches all the cells. By relaxing and opening up energy pathways, reflexology revitalizes the body and gives it energy on all levels. The body seeks its own balance as its systems begin to work in harmony again, and healing can take place.

"Skeptics?" says Alice. "Not many. Once they see the effects of the treatment, they come back for more."
- *Diane Floyd and Mar Goodman*

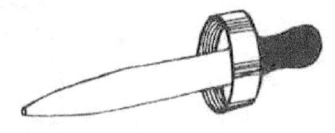

RETURN TO HOMEOPATHY

Homeopathy is a 200 year old system of medicine which is undergoing a renaissance in the '90's as people search for alternatives in treating illness and encouraging health. Homeopathy is based on the "Law of Similars" which means that a substance which can cause certain symptoms in healthy people can cure those same symptoms when they occur in an ill person. Homeopathic "remedies" are made from a variety of animal, plant, and mineral substances. Prepared by a special process of dilution and agitation, the remedies are rendered non-toxic and safe even for small children, yet have the capacity to stimulate healing on a deep level when matched correctly with the symptoms of the illness.

Homeopathy is used in the treatment of many acute and chronic health care problems on both the physical and the emotional level. When treating with remedies, it is more important to know the way the person experiences the illness than to know the exact causative organism. For example, sore throats can present very differently. One person may describe a burning pain that is only relieved by hot drinks, accompanied by restlessness, chilliness, and a coated tongue. Someone else may describe the sensation of a lump or plug in the throat worse from warm drinks, better eating solid food, and much worse if anything touches or constricts the neck. Each of these would respond to very different remedies.

In treating chronic illness, the remedy is picked by looking at the specifics of how the problem is manifesting in the person and also at the general tendencies of the person in food preferences, sleep, weather tolerances, emotional tendencies, etc.

Homeopathic remedies are commonly available in natural food stores and now many pharmacies (like Rexall in Ashland). Many are combination remedies using a variety of substances in one tablet to cover all the bases. Classical homeopathy prefers using only one remedy at a time specifically chosen based on the individual's symptoms. This method is my preference. The "C" potencies are preferable over the "X" potencies because they are more dilute and therefore more potent. (They are also safer.)

A great book for home use is Homeopathic Medicine at Home by Maesimund Panos, MD and Jane Heimlich. It covers common acute illnesses that affect us all and the way to choose the correct remedy. Deborah Frances, ND, from Grants Pass, is giving a Saturday seminar in October on the use of homeopathy in first aid situations (sprains, trauma, bites, burns, allergic reactions, etc.). Check with her for details at 474-0503.

- Mary Beth Burton , FNP (Family Nurse Practitioner) who practices Classical Homeopathy in Ashland.

HATHA YOGA: SPIRIT IN ACTION

We've all experienced an ache in a shoulder, a sprained ankle, or an injured neck or lower back. What do you do to relieve these states of dis-ease? Either ignore them (till they go away) or seek help?

Many of us have experienced a stomach ache, intestinal distress, lung congestion, dysfunctional bladder or kidneys. What does one do under these circumstances? Probably the same answer as before! We may have experienced emotional and/or psychological distress, i.e., anger, grief, "bad mood," "bad day," low energy, stress, stress, stress, overactive thought patterns, anxiety about the future. Again, what does one do? Ignore it?!! Have someone fix it??? Or, we can take responsibility for our health, physically, mentally, emotionally and spiritually!

Yoga offers a complete approach to all of these "life problems." The Western approach would be to look at the body as a machine. It breaks down; you fix it! But another way to view this body/mind/soul relationship is as a very subtle energetic system. Its energy flows relate to the organ systems, muscle, bones, nerves, emotional states, etc. These energy flows can become under or over-active, blocked, stagnant, or overly agitated!

What we look for is a way to balance these energy systems daily. In the Eastern tradition of martial arts there is Aikido, Tae Kwan Do, Karate Do. Do means "way;" a path or way of seeing life, meeting one's fears, finding compassion and strength with a gentle heart! So here we have Yoga-Do, an approach to unlearn and/or relearn ways to interact harmoniously with our world and within ourselves!

Patience, Practice and Perseverance are the necessary ingredients to do Yoga. Yoga asanas (postures), and breathing and meditation techniques are incorporated in this approach to look deeper within, to find silence, to cleanse and strengthen all the vital energy systems, to relax and heal the body/mind! Know thyself! Heal thyself! And all it takes is the doing! Namaste, *Chad Hamrin*

ALTERNATIVE HEALTH CARE

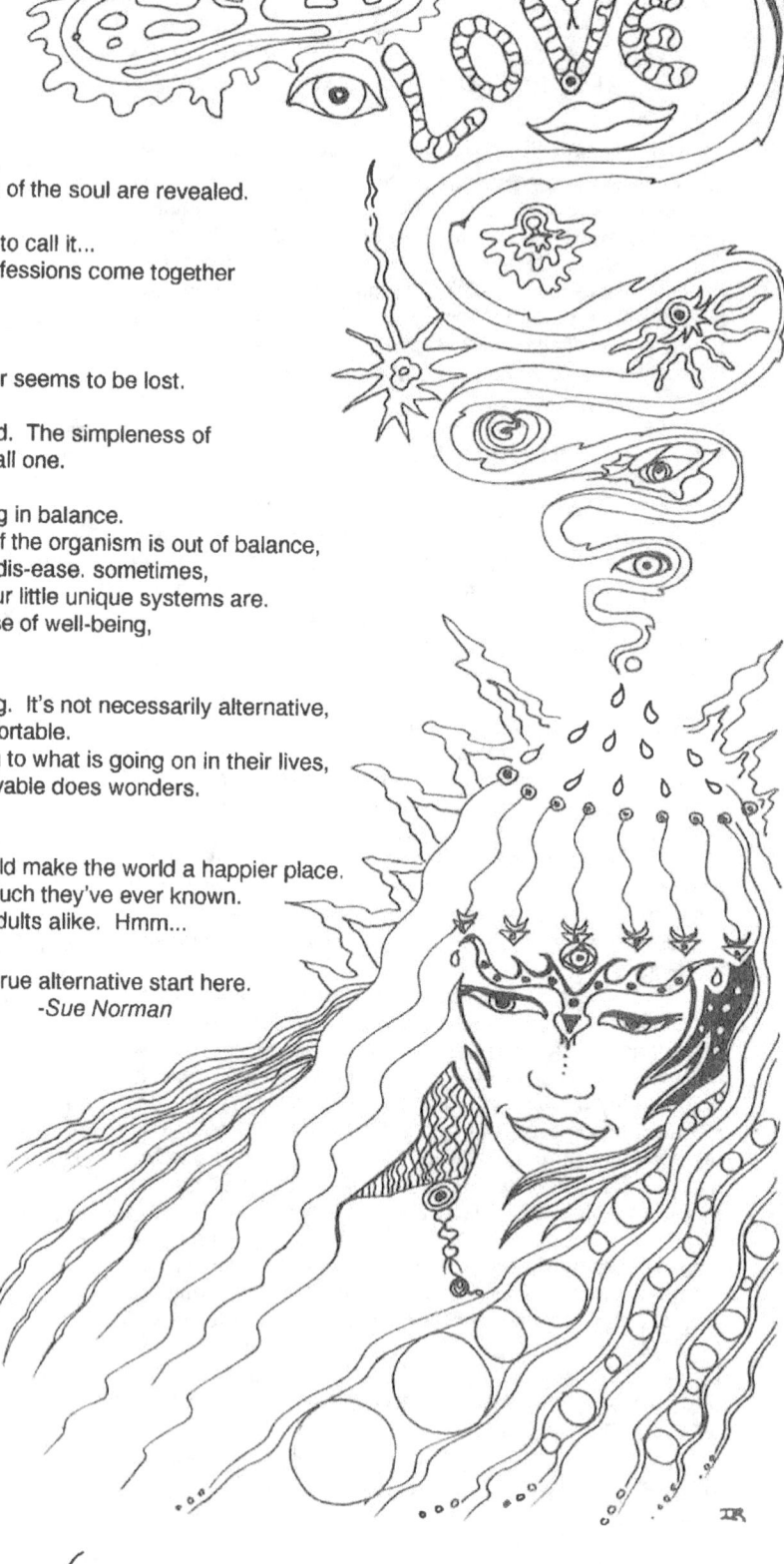

The similarities...
 Microscopically, we are all so much alike,
My work sends me into the microcosm of life.
 The cell...so small..connecting us all.
Life is a slow moving miracle.

We all come into this life with unlimited possibilities.
 As you gaze into a newborn's eyes...the depths of the soul are revealed.
We are all healers...
 Instead of Alternative Health Care...I would like to call it...
Co-operative Health Care, where all the healing professions come together
 for the soul purpose of relieving stress.

Love...really is the true healer.
 The connection with an all knowing loving power seems to be lost.
as we grow into human beings.
 We start as unlimited spirits and get transformed. The simpleness of
going back into the knowingness that we really are all one.

Healing...to shift from being out of balance into being in balance.
 The Mind and Body really are one. If any part of the organism is out of balance,
the domino effect takes place, making the cause of dis-ease. sometimes,
 hard to find. Forever amazed at how efficient our little unique systems are.
To bring back, through love and compassion, a sense of well-being,
 restores an opening for healing to take place.

I work in a clinic, and am part of a health care setting. It's not necessarily alternative,
 yet, I find a magic in making someone feel comfortable.
I find that giving someone a little bit of time, listening to what is going on in their lives,
 and, reminding them of the fact that they are lovable does wonders.
Simple as holding a hand.

Touch...to touch each other more, non-sexually, would make the world a happier place.
 To many...sexual connection is the only loving touch they've ever known.
So why is sex so important to our youngsters, and adults alike. Hmm...
 Let's touch more, love each other more...
 What a concept, and yes so easy to do. Let the true alternative start here.
          -Sue Norman

LITTLE CHILD
Little child, you of my blood and spirit.
What will you do when I am gone?
Shall you ponder over my greatness
or scoff at my weakness?
Shall you be great yourself
or just another citizen in a house
working 9-5 and on Saturdays
mowing your lawn?
I think that you,
little child,
will be great no matter what you do.
Never will you become that citizen
for you have my heart and that is what
matters,
little child.

-Mirya Holman

LIBRARY OFFERINGS

The Josephine County Library System has a large collection of books which deal with alternative health topics. Our collection dates back to classics like Adelle Davis's *Let's Eat Right to Keep Fit* and *Let's Get Well*. Since there are dozens of choices, I've covered just a few of the books published after 1989.

***The Healing Path; a Soul Approach to Illness;* Marc Ian Barasch,1994.**
Using his own experiences as a starting point, Barasch interviewed dozens of others for whom serious illness had become a catalyst for change.

***Healers on Healing,* Richard Carlson; 1989.**
Thirty-seven physicians, psychologists, nurses, metaphysical healers and shamans explore the complex nature of healing from a wide variety of viewpoints.

***Food - Your Miracle Medicine: How Food Can Prevent and Cure Over 100 Symptoms and Other Problems;* Jean Carper, 1993.**
Discusses what you should eat, and shouldn't eat, to prevent or re-
lieve a variety of symptoms.

***Ageless Body, Timeless Mind;* Deepak Chopra, 1993.**
Chopra believes that the aging process can be dramatically reshaped using the mind/body connection.

***Alternative Medicine and American Religious Life,* Robert C. Fuller, 1989.**
A look at the history of metaphysical healing theories in the United States.

***Disease Free: How to Prevent, Treat and Cure More Than 150 Illnesses and Conditions;* William LeGro Hoffman, 1993.**
Hoffman covers a wide spectrum of common health problems, focusing on prevention as well as treatment.

***Clare Maxwell-Hudson's Aroma Therapy Massage;* Clare Maxwell-Hudson, 1994.**
A beautifully illustrated guide which covers the basics of massage and the use of aromatic oils

***Healing and the Mind;* Bill Moyers, 1993.**
Moyers interviews physicians, scientists, therapists and patients in an exploration of how advances in mind/body medicine are being applied in the world of modern medicine.

***Water Birth; A Midwife's Perspective;* Susanna Napierala, 1994.**
Napierala guides the reader through the details of parental and midwife preparation, labor and birth, noting danger signals that must be heeded.

***The Complete Medicinal Herbal,* Penelope Ody, 1993.**
A practical guide to the healing properties of herbs, with more than 250 remedies for common ailments. Features 120 full-color photographs of medicinal herbs and explores both Eastern and Western approaches to natural medicine.

***Dr. Pitcairn's Complete Guide to Natural Health for Dogs and Cats,* Richard Pitcairn, 1994.**
A revised edition of a 1982 classic. Pitcairn covers pet ailments,natural diets and natural pet care products.

***The Allergy Discovery Diet: A Rotation Diet for Discovering YourAllergies to Food,* John E. Postley, 1990.**
A rotation diet designed to help reader identify which food (or foods) make them ill.

***Cancer and Nutrition; a Ten-Point Plan to Reduce your Risk of Getting Cancer;* Charles B. Simone, 1992.**
Dr. Simone discusses foods, exercises and supplements which provide the reader with a program for cancer prevention.

***Indian Medicine Power;* Brad Steiger, 1989.**
Medicine people from many tribes discuss how native American medicine can be used to get back in balance with nature.

***Natural Health, Natural Medicine; A Comprehensive Manual for Wellness and Self-Care,* Andrew Weil, 1995.**
A guide to preventaitive health maintenance with suggestions for treating ailments.

***Spontaneous Healing;* Andrew Weil, 1995.**
Weil turns away from the usual practice of Western medicine, which is founded on alleviating symptoms, to closely considering the healing process. Also included are case histories, diet, breathing exercises and suggestions for approaches to illness.

If any of these titles interests you, request it at the Illinois Valley Branch Library. If you are interested in further reading, you can search on our new public access computer terminals under the following subjects:

Alternative Medicine	Medicine, Popular
Mental Healing	Cookery-Natural Foods
Mind and Body	Diet Therapy
Naturopathy	Holistic Medicine

-Gail Warner

ACUPUNCTURE: TRY IT, YOU'LL LIKE IT

I don't remember when or how I first heard about acupuncture, but since my first treatment back in 1985 I've been a confirmed believer. I had just moved to Santa Cruz and discovered a low-cost acupuncture clinic at the Women's Health Center. I went mainly for what I thought was a superficial, physical problem: psoriasis. But right away healing began to happen on many levels. Having someone really listen to my litany of complaints and concerns—physical, mental and emotional—and not only accept, but address them all, allowed me to relax and trust both the doctor and the process. I felt encouraged by her picture of healing—not just a tube of something for my skin, but a journey toward wellness and balance.

It seems like almost every week for a year I lay on the table and as soon as the needles went in a well of grief would open up. My acupuncturist would say soothingly, "Crying is good; it softens the heart," and I would sob for a good, long time. The approach in Oriental medicine seems to be one of accepting what is, looking at how it got that way, and then working with the body's energy patterns to move, often gradually, back into balance. There's always something that can be done to help the body, and so fear can fade away.

Does it hurt? Well, yes and no. The needles are only about the width of a hair. Usually a point that needs stimulation will be tender when pressed, and occasionally I've experienced a quick, sharp pain as the needle's gone in, or a sensation of electrical energy radiating out from the point. Both of these sensations last only a second or two. More often, I've felt a dull ache around the needle, with a feeling of stuck energy in the area. After a while the energy feels like it breaks through, and I can sense it flowing up and down along pathways in my body.

The Orientals speak of health in terms of *chi* (chee), or life force, that flows along invisible channels throughout the body. These channels, called meridians, are governed by different organs. Needles are inserted at specific points along the meridians, facilitating the flow of "stuck" *chi*. This flow helps heal injuries and create harmony among the organs.

Along with acupuncture, Oriental medical doctors often prescribe herbs to assist the body—calming excesses, boosting deficiencies, or clearing heat,cold,damp, or wind. They will also often tell you ways to change your diet, sleep, or other habits to help in creating health. This is where I've tended to fail in doing my part! And after working in acupuncture clinics for 4 1/2 years, I can say that's true for a lot of us.

But in spite of *our* failures, I've seen acupuncture and herbs produce some remarkable results.Aches and pains sometimes disappear after one treatment. Headaches, sinus problems, digestive disorders, colds and flu, immune and circulatory problems, arthritis, addictions, allergies: all of these are recognized by the World Health Organization as being treated effectively by acupuncture. Because Oriental medicine works primarily with underlying causes on an energetic level, it usually makes a difference—sometimes in conjunction with Western medicine, and sometimes where Western medicine has been unable to help.

Lying on the acupuncture table, *chi* flowing into balance, I've gone into some the deepest states of peace and relaxation I've ever experienced. I've had incredible meditations, insights, and visual "psychic" impressions of what's going on in my body. Afterward, my body usually feels more balanced and life doesn't seem nearly as overwhelming. Not bad for an hour or so of being a human pincushion. Try it, you'll like it. And you'll probably get better, too.

NAET AND ALLERGIES

Speaking of remarkable results, I've been watching a process called NAET (Nambudripad's Allergy Elimination Technique) create amazing results for patients with allergies. Lori Paiken, acupuncturist at Three Harmonies Institute where I work in Ashland, practices the technique which combines elements of acupuncture and applied kinesiology.

The basic premise is that an allergy exists when the energy field of the body and the energy field of the allergen are in conflict or oppositon. If the brain and nervous system can be reprogrammed not to react in the presence of the allergen, the allergy can be eliminated—forever! The reprogramming is done using a chiropractic mallet to stimulate points along the spine, while the patient holds a vial containing some form of the allergen.

After the reprogramming, acupuncture is used to "fix" the treatment into the body. Then, for 25 hours, the patient must avoid the allergen completely. Usually, after the 25 hours, the allergy is gone, and the patient can eat, touch, or breathe the allergen without a reaction. I'm amazed to see people who've had deathly allergies to tomatoes, nuts, chocolate—you name it— go out and eat them in spades with no problem!   *-Carol Valentine*

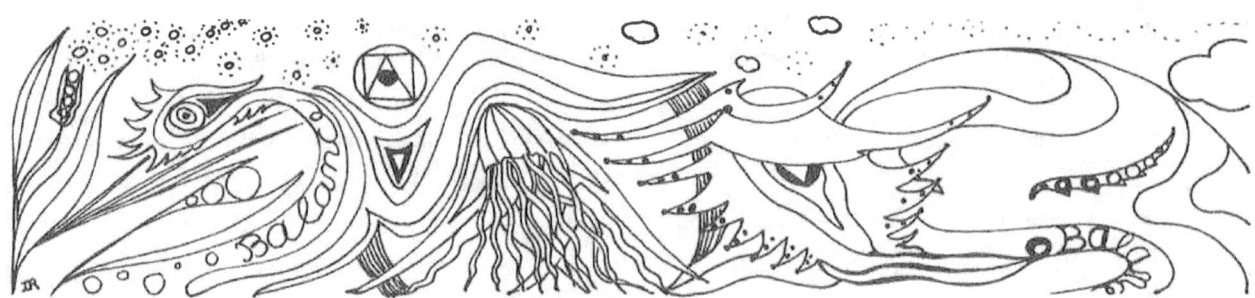

HOW TO HAVE YOUR DAIRY AND FEEL GOOD TOO

These two recipes use nuts to create rich, creamy alternatives to dairy products. While nuts are still high in fats, they also contain valuable fiber and nutrients. For those avoiding dairy's mucous-forming drawbacks or opposed to animal products, these recipes offer a replacement for custard and ricotta cheese.

ALMOND "PASTRY CREAM"

A filling, frosting, or custard alternative, this keeps for several days in the refrigerator.

1 cup blanched almonds
3/4 cup water (more if mechanically necessary)
1/4 cup honey or maple syrup
1 TB canola oil (optional)
1 TB almond extract (I like it very almondy. You may use less.)
1 TB arrowroot or cornstarch

Blenderize almonds and water until absolutely smooth. Add sweetener and oil. Blend to mix. Pour this into a saucepan. In a cup, mix thickener with a little cold water and stir. Add to almond mixture. Cook, stirring constantly, until mixture comes to a boil and thickens. Allow to cool. (You may wish to cover it closely with waxed paper to prevent the top from "clotting.") Stir in the almond extract after it is somewhat cooled. (Too hot and the extract's flavor may dissipate.) This makes a great base for fresh-fruit tarts, a decadent cake filling and even a frosting.

CASHEW "CHEESE"

The same technique can be used to create a delicious ricotta substitute from cashews. I've used this in eggplant parmesan, lasagne and vegetable moussaka. Substititute raw, unsalted cashews for the almonds. Omit sweetener, oil, and extract. Proceed as before. Add sea salt, garlic, or spices as desired. Spread the finished mixture into your favorite casserole in place of ricotta. For serving later, you can form the cooled mixture into "slabs" or "patties" on waxed paper and freeze. This cheese alternative is free of casein (a milk protein found in most soy "cheeses") and is adaptable to many uses.
-Kate Dwyer

ALTERNATIVE HEALTH CARE WORD SEARCH

Buried in a mass of extraneous empty calorie letters, the words you are looking for may appear horizontally, vertically or diagonally, forwards or backwards. Do not touch that junk food! Instead look for these health care possibilities: herbs, acupuncture, massage, chiropractic, yoga, exercise, tai chi, healing, humor, attitude, water, visualization, holistic, energy, endorphin, love.

Solution to Birds and the Bees in the 90's

V	H	R	H	E	A	L	I	N	G	L	C	T
E	I	E	E	U	M	U	N	Y	O	I	A	A
N	H	S	R	T	X	A	H	V	T	I	Y	T
D	O	T	U	B	A	F	E	C	C	X	H	T
O	L	O	W	A	S	W	A	H	R	S	P	I
R	I	T	S	D	L	R	I	S	P	T	G	T
P	S	A	T	G	P	I	E	Y	D	I	X	U
H	T	I	N	O	L	R	Z	N	O	Z	Y	D
I	I	Z	R	R	A	O	F	A	E	G	B	E
N	C	I	O	P	I	W	K	R	T	R	A	K
E	H	M	E	G	A	S	S	A	M	I	G	O
C	U	E	X	E	R	C	I	S	E	O	O	Y
H	A	C	U	P	U	N	C	T	U	R	E	N

With apologies for the numbering mistakes

NEWS FROM THE COMMUNITY

RACISM IN THE VALLEY?

The Illinois Valley Human Right s Alliance is investigating a series of incidents involving flagrant bigotry and discrimination that allegedly occurred toward members of OJ Ekmode and the Nigerian Allstars, an African World Beat band. Mixing business with pleasure, the band was visiting the valley in late August. While the Alliance found no evidence to substantiate most of the allegations made by band promoter Leslie McCombs, it remains "very concerned about a couple of the alleged incidents."

McCombs recently submtted an account of the incidents to the IVHRA. According to McCombs, "I urged this group to come home with me...I promised them a place to relax and enjoy some needed time off... I had no idea that there was so much hate and prejudice." McCombs says she "received several racial hate calls and threats during the time the band was in the valley."

According to McCombs, on August 23rd, Enika, a member of the band, was surrounded by white youth in front of Dairy Queen and "taunted with racial slurs." At one point they theatened to "take her around back to show her how they deal with N——— when they make the mistake of showing up where they're not wanted." She was able to kick her way free of the circle and ran as fast as she could to safety. According to McCombs, "it took us almost an hour to get the story out of her, she was (so) frightened and embarrassed. She said no matter how much she tries not to let it get to her, it still hurts." McCombs further noted, "all this took place in broad daylight,; no one offered any assistance." Members of the IVHRA are seeking further information from witnesses who may have seen the incident that day.

On their way to Williams, McCombs states that band members were turned away from service at three different businesses. The the Boarding House Restaurant in Selma, they were told there were no available tables. McCombs says that when she asked about tables that were empty, she was told they were reserved. According to restaurant manager Ken Adolphs, "There were table reserved for that morning," and "such prejudice would never be allowed at this establishment... in fact, I know the waitress (who has that shift) and she definitely is not prejudiced."

In Wonder, McCombs aleges that band members were not allowed entrance into the General Store. However, the store owner adamantly denied McCombs's allegations, stating, "We have never refused entry into this store in the 5 1/2 years that I've been here."

In a Takilma incident involving dogs that threatened the band members, McCombs alleges the owner of the dog claimed that, "The dog does not like black people, and (it) hates Jewish people and fat people." When questioned about the incident, the dog owner did not wish to respond to the allegations. In their Sept. 13 meeting, IVHRA members resolved to look further into the Dairy Queen incident. Members felt that the Takilma incident wa not a case of malicious intent, but rather showed a lack of sensitivity towards the need to respect diversity of people, regardless of race, religion or lifestyle. *-Dave Toler*

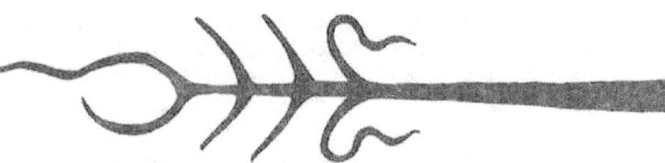

REFLECTIONS FROM AN OLD GROWTH CIRCLE

Up up and up we drive on the narrow and bumpy road and so do the trees grow up, up and upward toward the blue skies of late summer. Myray, our daughter of 3 years, grows more and more excited. "We are going to pray for the big trees," she kept announcing to the world, and yes, that is what we did do, pray for those beautiful huge and tall elder tree spirits that are mostly sprayed blue to be cut down by Boise Cascade Corporation. We camped overnight and relaxed and deepened our respect for our mother earth and realized as high in the skies as the trees reach, so do their roots go equally into the earth.

Oh I wish, I wish, I wish that more people would take the time to come into these ancient forests who are our relations and see the grandeur that abides. I'd love to see churches extending their congregations up into the forests where the natural cathedrals exist with no need for human interpretation. I see a direct link between the elder trees and the elder humans on the earth; a council circle of equals; perhaps the elder humans will give the elder trees a pure and loud voice in this world where corporations see trees as $$.

Myray sings spontaneously, "Kids love the trees, trees are spirits, and the trees cry when they are cut down." I encourage all and any of you folks to take a walk or a campout in the nearby forests before the cold and wet prevail, and before the sacred trees are logged. My family and many others are presently directly involved in a fasting and prayer vigil in the Sugarloaf sale units on our mother earth; that's the same mother that we all share, folks, MOTHER EARTH. I'll close with Myray's favorite song of this summer: "We're all brothers and sisters, some of us have brothers, some of us have sisters, and we all have the same mother, MOTHER EARTH!" (followed by hopping about and clapping, hurrah!!!!)

For my beautiful mother, Renee, and for my grand mother earth; i am Maya Many Moons Reames and family, end of summer 1995, Williams Oregon, or as Myray calls this place; Women's Orlygon. (Her brother's name is Orly.)

ho to all my relations, peace and love, i am *Maya*

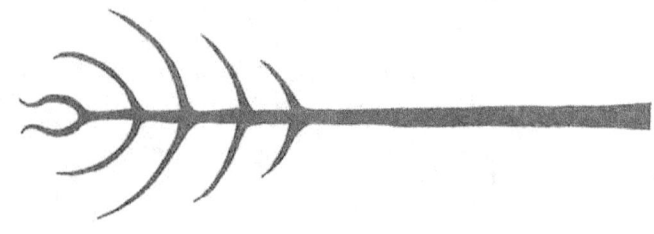

ANCIENT TREES ARE FALLING

After a 10 year struggle to save Sugarloaf, Boise Cascade, the Forest Service & the Josephine County Sheriff's Department closed the roads leading to Sugarloaf on September 8. They have begun destroying one of the last remaining old growth forests in the Siskiyous. On Monday September 11, I walked a mile with about 130 people, our flowers, children, and signs to the gate on the Williams side of Grayback Mountain. We had a very moving rally there where we were reminded that this is our Church, our sacred land. Nineteen of us decided, some spontaneously, to disregard their road closure and continued walking to pray on our land. We were arrested. They were pretty calm and not angry as they cuffed us. Boise Cascade taped the whole event and the Sheriffs took photos to identify us. Although they expected an arrest situation, they hadn't arranged for transportation to the Grants Pass Jail. They took us about 1/4 mile where we were handcuffed behind our backs with very painful wide black plastic cuffs, back to back and cuffed to a chain. The cuffs were always cutting into our wrists. We were placed in the hot sun and not given water for 3 hours when the vans arrived to take us to jail. At least one person's hand was still numb a day later. I cried uncle after two hours and they let me stand up to relieve my back but still cuffed behind. I didn't expect a picnic, but this seemed a little extreme.

When we arrived at jail and informed them no names would be given unless we got group arraignments they proceeded to check us into jail. Finally we got arraignments at the same time and gave our names. By this time we had been stripped of any jewelry and one woman had a large hunk of hair cut off, including a hair wrap. Mug shots were taken and two sets of prints, one for the FBI. They were mostly professional and really expressed gratitude for our cooperation. This really was police overkill. We are not "Dangerous Criminals". It feels like they are afraid of the truth. We don't need to cut every last ancient tree. We need to stop cutting them. In Josephine County we have a situation where many of the deputies have been laid off and they will not respond to most crimes but they have provided 69 deputies to protect Boise/Cascade. This seems wrong to me. The media captioned our peaceful gathering with reports of spikes found in forest. This was propaganda. It implied that we are dangerous and that's their excuse for this huge military type action. ACTUALLY, the bark had grown over the spike so it was probably done years ago.

Everyone was arraigned on Wednesday, September 13. On September 20 everyone will be pleading not guilty. Apparently someone higher up in the courts is sympathetic; one woman hasbeen sentenced to only a $25 fine and $50 court costs, which she can pay off in community service. Much will have happened before you read this but more help will be needed. We will maintain a vigil along Caves Highway to pass out information to the touristas. If you would like to help please call Debbie at 592-4459 or 592-3386.

ADVERTISING- WHAT DO YOU THINK?

To say that the Common Ground is a "non-profit" endeavor would fall short of accurate depiction. After all, most non-profits have people who are at least minimally compensated for their work (sometimes quite comfortably so). Common Ground relies on your support merely to cover material and printing costs. Labor is 100% voluntary. Unfortunately, we are not even covering our production costs.

The question has been posed to the Mud Council as to whether or not Common Ground should begin to accept display advertising. The Council has decided to first solicit response from our readers. Although it is I who presented the advertising proposition, I must admit having some serious reservations about depending on business for the bucks.

When I was the original co-owner of Ashland's Lithiagraph, it was the advertisers who first complained about my political writing not fitting well on their waiting tables, etc. Let's face it, the purposes of media as a tool are often very different for business than they may be for the publisher. And for the reader, it's nice to digest information and imagery without the indigestion advertising can cause.

One way to ameliorate some of the problems associated with advertising is to impose serious limits. For example, the Council could limit ads to no more than 10% of the paper. This would make it more tolerable for the reader and limit the influence business would have in the editorial room.

So why is Common Ground even entertaining the concept of advertising? One reason is that we are not keeping up with the cost of producing this paper. Improving the quality of this publication will obviously be difficult under our present financial limits.

The Common Ground is establishing itself as a legitimate voice in the Illinois Valley. Can Common Ground continue? Can we get more funding through other means? (Like more subscriptions!) The question is, what do *you* think?
-Dave Toler

134

A CALL FOR VOLUNTEERS AT THE IVHS CAREER CENTER

Volunteers are still needed for the IVHS career center. They fill a crucial gap in the educational process, helping students think about careers and education beyond high school.

"I find it to be personally rewarding work. The career center could be the key to making the high school a meaningful and valuable experience for many students. If you think you might be interested in coming in to the high school and working with students once a week for a couple hours, call IVHS at 592-2116 and check it out." urges Paco Despacio, who is helping to organize the volunteers meeting.

Common Ground thanks Norrin Stafford for his time and energy on the community photo.

Thanks to Diane Floyd for her help with issue #13.

We apologize to Geraldine Davison, whose piece "Geezers," appeared in the last issue without her name. We look forward to more of Geraldine's wit and intelligence.

Staff for this issue: Dave Toler, Kate Dwyer, Dave Hocker, Rachel Goodman(facilitator), Jack Dwyer, Gloria Stone, Laurie Prouty, Kerry Holman and Deb Murphy. Special thanks to Mar Goodman, who wrote, typed and solicited articles spontaneously. THANK YOU MAR!!

Submissions deadline for issue #15 will be Oct.23. The topic will be Takilma Rituals, facillitated by Laurie and Kerry.Please send materials to them.

SUBSCRIBE TO COMMON GROUND!

_____ $10 A ONE YEAR SUBSCRIPTION

_____ $25 A ONE YEAR SUBSCRIPTION PLUS AN ILLUMINATED FOOLS HAND PRINTED T-SHIRT. CHOICE OF COLORS (GREEN, BLUE, BRONZE OR PLUM) AND SIZE(S,M,L,XL)

NAME _____

ADDRESS _____

_____

TAKILMA COMMON GROUND
POB 2016
TAKILMA, OREGON 97523

BULK RATE
U.S. POSTAGE
PAID
CAVE JUNCTION
OREGON 97523
PERMIT #16

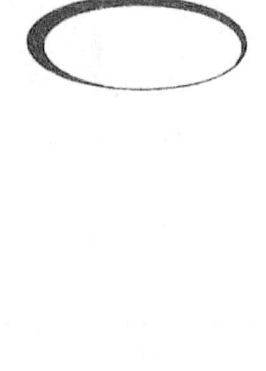

ho

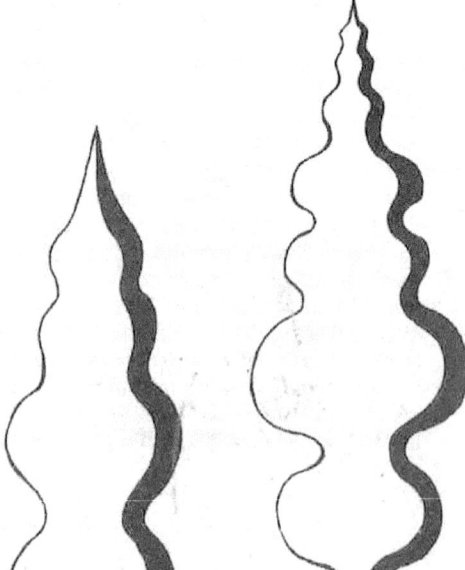

Takilma Common Ground

NOV-DEC '95

ISSUE #15

One person's ritual is another person's obsessive-compulsive disorder, no doubt about it; but what is it that distinguishes the two? When does rigid routine become religious rite? What is it that sanctifies repetition? How can we tell the difference between habit and ceremony?

Is it intent? The woman who can only open doors with her elbow, and who must wash her hands a hundred times a day may be no less preoccupied with the transformation of energy than the New Age groover repeating fervent affirmations on the way to work. Ritual is what we do to soothe ourselves in the midst of the chaos of existence. Rituals are the orderly, repetitious, self-calming behaviors of the entire species, and they range along numerous continuums from the self-consciously inventive to the mindlessly traditional; solitary to universal, secular to sacramental, malicious to benign.

Back in the 1960's, or even earlier for those beatnik types, a lot of time-honored rituals were unceremoniously dumped. Authenticity was the criterion by which we measured experience, and we had a keen nose for the bogus. Empty social gestures, hypocritical belief systems, doctrines of expediency and marriages of convenience were all rejected out of hand. We wanted Real and we wanted it Now. I myself fled from a culture deeply committed to the repetition of countless social customs and a family deeply committed to resisting change. This flight had a lot to do with discovering whether or not I even had an authentic, individuated Self, or if I was only a collection of rote observances in search of a place in pre-destiny.

Out here in the cultural free-for-all of the late twentieth century I have a lingering loneliness and nostalgia for the compelling rituals of my childhood. They get more distant, but no dimmer. There were the gorgeously predictable Christmases and Easters; haymaking in June and potato picking in October; the gathering of primroses and frog spawn in the spring, stubby handprints melted in the richly frosted window panes every nasty February. There was Ascension Day and Rogation Day, Harvest Festival and Guy Fawkes night, May Day and Whitsun, year after year after year.

Every Sunday morning at chapel my great-grandfather, Jabez Swan, would break the crusty loaf of bread apart - I still hear it tearing; the air was very quiet - and pour the chilly, red communion wine from a glass decanter. After taking a pinch of bread and a sip of wine — "this is my body.....this my blood..." - he would pass the plate, and then the cup, with unseeing eyes to the person sitting behind him. He chewed and swallowed as stolidly as his own cows in the field across the road. No-one made eye contact, no-one ever looked happy; it was a frozen moment. My relatives were dear to me around their own hearths, at work in their own barns, but they seemed to leave their hearts behind them at the chapel door. At this high point of their own creed they were caught in the icy grip of a blind faith. Their observance had no warmth, did not connect them to each other or the fragrant earth they tilled, but honored only the fierce justice of a common law. It was all ass backwards and I shunned the whole contaminated business for years, lamenting the dead center, wondering why we had the experience and missed the meaning, over and over again.

The use of ritual lies in its power to give meaning. Ritual allows elemental energy the opportunity to transform us. Its authenticity is measured, subjectively, by the felt responses of the participant. It is that odd conjunction of the active and passive, the creative and receptive, where we repeat meaningless phrases so that significance may occur, where we get in place in order to get out of our own way. It is the theater where we act out the truth and wear elaborate masks in order to become our real selves. Ritual is an act of faith; sometimes all you get from a trip to the medicine circle is cold feet; some days all you get from writing your journal are more dead trees.

I regret the passing of the grand traditions of our decomposing, recomposing culture. I can't help giggling at some of the neo-pagan reconstructions we come up with to replace them. I am overjoyed that there are people who retain their cultural connections to a vital magic. We know too much to be content with dead ways and we may not live long enough to be confident that the evolving rituals will really see us through, but we keep on keeping on, finding soul in the mundane and occasionally getting our socks knocked off by humbling blasts of unexpected transformative power. We do not do ritual; it does us.   -Felicity

The woman walks into the brush, armed with her bowsaw, crossing a manzanita grove where Life and Death mingle...With a prayer of thanks, she cuts a branch of dead wood. She searches for tinder materials, gathering dry, brittle lichen and milkweed pods. Passing by Big Pine Tree, she picks up balls of pitch, that are slowly dripping down the trunk.

Back at the lodge, she prepares the fire. The moon is new, coming into the sign of Scorpio, the water sign of deep inner Mysteries. As the sun sets, Women an young Daughters enter the Lodge, contributing their special pieces to the Altar. The four directions are set with a candle and symbols of their elements. East is Air, represented by bird wings, feathers and incense burning, scenting the atmosphere, illuminating the mind. In the South, a red candle burns brightly, the single flame of fire representing the direction of Lifeforce. In the West, a chalice of water sits among seashells; the direction of Introspection. The North has a bowl of sand, earth and salt, the minerals of matter, with owl statues pointing the way to the Elders of Wisdom. In the center stands a figure of the Great Mother, Goddess of the Harvest and of all Life. She represents Spirit and with Her shines the tallest candle. The smudging ritual begins, one woman waving smoke from an abalone shell burning sage and cedar, cleansing the aura, creating Sacred Space. The Welcoming song begins:

> Casting the circle of protection and light
> To guide us through this darkest night.
> Oh mother Kali, Hecate,
> Oh mother Kali, Hecate.

The Four Directions are called, welcoming the energy of each into our Beings. The candles are lit and the stage is set for an evening of sharing and magic.

Tonight there is a Firekeeper Woman, offering her Ritual of sparking the fire with steel and flint. She says a special prayer, asking for Air and Fire to come together. With a piece of charred cloth on the flint rock in one hand, she strikes the rock with a rod of tempered steel... The third strike lands a spark onto the cloth. Quickly, the nest of lichen, milkweed and dry grass is scooped up, the smoldering cloth is placed upon it. The Firekeeper's breath quickens to short spurts catching the flaming nest burning bright from her cupped palms, she carefully places the flame in the center of the firepit. A rattle is passed and each Woman offers a prayer, song or story.

Experiencing these Rituals is about raising Power and being creative and strong in our Path. We all need different rituals to nourish and empower ourselves. These Rituals are about Magic. Positive affirmations really work to focus our energy in the areas that need fulfillment. Rituals are about Fun! Coming together to laugh is one of the most healing energies I know. And finally , Rituals are about Connecting. To sing with one voice, to hold hands, to look into each others eyes and smile. To feel the Love and caring that women have for each other. Circling around a Fire is a simple way to share , create Rituals and feel LOVE. BLESSED BE!

-Bridge

Anyone who has lived here longer than a few minutes, and chooses to be involved has probably had the opportunity to participate in a Takilma ritual. They come in all shapes, sizes, rhymes and reasons. Some are adopted from ancient ways; others we've created to fit our needs and lifestyles.

I'd like to share how a Takilma process of the last six months had the feel of a ritual for me. Six months ago several Takilma elders convened to guide, support, and modify some anti-social behaviors of two of our youth. The many meetings, discussions, check-ins, and record-keeping, although not a normal description of what takes place in a ritual, did have a feeling of what I treasure about ritual. I appreciate gathering with people for a common purpose, believing what we are doing will lead to a higher good, and learning something important about ourselves. This sharing may be a first step toward creating a tradition of tribal justice.

As in life, there are no guarantees. The healing circle may not heal. The winter solstice burning ritual and relighting of candles may not purge us of the demons within. And the last six months of effort and guidance may or may not produce what we desired for these boys. Does that mean I would never participate again, or that as a community we should abandon goals of "doing it differently?" I truly hope not. I believe we have both a privilege and responsibility of continuing to redefine and recreate ceremonies, rites, and rituals.

-Gloria

CELEBRATING THE RETURN OF THE LIGHT

Ritual provides the bridge between inner and outer worlds; it creates a space to connect our souls. Unconscious rituals are a part of our daily lives, such as the morning coffee or tea, reading the bedtime story, sleeping in on the weekends, building the morning fire; all are important deeds for our emotional stability to feel balanced. Perceiving these everyday acts as being sacred makes them more special and empowering.

To consciously create a ritual with an intention is very gratifying. One that we have created honors the changes of the seasons. For many years now, we have been walking up to our ridge for sunrise at the Solstices and Equinoxes. Friends drive up in the early hours of the morning, sometimes still dark, seeking the balance and connection within ourselves, with each other, the world. We come with prayers, hopes, joy, sorrow, laughter and tears. When you see the train of people climbing the hillside, a pilgrimage is in sight. It is beautiful. In the winter solstice, we struggle to get out of our warm, snug beds and go for a hike in the cold, possibly rainy or snowy morning. Standing around our altar of various offerings, we honor the four directions, the earth, the sky, the Great Spirit and give our prayers as the sun rises over the mountain, connecting us with ourselves and relationships with others, consciously uniting us as members of a global family.

As darkness approaches, this being the longest night, we often join with family and friends and reflect on the past year and the inward searching that accompanies the season. To feel the essence of the longest night, we choose to burn candles and not to use electricity. Special foods of the season, such as root crops- potatoes, carrots, onions,all grown in the dark earth - are prepared and shared together. Joining in a circle around the fire, we each write down an aspect of ourselves that we no longer wish to identify with. When ready to release, the paper is burned in the flames, symbolically cleansed in the fire. As the flames flare up from our burning objects, the fire is fueled by the dark aspects of ourselves that we are releasing, thus we individually consecrate the return of the light and celebrate the feeling of renewal.

-Laurie

DRINK WATER FIRST

As a young adult in the late 1970's, I began traversing the nation with my backpack and toddler child, alternately camping in wilderness areas, visiting Indian Reservations, and attending Native American ceremonies. During those pristine days in the springtime of my spiritual life, Indian elders planted many words of wonder in my psyche which took root to later reveal their deep meaning and wisdom.

What is perhaps one of the most valuable teachings I carry into my daily life is also the most easy to share, and I hope everyone will try it. It is as simple as drinking a glass of water!

Many native prayer ceremonies have within their focus the presence or absence of water. Whether water is withheld, as in the four day Sundance ceremony, or whether it is prayed over before being used in sweatlodge or peyote meetings, this basic element of our earthly lives is never forgotten.

When I set out to make my permanent home in Oregon, far from my Indian relations, my Cheyenne dad gave me some sound advice. He told me that every morning when I arise, before I eat or drink or really do anything, I should drink a glass of water and give thanks for its presence in my life. He said that this way I would be connected to all the prayers that were said over water in ceremonies, no matter how far away. And even when there were no ceremonies in motion, the water would still bring blessings and slowly reveal its wisdom. "Daughter," he said, "always drink water first."

This simple "drink water first" ritual has had a strong effect on my life. We can all <u>say</u> that water is sacred, but to treat it as such every day can truly change our lives. Water has a very powerful and ancient spirit, and it can become your teacher, your cleanser, your healer, your friend. You can set a glass or a bucket of water in front of yourself, your family, or a group of friends and talk to it, pray over it, ask it to help you in your daily life, and it will. And then when you drink water with this special reverence, you may feel it cleansing and blessing you right down to your fingertips!

At sunrise the other day I was sitting in front of the wood fire with my morning water in hand. As I looked at the burning wood, a little voice from the fire seemed to talk. When I listened, it was really the water letting me know something... "Fire and water are not opposites. This wood that is burning needed water to grow into a tree. Even the fire owes its existence to me...."

-Oshana

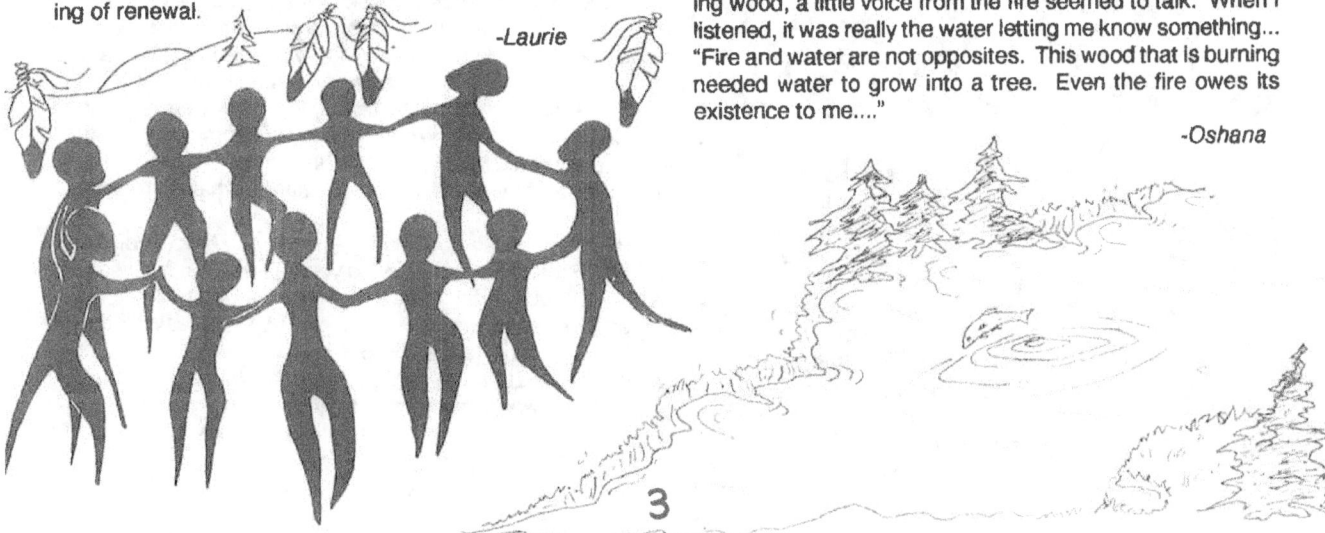

138

"LOVE IS MAGIC MAGIC IS THE TRANSFORMATION OF ENERGY" -Starhawk

I learned about ritual at a gathering of 2000 people during a civil disobedience campaign near the construction site of Diablo Canyon Nuclear Power Plant. I naively sat down in a small circle of women, some of whom were witches. Starhawk asked us to focus our awareness on the moment, evoking the natural elements of earth, air, water and fire to amplify our sense of connectedness with nature and one another. I understood that our circle of bodies, joined by our breathing rhythm and our mutual awareness of these elements, created a sacred space. In reverence, Spirit was called to enter this space, giving force to our intention of becoming clear and strong. We heard our names sung back to us, honoring ourselves; we chanted and drummed into a mild trance state. We acknowledged our fears by naming and releasing them, blowing them into a small cauldron of burning sage. We passed a bowl of sunflower seeds, imbuing them with the energy we had raised, and each fed a seed to the woman next to us. We offered some in thanks to the Spirits we had called to our circle, released them, grounded the energy by touching the earth and opened the circle with sharing of food and fruit juice. I felt transformed and I was hooked on ritual from then on. . . . .

For me ritual is about change; it's the way to shift the focus, the energy, the political conditions of my life. I emerge from the illusion of separateness, into profound knowing that we are all part of one Source; thus allowing change to be possible and immediate. The personal and the political are one.

Rituals don't require large groups, in fact some of the most powerful rituals are solitary events. Ritual may be incorporated into daily routines: the recording and honoring of dreams, drumming the sun up, yoga practice, meditation, taking a few moments to focus on your intentions for the day. Even the morning chores may be performed as ritual; a preparation and freshening of the altar that is your home...

Any act done with consciousness, acknowledging the beauty within and without, with awareness that the rational/concrete world is not all there is, is ritual....... -Kayla

Dear Community,

Thanks to the generosity and compassion of many, we are able to award scholarship money monthly to low-income families with children enrolled at the Dome School. Many of these scholarships are funded by the interest earned from the Asa Frank Parker-Shames Endowment Fund.

Anyone wishing to donate to this fund should know that the sum of the endowment fund is held in trust, with only the interest it earns being used to support Dome School scholarships. We are very grateful to the Parker-Shames family and all who have donated to this fund for the opportunity to disburse scholarships to young children.

-Oshana and Susan

ARREST AS RITUAL

On Monday September 11, seventeen people, including myself, were arrested as we crossed over a gate on public land. Since then 100 more have been arrested. The gate marked the boundary of a massive 35 square mile closure of National Forest and BLM land for the benefit of a multinational timber corporation, Boise Cascade, which was beginning to cut down 200+ year old trees on Grayback Mountain. Civil disobedience and non-cooperation against the corporate inspired poisoning and plundering of our public forest has been a tradition in our community since the time of the "herbicide wars." It is a commitment to hope and future for our community and a commitment against base exploitation, driven by corporate greed, which is anti-community. It is also a ritual where the "rubber meets the road;" that is to say, where symbolism meets the hard reality of authoritarian force. In this case, the agents of the state who are carrying out the force are the land management bureaucracies of the U.S. Forest Service and BLM. By the guns they bring with them the statement is made clear, they will use <u>any</u> means necessary to carry out the timber industry agenda. They become, in the final analysis, the private militia and propaganda arm of that industry. Just as obviously, by our attitude of peace and openly acting on our outrage, we make the statement that force will not intimidate us into passive acceptance and that we will not use violence to achieve our ends.

Ritual is often an affirmation of basic community truths or prayers to a vision for the future. It is through acts of ritual that we seek to empower ourselves and our community to live those truths or seek that vision. Civil disobedience in the defense of our remaining wild mountain forests is ritual in both senses. It is affirmation of our peaceful relationship to this place, of our connection to earth, and an offering of a new vision: a vision of sustainable communities, human and non-human, that is in opposition to the dominant juggernaut of ultimate resource exploitation for consumption; a vision of justice for all life in contrast to corporate class subjugation; and a vision of the many intrinsic values of our place in opposition to a single-value of materialism. This vision is not fundamentalist in nature, like say the wise-use or militia view, because it looks to a new future not to a revisionist past.

Since this ritual is direct action, the empowerment can also be direct, both on the personal and the community level, for the corporate states' power is challenged directly. In this and other ways we take power to change what that future may hold.

P.S. Dear friends, I will be leaving as Director of the Siskiyou Project at the end of the year. These last two years have been wonderful, especially all the support I have received from so many of you. While I will be leaving this position I will not be leaving our beautiful valley and I am looking forward to more garden time. Thank you, everyone, for your kind words, prayers, and love.

-Steve Marsden

THANKS AGAIN

Dear friends,   please brace yourselves a bit.
This gratitude—I tend to gush.
This hymn of praise for all you folks,
these honeyed words, might make you blush.
But if it does, you have it coming
for flooding my own heart and cheeks
with warmth and cheer and thus diverting
blood from brain. The words it seeks
it sought in vain that tongue-struck night.
I'll try again to say it right.

I'm awestruck by the friends I have.
I'm blessed to know you, living here
at this amazing time and place.
I clearly saw, despite the beer,
your rippling talents, wisdoms, jokes,
and at the bottom, sparkling clear,
your bedrock of integrity,
evoking what I might yet be.

I seem to need a wake-up call.
I must have been asleep or blind.
How did I get this old, this fast?
Bogged down in my daily grind,
overwhelmed by kids' requests
for energies I could not find,
too often busy or too tired
to seize what lay within my grasp.
Now I'm fifty, daughters grown;
those little hands I'd love to clasp
have other things to do than play.
Relationships I did not serve
have grown away, and my mistake
has always been a lack of nerve,
a fear indulged, that drove me to
pretend the days would always last
and so I let them trickle past
inconsequentially. . .
to show they spanned infinity.

It's clear I need to celebrate
the fleetingness of living's bounty:
an unoriginal refrain
on radios in every county.

But I forget it anyway,
as if the most important things
must promptly fade at end of day,
and vanish when alarm clock rings.
Like some caffeine for the spirit,
every morning I must hear it.
Yet this is hard when mired in mundane
matters like my dirty laundry,
and years I languished there in church
have put me in a silly quandary.
For I was taught the gap between
the fleshy realm and things religious
and so to cross to reverence
we all should have a creed to bridge us.
But ceremonies I grew up with
carried too much narrow baggage.
Browsing culture fusion stores,
hefting others' faiths like cabbage
seemed improper and contrived.
And so I found myself deprived:
without the proper vehicle
affirming what is visible,
not over-metaphysical.

But lately I've begun to do
a very simple ritual,
blessing meals with gratitude
that soon grows more habitual.
And so I'm slowly learning now
that any form for opening hearts
and joining us, commands a bow.
So I salute all loving souls
who learned before me all the uses
for occasions, celebrating
with the slimmest of excuses
seasons, births, exchange of kidneys,
rites of cultures there to borrow:
Whoop it up like no tomorrow.
Show me yet again the way,
and in turn I'll sing and say:
feel the joy,
stop to play,
flow the love,
caress the day.

-Jack Dwyer

IVHS CAREER CENTER UPDATE

The IVHS career center needs more volunteers! Thank you, Al Karger and Judy Taylor, who have recently started coming in to volunteer at the career center and soon will be advising students. Career center volunteers recently attended a training workshop in Medford on how to use the computer Career Information System to get information which can help students make decisions about career choices, colleges, trade schools, and scholarships. We were also introduced to a new model of career development based on transformation theory.

I'd like to share some of my thoughts about why I think the career center is important. Recently several bright young people I know have dropped out of high school. I still don't understand all the reasons for this trend, but from talking with a few of the dropouts I know they feel high school is irrelevant to their lives. In some ways, this is true. The school curriculum has not begun to catch up to the Third Wave (Information Age) realities that will shape their future (but neither have most of the other institutions in America, with the exception of a few industries and the military). Also the resources allocated to education by frivolously frugal voters leave the public schools lacking adequate staff and equipment to deal with the needs of today's students and the problems they face. Most of the people I have met who work in the high school are dedicated, hard-working, intelligent, competent people who are accomplishing a lot with the limited resources available.

Some of the students who come to the career center are getting a lot out of high school. They are proud of themselves for having met the challenges of classroom learning and use their school and community activities to enhance their self esteem and to create choices for themselves in the future. When I talk with these students I almost always hear about some adult who is taking an interest in them, offering advice, support, and recognition for their hopes and achievements.

I believe that caring, supportive interest from adults in the community can make a crucial difference in the lives of many students who are not getting enough of it. A dramatic example of the effectiveness of outside adult influence that I witness is the success of military recruiters and ROTC in bringing students to their programs. I hope that by getting a diversity of positive adult influences through the career center, students will learn about the many opportunities available in the world outside their small town, age-ghetto limited experience and discover the importance of learning and education for achieving their dreams.

Besides student advisors, I really need some help with my job of volunteer coordinator. Organization and administration are not my strong areas and I don't have time to plan some of the activities crucial to the success of this program such as job shadow, career fairs, college visits, and grant seeking for a paid career center coordinator. Anyone interested in volunteering call Paco at 592-4196.

CLING-TO-GREENS DRESSING

Feeling too physically fluffy lately? Well, why bother with the salad diet if it's got OIL all over it? Try this healthy oil-free dressing method for a truly low-calorie feast of greens.

Thicken 2 cups of your preferred liquid (orange juice, apple juice, vegie broth, etc.) with 2 Tbsp of arrowroot or cornstarch.

(Accomplish this by mixing the starch with a small amount of the cold liquid, then mixing this back into the rest. Heat over medium flame, stirring constantly. When it's just reaching the boil and thickens up, remove it from the heat.)

Let your mixture cool at least to only warm. In a blender, food processor, or with a whisk, mix in your flavoring ingredients, such as lemon juice, vinegar, mustard, pureed capers, spices, tamari, garlic, whatever.

I made an orange-honey-mustard dressing using this method for Gloria's Gala Equinox Party. People loved it and Gloria asked for the recipe.

This process yields a dressing with cling-to-greens body and is adaptable to many flavors. Bon appetit!

-Kate

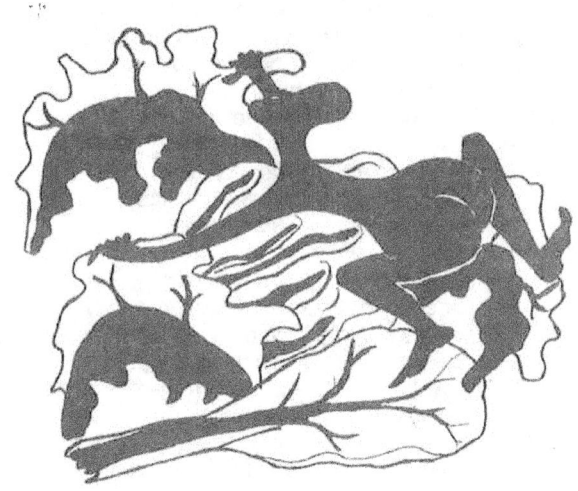

Common Ground is published to provide a vehicle for our community expression; ideas, feelings, and talents. We love to hear from you; we especially love to receive your opinions via 3" diskette (or typed double spaced). The theme for the next issue, #16, is "Work," in all its manifestations; joyous, painful, necessary. The facilitator will be Rachel Goodman and the deadline is Dec. 7. We would like to credit the following for their help on issue #14: Diane Floyd, Paco Despacio, Cedar Knoll, Chelsea and Austin Hocker and artists Cathy Hocker, Mr. Tracy, I. Rebelle, and Sue Terran. This issue #15 owes its gratitude to Felicity Elworthy, Kate Dwyer, Cathy and Dave Hocker, Jack Dwyer, Sue Terran, Rachel Goodman, and Jill Birmingham. Special thanks to artists, Chelsea and Austin Hocker. Kerry Holman and Laurie Prouty were the facilitators.

Common Ground is printed on recycled paper.

Here it is, the end of fire season, and I don't have a truck to take my modest pile of household trash to the dump. What shall I do?

Well, I thought I'd just pile it up and burn it. That'd be easy. But of course, I can't keep the smoke within my property lines, so I thought I'd investigate this option to be sure it's safe.

I called The Department of Environmental Quality in Medford (776-6010) and asked them to send me the laws about at-home burning. I found this under "General Prohibitions Statewide:" "No person shall cause or allow to be initiated or maintained any open burning of wet garbage, plastic, wire insulation, automobile part, asphalt, petroleum product, petroleum treated material, rubber product, animal remains. . . or of any other material which normally emits dense smoke or noxious odors." Oh, well, now what? My pile has plastic milk jugs, PVC pipe, some carpet and more.

I figured the government was just being picky and restrictive as usual, so maybe I'd just exercise my sovereign right to do whatever I please. First, though, I asked a few agencies just what happens when you burn these things.

According to information from the Massachusetts Public Interest Research Group, my modest pile could release into our air, any and all of the following: mercury, lead, sulphur dioxide, hexane, acetone, formaldehyde, chlorine, and, from that harmless-looking PVC pipe, DIOXIN, one of the most deadly chemicals known. All of this, in small measure, promised to waft windward from my burn pile. Also, the resulting ash is classified as hazardous waste, and its presence on one's property will lower the resale value.

Clearly, burning this garbage was not an option. Out of concern for my neighbors and myself, I had to make a deal, borrow a truck and haul it to the dump.

And I urge you, dear neighbor and reader, to do the same.

-Kate Dwyer

After numerous appearances on national media and talks to thousands of high school and college students throughout the country, Floyd Cochran was surprised by the "controversy" that surrounded his visit to Josephine County last April. The Three Rivers School District was the first in the nation to bar Cochran's message from reaching students throughout county schools.

A former leader of the White Aryan Nations, Cochran knows what hate groups thrive on. The list of those seeking his expertise range from "Good Morning America" to the FBI. His "Education and Vigilance" project takes aim at the key ingredients of a successful organized hate movement; ignorance and apathy.

Last month Cochran returned to the Illinois Valley to speak to students at Lorna Byrne Middle School and IV High. After several months of dialogue, members of the Illinois Valley Human Rights Alliance and school officials were able to agree on Cochran's visit to the schools. While the Alliance was "disappointed that most of the high school students would still not be able to hear Cochran's valuable message" they applauded the "willingness of school officials to rethink their position."

IVHS principal Linda Hoback and Superintendent Carole Ricotta sat in on Cochran's presentation at the high school. When asked about her response to Cochran's presentation, Hoback stated that "he has a good message; prejudice and bias are illnesses in our society that need to be stopped." Ricotta was unavailable for comment.

Weary from touring four states in the previous 12 days, Cochran was stirred by the caliber of questions he fielded from students. "When I talk to adults, unfortunately I get a lot of questions about the OJ trial. These kids didn't even mention that. Their questions tended to be quite intelligent!"

Recalling his visit last April, Cochran said he was "really impressed by the persistence of the Alliance. It's great to know this community has advocates of education and vigilance. When it comes to bigotry, it really is the key to prevention," If you would like to support the work of the Alliance, please contact Dave Toler (592-3908) or Barry Snitkin (592-4459).

-D. Toler

TAKILMA DAILY RITUALS

Try to match the ritual with the person. #1 is an example:

1. CARA
2. MENNO
3. ERIK
4. FELICITY
5. SALLY
6. DELLA
7. MEADOW
8. GAIL
9. LANCE
10. SHEILA
11. ALYCE
12. MARCY
13. PACO
14. SUE
15. SNJ

___ Before meals our family holds hands and we say something we're thankful for.
___ When we get together after our days work, we consciously commit to being there for each other. Before going to bed, I spend time drawing.
___ Wake up, build a fire, make tea and spend time writing and drawing.
___ Masturbate.
___ I stay away from ritual because it's so enclosed.
___ My husband wakes up at 5:15am, gets the fire going, makes coffee. At 5:30am, I get up, find my cup, pull up the wicker chair by the fire and begin to wake up.
___ I like to watch the sun come up, changing the colors of the leaves and trees-starts my whole day right..
___ I check to see if my Marjorie-thing is still there and if it's not-I put it on.
___ Putting the chickens to bed.
___ Taking out the compost-regenerate.
_1_ Going peep at my mom.
___ Just coffee and the daily b.m.
___ Best days start with a long hot shower- the shower comes before the coffee.
___ I have to write 3 pages in my journal
___ Brushing teeth. Love that fresh, minty taste of toothpaste. Don't forget the tongue.

TAKILMA CROSSWORD
by Dave

ACROSS

1. JFK beat this Dick
5. Y for women
8. Aye aye
9. Minora's big buddy
11. Feminine crumb-catcher
13. Elevator option
15. Hepburn or Roncalio
18. The whole enchilada
19. Steely ___
21. Boutros' org.
23. Credit card company
24. Tennis court divider
26. Bilbo's species
29. Thankful corpse ?
30. Eastern Daylight Time
31. Scared
32. Banners
33. Don't stop!
34. Mideast powerhouse
37. Florida Disneyland
40. Kayla, Linda, or Brenda
42. Discourteous
43. Popular CD-Rom game
44. Perfect concept
46. Stretch forth
48. Pointed hole-maker
49. Wrap up a meeting
50. Six point score

DOWN

1. Vampire's target
2. Mike Tyson's religion
3. Neighbor of Council Bluffs, Iowa
4. Belly button
5. Bear or Berra
6. Crane operator?
7. OR's southern neighbor
10. Premium Swiss cheese
12. He phoned home
14. Interviewer's tools (3 wds.)
16. What Perry White did
17. Sudden thrust
20. Come ___ you are
22. Computer type, often
23. Veni _____ vici
25. Good trade for tit
26. Health restorer
27. Awful homonym
28. Satiated and bored
32. Broke wind
33. Supernatural being
34. Woe ___ ___
35. Lower world river
36. Dread wearer
38. Restaurant shrimp
39. Reject lumber grade
41. Talking horse's name
44. Marriage vow (2 wds.)
45. Auditory organ
47. State near NY

SUBSCRIBE TO COMMON GROUND!

___$10 A ONE YEAR SUBSCRIPTION

NAME _____

___$25 A ONE YEAR SUBSCRIPTION PLUS
A HAND PRINTED T-SHIRT IN
YOUR CHOICE OF COLORS(BLUE,
GREEN, BRONZE OR PLUM) AND
SIZE (S,M,L,XL).

ADDRESS _____

_____

TAKILMA Common Ground
P.O. BOX 2016
CAVE JUNCTION, OR.
97523

BULK RATE
U.S. POSTAGE
PAID
CAVE JUNCTION
OREGON 97523
PERMIT #16

Risk the growth. Open to your power.
Incense and candle
Time made sacred
Unfold.
Affirm all is possible.
Get guidance in.
transform by fire.
by taking the space.
Faith in potential.

Takilma
Common Ground
- Tread Lightly -
Issue #16   Dec - Jan 95-96

WORK: A LOVE SONG

Work. The word is positively turgid with meaning. If we are suffering from some irritating personality aberration, our friends tell us that we should "work" on that. We exercise by "working out." We tend to refer to any endeavor as work the minute that it becomes laborious. For some of us, the realization that something is work is a signal to deepen our committment; for others, it is a signal to gracefully withdraw. I once attended a dinner of Gurdjieff followers who continually toasted "The Work." In that case, I'm not sure, but I came away with the impression that "The Work" they were referring to was the achievement of self-realization, or something in that genre. The work that this treatise is referring to is the work that someone is willing to pay us for, either directly or indirectly.

"If it was easy, they wouldn't call it work." I think that we are all set up by that concept in a certain way. The idea that work is a curse that only befalls peoplewho can't afford leisure makes it real easy to focus on the negative aspects of having a job, such as having to be there every day, putting up with percieved demeaning demands on your behavior, boredom, or, worse yet, actual physical exhaustion. I think that each of us has the option of looking at work as either a curse or a blessing. Personally, I have moments when I yearn for more leisure, bemoaning the fact that my financial responsibilities won't allow me to stop working. In those times, I think of all the glorious things that I would do, if just had the time to do them. I'm kidding myself when I think like that. I know how I am. I need work to keep me centered. When I don't have work, I don't do those noble things that I imagined I would. I become a couch potato, and the more I couch potato, the more I don't want to do anything but couch potato. Of course, not everyone is as devoid of personal ambition as myself, but we all depend on work, more than we realize, to keep us motivated.

Work defines us. We can be a parent, a volunteer fireman, a member of the bridge club and a motorcycle enthusiast or what have you, but if we are a teacher or a mill worker as well, chances are others think of us as a member of our profession, rather than one of those other sides of us. We think of ourselves in relation to the work that we do. Even the most ignoble job carries with it the pride of providing for your own support, and a lot of jobs earn the envy of other people. When someone skewers you with the gimlet eye and says, "What do *you* do?," we are most apt to reply with our vocation. However, I once read of a French painter who always replied, "I'm a breather," to that question. I had a friend that was into being a saint who always answered simply, "Good," to that question. But I think those are exceptions to the rule.

Work gives us all a chance to prove to ourselves that we can do something. We can make a contribution. We are not just taking up space. If we have a job, we feel better about ourselves in a certain way. Work is the supreme form of self-expression. Even the most menial task gives us a chance to prove to ourselves, and others, the depth of our committment, or constancy and our dependability. More exalted work gives us a chance to express every aspect of ourselves.

The dark side of all this is when all of these positive aspects of work take over, and work becomes an obsession. It seems to me that there is a fine line between being commmitted to work and being obsessed with work. A certain kind of a job can be a tempting seductress. It is often true that more ego gratification is obtained from doing one's job than from looking after one's home, or family, or relationships. It is not very often that someone comes up to you and says, "Ya know, I noticed that you are really doing a good job of keeping it together with your significant other." Or," You sure are being a good parent." The results of effort put into your job are more immediately evident, in most cases. I'm done now. I just know that everyone is going to read this love song to work and think, "Yup, I just knew that Delbert Kauffman was hung up on work." -Delbert Kauffman

WILL THE REAL JOB PLEASE STAND UP?

Work! Can't you just hear Maynard G. Krebs. Work is not necessarily your job. Work is hard, unpleasant sorta stuff, something someone else should surely be doing for you, if they had the decency to do so, graciously, of course.

Work! is crappy or no kindling. I am cursed with this blue collar ethic. Up before dawn like god herself will surely strike me dead if I were to lay about. First fire in the morning is my sordid ordeal. A heater that will hold a cinder of any consequence? Ha! This is work.

Bathrooms. Could I possibly be the only person with olfactory intact? This is a job! Other people's most personal dirt.

Personal grooming, definitely a job. Any time one must spend in front of a mirror is work. I'm old; I don't particularly like this constant primping and fluffing. Never could apply or buy makeup, had to wait for the girls to get old enough to help, and you know they'd rather make you look like a clown than take their last breath.

Exercise is work. When did our bodies become part-time jobs?

Sick people are work. Children are awful; husbands much worse. My Mike does sick not to be missed. The big ones will actually come home from college with ills acquired from roommates I haven't even met.

Jobs are not necessarily work. I, for one, have the most terrific stupid job in town. It only becomes a job on occasion. It's a job when I've asked you if you would like cheese with your sandwich, and I have to hear about your colonic flush or how long you've been a vegan. Please spare me the details, not only of your colon health, but why dairy products are the curse of all mankind.

Meaningful work is a joke. Keep it simple; it's work or it's play.

Holidays, work, work, work. Thanksgiving, pass the smallpox blankees, care for a little turkey we poached from your backyard? What are we celebrating here? Christmas, what other holiday do you send paper to people you haven't seen in years, and prezzies to folks you can't stand.

Until next time, get a job.   *-Geraldine Davidson*

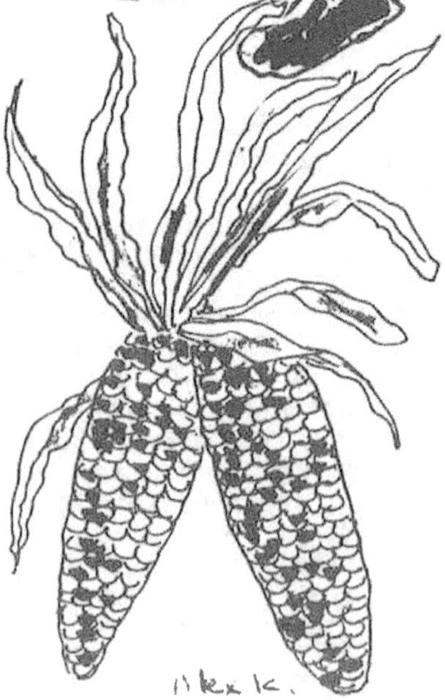

WORK, COMPULSION AND REST

A day of zero productivity.
-365 Things to be Happy About
And on the seventh day God rested
-Genesis

It's the winter solstice, that time when plant growth slows, Mother Nature takes a break from gardening, and we are offered the longest sleep of the year. It's a good time to think about how we work and how we rest.

Many of us were raised in some association with Judao-Christian religion, which mandates a weekly day of rest. Although most people only remember being dragged to boring religious services on that day, setting aside a day of rest does at least have the potential to be meaningful. It's true that Sabbath observances date from a time when subsistence living left no concept of leisure, much less a two day weekend. We are theoretically on a 40 hour work week, going home to a life of 20th century ease. The reality, of course, is that today many people are working as hard, or harder, than ever. Here in the Illinois Valley, we are a very mixed bag. While some have retained a life of voluntary simplicity and with it a lot of free time, others are coming home from 8 or more hours to do their gardens or work on their houses- often while trying to meet the needs of their children. Single parenting, long commutes, small businesses and/or the urge to be a homesteader while still needing income create very long work hours. Workaholism, a term created since leisure time became a concept, to many, also comes into play. There is no end to the projects that can be dreamed up by an imaginative homesteader. While usually valid and worthy, some use extra work compulsively. Sometimes it is easier to go into more activity than to slow down and feel one's feelings.

It's good that the creative imagination wants to make life better. Yet it is important sometimes to stop and regroup. Maybe that's why those days of rest were set aside originally. Whether a very intense agenda stems from necessity or compulsiveness, the result is the same- stress, which is overactivity of one part of the nervous system, allowing no time for repair, re-creation or looking at ourselves. Making a conscious decision to rest wait allows muscles to relax, and the fight or flight reaction to stop. Digestion and assimilation of food becomes possible, and major stress-related illness may even be prevented. It's nice to take a break when you can enjoy it, rather than having to get sick to feel you deserve it. Setting aside a time for emptiness and inactivity also allows sacred space into our lives, and through this can come change and growth.

When activity stops and we allow a contemplative, quiet time to occur, the same person will not resume activity. With even brief rest and repair things can be looked at differently. And that is a true Sabbath.
-Rachel Goodman

REMEMBERING LINDA TREE

A friend died this month, unexpectedly, in her sleep. She is at peace, but what of those left behind, her son Jesse, her friends, her acquaintances? Linda was a woman of substance, a woman with a warm heart. She had the ability to let me feel close to her, even though we might only see each other five or six times a year. There was always a kind word, a hug, a smile. Linda was a wonderful mom, involved, devoted and fun-loving. She could always be seen at Jesse's games, full of enthusiasm and encouragement. Linda recently moved to Eugene after getting Jesse settled in college at SOSC. She was excited about getting out there in the world, moving on in life now that her everyday parenting stage was over.

I will miss you, Linda. In my humble opinion, you died too damn soon. But who knows what is the right time to die? It certainly reinforces my belief in keeping a clean slate with all those in my life who have touched me in some way. Goodbye, friend.
Love, *Gloria*

You would know the secret of death.

But how shall you find it, unless you seek it in the heart of life?

The owl, whose night-bound eyes are blind unto the day, cannot unveil the mystery of light.

If you would indeed behold the spirit of death, open your heart wide unto the body of life.

For life and death are one, even as the river and the sea are one.

-Kahlil Gibran, *The Prophet*

OF RITUALS AND RESPONSIBILITY

The last issue of Common Ground, highlighting rituals, felt like an appropriate segue into the issue of air quality in our valley. As you've probably noticed, our deteriorating air quality is becoming a frequent problem, demanding prompt solutions lest we rival our toxic neighbors in Medford. Autos and industrials are not our primary source; wood stoves are. Due to its large particulate size, wood smoke is a major health concern, and as it becomes trapped in the tiny air sacs deep in our lungs it reduces both lung capacity and the functional ability to exchange oxygen and carbon dioxide. This can cause permanent damage at any age, but children are even more susceptible.

The first step in solving this problem is to recognize that this cherished ritual is ancient, stemming from a time when neither population nor air quality was a concern... but that was then. Now we need to be flexible and responsible enough to make necessary sacrifices for everyone's sake.

Here are a few suggestions to help lessen our impact: 1. When you wake on a cold morning in your abode, wait to strike that match. Pile on those winter clothes, and stoke that internal flame with hot fluids. (Hot H2O does wonders.) You'll be surprised how long you maintain a quality comfort level, and you'll find that cold air doesn't have to mean a cold body. 2. Save your $s and insulate. Energy, fuels and time will be greatly enhanced if you trap the heat you work so hard to create. 3. Intersperse down time with active periods to keep your blood circulating; i.e., walk, run, jump before being still for long periods...our bodies are very effective thermal units if we prime them.

Following these suggestions, you may find that you can delay burning till afternoon or evening, or even skip a day. Every bit helps our air remain clear. If burning is imminent, strive for complete combustion to help ameliorate smoking conditions. Use dry wood. A green log, smoldering all night, contributes significant smoke, which is trapped near the ground by the heavier cold air of the night.

While an efficient stove may be too spendy for some, there are many of you who can afford the initial cost--remember that you/we will save in the long run by burning less wood. Be aware of conditions outside; is there a North wind which will blow the smoke to the base of our mountains, trapping us in a toxic cloud? Or is there a no-wind condition, resulting in the same effect?

These suggestions enable us to examine the absurd notion that many of us seem to have about some inalienable comfort right to remain sparsely clad (T-shirts?!) throughout winter in Southern Oregon. This is not the tropics. Unless we, as individuals, are willing to make air quality a priority, we could find ourselves restricted by the same regulations already in effect in surrounding locations. I think we can avoid that.

So next time you're thinking of building a fire. stop a minute and consider that you are indeed part of the bigger picture...before striking that match.   -Sara Mayer

A ROVING REPORTER INVESTIGATES WORK

Work, some is a pleasure, some a real drag. Is money the driving force behind our workaday world? I interviewed several Takilmaites both east and west, and here is a sampling of their responses.

Question: What do you do for work? If you suddenly had an endless supply of money, what work would you do, if any? How would you spend your time?

Laurie Prouty- Sewing. "Gardening and travel. I would build a greenhouse and volunteer time to our many great organizations."

Ron Raven-Photographer. "Exploration."

Katherine Roncalio-Teacher. "Have another day off per week, more hiking."

Helen Kauffman-Teacher. "Easy question. I would do what I already do, or garden."

Jenny Mae Donnell-Theatre Arts. "Bring quality theatre to my community."

Leo Goodman-Carpenter, woodworker. "Build a shop and still do woodwork. I would hire more people in the community to help my child Ian. I would buy all timber sales and not log them, buy the Selma mill for appropriate wood use, work on alternative energy projects, and work to legalize hemp products."

Dan Heller-Road tapes, business consultant. "I'd spend half my time setting up organizations to benefit society through environmental matters, and the other half just having a good time."

Heidi Parker-Shames-Teacher, judge, policewoman, dishwasher, maid, nurse, psychiatrist--in other words, a mom."I wouldn't spent my time much differently. I would hire someone to be with the kids a little more of the time so I could go to school, study everything and see what pulls my interest. I'd also also do service work."

I believe that what I have gathered here, fellow Commongrounders, is a sense that many of us are pretty satisfied with our current line of work. Supplementary time for play, travel, philanthropic deeds and the freedom to create new possibilities appear to be the major thing lacking for most of the folks I interviewed. How fortunate that many of the people we know find joy and gratification in doing what they already do.

See ya next time,
Your roving reporter. *Gloria*

WITNESS

This late October morning
loud rumbles fill the sky.
To the South, just above
the orange and yellow of autumn
just above that mountain,
hovers the helicopter
poised above its prey.
It growls and strains and pulls
up the huge dismembered trunk
of our old friend.
It strains and groans
until both veer crazily
over the ridge.
Geese protest overhead.
The wind rises.
Cedars and firs, still safe
in the valley grove,
sway their ancient farewell.

-Alison Aldrich

Tonight, when you lay your head on your pillow, forget how far you still have to go. Look instead at how far you've already come.

PROTECTING THE FOREST

TAKILMA COMMUNITY ACTION NETWORK!!!

Steering Committee: To coordinate action of the other committees. Phone contact to be announced.

Peaceful Action: To plan and carry out only peaceful actions that will effectively assure the protection of our public forests. 592-4233

Media: Education and outreach to the general public about the proposed Waldo thin sale. 592-3508 or -4269

Cultural Resources: To collect public input concerning the cultural and spiritual importance of the public forests around us and to establish recognition of these values by public agencies. 592-6734 or -2549

Letters: To facilitate the accumulation of public input from the community. 592-6254

Tours: Guided tours will be arranged to better familiarize the community and the public at large with these forests around us. 592-4619, -2311

Management Plan: To develop an alternative forest plan that embraces the visions of the Takilma community, ensuring aesthetic viewshed, ecological inte grity, etc. 592-3908

Economic Alternatives: To develop an eco-touring/cultural arts- based economy that provides opportunity for 21th century Takilmaites, and is dependent on a healthy forest environment. 592-3908

Cumulative Effects Document: To record the ecological impacts that have already occurred within the Upper East Fork Illinois watershed, particularly the unknown effects of private logging. 592-2214

PUBLIC FORESTS AT RISK IN TAKILMA

Unless you've long since entered your winter dormant phase, you're doubtless aware of the proposed Waldo Thin timber sale on BLM lands near the very heart of Takilma. Roughly speaking, the lands BLM is considering include three basic areas: the steep slope across from the Green Bridge, an area part way up the Hope Mtn. Road, and a large block on the West side of our valley encompassing Allen, Sailor, and upper Scotch Gulches, and dropping over the ridge into Fry Gulch and the old Waldo town site.

Recognizing the need for some specific information on BLM's plans, Takilma Community Association (TCA) organized a community forum with BLM Resource Area Manager Bob Korfhage and three of his staff on Nov. 30. The meeting was a shining example of Takilma at its finest: over 150 people expressing themselves eloquently, in diverse styles but with a single-mindedness of purpose. The specific information we gleaned consisted of: (1)Bob cannot place our valley off-limits to logging; all he can decide is when and how it will be logged— however, he admitted this could include deferring logging for, say, 100 years, after which our descendants could try to delay it further; (2) BLM intends to do a thorough analysis for this sale, yet somehow expects to make a decision by next April or May; (3) Bob says only hard data from us about these parcels and their special resource values can influence his decision— a deluge of form letters will not sway him, nor will a bunch of emotional talk about how "we love these forests"— however, portraying our community as a "cultural resource," of which the forests are an integral part, and/or the forests as our religious sites, may hold promise.

So—what can be done to stop this sale? Start with a letter to the BLM: Bob Korfhage/BLM Medford Dist./3040 Biddle Rd./ Medford, OR 97504. Next, take a hike. Become intimate with the forests at issue, here. To facilitate this a guided hike is planned to Hope Mtn. and Allen Gulch on Dec. 30 meeting at SREP at 10:00 and then at Bill and Joya's at 1:30. If you indicated an interest in hikes on the sign-up sheet at the meeting, you will be notified of other hikes as they come up. If you can get together at least 4 people, we will try to arrange a date to take your group out. Call Romain, 592-3911, or Bill, 592-4619 for Scotch and Allen Gulches; Kerry, 592-3958 for Hope.; and Jonny, 592-2741 for Green Bridge area.

Dave T., 592-3908, will lead a tour of the Noreast BLM sale, on Jan. 6, at 2:00—meet at Dave's. People can see what a very recent marking looks like (it hasn't been cut yet.) Fred M., 592-3770 can give directions to the recently cut Moosehorn sale near Kerby. This is the one the BLM repeatedly urged us to look at as an example of their new, enlightened thinning practices.

Kate D., 592-2214, could use plenty of help determining—from county records and individual land owners— the extent of past timber cutting in our entire watershed, so as to present to BLM the big picture they still lack. We need to prepare materials for the press, including videos for TV. Anyone with expertise in this area can call any of the above people to get plugged in.

Red-tailed Hawk and Southern Oregon Siskiyous
(Buteo jamaicensis)
Broadly distributed throughout North America in open country. Eats mammals and small birds. Nests on stick platform in trees or on ledges.

Scout frequently for BLM vehicles near any of these parcels— recognized by the white U.S. Gov't plates. If you see one, by all means confront the workers in a friendly way (look for them in the stands) and talk to them at great length. Bring along your friends, too.

So you see, there are many ways to be involved here. With the energy, intelligence, and solidarity displayed at the community meeting, I feel we have an excellent chance to abort the sale. But it will require action, not just talk, on everyone's part. So plug in, and save our church!

-Bill Gray

The letter committee has a file at the Siskiyou Project for the purpose of documenting our community's strong support. Please send a copy of your letter to the file at:
Siskiyou Regional Educational Project
P.O. Box 220
Cave Junction, OR 97523
You can also drop your copy off at the Project's office, located Right before the Domeschool at 9335 Takilma Road. Copies of the data sheet on possible local BLM logging can also be picked up there.

-Kayde Mowery

TheSREP office has offered the use of their computer, paper, envelopes and stamps to anyone wanting to write a letter about he proposed BLM logging. SREP has has a special bulletin board for information pertaining to this situation located in the front porch of the building. Please come and write your letter!

We Come to Mourn the Ancient Trees

Betsey Jacobs

♩=100

C   Am   C   Am

1.Where once a great ca-   the- dral stood a   can- o- py of   green,   with
2.   though we've fought to   save them we are   los- ing by de-   grees.   Can-
3.   here we stand to-   geth- er now up-   on the ver- y   land   where

C   Am   C   Am

shafts of fil- tered   sun- light cast- ing   dia- monds in the   streams   where
not the truth be   heard at last and   change their des- ti-   nies?   When
once we thought we   had a chance to   make them un- der-   stand.   Let's

C   Em   F   E7

once there was a   wealth of life there'll   soon be stands of   trees   where
Mo- ther Earth has   gi- ven birth to   trea- sures such as   these,   oh,
all pre- serve the   im- age of the   gi- ants that re-   main;   and

C   Am   C   Am

crea- tures vie for   live- li- hood and   cower a- mongst the   leaves--   as
how can man dis-   turb her plan and   cre- ate such dis-   ease   as
let us mourn the   ones we've lost for   mere fin- an- cial   gain,   as

C   Cm   Ab   Cm

one   by   one   they kill the anc- ient   trees;   as

Ab   [1, 1 Cm]

one   by   one   we mourn the anc- ient   trees.   al-
                                                                So

[2, 2 Cm]   FIN.

trees.

8

To the editors:

The first "Takilma" style drum 'n dance fest brought on an evening of healing and fun. On my own personal levels, rewards were many. Drumming before men and women of my community, with my maestro Simbo, orchestrating a large group of drummers, and, of course, all the "Nice going, Miguelo"s, and "Thanks, Miguelo," were needed "strokes" for sure. However, the most significant reward for myself was this simple revelation: in a true community, one does not need to put out a large amount of energy to have a very positive effect on the whole. I wish to state here that it was the sum total of all our small doings that made the evening work. Together, we manifested some dinero for the Domeschool and stimulated the economies of some local pastry women- danced, drummed and sang like an eagle (thanks, Grey!). Simply put, we celebrated ritual, crossed ethnic and cultural boundaries. We acted in spontaneity; no attitude, no problems. We should all be pleased with our manifestation, and I for one wonder what other events are prancing around in our "inner space."

I believe that the same outcome would naturally follow any "solidarity" movement we would show. It's obvious "we" cannot count on "them" for anything, whatever that "them" be; BLM, Forest Service, or the law enforcement agencies. Our frustrations are sure to rise if we expect anyone to change who "them" are and become what we believe in. It's difficult for me to imagine calling on the same "cops" that fly over and intimidate us in Sept./Oct. if we have a driving too fast problem in Nov. through Aug., or to expect help in the "meth" arena. We need to solve our problems through our solidarity. The beautiful Illinois is the common denominator. I believe a good show of solidarity is to make a committment to not drive faster than 20 mph!! this side of four corners.   -Miguelo

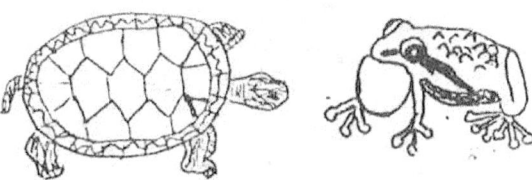

COMMON GROUND was created to present a forum for information and ideas on issues of concern in our community. Our theme for the next issue is one dear to our hearts- The Forest. We encourage you to write about what does the forest mean to you, your experiences, feelings, how you see our local culture connected with the forest and how our culture is supported by leaving the forest standing. The deadline for submissions is Jan. 20 and Kerry Holman, 592-2549, will be the facilitator. We would love to hear from many of you. Editing is available if you want or need. Please write!

We would like to thank Dave Toler for his great talent and skill for paste-up in issue #15. Issue #16 thanks **Facilitator:** Rachel Goodman; **Staff:** Dave Toler, Kerry Holman, Dave Hocker, Laurie Prouty, Sara Meyer, and Debbie Lukas at SREP; **Graphics:** Jill Birmingham, Alex Krupka, Cathy Hocker and Cara Rose. Common Ground is printed on recycled paper.

The Sun had a dream...
of the time of the Sun of Flowers: Heaven on Earth,
divine children dancing in the golden octave of creation.
Sojourner, come to the threshold of this new dawning!
From the Mayan Oracle

AHAU-ahow'-Lord of the Sun

We are the children of the sun, we circle for healing, for love, strength, death, birth, reunion. We are the children of the Sun, we pray together to varied manifestations of Creator; we pray on mountaintops, in caves, in sweatlodges; we pray with peyote, with sweet grass, tobacco, white sage, and with the sacred pipe that was brought to us from White Buffalo Woman on Turtle Island. We pray in many languages, tongues and minds. We pray with one heart.

We are the children of the Sun, we dance, we sing, we chant in celebration of our Mother Earth, of our oneness. In Takilma and Williams I especially see us dancing in the dream of harmony, health, happiness and the many varied spaces of realities.

We are the children of the Sun; we work to create a non-nuclear planet, we work to help the tree people be able to stand tall and alive on our Mother Earth. We work in ways that help our watersheds be pure and clean for our children and grandchildren. We work for the creator here on Earth. We are the children of the Sun; we honor the passing of the earth around the sun, solstices and equinoxes; we honor the new moon and the full moon and dark of the moon as far as planting in the earth.

We are the children of the Sun; we honor our elders in varied forms; human, tree, fossil animal and the Great Mystery. We honor the directions of the sacred hoop: East-dawn, South-child, West-sunset, North-elders' wisdom. We honor the Sky-our father, the earth-our mother, and Within-our-heart. We honor the elements; earth, fire, water and air. We honor our food grown within our mother, the healing herbs, the clean waters, the messages of the rock people. We honor the children and look seven generations a-coming as we are called to make decisions and guide our ship on Turtle Island.

We are the children of the Sun, and for all things that I have left unspoken I chant, om mani padme hum, and I sing out, love is the way...in peace I am *Maya Many Moons Reames*, dark of the moon, Williams, Oregon, indian summer's golden time '95.

CHILDREN LEARN WHAT THEY LIVE

Work was always one of those four letter words my parents so dutifully avoided when the kids were around. That might have been a factor in the state of shock I experienced when confronting the real world after school. But my parents didn't hold a monopoly on avoiding the work issue. Did you ever take basic economics in grade school? Even today, it's not offered. Yet what issue has more control over our everyday lives than money?

Unconstrained by the multitude of learned <u>assumptions</u> that afflict adulthood, children can be quite open-minded. Unlike their elders, children seem much more likely to base their assessments on personal experience. Perhaps that's why we avoid any serious explanations concerning our economic system. Perhaps many of these fundamental <u>assumptions</u> that serve to legitimize our economic system would come under heavy scrutiny through the open minds of our children.

For instance, have you ever tried to explain to your kid why fierce competition is the corner stone of our economic success? Don't be surprised if you get a look of dazed confusion. After all, they might still remember your most recent role in the last sibling squabble over who is the best, gets the most, or gets to be first. And don't think about those lectures on the virtues of cooperation; it'll only make you feel more awkward.

Then there's private property, a tenet of unquestioned faith by the time you hit 20. But for a kid who's trying to adopt the concept of sharing, it can really get a bit complicated. The desire to play with an idle toy or on a vacant lot is consistently superceded by the respect for another's property. It doesn't take long for children to figure out that ownership pulls a lot more weight than sharing.

At the heart of our economic system, the institution of profit may be the most difficult for youth to accept. I remember the kid down the block who used to hire some of us to cut and trim yards in the neighborhood. He owned the equipment; we did all the work. He felt he deserved a good chunk of our pay because he supplied the tools (or was it his folks?) All I know is , we didn't swallow his economic theory without some significant gag reflex. And I don't recall that he had too many friends, either.

I guess it takes some aging to accept as fair that 20% of Americans should earn more money than the remaining 80%, or that only 10% of households own 70% of the tools. Perhaps, as adults, we can recapture some of our youth and vigor to act on our experiences rather than the rigid assumptions we so dutifully learned to justify this insanity. Personally, I'm feeling younger every day.   *-Dave Toler*

Work is doing your part in relationship to other human beings. It is a means of connection to the whole community. If not compulsive or overdone, work will make you feel good and stay healthy.

As young human beings in our teen years, most of us prefer to avoid work. Work is just one more thing the older folks are telling us we have to do.

Work is a way for us to express our love and creativity. It also gives us a personal identity, as well as being a means to supply our basic needs and desires. Physical use of hands and body in doimg work is therpeutic in utilizing nervous energy, and will create peace of mind. Work is essential in living a stable life-style.   *-Al Karger*

If you want your dreams to be,
Take your time, go slowly.
Do few things but do them well.
Heartfelt work goes purely.
              -Donovan
      in *Brother Sun, Sister Moon*

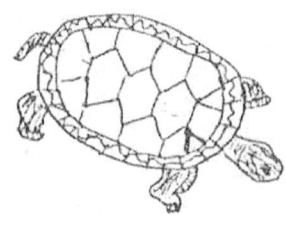

Common Ground Calendar

DECEMBER

SUNDAY	MONDAY	TUESDAY	WEDNESDAY	THURSDAY	FRIDAY	SATURDAY
17	18	19	20	21	22	23
24	25	YOGA PRACTICE TCB 4PM $1.00 26	27	28	29	LBMS & IVHS DANCE PARTY IVHS 8--12 $2.00 30

JANUARY

SUNDAY	MONDAY	TUESDAY	WEDNESDAY	THURSDAY	FRIDAY	SATURDAY
	FOOD BUYING CLUB TCB 10AM 1	YOGA 2	3	4	FULL MOON 12:51 PM 5	6
7	8	REFLECTIONS ART SHOW IVHS 5:30-7:30 YOGA 9	DOME SCHOOL BOARD MEETING 10	COUNTRY DANCE TCB 4-5:30 11	BAROQUE CONCERT NEWMAN METHODIST CHURCH GP 8:00 PM 12	13
14	FOOD BUYING CLUB TCB 3 PM 15	YOGA 16	17	PTA IVHS 6:60PM 18	19	CG SUBMISSION DUE NEW MOON 4:50 AM 20
21	22	YOGA 23	24	COUNTRY DANCE TCB 4-5:30 25	26	CHINA LEFT MEETING 592-3386 27
BEATLES CELEBRATION TCB 1-5 PM (SEE BELOW) 28	FOOD BUYING CLUB TCB3PM 29	YOGA 30	31			

1/28 BEATLES' MOVIE, SNACKS, AND SING-A-LONG.

CALL **DEBBIE** 592-2866 OR 592-3911   BEATLES' MUSIC & PARAPHENILA WANTED.

FEBRUARY

SUNDAY	MONDAY	TUESDAY	WEDNESDAY	THURSDAY	FRIDAY	SATURDAY
					HEADWATERS FOREST ACTIVISTS CONFERENCE 482-4459 1	2	3
CONFERENCE CONTINUED 4	5	YOGA 6	7	COUNTRY DANCE TCB 4-5:30 8	9	10

REMEMBER TO GET YOUR DOME SCHOOL 1996 CALENDAR. AVAILABLE AT THE SILVER LINING IN CJ.

CLASSIFIED ADS

Seeking spiritually minded land partner. 20 acres Sucker Creek frontage, forest, meadow. $45,000 cash. Must be financially secure enough to build up-to-code home. Send photo and biography to Deborah Lee and Alex, Box 1286, Cave Junction OR 97523

Feet Wanted for Reflexology. Let us touch your soles, to relieve stress and tension. Sliding scale $5-10.00. Call Diane 592-3908 or Mar 592-4436.

Looking for 1-3 people who may be interested in sharing living expenses in Chico, Calif., while earning money distributing U.S. West phone books. Work would last 7-10 days beginning Jan. 10. Call Al Karger, 597-2205.

Garden and yardwork my speciality. I follow directions well and can do other projects. Al Karger, 597-2205

Greatest dinners in town: 1000 Cranes Deli and Bakery. Every Friday night, reservations a must. 592-3436

Lost: At the W.A.L.L. action at Greyback Campground. Painting of mountains and tree, "honor sacred land" on cardboard. If found, call Marjorie, 592-6733

For sale: 1970 Volvo. Engine runs good, new elec. and steering rack, new battery. Parts car. $100, you tow. Marjorie, 592-6733

24 volt, 2500 watt inverter. Excellent condition, run washing machine/power tools/ computer with your own DC energy/batteries. Call 592-2311.

Lost: Guatemalan shawl, blues, greens, lavenders. Burn hole in one corner. Very attached to it. Joya, 592-4619.

DOMESCHOOL CALENDARS- The Domeschool has great new homegrown 1996 calendars for sale. They're full of cute art by the elementary students, packed with interesting dates and goddess festivals, and bound with plastic spiral binding. $4.00 at the school M-F 10:00-3:00 or call 592-3911.

Crossword solution

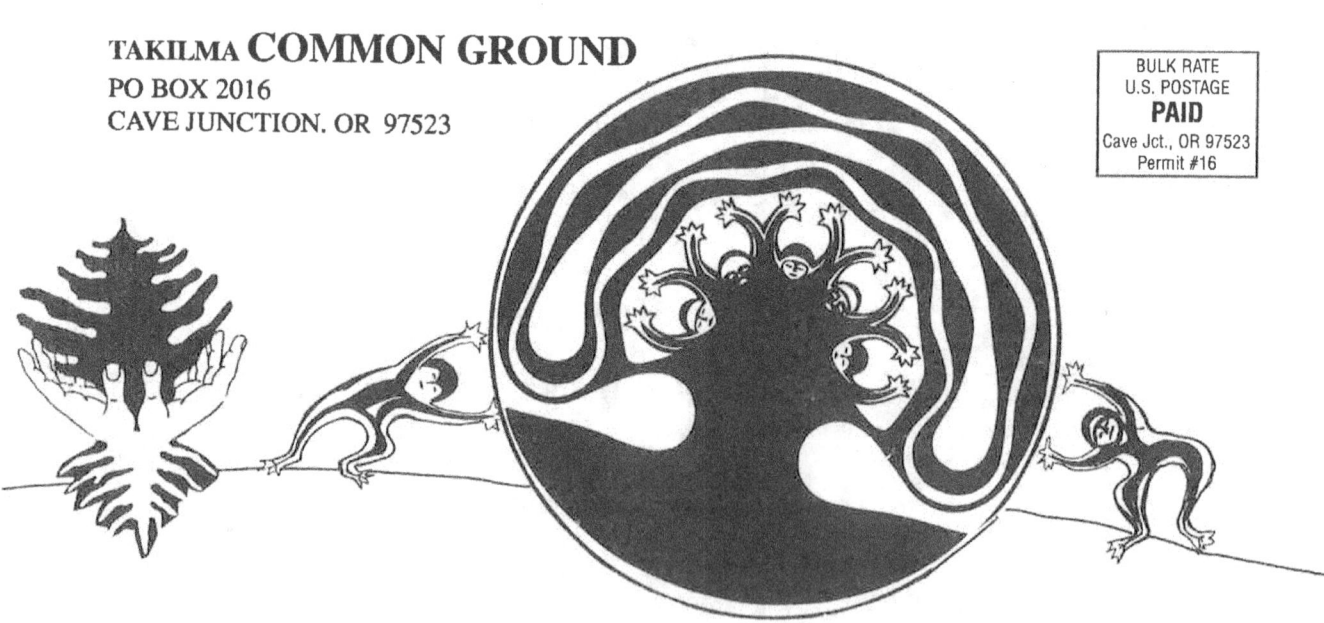

TAKILMA COMMON GROUND
PO BOX 2016
CAVE JUNCTION. OR 97523

ISSUE 17   CANDLEMAS '96

Takilma Common Ground

THE FOREST AROUND US ~ OUR SANCTUARY

WALDO THIN DROPPED - FOR NOW

"At this point there is no Waldo Thin timber sale for the 1996 Sale Plan." BLM manager Bob Korfhage's message to an ad hoc committee of Takilma residents has sent a deep sigh of relief rippling throughout the community. Korfhage met with the committee on January 16th in Takilma.

Korfhage first introduced the Waldo Thin Sale to the community in an open meeting held last November 29th. The proposed Sale area covered many of the foothills surrounding Takilma. Over 150 concerned Takilma-ites turned out for that meeting and spoke overwhelmingly against the Sale. In a subsequent Takilma community meeting held December 20th, and ad hoc committee was formed to meet with Korfhage in January.

Representing the Takilma community, the committee delegation carried with them a two-dimensional bottom line: No Cut! And No Timber Sales as long as the Logging Without Laws Salvage Rider exists. The Rider insulates BLM and Forest Service Sales from virtually all environmental laws and regulations.

At the January 16th meeting, it seemed evident that the November turn out had made an impression on Korfhage. He stated that *"after going to that meeting, I thought pretty long and hard about what was said at the meeting. I heard what was said there, and I thought there was room for pause in terms of timber sales."*

With a NO Cut objective in mind, several members from the committee searched unsuccessfully for a commitment from Korfhage beyond 1996. Unable to get anything more definitive, members of the delegation turned to the matter of the ominous Salvage Rider. To that question Korfhage responded that *"to the best of my knowledge, the lands (we've indicated) will not be affected by the Salvage Rider."*

Korfhage proposed that the Takilma community join with the BLM to develop land use strategies by the end of the year. It was unclear whether or not that would include some level of timber harvest. Korfhage did acknowledge that *"as long as any BLM lands are in the matrix, sometime we're going to be there."* The entire Waldo Thin Sale area is within the matrix.

The possibility of removing these lands from the matrix was held out by Korfhage. He made it clear that he needs relevant information in order to do so. *"All I'm looking for is that kind of data because I'm going to be politically pressed from other groups, you know 'how come you're setting all this stuff (aside) out in Takilma, those people got you all upset, they've got you scared' and that's what I'm gonna hear, but I want to be able to say, here's the data. I don't want to make decisions based on personal feelings."*

Referring to the rather contentious relationship the BLM has had with Takilma over the years, Korfhage appeared intent on forging a more positive relationship between the two in the future. Korfhage said he canceled the Waldo Sale because *"I felt that development of a good relationship with this community was worth the risk of what might happen in terms of my performance in putting up volume."*

Judging from the response of several delegates after the meeting, it appears Korfhage has been effective in gaining trust and a cautious optimism from many of the delegates. Typical of many responses was, "I think Bob might be sympathetic towards the desires of our community." Only time will tell whether a cooperative venture between the BLM and Takilma will produce a mutually agreeable plan for the BLM forest around us.

Meanwhile, several people in Takilma have noted how the Waldo Thin Sale has brought our community closer together. Once again we're reminded of the strength we derive from our solidarity. "Power to the People" -Dave Toler

The next town meeting concerning this issue will be February 8th, 7 pm, at the Takilma Community Building.

PAUL BUNYAN VISITS THE SACRED GROVE

Among the reasons to keep old-growth trees alive, the word "sacred" is often used. Deciding to explore what sacred trees are, I found a long story, beginning in myth, and progressing through history. The story concerned ancient goddess religions and masculine hero figures, and an old struggle to balance the masculine and feminine principles in the lives of humans on the earth. These ideas are alive today in our collective unconscious, and have a lot to do with the current conflicts between logging and environmental interests. The story begins once upon a time.

When religions of the earth and a mother goddess predominated, trees were important figures among the natural deities. Europe, in fact, was once largely covered by forests. Wild and uncultivated, the forests represented nature without any human interference. Their energy was powerful, and sometimes dangerous. Fairy tale children lost in dark forests can be interpreted symbolically, but they also represent facts. There was danger in the woods, and the purpose of some worship in the sacred groves was propitiation of that danger. A sacred grove was a group of trees, usually growing in a circle around a large old tree of acknowledged power. Occasionally, these venerable trees were oracular. Sometimes human sacrifices, or other offerings, were hung from them. Pleasing nature was often a violent game. At first the tree itself was known to be alive; later it was believed that a spirit lived in the tree. Throughout the world, numerous examples of this belief have been recorded; sacred groves with carvings of the Egyptian god Osiris placed in a tree; stories of the Greek Dryads; spirits that were seen leaving a tree when it was cut down. Some cultures believed that the spirit would die if its home tree was cut. A Greek cautionary tale describes a rich, powerful man who continued to hack at a forbidden tree even after it shed blood. He cut it down, and was visited by the goddess Famine. The permanent, insatiable hunger she gave him resulted in his financial ruin, as he had to sell all his property to buy food.

Belief in the power of a single tree also exists in Norse mythology. Yggdrasil was the World Tree which covered the earth, connecting heaven, the earth, and the underworld. Its roots separated three underground realms, and it grew from the body of an ancient hero. In England, the Druids venerated oak trees, and Buddha received enlightenment while sitting under the Tree of Immortality. And the biblical trees of life and of knowledge are well-known.

The Bible, in fact, made things more complicated for the mother earth religions and for trees. In Genesis, God gives humans "dominion... over every living thing..." (Genesis 1:28) Previously, people and nature were interdependent; now humans had a right to control nature. Continuing to the present, this belief has been acted on since about 4000 B.C.. At that time, warring Semitic tribes began their conquest of worshippers of the mother goddess, spreading the Biblical, father-based, monotheistic religion.

The traditional foil to the mother goddess was the hero, a young man who was often her son. Acting as a son does, he would have new ideas and leave alone on adventures. Of course, mother would remain at home, taking care of the natural world. This balance becomes warped by the Biblical belief that man and nature are separate, and European settlers brought this belief to the New World. From this concept developed the American hero, Paul Bunyan, he of great strength and logging ability.

Imagine, then, Paul Bunyan as he entered the sacred grove. The grove grew in the deep dark forest of fairy tales, and it had a powerful, primordial energy. It also sheltered wild animals and Indians. No wonder trees became pure resource, and tall tales were told of the number of "forties" it took just to stoke the logging camp fires. Meanwhile, some East coast missionaries cut down one particular Indian sacred oak tree. It was the only way to get that group to give up its religion.

From then until the present, traces of the mother goddess religions have remained. Mayday and other traditional European celebrations have featured tree worship. Jewish mysticism emphasizes the feminine principle, using the Biblical tree of life as a diagram of spiritual development. Jews still welcome Queen Sabbath on Friday night, while the Christian Mary strongly suggests remnants of goddess worship. Recently, the Gaia hypothesis, named for an early Greek earth goddess, suggests that the earth itself is an organism. Concepts like this help us humans be aware that we are interdependent with the other earth dwellers. They can help validate the people who intuitively feel that trees are sacred, keeping myth and mystery living concepts. We can rejoin the ancient belief in the importance of trees.
    -Rachel Goodman

Yggdrasill

Ratatosk the Squirrel

Well of Urd

Asgard Realm of the Aesir

Vanaheim Land of the Vanir

Alfheim Land of the Light Elves

Valhalla hall of the slain

Bifrost the Flaming Bridge

Spring of Mimir

Midgard middle world

Utgard Citadel of the Giants

Nidavellir Land of the Dwarfs

Jotunheim Land of the Giants

Svartalfheim Land of the Dark Elves

Jormungand the Midgard Serpent

Hel Realm of the dead

Spring of Hvergelmir

Niflheim World of the dead

the dragon Nidhogg

2

THE FOREST SPEAKS

So what's all the noise?

What's the eco-freakout about this time?

Let's get back to basics. Get that high altitude jet plane point of view. 500 miles per hour, looping along the West Coast of North America, sizing up the landscape. It's a humbling awareness hitting you in the face; the overwhelming expanse, the intricate detail. From the time lapse perspective of history we fast forward through geo-forces set in motion woven with sparks of biology. The hurricane of life arises giving power to this landscape. The Earth flexes its muscles and after a million years the Big Green Revolution has taken over with its perpetual motion dynamo of photosynthesis. The life support system is ON and it's a plants' planet. The plant world colonizes the rocks and water into a place to live. The atmosphere stabilizes, the sun is now more than just hot and bright, water is no longer just two gases temporarily caught between ice and steam. We are drawn to the lush greens and the waterways and the forest views of spectacular rocks. You and I have ourselves gravitated to these more temperate forests. Ah, the "F" word.

We live in the diminished leftovers of the post-glacial Pan American Forest that previously blanketed the continent for millions of years. That is the living legacy, the matchless treasure of this region, our neighborhood. We live in a true ancestral remnant with its unmangled groves of the Life Support System, a genetic terrain essential to the human experience, a birth place of consciousness.

"People often feel, upon entering a forest, that they have encountered something with integrity and volition, with consciousness. I would be more comfortable dismissing such feelings, which I have experienced, if we understood how our own consciousness arises from the tangle of neurons in our heads." -David Rains Wallace

The world is deeper than appearances. There's more to the wild lands than water, timber, mineral and grazing rights. There's more to the forest than beautiful ridgelines and fish in the creeks. It is a spiritual resource that speaks to our deepest identity. Wilderness is the scene where the prophets experience spiritual transformation. It is the wild place where the church of life is celebrated.

Our forest can tell us the whole story. It is the mother of all multi-level marketing schemes, the lesson of creation, the Big Model, the complete package, the real "world wide web." Birds, fungi, insects and rodents as a unit assist forest reproduction. It's a system increasingly complex, made all the more confusing whenever we look at anything less than its whole self. It's the tiniest brush strokes that paint the masterpiece of the Big Picture. The truth is humans may be expendable in this dialogue of creation and consciousness. We may be an unaffordable luxury, because the natural world doesn't need us to do anything but understand.

"Another hundred years of business as usual is inconceivable. Dogma and ideology have become obsolete; their poisonous assumptions allow us to close our eyes to our hideous destructiveness and to loot even those resources that properly belong to our children and grandchildren. Our toys do not satisfy; our religions are no more than manias; our political systems are a grotesque aping of what we intended them to be. How can we hope to do better?" - Terrance McKenna

For all the plunder there is still abundance beyond belief. Environmentalism is the life science of the Earth and the Earth philosophy of our lifetime. There is still a place for everyone on this living skin of Earth. It's the geography of mystery, the forest lesson of connection and cooperation, the majesty and joy of the directly personal forest experience, which in turn gives us insight, hope and compassion. This is the source of life and our souls can't be very far behind.

So when they ask you just what this 100 year old truly American movement of tree hugging preservationists is all about, you can tell 'em in 25 words or less: every square foot is irreplaceable. Water. Stable climate. Fresh air. The biological and spiritual fountain of life. It's saving the world and our own souls.   -Kenny Houck

FOREST EXHALE

Merriam Webster tells us that the word forest derives from the Latin *foris* meaning "outside." It defines it as "a dense growth of trees and the underbrush covering a large tract." A simple statement yet, for me, the word forest conjures up so much more. It is my home. It is where I choose to live because it is so alive. Nestled in "our" little tract I have learned great lessons about the wisdom, beauty and cycles of Mother Nature.

 I have been privileged to hear the owls hoot at night and watch the glorious pileated woodpecker swoop above me seeking food in an old, decaying tree.

Certain moments have captured me... a lustrous moon peeking through silhouetted firs or the dawn filtering through the branches outside my bedroom window. They touch places deep inside me, like nothing else does. Maybe it is the wilderness within me.

I recently returned from a trip back East. Landing at the Newark Airport is about as far as you can get from the forest. It is the antithesis of the natural environments. I don't think I breathed correctly for a couple of weeks until we came down the driveway on our way back home and I finally exhaled aaaaaaaaahhhhhh the forest.... -Deborah Colette Murphy

SPEAKING FOR THE FOREST
(THE INSECTS, DECOMPOSERS, SMALL CRITTERS, FLOWERS...)

When i was young, i had an awareness that something was wrong, on a global level. As i grew, this feeling took on many names: nuclear waste, ozone depletion, pollution... I had to **do** something, but what? I came to a major transition in college. Interested in simple living and ecology, i was seeking a "new myth" that would help our culture return to balance. I camped out, gardened, bicycled, and studied about the livelihood of the local native people. Something changed in me as i began to acknowledge and greet the beings around me, small flowers, blackberry branches, the "webwood tree" (a redwood covered in webs), mosses, salamander, cedar, fern... slowly they became my family, my relatives, my teachers. In the forest i felt refreshed, reborn, whole and holy.

In an "experiential education" class, taught by deep ecologist Bill Devall, we were instructed to **become** bears waking from hibernation. To survive, we had to cross the campus without being seen by (or seeing) a police car. There were several roads to cross, garbage cans to explore, caged animals to smell, etc. Snuffling along it was surprisingly easy to imagine the weight, curiosity and hunger of this magnificent creature. My nose led me around, and like most of the class i was "shot" by a cop. We did many exercises like this to develop a different perspective, a deeper awareness of living.

Probably the most revolutionary event for me was a weekend "council of all beings", held in a threatened old growth grove. After many exercises and rituals, each person prepared to represent different species meeting in a council. We gathered silently in the morning, wearing masks or face paint. After introducing ourselves, we shared our stories. The marbled murrelet spoke of the forests that were no more, of her exhausting search for a mossy old growth tree to nest in. The ancient redwood spoke of the wonders of the ages, of seeing bear cubs become full grown, small trees sprouting out of fallen old friends, of the swelling waters of Lack's creek, the dance of the seasons... some of us became humans at one point and listened to the beauty, anger, strength, sorrow and helplessness of the plants, critters, river... we were deeply moved by those voices that spoke through us. They told the truth so clearly, so fully, i experienced a tingling of ancient memory (so hard to express with words), a feeling of cellular knowledge, instinct. It was powerful and spiritual. I felt animal.

Later, when some of my class returned to this place, a road had been cut. I walked down it apologetic and in shock. The violence of slaughtered trees, stripped ravines, lost friends. I could feel the invasion in my bones, the disruption and taking of sacred life, and it rekindled a deeper loss and a sense of responsibility. Many emotions rushed through me as i swore to do every thing in my power to stop this war, this madness of my people. And if we never stop to listen to our relations, may they live on after we are gone.

Now, as i embrace my life, i speak for the voiceless ones. As i confront the destroyers, i see the delicate web of life. And i realize that we humans don't know much.-*Deb Lukas*

"BIOPHILIA"

Living in Takilma's surrounding woods for these many years I have experienced the wonderful feeling of falling in love and becoming very personally involved with a piece of the earth. I've discovered that this tendency to love and be deeply moved by Earth and Nature has a name, "biophilia." Well, now I know, there's an official name for what I've been feeling.

The forested land that inspires my passion, my biophilia, has a large radius, but the heart of my world rests here in Takilma's woods. Of course I admired the beautiful Takilma forests when I first came here years ago, but my deep love and admiration has grown and developed over the years.

As I have lived my life here, as I partied, prayed, and pranced around in the woods year after year, the characteristics of these neighboring forests became increasingly unique and endearing to me. There are places in these forests where very special things happened, where I camped when I first came here as a nineteen year old, where I rode my horses, where my babies played, where prayers were left, where awesome times were had, where ashes of old friends were spread. Happy and sad memories. When I walk through the forests around Takilma, I relive experiences and remember all these times. Through the years these woods have become a piece of my life, I have a very personal love for them.

My intellectual admiration for the Siskiyous has also increased through the years as I have read, studied, hiked and explored this unique bioregion. I feel like I'm just beginning to learn about the many trees, herbs, flowers, and plants in these forests and about how many of them don't grow anywhere else in the world. Animals, insects, even the rocks around this bioregion are very special.

Takilma's forests inspire my life; these forests are a part of my life. Biophilia is a new word, but deep and personal feelings for Nature are an ancient experience. I think this happens to everyone who takes the time to personally interact with, observe, and love a piece of the earth.

-*Katherine*

"TAKE A LOOK"

If you read the paper,
Then you won't be getting
Corporation spokesman,
Have a way of telling you
printed on the forest,
all of the news.
slickest shills you'll ever find,
they love what they abuse.

Take a look for yourself.
Take a walk in the trees.
Take a look for yourself.

None of us are pure.
We compromise and draw our lines
But who can look at what we've done
And claim we can continue doing
There's more we all could do.
in many different ways.
the last one hundred years or so
anything that pays?

Take a look for yourself.
Take a walk in the trees.
Take a look at yourself.

Those commie eco-terrorists
Hypocrites in wooden houses
Elitist no-job spongers,
Holier-than-thou types.
out to take folks' jobs away.
saying no more cuts.
scornful of the working class.
Environmental nuts.

Take a look for yourself.
Have a talk with some people.
And decide for yourself.

What then separates us?
Who sets us on each other
Who uses up the workers,
Who's making all the profits
Why do we find no common ground?
when we all have much to lose?
the trees the land the air we breathe?
while still singing us the blues?

Take a look for yourself.
Ignore the P.R. men
And think hard for yourself.

For the sake of children
For wondrous creation.
For reverence and beauty,
For peace of mind and tranquil heart and
and generations to be born,
many forms and yet one soul.
humility and selflessness,
spirit growing whole.

Take a look for yourself.
Take a walk in the trees.
And take care for yourself.

Note: I wrote this song for a gathering last summer, organized by Diane and Dave, to generate opposition to the pro-posed Rockydale cut. I'm not sure how well it holds up as a poem.

Anyway, it seems there is the potential for a much more broadly-based environmental movement, and this song was meant mostly for those who have a love of the forest but oppose what they perceive as "environmentalism". Many are caught up in the limitless frontier mentality, or are scared about their livelihood; considering local history and educational levels, and corporate domination over media, this is hardly blameworthy. Many, too, are insulted by a sweeping critique of their way of life, especially when delivered by those who seem convinced of their own moral and intellectual superiority. Finally, many think environmentalism isn't grounded in a realistic, viable vision for the future. If we want to promote thought rather than defensiveness, change instead of reaction, we have a lot to keep in mind. 　　　-Jack Dwyer

5 98

KID'S
SPEAK OUT!

from: Adam
Dear Bob at BLM,
    I'm a student of the
Dome School. Our school is
in Takilma Oregon. We
heard you would like to log
the forests in our area. Well
don't!!!
P.S. Trees die We die.

Dear Bob at BLM,
    These are not your tree's. It should be all our
decision, because we breathe oxygen and we breathe
out carbon dioxide, the tree's breathe in carbon dioxide
and breathe out oxygen if we did not have tree's me
and you would not be here.
    PS. How would you feel to be a living toothpick.
When the tree's fall we fall and no one will bury us.
From Amara B. Snitkin

Creatures of the sea
Just let them be.
Whales are mammals
and so are we.
    Amara, age 10

Cara, 10

Dear B.L.M.
    What do you do with your letters I do
not have the time for this. I would like
to say I am mad !!!! With you! When I
grow up I do not want to say when I was
about your age we had a beautifut thing
tree's. Good bye from: Amber James

Dear Bob at BLM,
    Do you care about oxygen? If you cut down the
trees we won't beable to live. For our kids, kids, kids
grandchildren, I want them to have a nice forest to. I
have lived all my life in the woods and when I come
back when I'm a grandpa I don't want to see it gone. I
am a student at the Dome school in Takilma, Oregon.
        Sincerely, Jessea Prouty Mucha

Dear Bob at BLM
    I'm a student at the Dome School. I feel the Trees
are part of my family. If you cut them down i feel as
though i'm losing part of my family I think The kids at
the Dome School feel the same way I do. Please do
everything in your power to prevent our trees from
being cut down. Thank you a Whole lot.
        Sincerely Kristine Kompas

Dear Bob at BLM
    We are students of The Dome School. Our school is
in Takilma Oregon. We heard you would like to log
the forests in our area. We would like to say please
don't cut our trees. We need our trees for our childrens
childrens granddaughters.
        Sincerly, Seton Caroline

    I started life as a small seed, in a pinecone
floating down a river. The river went down. I
fell on the ground and started growing roots. By
the time I was three years old I was five feet tall,
a strong little tree. It snowed on me all winter
and my branches on me all winter and my
branches got very heavy. The next summer
there wasn't much rain and I grew my roots
deep looking for water. By the time I was six
years old I was a lot taller. Birds nested in me,
raccoon climbed me, and opossums hang from
my branches. I was a very happy tree. But now
I'm ten years old, and some human is coming
towards me with a chain saw.
        Simeon

Dear Al Gore:
    I would like to Persuade you to stop the Cut of
Sugarloaf and other National forests.
I am 11 years old and I would like to save them for my
children and for my children's children and so on.
I have been protesting at Sugarloaf and I have been
watching logging trucks take very old trees out of the
forest. I am very sad to think in a little while there will
be no trees. I ask you to preserve the trees for other
people to see and love. Make a law to protect
Sugarloaf and other rare and old growth forests.
        Sincerely Sol

KIDS RESPONSES TO ..."WHAT DO TREES AND THE FOREST MEAN TO YOU?"

Phoebe Parker-Shames-age 5: "The trees should grow up strong and healthy like me. I think it's a really beautiful place."

Max Parker-Shames-age 5: "Me too. I don't like it when they cut the trees when they don't even need um."

Ry Heller-age 14: "I like the trees, the trees are good, I wouldn't want them cut down."

Leaf Hayes-age 12: "lived around them all my life, they help us breathe and keep us warm."

Telos Deosil-age 12: "It's where I live-dogs play in the forest."

Cora Madsen-age 14: " It wouldn't be the same around my house without trees."

Brynn Rose-age 8: "They make air, shade, good forts and hiding places. If no trees were left I would be bored, hot and wouldn't be living."

Rael Hirning : "Trees are one of the most important things in our lives- couldn't imagine living without them. When I've visited the cities I notice there are not enough trees- I look forward to them when I come home.

Adios mis amigos. Ya me voy para Cuba. See ya in 6 weeks. Love *Gloria*.

PROBLEM SOLVING BY THE TAKILMA HOME SCHOOLERS

Problem: The BLM needs Takilma's woods for building and paper but the forests are almost gone.

Hey I've got the solution 1) Use hemp for paper and lumber and food. 2) Use recycled clothes for paper. They do it in Japan. -*Rachel*

My solutions are: 1) Just take a few trees and not all; don't clearcut. 2) Re-cycle your paper and cloths. 3) Use re-cycled lumber. If the BLM considers other solutions rather then cutting all the trees down then we could have our needs and our forests too. -*Mike*

My soulution is: to take some of the trees, and leave some of them. We have lots of trees, and need to not cut anymore. Using recycled paper and lumber and using recycled cloths like they do in Japan for paper could solve this problem. -*Lorenza*

We are running out of trees. I have thought of some solutions, here they are: Stop cutting and recycle everything we already have! Cut what is already going to die, and only cut when you really need to, never clearcut. -*Cedar*

7

ORAL CHORUS

It looks as if we have a window of opportunity to convince the BLM and the powers-that-be that these forests are part and parcel of our culture. For a healthy river and village, we need a healthy forest.

Here are a few quotes, drawn from the oral histories I've been collecting.

"When I came here I felt the incredible verdancy of the area, just felt like I could feel the oxygen in the air. Felt like it filled a thirst in me to be somewhere where I was surrounded by large, happy, growing trees. This hillside here, the hillside they are planning to log, is where I hike at least two times a week, often three times. It's just my place to get away. I would be very disturbed to see it cut because when I go up there, I feel I'm communing with nature and every few years they come up and re-mark it. Sometimes they even blaze some of the trees. That forest up there has never been cut by anyone and the idea of "fixing" the forest by going in there and affecting it, seems totally alien. The little we have left of unlogged forest seems to me to be sanctuary and it seems necessary to save it for our children and for the heritage of the entire earth."   *-Lance Thorne*

"I feel pretty fiercely opposed to the cut. I feel that it is a grave insult to a community that holds the forest in such high esteem. To come after so many years of reforestation failures, and then have a 10,000 acre fire come through and severely damage our water shed, and then the ensuing salvage, so that now we are left with a very small area, percentage-wise, of live, healthy forest. For the BLM to come and look at 1000 acres of that low elevation virgin forest, including some old growth; for them to consider cutting that, in whatever new forest-health method that they can possibly devise, is still a grievous insult to me and to what our community does."   *-Beth Meadows*

"This has always felt like a sanctuary to me, and I attribute part of that to being born and raised in the country and then moving to the city where I felt I lost my identity with the surroundings. It seemed like all those years I lived in the city I needed a sanctuary. A place where I could physically kick back and feel comfortable, feel secure, and feel that I could center myself spiritually, where I could just kind of let myself go and I always felt that this area allowed that for me."   *-Kerry Whitehead*

"Certainly the trees give me a feeling of insulation from the rest of the world; they give me a feeling of protection, they give me a feeling of brotherhood. It's like without the trees I don't know if there is anything.

I can't imagine that anything can help a natural forest. That it actually needs our help. We can't even understand the ecosystems properly and every few years they change what they prescribe for the forest. It's obvious that they don't know what they're doing. The only thing that knows what it's doing is nature itself. It's just going to keep doing it."
-Lance Thorne

We are a village. We are a very diverse group of people and we each bring something special to our village. There are artists, writers, musicians, enlightened horticulturists, equestrians and general recreaters who use this valley, helping to create a community to preserve.

Together we are an amazing power to deal with. Honor diversity in the forest and in the village.

If you can write about how we use this natural backdrop in our lives, or if you would like to share an oral history, please contact Marjorie Reynolds, Cultural Response Committee 592-6733 or 4443 Waldo Road, Cave Junction OR 97523.

"The belief that nature can benefit from "management" is obviously untrue. This theory is merely a transparent rationale to sway public opinion and justify the exploitation and abuse of the natural forest. No amount of management will equal the natural order.
There is no forestry like no forestry. "   *-Eric*

ACTION ALERT

1. A proposed ballot measure would repeal Measure 18, which banned bear baiting and hound hunting of bear and cougar. It also supersedes all post-1975 wildlife laws, and bans all future initiatives. Letters to your newspaper editor in opposition might thwart this initiative.

2. Oregon Department of Agriculture has applied for a permit to use 1080 compound, an extremely dangerous toxin once banned by the EPA, in sheep collars. A study in New Mexico demonstrated that accidental puncture, improper disposal, and similar mishaps spread this poison into the food chain. Write Christopher Kirby, ODA, Plant Division, 635 Capitol St.NE, Salem OR 97310 (503-986-4635). Refer to docket #OPP-42075.

For more information contact Debbie Lukas (592-3386) or SREP (592-4459)

SavingWILD
Spirit WILD FORESTS NOT FOR SALE

Common Ground was created to provide a vehicle for expressing our ideas and issues of concern in our community. Opinions expressed here are not necessarily those of the Editorial Staff or Mud Council. Our theme for the next issue is *communal life*. The facilitators will be Felicity, Rachel and Dave T. The *deadline is March 1st* . We love to hear from you (A 3 1/2" diskette is especially welcome) . We would like to thank Ron Raven for his help on issue #16. Issue #17 owes its appreciation to **Facilitator:** Laurie. **Computer layout:** Kerry. **Staff:** Felicity, Rachel, Dave T., Dave H., Jack and Deb, **Graphics:** Jill, Alex Krupka, Cathy, and FLISS . Common Ground is printed on recycled paper.

ᶠNEᵂᴹ Our apologies for any misunderstanding caused by our subscription labels. We did go slightly wild with our new expiration stamp. If you are a subscriber, there is a number above your name on the mailing label. That number represents the last issue for which your subscription has paid. Our policy is to send to anyone who identifies themselves to us in the Illinois Valley regardless of payment or persuasion. Many local people have, however, sent in subscriptions. When their subscription expires, we stamp their paper with a notice to that effect. They of course will still get a copy whether they pay or not (we just can't resist asking for money). The notice is just a reminder that if they choose to contribute the time is now! Our only expenses for the paper are materials, printing and postage - there are no salaries. Currently it costs approx. $200.00 to publish the paper; 60¢ per copy. We are hoping to print on tree-free paper. The cost is more but we all agree we would like to see fewer trees cut down. Our publishing cost will increase so we would appreciate any contributions and support.

We publish eight times a year. Our goal, not always possible, is to have the paper in your mail box by these holidays: Winter Solstice, Dec. 20-23; Candlemas, Feb.2; Spring Equinox, March 20-23; Beltane, May Eve; Summer Solstice, June 20-23; Lughnasad, Aug.1; Fall Equinox, Sept. 20-23; Samhain, Oct. 31. These eight points mark the Wheel of the Year celebrating birth, growth, fading, death. Ideas are born, we give birth, we struggle, we laugh, we love, we grow, we suffer, we write, we read, we subscribe, we pay! Please let us know what you would like to read or write about in the Takilma Common Ground. Send letters to convince us that you are out there and you care. Thank you for your support for these past two years!

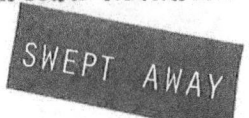

SISKIYOU NATIONAL PARK

FLISS

9

ANNOUNCEMENTS

Sponsors are Needed to pay $10.-$30. per month to help with rental of new adult/youth comm-unity center in Cave Junction. Would like to offer teen programs, classes, entertainment, Saturday morning kids program. Need your help, ideas, support and $$. Contact Tom Legay 592 -6824

Attention Landowners! Does your land have the river or one of its tributaries flowing through it? The Tree Planting Project wants to give free trees for riparian restoration. Call by Feb. 15, 592-2166 ext.244 or 592-6805.

The Dome School is thrilled to announce that it is a proud owner of a **new Macintosh Performa Computer** with lots of exciting software. Donated by a former Takilma resident, Larry Tesler. The computer has catapulted the Dome School into the computer age. YEA!!

1996 Community Calendar - by the Dome School
The Dome School elementary students have worked hard on illustrations and research to create this great calendar. They discovered famous and not-so-famous dates, holidays and festivals from around the world. When IS National Kazoo Day? When is it appropriate to celebrate Fornicalia? Buy one or two, they're just $4.00 and naturally all profits will benefit the Dome School. Call the school, 592-3911, or Deb Murphy. 592-2866. Calendars are also available at "The Silver Lining" in Cave Junction. Thanks Linda!
P.S. You will be challenged with a crossword puzzle based on the famous and not so famous dates.

Anyone interested in researching **local salvage sales?** There are plenty for all of us! Contact Debbie 592-3386 or 592-4459.

TR_{ans}FOR_{MATION}

We were woke up by a weird, rumbling, banging sound, "Is that the cats running around or what?" Mar smelled smoke and opened the bedroom door to find the hall filled with smoke. I sprang out of bed and we rushed down stairs. Throwing back the blanket that hangs in the stairway we were engulfed by thick, heavy, hot, acid smoke . "Quick, get the kids." Mar went into Ry's room and I went down the hall into the living room to see how bad the fire really was. I started to panic, thinking we were going to lose it all. I ran back down the hall and said "Where's Ian? I thought you got Ian." Mar said "I thought you got Ian." I ran into Ian's room, grabbed him and ran down the hall and right into Ry who was coming the other way, knocking him down. I don't even remember hitting him. Still freaking out I said "Quick, take Ian"and gave him to Ry so he could be with him outside in the cold night. My mind was racing. We've got to save some stuff from the file cabinet. I grabbed a couple of file folders; papers flying everywhere. I told Mar to get the buying club money and our stash. Mar requested that if I had to save anything, please get the computer. This all took place in the office which is the lowest place in the house and at that time relatively smoke free. The lights still worked, so we could see what we were doing. Having got that stuff safely outside Mar tries to call 911 but the phone is dead. So she starts the car to drive over to the Dunhams and the windshield is covered with frost. I yell "Hit the horn! Wake up the neighbors." Ry does this with Ian in his arms. Meanwhile there I am outside in the cold, buck naked. I immediately ran back into the house and went up stairs and grabbed my bath-robe and a handful of clothes and ran back downstairs to be greeted by that wall of smoke behind the blanket. I turned around and opened the window at the stair landing and jumped out . Once out side I regained my bearings, and looking in the kitchen window I thought I had a chance to put the fire out if I could get the garden hose hooked up. So I ran around the house and dragged the hose in through the slider. Damn, the nozzle is frozen. Quickly unscrewing it, I proceeded to spray water on the ceiling knowing it was crucial to keep the fire from getting into the attic. By this time it was spread-ing out from behind the refrigerator towards the back of the house and also from the stove towards the front and across the ceiling to the dining room.

Dave Kendall arrived just as the propane line to the stove flared and I hollered for him to shut off the valve at the tank, which he did. Then he rushed back in and gave the fire a blast with his fire extinguisher. That was a great help in knocking the fire down. Meanwhile I went into the mud room and managed to get my rubber boots on and threw the other pairs out the door. Having both doors open helped vent the smoke and breathing be-came easier. Something I was really not thinking about too much, just focus-ing on putting water on the fire. By this time Doug Kendall and Bill Dunham had come into the house and they removed a burning couch from the living room. We managed to knock down the fire some more and realized that the ceiling joists were on fire. I hollered for Dave to find something to tear the dry wall down so I could get some water in there. We were able to do this and it was about then that the fire department arrived. Having done enough I dropped the hose and went outside to see about Mar and the kids.

I am very grateful to Dave, Doug and Bill for their help and the risk they put themselves in while helping me fight the fire. The flashlights and fire extinguishers they brought were a big help. -Leo

reBirth

We Are Rising from the Ashes! As most of you have probably heard by now, fire broke out in our home the other night. Somehow, by the grace of God, we were able to get both of our boys out of their beds and to safety. And then, by another series of minor (yeah, right) miracles, Leo and Dave Kendall, Doug Kendall and Bill Dunham were able to extinguish the fire itself and save our house. Cathy Dunham and Susan Kendall became the calm voices of wisdom, cared for Ry and Ian, and helped me get clothes and boots on. The Fahrnkopf family ran over with clothes for Ry. The IV fire department arrived in force in what seemed like moments and took over. Myrica and Bruce held us up. Dan and Mary Beth threw open their doors and gave us a place to thaw out and get warm again. We stand in awe of this series of events that in such few moments changed the course of our lives.

The outpouring of love in countless forms has touched us deeply in these days immediately after the fire. Your offerings of love and support have really sustained us as we adjust to a different life. The bags of food and kitchen supplies, the sheets and blankets. The clean up crews, the dump crews, the salvagers, the voices of reason. The hugs and phone calls. The suitcase of shoes and hand lotions, the brand new quilt from the quilters guild. The bags of sponges and cleaning supplies. Piles of boxes. Fillers and movers of boxes and furniture. The financial support. More hugs. The demolition crews and the rebuilders (carpenters, electricians, painters, and plumbers). The talkers, the listeners. The prayers and the One who answers prayer. The town runners. The laundry brigade~oh the mountains of laundry! The meal offerings and dish doers. The Ian watchers. The cookie bakers. The organizers. The opinions and expertise you have all brought to the scene. We thank you all so much.

The experts say our refrigerator (an old one) over-heated and caused the fire. Is there a way to check on our old appliances and find out if they have problems? Is there maintenance that needs to happen? If you will, please do us a favor. Inspect your smoke alarms, and if you don't have any, get some installed right away. Ours were wired in but not yet installed. Their presence would have really changed the course of things for us.

It has been interesting seeing the evolution of our own reactions to this experience. What would have become tragedy in a few more minutes, didn't. It moved instead to a time of joy and thanksgiving. We woke up. We were able to get our children out of the house alive. We can breathe again. What more could we possibly ask for. And our house didn't burn to the ground. It can be rebuilt in a relatively short amount of time. Sure there are inconveniences; and yes, our minds go over and over t h o s e few moments, reliving the panic. But for the most part what was lost can be replaced. Many blessings to you all, and Thank You. Thank You. THANK YOU! -Mar

CLASSIFIEDS

Massage therapy at the Hair Station, next to the natural foods store. Deep muscle and energy work, ion pellet and magnet therapy. Questions or appts. Rachel Goodman, 592-3079, -6947.

Seeking spiritually minded landed partner. 20 acres Sucker Creek frontage, forest, meadow. $45,000 cash. Must be financially secure enough to build up-to-code home. Send photo and biography to Deborah Lee and Alex, Box 1286, Cave Junction OR 97523.

Tree-free paper! Quality paper is now available locally from non-wood fibers. For a free catalog call Karen Wood 846-6366 or write to her at Box 222, Williams OR 97544.

Wanted: Feet for reflexology. Let us touch your soles to relieve stress and tension. $10.00/session. Mar, 592-4436, -4263. Diane, 592-3908.

Garden and Yardwork my speciality. I follow directions well and can do other projects. Al Karger, 597-3436.

♥ SUBSCRIBE TO COMMON GROUND ♥

__ $10 1-YEAR SUBSCRIPTION.

__ $25 1-YEAR SUBSCRIPTION AND
A COMMON GROUND T-SHIRT.
CALL 592-4695 FOR SIZE AND
COLOR INFO.

__ $? BROKE BUT LITERATE, SEND ANYWAY.

NAME: _____

ADDRESS: _____

TAKILMA COMMON GROUND
POST OFFICE BOX 2016
CAVE JUNCTION,
OREGON
97523

Common ground

Communal Life

A Meadow of Dreams

March-May   ISSUE 18

Why would anyone want to live communally? Doing so can involve endless hours of meetings, interference in each other's freedoms, and much laborious coordination of activities. Not to mention the recriminations that can occur if one fails to perform one's cooperative duties to someone else's expectations.

One answer is that there is a power in group agreement that is far beyond the sum of its parts. This power is what enabled a rather spacey group of cruising hippies to coalesce into a tight extended family or minitribe. And to manifest its own quirky vision of a home where humans can live lightly and in relative harmony with the natural world. Sometimes the group head seemed to have a life of its own-- calling us to grueling meetings that no one wanted to attend. It was at meetings such as these, however, that we hammered out our goals and refined the vision. It was an ambitious one that none of us would have had the slightest chance of achieving on our own. But by sharing workload and resources it became possible. Not easily though; this is, after all, Amerika, and we are all products of its Marlboro-country-rugged-individuo-pioneer-bootstrap-capitalist culture. We once saw a photo taken in a town in China about the size of Cave Junction. Just about the entire population of that town was gathered proudly around the gleaming automobile which they all shared! We had a hard time sharing a couple of vehicles among twenty or thirty folks. The point is, some cultures have a long tradition of living and working closely and ours does not. Communal/cooperative living in America is not for everyone.

For those whose personalities lean in that direction, however, communalism does offer distinct advantages. How else can a person of modest means leave her gardens and orchard for weeks at a time and return to find them bountiful and well cared for? Despite what our consumerist media tells us, every family in America does not need to own its own chain saw, weed whacker, pickup truck, rototiller, and perhaps most importantly, land. Sharing land and tools can make it possible to afford them. Figuring out how to pay for them and fix them when they break are the tricky parts. Discrepancies in energy outputs are a major issue for all communal groups. We attempted over the years to set up various systems for dealing fairly with energy issues, such as hours per week expected from each of us in family related work (garden, tool repair, water lines, etc.). Or delegating specific areas of responsibility to each individual. Ultimately, these systems fell by the wayside, perhaps because of their cumbersome nature, or maybe due to latent anarchic tendencies. What finally does work is having an innate trust in each other's ideas of fairness.

Then there are the intangible benefits of living cooperatively. It's not unlike a kind of diffuse marriage. Living closely with others through the years reveals everyone's strengths, weaknesses and warts. Knowing that you can depend on your extended family in good and hard times means comfort, support and a sense of belonging.

There are many different degrees of sharing cooperatives. Some, such as the Oneida communities in 19th century upstate New York, shared everything from mates to money. Others may share only land. It seems, unfortunately, that communal groups with the highest degree of sharing have a low rate of long-term survival. None of the several communal groups in the Takilma area who chose to live together in one big house are still doing so. But there are tribal cultures who have been doing it successfully for thousands of years, so we know it is possible.

Besides luck, other factors that favor the survival of communities are the up-front sharing agreements of its members and a structure that meets regularly to deal with and adapt to physical plane realities. Both agreement and system seem necessary. One Takilma commune of some quarter century ago called "Omarshivalkin" (sic?) was founded on the premise that if a male and female of each astrological sign were gathered together to live in perfect spiritual harmony in one big house, then a flying saucer would land there to sweep them away to live in perpetual harmony on Venus or some such place. We heard that while waiting for the ship to arrive the well dried up and other inconvenient realities intruded.

To the approximately two hundred people who have called the Meadows home over the last twenty-five years we'd like to say a heartfelt "thank you." Your energy and ideals live on, and those of us who still live here strive to be worthy caretakers of both the ideals and this beautiful fold in our Earth Mother-- Scotch Gulch.   -Beth Peterson and Mark Kelz

Who Is We?

Common Ground was created to provide a vehicle for expressing our ideas and issues of concern in our community. Opinions expressed here are not necessarily those of the Editorial Staff or Mud Council. After working in a white heat to put out this current wonderful and huge issue, our communal process has not yet evolved next issue's theme. Submissions **deadline will be April 23** and we suggest, even implore, that you help create an interesting paper by writing on whatever concerns or inspirations you'd like to share. Although each issue of Common Ground centers on a theme that seems to invite essays, we'd also like to print more creative writing. Send us your poems, short stories, fantasies, imaginatively on or off the issue's theme. Please send original work not previously published.

The editorial staff for issue # 18 was Laurie Prouty, Dave Hocker, S. Dog, Robin Wren, Jill and Nicole Birmingham, Kate Dwyer, Miguel, Claire Sierra, and Nicole Rensenbrink. Felicity El worthy and Rachel Goodman facilitated. Artwork, facilitated by Jill Birmingham, was done by Cathy Hocker, Alex Krupka, Mr. Tracy, Jill, Kate, Gilda. Great thanks to Barry Snitkin for his computer layout work, and to SREP for sharing their office and computers. Takilma Common Ground has traditionally been printed on recycled paper. The paper market has been fluctuating wildly over the past several months. Last time we bought recycled paper we paid 3 ½ cents per 11 1/2 x 17 " sheet. Issue #18 is being printed on Alexandria bond, a blend of 70% hemp and 30% cotton. This tree-free paper costs over 6 ½ per sheet. Although we'll get a better price on our next paper order, we're open to any extra contributions until the day when kenaf is the norm (and as cheap as recycled paper). (Thanks, Kelpie)

We have no facilitator for the next issue yet. If this stirs your ambition to be a newshound, cum-typist-cum-temporary demi-god, contact a mud councillor before the beginning of April and make your presence known to us.

In Unpredictable Process

I don't remember ever aspiring to become a country hippie communard. On the other hand, it wasn't completely accidental. It was through some conspiracy of intention and serendipity that I came to live at Magic Forest Farm in the summer of 1975. Did it change my life? Like conditionally inheriting a fluctuating portion of an unspecified fortune from someone else's relative. For while there was clearly some value and privilege to moving on the land and becoming part of the group, there was no specific transaction or arrangement involved. The benefit lay in belonging to a dynamic process, not in owning a particular set of assets.

Systemic vagueness may not be inherent to all communal situations, but it has certainly been a persistent characteristic of "the Farm." Which is not to say there haven't been any rules, just that the rules tend to be unwritten and fluidly understood. And despite ongoing efforts to codify the terms of membership, concepts such as "ownership" and "responsibility" remain open to interpretation. The result is a rather flexible system which has more or less "worked" for three decades.

Despite the uncertainties, living communally afforded me (and others) many specific benefits:

Migrating to the Farm from San Francisco, quite impoverished, I instantly gained access to 33 beautiful acres, several unique structures, a small menagerie of farm animals, a mega-yard sale of tools, equipment, clothes, books and records, an awesome scrap pile cum spare parts department, and a scattered fleet of vehicles in varying stages of oxidation.

Supported by a communal income and the broad sharing of domestic chores for most of my first 12 years in Takilma, I was able to devote a significant chunk of my time and energy, with little or no monetary remuneration, to the early development of the Dome School and the creation of the Community Building. Being part of a large "family" which encompassed a wide range of talent, experience and personality, I had endless opportunities to learn- not just about milking a cow, canning tomatoes or building a house, but also about living in community (in rather close quarters) with a steadily evolving group of people. Although privacy was often elusive,"there was always a party in the next room."

Finally, and most significantly, communal life proved to be an extremely beneficial arrangement for raising children. Having more than two adults around not only eased the task of "looking after the kids," it also provided a broader range of role models and greater opportunities for the kids to interact with non-parental adults. Living and commiserating with other couples who were going through similar stages of parenting was comforting and sustaining. And the relationships which developed between the kids who grew up in the same "family" but with their own sets of parents are, I think, wonderfully unique and enduring.

Obviously, that's not the whole story. There are some thorns among the roses (no pun intended, Lance). Living with the uncertainties of group dynamics has its disadvantages, but from my current vantage point (having spent the last 8 ½ years in Ashland), the benefits of communal living loom largest in my memory and keep me looking forward to the day I shall return (approximately 530 days to go).

While writing this condensed description of my experience at Magic Forest Farm, I realize that much of it applies to my experience of living in Takilma as well; adding credence to the notion, shared by many who know Takilma only by reputation, that "it's just one big commune out there."

Do you know whose day it is today? Tell them I'll probably be home for dinner, and I might be bringing a few friends.
    –Jake

Down to the Valley to Pray

It was 1973 and I didn't know nothin'. What I thought I knew was the stuff I hadn't yet struggled for, the rest was suspicious because, well; it was the seventies and who could trust Nixon and society that tolerated him? I landed in Takilma and became instantly confused.

Those first few months in Takilma were like a whole segment of my life; like adolescence, or middle age, but compressed. I suspended reality, the way one does when you read a novel, but I was living the story. I phoned the hospital in Portland and told them I wouldn't be coming. I told my girlfriend things had changed. And then I just let stuff happen.

Magic Forest Farm was the earthy, accepting yet scolding, manic-depressive mother I never had. She opened her arms to me at a time I needed unconditional love. Heidi had already opened her arms to me and together we were ready for family life.

The kitchen at the main house was a place of great commotion. Around a small, circular, chipped red particle board table, a few feet from the blackened wood cook stove, Jose and Albie, wearing the most incredibly ragged clothes, would be designing geodesic domes. Visitors would blow in and share stories and good bud around the table. Deep discussions about the spark plug gap for our behemoth of a rototiller would be taking place while a few feet away Rabbitt and Darrel would be harmonizing obscure Grateful Dead songs.

Had I died and gone to heaven? The was what I wanted and needed; a family having fun, and as I later learned, a family with much to teach me.

It took some getting used to. I was in the habit of talking with my friends back in Philadelphia, those future psychotherapists, about *feelings*. But here we were mostly talking about *stuff*. It took me a long time to "get it." Like those incredibly dense students in the Zen parables who are always asking their teacher "what is the meaning of life?" and being told to chop wood for the umpteenth time, I was beginning to see that I would learn all I needed to know about myself, not from chatting, but by doing.

I learned all sorts of new country skills; cruising for firewood, milking, farming, carpentry. Never mind that my teachers were only a few months ahead of me on the learning curve. They spoke with authority, and authority was what I needed.

> Our work was our joy, unless we were stewing about some power struggle within that current communal exercise. I remember riding in the back of the Berkeley Glass Company truck singing a capella, "I went down to the valley to pray."

Mist hung over the mountains. We were dirty with wood chips in our hair. We were young and in love with ourselves and so beautiful.

Even though everything was a negotiation and therefore a compromise, it was okay with me. I knew I wanted to lose a little ego, and this was the way to do it. It was like joining a religious order (Brothers and Sisters of the Holy Farm). You were expected to leave your individuality at the door in order to gain the enlightenment that comes from suspending ego for the benefit of the group. And so nothing was really your own, not your clothes or your money. To some extent your ideas weren't yours either. Some visitors to the farm were freaked out by our loss of individuality. However, I feel I never could have made the personal growth that I did without a long stage of nurturing and coalescence in the group process.

Although I probably couldn't live like that at this stage of my life, I have few regrets and much gratitude for my communal years. I have many friends whom I hope to share the rest of my life with. Takilma and the Farm are my communities, my home, despite the fact that I find myself far from many of you.

-Jim Shames

3

Queens, Kitchens and the Temple of Love

I was twenty-two years old, some twenty-six years ago, and living in a decadent area above Hollywood, in an opulent house overhanging a canyon. I ran the estate as cook, bottle washer, gardener, house cleaner for the producers and directors of the Smothers Brothers and Pearl Bailey Show. I had arrived in Hollywood as Rex, and like everyone else was waiting for my big break into the motion picture industry. I discovered that I did not fit well into this world of crystals and gilt.

One morning, I was awakened by the rolling and pitching of the great house. The morning sun was just arriving, and the sky was full of fire and explosions, as the power lines broke and bounced from car to car. The sky was red and grey and full of smoke. I awaited the big flash and rush of hot air from what surely was the beginning of WW III. Someone had dropped the big one. It turned out to be a rather large earthquake, still on the books as a big one. The other occupants of the house were running around freaking out on the damage to the crystal chandeliers. What a scene, the two older queens flouncing around in their great house crying and screaming over the loss of material doohickeys. I guess it was at that moment that I decided it was time to move along. I had been to San Francisco a month before, and was filled with fantasies of love and adventure.

I announced I was leaving, explaining my decision with the story of Christ going into the desert for forty days, and took the next $25.00 commuter flight. I arrived in the early morning, and was hitchhiking to downtown SF, only I was going the wrong way on some street, when a truckload of beautiful hippies stopped and asked if I wanted to go to the nude beach at Devil's Slide. I had never been to a nude beach, but I was excited as at least three pairs of roving eyes tickled every cell of my body. I went home with Phillip that day. This was my introduction to Hunga Dunga, the home of sixteen of the most beautiful people I had ever met. Hunga Dunga was a three-story Victorian home at 18th St. and Church. This group of hippies had refined tastes and had made this house into a temple of love. I went from bedroom to bedroom and soon found myself staying. There were Lizard, Bobby Star, Little Richard, Sylvia, Michael, Phillip and a host of others. I was rather cute at the time, with long flowing hair, soft blue eyes, and a beautiful beard that gave me a Christ-like look. The house was known as a bi-sexual house, and I proved that to many as the days and weeks went by. This did not go unnoticed, however, and before long some jealousy flared up. I was accused of diving into many situations that others had been contemplating, and being as forward and full of love as I was (or was it just plain horny) I was often the first to welcome new brothers (or sisters) into the water sharing ceremony. I had just finished Stranger in a Strange Land, and took it as my own personal Bible.) This caused some problems in the house, as various members, including Phillip, wondered what I was still doing there some months later. It seemed like no one else had ever considered staying so long. Meeting after and meeting was held to discuss this issue. Now, coming to a decision was no easy task for a consensus group. There were at least two people who blocked each time a vote was taken, and the process led to a decision that as long as one person was willing to share their bed with another, no one had the right to ask that person to leave. The house was not really monogamous, but it was important to see where certain partnerships existed and move cautiously around them. I was not always that subtle. Aware of my instant love that would constantly pop up, I took advantage of what I thought was my duty to share this great love.

After about two years, the vote finally came down that exited me from my greatest love experience. It was a hard blow. I now look back and understand that it was more about my feeling over the evil of money than anything else. I simply refused to earn the black stuff, and took advantage of the sharing situation that existed in Hunga Dunga, the Church of Manna. It was so called because we took it upon ourselves to go to the Farmers Market , buy large amounts of produce, and distribute the food to some fourteen different collectives in exchange for food stamps or money. You took what you needed and gave what you could. The excess was distributed to poorer communes. This worked extremely well; there was always plenty left over and more than enough money to purchase more. The story of Hunga Dunga is in the Kauliflower News, a collective which still exists and whose library is open to all collectives.

I did my share of work. The kitchen became my sanctuary, as it was brought to my attention that so many people loved my cooking, it became my power.

I have met many people who remember me from Hunga Dunga and their first time receiving the sacrament of love. There were no regrets and many repeated sharings. I have so many psychedelic memories of this time and place. It changed my life forever. There are chapters and volumes I could write from this most perfect, sad and delicious time.

 -Robin Wren

"Instead he was enjoying living a life of non-stop pleasure few men ever experience."

Hauling Gravel

One damp spring day several years ago, I hiked to the top of Table Rock, outside of Medford. Above the parking lot was the trail head, graced by a sizeable pile of gravel, a sprawl of buckets, and a sign inviting hikers to haul their share as far as they could and distribute it along the muddy trail.

Cynical yet compliant, I grabbed a bucket or two and hauled it however far, wondering just how successful a volunteer public works project such as this might turn out to be.

The same idea has presented itself to me as I've puddle-dodged my way along the path to the Dome school/TCB. I've never verbalized it because I theorize; a) maybe other people relate to mud as organic/politically correct; b)who would pay for the gravel/sand/sawdust? and c)would any fool besides me haul the stuff?

Which brings me to the topic of communal living, a lifestyle which I have never experienced. Circumstances of my life may not have led me into a communal living situation, but it is equally possible that my concerns over who else would haul the gravel may have inhibited me from joining in an experience that could have done me a lot of good. Gradually, I'm exploring this aspect of myself.

Tellingly, the trail to Table Rock has been stabilized. It looks like the process worked. Maybe if we keep the faith, the gravel will be hauled.

-Dave Hocker

My Neighbor, Myself

We all live communally. Our borders and boundaries are illusions. Fences and property lines are the physical manifestations of divisions which really only exist in our minds.

As I search for a piece of land to "buy," on which to make our home, it becomes even clearer to me that we all live together. Denying this has some bad results. Would any commune on twenty-five acres allow thirteen dogs? I imagine they would recognize the threat to wildlife and chickens and compost piles that such an overpopulation of dogs would create. Yet, adding the property on which I live to its three immediately adjacent parcels results in that same number of fence-hopping, deer-chasing doggies on that small acreage.

Water and air, like dogs, are immune to our boundaries. My neighbor's habits affect my water table and air quality quite noticeably, as mine do his. Yet, strangely, we ignore each other with conviction. People dedicated to illusions of other sorts are generally referred to mental health professionals.

Even though we may want to very much, we cannot escape each other. Fences cannot create for us separate planets on which to reside, sovereign in our preference for immaculate or piggy conditions. Perhaps those folks who choose to face their togetherness and work on their relationships have it best. Certainly, that seems more real than our delusions of five acre nations. But we can't all be as fortunate as the most successful examples. Maybe the answer lies, for many, somewhere in between.
Recognizing that we all live in the same house is a start. Hi, neighbor.

-Kate Dwyer

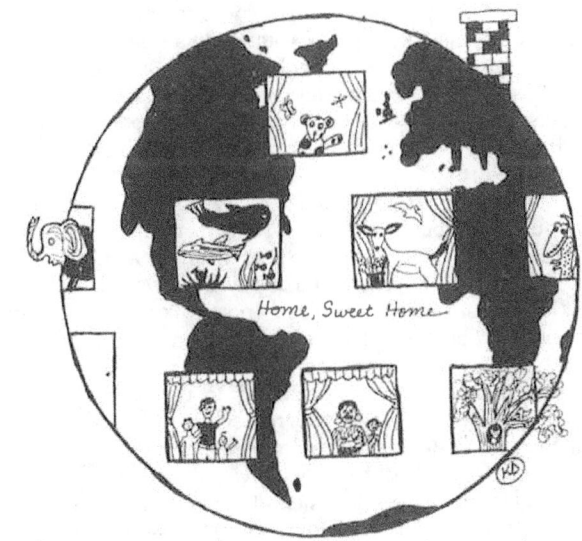

Home, Sweet Home

> Everything was owned together. Trying to work out the cars was always stressful. - Meadow Martell

A Balinese Perspective

Yesterday, Nyoman came by to tell me a neighbor of his had died in the night, and he would be busy for the next few days with the *naben* (burial). The place is a small-sized village on the island of Bali. Communal life here is an ancient way, and this death is another community affair. As I watch from my bungalow, early A.M., I see small groups of people, dressed in black and carrying offerings to the "death house." Everyone has something to offer-coconuts for milk, bamboo to assemble the carrying pallet, shovels to dig the grave, food for family and all the village that will come by. As I walk the trail from my house into the village, I pass by the family compound. I can tell easily which one it is, as there are stacks of Hindu palm offerings, and incense outside the doors. A line of squatting people 'hang out' outside, chatting and laughing as they keep watch with the family. In the street, everyone is wearing black and are on their way to some errand connected with the family death. And so it goes all day, comings and goings, preparations for tomorrow's burial.

On my return home after dark, I see the compound is full of people. Most will stay all night, sleeping on the floor together. No one is ever alone in Bali. Early the next morning, twenty or so of the men are off to the Puri Dalam (temple cemetery) to dig the grave. They said it wasn't that hard because there were so many of them. Meanwhile, at the compound, the priest and others are preparing the body for her journey, washing, anointing, praying, wrapping the body in cloth. All with many hands and constant chatter. Bamboo is cut and lashed to make a pallet to carry the corpse on. New offering pile up outside the compound, and visitors continue to fill the house. When all is blessed and ready, the procession ton the cemetery begins. Many hands make light work for the carrying of the pallet. Hundreds of villagers, who have known this woman all their lives, follow. It's not such a serious time for Balinese, as their belief is reincarnation, and death is only another step in a continuing process. So it's a rather lively procession, with neighbors visiting, sometimes laughing, and catching up with things.

More blessings, prayers and holy water and the body is placed in the ground where it will remain until the family can afford the cremation. Many are tired, as they have been with the family for the past two days without much rest, but it's O.K. because it's "suda biasa" (normal life). Even today, as I pass the compound, I see stacks of prayer offerings, and the house is still crowded with folks.

Communal life here is the norm. Most live and die never knowing much to be "mine," but rather "ours." It's rather chaotic at times for me in the family compound where I "hang out," with so much family all living their lives together, and yet I love to go and just sit and watch as the grandfather rocks the baby to sleep , or ten men work together on the new family temple, or it's time to just sit and "jaw" a bit. As I spend more time with these peaceful people, I understand a bit more where their acceptance and joy for life comes from. It is centered around the family and their Hindu religion. All is shared from birth to death. Love and caring for the community is a way of life.
-Roxy Sincerney

Communal Childhood

I was born on a commune called Magic Forest Farm (MFF) in Takilma, Oregon on March 8, 1982. From the second I came out of Heidi, I have been protected by love and freedom by my extended and birth families alike. The commune in which I lived from ages 0-7 was and is the specialist place I have ever been. There I had fifteen parents, twelve siblings, and countless cows, chickens, bugs, dogs, goats and cats. We made food together, gardened, played, worked, laughed and cried together. The kids I grew up with on MFF share a bond that I think no one else will ever have with me. We climbed trees together, swam, fought, imagined, laughed, danced, explored, romped, joked, made potions , played, worked, learned taught, changed and grew together, We went beyond friendship to a place of brothers and sisters. Even when the commune began to change and many people began to move on and be pursued by"real life", the bonds us kids had acquired remained.

The things that communal living have done for me are vast and important. I am extremely proud of who I have become, and I owe a lot of it to the place where I lived and the people I lived with. Magic Forest Farm is a place I love and will ALWAYS be connected to. The people who live(d) in MFF have gained an unusual respect for nature and a symbiotic relationship with it. This, and the family one gains from a commune, are the most important things I learned, things I will keep with me for the rest of my life.
-Kate Parker-Shames

Communal Life Remembered

In 1972, humanity had lost its sanity. Disillusioned with American politics (thinking the Vietnam war was endless), at odds with my family of birth, searching for an identity... out of place in the world, I arrived at the Mirage Garage in the Takilma dusk. Having hitchhiked the last seven or so unpaved, dusty miles, I found myself in a New World; a circus of odd, beautiful, terrifyingly colorful people out of step with the insane world. I had come home to acceptance, love community.

Over the course of the next few years, as the Illinois River spoke to me, while hepatitis ravaged our communal livers, with no T.V., telephones, newspapers, the messages from Mother Earth came through loud and clear. In the search for "non-judgmental" warmth to replace the *unacceptable* label stamped on me by my family and society, I unwittingly entered, via love , through the back door of the Magic Forest Farm communal family. The first years were not easy. Giving up private ownership of everything except what would fit on a 2x3' cubby was an exercise in monastery-like asceticism. Seeing a fellow communard wearing my favorite shirt out to change the oil in the rototiller was an enlightening experience. Neither the shirt nor I were ever the same again.

The whole process was akin to becoming a parent for the first time...a lesson in surrender. As with an overly lenient parent, the commune as spoiled child often ruled. Since we strove for consensus, those who objected most vocally or threw the loudest tantrums or tenaciously held onto their point of view often "won." Determined to make a

different world from that of my own parents' conservative, religious, "right" values, I often gave up too much advocacy for myself. And sometimes I exercised too much control. But, over the years, a healing occurred, a balance was achieved. I GREW UP! I felt ready to become a parent myself.

For rearing children, there was no better life than communal for me. I believe parenting in isolation is dangerous for the parent and the child. Having other adults around makes you more accountable as a parent. The interactions are cleaner because there are witnesses, as well as stimulation, support, new ideas, whether across the table or in the next room. The richness of the tapestry is enhanced because you're not only a part of your own child's unfolding, but also that of the others in the community. Over the weeks and years, you literally become FAMILY. The importance of community at either end of the life cycle is **vital**. Both with the joyously welcomed births of my children, and the sad, sudden death of one, I felt tremendous unconditional love and support, without which our family's survival would have been precarious.

Leaving Magic Forest Farm after 16 years was an extremely difficult choice, one that, as a family, we still question. I have come to believe over the years that a lot of society's ills stem from lack of community. We all need to be loved; we need "family" (genetic or chosen); we need roots; we all want to be known and valued; we need to share. At its best, community can give us all these things. Communal living is AGONY, it's ECSTASY, it's YIN, it's YANG. It is a part of my very rich past.

-Heidi Parker-Shames

The Good Life

When I arrived in Takilma in early 1975, I had the good fortune to be accepted at Cedar Gulch, an " end of the road" sanctuary with a fine group of people sharing the land. In the early days of Takilma, communes like the Meadows, Canaan, Magic Forest Farm, Doo-Dah, New Land, Sun Star, Cook Ranch and Talsalsan were like islands in our uncertain valley scene. Many people used these places as a base to find their own niche in the area and create the tapestry that we see here today.

Being natural hubs of meeting and living dynamics, these communes helped unite thoughts and energies that constellated into great services, such as the Clinic, Community Building, Dome School and Siskiyou Project. These thoughts also became the work efforts of Green Side Up and the Conehead reforestation opportunities. Lately, communes are providing beautiful places for children to grow up and sites for rituals. "Community" implies what we do together. If there is no interaction as a group, one only lives in a neighborhood.

Our recent skirmish with the BLM showed us some of the spirit that can transcend community and rise in tribal awareness.

- River

174

It's a Dog's Life

In looking back it seems that since leaving home I have always lived in some form of commune or another. As an art student in the Fifties, there was shared space, food, wine and conversation. A group of young women and men was devoted to Art, Bach, Sartre, Camus and what was then called **Free Love**. None of us could individually afford to rent the amount of space that we required. Economics and Philosophy were the glue for a proto-commune. We worked and partied together for a couple of years. It was wonderful while it lasted. It started to unravel when Walter, our black and beloved family cat, disappeared. We went to the pound together to look for him. Ushered into the cat wing of the pound, we walked down long aisles of caged cats. There were hundreds of them and half of them black. They all looked like Walter! They rubbed up against the cages meowing and purring piteously, trying to get as close to us as possible and all acting as if they had known us for years. We left the pound without Walter, not knowing if he was there, and not knowing if we were leaving him behind to his doom. Deeply immersed in existentialism as we were, the family couldn't survive our group inability to identify Walter. Within a month everyone had drifted off to other parts of their lives and into other stories.

I moved to New York in 1959, married, and shared a railroad apartment on East 5th Street with my wife and an assorted group of poets, artists, & druggies. We may have given the impression that we had chosen voluntary poverty as a way of life but we had no such intention. We were artists! We were poets! We had no time for jobs. Our days were needed for recuperating from glorious night! We were mostly stoned. I won't say on what. Sins survived need no enumeration. Our main communal effort after paying the rent was hustling the ingredients for the meals that my wife Donna and I would pick out of *Larousse Gastronomique.* The Family would hit the streets with their lists and head to stores all over the city: Fresh bay scallops and shallots for the Creme Saint-Jacques, tenderloin and port wine for the Tournedos a la Louis, strawberries and kirsch for the Tarte aux Fraises. Needless to say we had some accomplished shoplifters in our little group! Due to the chemicals that we were taking we would often sit down to six course dinners at 3 am. We were a commune based on cuisine, art, jazz, drugs and the prevailing philosophy of the day, Nihilism. The drugs introduced death into the family and at the end of a summer of funerals, we survivors scattered, seeking safe havens to cleanse the Lower East Side's dark pleasures from our veins.

Several years later Donna, our baby boy, Matt, and I found ourselves in San Francisco. It was the summer of 1964 and we had walked into a new era. Seeking a place to live near Golden Gate Park we hit the streets of the Haight-Ashbury. Following our keenly-developed noses we encountered George, an artist-rock musician, smoking a joint on the stoop of a house on Cole street. He introduced us to some friends who had a huge apartment on Ashbury street. Another proto-commune, this one based on rock and roll. There was a new element entering the picture. This family was linked to other similar families in the neighborhood. The extended family was being born. It was a strange place to find ourselves. Our idea of a concert was a box at the Opera or a night at a jazz club. There we were in a house filled with people forming rock bands. Three bands came out of that family. They all achieved various degrees of fame. The weight of

I like the little village sounds of waking up with everyone. It's lonely not living communally. -Jill

Communal life? It's how we met. The bathtub was the only place where other people weren't. - Menno

8

their own success broke up this household. They needed their own spaces. The greater extended family however had taken on a life of its own and would continue to spread throughout the neighborhood culminating in an all too brief explosion of love and pleasure in the summer of 1967. We returned to the lower east side in 1965 and rented a large loft on east 3rd Street. I soon was a bachelor again which after an initial period of grieving was not all that onerous. Promiscuity had become the rule rather then the exception. One evening a friend dropped by with a jazz musician, Steve, who was looking for space to live and practice in. He was a drummer and soon the place was filled with musicians. It was a large loft taking up the whole third floor of the building. We built bedrooms into various corners for myself, Steve and Herbie, a bass player who was a friend of Steve's. We had a rhythm section! Musicians, in town for gigs, would crash there. The place was always full of people. I would often paint into the early morning to the sounds of trios, quartets, quintets. By then our philosophy had been reduced to five words: "it is what it is." A proto-commune based on Art, Jazz, Sex and two new elements, politics and acid. It was a two year period that I know was wonderful because I can remember so little of it.

In the summer of 1967 I returned to San Francisco and into a world that dovetails with the lives of many of you who are reading this. The story of the summer of love and the diaspora that brought so many of us to our happy valley is well known. I moved into a crash pad on Clayton Street and became involved with the Diggers. We were older then most of the kids that were flocking into the Haight. The Diggers devoted themselves to housing, feeding, and politicizing flower children through what we called street theatre. The Viet Nam War was on. Politics was fueled on acid, fear, and despair over our inability to stop our government from burning children alive in a foreign country.

I've lived communally in one form or another since 1954. Most of these groups were by nature temporary. They all had shared goals. Getting the rent, finding the drugs, shopping the food, creating our art, getting the band to the gig on time, printing the flyers, organizing the demonstration; short term projects that kept us bound together. There was never a permanent commitment to a particular place.

It wasn't until I came to Takilma in the summer of 1970 that I found what it was to be truly part of a family. The extended Takilma family had the feeling of permanence and commitment to place that I had not realized had been lacking in my life. Walking into the Meadows was like coming home to a family that had always been **my** family, a home that had always been **my** home. Here I found a family that was committed to a place and to the people on that place. I found that commune is a verb, not a thing; a state of being, not an idea; a commitment, not a contract.

I am your family,

you are my family.

We shall all grow old together.

S.Dog

I've never had the pleasure! - Jack

I like sharing meals together, hanging out in the dining room, taking turns with dishes. -Holly

Are You My Sister?

We left Modesto, or wherever the heck that was, as the Whole Family. She named us after being stuck in the bus in the heat for a month, while he did repairs and smiled at younger and thinner ladies. I was Swimmin' Whole (19 and keeping cool); her seven year old son was Hey You! Whole; her baby was New Whole, she was Old Whole, and he was Any Old Whole Will Do.

They weren't the easiest of times.

Which was probably got her thinking of her mom and British Columbia and gathering some home turf advantage. Moms are good for convincing daughters we're desirable, even daughters who've had two kids, three miscarriages, and sunburst stretch marks which hang down to their vaginas. She changed a "Southbound" song to "Northbound" and sang it over and over again. As soon as the bus was fixed, we were off.

B.C. wasn't all that she remembered it to be though and he was uptight and hangin' around grouchy all the time because he couldn't work legitimately. She and her mom had a way of fighting that had them both in quiet misery a lot and I complained about being disliked as a Yankee. But the "Northbound" song had kind of taken hold. She soon made the shift to "North to Alaska" and we were off again.

We had enough money to get to Ketchikan. I'll never forget waiting up all night at the ferry dock, drinking my latest homemade alcohol concoction, while the others slept. I'd always envied Huckleberry Finn and this time I felt I'd arrived, and truly was "heading out for the territories." Peopleless mountains, water, trees and stars made for a spinetingling shift from Northeast New Jersey and I didn't want to miss a second of the hype.

She met lots of folks when we got there, like she always did. I met lots of folks because I was around, and people confused us at first. We were both tall and big, had brown hair and glasses, and loved to party. We got into a routine of taking turns hitchhiking into town every other day from the campground where we'd parked the bus. She'd go, I'd stay home and watch the kids; then I'd go, while she stayed home. Folks would pick up one or the other of us up and start going on midstream in conversations, obviously thinking they knew us. We never knew how to respond because it could be that a)they'd really picked up the other one of us, or b)they had us right, but we'd been too drunk to remember. We got picked up on one of our rare trips together once, and our (kinda drunk) ride asked, "Are you your sister?" She decided then it was a cosmic thing, and

that should be our explanation for any further confusion. I didn't really get it, but it sounded so warm and friendly that I wholeheartedly agreed.

She often met him in town as he'd gotten a job pretty quick, having good skills and being personable and all. They were having a great time together and he was being way more considerate so she decided to rename us the Dude Family. He was Dude Pa, she was Dude Ma, her son was Dude Boy, the baby was Dude Baby, and I was Slow Dumb Dude Sister, because I'd been celibate for at least a year. I told her I was recovering from a broken heart, but she didn't see what that had to do with it.

We moved the bus to someone's property overlooking the narrows and islands across the way. You could look out and see three or four rainstorms happening at once while the sky was blue overhead. Bald eagles dove for herring and seemed to stare at us from distant perches. Killer whales and sometimes gray ones cruised by. She'd bring out her saxophone and play like some ol' moose bellowing a joyful chorus. I'd get lost in the picture until she'd start hootin' and hollerin' at fishing boats heading for Dutch Harbor and points unknown. I'd take up the cry and she'd stick out her thumb, always eager for the next adventure.

Those were the days.

She took to wearing her dresses from the 1940s with combat boots and a Stetson hat. She developed an entourage of musicians and played informally at our favorite tavern. The whole bar would join in on late night renditions of her own nasty version of "Up Against the Wall, You Redneck Mothers." I stayed in jeans and got a job there as a janitor. We didn't get confused too much anymore.

He and I hung out at the sidelines. It was impossible to get too close though, seeing how we both felt about her, so he once again moved on to the younger and thinner ladies. Folks had a lot of sympathy for him now. She'd flirt with the musicians on stage and talk about hitchhiking fishing boats in front of everyone and though it made for some mighty great times, most folks agreed it was hopeless to love a tramp. The musician she brought home once was kinda nice to me so I moved into his place. They started fighting a lot . He bought the family a trailer. She got into throwing

I am so selfish. Living communally is kind of like being in a marriage; you have obligations. When I lived communally I couldn't stand the meetings - I mean, when someone's having problems, what do you DO?
- Marjorie

things. Usually pots and pans but plants when she was really, really upset. He topped everything by throwing their TV over a cliff, but that wasn't a big deal actually because it was only black and white and we all knew he wanted color.

She visited me once, years later. She'd hitchhiked several boats by then and was hollering some dirty joke into the door of the bar where I met her.

I was kind of embarrassed because I didn't want to be part of any sort of scene as I was working on being respectable. She was uptight because her latest plans had fallen through. She told me she had come down to the lower 48 to chase some fishermen and was taking medication for depression. I told her I was recovering from something that didn't work out and going to school to become a social worker.

She thought that was funny. "Are you my sister?" she asked.

-Nicole Rensenbrink

• •

Children's Poetry

A Far Off Place

It's a place where I can get away
Where it doesn't matter what I do or say
It's where I can go for a little bit
And when I'm gone my parents don't realize it

I like to imagine different places
Where I can see new things and different faces
I can go where the fish will swim
Or be like a monkey and swing limb from limb

I like to look in scary caves
Or go to the ocean and watch the waves
When I'm by myself I have so much fun
But I have to go inside when the day is done

-Elizabeth Johnson   13 yrs

Experiencing Community

My first community experience was in Canada at the Srawberry Fields festival in Ontario when I was sixteen. I discovered that I liked living communally. Later, in England, I met some musicians who needed a house with room for their band, Tallis, to practice. Splitting rent, utilities and food five ways, we rented a large house. It was fun! We moved to London. Economic hardships broke the band up two years later. Everyone went their separate ways. It was 1974.

I traveled to the Findhorn Community in the north of Scotland and came away with the gift of pregnancy. Moving to California, I gave birth to my child in the Islandia commune. It was in the redwood forests of the Santa Cruz mountains. I had found a supportive place to have a child. We bonded deeply yet I was restless. I returned to England and became involved in the Peace Movement, where I met the father of my second child. We lived in a tepee village in south Wales. When we broke up I made my own tepee and raised my children in the circle of other tepee families. I embraced single motherhood and learned.

The 1984 Rainbow Gathering attracted me. Folding our tepee cover, we flew to California. With the help of friends, we obtained a van and tepee poles. I met the River Spirit Folk in the Trinity Mountains. It was a beautiful wilderness paradise. We spent a very snowy winter there. Realizing that I wanted a partner to help me raise my children, I continued searching. That spring I settled in Williams. We had a new tepee on beautiful land and good friends. We were happy. I met David, a member of Sun Star. He loved children. He was into monogamy and was ready for a committed relationship. David was funloving, hard working and community minded. Sun Star is composed of separate households sharing a common piece of land. I moved in and set up my tepee. The bond here is ecology. We all have to work to sustain our lives. No one is rich, yet we have the priceless wealth of clean air, water and lots of trees. The wilderness is at our doorstep. We have each other. I have given birth to two more children with David. We are grateful for our healthy family. We have a place to sink roots and raise the kids. I have found a place to experience the joy and spirit in life. Give thanks! Blessed be!

-Bridge

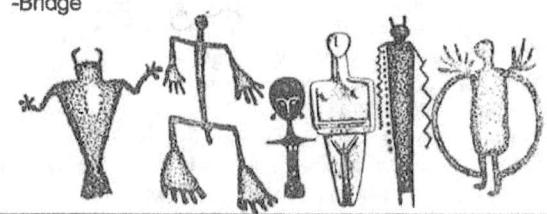

What do I like about living communally? Can't think of a single damn thing!(Just kidding). The emotional inter-support. There's always someone around. You always have the option of company. Earlier, you didn't have a choice and that was too overwhelming. - Lance

From England on the Tofu Wave

I always wanted to be a hippie. And I wanted to live on a commune. Despite the grooming of schoolteachers and the groaning of family members, I knew the real juice of the late 1960's was being squeezed from fruits not to be found down on Dad's dairy farm.

The first wave of back-to-the-landers started buying up the nearby deserted Welsh hill farms. They made ammoniac smelling goat cheese and sturdy furniture; they spun lumpy yarns from the flighty sheep which they tried, vainly, to shepherd without the aid of a dog. The Welsh sheepdog has a sophisticated intelligence, but understands no English and these were all " Sais" immigrants from the squats and suburbs of London and Brighton.

Although they smoked hash, dropped acid, gardened bio-dynamically, loved freely and voted Labour or Communist, if they voted at all, these were mostly people who maintained traditional, though fluid, family structures. There were notable exceptions. My now-neighbor, Bridge, lived in a locally notorious tipi village and my school friends and I used to spy on the haunted looking residents of the Silene Community, just up the road from the Drovers Arms. They dwindled to a sad faced menage a trois and we lost interest in them and their pagan ways. I left home soon after this and my own experience in the seventies was of living in England, Wales and Iran with groups of friends who shared living expenses. This was cheap and cheerful but not the communal experience I still imagined in the back of my mind. These households lacked fervency, focus, a philosophical raison d'etre that went beyond material expediency and good vibes.

The Tofu Factory gave me focus, in spades. Situated on the Flathead Reservation in western Montana, between the Bison Range and the Mission Mountains, it was the most unlikely location for a small commercial tofu production outfit, but we were undetered. Our collective passion for the mighty soybean knew no bounds and our (truly) superior product was trucked across three Western states, bearing a quaint lotus blossom logo.

Ten or twelve adults lived very close together in a three-bedroom, one-bath old log home and a one-room meditation cabin on the way to the splendid garden. No one was ever refused a place to stay or a free meal. We never asked residents or visitors for money, though people often gave. We attracted troubled young students from Missoula and Rainbow Family folks on the way to and from Gatherings. There were poets and tree planters, mystics and mountain women. Two visitors who never left were an Austrian military man and a permed secretary from Butte, who got our address from a package of tofu at Safeway. At one time we

hosted a group of three lesbian women and seven kids who turned the living room into a dormitory-cum-home school for a month while they fixed their school bus engine. We believed "what goes around, comes around" and it was our pleasure and purpose to give.

Not too surprisingly, some of us gave a whole lot more than others. Of the dozen or so regular Tofu-ites, five or six of us did most of the work, in exchange for ten bucks a week (and all the tofu you could eat) that we usually spent on chocolate malteds or the occasional luxurious beer. We got up at three a.m. to grind the beans so that the mop-up crew could finish steam cleaning the okara-spattered machines before nightfall. The others read, slept, got high, got sick, talked, laughed, meditated and watched TV until we came in from the shop and cooked dinner. We were all so high on the euphoria and exhaustion of constant, righteous physical work that it took a long time for most of us to resent the unequal division of labor. We were in the middle of achieving equilibrium, with surprisingly little rancor on any side, when the whole commune collapsed.

It's cheap. -Gail

I want to be alone! - Marcy

I like the way you can spread your depression all around the house. Seriously, I'm the Hermit, so if I'm having dark periods, I don't like to bring other people down. - Mr. Tracy

What dissolved us, finally, was not lack of focus, or enthusiasm, but our failure to define what we were really about. Were we a cottage industry or a healing community? Should we accept as members people who were crazy about tofu, or could we take on folks who were just plain crazy? Who was entitled to own shares and how many? How do you establish the monetary value of devotion? And while we were debating these issues, our sister company, a wholefoods trucking co-op, to whom we were joined at the hip, heart and bank account, went belly up and we all sank together.

It takes a rare breed of persons to navigate the whitewater of collective vision making and then translate their dream into a form that can flourish within a society that is indifferent, or hostile to the ideals of commune-ism. The Tofu Factory was a brief, brave introduction to the politics of togetherness that took me several strides closer to the open-hearted, diligent, process-oriented, fun-loving group of folks I live with now at Cedar Gulch. The politics are still there, still challenging, but I've arrived at the communal destination I was looking for. Now I can get on with the journey.

-Fliss

"CONFUSION"

WHAT SHOULD I DO? HOW DO I LIVE? WHICH WAY DO I NEED TO LIVE MY LIFE?

> I've always lived communally because of the theater thing. It's always amazing to think about how all the women bleed together in sync. The last show I was in was six women and by the end of the run we were all in line. -Jennie Mae

Before and After

Having lived most of my adult life in an intentional spiritual community (ashram) has given me much food for thought on this current topic of Common Ground. I have so many thoughts and experiences that I think I could fill volumes. I will attempt to give a broad overview.

Especially in the early years of the ashram, we spent almost all of our time together in eating, yoga, meditation, philosophizing, exercising and sleeping. Bonds and intimacy between people happened fast. I have never felt so profoundly loved and cared for, not even by my mother or father. The goal of our community was "internal " work. Search inside yourself for the love and goodness you are seeking. Be a scientist--study yourself. Question--how still can I be inside? How gentle and loving can I become? Explore--what is possible for human spiritual development? Everything in our community was geared so an individual could focus on their inner work.

As a man, I feel especially gifted to have lived where the soft and vulnerable places inside of me were so nurtured and held in deep respect. In general, I find it rare to experience sensitivity and vulnerability with other men outside of the ashram. I feel saddened by this. For me there is so much more power and strength in softness and love.

Through a series of scandals with out spiritual teacher and other philosophical differences, our community broke up. Hundreds of us were scattered like seeds in the wind. And so I find myself here in Takilma, sorting out the broken pieces that remain of my once utopian life. Once I thought that all that mattered in life was love. That is what I had been taught. Now I find that making money so that I can eat, have a car and a roof over my head also matters. Once I was very sure of my ability to love myself and others. Now I am not so sure of anything. My heart and my once deep sense of stillness are very disturbed. I experience great fear, insecurity and anger as never before. In my "clearer" moments, I see these things and this new life as opportunities for internal growth. At other times I just feel little and afraid.

Looking back, I am glad I had the chance to experience the love and tenderness that was so healing to me. I am also glad to have experienced the profound depth and beauty that meditation, yoga and the other healing arts can be. Looking forward, I await what new adventures life has to offer me. I pray my lessons will be gentle and loving. I hope that my presence in this community will be healing for myself and those I am in relationship with. Thank you for welcoming me into your hearts.

-Yogesh

> I like bringing up kids with other people and I like going shopping in other peoples' fridges. Sharing tools and wheelbarrows. Talking. And you don't have to brush your hair and go out in order to visit other people. -Laurie

Letters

To the editors,

Greetings from the Southwest. Managed to see the recent issue of Common Ground while passing through Tucson, AZ, and it felt good to get news of home. It has been a hot, dry winter in the desert. Even though this earth sees little rain, the wild beings are struggling this season. Few flowers will bloom, and the migrating birds are small in number. As I walk the trackless border lands, they are not so trackless. Once obscure paths are beaten trails. All footprints pointing norte, troubled times in Mexico too. As the bankers, politicians and corporations impose their programs of austerity, it is the poor that pay the price of our free trade. Walking down a desert canyon, the falling stream reminds me of home, and the sandy shore is crowded with willows, alamo and sycamore. Spring is coming. I can smell it. This little stream teams with native fish, and all 5 species are threatened with extinction. Here in the desert canyon, they're hiding out, waiting for the economy to pass. Overhead, jets scream by, barely 100 feet above the mesas, each one guided by a person just doing their job. I read the BLM area manager will not cut our forest, for now. He will be back, the plan states so. Who can blame him? Some say he is a good man. Good or bad, the plan commands him, his boss, his boss's boss. Good man or bad, does it matter to the stump? Probably only that the plan was followed and obeyed. Not much flesh and bone in those words. I will assume he is a good man all the same, and respect him. But I'm not going along with this plan and will resist. All resistance to him, his boss, his boss's boss, for the river is our blood, the forest our home. The mountains are crying out. Who can blame them?
Keep on, Steve M.

To the editors:

Now that we're talking communal life, there is an issue that has come to the attention of a few of us in the valley. Hammer's Model Market and the Thousand Cranes Deli need our help. Cash really would boost the viability of our much needed resource. Many of us feel that we must preserve this part of our community presence in town. Where else is there to sit down and eat fine food while visiting with your friends and neighbors?
So how about another benefit? I don't think so. What are the alternatives? Let's have an envelope parade, containing whatever you can afford, that finds its way to Robin and Chas.
-Tio Rio

> *All the different ideas. - Robin*

Announcements

I lost my prescription wire-rimmed eyeglasses, in hard gray case, at Gray Back Campground last fall at the WALL Sugarloaf protest. Contact Wapsu if found, please.

1st Illinois Valley Cribbage Tournament

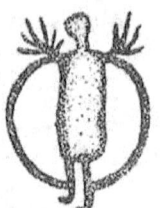

Adult and under age 12 categories.
When: Sunday, April 28, 1:00 P.M.
Why: Benefit for Common Ground
Luck of the draw pairings
Double elimination format
Bring your favorite crib board/cards
Where: Takilma Community Building

Preregistration special, adult or child $3.00, at the door $5.00 and $4.00. Ask about family rates; $1.00 rebate if you bring a card table. Mail registration to Common Ground, attention: cribbage tournament, P.O. Box 2016, Cave Junction 97523

Golden Bear Reunion

In a previous lifetime in the 60's, Helen and Delbert ran the Golden Bear club in Huntington Beach, CA. On March 23 at 8:00, some wild Golden Bear people will show up at the Takilma Community Building to entertain us and benefit the Dome school. Steve Gillette will play, Sylvia of Ian and Sylvia will be there, and there will be some hot entertainment surprises. $10.00 tickets are for sale at Hammer's, the Dome School and at the door. Meat and vegetarian bearball sandwiches and espresso will be available; if you can donate a dessert call Helen at 592-3911

The Dome School could use some more help with those benefits. Current parents and teachers are a little burnt out, and are calling on the community for help. Some of us have kids who got their solid, gentle start in Dome School, and then went on life on the larger stage. We can give back by baking something or even contributing some good store bought goods. Or help with setup or cleanup and get in touch with the school as it grows and changes.
Call Heidi at 592-2123 to plug in.

Takilma Old Growth for Sale
Buckhorn Timber Sale is being auctioned on April 1. Don't let it go without expressing your outrage. Call SREP 592-4459 or Siskiyou National Forest 592-2166.

> *People notice if you stay under the quilt for more than one day. - anonymous*

COMMON GROUND CALENDAR

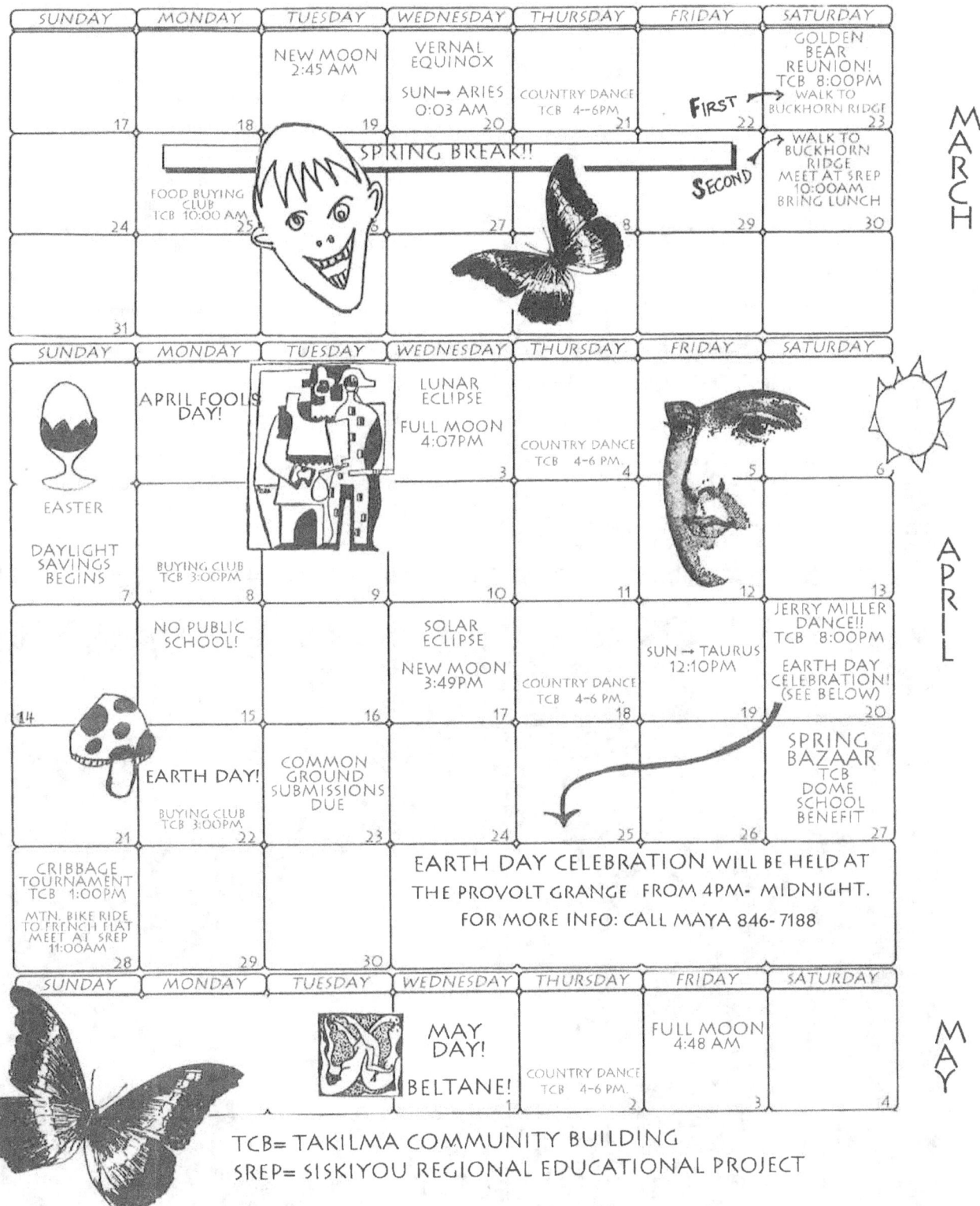

SUNDAY	MONDAY	TUESDAY	WEDNESDAY	THURSDAY	FRIDAY	SATURDAY	
17	18	NEW MOON 2:45 AM 19	VERNAL EQUINOX SUN→ARIES 0:03 AM 20	COUNTRY DANCE TCB 4-6PM 21	FIRST → 22	GOLDEN BEAR REUNION! TCB 8:00PM WALK TO BUCKHORN RIDGE 23	M A R C H
24	FOOD BUYING CLUB TCB 10:00 AM 25	26	SPRING BREAK!! 27	28	SECOND 29	WALK TO BUCKHORN RIDGE MEET AT SREP 10:00AM BRING LUNCH 30	
31							

SUNDAY	MONDAY	TUESDAY	WEDNESDAY	THURSDAY	FRIDAY	SATURDAY	
EASTER DAYLIGHT SAVINGS BEGINS 7	APRIL FOOLS DAY! 8	BUYING CLUB TCB 3:00PM 9	LUNAR ECLIPSE FULL MOON 4:07PM 10	COUNTRY DANCE TCB 4-6 PM 11	12	13	A P R I L
14	NO PUBLIC SCHOOL! 15	16	SOLAR ECLIPSE NEW MOON 3:49PM 17	COUNTRY DANCE TCB 4-6 PM 18	SUN→TAURUS 12:10PM 19	JERRY MILLER DANCE!! TCB 8:00PM EARTH DAY CELEBRATION! (SEE BELOW) 20	
21	EARTH DAY! BUYING CLUB TCB 3:00PM 22	COMMON GROUND SUBMISSIONS DUE 23	24	25	26	SPRING BAZAAR TCB DOME SCHOOL BENEFIT 27	
CRIBBAGE TOURNAMENT TCB 1:00PM MTN. BIKE RIDE TO FRENCH FLAT MEET AT SREP 11:00AM 28	29	30	EARTH DAY CELEBRATION WILL BE HELD AT THE PROVOLT GRANGE FROM 4PM- MIDNIGHT. FOR MORE INFO: CALL MAYA 846-7188				

SUNDAY	MONDAY	TUESDAY	WEDNESDAY	THURSDAY	FRIDAY	SATURDAY	
		MAY DAY! BELTANE! 1		COUNTRY DANCE TCB 4-6 PM. 2	FULL MOON 4:48 AM 3	4	M A Y

TCB= TAKILMA COMMUNITY BUILDING
SREP= SISKIYOU REGIONAL EDUCATIONAL PROJECT

182

Classifieds

Takima
common ground
BOX 2016
Cave Junction, OR. 97523

Bulk Rate US Postage **Paid**
Cave Junction 97523
Permit # 16

To

Common ground

ISSUE #19   BELTANE '96

KTLM - RADIO FREE TAKILMA

Fear not! Quality ear food, with heart and soul is coming to our radio dials. The simple beauty of local micro-watt radio is soon to be a reality. Micro-watt stations use small amounts of wattage to send their signals, 100 watts as opposed to 100,000. As a result they broadcast over a small area and cannot be picked up outside of the immediate vicinity.

Miguelo, Takilma's czar of the airways, and his assistants, Sara Carnahan and Aspen Farer, are going to bring micro-watt radio to the Takilma community. KTLM will be *our* radio station right here in our happy valley (Takilma East, eat your heart out!).

They have a vision for KTLM. They see an opportunity for a station with total community involvement. Young and old are invited to participate; as D.J.s with their own personal styles of music, as story tellers, as creators of children's programs. The possibilities are endless. A "Good News Only" program is planned and readers are encouraged to go out and make as much good news as they can for the show. Local events and important meetings can be broadcast. The big 4th of July game will be brought to you on the air, LIVE, this year.

People who want to share ideas, help, or want more information, call 592- 6902 or write to KTLM, P.O. Box 815, Takilma, Or 97523.

WHY IS THIS PAPER SO SMALL?

The elegant brevity of this issue of Common Ground is the result of two artfully synchronized events.

First, the Mud Council decided to do the right thing and print on tree-free paper, at twice the price. Now we have a golden glow of eco-correctness and a fragile three digit bank balance. Like the rest of America, we are now only a paycheck away from extinction.

DO YOU LOVE THE PAPER? THROW MONEY!

Secondly, of all the more or less crazed individuals who have facilitated the production of the rag in times past, none could be persuaded to take on this issue in anything but a severely truncated form. Fortunately, very few people write unless we beg, enrage or flatter them, so there wasn't much to facilitate.

DO YOU WANT THIS PAPER? WRITE SOMETHING! DO YOU WANT TO SEE YOUR NEIGHBORS IN PRINT? WORK FOR THE NEWSLETTER! THROW MORE MONEY!! CALL 592-4245 TO OFFER UP YOUR UNIQUE TALENTS!

SUBSCRIBE NOW!

A HEARTFELT THANKS TO ALL WHO HAVE AND CONTINUE TO SUPPORT US THESE PAST TWO YEARS ♥

_____ $10 1-YEAR SUBSCRIPTION   NAME:_____

_____ $25 1-YEAR SUBSCRIPTION AND   ADDRESS:_____
       COMMON GROUND T-SHIRT.
       (CALL 592-4695 FOR SIZE AND COLOR INFO)   _____
_____ $ BROKE BUT LITERATE. SEND ANYWAY

IT'S A NATURAL PROGRESSION FROM DREAMS TO REALITY...

Peace with Inn Healing and Renewal Center is open for a full spring and summer season of transformational events.

I did say this is what I wanted to do... and now it feels like it has a life of it's own! I find myself trying to keep up with the energy that is unfolding. Always reminding myself to breathe ... and remember that not only did I ask for this, but that it's just the way it's supposed to be. There are many wonderful things happening here this spring and summer. Some of our friends and neighbors will be teaching classes: Paco and Marcy will be sharing a "Conscious Breathing Daily Program", Carol Valentine will be facilitating "Singing From the Ground Up," Francis Warner, from the Chopra Center for Mind Body Healing, will be teaching "Magic of Healing" and "Primordial Sound Meditation and possibly a Afro-Caribbean dance class. Clearysage will be doing an "Acupressure for Women" workshop, Marcy will facilitate an "Artists Way" group and Sue Krisa will hold a gourmet and medicinal mushroom cooking class.

My vision for Peace with Inn is to provide a space for transformation, healing and renewal, for myself and our community, and to offer visitors a reason to come and experience the beauty and richness of this place we call home.

As Peace with Inn evolves, we will have several therapists offering their services here. Stay tuned, and get involved, we're all in this together.   With Love, *Myrica*   592-4209

IT TAKES A WHOLE COMMUNITY TO RAISE OUR CHILDREN

Many thanks to all the good folks who have offered their time and talents to the children in our community. Just to name a few of the wonderful workshops that have been offered to our children by community members: jewelry making, botany, science, ecology, astronomy, hiking, camping, mapping, drumming, dancing, tile mosaics, languages, woodcarving, knot-tying, basketry, tree-climbing, biking, acting, game-playing, writing, storytelling, mask-making, and marimba playing. Way to go Takilma! People have come to the Dome School and offered workshops, they have come out to our homes, taught from their homes, in the Community Building, in the mountains, at the river....anywhere seems to be a good place to learn! The children are very comfortable learning from their friends and neighbors with our relaxed community formats. Again, thanks to everyone that has taken their time to be with the kids.

If you love what you're doing and would be willing to work with small groups of children, please get in touch with *Katherine* at the Dome School.   592-3911

A MOTHERS DAY MEMORY OF A CHILD'S EASTER IN HOLLYWOOD

It was early and Mommy and Granma were still sleeping when I entered the living room. The Easter bunny had left a big basket! I could see the chocolate eggs and the brightly colored candies through the emerald green cellophane. Then I saw *him*.

I just got a glimpse as he ran past the window. Plump and as big as an adult, he was white all over with long ears that hung askew on either side of his head. "It's him! It's the Easter bunny!" I was stunned. He scurried past the concrete lions that framed our front steps. I ran to the door. "Mommy! Granma! By the time I got outside he was gone. Granma, in her old green robe, was peering out at me when I came back. "It was the Easter bunny, I saw him! He was this big and, and ..." "You did! He was?" She hugged me. "That's because you're such a good boy. He only lets the nicest boys see him." My mother joined us at the door. "I wish I had been here with the camera, I would have taken his picture and sold it to the newspapers!" I held the basket up. "Look what he left!" They both yummied over the chocolates and candies. Feeling rich and magnanimous, I passed it around. Mommy had a red jelly bean and granma took a green one. "It's Irish," she explained. I liked the green ones too.

Then Mommy had a really good idea, "Sometimes he hides eggs for very special boys to find." She was right. She's so smart! He had hidden them everywhere, under the couch, behind the legs of chairs, even under a fold in the rug. They sat at the table, smiling and watching me search. I ran to them, breathless with each new discovery. They smiled and cooed and exclaimed and enveloped me in their love. I could weep with yearning for such happiness.

I don't know who or what it was that I saw that day. It was probably some poor actor, earning some extra money, playing the part for some store or party.   I do know that when I was too old and sophisticated to believe in Santa Claus anymore, I still believed in the Easter bunny. I had seen him with my own eyes! My friends thought I was weird. There is still a part of me that believes in him to this day.   *-Dog*

Dear Common Ground,
Really enjoyed the Communal Life issue of Common Ground. Although I didn't live on a commune, I was a guest at several and experienced the anxieties, hopes and revelations of growing up in the 60'-70's as written about in the last issue.   -Al Karger

Thank you to Deb Murphy and all the other Women who did such a fine job of the Women's Cafe this year. It was a very enjoyable event.   -Anonymous

MERE ANARCHY

Dear Takilma Family,
I loved the last issue—so much heart and wisdom and humor. I'm grateful that I was a part of your world for 10 years and that I can be a long distance family member even now.
I have one little clarification. It's about the word "ANARCHY". The authors referred to 'latent anarchic tendencies' in theorizing why work systems often fail in communes.
In the U.S., the word anarchy has come to be synonymous with disorder, chaos and terrorism. However, the word originally meant "absence of government." Anarchy is a utopian vision of a society of individuals who enjoy freedom from imposed authority. Most of us were socialized under systems of authority and find ourselves in a social setting that values freedom from coercive authority. We are often ill prepared to accept the personal responsibilities essential for voluntary cooperation to work.
Takilma is closer to the ideal of anarchy than most communities I have known. A community/village has emerged that developed its own educational, health care, food production and distribution, political, and social infrastructures. Under the true definition, many of us are anarchists.
Somehow, it is hard to live these principles. Some are always doing the work of others and are tempted to impose rules of fairness; others are evading chores, perhaps still rebelling from the imposed authority in their original families. It takes motivation and re-training to learn to live in anarchy.
-Kayla

YOUTH TO COMMUNITY:

Hey friends and neighbors,
The question of the youth problem has been a big issue in our community lately. We (Sara Carnahan, Sara Hodges, Oona Dean, Ida Madsen and Sequoia Alba) have figured out a solution. We've been thinking of opening a small youth cafe/coffee shop, an alternative culturally targeted in the old Silver Lining.
But we cannot do it ourselves. We need help getting it started: chairs, tables, dishes, services, money, anything you can donate would be greatly appreciated.
Your first reaction may be "Nice dream" or "Silly kids," but we are very motivated and tired of having no place to go. We really want to do this. This is a time to show why Takilma is such a wonderful community. It's time to look into your hearts, reach into your pockets, get together to help us make this happen. If you have any input, donations, or services contact   Sara Carnahan 592-3835; Sara Hodges 592-6307 or Sequoia 592-6733.

BLM-ISHED OPPORTUNITY

Hey friends & neighbors,
This timber sale issue is not dead. BLM wants to push forward with the planning process soon. Keep those letters flowing to BLM. Here's one I just sent:
Dear Mr. Korfhage:
After much soul-searching, I have respectfully declined the opportunity to perform the rare plant survey contract for the proposed Waldo Thin timber sale in and around the community of Takilma. It is, for me, a conflict of interest. While it would be very convenient for me to be able to earn my living this season working so close to home, nevertheless, I must stand in solidarity with my community.
At this point, due to their atrocious mismanagement of our public lands for decades, neither the Forest Service nor the BLM can be trusted to carry out a truly environmentally benign timber sale, all "new-agey" rhetoric notwithstanding. Thus our opposition to any cutting on these lands. And we feel that even the gathering of this important biological information is only facilitating the violation of our church and source of inspiration, namely the virgin public forests of our valley. We will oppose this sale in all its various incarnations as we work to permanently remove these lands from the Matrix.
Although the plant survey will presumably be done by others anyway, let it not be said that Takilma consented to desecration of its sacred forests in exchange for money or jobs.   Sincerely, Bill Gray

The BLM has now scheduled the Waldo Thin Sale to go on the auction block in May '97

186

THE TAKELMA RIVER

A message came to me and coalesced in my mind until deadline time for the "Common Ground." I thought, or felt, that the river was talking to me. It said,"I want to be called the Takelma River from now on." This really resonated with me. For as long as I have been here, I've felt it odd to have a river and mountain, the Illinois and Chicago respectively, named for things back east that already have names. Well, I state that this river, our river, already has a name. And that is the Takelma River. The mountain has another name as well; I don't know that name.

I feel that this message came to me about the time that Grant Pilgrim passed on, and that it came from him. So, in his honor, and Agnes', the last surviving tribal member of the Takelma Indians, let us dedicate the renaming of the Illinois River, to the Takelma River. Maybe name the mountain Pilgrim Peak - sounds good. -River

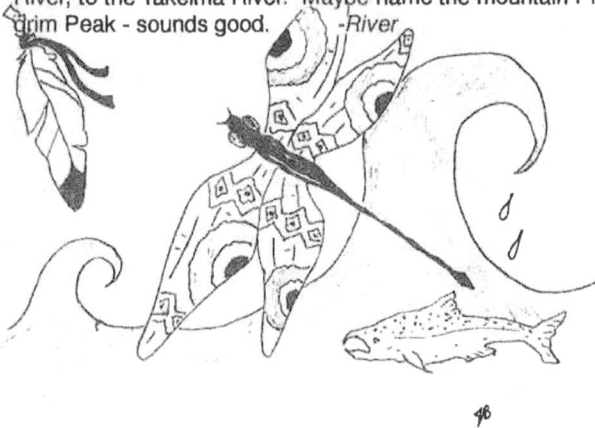

SUBSCRIBER ALERT

Our mailing list is occasionally requested by groups such as SREP, Le Show or The Dome School. We review these requests and do sometimes lend the list for one time uses.

If you are vehemently opposed to us releasing your name and address, you must notify us in writing. Drop a note to PO Box 2016, Cave Junction, Oregon 97523. Thank you.

UNDER THE TAKILMA INFLUENCE

From Russell Kauffman, the first Takilma kid who went to Illinois Valley public schools(and now holds a Ph.D. in Physics), to Ty Houck, an Evergreen Elementary School student who recently tied for first place in a county-wide spelling bee, children from the Takilma community have excelled academically.

I was struck by that recently when I attended the Academic Masters finals at Grants Pass High School. Madera Allen and Melissa Gustafson were representing IVHS. Two of the three announced judges for the music category were also from Takilma, Jim Rich and Pat Mersman. In the program the first past winner listed was Steve Mason. I want to compile a list of all the Takilma kids who have accelerated in the larger community, but space just doesn' t permit it.

Takilma has also provided the valley with many outstanding teachers: an entire parade at Dome School, led by Helen Kauffman, who for a quarter century has been teaching the very young of us to enjoy learning.

Then there's Della Meengs teaching first grade at Evergreen while Cathy Dunham teaches children to love and respect books. Trish Kenney gives kids a Head Start. Alyce Kendall helps the alienated at Lorna Byrne through the Alternative Center while Bill Dunham gives middle schoolers an appreciation of history and Gail Borod counsels them toward greater goals.

Lisa Kelz, with help from Jennie Mae, has founded a teen theater group at IVHS that enlightens the community about the serious problems teenagers face .

Takilma community kids have peppered the honor rolls at both Lorna Byrne and IV High. An outsized number have gone on to, and earned degrees from, college.They are making significant contributions to the world, and making it a better place.

It takes a whole village to raise a child, and our village has raised, and continues to raise, some outstanding children. Ultimately, that may be our greatest contribution toward inflicting upon the world all the change we so desperately set out to make when we founded our country community lo those many years ago. -T.A.

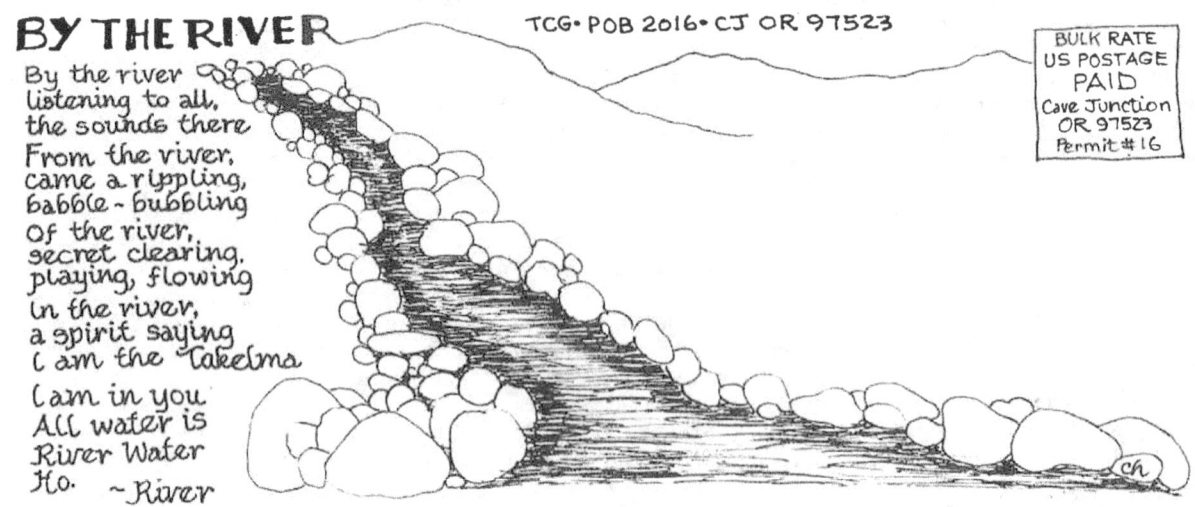

BY THE RIVER

By the river
listening to all,
the sounds there
From the river,
came a rippling,
babble - bubbling
Of the river,
secret clearing,
playing, flowing
In the river,
a spirit saying
I am the Takelma

I am in you.
All water is
River Water
Ho. ~River

TCG· POB 2016·CJ OR 97523

May 1996

Sunday	Monday	Tuesday	Wednesday	Thursday	Friday	Saturday
TCB = Takilma Community Building SREP = Siskiyou Project			1	2	3	4
5	6	7	8	9 Siskiyou Project Camp Out Hogues Meadow for more info: call 592-4459	10 Osgood Ditch Trail Hike meet at Hogues Meadow 9:00am SREP Open House 1:00-5:00pm	11
12 Mothers Day! Takilma Bird and Flower Hike meet at SREP 8:30am	13	14 PTA meeting IVHS 6:30	15 Country Dancing TCB 4-5:30 $2.00	16 Dome School Open House 7-9:00pm New Moon 4:46am	17 Marimba Band TCB 9:00pm Laser Light Show at IVHS Crazy Peak Hike-meet at SREP 10:00am	18
19	20 Buying Club TCB 3:00 Sun →Gemini 11:23am	21	22	23	24	25 Serpentine Ecology-Hike in the Canyon Creek Watershed meet at Visitors Center in CJ 9:00am
26	27	28 Community Building Clean-up 10-3pm	29	30	31 Phone book recycling 5-11 Select Market	

CLASSIFIED:

1000 CRANES CATERING All events – 2 to 1000! Call Robin 592-3159.

3rd ANNUAL SPRING OPEN HOUSE at Hope Mountain Nurseries on May 18th and 19th from 10 to 3. Gardeners don't miss this one. We're only open to the public for one crazy weekend a year. 592-4769 8685 Takilma Road.

GOLDEN DAWN GARDENS bedding plants, vegetable and herb starts, container gardens, cut flowers. Connie Hayes 592-6312.

JEWELRY LESSONS Fabrication and stone setting or cloisonne enameling. Individual or up to 4 kids or adults. Marjorie 592-6733.

CATCH THE VIBE! River will offer didjeridu lessons for beginners starting May 15th and continuing for the next two Wednesdays, the 22nd and 29th, 8pm – 10 ish. Instruments provided. $5.00 per class. Call 592-6889.

LOST: Old family salad tongs, silver plated brass. Left at some potluck in last 4-6 months. If you've seen them **PLEASE** call Marjorie at 592-6733.

OPEN HOUSE: SREP will be holding an Open House on May 11th. The Illuminated Fools will perform at 3:00 p.m., a raffle at 4:30 and a Sugarloaf slideshow at TCB at 7:30. Pat Mersman will play her harpsicord. Come join the fun!

THANKS TO: Dog, Linda, Rachel, Dave T. Jack, Fliss, Jill, Kerry, Laurie, Cathy and Dave H. for creating this issue. The theme for issue #20 will be "How did you arrive in Takilma"? due June 5th.

A RABBIT IN THE MOON

The man said to the rabbit in the moon, "How did it come about that you appear on the moon?"

"Well... many, many moons ago I was hopping from star to star and I hopped right onto this huge white thing of a ball. And a beautiful lavendar light appeared. Then... ahh.. another. A

June 1996

musical voice spoke, "Who is that hopping on my nose?" "It isss me... Rabbit," I said, feeling a bit frightened.

I was looking right into the eyes of the moon. Here I stayed tumbling and twirling, twirling and tumbling through the atmosphere of life.

The rabbit looked into the eyes of the man and said, "If you listen carefully, you will hear our laughter echo throughout the land." This is how the Rabbit became one with the moon.

~ Sally Clements

I have been affected by the moon, watching it explode up from the East behind Little Grey back. Eighteen years and many seasons have gone by and still this majestic ritual, the swelling of this heavenly body, touches my senses. One evening I was so inspired that I wrote this little story. View the moon when it is full and look for the rabbit hunkered on its legs sitting straight up.

Sunday	Monday	Tuesday	Wednesday	Thursday	Friday	Saturday
						Full Moon 1:47pm Calif. Grayback Hike- Meet at SREP 10:00am 1
2	Buying Club TCB 10:00am 3	4	Common Ground Submissions Due Theme: How Did You Arrive in Takilma? 5	Country Dancing! TCB 4-5:30 6	7	Dunn Creek Headwaters Forest Hike Meet at SREP 10:00am 8
9	10	11	12	13	14	New Moon 6:36pm Piersoll Peak Hike Meet at Selma Market 9:00am 15
Fathers Day! 16	Buying Club TCB 10:00am 17	18	19	Summer Solstice Sun → Cancer 7:24pm CountryDancing TCB 4-5:30 20	21	22
23	24	25	26	27	28	29
30	TCB = Takilma Community Building SREP = Siskiyou Regional Education Project Please remember to wear appropriate hiking shoes bring a lunch and water for all the great hikes planned. Call 592-4453 for info.					

TAKILMA

COMMON GROUND

TAKILMA 29 SPEED LIMIT

SUMMER SOLSTICE '96 ISSUE #20

THE BILL AND DONNY SHOW

My first arrival in Takilma, and Oregon for that matter, was through the back door. Happy Camp Road in mid-July of 1970 was an unpaved single lane. Mark and a few other passengers were along. The vehicle was an old Dodge panel truck, orange in color, named the City of Azusa, and it still bore the city's official seal on its driver-side door. One of the truck's tires (I forget which one) was dangerously low and Andy, an old transplanted Mississippian who owned the store, helpfully filled it with air as soon as we pulled in. He gave us a friendly first welcome to this town that we'd decided to visit. About a year later, the City of Azusa, driven by Donny Rogers, would hit a wooden pillar supporting the roof over the store's gas tanks and the roof would collapse; but that's another story.

As one might imagine, approaching Takilma from Happy Camp might give a first time tourist the impression that Takilma is way back in the woods. At that time, before stop lights had found Cave Junction, the setting was decidedly more rural but we soon found that Takilma was a thriving, well populated community. As I faintly remember, we hunted out a former acquaintance, Aries Jerry, and he directed us to where Donny and Bill were staying. The place was already called the Meadows and I can still see, in my mind's eye, the imprints in the tall grass under big ash trees where Bill and Donny laid their sleeping bags - the bent over grass marked their camp.

I'll back track a bit and explain how Mark and I chose Takilma as a place to visit. I had been living in San Francisco for a few years. The city was getting rougher and tougher. Hard drugs and rip offs were at epidemic levels, race relations were becoming rockier and the overall city mood was verging on ugly. The logical remedy was a move to the country. At one point, toward the tail end of 1968, a bunch of us tried to find a place along the Mendocino Coast. It's hard to find a landlord/lady who'll rent to eight or nine dirty hippie types and we had no luck after months of searching. We were finally able to rent a place in downtown Ukiah (First Hippies in Ukiah award?) as a base camp to search for a more ideal rental. We decided to search inland. The coast was where our type of people (hippies) lived but the scenery and the climate of eastern Mendocino intrigued us and we located a house on the edge of Covelo in Round Valley. We had arrived in paradise, spring was bursting, a garden was started and we made friends with several of the locals. We were oblivious, however, to the sentiments of many townsfolk. After two months a segment of the town decided that a bunch of racially mixed and unmarried outsiders were too much. We were driven out of town by force and, to add insult to injury, the high school kids did the work.

Back to the city — but not for long. The following summer, with my friend Mark, I began to camp on the Navarro River near the Mendocino Coast. Gemini Bill and Donny Rogers were two of many new friends. Bill and Donny were a team of traveling minstrels. Donny had a great store of songs and played with wild abandon. Bill would attempt to tone Donny down and refine their act. Bill would complain and Donny would ignore Bill with broad smiles and crack jokes, "Hey, lighten up Bill".

Bill and Donny were leaving the Navarro River to check out Oregon. About a week later at a 4th of July music gathering at Hales Grove (north of Fort Bragg), we bumped into Bill and Donny. Takilma was a great place, they told us. Plenty of camping and a good swimming hole. What really appealed to me was that the place was inland enough that we'd have hot summers instead of that windy, foggy coastal shit. I imagined it as Covelo North. We said we'd be up there soon but first had to take care of some business in San Francisco.

Just a few days later we were off on an adventure, with Takilma as our destination. We traveled inland from Arcata up Hwy. 299 and camped along the Klamath River. When we arrived in Takilma, we searched out Bill and Donny and, in so doing, found our home.

Donny died in a tragic canoeing accident only a few days ago. He was so vibrant, optimistic, good natured - a real "don't worry, be happy" kind of guy. Donny visited Takilma last summer (Green Side Up reunion) and he hardly looked different from "the old days" when he spread around his music and good cheer. We'll miss you lots, Donny. *cont. page 2*

BILL AND DONNY from page 1

Bill is in prison for a pot growing bust. Hopefully he'll be out and back home soon. We love you, Bill, and are waiting for you. What a colossal travesty of justice and misuse of the law enforcement and justice systems.

What amazes me is, despite incredible knowledge, how little people really know about how life works. Are hundreds of people absolutely essential ingredients that have brought our lives to where they are now? Would I be living in the Meadows or in Takilma at all if not for my friendship with Bill and Donny? *-Romain Cooper*

Gemini Bill would love to receive mail; his address is William J. Schneider, #59208-065, POB 6000, Sheridan, OR 97378.

MY MOTHER STANDS STRONG

my mother stands strong
despite the weight of insecurities
accumulated over the years
and stored in a corner
like a stack of old papers
that might be important
someday

I slouch and then stand erect
confident in my youth
uncertain in my future
and I step on the cracks
just to see where I'll be
in twenty–five years

and my mother stands strong
supported by a body
sometimes too round
but never imperfect
and she still feels the presence
of a child around her leg

I walk proud but with hesitation
my body is lean
and it carries me swiftly
and sometimes
I'm mistaken for
my mother

-Shanie Mason

NORTH TO ALASKA

It began in the summer of 1970 when I saw a young woman carrying groceries up Larkspur street. Her thin cotton dress, like the overfilled bags, looked ready to burst at any moment. What's a Dog to do? I helped her. Two weeks later we decided to move to Alaska. "There is no privacy here," she said. Whenever they saw us, the boys upstairs had started calling, "More ,Dog! More!" She was a noisy lover. I found this funny but she wasn't amused. We loaded my old '52 Plymouth van with her baby boy, a broken rake, and eighty dollars worth of food stamps. I replaced the van's hood ornament with the head from a broken hobby horse and we followed its smiling horsey face up Hwy. 1 North.

A friend had told us about Takilma. "It's a great party," he said. After days or aeons of travel (time was more mutable then), we reached the Mirage Garage, a one room cabin with a sleeping loft on Takilma Road. It reeked of marijuana. Harold, a short stocky man, with stylishly unkempt long tangled dark hair, greeted us with a joint. He and his wife Dolores were the pater and mater familius of the place. Nobody owned it, but they made it clear that it was they who "kept things together." After a couple of days Harold started getting irked with us. Their daughter Laura, a pubescent girl with flaming red hair, had taken to calling from behind bushes, "More, Dog! More!" We were a bad influence. We drove across the river and under the trees to check out the Meadows.

In the Meadows, people were preparing for winter in an amazing array of styles. There were tree–houses, tepees, bark lean–tos, dugouts and cabins. I liked the people who were building one of the cabins. They were into organic gardening and self sufficiency. They had a dream for the place that actually seemed achievable. I was impressed. Achievability was not an important part of people's dreams those days. Other dreamers were digging a dugout in a well-watered thicket. I wondered if it would flood in the winter. I could see that I was bumming them out with my negativism so I didn't bring up ground water. We wished them well and walked on.

We found a couple fixing up an old miner's cabin. It was a beautiful spot with a view across a rolling meadow to a line of trees that masked the river. Beyond the trees lay Hope and Page mountains. Rivers and currents of air moved through the forests around us. A barely audible unending sound of the earth's breathing filled the quietness of the long summer's day. "What a beautiful place to build a house," I said. I did not know then that, someday, a quieter woman and I would eventually have a house on this spot. It is where we live today.

Alaska? Some day perhaps. Who knows where the trip ends? *-S .Dog*

THE LAND OF MILK AND HONEY

In looking back to how I got to Takilma, it is all too tempting to write a romanticized version of that story, just another fun-filled road story...akin to "Lucy and Ethel Hitchhike the West Coast"...the too-cute bumbling antics of a completely dysfunctional alcoholic, his large white dog, and li'l ole me, six months pregnant and full of determination. Sure, parts of this migration story have all the makings of a good counterculture sitcom, but most of the journey is tinged with that special despair that surrounds the lives of addicts and the people around them.

It was with a feverish case of greener–grassitis that Ron and I began that journey out of Albuquerque. The minute we stepped onto that on-ramp, Takilma became more and more magical. He had already lived in the valley, and assured me it was the land of milk and honey, the land of green buds, birthmobiles, and easy living. All along the way we dreamed our own versions of the promised land; while Ron anticipated bottles of green death (Rainier Ale) shared with old friends, I imagined white picket fences.

The road trip included the most fascinating collection of unique personalities...it's not the average bear that will stop for two hitchhikers, their backpacks, and a large dog. Interestingly enough the two most memorable rides were both headed to Oregon. The first one began outside Flagstaff. The driver was a fluttery fellow, on his way to Ashland full of high hopes. He thought Ron was fascinating. Besides the irritating fact that Ron was basking in the attention, we also stopped at each and every rest area between Flagstaff.and Berkeley to "cool down the tires." This ritual required pouring water over each tire until it felt cool. When we reached Berkeley I was more than ready to part company. After a few days with relatives, we hit the road again.

It was just north of Sacramento when the most cosmic ride began. I was becoming disenchanted, tired, and worried about having to live in this place with only a Denny's and a gas station. It was then that an old faded station wagon with a Texaco emblem on its door stopped for us. We pushed the dog, our packs, and ourselves into that vehicle as if it were the last train out of the station. The driver was a man with a kind face. He was traveling with his family, in two cars, to Oregon...to Southern Oregon...just past Grants Pass...outside Cave Junction...to Takilma! And so we were on our way and had arrived all within the same time. We traveled with them to Cave Junction, and because it was late at night, decided to stay in town. We spent the night on the back porch of the old building that later became the visitors' center; somehow appropriate, I suppose. The next morning we got a ride from an old friend of Ron's..."Hey, brother, remember that time we bailed you out of jail in Canada?" We went to their house to watch a movie and share food. The movie was 'Easy Rider' and we had arrived in Takilma.

There is/was so much more to the story, it is difficult to do it justice in the framework of just so many words. I do feel that I should acknowledge the fact that Ron died last summer, the addictions that caused him to lose the support of his family, and the respect of his children, those same addictions that were draining his sanity, finally rose up to extract the only thing left, his life. If I am thankful to Ron for anything I suppose it would be for bringing me to Takilma. Because as much as I have whined about the cliqueishness, and the hipper–than–thou attitudes that thread through the counter culture, I have also experienced the spirits of compassion, empathy and friendship on a level that has made my life a rich and rewarding thing...getting through the hard stuff a little easier, enjoying the good times a little bit more. *-Sherri L. Hopper*

TIN SOLDIERS AND NIXON'S COMING

In the late 60's I was a student of the U of W, majoring in biochemistry. The next ten years of my life were mapped out; graduate, get a good paying job, step into the fast lane. As I became aware of what we were doing in Vietnam, the lustre of that "good life" began to fade. On May 4, 1970, when our soldiers killed four students at Kent State, my dream was over.

From then on I began to save all the money I could. I traded in my TR4 sports car and bought a 1960 VW bus. I started looking for somewhere to go. Canada seemed attractive but the border crossing was a different story. "How much money do you have?" said one Customs official. Hippies were moving to the hills outside of Seattle but I needed to go further. A traveler, Black Barry, appeared at our communal house in Seattle and said the magic word "Takilma"- where hippies lay naked on rocks by the river, smoking pot and making love.

The next weekend my VW bus was heading south.

I spent my first night at Steve and Eve's log cabin on Waldo Road, where I met Chris Kentris. We became friends and, a few weeks later, land partners when we followed a handwritten note - pencil on a brown paper bag - posted in the window of Andy's store: " 80 acres with house, must sell, see Beaver". *-Kerry Holman*

INTERVIEW

COMMON GROUND: What brought you to Takilma, Michael?

Michael Garnier: I was from Gary, Indiana and got out of there as soon as I was able. A guy I met in the service told me about Oregon. He was from Medford. He said that there was clean air, mountains, and bridges that you could jump off into clean water.

C.G.: Why did you pick the Illinois Valley?

M.G.: I looked at a map. I was looking for a place that I could get a job. I had been a medic in the Special Forces with airborne training and Cave Junction had a smoke jumpers base. It also had a lot of roadless areas and if World War III came, it seemed a good place to survive it. First I went to Portland, I wanted to go to the Physicians Assistant school there. Then I met Jim Shames. He asked me to come down to Southern Oregon with him to check out a clinic. As soon as he mentioned Cave Junction I said yes!

C.G.: What did you find when you got here?

M.G.: We went to the Farm. The people were more interested in the doctor than in me. It was my birthday. I walked the back trail until I came to a big meadow. I walked across it to a big oak tree. I thought, "That's a nice tree." There was an old Quonset hut there and I wondered if someone could live in it. Two years later I owned it.

C.G.: Why did you decide to stay?

M.G.: I found the people interesting. People who would give me shit, but still be my friends, mentors. I was young. I still wanted to change the world . The people here would let me make my own mistakes, they would advise me and still be my friends even when I wouldn't listen. I wasn't always wrong, but then they weren't always right.

C.G.: Do you still want to change the world?

M.G.: I still want to change it, but only as it applies to me.

C.G.: A final thought?

M.G.: I'm not going anywhere. I like it here.

IT'S IN THE STARS

The destination had been Colorado or further west, myself very comfortable in the mountains. I like the water to run cold, snowy reminders of the winter. Yet I drove a dilapidated VW diesel Vanagon that loved the mountains like emphysema loves cigarettes; an agonizing sputter abounded.

Gail and I cruised through a beautiful two week stay in Telluride, Colorado, interrupted by a four day hike to Silver Lake at 12,000 feet. Sittin' on top of the world, free from school, escaped from the mad eastern rush of our pasts. But T–Ride was not to be home so we drove back to Boulder for a stay with another friend. Killin' time, trying to decide where to try next.

Gail woke in the morning and told me of her dream. I yawned in dull appreciation for her continual efforts. I did not ever remember dreams. I rubbed my eyes in anguish as she repeated, "I dreamt that Melissa Chauvin called and invited us to visit her at her dad's commune and we went and stayed there and lived there."

Melissa had been a college friend of ours. She had shared some stories of her youthful home; Gail was intrigued. I cannot recall my emotions.

"Oh, God, all I need, to move to Oregon and live on a commune with a batch of old hippies. Please!" Now emotionally set and stubborn, Gail had often spoken of Eugene, The Country Faire and the hot springs. I had loved the sand dunes and redwoods in previous adventures, memories, memories; but to follow a pipe dream.....?

"It's just a dream, don't get so defensive and cynical." She smiled. OK. That afternoon there was a lunar eclipse. We watched it from a parking lot, carefully staring into a tiny puddle evaporating from the intense heat. It truly was glorious, a sight of magical penetration, a glimpse into the unknown, blinded, light side of the universe, a subtle truth that perhaps we have all realized, that secrets in life are often obscured by their very own source of illumination.

Melissa called that night, somehow tracking us down in our smoke–filled guest quarters in Boulder. She invited us to visit. After another ten days on the road, a wild Garcia show on the Eel, 1000 miles of dust, the slow diesel winding up the Smith River Canyon, sun so hot it made rocks shine through transparent aqua water below, we pulled into the O'Brien Store for a soda and directions. Lou told us the way and, bleached by sun and desire, we arrived at Doo–Dah. Melissa was not at home but Lou led us to the Community Swimming Hole and we smiled at four naked children and got undressed.

That night, after eating tofu enchiladas, spiced brownies and laying out two giant blankets in the meadow, we were drawn in, transfixed, by the Pleiades meteor shower. Celestial guidance, clean cold water, random chance, romance, community, or cheap rent? No telling what made us stay....but here I sit and type at magical Doo–Dah, wondering when our dreams began to come true.   -Jon Jeans

HIPPIE INVASION

Alvie Blackmore is now 86 years old and was living in Takilma when the Hippie Invasion began.

There were only three people in the valley when I first lived in Takilma. Whenever I heard a vehicle I used to run out to see who was coming up the road. I had fifty acres that ran from Page Creek Road to Duval's ranch. During the flood of '64 I was living at what is now Jonnny Klein's place. We couldn't get across the river for forty-eight days. I grew grain in the meadow below Jonny's house. We had a big garden and raised everything we needed except some staples. We had to go to the store for them.

Curly owned the old Takilma Store then. It was a nice little grocery store. It was also a post office and we'd pick up our mail there. We used to go over there and sit around the big old stove and talk and spit. Them old guys chewed tobacco and snuff. When they spit, that old stove would boil.

We had a good time until those guys from San Francisco, the Haight-Ashbury, came. They wanted to take over the whole country. They were tough hombres. The police were afraid to come out there. They had shoot-outs every once in a while. One guy got shot in the belly with a shotgun right around the curve from my house. They would block the road to keep the Sheriffs out. They'd dump boulders, trees, anything across the road. I couldn't even get out myself.

The Mirage Garage was catty-wumpus from our house. The son of an engineer owned it. I met his dad when he came for a visit. He couldn't believe that his son would have such a place. "They just pee off the porch!" he said. "I sent him to college and worked hard to give him a good education, and this is what he turned out to be." I told him, "That's what happens sometimes."

It was shocking, the things that they would do. They'd run up and down the road stark naked. They'd try to block log trucks. Sometimes they'd steal my wife's flowers from our front yard. I'd say, "What are you doing?" They'd say, "These are God's flowers." One time a bunch of them lay across the road and blocked it. My wife couldn't get home. She finally managed to squeeze by. She was scared. It was a wild time, they'd do anything.

They never came around to visit, so we didn't get to know any of them. They stayed down by the river mostly, and kept to themselves. As long as they didn't bother us, I didn't bother them. We didn't care what they did.

ME AND BOBBY McGEE

It took a full three days for Rainbow Bob and me to hitch from Marin County. I had thrown in with Rainbow not only because of his tales of free land up in Takilma and pot-lucks in Wilderville but also because his Bobby McGee image of nothing left to lose had inspired a continuing youthful wanderlust.

We drank our daily breakfast wine and narrowly escaped being kidnapped by Jesus-Freaks in Eureka, by that time we turned off the highway in O'Brien. My heart raced with excitement. Rainbow had promised the driver of the yellow van unlimited rewards of sex, drugs and rock & roll if he'd just turn off into Takilma.

We zipped up Takilma Road in a cloud of dust- the road wasn't paved then- and pulled in where Rainbow indicated at the Mirage Garage. As we all slid out of the yellow Econoline, a parade of hippies began to emerge from the small cabin. They were introduced as Billy Gulch, Brian Bones and so on by Rainbow, who had now somehow conned the driver out of a lump of hash. The last one to tumble out the door was a Charlie Two Shoes who exclaimed, as if continuing a conversation: "Who did put methadone in the orange juice anyway?"   *-Robert Hirning*

THE INVOCATION

Strike the flame, ignite the candle,
Wield thy sword by hilt and handle.
Stand within the circle old
Face the north wind blowing cold.

Reverence under stars and moon,
Boldly wield the spoken Rune.
Bearing Air, Earth, Water, and Fire
To sanctify thy heart's desire.

Powers of north, south, east, and west-
Invoke them in to be your guest
To bless and caress thy purpose sought,
The ancient forces of Nature wrought.

Merry Solstice!

-Tom Yattaw (aka Charles Pullen)

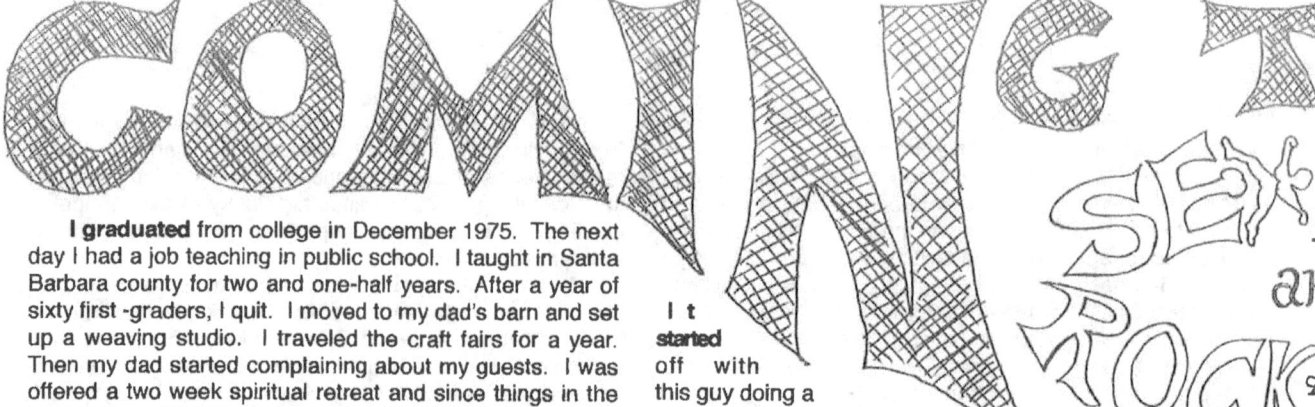

COMING T SEX an ROCK

I graduated from college in December 1975. The next day I had a job teaching in public school. I taught in Santa Barbara county for two and one-half years. After a year of sixty first -graders, I quit. I moved to my dad's barn and set up a weaving studio. I traveled the craft fairs for a year. Then my dad started complaining about my guests. I was offered a two week spiritual retreat and since things in the barn were getting confusing, I went. I spent two weeks in prayer and meditation. A twenty-four hour prayer vigil on any request was offered. My request was for a new home. After the last two days of the retreat in total silence, and my request prayed over for twenty-four hours, I left knowing I would find a new home.

The next week I went to Santa Barbara. The end of the day found me at the harbor watching the sunset. A guy who looked to me like a leprechaun flew down the ramp and embraced me. I said " I don' t think I know you."

He said " Come to my boat and watch the sunset." The sun set to songs on Michael' s dulcimer. Michael said, ."I live in a community in N. Calif./So.Oregon, do you want to go?" I said "Yes".

We left the next day.

We arrived at Sunstar and I was taken in by all its beauty. In the meadow below Michael' s house I gave my thanks for a safe journey. Then I was told " This is your home"

Wait a minute; I had just met Michael, I knew no one at Sunstar, yet the message was loud and clear. 'This is your Home. "

I stayed, spending the first year on my own, growing a garden and communing with the nature spirits. Sunstar has yet to be what I had envisioned a community would be. The beauty and peace remain and so do I. I' ve been growing a garden for eighteen years now. The quiet I once had has been replaced by five happy voices that make finding silence a task of its own.

Prayers are answered. Each day I give thanks for my family and home. Life is truly a blessing. -Alison

It was 1980 and I was pregnant with Tao. I was living in Santa Cruz and knew I wanted to give birth in the country. My friend and roommate, Mark Wood, told me about Takilma. I packed up my '52 GMC panel truck , complete with tepee poles on the roof and moved to Takilma. Tao was born 16 years ago in July, at Long Gulch.

I moved to Hawaii and Williams from 1982-86. I returned to Takilma when Janaki was four months old and chose to make Takilma my home because of the diversity and strength of the community. -Rebecca

I t started off with this guy doing a community magazine out of Berkeley in 1966/67. I was involved with a woman who was part of a group of people looking for land in the country. The original Magic Forest Farm, which at that time was called 16 acres, was conceived from this same group. We searched the Strout Catalog and the United Farm Catalog and discovered the property which we now call Talsalsan. I bought in with seven adults and twelve kids and came up to So. Oregon in the spring of '68. I went back to Berkeley only to realize I had to leave the home I was in. In the summer of '68, I packed my bags and moved, in my Borgward and a VW truck filled with goods. I stored my Daimler in a garage in Oakland.

We had no idea what this area was like and we were surprised to find a few hippies already here. I initially wasn't taken all that much with the land or the place, but after 28 years, it certainly has grown on me. -Jonny Klein

I was in my small cabin in Santa Cruz and this little blue light came to me. It was Emma, the spirit of Maya and Snow's first -born. She spoke to me "Why aren't you in Takilma with your friends?" I walked to many springs in Takilma- the fresh beginning- where the community starts. I was home when I got here. -Marjorie

I came to Selma with Jonathan after a long hot summer at the 1984 California Rainbow Gathering and on Mount Shasta. Elishua was a year old and soon it began to rain. Being a Brit, I felt at home in the downpour and we rented a house on Deer Creek Road. Jill and Mike Birmingham moved in to the lime green house across the street and both our second-born children came into the world at the Takilma People's Clinic. As soon as I heard about the Clinic I knew Takilma would be my home! I loved the way the clinic bartered back in those days; roto-tilling for pre-natal care, on-call for medical insurance! I met Kayla when I was training for on-call. We sang nursery rhymes and Sunday School choruses to the kids; we were intrigued by each other's peculiar minds. Later, I moved into Kayla's cabin, and fell in love with Lance and found a soul sister in Laurie, all in the same summer. Kayla took me to Cedar Gulch, to Janie's house, and said "Wouldn't you like to live here?" Some dreams do come true, so I took up residence in the next best place to Paradise, and have stayed, because love made me. -Felicity

It was November '94. I had packed up my home into storage and put a few treasured belongings in my car to embark on what I imagined to be a three to six month journey. I headed west with thoughts wandering aimlessly only to realize that Thanksgiving was soon approaching. Images of Thanksgiving alone in Wendy's inspired strong actions. After many long days and nights of driving I arrived in Selma where my sweetheart ,Yogesh, was waiting. I had no definite plans to stay or go. Yogesh was housesitting and the arrangement was convenient, easy and free. Somewhere along the way I guess I decided to stay. We began the search for a more permanent home. We heard about Takilma and set our sights here. Yogesh met JD while he was helping on the Dome School addition. A serendipitous encounter, as JD was setting up for his band's gig that evening. He needed a caretaker and the housesitting situation ended earlier than we expected. We called JD and moved in one week later, Christmas Eve 1994. It's been wonderful, a total blessing on so many levels to be here. A thousand thanks to JD for sharing his home with us and in a very real sense, making this next chapter of my life possible. And thanks to you all for making this such a rich vibrant place to come home to. -Claire Sierra

The memory of my coming to Takilma is a very good one. I was living in an urban commune in Eugene when a friend of mine from Seattle came by for a visit. He found my address from a letter that I had sent to friends there. His back was hurting him and he wanted me to accompany him to Ukiah, Calif. to find a healer who lived there. Well, of course that sounded good and off we went, hitchhiking south. We made it to Grants Pass ok, but we had to walk all the way through town and plunked down our packs on Hwy 199 .

It seems like everyone in Takilma owes their being here to someone and Laurie Prouty was that someone for me. She picked us up and had us loading her old VW pickup with horse shit within the hour. From talking with Laurie, my friend Bob found that a preferred healer, Weird Harold and his wife Jeanie, lived just past her land at a place called Sunstar. Laurie drove us all the way there! Thank you. The next day we walked to Cedar Gulch. I still remember the first time I walked down the long driveway, twenty-one years ago. I felt like the guy who closed the gate behind him in the movie called "King of Hearts". -River

It was 1972 and my sister Penny and her two kids, Shane and Marin, and myself, were all living in Humboldt County. I came home after a wild weekend and Penny told me about these two great guys she had picked up hitchhiking, Kerry Holman and Chris Kentris. She brought them home and fed them breakfast before they took off on their journey.

Kerry came back down from Takilma and asked Penny to go to Colorado for two weeks. Penny and Kerry continued their Or/Calif. relationship. In the summer of 1972, Penny and I hitchhiked to Takilma. Janie Rabbitt, driving the Berkeley glass truck, picked us up in O'Brien. I think she had been delivering milk or picking it up; I forget. She kept looking back at Penny and I, laughing and having a great time (our ride from Humboldt County had provided us with some great mescaline). She was so entertained that she drove us all the way to Cedar Gulch. When we arrived, Kerry, Eric Martin, Steve Fanger and Chris Kentris were all living there. What a bachelor pad! Kerry had just gotten hepatitis and was really sick. Welcome to communal living.

We came up again on Thanksgiving along with about 50 other people. I think there was a pie for everyone. We were liking this place.

In January of 1973, Penny and the kids packed their bags and moved up to Takilma. I would continue to hitchhike up here to visit until I moved in June. I still remember getting butterflies in the tummy every time I came up the driveway. I was excited and never knew just who would be there, what drugs to take or who to sleep with. Always an adventure! Twenty-three years later, I am still enchanted with Cedar Gulch. And I do know who I am sleeping with these days. -Laurie

How I got here? You can blame Paco for inviting me, Maya for making sure I had a place, and everyone else for keeping me here. -Robin

I was playing music at the healing gathering in Trillium in 1985. After the show, I met Maya Many Moons (at that time Maya Despacio). I told her I was planning on moving to So. Oregon. I was currently living in Portland. Maya told me to check out Takilma. In March/April 1986, I was headed back north from Mexico with my three children. I stopped by Takilma and met Maya. She took me to Cedar Gulch where I met Laurie who was pregnant with Jessea. She talked Kerry into renting his house to me. I moved into Cedar Gulch in May where I spent my first year in Takilma.

Landing in Cedar Gulch hooked me on Takilma from the get go. I would often spend 5-6 days at the gulch and not go anywhere. -Newman

PARADISE - LOST AND FOUND

In the spring of 1968, Oregon looked like a good idea. I had run out of options in Southern California. My business had gone bankrupt. I had been through a series of jobs in the couple of years since the bankruptcy, and none of them had worked out. I wasn't helping myself any by dabbling in drugs. I was into taking a lot of speed, smoking a lot of grass and hash, and taking LSD once in awhile. I was becoming more and more preoccupied with spiritual development. Looking back, it seems to me that I should have had a little trouble reconciling drug usage with spiritual development, though it didn't bother me a bit at the time. In fact, I looked upon the drugs as tools that I needed to help me in my quest. That was a common attitude among the disenchanted underground at the time. To top things off, my wife became pregnant with our third child, and was going to have to stop supporting us. Things were getting serious.

Naturally, I blamed it on the rest of the world. It was that materialistic, selfish, middle-class bunch of hypocrites in Southern California who were the problem. I reasoned that everything would be all right for me and my family if we just escaped to the country and joined up with some groovy people in a commune. I felt that the only way to turn the world around would be for us to start living lives of total giving and love.

I had a friend who was also experimenting with LSD. He and a whole circle of people. They were very serious about it. None of this "tripping" like the majority of acid heads. These people had "sessions". They all had jobs, homes, and cars—sort of middle-class hippies. My friend Frank was sort of the leader, or guru, if you will, of the group.He had taken on this other guy, Bob, as a project.He was trying to help him find his way out of alcoholism.

It worked, in a way, but Frank discovered that Bob had given him all the marbles, so to speak. I think that what the psychologists call it is "transference". I remember Frank complaining that Bob would wash up on his doorstep every few days in pieces. Psychic pieces, but pieces, nevertheless. He always expected Frank to put him back together, which Frank attempted to do, with less and less enthusiasm, and after a few episodes, he began to have the scary feeling that maybe he was missing some parts.

Alienation was going around in 1968, and Bob caught it. He came to the conclusion, along with a bunch of the rest of us, that Southern California was just no place for an enlightened hippie to live. Bob made good on it. He picked up his family, all six kids and his wife, Margaret, and headed for Southern Oregon. He got a job in a gas station in Cave Junction and rented a log cabin in Takilma.

Bob promptly started writing letters to his guru, Frank. He put 'Paradise' as the return address. He described in great detail the box of free food that poor families received, just by going to the commodity food office and saying, "I'm hungry." I was visiting Frank, and I read his letters from Bob. Sounded like the perfect place for me and my family.

Months later, things were going badly for me in Oregon and I was over at Bob's house, complaining that I wouldn't have come here if he hadn't written those glowing letters to Frank. Bob replied that it served me right for reading someone else's mail.

We began lightening our load so that we could move North. Helen, my wife, was a practical person who had not elevated her consciousness with an assortment of drugs. Therefore, she saw nothing wrong with selling our discarded possessions at a garage sale. I allowed her to do it, but I was not enthusiastic. Selling things did not fit with my image of myself as a loving, giving person. After all, we had $400 left after we paid all of our bills out of Helen's retirement pay. When we got to Oregon, we were going to be welcomed with open arms into some groovy commune full of enlightened people. What did we need money for?

Finally, around the end of May 1968, we headed up the highway. We had everything with us that we could stuff, or pile on top of, our 1951 Plymouth, plus a guy named Tom Campbell.

So we were in the wind, God's own dropouts, looking for nirvana. On our own private "Journey to the East". Helen and I, our three boys, six, three, and 3 months; Tom, and Tom's two German shorthaired dogs, Mogert and Lilly. Those dogs were undisciplined mutts. It was hot, so we traveled with the windows down. Every time the car stopped, those two dogs bailed out the windows, right over the top of everybody.

We had a tent that we pitched every night. It was great fun. When we got to Oregon, we pitched the tent for a few days in Bob's back yard. We were in heaven. It was June by this time, and it got so hot in our tent, during the daytime, that it melted our candles. We didn't care. We had found paradise.

Now, when people ask me what brought me to Oregon, I say, "Free peanut butter sandwiches". -*Delbert Kauffman*

8

LETTERS:

Dear Common Ground,

The first indication of where my homeland lay was six years ago; early 1990. At a local pub in Indiana, I recognized Lou Gold while I was selling beverages.

Since that moment of recognition and introduction, Lou Gold's vision of saving ancient (all) forests, through widespread education and awareness, has remained a motivating force. Saving and preserving forested lands is an action for us all. The forests and myriad ecosystems of Oregon are priceless. They must not be lost to corporate interests.

Over the years, paths of various origins converged; conveying a burgeoning wilderness consciousness onto the Oregon Trail. Last summer, I found myself staring often at Oregon maps, my eyes drawn to southwest Oregon, yonder to Takilma/Williams.

The energies linked! My partner and I spent the winter (our first here) finding our Oregon home. Surely it was a gentle hand that guided us to rest along the banks of the clear blue Takelma River. So ancient, as it flows into the Kalmiopsis Wilderness!

The discoveries Oregon holds, especially in this area, are vast. I am in love with and in awe of the natural history of the Kalmiopsis and the Siskiyous.

Last night was the Full Rose Moon. Wasn't it glorious?! That evening was my first summer night out in Oregon...Takilma. Strains of Jah Levi floated and reverberated through the air as I sailed high in the swing, touching the moon with my toes.

Thanks for being what you embody, Takilma. It's so fine to be among you! Most sincerely   -Tiffany Jenkins

FOR THIS ISSUE:

Facilitators: S.Dog, Linda, Laurie
Computer Layout: Kerry
Staff: Fliss, Jon, Gail, Robin, Dave T.
Graphics: Cathy, Fliss, Sheila, Robin, Ina

If this issue has inspired you to write your own story of how you arrived in Takilma, please don't hesitate. We'd like to publish more of these tales from time to time.

For our next issue we'd like to hear about those favorite places you're willing to share. All kinds of places - geographical, spiritual, relational, anatomical - you name it. We hope you'll include instructions, directions, invitations and revelations. Let us jump right in there with you; join you vibrationally or pick up a vicarious thrill. Submission deadline is July 25th.

Please mail your submissions to POB 2016, Cave Junction, 97523 or email holmans@cdsnet. net

Opinions expressed here are not necessarily those of the Editorial Staff or Mud Council. Common Ground is printed on 100% tree free paper, except for once in a Blue Moon, when it's not....

Hello Common Ground,

My name is Fred and I lived in Takilma from 1976 to 1986 and now it's 1996. Ten Years After ? Ten years in Takilma? I have lots of memories about Takilma. Some are good and some are bad. So I am not going to talk about the God Damn trees and I am not going to talk about the kids at the Dome School or Takilma VS the fucking law.

I am going to tell you about my experience with most of your women in your society. My experience is very painful and sad. As a physically deformed man or Handicapped, crippled, etc.

I am going to point out to you women of Takilma that you are doing your part in Handicapping America. This is what it was like dealing with you. You did not see me, you did not hear me, nor did you look to find my abilities, my interests, and what I love. Not one of you.

Every time I tried to reach out to one of you, you got mad at me or you patronized me or you dismissed me. So these reactions from you made my Social Relations with you very difficult and they still are. Tell me something, would you have treated an African-American Man that way? No, you would not! Because after all you are not Racist! But to me you are!

Because you had labeled me and categorized me apart from normal men, somehow less than the Takilma man or woman who is more deserving of the opportunities and liberties that he or she so freely take from you and it's for granted! HOW SAD!

That's why I retreated from social interaction with you five years before I left Takilma. Now my visits are down to one or two times a year, if that.

Sometimes I come to see my brother, sometimes it's for the music at the Dome School. When I go to the Dome School for the music the energy from you women is still the same as it was fifteen year ago and some of the men have this energy too. The faces have changed and the names but the energy is still there.

I have you know that Men and Women like me live worthwhile and meaningful lives that you will never know about because you do not become our friends, our girlfriends, our wives, or our lovers.

You need to work on your prejudice against the Disabled. Read about Elizabeth Barrett Browning, she was an INVALID and she made a superb contribution to her society. Maybe your society of women doesn't need People like us and THAT'S COOL. Because we can't change you anyway, but we can help point the way if there is one for you? So how does it feel to be labeled and categorized?

I am telling you about this for me not for you and it has to do with healing part of my spirit by freeing it from a very bad memory.

-Frederic Janssen
PO Box 1392
Grants Pass, OR 97526

SLICES OF TIME . . . THEN AND NOW

It was tall tales and a hand-me-down, hand-drawn map that lured me from the counterculture/student ghetto of Isla Vista. Having never been farther north than Marin County, I hit the road two days before Thanksgiving. With the best of hitchhiking luck making quick work of the 600 odd miles, I stepped off highway 199 at the O'Brien store. I stumbled along Waldo Road, lost but lucky, in pursuit of a place called Sunstar. That was 1974, I was 20. Good bud and communes, tall trees and clear water— it was the chance to lay claim to a little piece of some remote backwoods paradise that snake charmed me— me and those other eccentric (hopefully rugged) refugees from Nixon's America and the ugly head of Disco rising. That four day trip provided enough of an inspirational glimpse into the future to hang my hat on. Two years later in '76 I put some money down on an acre of the jig saw puzzle that was Sunstar Country Club. For several years the only contact I had with this Southern Oregon / Northern Cal ace in the hole was through occasional postcards and even less frequent land payments.

When Marilyn and I fell in love during the summer of '82, it was time to play that ace. Marilyn was six months pregnant with embryonic Tyrone the first time she drove through the Takilma gauntlet and out the dusty road to Sunstar. The prospect of actually living here, clearing land, building a house, making a living, was reduced from frighteningly monumental to merely exciting by our blissful ignorance.

The rest, as they say, is history/herstory, but it's a story that's still being written. The allure of our backwoods paradise, this quiet safe haven, has been overtaken by events so predictable that the only surprise is in our surprise. A once-idyllic oasis has been sucked through the looking glass and our private little lives are increasingly yanked into the bigger world by challenges too insistent to be ignored. We have been making a difference, for better or worse, for decades. From the nuts and bolts of self-sufficiency, to family raising, to coping with our own versions of American schizophrenia, it is we who are holding little pieces of the future. This isn't a call for frenzied burnout, no guilt tripping, it's just me wrestling with the obvious. Whether it is called Sugarloaf or Canyon, education or politics, health care or sanity, China Left or Waldo Thin, the truly great issues of this era have unerringly come to roost right here, right now. While we may not be as many or as strong as we would hope, neither are we a fearful few.

Blissful or not, our ignorance evaporates leaving us holding the hot potato of life's responsibilities with scorched hands. We all want to spend our summer in the garden or soaking up good times down by river, but existence is begging us to do a little bit more. We really have no choice.

-Kenny, Marilyn, & Tyrone

JUST PASSIN' THROUGH–NOT!

Kentris brought me here. One of the original co–owners of Cedar Gulch, he was notorious in these here parts, but he is another whole story! Chris was a former neighbor of Mannix, my husband, and a former boyfriend of my dear friend, Kathy. He kept telling us to go to Oregon when we were still in New York planning our great "Westward Ho Adventure."

Kath and I were tripping around the country that summer and were on the verge of **BIG CHANGES IN OUR LIVES**. We were visiting with friends, and friends of friends, all over the country for free and easy places to stay. The Redwoods were on the itinerary of "Things We Must See." There were college friends in SF and a cousin in Eugene. The Redwoods lay betwixt those two destinations and CJ seemed to be on the way as we were passin' through.

If Kentris told me once he told me a dozen times, "You'll just love my friend, Bob Mannix." And like some gypsy fortune–teller predicting my future, he was right!

I fell in love, head–over–heels, to the core of my being, like some sappy movie. I can close my eyes and still remember so many golden moments from those first few days. Gold was the color of the August sun in the woods of Oregon. Gold was the color of my lover's hair as he bent to pick veggies from the garden early in the morning. Gold was the color of the gargantuan African marigolds he grew that year. We feasted on blackberries as we lounged in the sun on the sandy banks of Sucker Creek. We bicycled along backcountry roads. As we cruised to the Oregon Caves, I hung on for dear life as Mannix careened his way around those curves on his motorcycle . I luxuriated in the splendor of each day.

I meant to pass on through. I cried all the way to Eugene. I turned around and went back possessed with a passion for the sanctuary in the woods, obsessed with a passion for the man with the golden hair. A new life beckoned; three thousand miles away from family, friends, and career. I stood on the edge of turning thirty and on the edge of creating a new life. I held my breath and leaped. I've landed on my own two feet. When others ask where I come from I say I am from New York but I LIVE my life and LOVE my life in the woods of Southern Oregon   *-Deborah Colette Murphy*

CHAUTAUQUA

During the late 19th and early 20th century there existed hundreds of touring "Chautauquas" presenting lectures, dance, music, drama, and other forms of Cultural Enrichment. Performing in tents across the country, Chautauquas were once called "the most American thing in America" by Teddy Roosevelt. Alas, this form of outreach has all but died out.

On July 19th the New Old Chautauqua will come to Takilma Dome School straight from the Country Faire. The show will include: Faith Petric, with her special form of song and story telling, jugglers, magicians, dancers and musicians to delight the whole family. On Friday at 7 p.m. a parade will march through downtown Takilma. Anyone with a bike is invited to decorate it and ride in the parade. There will be prizes for the best, funniest, most creative decoration. If you have animals who like to perform, bring them! The show starts at 8 p.m. Friday, July 19th. The next afternoon will be filled with activities for the whole family. Workshops are offered free of charge on Saturday, July 20th from 10 a.m. until 2 p.m. They will be for all ages and include juggling, dance, drumming, children's mask–making and more. Saturday there will be a children's carnival. Don't miss the event of the summer! For information, or if you would like to perform or parade, call Robin 592–3159.

DID YOU READ CAREFULLY?

MIX AND MATCH:

1. Hobby horse head — A. Rabbitt
2. Under the Borgward — B. Michael Dulcimer
3. Leprechaun — C. Paco
4. Driver of Texaco truck — D. Jonny Klein
5. Driver of City of Azusa — E. Delbert
6. My mother — F. Sheila
7. Man with golden hair — G. Penny
8. Travels w/ Kerry to CO — H. Robert Hirning
9. Driver of Berkeley — I. Rebecca
10. Read another's mail — J. Romain
11. # of Chris Kentris refs — K. 3
12. '52 GMC panel truck — L. S. Dog
13. Hitched with Rainbow Bob — M.5
14. #of hithhiking refs — N. Mannix

THANKS MIGUELO

The First Annual Cribbage Tournament was a tremendous success, raising much needed funds for COMMON GROUND to the tune of TWO figures!

Austin Hocker won first prize in the youth division and tournament organizer, Miguelo, walked away with the adult trophy.

Those who participated had a great time, and look forward to doing it again. Did you hear that, Miguelo?

You have probably not noticed the $ubtle appeal$ in pa$t i$$ue$ of COMMON GROUND for money. Like the re$t of u$ you probably give little thought to $uch a cra$$ $ubject. Please give it $ome thought now. Our unpaid volunteer $taff cannot produce thi$ paper on good vibe$ alone. For a mea$ly TEN DOLLAR$ a year you can help us to keep thi$ rag alive. If you enjoy COMMON GROUND, $ubscribe today, now, immediately, forthwith, in$tantly, and at once. We can't do it without *money*.

SUBSCRIBE NOW!

___ $10 1-YEAR SUBSCRIPTION.　　　　NAME: _____

___ $25 1-YEAR SUBSCRIPTION AND
　　　A COMMON GROUND T-SHIRT.　　ADDRESS: _____
　　　CALL 592-4695 FOR SIZE AND COLOR INFO.
___ $　BROKE BUT LITERATE, SEND ANYWAY.　_____

SALLY CLEMENTS TO EDIT YOUTH PAGE!

I would like to start a YOUTH PAGE for COMMON GROUND. My goal is to get our youth involved in the paper through their writings, drawings, poems, and ideas. I would like to give them the opportunity to edit and produce their own page. *Their* page, a page to share their thoughts on any subject. By youth I mean those who are 19 and under.

I need help to get us started on this first page of youthism. Kids, teens, send me writings and drawings. Send me your poetry, dreams and doodles. Parents, send me some of those darling treasures that your kids come up with.Just keep in mind that COMMON GROUND prints in black and white and works in color will not reproduce well. Most of all I want your ideas! What should we call it? What should we do with it? Let me know. Sally, 592-3095. POB 2016, Cave Jct.

CLASSIFIED:

It's your birthday, anniversary, or time to see just how many friends you really have. You want a party, but don't have the time or inclination to do the work. Let us do it for you. We will set the mood, create the ambience, design the food, from the ridiculous to the extravagant. We do the work you have the fun. Call Sheila and Robin 592– 3159 or 592–3958.

A Takilma Web page on the internet is in the process of being born. Delbert and Jim Gurley have been designing the page. They are seeking local crafts people and artists who would like to display their product on the internet. If interested call Delbert, 592-2327, email kauffman@cdsnet.net

For sale: 24 volt, 2500 watt inverter. Excellent condition, runs great. Change your DC electicity to AC and run power tools, washing machines, computers, etc. Reasonable price.Call Romain at 592-2311.

Wanted: Feet for Reflexology. Let us touch your soles, to relieve stress and tension. $10 per session, Mar 592-4436, Diane 592-3908.

TCG
PO Box 2016
C.J. OR 97523

PHOENIX RISING

Out of the ashes flies the newer, better "It's A Burl". Harvey and Joy Shinerock, with the aid of Stanley Dalegowski and friends, have created one of the valley's most stunning structures. The new gallery will be the venue for a community party on Friday, June 21st from 6:30 'til 9 p.m. The event will be catered by 1000 Cranes, those other folks with flair, and Wiz Kryssa's music in the Garden Gallery will make this the Solstice celebration you won't want to miss.

ANNOUCEMENTS:

The Takilma Community Building's beautiful oak floor is due for refinishing. We have scheduled July 23rd to have Rob Caldwell come and apply the finish. The cost will be around $500.00. We need money! Please make any contributions to Beth Meadows or Laurie Prouty. Let's keep our floor the best dancing floor in the valley!

The 4th annual 4th of July softball game will again be played at Out 'n' About. Only this time it will be Saturday the 6th, first pitch at 1:00. The teams will be practicing, call Miguel 2-6902 if over the hill, call Jon 2-4615 if still searching. There will be a second less-serious game to follow. Event includes tree house stress test and will be covered by Radio FreeTakilma.

Early Head Start is a non-profit program for low-income families residing in the Illinois Valley area. Families must be expecting a baby, or already have a baby in order to be eligible. Like Head Start, the program provides comprehensive health, nutrition, child and family development services - to the littlest children. For more information and an application, please call 592-3259 or 1-800-866-9674.

Free Chocolate! Community Building. Workday- Sat. June 23rd, 10-2. Picnic/Potluck. Bring your family. Lots to do- Let's Party!

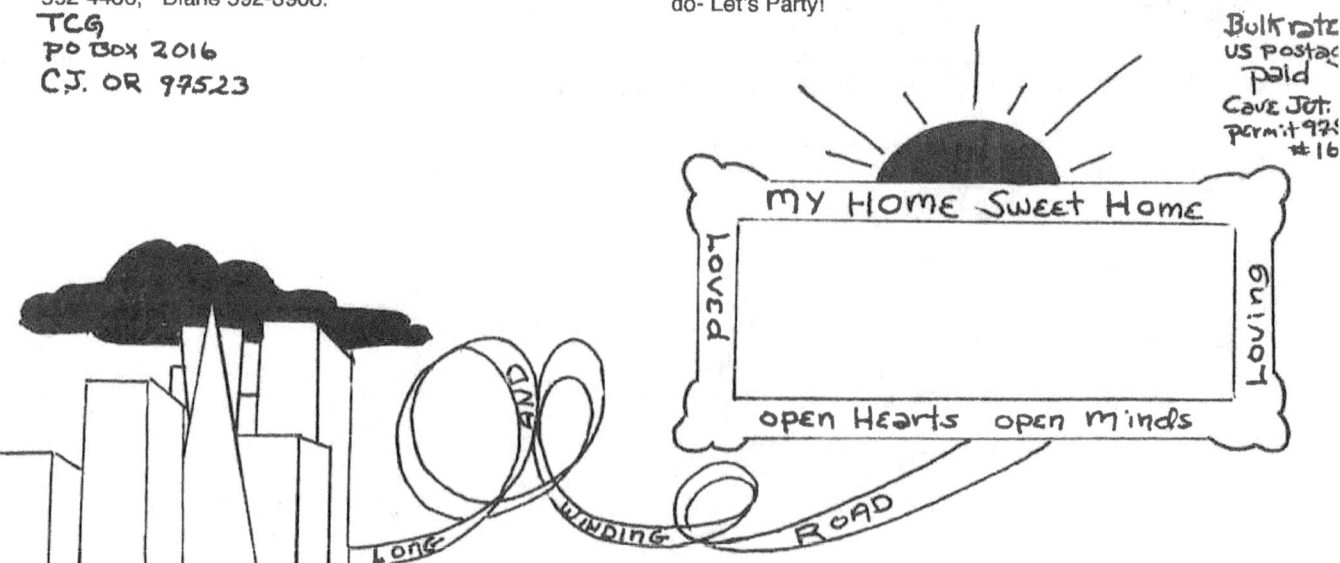

MY HOME SWEET HOME

Loved

Loving

open Hearts open minds

Long WINDING ROAD AND

ISSUE #21

AUGUST 1996

CHINA LEFT BLOCKADED! SISKIYOU FOREST DEFENDERS OCCUPY ROAD

On July 1st, forest protection activists from the Siskiyou bioregion took action to prevent further clearcut logging of ancient forests at the China Left Timber Sale, located in the Siskiyou National Forest near Cave Junction, Oregon. Using their own bodies and a number of blockades and lockdown devices, the Siskiyou Forest Defenders (SFD) have taken over the logging road leading to this controversial sale, beginning a sustained Warner Creek-style occupation of the area. Last fall Rough and Ready began cutting hundreds of acres of ancient forest in, and adjacent to, the Kangaroo Roadless area, a critical wildlife corridor in southwest Oregon. The units that remain unlogged lie within the headwaters of the Left Fork of Sucker Creek, home to one of the healthiest steelhead runs in the upper Illinois River basin. There is also a spawning population of threatened coho salmon in Sucker Creek just below the sale units; these salmon are in imminent danger of extinction due to the erosion and loss of canopy cover caused by the proposed China Left clearcuts. Also present and at risk are mountain lions, bears, foxes and bobcats. This 12.7 million board foot sale consists of 16 "units" that total 530 acres; 274 of these acres are clearcuts.

Actress Alexandra Paul, who plays Lt. Stephanie Holden on television's "Baywatch" series, visited the blockade on Thursday, July 18. Ms. Paul took a Lighthawk flight over the area before visiting the blockade. During interviews with news reporters, she confirmed that the world is watching the northwest forests. "Everyone knows about the logging in Oregon," she said. "We need to do everything possible to stop it: letters are needed, lobbying is needed, and blockades are needed. We need to keep telling President Clinton that we want our forests protected."

Saturday afternoon hikes and potlucks are a good way to get involved. Meet at the base camp (about 1/2 mile past the blocked gate) at 1pm. Bring water, food, good shoes or boots.

To get to the site: From Hwy 199, in Cave Junction, drive east on Caves Hwy (Hwy 46) nine miles to FS road 4612. Follow 4612 for another eight miles until reaching FS road 080 on the left. Walk 1/2 mile up 080. For more information, call: (541)732-3101. Send contributions to: Siskiyou Forest Defenders, POB 400, Williams, OR 97544. Wish List: More people! Come for the day, or stay a while! Foods: (most activists at the site are vegan) tahini, tamari, olive oil, Dr. Bronners, maple syrup, soy or rice milk, tofu, bread, pesto, FRESH FRUITS AND VEGGIES, juice. Non Foods: big buckets w/lids, crates, shelves, Hi 8 video film, bikes, AA batteries, flashlights, cooler, blankets & pads, garden cart, masseuse, tinctures, organic fertilizer, cover crop seeds.

-Debbie Lukas

OUR OWN LITTLE PRISON?

The City Council of Cave Junction has expressed to the state its interest in being the location for a MAXIMUM SECURITY PRISON.

Despite our troubled infrastructure, our workforce not trained in "corrections," the myriad of troubles experienced by Crescent City, the morally bankrupt nature of the human landfill system, and our fragile and endangered environment, AND common sense to the contrary, the Council "thinks" this is a good idea because it "would provide Jobs." (Always capitalize a deity.)

What Jobs and for whom? Imagine the dignity and productivity of working in a prison. Imagine this for your children. Imagine our welfare system and clinic after the families of inmates move in. (Our clinic has already experienced this phenomenon as Pelican Bay inmates' families seek care here.) Imagine the impact on our psyche, our river, our crime rate, our valley's beauty. *Continued on page 2*

Letters

Dear Common Ground

Did I miss an issue? I've been looking forward to the "How I got to Takilma" stories, which haven't yet arrived. Send me a copy would you?

Thanks to all you Mud Councillors for an ongoing great job - I feel like each issue of TCG is a letter from home.

Happy Lughnasad!

John Whiteside, Cambridge, Mass.

Dear Folks

Enclosed please find $25 to insure our uninterrupted pleasure that comes from reading Takilma Common Ground.

Part of this money is for a subscription to our transplanted brother/sister, John Jones and River. Please begin their mailing with issue #20, my favorite so far.

Thanks, and all your efforts are appreciated,

Don, Sunstar

PRISON? continued from page 1

Because the city has alerted the state to its interest, the state could now stick us with the prison above any protest we make on a city level. We must now take our opposition to the state as well.

Here's the address to write to: Zadean Auer, Facilities Siting Coordinator, Department of Corrections, Facilities Division, 470 Lancaster Drive NE, Salem, Oregon, 97310. Calls to: (503) 373-1572 ext 229. Fax to: (503) 378- 6536. NOTE: This person doesn't want to hear "why prisons are bad." That won't help. Focus on "why Cave Junction would be a poor choice."

On the local level: City council Office, City Hall, P.O. Box F, Cave Junction, Or. 97523. Calls: 592-2156, leave messages with the Recorder, Jim Polk. If your number is hard to find and you wish to be on the phone tree for any rallies or protests on this issue, leave a message for Kate at 592-2214.   *-Kate Dwyer*

Sports

POTATOES, POTATOES, POTATOES OH YEA!!

On July 4th, under mercifully partially clouded skies, the Under-35 Potatoes successfully defended their softball crown by edging the Geezers, their elders, by the score of 10-9. For the third year in a row the game was decided by one run, and wasthe first to end after nine innings. The Potatoes now lead the series, 3 to 1, leading to conjecture that the one loss was merely a fluke.

The game.... The Geezers were steady, Donny Shaw unstoppable at the plate, Miguel talking trash from the mound and constantly appearing at second base, Sue Zook a magnet in right, Steve Marsden earning a gold glove in his return from retirement. But it was not enough.

The Potatoes played solid defense, scored big in two great innings and held on to win. "The team was more cohesive this year," said captain Jon Jeans. The Doo Dah teen trio was stellar, Jessame Kendall adding professional flair. New resident Scott P. was a vacuum at third base, Jude scored two big runs in her softball debut, and youngest but quickest spud, Rael Hirning, darted over, concentrated, and caught the final out on a deep fly ball to right. If it had fallen, the Geezers would have won.

But the true story was the double ceremony. The sun dance to the north, drumming, chanting, ropes attaching chests to pole, screams of release, celebration and suffering. Softball to the south, devious, playful, colorful crowds, "beer here", hot dogs, and Hendrix's National Anthem. Side by side, separated by a dirt road. Opposing methods of community ritual that did not compete. Rather they somehow merged in the rising and sinking of volume.

The softball crowd happy and loaded, biased early in favor of the home town Geezers but eventually warming to all. Folks in the shade, eating dogs washed down with Oregon beers, keeping Kate busy. Kids rooting for Potatoes, dreams of future glory in their fragile minds. Someday it will be yours. Beth Meadows told me, "It was just so fun and exciting. We rooted for everyone, for a good hit, a great catch. We just loved everyone out there." Thanks, and we love everyone who keeps coming out and being a part of the game. Special thanks to Neil for umpiring, no longer a thankless job. See you next year,. and it's root root for the "home team." *-Jon Jeans.*

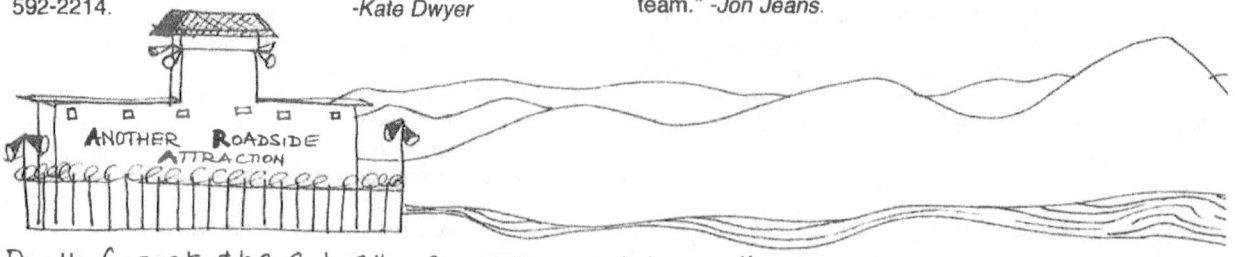

ANOTHER ROADSIDE ATTRACTION

Don't forget the C.J. City Council meeting — Monday, August 12th at 7:30 p.m. Ask questions! Listen closely!   Say NO! Just say NO!!

Favorite Places

LAKE TIARATI, AGE TEN

We usually played what I wanted to play because I wouldn't play if we didn't. I liked to play this one game I called "kids" a lot. We could be any kid we wanted but everyone had to work around me being Huck Finn. I knew I was off a bit because I always led the gang like Tom Sawyer instead of taking off into my own thing like Huck really would have. Not that anyone else knew how it was supposed to go. I tried to be Tom once, but I couldn't stand that he had so many social things he had to deal with so I switched midgame. The others were sorta mad at me, but they let it go when I threatened to quit.

I remember once Debbie Babcock played Becky Thatcher and did a really good job of it. I wanted to play Becky then too because Becky was desirable. I tried being Becky myself another day. I didn't get what Debbie had done to make Becky desirable though. Becky didn't *do* anything. I got real frustated about it and I think I made the others nervous because they didn't complain when I switched roles that time.

My friend Carol Rubio and I made up our own newspaper. We called it the *R & R Daily News* even though we only wrote it once and it took us a week to do it. We thought adults were really weird for always going on and on about obvious things so we made up some pretty good jokes about that. These are a few of them:

Are you worried that you are getting fat? Then don't eat so much!

Do you feel exhausted at the end of the day? Then take a nap!

Our parents didn't think any of our jokes were funny. Me and Carol thought that was really strange.

The Diggidio's hung out at my house a lot after their stepdad moved in. Buddy always wanted something to eat and his stepdad put a big chain around their refrigerator, with a padlock on it. I thought his stepdad had a good plan, seeing how Buddy was kinda fat. I liked to go to their house and look at it. I played doctor with the Diggidios in our big bush. It was sorta exciting but I was glad when it was over because I didn't like the thought of getting caught.

Timmy McGillicutty's best friend took my hat once and wouldn't give it back when I asked. The others sang that KISSING IN A TREE song about me and Timmy. I don't know about that but I do know I liked eating Jello out of the box with him in the dog house. Anyway, I got mad at his friend and I fought him. It was a great fight. I didn't win, but I didn't lose either and since I was a girl and we were the same age, I got lots of glory. My dad was really proud.

Me and the Diggidios were the only kids on the block who could play with JJ Babcock. I think the Diggiddios could play with him because they had dirt instead of a lawn. They couldn't afford to be choosy. Our lawn wasn't so good either but at least my dad threw down grass seed and roped it off.

Another reason I could play with JJ was because my dad liked people to be a little bad. Most kids couldn't play with JJ because he got in lots of trouble and his dad was always yelling and cussing at him. It'd be past time all the rest of the block was in for dinner and there'd be Mr. Babcock on the front porch yellin for JJ: JAY! JAY! JAYJAY!!! JAY! YOU GET THE **FUCK** HOME RIGHT THIS **GODDAMN** MINUTE!!! My dad would look out our front window when Mr. Babcock did that to check the neighbors' reactions.

My dad always noticed weird things about people. We'd go down to the Jersey Shore every year for vacation and he'd point out all the drivers that picked their nose and ate it while we sat in traffic. It always surpised me how many he could find. He'd act like a sports announcer and narrate each booger getting dug out and chewed up. He embarrassed my mom all the time.

I got a lot of ideas when I was with my dad. We'd cruise Bergen County during lunch time in search of the perfect milkshake and he'd talk about the world and all the stuff he paid attention to. I argued so much about the Kent State killings with my fifth grade teacher that we ran out of time to do math. The school kids usually weren't happy about me arguing so much but I was popular after that.

I got my best ideas when we weren't talking, up at Lake Tiarati. My dad would find a sunny spot, pull out a yellow pad, and write his poetry. There were terrific boulders at Lake Tiarati to climb and the woods were just right for walking through and hiding out. There were always lots of frogs going "ribbit" at the shore. I could even go part way around the lake and still see my dad. I could dream things up without explaining myself all afternoon. My dad and I would come back like great explorers and that's what gave me my power in the neighborhood. Most kids would've liked to have adventures like I did.

It was pretty cool to be so lucky. *-Nicole Rensenbrink*

Favorite Places

ANOTHER POTATO HEARD FROM

"Favorite places we're willing to share"? Makes me shudder. I helped come up with this issue's theme, in the naive hope that by reading and memorizing the collective lore of wilderness connoisseurs and river tribespeople, I could find camouflage for my inadequacy. Instead, the thought of writing on this subject brings me face to face with my own worthlessness.

I've seen this face before. In the spring of '95, I tagged along on some poetry picnics. Led by beautiful people who don't need to find all their poetry in books, we took some lovely walks to magical spots. Some well–meaning person suggested I lead a future hike to one of my favorite spots. I secretly cringed. Where could I lead anyone?

Twenty–four years in this valley, and I still don't have a rich private collection of swimming holes, pack trips, or sylvan glades. I love those wild spots, but I don't go to them often, and it's always someone else's place. What inner failing has prevented me from seeking out my own? Where have I been all these years?

Actually, I know exactly where I've spent a big chunk of time. I'll disclose my favorite place, but I'd like to make some excuses first.

I'm a working stiff who spends too much time away from home as it is, immersed in people. I choose to teach adolescents, and I love them, but they sure fill my space up with needs and noise. So when I'm off, I don't seek out crowds of people! I race home.

Home is in Selma. It's not wild here. Walks are either along the road or through the private property of neighbors I've not gotten to know. Driving to a spiritual place seems incongruous. So I usually stay on the property. That's fine; there are several places—by the creek, the pond, under the cedar trees—where I can commune with nature and feel vaguely Zennish. But measured by frequency of visits, average or aggregate impact on my psyche/soul, or the less quantifiable me–ness of these places, none is my favorite spot. They are treats, not refuge.

As a refugee from work, where self has been subordinated to other selves, I need to be surrounded by my stuff, not the otherness of nature. And so I plop down at my favorite spot: my couch. Here I sit, feet up, surrounded by my magazines and books and musical instruments: hard evidence that I have a life beyond work. Here, in ten to twenty minutes, I shift identities, letting Mr. Dwyer rest until the morning alarm.

The couch. That's why I live in this beautiful valley, right? While others have pushed through green trails and plunged into crystal pools, I've been molding the cushion to fit my butt.

I'd like to say I meditate. Despite the couch, it might make me look more spiritual, less tuberous, if I were meditating. But I don't. Nor do I achieve transformation by reading the Nation or playing the banjo. I need something to absorb my buzzing mind energy while leaving my soul untouched. So what I do is read the sports page.

Reading the box scores on the couch, I find inner peace.

Note: I am not into "sharing" this place literally; there's one best place with a footrest, end table, padded arm, and I want it. Rather, "sharing" here means "telling," as it usually does these days. I shared this to encourage others like me. **Are** there others like me? If so, take heart; you are not alone. Please write me so I can take a little heart, too. The more there are of us, the more average we'll feel: a bittersweet comfort, but better than feeling weirdly commonplace. Remember to send your replies to me, not Common Ground. Not everybody wants to read your banalities. -*Jack Dwyer*

GREATER TAKILMA

How silly, i feel like i'm back in the second grade. OK, i'll play along. Oh yes, it must be my garden on a warm summmer's morning. Or...maybe it's my bed on a cold rainy night. No...perhaps it's the ocean during a huge winter storm. My indecision could ruin this article. How could i feel so ambiguous about my favorite place? Then it became clear- no one location could be favored. My community creates the feeling, not the physical space.

Somehow i've always known this; however, since Janie became ill the feelings have crystallized. My garden, Janie's garden, Ashland Co-op, the community building or the Oregon Country Fair. All can produce in me a potent sense of a common bond and a favorite place, along with a complete appreciation for those people whose lives have both touched and altered mine in a myriad of ways. This last month has been an enormous time of reevaluating my priorities, reaffirming old friendships, and remembering how fragile and sacred life is. Any of us could be extinct tomorrow. My ideal is to grieve without guilt, clean up the old stuff, and not fear speaking from my heart.

I'm amazed how catastrophic illness has prompted a yearning for the present and a desire to surround myself with favorite places that are only enhanced by all of you   -*GloriaStone*

Favorite Places

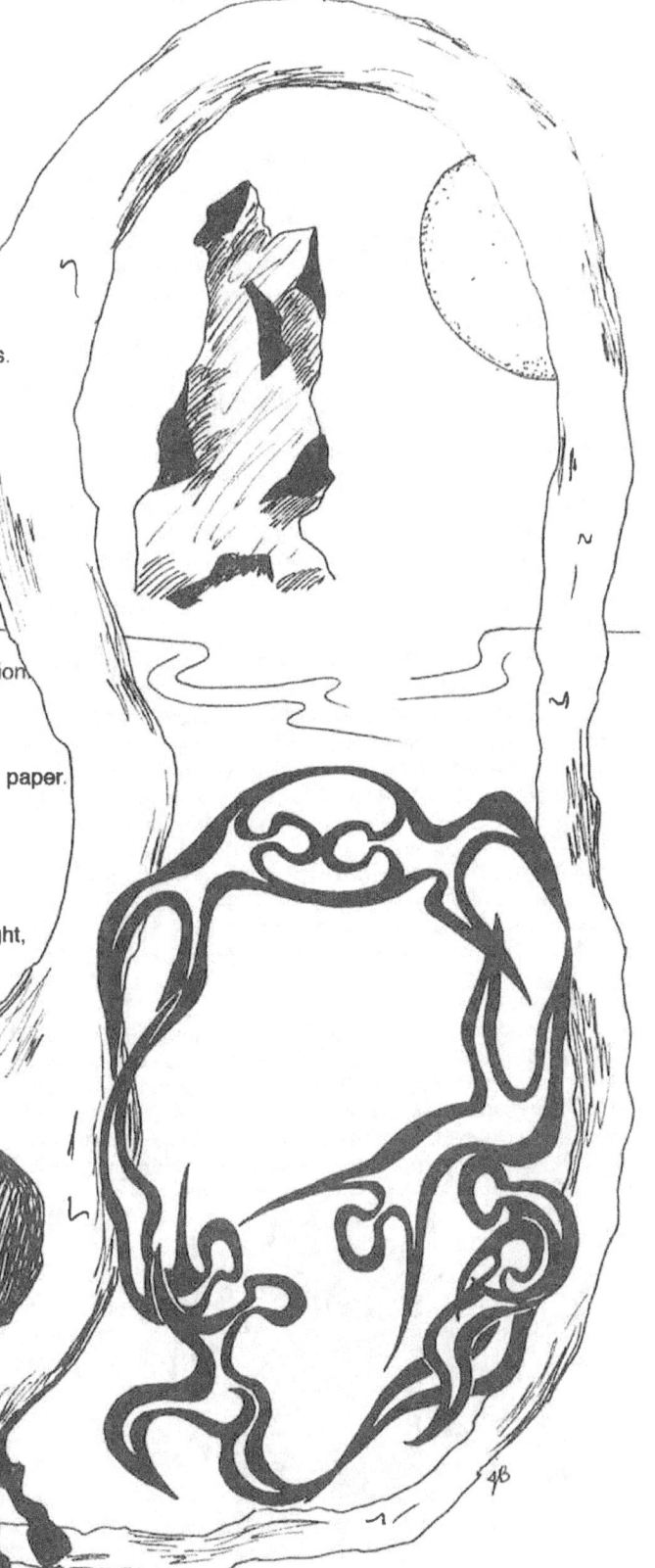

BEACH BUM PILGRIMS

We come here yearly, beach bum pilgrims;
And though our gifts are meagre
(Altar cairns and kelphorn bugles),
We leave, always, with more
Than we had bargained for.

The swooping trail is dark as church, sworded with ferns.
Juicy plants are jostling high on either side
And birdsong glints, like little silver coins,
Falling from a great, slow height.

Lurching under neon loads of tarps and food,
We burst on stage, into our mystery play.
Clambering across the driftwood footlights,
As the huge Pacific greets us
With unconditional applause.

At once, the grand emotions surface
As we assume our roles in this wild, improvised production.
Nameless tragedy consumes my child;
Mouth rectangular with rage, he howls into the sun.
The North wind, steady as a steam train,
Plucks the words out of our mouths like pieces of ripped paper.
We yell among the dunes, impotent as dreamers,
And laugh for joy, at nothing, in the golden noon.

Day after gusty day, we persist in outdoor domesticity,
Sloping at thirty-five degrees from vertical.
Sand blasts our shins, abrades all usual planes of thought,
Until dusk shawls around the camp
And the air stalls.

We stand silent as the monolithic rocks
Gazing out to sea.
Anthropomorphized, crenellated, Gothic -
Their feet in the teeming ocean,
Their minds gone all the way to China,
Empty, black-inked on the sky,
Devoid of ideas,
Rich with definition,
Mystical and heartache old.

The miraculous ice in our gin-and-tonics,
Buried in sand for several sunburnt days,
Refracts the plummeting sun like diamonds.
We grip the dripping glasses
And crawl towards each other
Through the soft, metallic sand,
Grinning like Buddhas.

-Felicity Elworthy

Favorite Places

WITHIN YOU AND WITHOUT YOU

I'm not really playing devil's advocate when I say that my favorite place is ... Manhattan. Or maybe it's just one of my favorites. But, in all seriousness, what with the city's constant adrenaline rush, hordes of people living life for you, home a tiny refuge where the life of the city pours in through every window, it's a perfect place to escape-- to escape oneself.

When I was a kid in the city, my instincts did attract me to the natural world, and as an adult I moved far back on a rural road, part of the mass migration looking for freedom from urban distractions. Beautiful lush meditative spots by bubbling water definitely became my favorite places. I was sure I'd never want to be anywhere else. But surprisingly, away from streets and phones and jobs and electricity, the distractions of my own mind emerged. Some of those shadows in my psyche weren't too likeable. In the simplicity of the country, I kept bumping up against a strange new person, myself. Maybe nature wasn't my favorite place after all. This love affair with the country was getting way too personal. While the Evil City was a possible temptress, it wasn't really what I wanted either. What to do?

During a visit to Manhattan, counting the days till I got to go home, I learned that it doesn't matter which place it is. I sat by a window, sixteen flights up from Mother Earth. Sirens shrieked, and yells and laughter and anguish came from the street in a tidal wave. Trapped in that terrible, inseparable community, I experienced another place. I could feel Oregon, I could feel the country. It was not far away. I was there too. Nature was still there, the city was still there, and my mind was quiet. So with a quiet mind it didn't matter where I was, and that was the favorite place I had been looking for. With that awareness, I might even get to live in the country after all.

Recently I walked outside into a warm, quiet summer night. Lying on the grass, I listened to the creek's soft sounds and looked up into the interlacing branches of trees and the patterns of sky between them. In that moment I was again fully present, inside and out. It's been a long time learning how to find my favorite place. It could be anywhere. I'm glad it can be here. *-Rachel Goodman*

GERALDINE'S FAVORITE PLACE

I couldn't be happier about this month's theme, favorite places.

Mike and I were fortunate enough to be in Portland during the Imperial Tombs of China, at the Portland Art Museum. If you have to walk, crawl, hitchhike or drive, get yourself there before September 16th.

Portland was the only west coast city chosen because of current trade negotiations with China. Much larger cities in the east and Midwest were so honored for size and population, so we are fortunate indeed.

A legion of volunteers are necessary, which immediately fills the atmosphere with good will. Tickets are necessary in advance. You may call in advance or order from Ticketron, or Target Stores.

When you enter, you'll be given complimentary audio cassettes, with headphones; don't be put off, the noisy kids and tourists now will not interrupt your tour. Each room is dedicated to a different tomb,and time period. If you wish to linger you simply press stop, then proceed by following the directions, clearly given on the tape. This system was a first for me and I found the quiet and the dissertation perfect. But I'm easily distracted.

The 6,000 terra cotta soldiers and horses unearthed in 1990 were a particular favorite of this equestrian enthusiast. Every soldier has distinctly different hair and facial features. The horses stand 6 1/2 feet tall, with manes straight up, and are perfectly shaped in every aspect.

The Chinese perfected porcelain, and exquisite pieces were exhibited throughout. The lacquered wood objects, also a Chinese accomplishment, from as long ago as 1,500 years, were remarkable. A book the size of my truck, with every family member carefully recorded therein-- a throne, so ornate, I'm sure I'll have to visit again, to see again the detail- the complete burial armor of four inch jade squares, joined with gold wire. You could not move away.

One of the reasons we are able to enjoy these objects today is not pleasant to reflect upon. As with the Great Wall of China, one member of every family would be selected to serve for life at these ornate burial sites. With the terra cotta soldiers, your entire family was hauled to the site so that none could return to tell of this fabulous fortune, probably the reason it remained such a well–kept secret.
-Geraldine Davidson

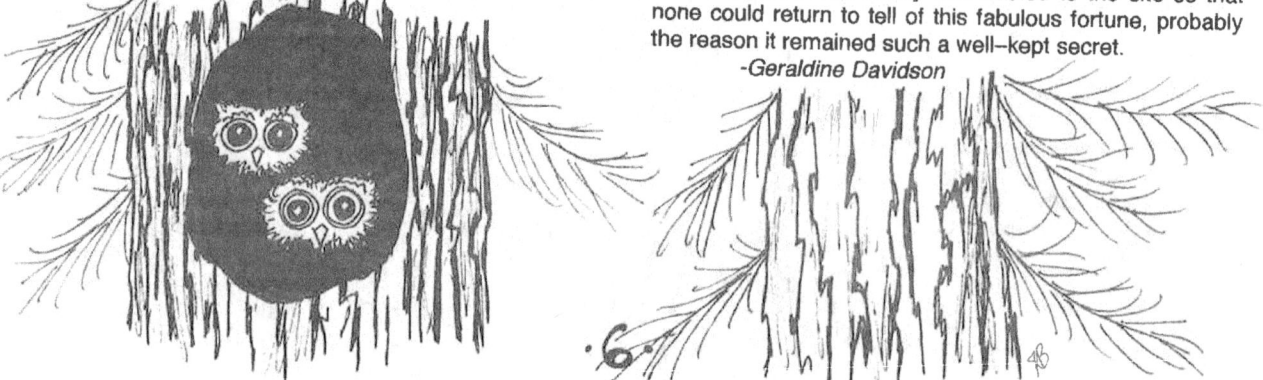

Rockin' Youth Page

I'D LOVE TO BE A FAIRY'S CHILD

Children born of fairy stock
Never need for shirt or frock,
Never want for food or fire,
Always get their hearts desire,
Juggle pockets full of gold,
Marry when they're seven years old.
Every fairy child may kept,
Two strong ponies and ten sheep:
All have houses each their own,
Built of brick of granite stone;
They live in cherries, they run wild.

Lily Maxfield likes to pick flowers in spring. She likes to pick the roses that climb up the wall. But lilys are her favorite kind of them all in the whole world, becaues of her name lily. Do you no what this story is about it is about flouers beautfel flouers. Like Lilys, Roses, Violets, Butter cups, Daisys and iris.
By Lily Maxfield

One day the babsiter came into my room 1 hour later he was gone. The next day anoter one came 1 hour later she was gone. The next day my mother came home she said, "how was your day?" I said, "yummy."
By Jonathan Bradbury

SMILE!

Drawings By: Mason Madden, Austen Hocker, Gabriela

Editors
Holly Moon and Katie Davis
Send your stories, drawings, and thoughts to Common Ground, P.O. Box 2016, Cave Junction, Oregon 97523

TAKILMA COMMON GROUND is brought to you by a clique (or so we keep hearing) of beleaguered print freaks. We are constantly cruising the neighborhood in search of hot news, community debate, startling graphics and edgy prose. If you would like to fan the flames of controversy or display your doodles, send us your stuff. We love 3" disks accompanied by a printed copy. We also read trash, but make it funny will you? Get radical before we die of heat <u>and</u> boredom.

THIS ISSUE:				
Facilitators............	Felicity and Jack		Calendar/Mailing ..	Laurie
Computer.............	Kerry		Paste-up...............	Robin
Graphics..............	Cathy, Jill, Felicity, Ina		Significant Other....	Hocker
Typists/Editors......	Linda, S.Dog, Kate, Rachel, Jon, Sally			

Naturally enough, the Editorial Staff and Mud Council do not necessarily support any of the opinions expressed in this issue. We thank all our contributors. Thanks!

NEXT ISSUE: THE ARTISTS' WAY, an issue devoted to graphic art. Deadline September 7th. Give us cartoons, political comix, serious art, graphic extravagance, collages and montages, in black and white pen and ink. Creative writing's good also, no more than three paragraph fiction or non-fiction vignettes, but this is an issue about VISUALS.

TCG, P.O.BOX 2016, CAVE JUNCTION, OR 97523. email holmans@cdsnet.net

Printed on tree free paper this time.

SUBSCRIBE NOW!

_____ $10 1-YEAR SUBSCRIPTION

_____ $25 1-YEAR SUBSCRIPTION AND
COMMON GROUND T-SHIRT.
(CALL 592-4695 FOR SIZE AND COLOR INFO)

___ $? BROKE BUT LITERATE, SEND ANYWAY

NAME:_____

ADDRESS:_____

_____

#21

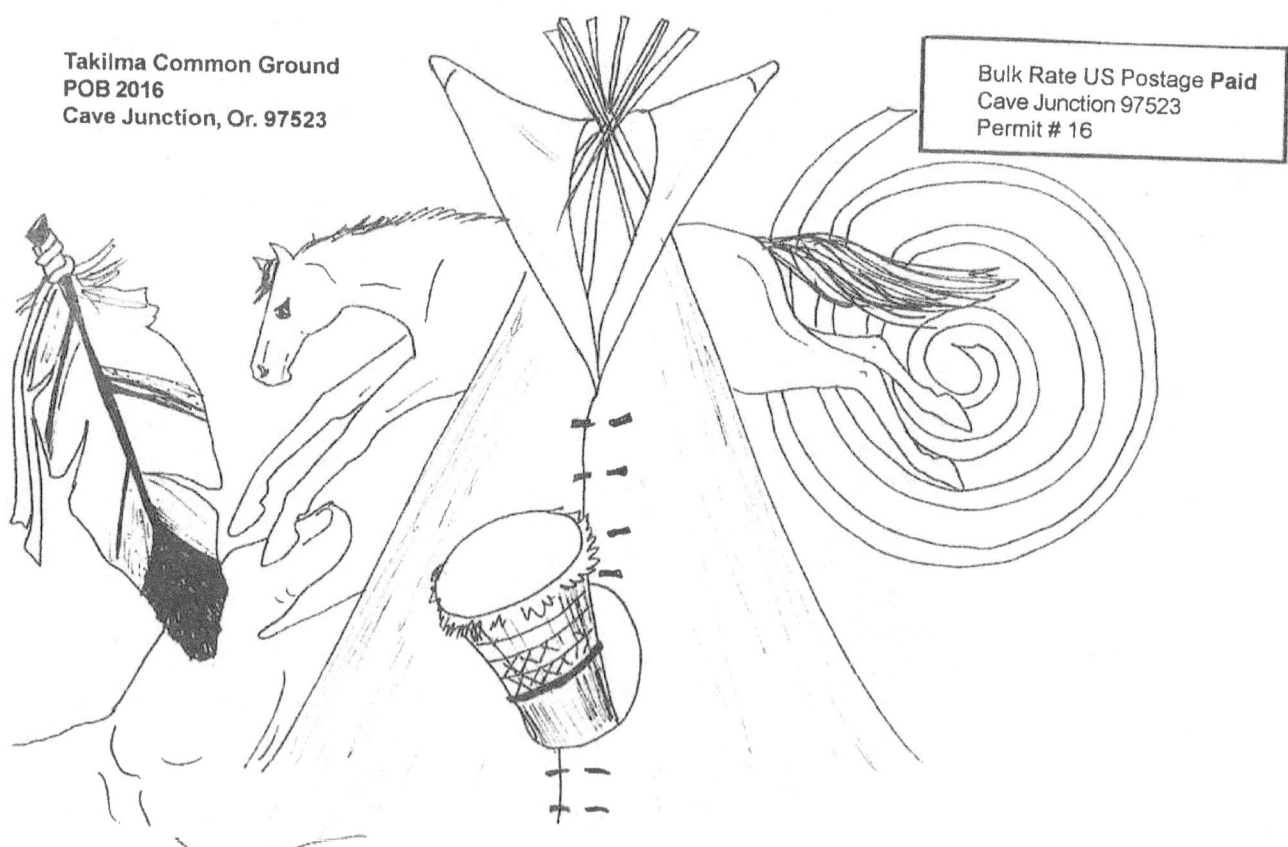

Takilma Common Ground
POB 2016
Cave Junction, Or. 97523

TAKILMA COMMON GROUND

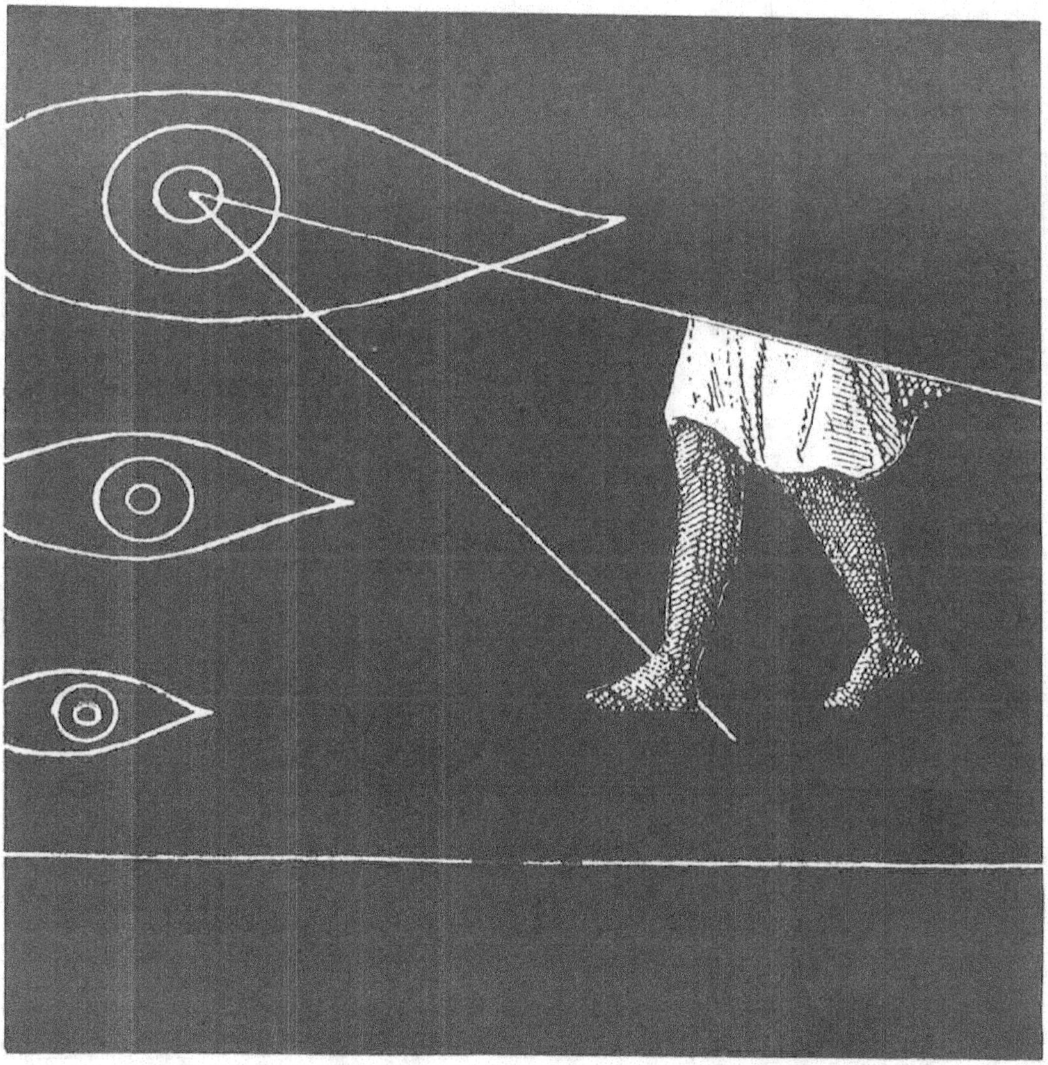

Fall * Equinox * Issue * 22

STOP THE PRISON:
GET YOUR PEN OUT NOW !!!

Calling themselves "People Reviving the Illinois Valley's Declining Economy (PRIDE), a group of approximately thirty Illinois Valley residents are applying to the Oregon Department of Corrections (ODOC) to place a 1635 bed state prison here in the Illinois Valley. The group is being assisted by County Commissioner Irv Whiting and the Josephine County Sheriff's Department.

The Citizens for a Liveable Illinois Valley (CLIV) and the Rockydale Neighborhood Association (RNA) have been spearheading opposition to the prison to "retain our safe, rural community". RNA and CLIV made sure that an ODOC Public Forum on August 8 turned out to be perhaps the largest public meeting in this Valley's history. Approximately 500 people braved the sweltering heat at IV High, with about 80% opposed to the prison. CLIV and RNA held a subsequent meeting on August 26 where 200-250 people attended, all of whom were opposed to the prison. Although the pro-prison group claims to represent the "silent majority," they have yet to hold any public meetings.

More likely the silent minority on this issue, the pro-prison group does possess some powerful assets which greatly enhance their chances of bringing this mega-prison to our community. The most significant asset is a very powerful state bill, HB 2214, which allows the state to completely ignore the wishes of a community in siting a prison. Under HB 2214, Governor Kitzhaber will receive a list of approximately 28 sites around the state. From this list, the Governor will choose sites for 7 prisons. So far it appears the Illinois Valley site will be one of those 28.

The sad thing about this whole issue is that many of the people who are for the prison will be very disappointed if indeed a prison is built here. Many of these folks have good intentions and only want to improve our community. Unfortunately, they are being duped by the ODOC with information which glosses over the problems associated with large prisons. The ODOC and Justice Department officials have a clear agenda- to build these prisons ASAP ; they are not a good source for the kind of accurate information we need.

Hundreds of letters pouring into the governor's office may be the only thing that will stop this run-away train. Letters should cover issues such as our limited water supplies, the fatal blow this prison would deliver to our economic development Strategic Plan, the endangered species which swim our East Fork Illinois, our already overwhelmed social services (health care, law enforcement) and schools, our limited transportation infrastructure (Hwy.199!), the conversion of scarce choice agricultural land to concrete, and the high operating costs of operating a prison in this remote area.

Apathy is perhaps our most potent enemy. Many who oppose the prison simply refuse to believe that it could possibly be located here. These folks need to realize that due to political factors, our odds are probably better than 7 to 28 for being chosen. These are not exactly comfortable odds. If you think this is a reasonably quiet, peaceful, rural community and you'd like to keep it that way, we recommend you pick up the pen now, before it's too late. If you'd like to see a prison town where crime dominates our economy and culture, don't bother. This is a call to all of our friends in East Takilma and elsewhere. This prison will devastate the place that many of you still call home.

> WRITE TO: Gov. Kitzhaber, 2575 Center St., Salem, OR. 97310
>
> cc copies to Sen. Brady Adams, State Capitol S-203, Salem ,OR. 97310 and Bob Repine H-496

Silas and Punchy Go to Prison
By Aspen Farer

PƏM R

MORE TAKILMA HISTORY

After reading the last issue of Common Ground and enjoying everyone's story of how they got to Takilma, I decided that I would really like to share my story too. Although I don't live on a commune, I feel I am a part of something even greater: a community. It gives us all the freedom to be what we want to be and yet still be interconnected to a bigger tribe. I met my ex-husband Jim at Brown's Hot Springs near Lake Arrowhead and we lived at a commune together in Reche Canyon before deciding to move to the country. Jim had just graduated with a degree in sociology and was studying communes as his personal quest. We traveled around the west in our old camper visiting communes in New Mexico, Arizona, and northern California. We ended up in Atascadero where Jim was learning the trade of shoe repair. In the summer of 1979 we took two weeks vacation in Oregon. We had the number of a friend at Sun Star and we decided to visit. He wasn't home but as we drove back through Takilma, we fell in love with the canyon beauty. Back in Cave Junction, we ran into an old man who wanted to retire and sell his shoe repair equipment. Within a week we had moved to Cave Junction and started to set up shop in the little house next to the Pizza Deli. Business was good right off the bat and we prospered. We expanded our shop with Birkenstocks and moved downtown. One day Jim heard of some property for sale in Takilma on the river. It

was perfect for us. He took me out there and we hacked our way back to the river through a jungle of vines and poison oak. Under all that we could see was a very nice little homestead. We bought it the next day and moved our old green trailer on it. It was October of 1980. It was the beginning of a new era for me. In two months my world would be shattered by the assassination of my idol John Lennon, who did more to create love and peace in this world than anyone. I was too busy to cry for long as we worked to build our cabin with the help of Blake Topping. We had two small children, Darshana and Jayke and winter was coming soon. We built a basic small cabin with hippie siding which reminded me of the little house on the prairie, complete with outhouse. It was all we could afford and we lived a very simple life. I enrolled my kids at the Dome School right away and that's where I began to get to know my neighbors in Takilma. For a few years I was known simply as "the cobbler's wife" but very slowly people began to know me as Kindi, my nickname from the day I was born in Friedrichsdorf, Germany. I was the quiet child-woman and indeed being a mother and gardener suited me just fine. Those were the good years in Takilma when folks still had abundant money and herb. I had the time to dance and make beaded necklaces on the beach. I had fallen in love with Takilma and its wonderfully eccentric people. There were many celebrations, parties, and strange and unusual events. In 1982 my second son, Mikael, was born at home and just barely attended by Lisa and Dr. Jim. Two years later my husband, Jim, was diagnosed with a rare form of leukemia apparently caused by prolonged exposure to the shoe repair glue and chemicals. He was ill for some time and tried various new age cures, until finally he made the decision to move to LA and stay with my parents. He enrolled in an experimental program at UCLA Medical Center, which administered a new drug, interferon. Within a year he was much better and working as an orthopedic technician in Los Angeles. Unfortunately our marriage had fallen on the rocks after so much stress and separation. On Halloween night of 1985 I met my current partner, James. I was the Queen of England and he was a rainbow warrior. He was the knight in shining armor I needed to save me from loneliness and neglect. He gave me back the gifts of joy, laughter and self-confidence. He was a refugee from the Grateful Dead Family in San Francisco and his zeal for living excited me. I had always been a part of that hippie family but I didn't know it. The early years were one long party only partly interrupted by police harassment. In 1987, our beautiful daughter Serena was born, and James started to settle down, a little. We had our ups and downs but found our love was strong. To this day, we find ourselves to be, surprisingly, the best of friends. My particular philosophy of dualism is reflected in my life and in my song, "Living in a canyon...with two sides". I've had two partners named James, two Gemini sons, two lovely daughters (the first of which was a twin), two best friends named Lora, two Chevy trucks, and two oak trees in my front yard. The many other eerie dualistic coincidences are too numerous to mention. All I know is that this is my home and I am still learning to grow food and raise my children. I am still growing into the person I am destined to be. I am very glad to be close to so many other self realizing people of similar beliefs. I am proud to be a part of a very diverse and talented group of good people. I hope you all are making your dreams come true as I am. We must survive, strong and resilient, throughout these troubling times. My heart is with you all in spirit. Takilma is my favorite place on this earth.

Love . *Kindi*

CONFRONTING THE COMMUNITY SHADOW

We each, as individuals, have our shadow side: our pains, frustrations, disappointments, abuses, our craziness. So, too, each community has its shadow side that is in some way a collective manifestation of the shadows of its individual community members. One way the community shadow reveals itself is when a particular individual's shadow erupts into the community by what we call a psychiatric disorder or behavior problem.

Sometimes the community shadow merely takes form as curiously eccentric or moderately bizarre appearances or behaviors. This kind of shadow is worn by individuals who create little friction in the community and who are basically content with their often marginal role. They are testament to the wondrous diversity and iconoclastic spirit that every thriving community would support and inspire.

Other times, the community shadow may explode dramatically, in the form of dangerous psychosis or violent acts, or both. These behaviors and the individuals who embody them reveal, and are testament to, the most frightening shadow aspects of each of us - extreme frustration, despair, terror, rage and vengeance; states in which we are almost literally "out" of our minds. The results can be verbal abuse, fearful threats and harassment, property destruction, assault, suicide, and gruesome murder.

What might a community do when such frightening shadow aspects erupt in our midst? What might be some effective community attitudes and strategies to reduce the likelihood of violence? And how effective can any community be in changing a particular person's potentially violent behavior?

It frequently—though not always — helps to better understand the origins of these kinds of fearful eruptions. Most individuals who are considered dangerous to self or others have a psychiatric disorder based on deficiencies in both nature and nurture. There is often a biochemical imbalance in the brain that could have originated genetically, or pre-natally in-utero, or from physical or emotional trauma in childhood, or from substance abuse, especially methamphetamine, at any age. In addition, there is frequently a history of subtle to severe parental neglect, or rejection, or overt abuse in many possible forms. The combinations and proportions of biochemical problems and family problems are extremely variable. In addition, socio-economic stressors, such as poverty, joblessness, homelessness and low social status make it much more likely that potentially dangerous individuals will fulfill that potential.

O JOYOUS DANCER
THE COSMIC SEED TAKES ROOT
IN THEE
TO FOLLOW THY JOY WILL SET
IT FREE..
AROUSE CREATION WITH TEN-
DER GRACE,
REVELATION OF THE BELOVED'S
FACE,
MYSTIC REUNION DIVINE.
BE ONE.

Although these factors do not lessen a person's responsibility for his or her behavior, it is important to remember that these individuals are usually suffering intense and debilitating emotional pain. In this way through our own pain we know them. Their shadow is ours', they are us, we are them.

Finally, what are our limits? How much can we really help another person? If someone is in a near total shadow state, absolutely compelled to suicide or murder, probably no one and no community can prevent that. And sometimes, with imminent danger, the authorities must be called because their resources are more total or more efficient. Most individuals, however, even when their shadow is erupting, maintain some light. They are in fierce internal struggle, with despair, hope, rage, guilt, hate, fear all competing in turmoil. If we compassionately acknowledge and accept these shadow feelings, and gently support the light feeling, help will be happening. Although we usually think of help as meaning "improvement"—facilitating the experience and expression of more light — often it means merely preventing more darkness, or guiding an irreversible darkening into a safe and healing environment where trust and inclusiveness might be able to be experienced again.

So what can be done?

Sometimes a show of force, designed to inspire fear of painful consequences in the potentially dangerous individual, is appropriate and effective. The less this show of force is enacted by one of a few individuals, and the more that it has the weight and sanction of the community at large, the more likely it is to inspire respect and fear. But a show of force is more often likely to polarize and escalate the situation. Like power struggles between

6

215

WODAHS YTINUMMOC EHT GNITNORFNOC

individuals and nations, this approach is quite risky because it may easily backfire and increase the danger of violence, rather than reduce it. It is usually best considered a last resort strategy.

I believe that generally the most effective strategy is "community support." This approach recognizes that the individuals who are embodying the community shadow are mostly in need of help rather than confrontation. Their lives are in turmoil, their material resources are usually meager, they have alienated friends and neighbors, their internal coping skills are eroding, their sense of self·is fragmenting, and their shadows are erupting.

I work for the county mental health program on a team of eight clinicians called the Community Support Unit. From the point of view of our program, community support means linking people who are experiencing psychiatric disorders with as many community (read "government") resources (read "subsidies") that they are eligible for. It is surprising how many people are either ignorant of these programs, unable to negotiate the bureaucracy, or unwilling to. When needed, our unit assists qualifying individuals in obtaining General Assistance, Food Stamps, disability benefits, HUD housing, medical, dental and prescription benefits, transportation, crisis care, day treatment, foster care, alcohol and drug treatment, counseling and psychotherapy. This is community support at the state and county level.

But at more local levels even more can be done that government or private agencies can't do. What would REAL community support look like in the communities of the Illinois Valley?

If it is true that ultimately we are them and they are us, we must realize that when we go into our extreme shadow states we completely forget that truth. Two characteristics of the shadow state stand out: the shadow does not trust; and the shadow does not feel connected or whole, it feels isolated and alienated.

Real community support would have as its goal the reattainment of trust and wholeness. It would reach out to its shadow not so much through selected experts in the community, but through the heart of the community at large. It would rebuild trust and wholeness by welcoming the shadow-driven individual with appropriately sensitive ceremony back into inclusion in the community, rather then isolating him or her out to the dangerous edge. It would be a welcome of unconditional regard for the person, yet only conditional tolerance of that person's behaviors. That discrimination must be clearly communicated.

In addition to the obvious compassion and genuine heartfelt welcome that this approach requires, another important healing step would be to offer material support to reduce the intense stress of unemployability or homelessness. In effect, the community would in these ways be redistributing its wealth—material and emotional—from the haves to the have-nots, out of recognition that socioeconomic disparity only lengthens the community shadow.

Sometimes even this strategy may be ineffective. Some shadows are so dark that they cannot take in the light and they push it away. Others, when they get a little light, demand more and more, and always feel insatiably deprived and deserving.

For these, neither fear not love alone is effective. The art of supportive confrontation is called for, in which the individual feels just enough trust and understanding from the community to be able to tolerate the uncomfortableness of being challenged to look more closely at his/her pattern of shadow behaviors. There must be genuine love and compassion from the community, and also a firm willingness to enact restrictive consequences if the shadow continues to abuse the generosity and dignity of the community. This dance is tricky and demanding and may require training and practice. Mostly a willingness to practice and more practice and not give up. Giving up on the shadow, paradoxically, keeps it alive and thriving. Whenever we give up on the shadow-driven individuals in our community, we just lengthen and darken the community's shadow.   -Pedro Tama

7

216

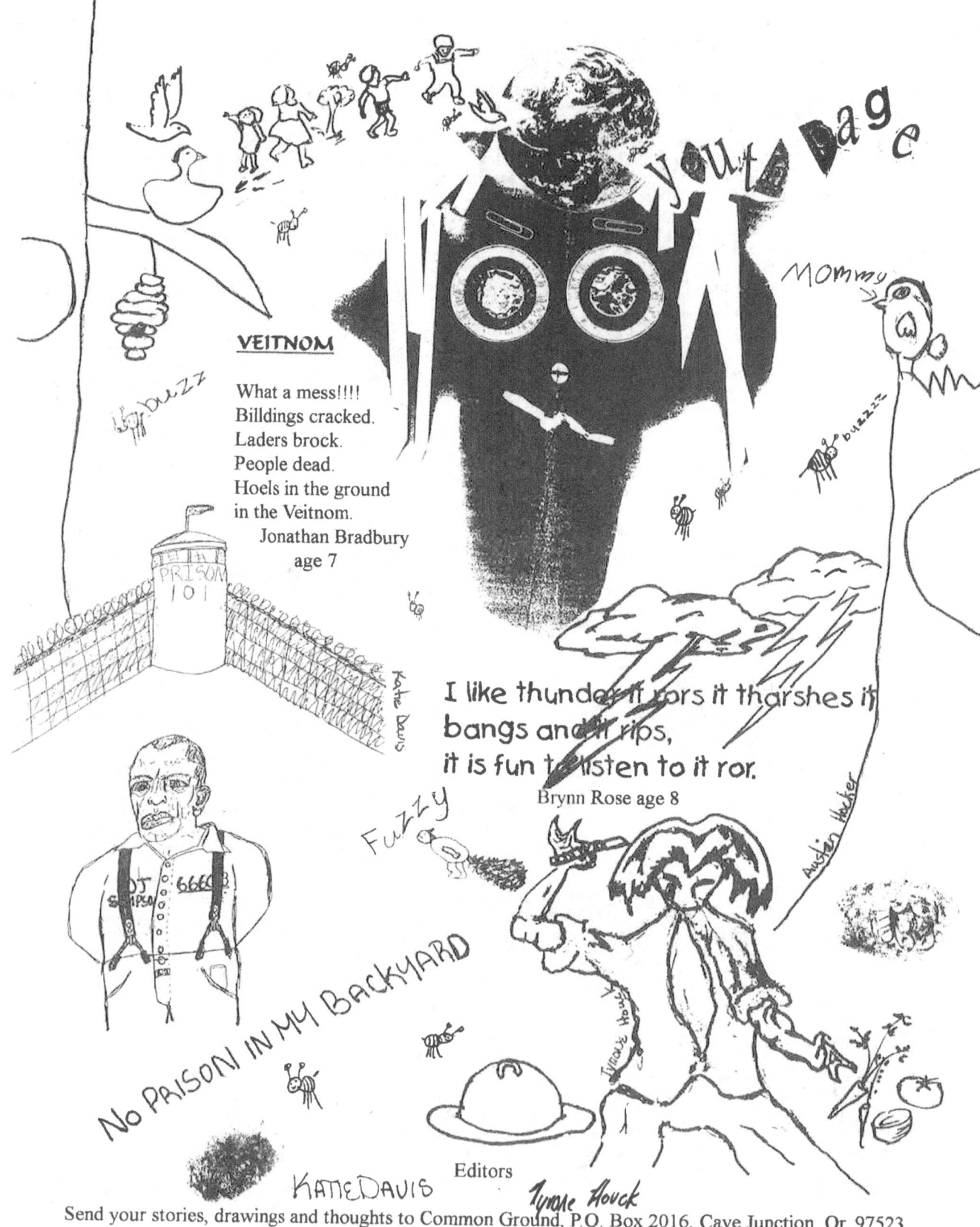

Youth Page

Mommy

VEITNOM

What a mess!!!!
Billdings cracked.
Laders brock.
People dead.
Hoels in the ground
in the Veitnom.
    Jonathan Bradbury
    age 7

PRISON 101

I like thunder it rors it tharshes it
bangs and it rips,
it is fun to listen to it ror.
    Brynn Rose age 8

Fuzzy

No PRISON IN MY BACKYARD

Editors
KATIE DAVIS   Tyrone Houck

Send your stories, drawings and thoughts to Common Ground, P.O. Box 2016, Cave Junction, Or. 97523
or e-mail Clemshaw@cdsnet.net

8

LETTERS TO THE EDITOR

Since the last issue of Common Ground, I've come to wonder about "community Justice"! Where does it start? How do we as a community enact such justice? Do we as a community have the desire, the skill s or need to pursue such Justice? Is Justice to one the same as Justice to another? Are we strong as a community? Weak? Or just full of shit in a politically correct way? When sick or frustrated individuals tamper with community dreams and ideals (be it spray painted slanders or clear violations of our childrens' boundaries) should we tar and feather? Should we ignore? Should we start the rumor mill spinning and possibly promote more community demise? When does Common Ground address these community issues? Where does individual freedom end and community well being begin? When do we put aside our anarchistic preferences and became "one in strength and spirit"? If you are also concerned with the above , write and respond with your opinions and concerns to Miguelo c/o Common Ground. -Miguelo

HELLO COMMON GROUND, Thank you for sending me the recent issue via our good friend Don Shaw. We are now living in Tonasket, Wa. And are enjoying this very alternative community here. I am once again teaching in an alternative school and River is working at the Co-op. We are helping with the Community Center and the Original Barter Faire. Come join us.....

Thank You Very Much in dealing with an unworthy community member..

We appreciate your efforts..
John and River Jones
1-509-486-2479

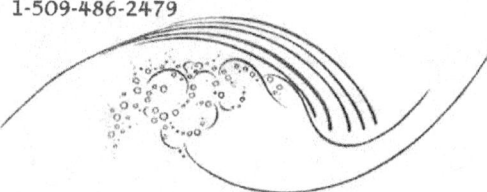

even MORE TAKILMA HISTORY

Where do I start...for me it was 1965, LSD, the Airplane and Country Joe. I was disenchanted with the PhD thing, the system reeked (still does) so I opted for an easy M.A. in marine biology, got a job as a diver-biologist, a very stoned one, but even that got old.. So we hit the road along with the rest. Festivals, fruit-pickin', lots of fun. California was getting extremely weird, and I wanted a healthy, pastoral life for my family (we had three sons). We covered the West, and landed in Takilma in a broken-down school bus, towed in by Delbert, with Billy Gulch, Charlie Two Shoes, and Brian Bones co-piloting. I talked with Stan Ivec about buying his place, but it was a little risky, deed-wise. Later a bunch of early Deadheads moved in there. Up the road, Electric Michael had a cool little cabin in the Riverbed. The Riverrats ranged from friendly to furtive to downright dangerous, but we made good friends, for life. Brian was always getting us in trouble, Charlie could charm us out of scrapes, and Billy (bless you w. arroyo) held the stash. Michael wanted some cash to finish his boat. Of the four boats that were built in the Riverbed, only Michael's survived launching and he made in to Monterey Bay where the boat was found up on the

beach, no sign of Michael. Hope he made it to the land of cheap mahogany. My down payment was from a liberated army payroll check, and a T-man came to my door several years later. We talked, sort-of. He looked around at the neighbors, decided I was too brain-damaged to be responsible, and wrote it off. Takilma was heaven, one long celebration. I felt grounded and I put together a five year plan for self-sufficiency. We moved to Ashland in 1977; my boys had better high schoolin' there than I.V. High at the time, and I worked for the Silviculture on the Rogue Forest doing reforestation plans, tree disease studies and endangered species surveys. Later I would "retire" in Puna, along with some other Takilma folk; the Terry Davis clan, Sabina, Debbie and Ivy, Theo and Sandy, and some Santa Cruz people I knew, plus numerous progeny. But my heart was still in Takilma, where I could always seek solace at the Underhill Abbey and Quail Sanctuary (original Tokay Heights).

Here, along the Illinois' sparkling east fork, beaver played, steelhead ran, serpentine endemics abound, and to the Abbey I shall ever return. -Andy Kier
POB 491
Pahoa, Hawaii 96778

the atomic museum

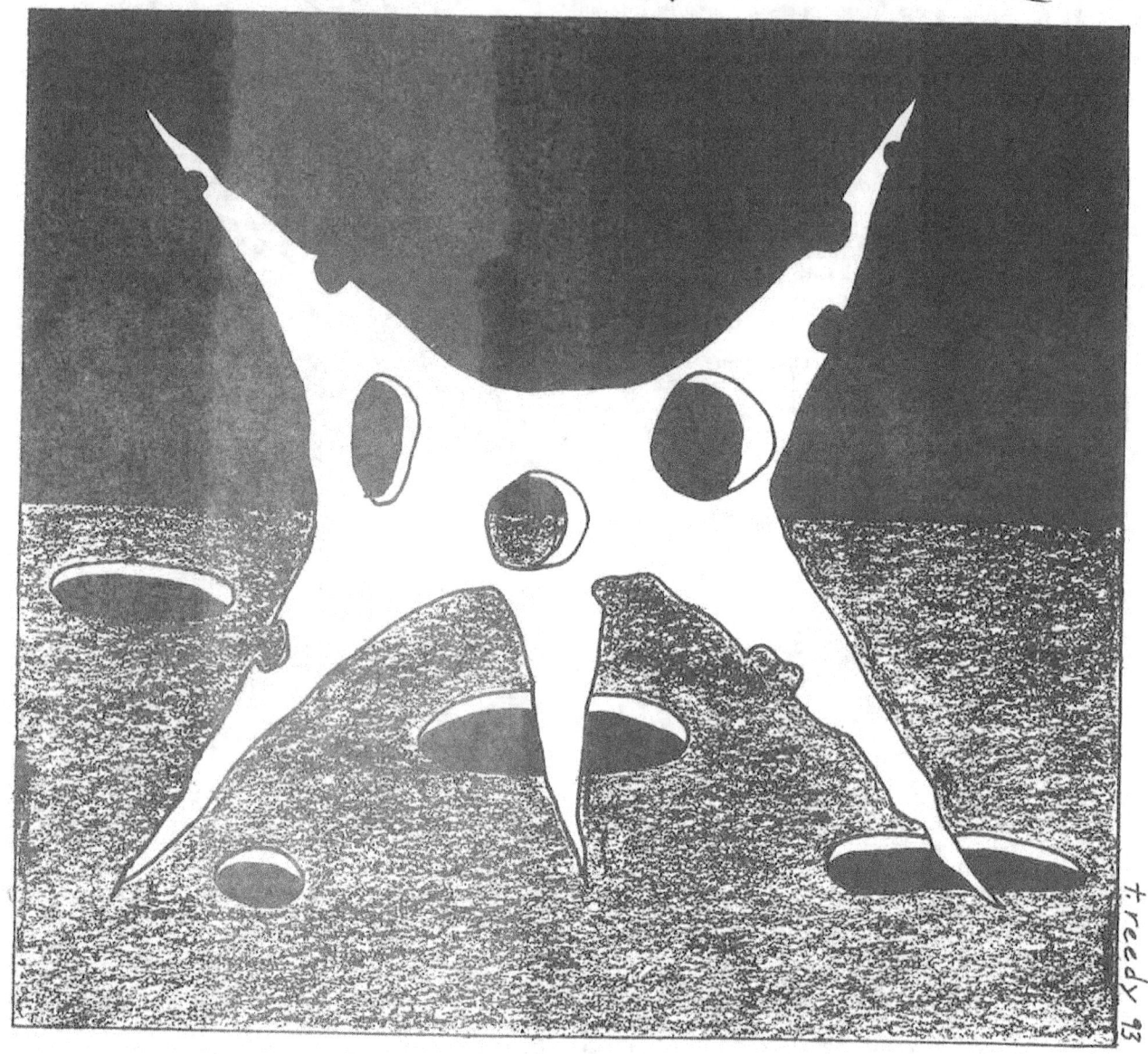

is full of holes.

10

Announcements

SALMON CEREMONY

On Oct. 20th at 2:00p.m. Agness Pilgrim will give a Salmon Ceremony at the Dome School. This is an invitation to a wonderful event. Donations will be requested and bring a favorite dish for all to share and your own eating utensils.

Presently we are collecting donations from the community to purchase a headstone for Grant Pilgrim's grave. The headstone will cost $650.00. Any and all donations will be gratefully accepted.

Agness will be traveling to Australia in mid November where she will attend a gathering of aboriginal and indigenous leaders as ambassador of good will from here. Her airfare and boarding have been taken care of but donations to help her with other costs are needed. This is an excellent opportunity to express our gratitude and thanks for all that Agness and Grant have given us. Let's help launch Aggie's new mission as an international ceremonial elder and earth ambassador. Donations can be sent to:

Agness Baker Pilgrim
369 Shan Creek Rd
Grants Pass Or.
or give to Barry or Lou at the Siskiyou Project.
Info: 592-4459

The play "Lost in Yonkers" by Neil Simon will be presented on Thursday, September 26 at the Barnstormers Theatre in Grants Pass. Outrageous desserts will be available at 7:30. Curtain time is 8:15 pm. The tickets are $15 each. It is a benefit for the Josephine County Library Foundation so $9.80 of the ticket price is tax deductible. For further info call 476-6677 or Deb Murphy 592-2866.

It's time for **The Dome School's Annual Bike-A-Thon**, October 8th. This is a great fund raiser as the kids are the ones making the money! Find a Dome School student and make a pledge.

The Human Rights Alliance presents a talk on local **Archeological** sites with Kate Winthrop at Options in Grants Pass, 1215 SW G ST at 7:00pm.

Siskiyou Project needs you! Come help us in the office or in the field. Contact Deb or Cathy at 592-4459 if you can help one day a month.

Volunteer Fisher Study co-ordinator needed. Contact Deb at 592-4459 if interested.

Found: Black dog (large puppy?) downtown Takilma call 592-3386.

Free: Working hand-crank mimeograph machine with chemicals and paper. Call the Dome School 592-3911.

RENEW YOUR SUBSCRIPTION NOW

CHOICE POINT WORKSHOP

You can learn transformational techniques for making conscious choices when Alex Merrin brings her Choice Point Workshop to Peace With Inn on Oct. 12th. Alex is a senior trainer for the Hendricks Institute and, in addition to her private practice, co-facilitates, with Kathryn Hendricks, the Hendricks Institute Body Centered Transformation and Corporate Transformation training.

The workshop includes an in-depth exploration with breath, movement and other body centered tools to learn and experience: *WHAT PERSONAL OBSTACLES AND PATTERNS ARE KEEPING YOU FROM HAVING WHAT YOU MOST WANT.HOW TO USE YOUR CURRENT ENERGY, INCLUDING RESISTANCE. HOW TO ACCESS THE CREATIVE GROWTH OPPORTUNITY IN EVERY OBSTACLE..HOW TO RECOGNIZE AND CELEBRATE YOUR CHOICES.*

Paco Despacio and Marcy Tilton have been taking workshops with Alex during the past year and are delighted to recommend her workshop to anyone committed to personal growth. Cost $75. Time 10am -6pm...call Marcy and Paco for more info. 592 4196 or Myrica 592-4209.

THANK YOU 88.5

Attention Thespians! We need to hear from you soon if you are interested in performing in Le Show next April. Come and be a part of the fun. All acts welcome. Your creativity is legendary. Start early and plan ahead. For more information call Robin 592-3159 or Jennie May 592-4344. Remember if you don't volunteer you may receive one of those special little slips in your invitation, volunteering you....

Home again, we're home again. One more time, we want to say thank you to all who helped us after our fire last winter. We just couldn't have done it without your loving assistance. But here we are, home again, and the house is way better than it ever was. A couple of things were left here, by the way, so if you're missing an 8' black extension cord, a 25' black extension cord, or a couple of halogen construction lights, come on by and get them. Again, thanks for reaffirming the meaning of 'community' to us. -Mar, Leo, Ry and Ian

Celebration of Diversity! Come join the fun at Riverside Park on Sat. September 28. The Parade begins at 11:00am, followed by entertainment galore. Takilma will be well represented by the Illuminated Fools, Jim Rich and Pat Mersman with the Jefferson Baroque Orchestra, Lisa Kelz and her local teen theater group and Donna Bell's Brier Rose Dance Ensemble. There will also be story telling, poetry reading, mural painting and soccer games. Green Salsa (Afro-Cuban style drumming), will start the day rockin' at noon on the main stage.

CLASSIFIEDS

Writing, editing, graphics, murals (in and outside), signs, I type 117 wpm. call Pam 592-6832 evenings or leave message.

New Artist's Way group forming, starting in Mid Nov. Call Marcy for more information. 592-4196

WANTED : Feet for Reflexology. Let us touch your soles, to relieve stress and tension. $10 per session. Call Mar 592-4436 or Diane 592-3908. (note from the editor...this is most wonderful)

1000 Cranes Catering serving the Illinois Valley. Unique, exotic, ethnic, and just plain old good food for all occasions. For your next party or a romantic dinner for two call Robin 592-3159.

FOR THIS ISSUE
Facilitator: Robin
Computer: Kerry
Staff: Felicity, Laurie, Dog, Linda, Sally

For our next issue we'd like to hear from you concerning AGEING. Any opinions on ageing, fears, health, hopes, etc. Linda and Felicity will facilitate. Deadline for submissions will be Oct. 18th. Please send your submissions to P.O. B. 2016 Cave Jucnction, Or. 97523.

Opinions expressed here are not necessarily those of the Editorial Staff or the Mud Council. Printed on 100% tree free paper. email holmans@cdsnet. net

PEACE WITH INN

Sept. 28-29 Ancient Echoes of Tribal Dance weekend for Women, where women can reconnect with themselves and connect with other women, while learning to reduce stress through movement. Sliding scale $125 -$175 includes lunch and dinner camping.

Oct. 18 Cooking with Gourmet-Medicinal Mushrooms. Sue Krisa will be sharing a wealth of information about gourmet/medicinal mushrooms, many of which grow in our own backyard.

Nov. 2-3 Chi Gong very similar to Tai Chi but much easier to learn and remember. Rob Pell will help you learn to increase energy, reduce stress, and relieve pain through the ancient Chinese movement. $50.

Nov.9 Acupressure For Women. Clearsage- acupressure teacher and practicing acupressurist will share acupressure points to balance the female system. Help with PMS, endometriosis, fibroids etc. $30. 12-3pm

You can reach Myrica at 592-4209 or e-mail bliss@cdsnet.net

Special thanks to the Artists: Jeffery, Aspen, Pam, Gilda, Ina and Tracy.

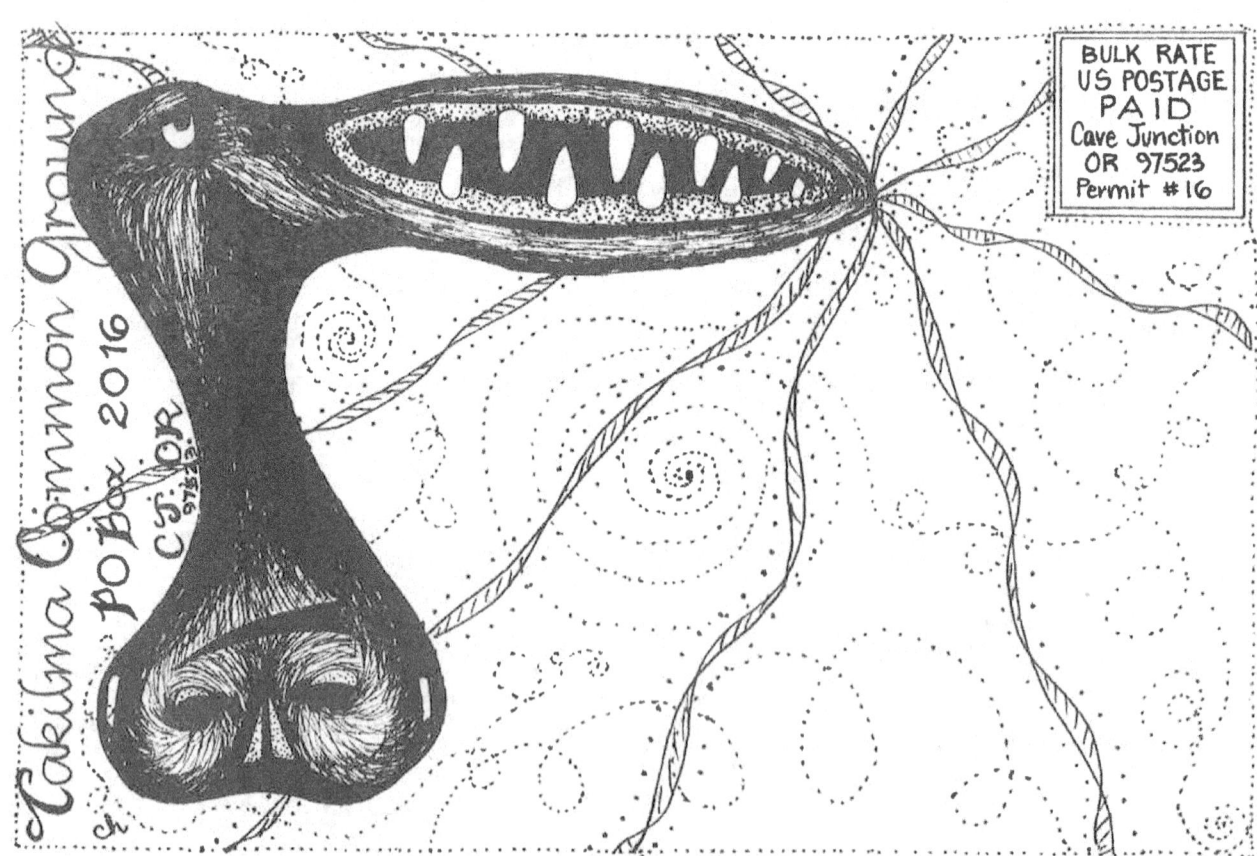

BULK RATE
US POSTAGE
PAID
Cave Junction
OR 97523
Permit #16

Takilma Common Ground
PO Box 2016
CJ, OR
97523

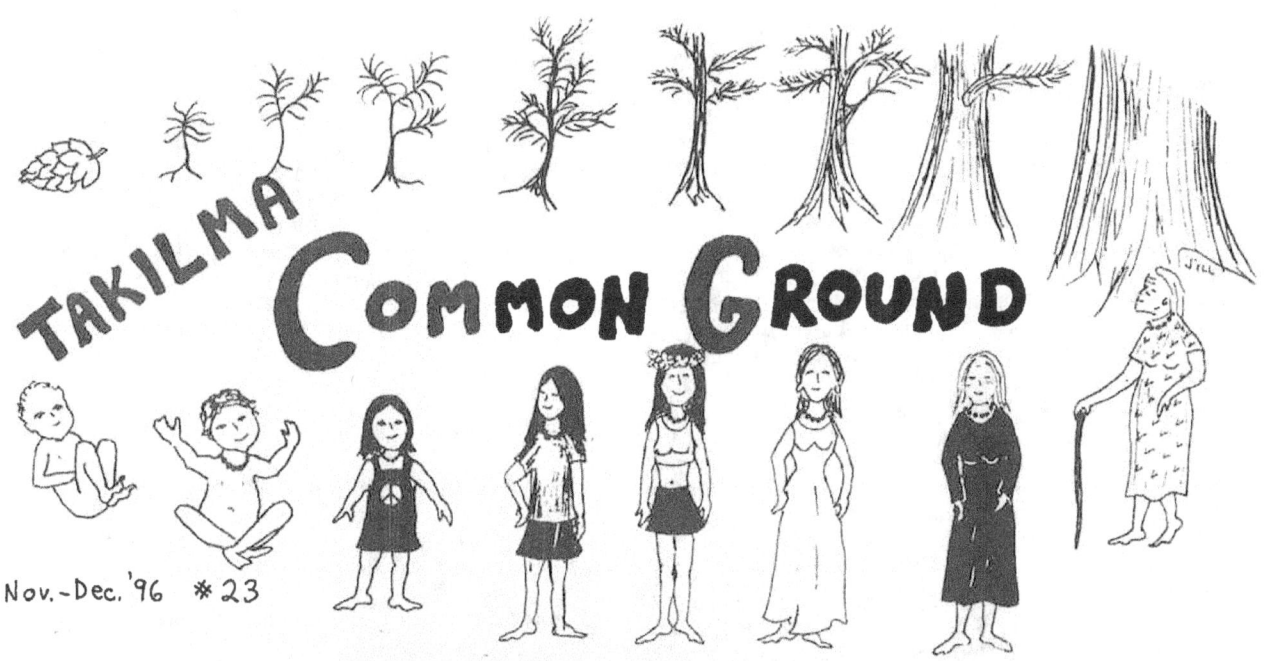

TAKILMA COMMON GROUND

Nov.–Dec. '96 ✳ 23

IF YOU WANT TO KNOW ABOUT AGING, ASK THE AGED

"The only way I'll ever die is when a jealous husband shoots me in the back as I jump out the bedroom window" said John Clayton Cory, still a handsome guy with sparkling eyes at eighty–five years of aging. John had been working a ranch out near the Ruby Mountains in Nevada, bought when he turned sixty–five, with a four–horse team and more spunk than most people ever have. Ever since J.C. Cory had been run out of the Owens Valley by L.A. Water and Power he had wanted to find a good place to ranch, a safe distance from thirsty Los Angeles.

His friends Lou and Margaret had found a little valley in Oregon and started ranching right here in Takilma back in the late teens. It was John's suggestion that I visit them which brought me here. It turns out that they had fought the good fight, together with others, back in Owens Valley. Being resourceful types they knew how to place the stuff for maximum effect. Yes, L.A. won that war, but these three and others went on with their lives, with a good story to tell, the self–respect that comes only with righteous action and none of the bitterness that seems to afflict the old ones who complained rather than acted.

Bill Ormsby is another example of how to age. Back about fifteen years ago, I helped him get his little 5 KW hydro system going, and got to know him pretty well. He told me that when he was about fifty his doctor said he didn't have long to live unless he really changed his ways. That brought him to Long Gulch and gave him a bonus round of good years, some of which he spent doggedly pursuing his goal of hooking-up that dang 1906 Pelton Wheel. He bought it at a garage sale for $5, and knew it to be the wheel that used to run up at Bill Mortenson's ranch (Sunstar today).

Otto got the shaft and stuff fixed–up and I ran interference with the power company. After I convinced Bill he had to take all the pipe apart and put it back together, only with glue this time, the system turned on and ran. Bill was so proud of all that effort that when he died his ashes were placed in a big rock next to the wooden power house. When lightning struck the Rough & Ready logging show, up at the top of Long Gulch, and fire swept down upon the little power house, it should have been the end of this story. But there it stood, a monument to forces we truly do not understand, in the midst of a completely charred moonscape; unsinged, untouched, unblackened, with Bill's memorial marker shining in the sun. With a new pipeline installed, it turned on and ran. I like it when things defy the laws of physics.

One of those laws of physics states that things must proceed towards a state of disorder and decay, which pretty well describes the aging process. But as we have just seen, sometimes laws get broken. Aging occurs when we fail to allow our spirit to exceed the limitations of our bodies and minds, for it is only our spirit that is exempt from physical laws. Violence, divorce, bitterness, depression, unresolved anger, unlived lives and overwork, are what grind us down, not the passage of time. John, Lou, Margaret, Bill and the many old ones who show us how to properly age are people who found their power, their partner, their place and their people. See you all at the Rockin' Rest Ranch.-Charley Greenwood

EDITOR'S NOTE: The British spell it "ageing" and the Americans spell it "aging". No matter how you write it, time marches on. You will find both spellings in this issue.

HOW A FOREST AGED THIS YEAR

I had the opportunity to visit one of my favorite places yesterday. It's an old forest below Mt. Elijah, at the top of Limestone Creek, not too far from the Oregon Caves. In that forest there is a population of trillium plants that I've been studying and really getting to know over the past five years . I once mapped all 56 plants in the 20'x30' population on a grid and began to watch them through a few years — seeing how many died, how many seeds they made, and how many babies they had (i.e., seedlings). I also found out how old all the plants were. Trillium are easy to "age" without killing, simply by digging up their underground rhizome, counting the annual rings on the outside and then re-burying. The oldest trillium I've found was 72 years old. That population up near Limestone Creek had a lot of older plants.

I wish I could show you that forest. It's very special. It took me two summers of hiking around the area near the Oregon Caves (Sucker and Grayback watersheds) to find eight trillium populations like the one in that forest. For my trillium study they all had to be in old-growth forests, between 3000-4500 ft. elevation, and have a distinctive community of other plant species. This community is a rich one — having calypso orchids, phantom orchids, baneberry, wild ginger, etc.... so many beautiful herbs in one place. It's the kind of place that people who visited there with me would inevitably sit down on a log for a while and just stare into the open, cathedral-like understory, so full of blossoms and fruits. These plant communities are lush and green and moist all summer long.

And they are hard to find. Walk through a forest in New Hampshire with trees only 60 years old and you will probably be impressed. Moist summers make most forests there a great place for all kinds of wildflowers. But here, with our dry summers, it takes a long time for young forests to become moist and cool places for those special plant communities.

When I found the age of all those trillium I realized that there were very few young plants in the population. And after some attempts in the role of "scientist", I discovered that very few plants had been born since 1970, when a clearcut was cut 300 ft. away. The same pattern holds true all over our forests. Even those trillium plants you see in old forests, if they are near clearcuts, will have probably stopped reproducing very well since the time of cutting. The plants you see have been there since before the cutting and will eventually die, leaving the forest a little less rich. So, the logging doesn't just alter (or destroy) the forests that are cut, but the forests that remain.

This spring the forest with the trillium at the top of Limestone Creek was logged as part of the China Left timber sale. I don't object to cutting a tree, but I want to tell you how ungraceful I feel the death of this forested community was. Where I walked through a carpet of herbs there is only slash, empty plastic bags, and five-foot deep gouges in the soil from dragging the trees up to the landing. Where the plants were a botanist's dream, there are already several non-native plants invading. Where the canopy filled 95% of the sky, there are now just a few trees per acre. And even yesterday, with cool autumn air, I was aware how hot that exposed ground would get on a summer day. All those herbs will get hot, maybe hanging on for a few years in a futile attempt to grow in an alien habitat.

This is how a community aged and died. And we all realize after reading this Common Ground issue that aging and dying is not so unusual. Only there is certainly little grace in the death of this forest. Certainly no respect. Certainly no justice. Certainly no love — for the forest, for the trees, or the young community of people down here below the forest
-Erik Jules.

OUT OF THE MASON JAR

I was only twenty–four when I came to Takilma, twenty–five years ago on October 12, with two small children. My children are now thirty and twenty–seven years old. Where did the time go? I still feel young in my heart and soul. It's my body that really fooled me! Years of moving rocks, dirt, and tree planting have caught up with my body. Sometimes I wonder what happened?

Some people the same age look just the same but some of us have changed a lot. I stand in front of the mirror with hands on wide hips, stare at my white hair and pot belly, I shake my head and smile saying "Well, you still got nice legs and everything is still working" and laugh. Kerry walks by, stops, looks at me and says "You're beautiful." I give myself a little lecture that it's being healthy that counts and being happy. Aging has taught me to give and to play (more LeShow coming soon) but what I love the most about aging is you get to experience history as it's happening in your lifetime.

You can listen to a group of some of us tell tales of the old days in Takilma (1970 on). I sometimes see old friends from the early Takilma days and remember how thin and young we were and what hair we had. What history we make. I see age more on some than others but with the same eyes and the same beautiful smiles and everyone still acts twenty–four! What lovely hearts and souls.

I have raised two wonderful people in the last twenty–five years and that is my history. Found my soul mate. Built a beautiful home with my mate. Carved totem poles. Sculptured walls and many other objects. Discovered sea kayaking. Aging is wonderful or should I say making history is wonderful and it takes time.

Truly, aging is about our history and not just the history of our bodies. I can't wait to be sitting around telling stories of Takilma when I'm in my later history time (90's)! I'm sure we'll all have a few. Enjoy your history time. -Sheila Mason

It's Relentless!
-Bill Haynes

PROCESS

Age is too big a concept to be contained in just three letters. I've certainly run the gamut from A to Z in one short lifetime. I think of my childhood. I can recognize that child, but would he recognize me?

My granma raised me. My parents were divorced and mom had to work. I was the only kid in my school with divorced parents. It was rare in those ancient times. Granma was devoted to me, the Pope, and F.D.R., in that order. When Roosevelt died she was sure that he had made a deathbed conversion. She couldn't imagine a heaven without him.

I could spot her in her old black and white checkered coat as she wandered the neighborhood looking for me when I was gone too long. Her coat was visible from a block away. Sometimes I would hide if I didn't want to go home yet. I would watch her small figure walk away. I knew her feet hurt her. Finally, overcome by guilt, I would hurry after her. The image of that old woman limping down the street in her old coat is one of the ghosts that I have carried with me throughout my life. Not all ghosts are malevolent.

As an Irish–Catholic boy life was simple, the future clear. I would finish high–school, enter a seminary, and become a priest. None of this happened.

At the end of the tenth grade I lied about my age and went into the National Guard. It sounded great. We would go off to camp for two weeks every summer, shoot guns, and get to drink beer. We went off to Korea instead.

Dreams of priesthood died, along with religion, one snowy night of that war. My friend Carlos and I lay in a snow-bank. He would scream now and then. His intestines pulsed between his fingers as he tried to hold them in. They were shiny in the weak light the searchlights reflected back from the clouds. He was trying to say something and I leaned closer. He wanted his mother.

That morning I pulled off the rosary that granma had put around my neck and hurled it out into a no–man's land of tangled wire and frozen Chinese boys. Boys who also died wanting their mothers. I no longer knew who or what God was, but I did know that he wasn't my friend.

A few weeks later it was Mother's Day. All of us had wired flowers and reassuring messages home. I thought of Carlos' mother standing in her doorway with a bunch of dying flowers in her hand. That woman whom I never met is another one of my ghosts.

The young boy who had viewed life as a progression to heaven no longer wanted God's salvation. He could have it. Our parish priest came to the house with all of the rationalizations that priests and ministers use to explain the existence of evil in a world ruled by a benevolent God. None of it justified that dying boy or that weeping woman. It all seemed absurd. An almighty being testing little insignificant creatures for worthiness? The all–knowing creator of the universe getting upset because little children played with themselves under the blankets? Give me a break.

I went to college. Like an unexpected ray of sun breaking through a gloomy winter sky the thoughts of people like Camus and Dostoyevsky dazzled me. Humans could be creators also. I heard Bach for the first time and realized that humans were capable of God–like work. This was not like listening to Teresa Brewer singing "How much is that Doggie in the window?" Art became my new religion.

The Vietnam war jolted me and many of my artist friends out of this self absorbed apolitical existence. The smell of burning babies clogged our nostrils. Now we were killing the mothers too. Once again religion dissolved into absurdity. What did art mean in the midst of all of this carnage?

Politics became a major topic of conversation in my Lower East Side loft. New concepts turned everything upside down. It was so simple; we only have to work together, consume less, share, and destroy the establishment. We didn't accomplish all of these goals.

Today I live here, in a place, in that ephemeral moment that we all share and call life. We've always been here. I have come the full circle, but not back to the egotistical immortality of the self that they call the soul.

Immortality was always here, beneath our feet. You only have to look at the composting debris of the forest floor to see this. Life never ends, it only changes. We are part of a process. I can live with that.   —Dog

"As a white candle
In a holy place,
So is the beauty
Of an aged face."
    -Joseph Campbell

SHEL'S SLANT...NOT YET DOWNHILL

Webster's defines age, or aging as "to show the effects or the characteristics of increasing age; to become mellow or mature." The last definition seems to be used more for cheese than people.

I'm lucky that I grew up in a Midwestern farm culture at a time when there were lots of old people in everyday life. Many of the dearest faces of my young life were old and wrinkled, and bodies were fat and lumpy, and I got to experience all that as beloved and familiar. Notice how much more segregated we all are now, how older people have their own spaces and aren't just part of everyone's daily life?

An amazing part of aging for me has been surprise. I'm surprised that I'm old. I noticed a couple of years ago, when I did my 50th birthday ritual, that a big inner part of me still thinks that I'm 26 and hasn't changed my plans for when I grow up. Where did the last 20 years go?

I notice constantly our cultural bias against aging. A young friend was very surprised when I told him that I was not complimented by being called a "young lady." Grown up women are called girls. People are being nice when they tell you how young you look. How **are** you supposed to look? You shouldn't be fat and round and comfortable like my grandma, I guess.

Karma. You see it in old people's faces. Especially old women. Bitterness, disappointment, refusal to let go of who you used to be. The body begins to reap the consequences of all the bashes, abuse, and lack of care. The whole life settles into the body.

Did you know that, when they studied the two populations in the world where people regularly live to be really old (120-145), the one element they found in common was the high esteem that age conferred? In both Ecuador and the Circassian Mountains, people look forward to getting older and older. They smoke tobacco and drink, by the way, and are physically active almost all their long lives. In this country, the focus of age seems to be Medicare and cable TV.

The scariest part about getting old for me is being old and poor and alone. When I see some of the old people around town who have nowhere to go, no resources, failing health, sad and frightened eyes, I find myself averting my eyes. Hey Paco! Get that retirement home for old hippies together, won't you?

Finally, I am happy to report that I am beginning to experience that ineffable release that comes when you don't really give a damn about what other people think. Not the way I used to do it; you know, hunched shoulders and a mean look and balled fists. Just, at the best of times, a mild curiosity and continuing along my way. It gets better, I think. I'm just starting this journey into the age of my life. Funny, it doesn't seem to be downhill yet.   -Shel Anderson

"Education is the best provision for old age"
    -Aristotle (384-322 BC)

AGING

Now, in the middle of my fiftieth year, I am aware of my body aging. It has been a decade since I experienced the cycle of weight loss and gain that characterized my early adulthood and now I remain in a state of mild overweight. My hairline has been marching slowly, relentlessly, away from my forehead. I am more careful about jumping when I dance, to avoid being sore for days afterward. I tire sooner at dances and have to sit out every third or fourth rock and roll dance. My desire for sex has not diminished as much as I thought it would, but the priority I place on satisfying my every sexual impulse has taken a giant step backwards, behind my desire for relatedness and compassion and safety. I am more interested in taking care of my body and keeping it healthy into old age. Recently I discovered how my practice of yoga can reverse the direction of many body problems I had started experiencing. Aging is not exactly what I thought it would be.

I find myself thinking about old age more and feel it nearer, like I feel the approach of winter in the turning of autumn leaves. I feel the cycle turning in me. When I shave my face, I see my father in the mirror. I have never looked so much like him. People tell me I look younger since I started shaving two months ago, but in my shaving mirror I see myself as my father's age, 76. I wonder how I will live in 2021, if I am still alive. I am getting more familiar with death.

Change has not slowed down for me though now I manifest it differently. I don't change lovers the way I used to. I now feel change in the way I want to relate to my lover and the way I conceive of myself as a lover. I don't find it as easy to dismiss contradictions in my behavior as temporary accommodations. I am more concerned with my integrity. I feel that major change is happening within me in preparation for a new phase of my life. I welcome change as much as I ever did. At 27, my first Saturn return brought major change in how I expressed my individuality and separateness. As my next cycle approaches, I am ready for change in how I express my relatedness. I am learning to see myself in "them". I am learning to accept my fear and weakness. I'm more likely to challenge internal limitations than external ones. I have more faith in will, and less in force. I feel like I've come to the end, the reductio ad absurdum, of some assumptions I've held since childhood about money, responsibility, and love.

I don't know where to end this story. I can't separate what's aging from what's me. I still sometimes see with the eyes of a child. I am happy to be aging in and with this community.   -Paco

PILGRIM'S WAY

We asked Agnes Pilgrim to share with us some of her history and her wisdom on the subject of aging.

In the beginning we were given the four bundles, the four Chiefs: Land, Air, Water, and Fire, to take care of them and to use them in moderation. I teach that way to my children. I feel that I am a bridge of understanding between the Indian world and the non-Indian world. I feel like I am a pendulum that swings from the Indian world into the non-Indian world. I can take the best of both worlds and walk in balance that way.

I am not into the ego trip but I want to set footprints in front of my grandchildren and great-grandchildren and the yet unborn so that when I am gone from this world and am in the spirit world I will leave those footprints. They will guide my children's children's children in time to come. No matter that I am crippled, I am certainly far from handicapped. My hands are injured but I still continue to keep occupied using them.

All of my life I was proud of who I was. From 1953 to 1977, the government had terminated us as a tribe. It was a frightening time. It was a floundering time for feeling and patience. For twenty-four years, we did not belong. They wanted us to be called Caucasians on our I.D. cards and I said "I refuse, I am an Indian." We finally got reinstated on Nov. 18th, 1977. What a beautiful day that was! We were finally recognized as a tribal people. We are Indians, we are Native Americans and a piece of the puzzle was back and it fit.

I think that, looking ahead, I still have a lot of things to do. If you want something you have to work for it. I think that has a lot to do with keeping your body joints functioning and agile. I am getting creaky now and I always want to believe, like my grandmother, that my body might shrivel up like a prune but my heart is going to stay young!

One of the things I believe is that you have to be determined, to accomplish tasks every day, to keep going, and try to set obtainable goals. For example, if my back is bothering me then I can do research while lying down. I can read some of the history of my people and still be working. If I am able to sit up a while then I have hobbies like beading, sewing, or writing. I try every day to accomplish something or finish something. I think that the durable part of life is wanting to live, wanting to obtain something in life to make your mark upon the world.

There have been terrible changes in our environment. We are moving too fast technically. The world is slowly getting destroyed and it hurts my heart to think what will be here seven generations ahead for our grandchildren's children. Even my great-grandchildren; when they are great-grandparents; what will they have here? This is what those two-leggeds should be trying to preserve. We have to put a stop to the destruction. Everything is off balance. There is a better way to take care of our Mother Earth.

This issue of Common Ground was put together by: Linda, Dog, Felicity, Jill, Laurie, Kerry, Rachel, Deb, Ina, and Cathy. Limited space excludes editorial rambling. Common Ground is printed on tree-free paper.

"GROW OLD ALONG WITH ME THE BEST IS YET TO BE."

These well-known lines were written by the famous poet Elizabeth Barrett Browning. There is much truth in the poem and yet there are often circumstances of life and personal attitudes that determine what happens in our "golden years." Were we raised in a home where love and laughter prevailed? Did we early in our life learn about the love of God and His Son, Jesus Christ? If we believe in them, we do not have to fear the end of life on this earth, because we know that "the best is yet to be."

Perhaps these blessings were not a part of your past years. However, it's not too late to make them a part of our present time. We read in the Bible in I Corinthians 13:13: "and now abide faith, hope, love, these three; but the greatest of these is love." Is love the by-word in our home? My family's love and concern for me is one of my greatest assets. Do we show real love to our children and grand children? How about our neighbors? Does our love spread to others in need?

I believe that one more thing has a great effect on our happiness and peace of mind. Is our mind filled with thoughts of the beautiful world that God has given us? Do we try to find some degree of contentment with our circumstances or do we stress the negative side of things?

Many years ago a very wise man said, "Rejoice! Let everyone see that you are unselfish and considerate in all you do." If you do this, you will experience God's peace, which is far more wonderful than the human mind can understand. His peace will keep your thoughts and your hearts quiet and at rest. Fix your thoughts on what is true and good and right. Think about things that are pure and lovely, and dwell on the fine good things in others. Think about all you can praise God for and be glad about. (Try this at night when you can't sleep!)

So these are some ways to find peace and joy. Let's try them so we can also say with the poet:

"Grow old along with me
The best is yet to be" *-Gertrude Meengs*

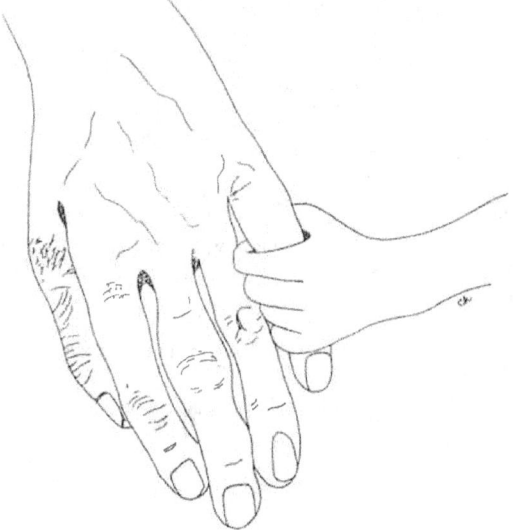

ETERNAL INSURANCE

"You mean I don't have to think about it anymore?" Ethel asked.

"That's right, Mam. You can put all that energy into something else now."

"Oh, my." Ethel's broad bottom hit the seat of the chair. "I feel so relieved."

She stood up again and grabbed the young man by the shoulders.

"You mean, no more planning and scraping, no more worrying about meeting that monthly payment?"

"No, Mam, you can put all that above, I mean behind you now. You can even sell what you have and...say, why not buy yourself a new wardrobe, or do some remodeling." He looked around the dark room, saw other dark rooms squatting beyond doorways.

Ethel didn't reply to the young man's suggestion. Instead she asked, "When does the first load take off?"

"Oh, let's see." The young man pulled a small red book from his shirt pocket. He licked his fingers and began thumbing through the pages. "Well, they figure sometime next year, say about May. So, by the time you go...well, that is, when you..."

Sitting at the table again, Ethel looked out the window. "When I go." she said softly.

The young man looked at the dark velvet curtains and smiled.

"Yes, Mam, you could do a whole lot around here with what you'll be saving."

"How much are the coffins?" Ethel asked.

"Coffins, Mam?"

"Yes, coffins. I want to know how much the coffins are. I'm sure they're specially built, aren't they, for this type of thing?"

"There's no coffins, Mam." A muscle jumped in his cheek.

"Well, then, how on earth do I get there? Is this some kind of scam?" Ethel glared at the young man.

"Uh, Mam, you get cremated."

Ethel slammed her fist down on the table top and stood up.

"You mean when I die they're gonna burn my ass down to fit into a capsule? Is that what you're saying?"

The muscle in his cheek jumped again. The young man pulled the contract out of a pocket deep inside his jacket and held it out to her.

"Yes, Mam, that's what happens. Now if you'll just sign right here, let's see, on this line here, your future will be secured."

"So what happens is they burn you up, right?" Ethel

looked at the young man. Her eyes poked and shoved their way into his own. Looking away, his eyes watered from the intensity of her stare.

"Yes, Mam, that's right."

He slid the contract towards Ethel's side of the table.

"Then they burn you up some more, right?" Ethel asked. "Get you down to just a teaspoonful of dust, RIGHT?"

"Oh, I think it's about a quarter-cupful, but, that's about right, Mam. Now if you'll just sign here."

"Then they pack you into a little capsule." said Ethel. Indignation made her body look larger.

"Yeah, yeah, that's right, Mam. Two inches long, five-eighths around. That's the size of it." His eyes darted beyond Ethel's to the door, then snapped back again.

Ethel narrowed her eyes together until the eyelashes formed a veil in front of her pupils. "You got another thought coming, Buster." she said quietly.

"Mam?"

"I said you got another thought coming."

"Well, Mam, uh, you...you think about it a few days and I'll drop back by." He started a side-shuffle towards the door.

Ethel's big body followed the young man. "So, you think you can come in here and sell me on a plan like that. Get the hell outta here! What kind of lady do you think I am?"

He hit the door, jerked it open, and ran out. His knees pumped a full four feet off the ground as he sped across the lawn. Ethel stood in the open doorway. Spittle seeped out the corners of her mouth. Her eyebrows danced and the fat under her first chin quivered.

She yelled after the young man. "If you think I'm gonna be some friggin' suppository up a rocket's ass just to be dumped out in space, you gotta be kidding!" Ethel stood and watched the man run down the street. Her voice cracked the quiet afternoon in the smooth neighborhood.

When the young man was out of sight she turned and waddled back inside the house. As she passed by, she flipped over the sign that hung on the front door. The sign swung back and forth on its chain. The lettering on the sign read: "Dixon's Freedom Mortuary." *-Doris Lavoris*

We would like to thank our community for their support and wild abandon at the very successful Halloween benefit. We profited both financially and spiritually. A big thanks to the band "Altered States" for their excellent performance; Wild River Brewing Company, Foris Vineyards, Coffee Heaven and IV Printing for their generous support. Party On!
-The Dome School

THE AGING OF A HOYA

The Hoya grows slowly. Its leathery leaves and vine–like tendrils take many years to mature. Eventually, with proper care, much love, and wishful thinking, the Hoya produces one of nature's most incredible flowers. Each flower is bold, yet delicate, and exudes a nectar sweeter than honey. This year, after twelve years of nurturing, my Hoya surprised me with about six blooms! Aging and blooming, plants and humans, I delight in seeing the similarities between us. Thank you sweet Hoya for your gift.   *-Gloria*

TWENTY SOMETHING

In response to her age, she says,
"Will I ever have grandchildren?"

The presence of the years
outlined by crows feet
assures her that it's time

Time to be a grandmother
time to demand her expectations
be addressed

Just yesterday
I swear she said,
"Don't rush into anything, you're still
young."

Yet she's rushing, with
the impulse of a teenager,
to satisfy a need only
she has.   *-Shanie*

ALEX

"You think it horrible that lust and rage
Should dance attention upon my old age;
They were not such a plague when I was young;
What else have I to spur me into song?"
     -William Butler Yeats (1865-1939)

I hate Britt

What a Bunch of Nits
Bands that need Donations
Instead get standing Ovations
But I have a Plan
Good as any Mans
I'll take my Spam
Right From the Can
I'll have curlers in my Hair
Sit in a tall lawn Chair
My husband will be There
Being such a Square
Belly hanging Out
He'll be the perfect Lout
People will shush Us
Then they will rush Us
Out to the Gate
Where we'll meet our Mates
There we'll maybe Litter
Just to see them Bitter
What a bunch of Twits
I hate Britt
          -Geraldine Davidson

TO MRS. SHEILA WHITEHEAD

I have thirty two grey hairs
I blame my mother

think about it
                 -Shanie

SPORTS

At first all of the players were older than me.
Then just some of them.
Next all of the coaches were older than me.
Then just some of them.
Now only the officials are older than me.
They used to look ancient.   *—Mike Hohm*

·7·

229

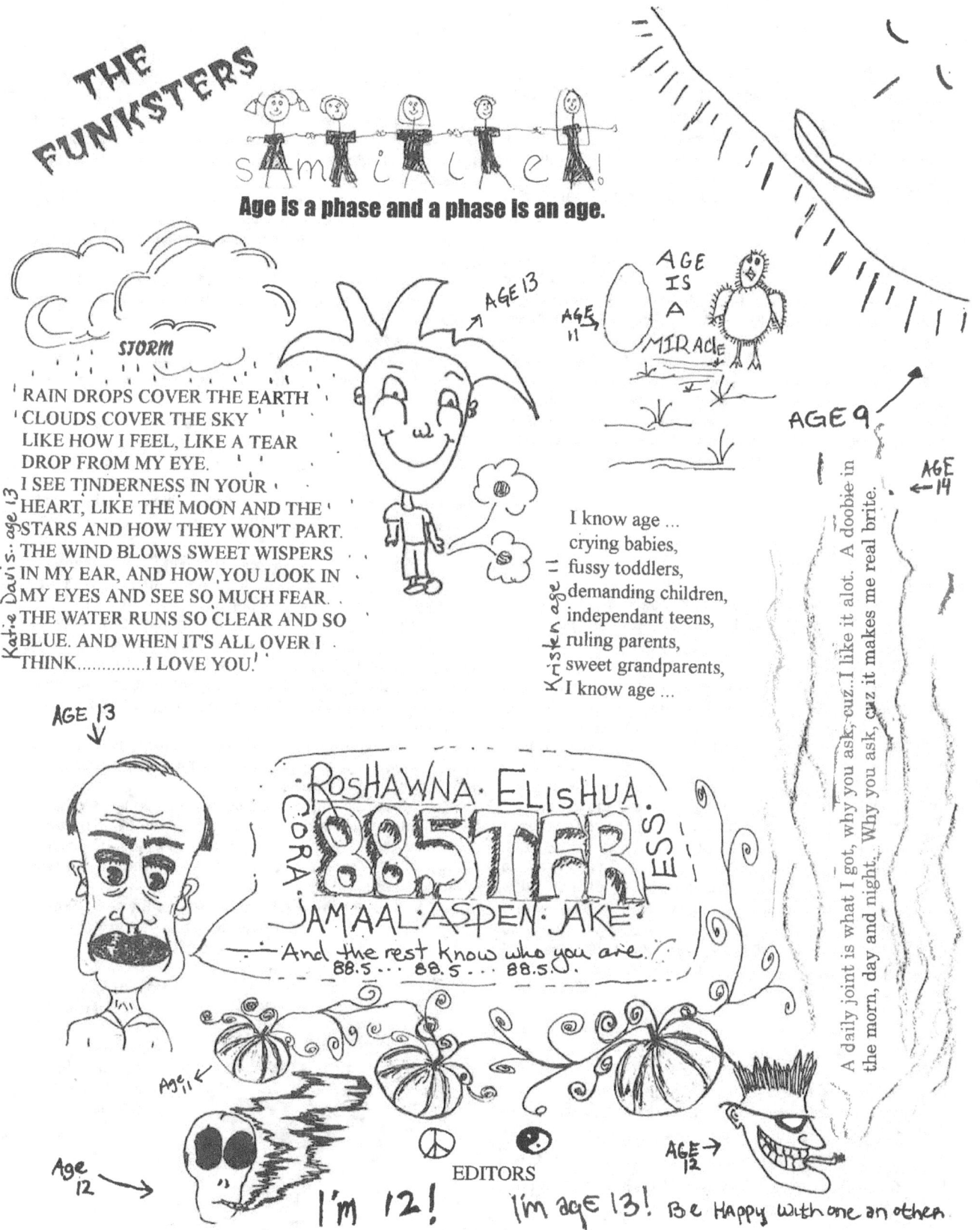

THE FUNKSTERS

sAmiilieA!

Age is a phase and a phase is an age.

STORM

RAIN DROPS COVER THE EARTH
CLOUDS COVER THE SKY
LIKE HOW I FEEL, LIKE A TEAR
DROP FROM MY EYE.
I SEE TINDERNESS IN YOUR
HEART, LIKE THE MOON AND THE
STARS AND HOW THEY WON'T PART.
THE WIND BLOWS SWEET WISPERS
IN MY EAR, AND HOW YOU LOOK IN
MY EYES AND SEE SO MUCH FEAR.
THE WATER RUNS SO CLEAR AND SO
BLUE. AND WHEN IT'S ALL OVER I
THINK.............I LOVE YOU!

Katie Davis.. age 13

AGE 13

AGE IS A MIRACLE

AGE 11

AGE 9

AGE 14

I know age ...
crying babies,
fussy toddlers,
demanding children,
independant teens,
ruling parents,
sweet grandparents,
I know age ...

Kristn age 11

A daily joint is what I got, why you ask..cuz..I like it alot.. A doobie in the morn, day and night.. Why you ask, cuz it makes me real brite.

AGE 13

ROSHAWNA · ELISHUA · CORA 88.5 TFR JAMAAL · ASPEN · JAKE TESS
And the rest know who you are.
88.5... 88.5... 88.5.

Age 11

Age 12

AGE 12

EDITORS
I'm 12!   I'm age 13! Be Happy with one an other.

Send your stories, drawings and thoughts to Common Ground, P.O. Box 2016, Cave Junction, Or. 97523 or
e-mail Clemshaw@cdsnet.net

LISTEN HERE!

We at 88.5 are creating an alternative to the F.C.C., the Free Communication Coalition. The Peoples F.C.C. would like to see community issues addressed and resolved at community levels. We hope to create a talent and resource pool of individuals who can provide the necessary expertise in their personal spectrums to establish micro-broadcasting as a fully functioning entity with the purpose to break the bureaucracy's strangle hold on the free flow of info, ideas, news, culture and art.

On Saturday Oct. 19, the Takilma Community Building once again became the commuity happin' spot as Free Radio Takilma 88.5, had its first benefit since broadcasting began four weeks ago. A broad spectrum of individuals attended the gathering of food, music and dance. A crowd of 100-150 came, saw and conjured. A special thanks to all the bakers, musicians and those who kicked down some much needed dinero for the cause. On a scale of 1-10, the Radio Man gives it a Takilma style 10+. The funds will go for building, heat and equipment upscales. 88.5 is reason to stay home.

-RadiO

Dear Common Ground,

Well once again the holiday season is upon us, and due to our brain-washed minds we welcome it with open arms. Hallmark tells us to, after all, and since they're a corporation THEY MUST BE RIGHT.

Thanksgiving is the murderous event that plays upon my mind. That we numbly celebrate year after year, like programmed robots. Our "trusted" government, with the help of Hallmark, has taken this event (a masssacre of hundreds of natives, not to mention the innocent animals as well which some how got wrapped up in this mess) and have transformed it into a family event of togetherness and thanks.

Though it's too late to right the wrong, we can still make the conscious choice to not participate in this cornpone scam, which is just another Government cover up. Take this day to educate both yourselves and others, stop the destruction of the earth, free the animals, shut down the corporations or if you have been doing this all year then ok take the day off and enjoy what it is you want to save. This should be a day about asking forgiveness not about giving thanks. -Kim Marks

The theme of issue # 24 is "Parents and Children," facilitated by Rachel Goodman and Deborah Murphy. Children and parents are encouraged to submit their thoughts about this relationship, whether past, present or future. Submissions are due Dec. 3.

DEADLINE ON AGING AND OTHER THOUGHTS
(Dedicated to my favorite 90-year old, Nola Jay.)

I've always had a terrible time with deadlines. If your reading this, it means I just barely made deadline for this newsletter. Might there be a deadline on aging? It's all how you look at it.

With feet wide apart, I like to bend over and put my head between my legs, look at things from that angle to gain a different perspective. If I look at the world that way, why not aging?

Thus 60 (the age I become this winter). 60=09?

My mom always said I'd be late for three major events in my life:
    —graduation(I was)
    —my wedding(I was)
and I forget what the third was. D'ya s'pose she meant death?

Little difference between the heavily made-up woman with sagging face and wrinkles, desperately dyeing or bleaching her hair, and the man who says with every effort he makes, be it stair climbing or _____, "Boy, I'm getting to be an old man." or, "I'm too old for this any more." The one is in denial, the other so fixated on aging that his prophecy will be rapidly fulfilled.

Reaction to my dismay on looking in the mirror at new facial sags: What about that Super Glue, the stuff that can make your fingers stick together? Would that help?

What helps is acknowledging the amazing trade-off possible in the so-called aging process, taking yourself less seriously, willing to be who you really are (or if you're not sure, not worrying about it), and recognizing at last the same old destructive patterns when they start to rear up again. That priceless, " ah ha!"

One thing is certain, whatever one's habits, tendencies, attitudes now, they only become more entrenched with age. Moral: Get it together, now!

"Keep moving!" I've told my older dance students. Movement punctuated by moments of utter stillness (and I don't mean sleep) — thereby achieving inner motion, enabling energy, wonder, spontaneity, and awareness (both of the field and of the self).

"In our wonder, we're closer to the truth than in our answers" —John Robins

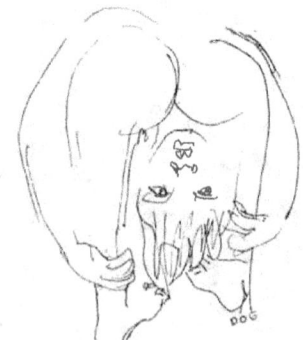

-ACCEPTANCE
    -BALANCE
        -GRACE

– Isn't there a lovely soft–C sound to all three? Time to learn our ABGs .
-Terry Cain

PRISON THREAT GROWS

The Illinois Valley has been shoved another ominous step closer to becoming a prison dominated community. The Oregon Department of Corrections has nominated the Martin Dairy site (off Rockydale Road), along with approximately 10 other sites across the state, to house one of 6 new medium security prisons. The nominations now go to a five-person Siting Authority panel that will assess the sites and rank them. The ranked list will reach the Governor's desk by early December and he will make the final decision before the Christmas holiday.

While the situation appears bleak, there are some solid reasons for optimism. First of all, just what are our odds? There is convincing evidence that the state will place a prison in southern Oregon. The Martin Dairy site is only one of four southern Oregon sites nominated by the ODOC. Two sites are in the Medford area and one in Klamath Falls. While the initial cost of land is likely to be less, both here and in K Falls, lower operating costs make the two Medford area sites more cost effective in the long run.

Secondly, Citizens for a Livable Illinois Valley (CLIV) has built a strong case showing that ODOC has failed to follow the process mandated by the Super Siting bill (HB 2214). CLIV has made the case that the Martin Dairy site fails to satisfy at least two of the mandatory siting criteria established under HB 2214. CLIV is currently searching for effective legal counsel to help refine these arguments should an appeal to the Oregon Supreme Court be necessary.

Third, one of the five members of the Siting Authority panel is Josephine County District Attorney Tim Thompson. Thompson is well aware of the widespread concern being voiced around the county. He has had close exposure to the reasoned arguments being put forth by CLIV and individual residents throughout the county. By ensuring that the siting process is in fact following HB 2214 guidelines Thompson will be protecting our community, which he represents.

So what can the people of the valley do to help stop this insanity? The only public hearing scheduled for our community by the Siting Authority will be held Wednesday, November 13, 7:00 p.m. at the IV High School. We aim to fill the school to overflowing with our presence and No Prison stickers. Our objective is to turn out 1000 people for this hearing.

Meanwhile if you haven't already written Governor Kitzhaber and Tim Thompson, do it now! Mention the water issue and the devastating impact this prison will have on our fisheries. Let them know that our schools, roads, and clinic will be devastated by this prison. If this issue is about saving a place very dear to you, if it is about protecting your home, don't wait any longer. Help is needed to raise funding for attorney fees and to ensure a massive turn-out for the Nov. 13 hearing. Do it now- before it's too late !!!!!

For info. call CLIV @592-3908. Donations can be made out to Rockydale Neighborhood Assoc., POB 966, CJ,OR.

NOW OR NEVER!

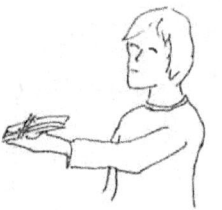

We received this letter from Robert Korfhage, BLM Area Manager, addressed to the Takilma Watershed Council:

Dear Friends,

Thanks to everyone who attended the coordination meeting in Cave Junction on September 20th. I thought the meeting was excellent. I am confident we can work together on projects and issues concerning public lands in the Takilma area.

I wanted to follow up on our discussion about the proposed Waldo Thin Timber Sale. The proposed timber sale has been eliminated from our 1997 timber sale plan. As a result of our scoping process, part of which involved the public meeting in Takilma, I made the decision to defer future timber management activities until a more thorough ecological evaluation of the watershed was completed. I will be asking the Illinois Valley Stewardship Team, with you assistance, to develop a "mini" watershed analysis for the East Fork drainage. Using the analysis, I will ask them to develop some alternatives and make a recommendation regarding future forest management in the East Fork drainage. We will not be initiating any future timber harvest planning until this process has been completed.

I have also notified my staff about early notification of field work in the Takilma area. We will do our best to keep you informed when inventories, projects, or other field work is taking place.

88.5 Weekly Schedule

	Sunday	Monday	Tuesday	Wednesday	Thursday	Friday	Saturday
8am-noon	Devotional Hour (7:00-8:00) The Dead w/Prankster	On the bench w/ The Coach	Aunt Ruby	The Doctor	Sherrie Lew	Good Morning Takilma w/Newm	Marco Polo
noon-2pm	Nick at noon or Goldilocks or Happy Camper	Takilma District	Newm at Noon	Newm at Noon	Takilma District	The Phil & Bill Show	Lisa Roots, Rock & Reggae
2pm-4pm		Pearl Drops Reality Check	Pearl Drops Reality Check	Pearl Drops Reality Check	Pearl Drops Reality Check	Pearl Drops Reality Check	
4pm-6pm	Doris Lavoris	Cesar y Gabriella	Club Cory	Lacy & The Energies	Ross Welcome or River Rox	The 'E' Man or Happy Camper	The 'E' Man
6pm-closing	Newm Fool	Mr. Tracy or Tri	Live or Else w/JJ	River Rox or Lunatic Fringe	Bird's Eye View	Hemp	Aspen (8:00)

SUBSCRIBE NOW!

A 1 year subscription is only................................$10____

A 1 year subscription and a Common Ground
   T-shirt (block-printed by Fools)...................$25 ___

Takilma Common Ground
P.O. Box 2016
Cave Junction, OR

BULK RATE
U.S. POSTAGE
·PAID·
CAVE JUNCTION
OR 97523
PERMIT #16

"The Aging of Aquarius"

GRANMA!! GRANPA!!

Phil Frank

In Our Humble Opinion...

#26 The Vindictive Justice Constitutional Amendment. This is another get-tough-on criminals initiative. We are appalled by people who kill or maim for fun or thrills, but should we make changes in our Constitution which affect us all. on the basis of our reaction to a few people? **VOTE NO!**

#30 The State pays the cost of State Mandated Programs Constitutional Amendment. This measure sounds reasonable but it will absolve local government from the joint responsibility it holds for educating its children, providing for health care, or protecting Oregon's environment and natural resources. If this passes, we all lose. If this measure been in place five years ago, Josephine County youngsters would still be without kindergarten. For responsible local government, **VOTE NO!**

#31 The Obscenity Constitutional Amendment. In regards to free speech issues, Oregon's Constitution is darn-right modern. It says that folks have the right to speak, write, or print freely on any subject. Period. This measure would take us to a standard that wavers according to the political whims aof the day. Do you want Haugen or Whiting setting the standard? How about Tefteller? **VOTE NO!**

#34 The Killing Bear & Cougar Cruelly Initiative. There is nothing sporting about baiting and hounding bears and cougars. It is cruel. In 1994, we voted to outlaw these practices. There are no good reasons to change our minds now. Opposed- Humane Societies, SPCA's, enviros and ethical hunters. **VOTE NO!**

#36 - Raising the Minimum Wage. The arguments against this measure are that raising the minimum wage will fuel inflation & cause lay-offs by small businesses. A comparison study done between NJ and Pa. after Jersey raised its minimum wage found more job creation occurring in Jersey. We raised the minimum wage in 1990. There was no proportionate increase in inflation. The minimum wage debate is truly a question of fundamental philosophy. Is it right for one person to work hard 40 hours a week and still be in poverty while a corporate CEO makes $2-3,000\hour? **VOTE YES!**

#37 The New and Improved Bottle Bill. This is a no-brainer. Vote with the statistics- 93% of deposit bottles get recycled as opposed to 28% of the non-deposit bottles.. **VOTE YES!**

#38 The Clean Streams Initiative. The bottom line is that salmon, and steelhead populations have taken a nose-dive in almost every Oregon river. Measure 38 is not Draconian. It gives land owners until 2002 to get their cow manure out of our rivers. It gives preference in obtaining funds to people required to comply & it allows citizen law suits if the agencies refuse to enforce the laws. In favor- the fishing organizations, the enviros, the tribes and some doctors. The anti's are a who's who list of water abusers. **VOTE YES!**

#39 The Health Care Freedom Constitutional Amendment requires insurance companies to cover all categories of licensed health care including chiropracters, naturopaths, acupuncturists and massage therapists. We'd rather it not amend the Constitution but **VOTE YES!**

#40 The Expanding Police Power Constitutional Amendment. This is especially bad. It undercuts everyone's rights to privacy, protection from unlawful police scrutiny, right to bail, and would increase the need to spend limited revenues on more prisons and detention centers. **VOTE NO!**

#42 The Additional School Testing Constitutional Amendment. With today's limited resources an expenditure of over $5 million to increase student testing must be carefully weighed. Already the state of Oregon mandates testing students in grades 3, 5, 8, 10, and 12. Will additional testing improve the education of our kids. It seems unlikely. Oregon Education Association & PTA agree, **VOTE NO!**

#44: The Tobacco Tax Initiative This is a regressive tax, which means that poor people will pay a higher percentage of their income than rich people. But it is a consumption tax. and it benefits the Oregon Health Plan which benefits poor people. **VOTE YES!**

#46 The Non-voters Constitutional Amendment. This measure would grant non-voters, more voice in their community than those who actually care and are involved in local activities. Democracy requires participation. Those seeking to discourage participation hope this passes. **VOTE NO!**

#47 The Next Tax Reduction Constitutional Amendment. This measure would reduce and limit property taxes, limit local revenues & replace fees. Who loses if this measure passes? All gov't services- schools, public safety, parks, programs for clean water, safe food, the Oregon Health plan; essentially all the tax-supported services that benefit most of us. **VOTE NO!**

1996 Voting Guide

This voters guide has been put together and written by Barry, Shel, Dave, Barbara & Rachel. We invite you to take this with you on election day. We hope it helps. We join with other progressive groups in urging you to **NOT** lightly amend the Oregon Constitution. We have therefore recommended yes votes only on 2 constitutional amendments.

All state laws are measured against the constitution, which should continue to be the broad framework amended only after careful thought and crafting of language. Some of these initiatives would put very bad laws into our Constitution, where their effect will be even greater. Look at Measure 11; people voted for a get-tough-on-crime law and now it requires state resources urgently needed elsewhere to be spent on prisons. Our collective voice is needed so please remember to vote. **Good luck and good voting!**

Ballot Measures

 # 26 NO *Constitutional Amendment*- - Changes the justice system from reform to vindictive justice.

 # 27 NO *Constitutional Amendment*- - Requires legislative action for agency rules to remain in effect.

 # 28 YES *Constitutional Amendment*- Expands eligibility for veterans' home loans.

 # 29 NO *Constitutional Amendment*- Sets a time-frame for the replacing the governor's appointees.

 # 30 NO *Constitutional Amendment*- Requires state to pay for programs it mandates.

 # 31 NO *Constitutional Amendment*- Would trample our free speech protections.

 # 32 NO $375 million for light rail, $375 million for roads.

 # 33 NO *Constitutional Amendment*- Restricts legislature from changing or correcting mistakes passed by voters in past initiative measures.

 # 34 NO Save cougars and bears from dogs!!!

 # 35 NO Limits doctors and clinics ability to be paid.

 # 36 YES Raises the minimum wage to almost a live-able wage.

 # 37 YES Expands the bottle bill. It's about time!

 # 38 YES Prohibits live stock from certain polluted waters. Allows for citizen law suits.

 # 39 YES *Constitutional Amendment*- Expands health insurance to include alternative providers.

 # 40 NO *Constitutional Amendment*- Expands the already intrusive police powers.

 # 41 NO *Constitutional Amendment*- Mandates how public employees' earnings are expressed.

 # 42 NO *Constitutional Amendment*- Requires more school testing. Not necessary.

 # 43 YES Amends collective bargaining law for police and firefighters.

 # 44 YES Uses cigarrette tax to fund Oregon Health Plan. No ifs, ands or butts.

 # 45 NO *Constitutional Amendment*- Raises retirement age of pub. employees to 65.

 # 46 NO Counts non-voters as "no" votes on tax measures.

 # 47 NO *Constitutional Amendment*-Cuts taxes, destroys schools, ends local control.

 # 48 NO *Constitutional Amendment*- Instructs legislators to support congressional term limits.

Commissioners & Local measures

Position 2- Laird Funk... do not forget to darken the circle and **write in** his name.
Position 3- Jim Brock
I.V.Soil and water- write in Erwin Sawall
17.58 YES Funds the 4-H Extension Service.
17.59 NO Another unconstitutional measure by the Paul Walters gang to gum-up the works.

State and Federal races

Most of us will vote **against** the Smith Brothers and for Bruggiere and Mike Dugan. Some of us will vote for Ralph Nader. However, if you are looking for fundamental change, you might want to look at the platform of the Socialist Party. It speaks more to our long term needs than the others.

TAKILMA COMMON SOLSTICE GROUND

IT TAKES A VILLAGE TO RAISE A CHILD AND TODAY IT'S YOUR TURN!

ISSUE # 25
DEC-JAN 96/97

INVASION OF THE TEENAGE MUTANT BABY SNATCHERS

Many of us are watching a metamorphosis. Just yesterday, a dependent, crying baby needed us and us only. A chubby little hand trustingly took ours. A child whined for bedtime stories and reverently listened to our answers to their endless questions.

Just when we had absorbed that role, adolescence changed it. The demands became different and accelerated. Soccer shoes, soccer camps. Rides to "away" games, their own car. A far cry from cute little books and carefully doled out shopping trips. Huge new people have appeared in our children's rooms. Yes, our kids are growing up. And along with the increase in complication and expense comes an apparent lack of love and appreciation of their parents. We bonded with them as we slaved to change their diapers and provide them with their own rooms. Suddenly the closeness seems one-sided. After all, they rarely obey us anymore, and all our once venerated instruction is now supposed to be wrong, stupid, irrelevant.

Many parents feel frustrated or even abused by the offspring they love and are still responsible for. If the parents are split up, it often seems a good time for the child to live with the other parent. After all, it certainly seems like he/she doesn't love us anymore. The constant arguments are hard to take, it takes more energy to get chores done than to do them yourself, the kid's never home anyway... But don't throw away your mutating, gangling, junk-food-eating baby just yet. They are just in an essential process of separation. They have to do it, and so did we. For those who resist this scenario as much as I do, it's good to think about our own growing up.

Remember those hopelessly boring parents who didn't understand you? We, of course, are totally different. We offer our kids an atmosphere of freedom and enlightenment.

But that doesn't seem to alter the basic process of adolescence. Kids have to separate from the people they're closest to (still us) so that they can learn who they are. We would have had to do that even if our parents had been ideal, and our kids have to do it no matter how groovy we are. Some kids separate more gracefully than others, but it really is the same thing we went through. It's rough, it's awkward and it can be heartbreaking, but it does come to an end. There are even moments when many of us find that we really do have good relationships with our children. We sowed communication and attention when they were small, and we still sometimes reap a sweet moment of connection amid the chaos.

What kids seem to need most at this very obnoxious stage is unconditional love. It is not a time for parents to stand on their egos and act defensively or feel neglected. It is a time to be very fair and adult, not to respond to their energy by regressing. While this sensitive time is bringing out our personal insecurities, the teenager is asking for an invincible wall, for freedom, for restrictions, for implicit understanding. As our own Linda Hoback says, "Don't miss this opportunity for dialogue." Short of the parent spy network, it's the only way to get a clue about what they're actually doing.

My hope is that, as parents reflect on their own metamorphosis, they won't resent their kids' as much. It's not exactly why any of us decided to have children, but apparently it comes with the territory. Remember, while all those innocent parents of 5 year-olds are living through the teenage years, you will have gained adult friends. They probably won't hold your hand to cross the street or beg for bedtime stories, but their presence will treat you to a new version of the rewards of parenting - and they'll enjoy terrifying you with stories of what they were really doing when they were teenagers.

-Rachel Goodman

236

ON FAMILY VALUES - CAMPAIGN '96

Sure, I heard the rhetoric, even way out in
Silver Lake, I heard Bob Dole, outspoken over
radio waves:
I SAY IT TAKES A FAMILY, he roared.
As if there are two sides.
So, who does it take to raise a child?
 A family? A village?

It's a false dilemma.
It begs the question -
to what extent does a child raise himself?
How much is ordained by
simple genetics or hallowed destiny
How much depends on culture?
How much depends on you?

Sure, times have changed, the
engines of mass media crank
My son is barrelling down the superhighway
still, he gets the lens from which he views the world
from me
There are many ways his core values mirror mine
He observes every aspect of my integrity
There are beliefs he does not question,
 because I hold them so dear.

I understand how you feel,
Mr. Republican
I don't want no government raising
my child.
"The Man" coming down on
radical thought, cloning our children in public
school, shoveling politically correct
bullshit of any stripe into their
growing minds
I remain leery of centralized power,

No, I do not want Jesse Helms raising my child
Sure, I have some libertarian instincts.
Discipline über alles

Rugged individualism
What I do is none of your damn business
I take care of my own.

So, I do understand, Mr. Republican
You are a hypocrite.
People are flawed, Mr. Republican,
You are flawed.
You may have a child you don't know about,
maybe you stuck it into someone, maybe she
had an abortion, maybe you have left your
child for your wife to raise,
maybe you are rich, but your spirit
is bankrupt, your children inherit
a foul legacy.

Who is going to pick up the pieces
When lives get fragmented? Who else but the
village.
I applaud the tireless counselors who promote
self- esteem in children battered by
circumstance. The coach who promotes self
respect, striving for the best, grace in defeat.
The musician who proudly leads the
community band. The butcher, the baker, the candle-
stick maker - The village.

It is a false dilemma! It shows your lack of
character, Mr Republican, even to suggest the
debate. You slam Hilary because you hate
liberals. You discredit her with sleight of hand
and I ain't buying it.
We are all in this together.
We cannot waste our energies
fighting biblical battles
over and over
fighting over false choices.
We are all in this together
let's live like it.

-Rochelle Desser, Nov 96

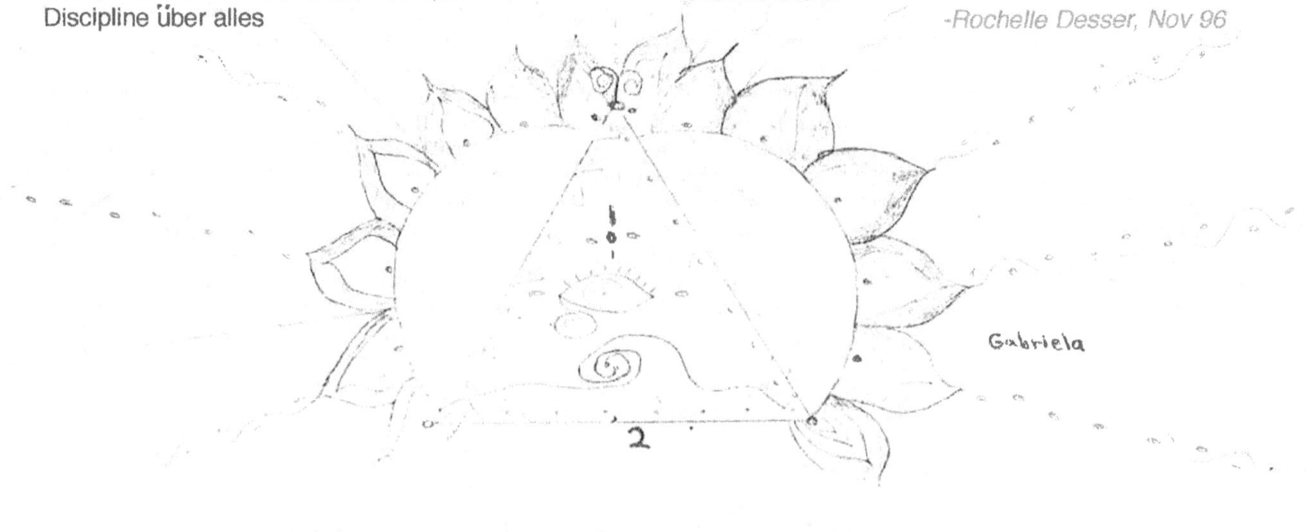

Gabriela

2

HERE COME THE BRIDES

Mike Hohm and Geraldine Davidson are pleased to announce the wedding of their eldest daughter, Chavi Hohm, on Saturday, October 26, 1996.

Chavi is currently residing in Seattle, Washington, and is employed as a professional fundraiser for non–profit corporations. Chavi wore a full length cream colored backless gown, with a celery scarf of considerable length.

The bride is Mara Collins from Sweet Home, Oregon. A graduate of Sweet Home High, she is currently employed with Washington Mutual Bank as a data entry specialist. Mara wore her deceased father's tuxedo, with silver bow tie and matching cummerbund.

Ceremonies were provided by Christine Pulver, a one–time Bible school friend of Mara's. Ms. Pulver is an Epis-copalian minister. Accordion music by Enid Gaof of Tucson, Arizona made it a lively event, as you can well imagine. The theme was Bedouin Carnival. The brides were registered at Chicken Soup Brigade Second Hand Store, very upscale, I assure you. The ceremony took place in Volunteer Park at 10:00 A.M, followed by a reception at the Wood Center, 7:00 P.M.

Chavi assured her daddy that he would be surrounded, no inundated, by healthy and confident heterosexual males, while he cooked the ceremonial Hohm turkey. There were sports galore from the television.

Mummy Geraldine attended to Grandmama Mayberry, joining us from Sacramento, California, who, I might add, was shamed into attending this ceremony by none other than Aunt Elaine, who pointed out to her that she would cross burning sands, scale mountains, to attend her elder daughter's wedding to her live–in electrician, good rent deal in San Fran-cisco, boyfriend, if the occasion should ever arise, that is.

A reception for the newlyweds took place at the Hohm residence.   -Geraldine Davidson

DOIN' THE DANCE

Nine years ago I became a mother, the most won-derful and most challenging role of my life, thus far. I will al-ways be indebted to the women who came to my son, Trevor's, birth. They supported me, rubbed my back, and breathed with me.

Trevor came into this world, in my bed, in a room full of love and caring. Within hours my Mom and Dad were there, then friends and neighbors.

I remember it all so clearly. It was a warm and sunny day and I felt magnificent. I glowed, bursting with life. My arms and legs had gotten thinner and thinner as my belly burgeoned with baby.

It was to be a girl, of course. How could I birth a male? It seemed incomprehensible. I was to birth a daugh-ter, like my mother and grandmother before me, yet there HE was! I saw that little penis and exclaimed in shock, "Oh my God, it's a boy!" And visions of purple velvet dresses danced away...

I changed in one split second from being the child to being the parent, with all the ecstasy and exasperation that that entails.

It has meant so many changes, mostly good ones, sometimes hard ones. It is tricky to be the parent, instead of the child, to have to look ahead and try to see what might be best in the long term.

It has meant being the one up in the middle of the night with a child that could hardly breathe, a truly terrifying experience. It has meant snuggling in bed with a favorite tale... what greater joy?

My son has also shown me how to be a child again as well, to play, to pretend, to notice the beauty in the small-est of things.

His discoveries and wonder have made me see again as we dance this delicate dance of love between parent and child.   - Deborah Colette Murphy

Editors' note: When asked by a CG reporter if he had been surrounded by healthy, confident, heterosexual males as he stuffed the bird, Daddy Hohm said, "I don't know if they were heterosexual. They were males." Upon further ques-tioning he also revealed, "They seemed healthy."

238

ANOTHER TAKILMA STORY

Dear Common Ground,

I'm sitting here in the little town of Rabinal, in the Department of Baja Verapaz, Guatemala. I just finished issue #20 of Common Ground and I'm thinking about how I first came to Takilma and wondering if I want to tell that story. It was not a totally blissful meeting - pain, joy and love were inextricably mixed, and something is always lost when the heart attempts to explain itself on paper.

During the winter of 1973, I was traveling with my lover, Bruce Galbraith. I was 29, he was 17, and my son Asa was 5 - all three of us born under the sign of the monkey. It was an amazing six months. While we were camping in San Blas in our '68 VW van, we met Doug and Julie with whom we shared certain adventures, and we became friends. When we parted, they gave us their address on Rockydale Rd. outside of Cave Junction, Oregon, and we made a solemn promise to visit the next summer.

After our crazy Mexican holiday, I found myself pregnant with Billie Rose and working in a hippie-operated leather coat factory in San Francisco. One long holiday weekend, Bruce, Asa and I decided to hitchhike up to Oregon to visit Doug and Julie. We found them on the bank of the Illinois River, naked and smoking pot on their illegal mining claim. We stayed a few days. I wasn't much impressed, but Bruce was. He wanted to live in the country. I was happy with San Francisco, but I thought maybe Stinson Beach was a good compromise. However, it was almost impossible to find a house, and the rents were astronomical. We finally found a vacancy, but an hour before our interview with the landlord Bruce dropped five hits of windowpane, and for some reason we didn't get the house.

Bruce went back up to Oregon with Asa, while I continued to work and look for a house in San Francisco. As far as I know, Bruce had a great summer staying stoned and drunk (and becoming known as "Lefty" in the process). Julie looked out for Asa when she was able to, until September when he joined me in San Francisco. As winter approached, I just got bigger and bigger, and still I couldn't find a place to live. Half the house I was staying in burnt down and my friend needed my room back. It was October, and Asa and I were sleeping on a mattress on the floor of a friend's enclosed, glass-walled back porch. We were feeling cold and lost. I was seven months pregnant and homeless. Lefty kept calling and writing - you have a home here, I want you here. Finally I gave in. Although moving to Oregon in winter seemed foolhardy, we packed up and went - what was our choice?

We arrived on Rockydale Road in a rainstorm two weeks before Thanksgiving. When we arrived, we were told that two Takilma guys had been found decapitated across the road from our land the week before. It didn't feel auspicious.

And so began my schizophrenic relationship with Takilma. I made friends immediately with folks at the Takilma People's Clinic. The people who delivered my baby on a cold January morning in 1975 are still good friends today. Yet I lived with someone whose life was absorbed by the drugs and alcohol that finally killed him last November (not a totally original ending for some Takilma residents).

I loved my clinic friends and often stayed with them at the Magic Forest Farm when things got tough at home. I owe my career in medical administration to my start as part-time receptionist, billing clerk and midwife assistant at the Clinic.

I never became a full-time Takilma resident, however. Though I was involved in Greenside Up, the Dome School, the buying club and the Clinic, I always kept a certain distance, finally moving to Ashland ten years ago. And yet, part of my heart is there still.

When my friend Kim sends me Common Ground here in Guatemala, where I'm working for the Peace Corps, I sit down with it immediately and read each page, hungry to hear news of old friends. I am still somehow connected. I have had welcome dreams of being at Takilma parties and talking to friends. I think love is the connection.

I always wonder if my path will meet again with yours in Takilma. Who knows? Although my story looks like a linear progression as it's written, there are wheels within wheels - an infinity of stories taking off from this one - and the wheels are still turning.

Con much carino,
Leslie Van Gelder
Cuerpo De Paz
Rabinal, Baja Verapaz
Guatemala, Central America

FOREVER

Two different magnets,
That come together and separate,
Different in looks,
Different in shapes,
But still alike in many ways.
You and me,
Me and you,
That's who we are,
That's who we'll always be.

-Tess Anawalt

THE KEY TO LIFE

The key opens the door to the side of the world.
The world is made for us.
We need to take care of the world, so we can be happy and have a better life.

-Shanti Birmingham

4

FATHERHOOD

For me, fatherhood could only be a hands-on experience, guided by the values of a more open and just world. So much for chasing the full time career while mom suffered from severe burnout. Fatherhood is a long and winding path, each successive turn providing unseen perspective. So much for the preconceived notions. Fatherhood has taught me to appreciate the simplicity of spontaneous play and interaction, for these are the truly special times. So much for planning "quality time".

From these eyes, the lines of distinction between the various relationships; friends, spouses, or parent-child have always been somewhat blurred. Certain fundamental values are essential to every loving relationship. Establishing open communications is more important than enforcing authority. Responsibility and growth is encouraged even if it means more independence from me. Respect is derived from my actions, not my age or gender.

Unfortunately, the ego provides a serious stumbling block to maintaining these values. Fatherhood has not been as easy as I thought it would be. When my kids were younger I used to say to Diane, "I'm not worried about teaching them the b.s. they'll need to know in the real world. They'll get plenty of that when they're in it!"

Still, the influence of the real world has blown me away at times. While I always thought the teen years would be relatively easy, often it feels as if the "real world" has shown my daughter how to interact with a generic parent that I can't even relate to! Likewise, I sometimes catch myself imagining that generic teen instead of the daughter I have spent so many wonderful years with.

While the values that form the foundation of a healthy, loving parent-child relationship are similar to other types of relationships, the challenges are truly more awesome. We cannot divorce our children, we cannot walk away from them. Parenthood is not for everybody, and I think we need to question our assumptions that it's an experience everyone should have.

Fatherhood has given me so much in my life. It is truly beyond verbal expression. Will my kids and I establish lines of communication that go beyond the confines of our generic parent-teen culture? I hope so. Meanwhile, every time I reflect on these two young people Diane and I have raised, I can't help but let those joyful tears flow. Yes, I am a very proud dad.

There once was a princess who had a very mean dad. She always had to work for her sisters. Whenever she had free time, she would go for a walk and visit her animal friends. One day, she went for a walk and got lost in the forest. She had to walk 25 miles to get to the highway. Since she had nowhere to go, she had to hitchhike. Then someone in a black car pulled over and said, "Do you need a ride?" And she said, "I could sure use one." So she got in the car and said, "I need to go to the castle 25 miles down the road." So he took her to the castle, and when she got there, everyone was happy to see her and she never had to work for them again.   -Nina and Shanti

YOSEMITE CLIFFNIGHT

Granite wall to heaven
Soaring out of view
Mingling with the stars
She reaches out to you

Bared breast of Lady Earth
Stripped of her green gown
Nude rock in glow of moon
Gently lays you down

Hands caress ancient stone
With joyous lover's feel
Lips touch mineral smoothness
Seduced by earth appeal

Lying against each other
Energy flows between
Kindred spirits wait for dawn
Forever felt, but never seen

-Tom Ness

WHEN I'M READY

Parents and their children, or is it children and their parents? Perspective and experience continually alter our lens from which we view such relationships. Bottom line, we have all been children. Many of us still are. All of us have parents in one form or another. At the least opportune moments, a mother will and slobber all over you. A father constantly creating projects which are always an obstacle to what is most important, anything besides chores! Some of us are lucky enough to have sets of parents. If you get bored with one set, there is always the other to keep you occupied. Some of our parents are totally absentee. In that case, you might have one parent. Single parenting is a difficult job, but being only parent and child you become a very cohesive unit.

Only a select few of us are allowed the opportunity to become parents. How well we function in this role is another subject altogether, but the connection between us is undeniable. As children, we believe there is a certain glory or attained status in becoming a parent. Most parents will tell you that to some extent this is true, but reality always differs from the ideal. I have never had the opportunity to change a foul diaper full of fecal matter nor experienced the agony of continually reminding my child to keep the porch stocked with wood! Reality is so harsh sometimes. As parents and their children look back on their experiences growing up together, good and trying, those tribulations can only strengthen the relationship and give a reference point from which to measure the progress.

As I grow older, I look forward to trying the parental role. I have visions of my child eclipsing all my achievements and making a substantial difference in the world. Yet, I still find it difficult to take care of myself at times and I shun any kind of constant responsibility. I fancy getting a dog, but the prospect of vet bills and the daily regimen of walks seem overwhelming. In time, when I am ready to walk the dog, this child may become a parent.   —Oliver R. McCoy

CHILDREN AND PARENTS GROW TOGETHER

I believe that peace and well-being are seeds to be planted in our homes, our temples. The flourishing of these seeds is nurtured in our bodies. These make up our family's and my connection to myself. My whole self is to first keep my body and mind healthy and whole. Next, i reach out to my children who are like the limbs on a tree trunk, for they grew inside me, the mother vessel. If i am healthy in body, mind and spirit, then they are too.

Holy day greetings to all you tribal folks and here i am with Maya pinions about parents, kids and family. This subject is so vast and filled with the ebb and flow, push and pull of consciousness. I am here now talking on my experience as the mother of a teen young man, Orly, who is 15, and a young lady, Myray, who is 4 1/2.

I chose to stay single through the late '70s, and had a great big dose of "myself." Heading into my first Saturn return, i started to feel the pangs of family-mother, babe, husband and home. So off to Oregon with baby Orly, dad Paco and brother Rambo who was with us for the summer. We camped on Paco's land and cooked on an open campfire, and my folks visited to see their grandson. They were scared for me and yet our love deepened through Orly's presence.

Seven years flew by quickly- a lotta love, tears, unfulfilled dreams and growth for me. Orly taught me about companionship. We had so much fun together. He was riding a bike before he was 3!!! We swam together in the river. But then some very negative transference parenting patterns would pop out of me, mostly all around anger, verbal yuck that i laid on Orly that is a BIG heartache for me. When i ask Orly for forgiveness for my abuse, he gives to me, "Forgive yourself." Maybe this kinda stuff doesn't arise until late in people's lives. I am ready when and if Orly comes to me with his pain from his past to openly look and feel and heal together.

Living in Williams, and seeing Orly once a month at best, i miss him!!! I think of him and visualize him being safe and happy. I also do worry about his safety driving around in cars on stormy nights kinda stuff!!! In moments i just want to hug him, and yet i created this by deciding to marry a man who lived in Williams. Orly had a choice, a rotten one for him, leave the Illinois Valley, his home, his friends, his world. No, not Orly... I just recently forgave myself for this life i have created for us. Myray has a hard time with her brother living so far away. She loves him dearly.

Myray and i have a blast. We sing, we do ritual, we take saunas, we cook, we make up rhymes, we shop, we dance, we drum. Anyone who has a daughter knows the relationship i am grasping to communicate - females living together are fun!

I have birthed my children with much space and time between, which allows for lots of focus, lots of attention, lots of love. I am a stern teacher at times, and a goofy mom at times. My most fulfilled moments are when Orly and Myray are with me. This summer we all went together to the beach for a few days and full moon nights. I cherish the threads of our lives' tapestry weaving over and through one another. To me this is ritual in its highest degree.

I very much honor my daughter in spirit, Emma Whitesage, who was born without breath and whose feet never walked the earth. I feel her presence in my life and so does Myray. She calls her spirit sister. I learned some hard lessons and some huge spiritual truths through her birth/death/rebirth.

With these rocking chair memoirs i am closing this chapter in my heartmind on parents, kids and family. I give to all peoples guidance towards meditation. Silence is a wonderful gift that only each one of us can sit and give ourselves to. See ya in the light! I am *Maya Many Moons Reames*, comin' on full moon, late November '96.

GLORIA AS PREY

Do your children tease you, notice your imperfections, make jokes and not let you get away with much? I suspect that if your offspring are not behaving in this manner they're either so young they still believe you're flawless, or teenagers who often don't have much to say to anyone.

My heirs, both adults, often have open season on their Mom. It's most relentless when we are all together. I am an easy mark.

In the past few years, we have been able to talk, cry, and heal some old and painful wounds. Lately we're settled into an intimate and comfortable place, opening the perfect opportunity for a son and daughter to shamelessly torment their Mom. Although their father and I have been divorced for almost 30 years, we have all recently enjoyed some holidays together. I had hoped the teasing would now be evenly divided; oh no, I still remain the favored prey.

I must admit I like it. It's never callous. It just reminds me of a verbal caricature, and if I choose to listen carefully I can always learn something. Oh boy, I can hardly wait for Solstice.
                                                        -*Gloria Stone*

Dome School Kids and Parents

Me and my Dad like to go to
the Dairy Queen in L.A.- Forrest

I like to stack wood with my Mom.- Kiley

I like to play baseball with my Dad.- Ian

I like to play catch with my Mom.- Jessea

Me and my Mom play with our dog.- Orion

I like to bake with my Mom.- Eileen

We read together.- Jacob

I watch TV with my Dad.- Trevor

I shake hands with my Dad.- Lukas

I like to bake with my Mom and
watch "Baywatch" with my Dad.- Jolene

I like to sit on the couch with my Dad;
my Mom gets jealous because
she is doing the dishes.- Spencer

I like to play board games with my Mom.- Mish

I like to open presents with my Mom.- Nolan

Me and my Dad play Nintendo.- Osha

7

A TRIP WHICH WILL CHANGE MY LIFE FOREVER

When this is published, I will be in central China, joining my life forever with that of a tiny girl I have never met. I am adopting a baby from Jiangxi Province, People's Republic of China. Just writing those words brings me to tears. I am thrilled, excited beyond belief, and terrified. People have asked me how long it has taken. The answer is two-fold; ten years or about one year. I have thought about adoption and single parenthood for at least a decade. I prepared my conservative, traditional parents for the idea at least that far back. But I went to my first pre–adoption class in October 1995. The two day workshop, which focuses on clarification of issues about parenting and adoption, is required by the US adoption agency I worked with.

I applied in January, 1996, and began the home study and immigration clearance process. Never have I opened my life up so completely to "strangers." The home study which is developed with the agency social worker looked at my entire life, my social, religious, and cultural values, as well as my parenting knowledge and beliefs. We began this on a rocky footing, with the social worker leaving after the first meeting with the comment, "I have to ask my supervisor if this is going to work. If not, I want to give you your money back." What was wrong? Ten years ago I purposely was arrested in a series of anti–nuclear and environmental protests. I live with roommates unrelated to me, and I am overweight. I was astounded that any of these choices could cause me to be considered unfit for adoption! Devastated, I began the year long emotional roller coaster this process would become. Fortunately, the social worker called the next day to say everything was alright and we would continue with the process.

On August 2nd I got "the call" from Melinda at the adoption agency. I had been assigned a child. Fu Guang Ying was four months old, tiny but healthy and in a small (by Chinese standards) town in central China. I was told it would be one to three months before I traveled there to get her.

A month became three months, which could stretch to at least six. That would put my travel into January 1997. My heart sank, especially since I was attached to having her home by Christmas. It is impossible to describe how hard the waiting is.

As winter began, it was more and more difficult not to be depressed about the indefiniteness of the situation. How could I become so in love with a two inch picture? I set activities and projects at intervals to keep me going. I collected the amazing amount of equipment and items needed these days for a baby. I hunted for child care in Ashland. I planned what I could for the trip.

On November 13th, Melinda called me at work. It didn't click right away. Melinda doesn't call unless she has something good to tell you. She said they had tentative travel approval for early December, and I should reserve my plane flights and get my Chinese visa. I still had to wait for official approval which could take until the day before we left. Fortunately, it came much faster than usual. I bought my plane tickets and and sent off for the Chinese entry visas.

The last two weeks have been a blur. Trying to work full time, get all the things I need to take to care for a baby for two weeks in China and my own needs, cover the details at home, deal with holidays and a million other details has been a monumental task. There is so much I could not do until I really knew I was going.

I stop every day and realize what a huge step I am taking. Raising children is the single most important endeavor we can undertake. I ask myself, "Can I do this?, Will she like me? Will she be healthy? Can I make a happy life for her?," and many other questions. I will know soon enough.

I leave for Hong Kong December 3rd, and will spend several days with friends there before meeting the group of other adopting Americans in Shanghai. The group includes two other single women from the East Coast, a couple from England, and a couple from Ashland who live just a block away from my house. We have become good friends through this journey, and it will be delightful to share the travel adventure with them. We will all go on together to NanChang, Jiangxi where on the 10th or 11th of December I will meet my baby girl. Just a few hours after that I will become her mother. We travel on to Guangzhou (Canton) to get the US entry visas from the Consulate and then back to Hong Kong and home by Christmas. Happy Holidays, everyone. Thank you for all the love and support my Takilma friends have provided through this journey. I'll return the last week of December with a new member of our community.   –Kim Blackhawk

MY MOTHER

You may know her, although she is kind of a hermit. She gave me life and protects me from it. She works to make this world a better place for me and my children. She lives a simple life, she lives right livelihood. She tries to provide me with the material things that I need and at the same time teach me that you do not need these things. And even though she is my mother, I know that she is a person too, with insecurities and desires. I love my mother and want to thank her for always being there when I needed her, even when she may have needed a mother too.

Marjorie, Thank you.   -Sequoia Alba

OUTRAGE

I've just recently retasted what might have been the original Forbidden Fruit. I took a big bite of moral outrage, aka righteous indignation. It was bittersweet, as Eden's "apple" must have been. It yielded its familiar high rush. But this time, I felt its aftereffects almost immediately, as if, as I swallowed, my guts were already beginning to twist.

My moral outrage experience was triggered by the how–great–it–is–to–get–loaded–every–day poem in the last CG. I hated it. It was place on the "Kids' Page" where young readers were most likely to turn. Signed by "14 year–old," it was invested with all the authority that a fourteen–year–old has for the elementary school bunch. How could CG run such destructive drivel? What could the editors have been thinking? Were they too hip to censor, too afraid of offending their kids to function as elders? Did this reflect some blind spot of the community, a tendency to condone in adolescents those types of injurious behaviors that their elders shared? I girded my loins and prepared to fight with Error at the next Mud Council meeting.

There I quickly discovered that almost everyone agreed the poem's inclusion was inappropriate and regrettable. Further, no one listed in the editorial credits had seen the Kids' Page until the issue was published. In short, it was a mistake.

On the one hand, I was relieved that CG people, good folks, shared my concerns about the poem's message and location. But as my moral outrage rapidly detumesced, I was keenly aware of the letdown. It had felt so good! I'd been energized, focused, filled with high purpose, fraught with universal significance.

What a heady drug moral outrage is! No wonder the Religious Right is strung out on it, so grateful to demagogues for presenting vivid caricatures of Leftist Demons, ready–made to be denounced. It's epidemic, and not just among the right wingers.

Did any CG readers, upset about the pro–dope poem's inclusion, feel a letdown when they learned it was a regrettable accident? For some, it might have been a welcome opportunity to characterize the CG community as applauders of adolescent substance abuse; for others, who knew better, (like myself), it was still a chance to correct someone else's lapse of judgement.

How sweet the ego boost we get correcting others! But moral outrage has other, more valorous results such as energizing movements for peace, civil rights, and environmental protection. This taste of it got me thinking hard about my generation's responsibilities as elders, filled me with self–assurance, and galvanized me into action. This all seems good, even though I was tilting at windmills.

Perhaps we elders need some moral outrage to bolster us in our struggle to help the next generation. We need strong convictions and determination to function as mentors and protectors, roles filled by elders in more healthy cultures. We can't abandon kids to all the messages they are bombarded with, whether from governments, corporations, hate groups, or exploitive culture peddlers who pander to their angers and prejudices, or their misguided peers.

It's easy to get worn down or drowned out by these messages. We elders learned to despise authority early, so we're uncomfortable with it. We deplored hypocrisy, and we've made mistakes, so who are we to condemn anything? We turned away from our parents and struck out in new directions (or at least we thought we did), so exactly when should we point the easy way for our kids? We live on the periphery of American culture because we chose to, because we disdain the mainstream, but doesn't this culture tell us incessantly that we are wrong, ridiculous, insignificant, and don't we sometimes wonder if we are? Our kids do.

Moral outrage/righteous indignation, if used judiciously, can steel us against crippling self–doubts. Of course, there are dangers. Just as it fueled the Civil Rights Movement, it fueled Desert Storm. It is rage, after all. It is much more safely targeted at injustice than at living creatures. And while it might be very helpful in guarding our kids from external danger, it is a deadly thing to direct at the kids themselves.

Eden's Tree might have been like those fruit cocktail graft jobs you see in seed catalogs. There are many varieties of good and evil, but I have to think moral outrage was hanging there, with all its tart promise.   - *Jack Dwyer*

I SURVIVED LIFE THEN, I LIVE LIFE NOW

I think because it was my first marriage, I didn't have anything to judge it by. I knew it wasn't good, but I figured, you make your bed, you lie in it. The abuse started out slowly. He'd get angry about little things. It got to where, if the phone rang, he'd look at me in disgust. He'd make my world small. People wouldn't want to come over. He'd be rude, but in a small way. I'd think, I can live with it. It escalated to yelling, blows, knives, the police. In the end, I had given all of me away. No self-respect, no determination. I stayed because he owed me a life. But I never got it from him.

I was afraid to leave because I thought I wouldn't be able to take care of my kids. But I wasn't taking good care of them at home. I always thought I was a good mother. I didn't know that I could be a better mother, just by leaving. By staying, I gave control to the abuser. By doing nothing I said, "It's okay to do this to me."

The shelter statistics say it takes three trips to learn, and it did. I took a year off from relationships, just putting my life together. I went to school, learned about self-reliance, learned there are normal people out there who don't degrade and abuse. I found out that I have a choice about who to have around me, and that I have to choose to keep abusive people out of my life. I found out what I'm made of and what I'm capable of.

My kids are dealing with what we went through. The older two were more affected by the marriage than the younger ones. If they are around abusive people, they revert and get inhibited. The younger kids, who have more assurance, say, "I am worth this," while the older say, " I think I am." The kids see that the mother doesn't love herself enough to leave, so why should the kids love themselves? They are less likely to have good careers because they have learned they aren't worth it.

The kids are discovering that they have responsibility and choices. They can learn from their mistakes. Before, they were just dictated to, or yelled at. It's not like that now. They don't punish themselves the way they used to. They used to call themselves stupid, degrading themselves. They had highs and lows; they didn't know how to vent frustration. Now they know that expressing true feeling is always an option. They used to quiz me: "If I burnt off my sister's hair, would you still love me?" As they become more secure, I hear those types of questions less often.

The most important thing a parent can do is raise good human beings. That's hard in an abusive home. The child loses respect for both parents, since the abuser doesn't stop and the abused parent stays. Kids wonder if their mother is a bad person to deserve this treatment. Are they? When you stay in an abusive relationship, it becomes familiar. They learn that this is life; disarray, no hope. When they are raised without respect, they don't develop a conscience. Why should they have to be any different at 18?

So, they find mates who create a familiar environment, the insecure, angry environment they had growing up. They find a mate as insecure and hopeless as they are. The result is generation after generation of abusive relationships.

Changing that is the one accomplishment of my lifetime. If I do nothing else, I broke the cycle. I can always fall back on what I did. I have control over my future and my present.

Sometimes I don't know how I got from there to here. How did I get from 21 and on my own, to 31 and hell on earth with no control over anything? Now I'm 35 and I have a voice. I have hope for my future. It's nothing anyone else can give you. No one can promise it will be like that. You just have to know you can do it today. I walked away with no hope. Hope can come from someone else "making it". Maybe what I say will help another child, another parent, get out. Maybe someone will read this and borrow my hope.   -Kim Van Skyock

FROM COMMON GROUND....

If Common Ground's role is to be a vehicle for discussion of the issues closest to our hearts (and perhaps a few raw nerves), we seem to be succeeding.

In our last issue, the Youth Page stirred up plenty of passion about youth and drugs. *While the Common Ground in no way condones the use of drugs by our young ones, we also recognize that these are real-life issues that can not be swept under the rug. Denial is but a false foundation for complacency. The line between responsible boundaries for our children and freedom of speech is a fine one that we will continue to walk ever so delicately.*

Opinions expressed in this issue are not necessarily those of the editorial staff.

In this issue, Common Ground continues to delve into our sensitive dimensions with a look at Parent-Child Relationships. Staff was Jack Dwyer, Daves Toler and Hocker, Sally Clements, Laurie Prouty, Cathy Hocker, Sitting Dog, Linda Starr, Felicity Elworthy, Rachel Goodman, Deb Murphy and Joya Feltzin. Thanks to Kerry Holman for the computer layout and Dave Toler for pasteup. Also, thanks to Jessea Mucha and Vegas for help at issue #23's folding party. Thanks to artists Alex Krupka (issue #23), Eydie Solis, Jill Birmingham, Cathy Hocker, Ina Krippana and many Dome School students for this issue's art. Get well soon, Alex!

The theme for issue #25 will be "How We Play," facilitated by Barry Snitkin and Mike Birmingham. Submissions deadline is Jan. 17. Let us know how play fits into your life! This time **artwork** should also be submitted on Jan. 17. Send submissions to Common Ground, P.O. Box 2016, Cave Junction OR, 97523.

"ANTI-PRISON TEAM IMPRESSIVE IN LANDSLIDE VICTORY"

On Wednesday, November 13, at the Illinois Valley High School, before a standing room only crowd, the Rockydale Neighborhood Association overwhelmed the minority team of Pride and kept the State's Prison Siting Committee on the edge of their seats during a raucous meeting.

It brought to mind the theme song and rallying cry of the great Pittsburgh Pirate teams of the late '70's, "We Are Family." The anti-prison side's enthusiasm, eloquence, bravado, research and depth, coupled with the articulate and polished starting lineup, contributed to a clear-cut victory; an emotional one at that.

This was as close to a shutout as you'll get. The Pride Minority only sent five people to the plate and few, if any, were successful. On the other side, the players that helped carry the team came up with strong performances, and set the stage for the supporting cast to score factual and emotional points.

The strong lineup began with leadoff speaker and co-captain Dave Toler who immediately drove one deep and to the point, quickly opening the eyes of the committee. The other co-captain, Kate Dwyer, delivered that controlled Irish Fury, backed up by strong facts. Next up were the Professors from Agness, or "Keepers of the River," who bowled them over with a steady stream, reinforced by years of experience. At that point, the rally was just beginning when Michael "Good Dog" Baldwin, entertained, schmoozed and finally told everyone how bad an idea this Prison was. As time expired, with a fresh clock, the veterans were called in as representatives for our river and its inhabitants. Beth and Mark touched us with their "straight from the heart" defense of our most treasured resource. Next up and "all business," was the Greenwood Engineering Team, who, while over-qualified to speak to the committee, nonetheless demanded overdue responses from an inept Corrections Department.

The Rockydale Neighborhood squad, at this point bolstered by an overflow support team, sent out Bill to serve up a very calm and collected "reality check bomb," seemingly delivered with a silencer. The arena got real quiet, and all the cops present, uniformed, plainclothes and off duty, stood by defenseless and bug-eyed. As they passed through the meat of the lineup, the team seemed to gain momentum as Meadow, Doc Kathy, and Lisa presented professionally, although with great feeling through personal experiences, a barrage of facts and figures from the health care standpoint. Nancy, with a timely move, asked for a show of hands for and against. That sent the score keepers scrambling for triple digits, as the tally unofficially numbered 680 to 20. We'll never know the official score, due to the fact that our local " journalist", Bob "I'm just an Ambulance Chaser" Rodriguez, continues with what seems a calculated censorship of the anti-prison views. No surprise to the bench though, cause he's been showing these colors all along. He's JUST another member of a small group of short-sighted, so-called business people who are willing to sacrifice a unique and beautiful place to sell a few more overpriced, weekly rags or speculate on some low-income housing, or whatever their tiny minds have cooked up..

Moving along very smoothly and virtually at will, Barry added to the lead, which took on the snowball effect. Repeatedly firing strikes with Jennifer, Linda, Debbie, Jack and Sally added to the pointed, no nonsense shots that had all the signs of a rout, erasing any memory of the feeble fence-walking jobs done by Haugen, Borngasser and the clueless Tom Green.

At this point, feeling confident and relaxed, the Rockydale Gang sat back and marveled at the grace of several of their elder members, fortified by an insightful message Linda brought from our elder, Agnes Pilgrim. But when surprise pinch-hitter Steve "been there, done that" Lyons, unleashed some first hand knowledge in a booming voice, the edges of all the seats carried the weight once again, and a buzz went through the crowd like the wave. Subsequent participants reiterated and colored in all the important points, with cleanup hitters Margaret Bar-Ha Cohen and Kenny giving final shape and prose to an already convincing case.

Other contributors, too many to list, backed up clever relief man Dave Hocker, agreeing that the Prison has only one fitting place and that's, "where the sun don't shine." That left Cowboy Larry Winn still trying to answer the timely gallery question of, "Were you living on that property in 1964?"

From the Bench — *The Coach*

"Empowerment to the People"

Uniti

Gabriela

SLIP SLIDIN' AWAY

My Dad was a brilliant, articulate, funny man, probably the most significant person in my life. He is in the beginning stages of Alzheimer's Disease and is beginning to lose his words; it is akin to Superman becoming a paraplegic. This one's for you, Dad.

The Fade Out

You have been like a star burning bright
who's run its course
and fades into the black night

In my life you have been a guiding star of light and love
I feel you slowly dimming
I reach out, but
I cannot save you, nor even slow your journey down
Good-bye, Dad

I will love you through eternity
I will meet you in the place beyond the stars.

-Deborah Colette Murphy

BULK RATE
U.S. POSTAGE
·PAID·
CAVE JUNCTION
OR 97523
PERMIT #16

Here comes the sun

Takilma Common Ground
P.O. Box 2016
Cave Junction, OR

Home Field

Autumn winds, still light, swirl over and across the graying water, nicking the short white caps rolling into the bay from the north. The water smells of change, the sails have been bagged, and only a few bobbing yachts await their last cruise to Sister Bay for winter storage.

The tourists have left for the cities, begrudgingly going back to assume their duties, in their place of work or school. The lavish summer homes sandwiched between the sheer limestone cliffs and the bay, along Cottage Row, have been boarded and winterized, starting their winter hibernation. The art galleries, gift shops, ice cream shops, and summer hotels are closed. The small bay town of Fish Creek has once again survived the summer metamorphosis.

With the start of fall the air always seemed chillier, more pure. The scents drifting across the water, earthy and natural. Gone are the odors of 2-cycle mix and suntan lotion. Gone are the sounds of 400 cu. in. marine diesels and the down rev's of ski boats. The bay returned to her natural rhythm, lapping her swells against the dock pilings and sand beaches. The gulls rested more peacefully.

Eight boys, me being one of them, half walked and half trotted down the narrow alley between the Alibi Bar and Dick Wiesgerbur's house. We headed towards the bay, shoving and butting one another. In the air, behind our backs, and under our crotches, a football exchanged hands. The end of the alley opened up onto the small parking lot of the town pier. To the west of the lot, our destination.

We stood there for a few minutes gazing upon the lawn. Our faces red from walking into the north wind, sniffing

back the occasional snot that ran from our noses. We took in the bay, the trees lining the park, the low rock wall mortared along one length and the opposite end from where we stood. Our hearts raced a little faster. Before us, our playing field; Dog Shit Park! It was once again ours! Home field!

From this first weekend after Labor Day until the tourists returned in early June this gridiron would host some of the most spectacular football anyone could ever imagine. Measuring 30 yards wide and 50 yards long, the only other field that rivaled it was Lambeau Field in Green Bay, 70 miles to the south. Our field was raw and exposed to the elements. We played here in all weather, and with street lights on all four corners and one on each side halfway down, it was also perfect for night games.

Our games were not for sissies. Never touch or tag where you pulled a cloth out of a belt. Our games were always TACKLE! No helmets no pads. Four on four. The ground was hard and we gave no mercy to one another. There was too much at stake. Bloody noses, twisted ankles, and an occasional cracked rib were always to be expected. The ability to take the pain was a rite of passage showing worthiness to play the game.

We would play for hours. Passing slants, hooks, running handoffs, defending receivers, blocking for handoffs, fading back to pass, kicking off, punting and tackling. Visions of our Packer heros drove us through the games. We personified all of them depending on the magnificent and impossible plays we would pull off. Bart Starr, Paul Horning, Elijah Pitts, Jerry Kramer, Boyd Doulder, to

continued on page3

Enough?

For me, it's not how we play, but do we play enough?? Our lives seem busier and busier. Here are a few quotes that I find relevant.

"Nobody ever went to their deathbed wishing they had spent more time working."

"Constant work is as abnormal as constant sleep."

"Goddess respects me when I work, but she loves me when I sing." (Thai proverb}

"I meant to do my work today but a brown bird sang in an apple tree, a butterfly flitted across the field and all the leaves were calling me."

Gloria

Have Fun

Some of the most fun times I have had lately are times spent in the sauna with my sisters. We raise our voices together in joyful abandon. Our fears melt, our hearts open, and spontaneously improvised renditions of old favorite songs and chants emerge. We are able to laugh at ourselves, stretch ourselves, and merge our boundaries a little as our voices become the one voice.

Awhile back, I was pondering the difficulty of being with people and remaining in the present. Present-time consciousness, that is. So often when we are together the conversation revolves around stories of the past, or fantasies about the future. It occurred to me that singing together is a wonderful way to commune with each other while remaining focused totally in the present. In fact, we are usually acutely aware of ourselves in that situation. We feel the tightness in our throats, the awkwardness of raising our voice in song at all! And the glory and grace of the moment when we let go of our considerations about self long enough to truly join together with others. Magic happens in that moment when we are together in the present.

I invite you to explore yourself and each other in the realm of the present while joining together in song. The only prerequisite is to remember to HAVE FUN!

Myrica

True Essence

What is the true essence of fun or enjoyment? For many of us, a fun activity is one that is not associated with tedium or work. Not many of us grind away Monday through Friday from eight to five because we find regimen and a paycheck exciting. Always work has been a matter of maintaining a desired lifestyle and setting time aside for leisure activities. Examining that hypothesis further leads to an interesting discovery: tedium and suffering now, in exchange for the possibility of an expected future reward. Unfortunately, we never know where our paths may lead.

I say, "Gather ye rosebuds while ye may," because in craning our heads toward the horizon, the world on which we are grounded is forgotten in the pursuit of an apparition. To hell with experiment. Now and each passing moment is but another opportunity to dig my hands deep in the earth under my feet. To cram clay beneath our fingernails, to feel the sun's hot kiss upon my neck, and to be touched by a gentle breeze as it nudges its way through my hair, that is fun!

Yet, to stop, step back, and suck the marrow from this world's experiences is work in itself. True enjoyment, pure fun, is hitting the ball in that sweet spot, and watching it hiss as it hits the back of the net. It is not for us to ponder upon the grace or skill it took to perform such an act, but, with arm raised in the rush of celebration, there is true joy in exaltation.

Ollie

"You don't see no hearses with luggage racks" Don Henley from "If Dirt Were Dollars"

Adrenaline

Playing by and in the river has been the source of some of my greatest moments of fun in the Siskiyous. Being fortunate to have so many wild and scenic rivers, I have floated, snorkeled or swam on the Illinois, the Rogue, the Smith and the Slammin Salmon. I must admit however, that I do not play enough. Life is too short and I think we all need to enjoy our lives more. We get old, we read or watch movies. But do we play enough? These rivers offer the possibility of adrenaline rushes as well as moments of beauty and calm unbeknownst to most mortals. The roar of the impending rapids brings chill to my bones. I use it always as a test. Can I be calm and clear? Can I focus through the white water?

I look forward also to the long moments of absolute silence, the flowers, the trees. Of course, the thrill of deer, bear, salmon, herons, eagles and osprey reminds me I am but a small part of this glorious place. So come spring or summertime, y'all might find me in a wet suit or stark naked, in the river. But if you aren't near the river, you'll miss me.

Barry

photo by Mark Thomas of Barry in the Smith River Gorge

continued from page 1

name a few. All coached by the great Vince Lombardie. We lived and breathed the Packers. They were our team. These were their glory years and they were the best in the world. Growing up, isolated in Door County during some of the harshest winters known, they gave us an identity.

By dark we were exhausted and chilled by the wind, after hours of burning off energy. With our clothes stained by grass and mud, ripped and sometimes reeking of dog shit, (a few missed piles) the games would end. Bruised and sometimes battered, we would confirm our friendships by a crack on the ass or a slap on the back. We would gather and boast about our individual plays and concede to our failed attempts, knowing there would always be another game to save face.

Our backs to the bay, the wind pushed us gently up the alley. In the air, behind our backs, and under our crotches the football exchanged hands. We talked of the next big game and laid plans for the night after we ate supper.

It was the first weekend after Labor Day. The tourists had gone. Fish Creek quieted into its long seasons of rest. Eight boys gathered on the stone wall near the town center outside Virginia Kinsey's house. The night was dark, quiet, and crisp. The boys were giddy with excitement. Fish Creek was once again THEIR TOWN!!

Michael

Rudimentary Fun

Some 55 years ago I began having fun on this planet when I discovered that by wetting my diaper I got me some quality time with a woman.

A year or so later I began walking around peeing on our house, our shrub, our tree, our car. That's seriously the only real fun I can remember until six-seven years later when my kid brother and I began years of piss contests.

Moving water good distances! Defying gravity! That little prick could whiz out an arch twice my best efforts. Mother was never impressed by our golden arches, but my little sister Judy was. It wasn't until I was 33 or so that the Gods of Love finally sent me a female who too knew the fun - cheap thrills of urination. Talk about bonding!

I'd guess a good 90% of Earthlings no longer know how to have fun. Thus our divorce rate, our drug culture, our suicide rate. Our Nipponese brothers and sisters travel 8,000 miles plus to stand in line at Disneylands. Decades ago, television moguls knew we weren't having fun and created "canned laughter" to tell us when we were. And then came sno-mobiles, Nintendos, jet skis, Internet sex, and the tragedies of gambling meccas.

Fun, sports fans, is simple. Fun is water, air, fire. I can't remember if I'd even learned to walk when I discovered the mystical magic of a Made in Ohio "Diamond" STRIKE ANYWHERE! match. I do remember getting serious discipline for this new FUN discovery and the quick skills I developed searching out my parent's match

4

stash. Just the blue-red-white dotted tips of those wonder-filled matches were mesmerizing. The sulfur stink forever, unforgettable. The tiny puff of smoke, the instant oval of FLAME!

Ah...! Fun! Fun! Fun! Fire, Air, Water.

At around four I "ran away" from my New York home and miraculously survived four-five blocks of traffic to visit my first fire station. Oh! To this day I have my own 200 foot fire hose and thousand gallon a minute Fire Red pumper.

And then Air! (Without which of course NO fire.) Air... To suddenly awake in grade school to witness aerodynamic perfection - The Paper Airplane! Defying fucking Gravity! Hovering magically over some bizarrely garbed no-nonsense Roman Catholic nun's shaved head- dive bombing the poor red haired freckle-faced lady scholar I am still obsessed with to this day. And on to spitballs! Peashooters! Bicycle tube slingshots! Fuck-you Goliath you clod! Fuck-you Mother Gravity!

That wonderful little brother and I did all that and then started cutting up our mom's sheets to make parachutes. Beautiful little ones with thermos bottle corks for weights, dropping them off fire (!) escapes in joy and awe of what seemed an Eternal Descent with thrilling sudden stalls and side dances. One day the moon surely full, the lil'bro' decided to snag the whole sheet and jumped out of a second story window like he was fucking Batman! Wow! Whew! Air indeed! And of course, even then the Gods protected lunatics and space pioneers and positioned a big bush beneath that window and my Bold Ass Brother dragged his Percale 'Chute out of it unscathed and grinning like a True Fool having Too Much Fun!

I suspect humankind discovered kites before fire. And wow- with fire, Thermal Updraft- hot air balloons that crazed celibate clerics judged ungodly- from Satan! Air. Clipper ships! Match stick masted paper boats, such simple fun.

And then we learned to swim. Suspended in water as we were in the Womb. We learn to defy gravity again and skip sweet feeling fun flat stones across ponds, rivers, bays, lakes, and bayous. Fun! Magic! We luckily luckily moved to the country and instantly learned the fun of

continued on page 5

continued from page 4

getting soaked to the balls diverting water. Constructing dams! Bringing little sister home so wet and muddy we got our asses whipped.

Then suddenly, we're 56 years old in southwestern Oregon, and still Fun. Fun. Fun. Soaked to the balls that have magically, miraculously, hung in there five plus decades. Expertly diverting H20 around your house, your hay, your shed with a lifetime of good stuff in it. H20 down your collar out your sox, oh...

Then you stop or give up Fun Diversions and go in and kneel in front of your almost as old as you are pig-iron woodstove and, yet again, play with strike anywhere matches.

With Air! Combustion! Updraft! All systems, Go!!

Your cock unshrivels. The coffee perks. You walk buck-naked out onto the porch, and add your steaming piss to Mother's Deluge. (O my little brother. Wish you were here...) Eyes wide, you watch water rush and rock 'n roll down your 'seasonal' creek. Floating the kids' made-in-Taiwan yard toys down into the pasture, maybe to the Illinois River. Gold Beach?

Fun. Water. Air. Fire. Eternal Fun.

Tony Nye Haynes

Play Time

The play of life goes on until you die. When I was very young I played endlessly in fantasy worlds of my own making, which I acted out with siblings and friends. As I got older, play was living and every day was an adventure. I traveled and learned a lot about myself, others and the world.

When I had my first child, I played with my baby and for the first time my focus shifted from myself. I played a lot with my 4 children, in all their stages, as they grew up. Mostly, I allowed them the freedom to play and to live in comfort with the security of unconditional love. They taught me as much as I taught them. We grew up together and suddenly I realized I was old and I finally found out who I was and what I really wanted to do. Yet, by then, I couldn't play anymore. I had all the responsibilites on my shoulders. I worked at a job I considered fun for six years.

Now I'm ready for a change and I'm as excited as a teenager. I wonder if people ever grow up. Seems like I'm still the same inside, even though the outside has changed. Age won't stop me from doing the things I dream of. It will actually give me the strength and experience I need to accomplish them. The years ahead could be the best times of my life.

Kindi

Slip Sliding Away

Body to body
Surrender to the abyss
Heart and soul set free.

Jill

Thinking

I have listened to bumble bees whisper about moonlight tickled flowers

I have watched foam tipped waves die on snowy white beaches

I have tasted the bitter sweetness of truly happy laughter

I have smelled a green tree breeze

I sensed the pain of a mother when her child is taken away to fight someone else's war. War with no cause and great effect

I have listened to the bumble bee's dying cries

I have seen once white beaches turn brown with human waste

Laughter is now a delicacy that only the rich can afford... and even then it's an imitation

I have smelt brown tree stump breezes

All of this is because someone didn't think: Maybe it's you... Maybe it's me...Maybe it's everyone

But do the world a favor and contemplate before you leap

-mirya R holman

Me and Morning

It's a bicycle morning which plays with my soul
Dipping and swaying in glistening gold
Sing merry children, a blossoming song
Clouds block the sunlight for moments too long

Emerging from flowers the buzzing of bees
Flying over branches the birds in the trees
I journey slowly with bicycle ease
Myself, I am one, I am merely a breeze

Up and down hillsides of shimmering haze
Below me the ocean and rooftops in a maze
Welcoming feelings that drift in the air
I follow directions from my bright, windblown hair
Journey in a dream, soft smile to unfold
Life is just something, I'm learning how to hold.

Kindi

Dedicated to Chester

I love Chester, she was my dog.
She jumped, she played,
She was my dog.
She barked, she ran.
I love my Chester.
A dog can play, a dog can laugh.
Only Chester can be my dog.

Died... January 13, 1997, 9:40 p.m.

Amara Belle

CORNER

The Journey

As I wade into the deep cool pools of the river
As I walk thru the thick forest feeling the life around me
As I sit in a meadow watching a flower open
I smile, seeing the child within, coming out to play
With eyes and heart wide open.
Seeing a hummingbird shower in a small waterfall
A bear romping thru the forest
A deer dancing in a meadow
I find I am not the only one who likes to play in the woods.

Ron Raven

I Know a Lady

I know of a lady, so proud and strong

With hundreds of followers, tagging along

When you see their faces, yellow, red, black and white

All united by one, it's a wonderful sight.

My rainbow warriors, she'll smile and say

For I know our Creator truly wants it this way

Each are his children, and family to me

For all are offsprings of the Great Mystery

Her works are endless, through dusk and through dawn

Though tired and sickly, she still carries on

Loved by so many, and maybe scorned by a few

But her love for them all, like a beacon shines through

Buckskins and moccasins, she does proudly wear

With a small basket hat, perched on her grey hair

She teaches of love, and of true harmony

The sharing of cultures, the way it should be

The light of her fires, she spreads far and wide

And no one that joins in is casted aside

This lady I speak of, to many you see

Is fondly referred to as Grandmother Aggie

Sun Bear

To Common Ground

I want to say thank you from the bottom of my heart to everyone who attended the Takelma Salmon Ceremony. What a wonderful day we all shared! It is absolutely beautiful how our Creator blesses us!

Also, I wish to thank everyone who contributed and helped. What a great job Jan Patton and Barry Snitkin did cooking the salmon. Just keep up the good work! What a great bunch of extended family I have in Southern Oregon in the land of my people.

Bless you all for your giving spirit, your donation. You all have made my trip to Australia a memorable one. Such love! Such greatness! May Our Creator bless each and everyone of you in a special, special Way!
Aho, Konoway Nika Tillicum.

Agnes "Taowhywee" Pilgrim

From Common Ground

Why issue 25 1/2? Although we assumed that most folks contributing to our ever rotating staff were schooled in basic math, logical numerical continuation should never be taken for granted. (what happened to #24?) What should of been wasn't. We managed to accept hearsay as fact. What can we say? We blew it. So we did what most honorable institutions would do. We called an apple a Mac, thus issue #25 1/2!

Opinions expressed in this issue are not necessarily those of the editorial staff. Common Ground in no way condones romanticizing the reckless use of matches or the silly practice of pissing contests. In our ever demanding role as parents and guardians, one of the basic rules we try to instill upon our youth is NEVER PLAY WITH MATCHES. However, we recognize in real life many unsuspected disasters are doused just in the nick of time by the urinary games of mischievious play.

From last issue... thanks to Dave T. for the Fatherhood article and to Dog & Gabriella. Many thanks to those who helped put this issue (#25 1/2) together- Ellie, Pat, Rachel, Oshia, Jill, Dave H, Robin, Cathy, and all others who submitted articles and artwork. The submissions deadline for the next issue is Feb. 26th. At this time, we have no facilitators and no theme. **Volunteer!** E-mail your submissions to holmans@cdsnet.net or mail to Takilma Common Ground, POB 2016, C J, Or. 97523

Barry Snitkin and Michael Birmingham
Co-facilitators and computer layout

In Memory of Joe

Joe Dominguez, the "father" of the frugality movement and co-author of the book <u>Your Money or Your Life</u> passed away at home on January 11 after a rapid illness, at peace with himself and feeling complete in this life.

> "..it doesn't always take money to have a good time and sometimes the best things in life are free! So let's enjoy every precious minute we have with our friends."

Joe, a dear friend, along with Evy, Monica, Marcia, Vicki and Marilyn (other members of the New Road Map Foundation) have had a profound impact in my life. They taught me about living in integrity and also taught me about changing my relationship with money. (*Am I making a living or making a dying?*)

There are lots of people out there with good ideas about how to make this world a better place. Joe, and all the New Road Map Foundation folks, live what they teach. That is real honesty. They taught me a lot about playing; that it doesn't take money to have a good time and sometimes the best things in life are free! So let's enjoy every precious minute we have with our friends.

Although it's been a few years since I last saw Joe, I miss his sharp wit and humor. He deeply touched my heart, and in that respect he will never go away.

Meadow

Announcements

1. The New Chautauqua Lecture Series will kick off its first season with three noted Western writers which will address the question "Who Owns The West?" at the newly remodeled Craterian Theater in Medford.

March 13 7:30 p.m. **Bill Kittredge,** a Wallace Stegner student, wrote the essay "Who Owns the West?" His family homesteaded in the Warner valley east of Lakeview and spent many years working the family spread before and after his graduation from OSU. He wrote of them in his first collection of stories, <u>Hole in the Sky</u>. He teaches at the University of Montana and is an eloquent spokesman for the common man in environmental and political matters.

April 10 7:30 p.m. **Terry Tempest Williams** is a superb writer and a Naturalist in Residence at the Utah Museum of Natural History in Salt Lake City. <u>Refuge</u>, her most popular book, speaks of healing, family and environmental issues. A feminist and engaging speaker, she addresses the concerns of all Westerners and through them all humankind.

May 1 7:30 p.m. **Ken Kesey,** who resides in the Willamette Valley, is a native Oregonian. His books, <u>One Flew Over the Cuckoo's Nest</u> and <u>Sometimes A Great Notion</u> are landmarks in Western literature. Kesey, also a Wallace Stegner student, will gather his fellow travelers on the bus made famous in Tom Wolfe's <u>Electric Kool Aid Acid Test</u> and steer it into the Rock and Roll Hall of Fame in Cleveland, Ohio immediately after this lecture.

Tickets are available at the Craterian Ginger Roger Theater box office and at locations in Grants Pass and Ashland. All seats reserved. Please phone 779-3000 for ticket info or call Dan Heller 488-2360 for more info.

Individual Tickets: $10	Series Tickets: $25
Student: $7.50	Student Series : $15

2. The Dome School's Annual Women's Cafe will take place on Saturday March 8. From 10 am to 2 pm there will be a workshop: "Create your own *nicho* or personal altar." Creations will be on display that evening. A group piece will become a community work in progress. Sliding scale fee: $3 - $5. The Cafe will be offering food from 5:30 to 7:00. The fine and performing arts show will begin at 7:00. For information or to donate time, talents, energy or food contact Deborah Murphy who

desperately needs your help and support @ the Dome School: 592-3911 or @ home 592-2866. P.S. Young children are discouraged due to mature subjects, delicate artwork, and the late hours.

3. A Dome School benefit at the Barnstormer's Theater in Grants Pass. Neil Simon's play, "I Ought To Be In Pictures" will be presented on Thursday, April 17, 1997. Refreshments will be served at 7:30pm. Show time 8:00 pm. The Theater is wheelchair accessible and tickets are $8. For further info call 592-3911.

4. Please join Agnes Taowhywee Pilgrim at the Takilma Community Building at 3pm on February 9 for a pot luck celebration. Agnes will share her adventures in Australia. Drumming, singing and other forms of sharing are encouraged. For more information call Barry at 592-4459

5. The First Conference on Siskiyou Ecology will be held on May 30 - June 1, 1997 in Cave Junction, Oregon. Coordinated by the Siskiyou Regional Education Project and cosponsored by the SOSC Biology Department and the Oregon Caves National Monument, the conference will bring together people interested in or working on various aspects of the Siskiyou Mountain region.

Presentations will cover topics, including past and current research on regional flora and fauna, the botanical significance of the area, unique geological features, and historical changes influencing the ecological integrity of the region. There will also be workshops and field trips to areas of ecological interest.

Anyone interested in presenting talks or posters at the conference should send an abstract of 300 words or less by March 1 to: Jennifer Beigel and Erik Jules, Conference on Siskiyou Ecology, c/o SREP, P.O. Box 220, Cave Jct, OR 97523, or email ejules@umich.edu.

If you would like to volunteer or could house a participant in your home please call Debbie at 592-4459.

6. Steve Gillette and Cindy Mangsen, the headliners of the Golden Bear reunion last March will be in concert at the Dome School at 8pm on Saturday, March 1st. Steve, a folksinger, is the author of a couple of dozen folk songs, a few of them hits, such as "I'm Back on the Street Again," and "Two Ten Train." Cindy Mangsen a song writer and performer. Proceeds go to the Dome school. $8. Admission.

7. The Illuminated Fools will perform their newest play, "A Scary Tale," at the Headwaters Forest Activist Conference on Saturday, Feb. 15 at 9:00am at SOSC Student Union.

8. When people rent the Takilma Community Building, their fliers should state that as the location, not "Dome School". Thanks.

9. Big, black, friendly male dog needs a good home. Free collar, leash, bag of food. Will share cost of shots and neutering. 592-3386.

10. A workshop: "Women in the Classroom, Women in the World" at SOSC, Saturday, February 8, 1997. For info call Deb Murphy, 592-2866.

11. The IV PTSA has invited school board candidates Dave (NO PRISON) Toler and Dodie Vandermark to speak on Wed., Feb. 19th., 7:30 at the Pizza Deli.

Classified Ads

The following classes are offered by **Peace with Inn**, Box 1154, Cave Junction, OR 97523 541-592-4209 fax 541-592-4863 email to: bliss@cdsnet.net

Starting Jan. 6th, each Monday, Kundalini Yoga. Alyssa Monnie. This class introduces you to Sadhana (daily practice), which, when practiced, moves us closer to cosmic awareness and Self-realization. $6 5pm-6:30pm

Starting Jan. 16th, Creativity at Play. A 13 week adventure exploring your natural creativity and play-full-ness. Marcy Tilton using the structure of Julia Cameron's The Artists way, Adriana Diaz's Freeing the Creative Spirits. $10/wk. includes materials for weekly art project. 10 am - noon Thursdays, please pre-register.

Starting Feb. 3rd Carolyn Myss Video series. Carolyn Myss is a medical intuitive and pioneer in energy healing. $5 7:00 pm

Feb. 22nd., Monthly Vegetarian Cooking and Feast. Join Robin Wren, famed chef from A Thousand Cranes, as we journey through the China Moon cook book. Spend the day cooking with friends, then enjoy the feast. Pre-registration by Feb 15th is a must! $20 11am- 5pm Feast only $12

March 8th & 9th, Reiki II certification. Loretta Hill, Reiki master, will guide any who have successfully completed Reiki I. Since this is a sleep-over class, we will be enjoying Sat dinner and Sun breakfast. Bring food to contribute. 3pm on the 8th-1pm on the 9th, $50.

March 15th., Monthly Vegetarian Cooking and Feast. Join Robin Wren for a journey into pastas and other Italian delights. Spend the day cooking with friends, then enjoy the feast. Pre-registration by Mar. 8th is a must! $20 11am- 5pm Feast only $12

March 22nd., Marbling Magic. Myrica will take us on a journey into the magic of color, design, and surprise. Fun and messy! Bring an apron or old clothes . 12 pm -4 pm $25 includes materials. Pre-registration a must!

March 29th., Bookmaking workshop. Marcy Tilton. Learn to make 3 simple books with ideas for how to personalize them. Bring your own scissors and embellishments (measuring tools, glue, beads, ribbon, thread, cord, stamps). 11am - 4pm $25

April 26th., Healers Networking Conference. Healers unite! Tour Peace with Inn, enjoy the hot tub, the river, & sing in the sauna. Vegetarian lunch provided. Pre-registration required. $40

Wanted: Feet for reflexology. Let us touch your soles, to relieve stress and tension. $10/ session. Mar 592-4436 or Diane 592-3908.

Garden and yard work my specialty. I follow directions well and am able to assist with other projects. Al Karger, 597-2205.

Classifieds continued on page 12...

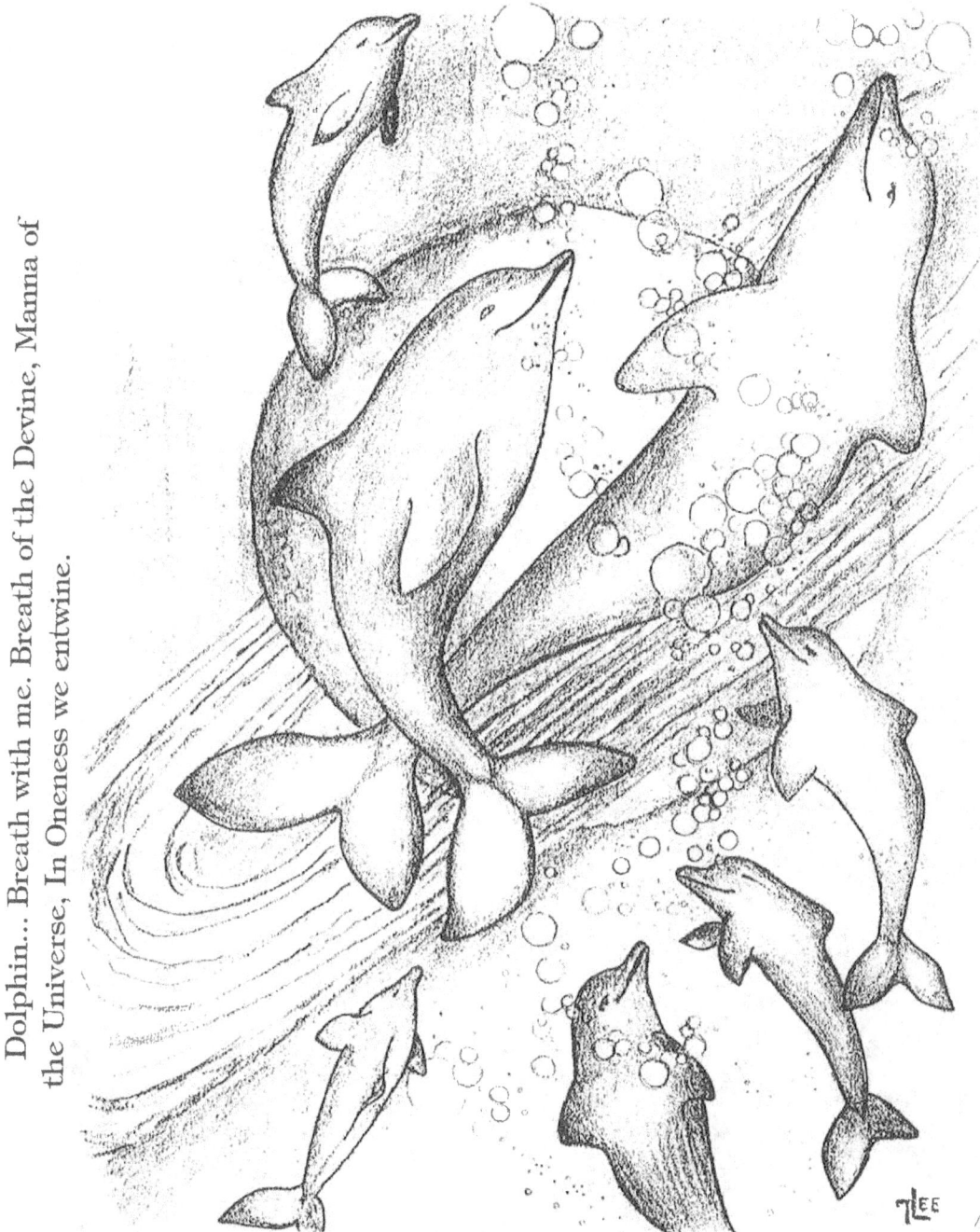

Dolphin... Breath with me. Breath of the Devine, Manna of the Universe, In Oneness we entwine.

Dolphin... Leap in freedom and joy. Playful, intelligent, messenger of the Dreamtime, We Honor you.

!!Subscriber Alert!!

Takilma Common Ground is courageously planning to publish this year, despite a rapidly dwindling bank account. If your subscription is due, if your ship has come in, or if you have an opportunity to forge someone's signature on a four figure check, please remember us with your charitable gifts. TCG Staff

258

Classified continued...

Taiji instruction; acupuncture, herbal remedies: Contact Dan Grossberg, Earth and Sky Cauldron, 592-4921.

Lunar Wall Calendars greatly reduced prices; beautiful and accurate. Call Gloria 592-4269 or 482-5156

moonlight calendar	16x36"	$6.50
moonshine calendar	18x24	$12.00
graphic time table		$6.00
century luna calendar (1)		$13.00

Little Treasures Quality Resale Boutique has kids wear, sizes birth-preteen. Mother wear, gifts and toys, too. We buy or trade for quality items. Open Wed-Sat Noon - 5:00 p.m. at 223 N. Redwood Highway in the Redwood Service Center. 592-2466. Kids day is Wednesday.

Takilma Common Ground
P.O. Box 2016
Cave Junction, Or. 97523

Prison- Takilma Style

Good news, we will not get a prison here. Now that the pressure is off, I decided to imagine what a prison in Takilma might be like. What if the prisoners had to live like many of us? What if they were made to participate in country ways? The conversation could go something like this:

"Hey, man, I just did some time in that joint in Takilma. Boy am I glad to be out of there. It was the worst. The food was all fresh and they served this weird shit called Tufu, or something like that. After we were done eating we had to go outside and put our leftovers into a pile. Weird ... You should have seen the shitters; they were buckets and you had to squat over them. Did you check out the new prison guards? Very strange uniforms, and they kept asking us how we FELT about things. Wanted to know about our INNER CHILD. Told them I wasn't pregnant so I couldn't tell them about anything like that. The worst was early on Saturday morning they wanted us to do something called Yogert or somethin'. I'm telling ya the place was wacko. I can tell you I'll do just about anything to NOT go back THERE again. It was really hard core..."

Gloria

Bulk Rate
US Postage **PAID**
Cave Junction, Or.
97523
Permit # 16

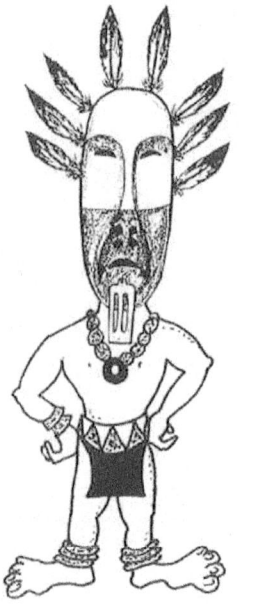

www.ingramcontent.com/pod-product-compliance
Lightning Source LLC
Chambersburg PA
CBHW081227020726
47503CB00011B/2936